GANGS

AN INTRODUCTION

Bill Sanders

SCHOOL OF CRIMINAL JUSTICE
CALIFORNIA STATE UNIVERSITY, LOS ANGELES

NEW YORK   OXFORD
OXFORD UNIVERSITY PRESS

Oxford University Press is a department of the University of Oxford.
It furthers the University's objective of excellence in research,
scholarship, and education by publishing worldwide.

Oxford New York
Auckland Cape Town Dar es Salaam Hong Kong Karachi
Kuala Lumpur Madrid Melbourne Mexico City Nairobi
New Delhi Shanghai Taipei Toronto

With offices in
Argentina Austria Brazil Chile Czech Republic France Greece
Guatemala Hungary Italy Japan Poland Portugal Singapore
South Korea Switzerland Thailand Turkey Ukraine Vietnam

For titles covered by Section 112 of the US Higher Education
Opportunity Act, please visit www.oup.com/us/he for the
latest information about pricing and alternate formats.

Published by Oxford University Press
198 Madison Avenue, New York, New York 10016
http://www.oup.com

Oxford is a registered trademark of Oxford University Press

Library of Congress Cataloging-in-Publication Data

Names: Sanders, Bill, 1972– author.
Title: Gangs : an introduction / Bill Sanders.
Description: Oxford ; New York : Oxford University Press, 2016.
Identifiers: LCCN 2015050547 (print) | LCCN 2016002048 (ebook) | ISBN
    9780199948598 (paperback) | ISBN 9780190608439 ()
Subjects: LCSH: Gangs. | Juvenile delinquents. | Juvenile delinquency. |
    Criminology. | BISAC: SOCIAL SCIENCE / Criminology.
Classification: LCC HV6437 .S26 2016 (print) | LCC HV6437 (ebook) | DDC
    364.106/6--dc23
LC record available at http://lccn.loc.gov/2015050547

Printing number: 9 8 7 6 5 4 3 2 1

Printed in the United States of America
on acid-free paper

For Pops!

BRIEF CONTENTS

CONTENTS

PREFACE

This is a textbook on gangs. Its target audience is students, although academics, researchers, and those in various professions who work with gangs will find it useful. The overall aim is to provide a comprehensive overview of gangs by drawing from gang-specific material conducted over many years. The 13 chapters are based on pertinent themes that together provide an inclusive and thorough understanding of the topic. In the following ways, this book is different from what has previously been published on gangs.

- Topics that have received scant attention elsewhere, such as race, females, style and media, desistance, prison gangs, and public health aspects, each have a chapter dedicated to them.
- The writing style is clear and free of academic jargon and technical terminology. This book is written so that everyone can understand the material.
- Many interview excerpts from gang members, young offenders, and adults who work with gangs are provided from two original ethnographic projects: the Los Angeles Study and the London Study. Details about these studies are provided in the Appendix. The objective of the excerpts is to stress a particular point about gangs as indicated by the members themselves or those who work with them.
- Each chapter contains a section called *Media Check!* These are lighthearted takes on media-related aspects about gangs, such as movies, documentaries, television shows, and music, that reflect the theme of the chapter.
- Dispersed throughout are sections called *On Trial.* These are real-life court cases offering the prosecution's and defense's arguments as they pertain to gang enhancement statutes (i.e., laws that increase the penalties associated with a crime committed on behalf of a gang). Major details have been altered to help ensure confidentiality.
- Unique contributions to the gang literature are offered. These include a theory that helps capture why gang members are the perpetrators and victims of violence (at the end of Chapter 6) and another that calls for a public health agenda for the study and approach of gang youth (at the end of Chapter 11). Additionally, an argument is offered

that questions whether or not US-style gangs are present in England (toward the beginning of Chapter 12).

- Noncriminal aspects about life in the gang are presented, including everyday life, positive and negative aspects of membership, employment and family prospects, diet and exercise, and access to health care.

A key objective of this textbook is to *present* the data on gangs and not offer support for any one particular definition, theory, program, or policy. An additional attempt here is to *proportionally* represent the gang literature. Hypothetically, assume three camps of gang researchers are evident in the United States—Camps A, B, and C—each defined by mutual research collaborations, publications, professor–student relations, and points of view. Then assume that the total gang research conducted by Camps A, B, and C is 50, 30, and 20%, respectively. This book would then aim to ensure that 50% of the material within was from Camp A, 30% from Camp B, and 20% from Camp C. This does not indicate favoritism for any one camp, but rather proportionality. A final endeavor of this textbook is that it covers research *specifically* on gangs and not crime and delinquency more generally. Parallels are drawn between findings from data on gangs and similar findings from non-gangs, but the reverse is not true. For example, a point stressed in Chapter 5 is that gang members have differential attitudes toward hard drug use—just like many non–gang members who use drugs. This is an apt comparison. However, if a particular characteristic about crime and delinquency among non–gang members *has not* been reported among gang members, this book does not hypothesize how they *might* behave similarly. That would result in a much longer book.

The preface and introduction are important to read first. The remainder of this book is organized so that it can be read in any order. Each chapter begins with a series of key words, followed by the chapter learning objectives and then a brief introduction that outlines the forthcoming information. The end of each chapter has a summary and then links to select articles.[1]

The introduction argues two points. The first is that what are considered gangs are an old phenomenon and the second is that current estimates of gangs are unclear because of the various ways gangs are defined.

Chapter 1 is about early research and perspectives from the late 1920s until the early 1970s. The point of this chapter is to offer a chronological outline of the development of the study of gangs. Journalistic accounts appeared in colonial America. Then, as now, gangs from different nearby communities fought each other, participated in rituals, and possessed symbols. Their formal study did not begin until the early 20th century. Then, social scientists began to provide competing definitions and explanations. In the 1950s and 1960s, a few criminological theories were developed on gangs and their behaviors. Other theories focused on cultural aspects of gangs, the various roles they occupied, or the outreach services provided to them.

---

1   For best results, copy the link and paste it directly into the address bar of a web browser. At the time of publication, these links led to the articles; however, such links have a tendency to change. If they do not work as is, type the name of the article into a web browser and the results will likely lead to that article.

Chapter 2 is about sociological and legal definitions, interrelated dynamics, daily life, and risk and protective factors. In the 1980s and 1990s, gang membership increased rapidly. So did public attention and research. Laws emerged that targeted members and their activities. Defining the term gang became a study in itself. Researchers conducted a number of ethnographies that asked gang youth about sensitive topics, focusing on the meaning of membership, the extent to which gangs were organized, and criminal patterns. Different types of gangs emerged as distinguished by these qualities. Also, a series of important longitudinal studies began. This research was more sophisticated in that it sought differences in background characteristics between gang and non–gang youth, as well as what prevented youth from joining gangs.

Chapter 3 is about race, migration, and immigration. Race has become a critical variable in understanding why modern gangs first emerged. For years, researchers downplayed the importance of race, arguing that other variables were more critical in understanding gang etiology. A close examination of how minority communities first became socially disorganized underscores the centrality of race. Patterns of immigration and migration are also linked. Many parallels exist in the experiences of African Americans on their arrival to various cities across the country and those of Latino/Hispanics and Asians entering the country. Although gangs were once solely the product of immigrant Europeans, all-white gangs today are something of an anomaly. Gang activity has increased among Native American populations since the 1990s, paralleling a general increase in ganging.

Chapter 4 is about female gangs and members. As with race, discussions about gender/sex in relation to gangs have historically been sidelined. Females were once viewed as sexual auxiliaries to male-dominated gangs or tomboys that affiliated with them. Researchers figured such involvement centered on sexual dysfunction or mental health impairment. Although the overall crime rate dropped during the 1990s and 2000s, female crime and delinquency soared. Paralleling this was a rise in female gang members, and during this time period research on the topic matured. Contemporary portraits indicate that some females who are more like males in terms of crime and violence belong to autonomous gangs. Novel and important insights gained through research have advanced the understanding of why females participate in gangs and how membership impacts them.

Chapter 5 covers drug use and selling. Members use significantly higher amounts of alcohol and illicit drugs than non-gang youth. Alcohol and marijuana play an active and recurring role in the lives of gang members. When hanging out and doing nothing—two of their most everyday activities—substance use is common. Use becomes amplified during parties, and the types of drugs used may shift toward PCP, ecstasy, cocaine, and crystal methamphetamine. Older users may slip into heroin addiction to cope with the drama of life. Many myths surround drug selling. One myth, *Don't get high on your own supply*, often does not stand up to reality. Many drug sellers are drug users. Also, few drug sellers will become wealthy or successful, although many are incarcerated or killed.

Chapter 6 discusses violence and victimization. Violence serves as a way to enter a gang, such as getting jumped in, and as a way to leave, such as through violent death or getting beaten out. Gang violence takes many forms, from one-on-one fights, to surprise attacks involving several antagonists and one or two victims (i.e., getting jumped), to group rumbles, drive-by shootings, and gang-related homicides. A close look at the offender/victim relationship reveals that many members who commit high levels of criminal and violent acts are also victims of crime and violence. The high rate of victimization among them helps underline a fatal irony: that youth join for protection.

Chapter 7 is a contribution to the cultural criminology of gangs. The chapter begins with an introduction to the history and focus of culture, crime, and media. From here, gang style is explored, such as the meaning and significance of graffiti, clothing, symbols, and music. Youth must look and act like members to convince others and themselves of their identity. They can "do gang membership" by listening to gangsta rap, wearing baggy clothing, slouching as they walk, and displaying a grandiose demeanor. The second part of the chapter examines gangs in the media. Gangs are media darlings because they provide an endless source of entertainment. The media are also complicit in creating moral panics about gangs and blowing things out of proportion, making the threat of violence seem imminent and everywhere. The Internet is a cultural phenomenon that has impacted the world of gangs.

Chapter 8 covers theories on gangs and gang behaviors. For most of the history of the study of gangs, major criminological theories have been applied to gangs, members, or their behaviors. In fewer cases, these things are explained using other, noncriminological perspectives. Theories developed specifically about gangs or gang members rarely emerge. This chapter largely focuses on such theories. It concludes by introducing a theory aimed to help explain why gang members are the victims and perpetrators of violence.

Chapter 9 is on prison gangs. Data on such gangs are relatively scant although they have become major concerns within correctional facilities. This chapter offers a near-exhaustive review of prison gangs, although some data are decades old. This reflects an overarching problem within the field: conducting research on prison gangs is difficult. Nonetheless, the available data offer important clues. In some cases, many similarities exist between prison and street gangs; in others, they are radically different. Prison violence largely occurs between members of different racial/ethnic groups, but street violence is the opposite. The number of prison gang members is uncertain because members are secretive and officials may be embarrassed about revealing such information. Such members commit a disproportionate amount of institutional infractions. Some evidence has emerged that gangs are being politically radicalized or targeting others for radicalization.

Chapter 10 is about desistance from crime in general and leaving a gang in particular. Getting involved in a gang is a simple process that can happen in a moment. Getting out is less clear. The first part of the chapter discusses in depth how and why people stop committing crime and move on to positive lifestyle choices. Many similarities have emerged between desisting from crime and leaving a gang. Leaving can be punctured by relapses—regressing back to criminal/delinquent activity or back to the gang life. Conveying to outsiders that individuals have relinquished their gang ties—particularly to law enforcement—is a difficult task.

Chapter 11 is about public health aspects, approaches, and programs geared toward gangs. Such youth come from backgrounds that public health officials recognize as putting them at risk. As members, they participate in risk behaviors at higher levels than nonmembers, such as violence, drug use, and unsafe sex, all major public health concerns. It stands to reason that youth with a heightened level of participation in risk behaviors should be at higher risk themselves. Symptoms of mental health illness, homelessness, injuries, and access to care are additional public health–related aspects discussed in this chapter. The chapter concludes by forwarding a public health agenda and approach to gangs and their members.

Chapter 12 is about gangs outside of the United States. For many years, gangs were thought to be only in America. At the turn of the 20th century, more cross-national comparisons emerged, and U.S.-style gangs are now found in various other countries. England has been a particular focus of research, but gangs have also been located in several Western European countries. Gangs and ganglike behaviors have been evident in Latin America for many years, and they are often linked to political parties, the military, and/or drug cartels. Gangs are also found in Australia and China. An important point to stress about this chapter is that the data provided are limited to that published in English. Moreover, the focus here is on empirical, academic research—not journalistic accounts.

Chapter 13 is about suppression, intervention, and prevention or a combination of the three. Of these approaches, more financial support and effort goes toward suppression. Examples include enhanced penalties for members and gang-related offenses, specialized prosecutorial and police units, and gun control. Intervention takes many forms, including programs that promote behavioral and attitudinal change, referrals to various services, and/or involvement in sports programs. Interventionists, who are often former (and sometimes current) gang members, play key roles in these efforts. Education is an important aspect of prevention. Over the course of several weeks, youth are provided grade-level curricula that warn about the consequences of gangs and/or involvement in general delinquency. At times, citywide and other approaches employ a variety of suppression, intervention, and prevention tactics.

ACKNOWLEDGMENTS

Thanks to the following who have helped over the course of my career studying gangs so far: Debbie Baskin, Dave Brotherton, Scott Decker, Karen Hennigan, Geoffrey Hunt, Mac Klein, Jim Short, Ira Sommers, and Lalo Valdez.

Data from a small research project on gangs in Los Angeles are presented here. Thanks go to the National Institute on Drug Abuse for funding this study (Grant R03 DA020410: Principal Investigator/Interviewer, B. Sanders). The views expressed herein are the author's own. Thanks also to Steve Lankenau (co-investigator, Drexel University) and Jennifer Jackson Bloom (biostatistician, Childrens Hospital Los Angeles). Thanks to Mac Klein and Penny Trickett (project consultants, University of Southern California). The assistance of the following community members is greatly appreciated because without their help, this research would not have been possible: E. Banda, outreach coordinator, St. Joseph's Center; R. Cortez at Clare Foundation; M. Diaz, director, Outreach Services for the Southern California Counseling Center, and founder and director, CleanSlate, Inc.; O. De La Torre, founder/director, and Y. De Cordova and M. Jackson, Pico Youth & Family Center; Father Greg Boyle and all the homeboys at Homeboy Industries; Skipp Townsend, founder/director of Second Chance at Loving Life (2nd Call); Virginia Avenue Teen Center, the City of Santa Monica; A. Diaz, director of operations, and J. Powell, outreach coordinator, Boys and Girls Club of Venice; F. Gutierrez, D. Gullart, and J. Godinez, Soledad Enrichment Action, Inc.; K. Shah, founder/senior advisor, & D. C. Staten, intervention specialist, Stop the Violence, Increase the Peace Foundation.

A final acknowledgment goes to the key players in making this book happen. First, to my super wife, Cheryle: you are totally awesome. Thanks to Sarah Calibi and Steve Helba and everyone else at Oxford. Thanks to all my Cal State LA criminal justice students who sent in photos and provided encouraging support. Thank you, Ben Tovar, for all your photos.

And a shout out, big ups, and thank you to all the young people who have shared their lives with me.

Bill Sanders
December 2015
San Pedro

ABOUT THE AUTHOR

Bill Sanders is a sociologist who was born and raised in Southern California. He is a professor of criminal justice at California State University, Los Angeles. Dr. Sanders has conducted ethnographic investigations on young people and crime in Los Angeles, New York, and London. He has published on a range of topics related to gangs, drugs, and public health aspects about criminal justice topics. Dr. Sanders is currently working with an intervention agency to help measure their program and capture the processes of desistance among serious juvenile and adult offenders. He is also interested in resiliency, specifically how youth from high-risk neighborhoods avoid gangs and drugs. During his free time, he enjoys surfing, snowboarding, reading, and traveling.

INTRODUCTION

This introductory chapter serves to stress two points that are important to keep in mind when reading this book. First, gangs—or groups of youth in urban areas engaging in various types of offending—have been around for a long time. What waxes and wanes over time is the public's attention toward them. The second point concerns how many gangs and gang members currently exist. If gangs are simply a group of people who offend together, then many are likely. If, on the other hand, gangs are semiorganized collectives that regenerate over time by recruiting new members, then perhaps the number is lower. The lack of a uniform definition fogs accurate estimates.

A HISTORY OF RESPECTABLE FEARS

Pearson's (1983) *Hooligan: A History of Respectable Fears* is a seminal text within British criminology and its arguments fit into the American context. Pearson contends that when different types of youth crime emerge over time, society tends to view it as something new, a radical departure from past traditions of stability and decency. As the subtitle of Pearson's work suggests, however, this is not true. The history of respectable fears is that for hundreds of years, youth crime and violence have been a focal concern. New forms of young offenders emerge each generation. The older generation tends to forget the concerns expressed about offenders when they were young and, instead, remembers a make-believe past golden age of tranquility and order. Thus, the following cycle emerges:

1. Groups of youth are demonized because of their particular offending patterns, often linked to a specific style or image;
2. These youth then age and become adults;
3. As adults, they look at the current cohort of youth and then declare things are now out of hand;
4. While doing so, they forget that adults said the same things about them when they were young.

Pearson (1983) notes that societal anxieties utilize the same rhetoric for each new cohort of young offenders. The current generation has a lack of respect for authority—parents, teachers, law enforcement—that is much more severe than in years past. The focus is typically in poorer communities, cultures of the underclass, the dangerous classes, or immigrants/refugees, who are held responsible for the moral decay (Krisberg 2005). The offenders consistently become younger, and parenting is noted as a principal cause of the new disorder. Each wave of young offenders is associated with a particular style, which becomes linked with criminality via the mass media. Substance use is also mentioned as a contributing factor, whether alcohol, cocaine, marijuana, ecstasy, or prescription drug misuse. So, too, are aspects of popular culture, often music or entertainment. Penny arcades, jazz, rock and roll, television, music videos, raves, gangsta rap, video games, and the Internet all represent aspects of popular culture that have been perceived as causing a new rise in youth crime at some point. Pearson notes that youth crime does change in form, type, and frequency, but the vocabulary used to describe it does not, nor does the overall reaction. Pearson argues that golden ages of law and order have more to do with nostalgia than reality, with the older generation wistfully yearning for yesteryear when, they believe, life was better.

If, for example, in 2010 people reminisced about bygone times 25 years past and declared things were better then, they would be repeating the cycle that Pearson describes. Murders in the mid-1980s were much higher than in the mid-2010s. Between 1985 and 1993, youth homicides (ages 10 to 24) increased 83%, but then decreased 41% from 1994 to 1999 and declined another 1% every year from 2000 to 2010 (David-Ferdon et al., 2013). The period from around 1994 until the beginning of the 21st century has been considered the Great American Crime Drop (Blumstein and Wallman, 2000; Zimring, 2006). Levels of youth homicide in the 2010s were lower than they have been for several decades.

Gangs are a long-standing concern related to youth crime and violence and have been deeply enmeshed within society for generations. Pearson notes that respectable fears will not go away with quick-fix solutions. What is required, he suggests, are long-term measures directed at encouraging more social inclusion that focuses on family, school, and community. Pearson says the system is not broken as is, but was never fixed in the first place. A key point of his argument as it relates to gangs concerns fear. In a review of 100 years of reporting on crime and disorder, Pearson found that the news bore little resemblance to actual events. The mass media were complicit in fearmongering about the severity and ubiquity of young offenders, indicating that anyone at any time was threatened. The reality was different, however, and youth crime and violence were not as widespread as reported. Societal fears did not match the genuine threat. In a similar vein, more reportage on gangs has emerged than genuine gang-related events.

The Crips wear blue and the Bloods wear red: most people with a passing interest in gangs know this. What is less apparent is that groups of young men in urban areas that have names, colors, and symbols have a long history of fighting similar groups. Pearson (1983) notes that in the 17th century, organized gangs terrorized many British cities. They were called the Dead Boys, the Mohocks, the Blues, the Roysters, Tityre Tu, and others. They committed particular types of crimes, such as "slitting the noses of their victims with swords, rolling old ladies in barrels" (Pearson, 1983, p. 188). These gangs did not always consist of uneducated youth from the slums; some were from the more affluent classes. For example, the name Tityre Tu was adopted from an opening passage in a Virgil eclogue[1] (Pearson, 1983). The gangs of pre-Victorian and Victorian England also distinguished themselves by wearing certain types of clothing and appropriating different colors. An observer in the late 19th century commented on the attire of members of a gang called the Scuttlers:

> A loose white scarf would adorn his throat; his hair was plastered down upon his forehead; he wore a peaked cap rather over one eye; his trousers were of fustian, and cut—like a sailor's—with "bell bottoms" . . . designs [on their belts] include figures of serpents, a heart pierced with an arrow. . . . Prince of Wales' feathers, clogs, animals, stars . . . and often either the name of the wearer of the belt or that of some woman. (Pearson, 1983, p. 96)

A good question to ask is, What is the next big form of youth crime and disorder? When and if a new type of youth crime replaces gangs as the next big thing, society will likely once again wish for the good old days when they believe life was better.

ESTIMATING THE NUMBER OF GANGS, GANG MEMBERS, AND GANG CRIMES

What is a gang? This simple question has been at the center of debate for decades. Age range, gender, size, longevity, commitment to delinquency, use of symbols and terminology, and other considerations have all shaped what defines the term gang. To date, sociological definitions, legal definitions, and definitions utilized within national surveys all differ. These varied definitions make it difficult to approximate the amount of gangs, gang members, and gang crimes. A chronology of how gangs have been counted follows.

Pre–Civil War Philadelphia was "plagued" with gangs (Haskins, 1974, p. 34). By the mid-20th century, the city was "swarming with gangs" (Howell, 2012, p. 7). In New York City by the mid-19th century, 30,000 gang members were believed to exist (Haskins, 1974; Spergel, 1995). Thrasher (2000) counted around 25,000 gang members in Chicago in the early 20th century. These numbers are guesses, however, not accurate estimates.

Only in the mid-1970s did efforts begin to offer more precise measures (Curry and Decker, 2003; Egley et al., 2006). W. B. Miller (1975) was the first to attempt to do this. Based on media accounts, reports from various agencies, telephone calls, and other sources, he found a link between the size of the city and the likelihood of gangs. Miller was careful to distinguish cities that had formalized gangs from those that reported the more common street groups. Of the 12 cities examined, strong evidence emerged to indicate that half contained gangs. The gangs were distinguished from street groups based on five criteria: (1) crime and violence are a major activity; (2) organization included roles and vertical hierarchies; (3) leadership was clearly defined; (4) recurring interactions happened between group members; and (5) territorial claims were made. This led W. B. Miller (1975, p. 32) to offer the following definition of a gang:

---

1   Virgil is a Latin poet who wrote the Eclogues in 37 BC. The name Tityrus appears in the First Eclogue.

A gang is a group of recurrently associating individuals with identifiable leadership and internal organization, identifying with or claiming control over territory in the community, and engaging either individually or collectively in violent or other forms of illegal behavior.

W. B. Miller's (1975) study also captured various details about the gangs in terms of ethnicity, sex, and contribution to delinquency rates. The age of members ranged from a low of 8 to a high of 22 years old. Participation in gangs was largely a male phenomenon, and Miller reported that perhaps 10% of all members were female. Most members were either African American or Hispanic, with whites comprising less than 10%. Youth in gangs were responsible for 10% of all juvenile arrests, but nearly one-third (31.5%) of all violent arrests.

W. B. Miller (1982) and others (Needle and Stapleton, 1983) conducted subsequent surveys in more cities and areas in the late 1970s and early 1980s. Miller found 2,300 different gangs with approximately 100,000 members in 300 cities and towns. Similar to his previous study, he noted that close to two in five of all serious and violent crimes were committed by members, as were approximately a quarter of all homicides. Needle and Stapleton (1983) surveyed law enforcement in 60 cities with at least 100,000 people, just under half of which (45%) reported gangs.

Several researchers in the 1980s sought to more accurately gauge estimates (Spergel, 1995). These estimates have been achieved using surveys of law enforcement agencies. One survey covered 45 cities and found 1,400 gangs and 120,500 members (Spergel, 1995; Spergel and Curry, 1990). Other surveys indicated the existence of 4,800 gangs with 249,000 members in more than 100 cities and then later estimated that at least 8,600 gangs with 378,500 members were active across the United States (Curry et al., 1994, 1996). Klein (1995) found that 9,000 different gangs containing 400,000 members were active in anywhere from 800 to 1,100 cities. W. B. Miller (2001) reported on the dramatic rise in membership over about a 30-year period. In the 1970s, as noted by W. B. Miller (2001), less than half of all states had youth gangs and no more than 300 different gangs existed. By the end of the 1990s, however, gangs were evident in every state (as well as in the District of Columbia), with more than 2,500 different groups. The number of counties that reported activity increased by more than 1,000% over this time (W. B. Miller, 2001).

This rise in the number of gangs contributed to the development of the National Youth Gang Center (later the National Gang Center) established by the Office of Juvenile Justice and Delinquency Prevention in 1994. A major role for the National Gang Center is collecting data via the National Youth Gang Survey (NYGS). They draw their data from a nationally representative sample of 2,500 to more than 4,000 law enforcement agencies in urban, suburban, and rural areas (Egley et al., 2006). The first NYGS was in 1995. The results indicated that youth gang should be defined as follows:

> a group of youths in the [respondent's] jurisdiction, aged approximately 10 to 22, that the [respondent or other] responsible persons in the [respondent's] agency or community are willing to identify or classify as a "gang." Motorcycle gangs, hate or ideology groups, prison gangs, and adult gangs were excluded. (Bilchik, 1997, p. xi)

The definition changed in 1997 when NYGS dropped the phrase "aged approximately 10 to 22" (J. P. Moore and Terrett, 1999). The following year, the definition was revised again, when "youths" replaced "youths or young adults" and "exclusively" was added before "adult gangs" (this was removed for the 2000 version but reinstated in 2001; Egley and Arjunan, 2002; J. P. Moore and Cook, 1999). The term "[respondent's]" and the like were also removed. The 2015 iteration employed in the NYGS is as follows:

> A group of youths or young adults in your jurisdiction that you or other responsible persons in your agency or community are willing to identify or classify as a 'gang.'" Respondents are requested to exclude motorcycle gangs, hate or ideology groups, prison gangs, and exclusively adult gangs from survey responses since these latter groups are characteristically distinct from youth gangs.[2]

Table A illustrates the numbers of gangs and their members for all NYGS up through the 2012 survey (Egley et al., 2014). NYGS data from 1996 to 2002 indicate significant decreases in the number of members, with a drop of more than 100,000 and a decrease of 10,000 different gangs. The number of members then began to swell, but by 2009 returned to 2002 levels, despite an increase of approximately 8,000 gangs. From 2001 to 2009, law enforcement agencies in large and small cities and suburban and rural areas reported an increase in the number of gang problems (Howell et al., 2011).

Klein and Maxson (2006) contend the NYGS definition lacks clarity, which has resulted in the inclusion of groups that are not gangs, including graffiti taggers, Satan worshippers, terrorist cells, stoners, and/or posses and crews. Klein and Maxson (2006) note that the NYGS also found more white members using this definition. When Klein and Maxson provided another definition that was closer to the one they helped develop (i.e., the Eurogang definition), they indicated that the NYGS overestimated the number of jurisdictions with gangs by 12% and the number of overall gangs by 26%. This means that the NYGS has overstated the number of members by 175,000 to more than 200,000 individuals depending on the year.

The NYGS is one estimate. In 2011, the Federal Bureau of Investigation (FBI) reported a total of 1.4 million members in the United States from approximately 33,000 different gangs (FBI, 2011).[3] The FBI indicated that gangs are responsible for about 50 to 90% of all violent offenses in various jurisdictions and are increasingly involved in nontraditional crimes, such as human trafficking, identity theft, and mortgage fraud. According to the report, gangs are also becoming more sophisticated, employing new technology and recruiting youths nationally and internationally.

Pyrooz and Sweeten (2015) offer yet another approximation. They used data from the National Longitudinal Survey of Youth 1997, a representative sample of individuals born between 1980 and 1984. Youth in this study were asked whether they were gang members.

---

2   Retrieved from https://www.nationalgangcenter.gov/Survey-Analysis#SurveySampleAndMethodology

3   Data from the FBI's 2011 National Gang Threat Assessment Issues, October 21, 2011. Retrieved from http://www.fbi.gov/news/pressrel/press-releases/2011-national-gang-threat-assessment-issued/.

TABLE A. RESULTS FROM THE NATIONAL YOUTH GANG SURVEYS[4]

Year	Gangs	Gang Members	Year	Gangs	Gang Members
1995	23,000	660,000	2004	24,000	760,000
1996	31,000	846,000	2005	26,000	790,000
1997	30,500	816,000	2006	26,500	785,000
1998	28,700	780,000	2007	27,000	788,000
1999[5]	26,000+	840,500+	2008	27,900	774,000
2000	24,500+	772,500+	2009	28,100	731,000
2001[6]	~23,500	~700,000	2010	29,000	756,000
2002	21,500	731,500	2011	29,900	782,500
2003	NA	NA	2012	30,700	850,000

Pyrooz and Sweeten then combined this response rate with population age estimates from the 2010 U.S. Census. Using this methodology, they estimated that, among youth between the ages of 5 and 17, in 2010 approximately 1,059,000 self-admitted membership, approximately 2% of all youth in this age range. The authors highlight the high turnover rate of members, with nearly as many leaving and joining gangs annually.

---

4   For 1995, see Bilchik (1997); for 1996 and 1997, see J. P. Moore and Terrett (1998, 1999); for 1998, see J. P. Moore and Cook (1999); for 1999 and 2002–2003, see Egley (2000, 2005); for 2000, see Egley and Arjunan (2002); for 2001 and 2002, see Egley and Major (2003, 2004); for 2004, see Egley and Ruiz (2006); for 2005, see Egley and O'Donnell (2008a); for 2006, see Egley and O'Donnell (2008b); for 2007, see Egley and O'Donnell (2009); for 2008, see Egley et al. (2010); for 2009, see Egley and Howell (2011); for 2010, see Egley and Howell (2012); for 2011, see Egley and Howell (2013); for 2012, see Egley et al. (2014).

5   For 1999 and 2000 surveys, the actual number of gangs and gang numbers was preceded by the words "more than."

6. For most years, the number of gangs and gang members are reported in the highlights of the survey. For 2001, this was not the case. These figures are derived from Egley et al., 2006, pp. 26–27.

CHAPTER 1

EARLY RESEARCH AND PERSPECTIVES

KEY WORDS

Anomie: In relation to crime and delinquency, anomie refers to a condition of normlessness in which individuals are uncertain of their expectations and appropriate ways to behave. Merton used this concept to explain why crime was concentrated within the lower/working-class strata in the United States. He argued that such individuals felt greater pressures or strains to achieve conventionally approved goals (e.g., money, success) through conventionally approved means (e.g., hard work, diligence). These strains might cause such individuals to offend. This is the foundation for strain theory and general strain theory.

Chicago School, the: A period of ethnographic research largely conducted in the 1920s and 1930s within impoverished, inner-city areas by sociologists from the University of Chicago, including Thomas, Park, Burgess, Shaw, McKay, Sutherland, and Merton. The theories they developed or contributed to include social disorganization, differential association/social learning theory, and anomie/general strain theory.

Delinquent subculture: A theory developed by A. K. Cohen that argues that working-class boys suffered from status frustration because of their inability to achieve culturally desired goals. As a result, they formed subcultures committed to delinquency. Such delinquency is malicious, negativistic, and wanton, but by behaving this way, the boys were able to gain status among themselves. The delinquent subculture was their solution to problems of obtaining status.

Differential association: A theory developed by Sutherland that indicates that crime is a learned behavior, like any other behavior. Prior to offending, an individual must be taught how to commit the offense (e.g., the physical properties involved in successfully completing the offense) as well as when, where, and which offenses are appropriate to commit. Offending resulted when definitions favorable to law violation outweighed those unfavorable to law violation. This is the foundation for social learning theory.

Differential opportunity theory: A theory developed by Cloward and Ohlin that extends A. K. Cohen's argument by positing the existence of three delinquent subcultures. The character of delinquency within each subculture depended on youth's access to opportunities to commit certain types of delinquency. In criminal subcultures, youth gained status through economic-oriented crimes. In conflict subcultures, status was obtained through violence. In retreatist subculture, youth gave up chasing status and instead retreated into alcohol use, substance use, homelessness, and the like.

Group processes: A theory developed by Short and Strodtbeck that argues that much of gang delinquency is spontaneous and occurs when the right individuals in particular circumstances come together. How gang boys interact with one another when these circumstances arise explains much of their delinquency. Gang boys focus on things that have little relevance to the outside world, such as their appearance and violent prowess, but make them of paramount importance because of their overall lack of ability to obtain conventional goals. Through these "group processes," gang boys transform such cultural traits into important and meaningful events and abilities.

Near-group: A concept developed by Yablonsky to discuss gangs as a social collective. Youth in near-groups were sociopathic, especially the leaders. Membership was fluid and no clear goals were apparent. Youth within these groups had delinquent values, and violence was committed against in-group members and outsiders for no apparent reason.

Social disorganization: A theory developed by Shaw and McKay which posits that crime is a result of the characteristics of an environment. According to the theory, crime is concentrated in parts of the city with the characteristics of poverty, rapid growth, no stability in the population, and heterogeneity (e.g., people of different races, cultures, religions, and nationalities all living in the same area). If an area exhibited these characteristics, that area was said to suffer from social disorganization.

Chapter Learning Objectives

- Acknowledge major milestones in the early history of gang research.
- Understand initial theoretical perspectives on gangs.
- Identify definitions of gangs.
- Outline characteristics of gangs.

INTRODUCTION

A well-known point within criminology is that juveniles offend in groups. Society has always had groups of young offenders, which have been referred to as gangs. Gangs were once viewed as a natural, inevitable aspect of inner-city life and something that youth did prior to assuming adult roles and responsibilities. Over time, however, this perception changed. Gangs became an important sociological focus in the United States in the mid-20th century and have since remained. They are now equated with violence, disorder, and fear. Significant amounts of money and effort are spent trying to combat gangs. Acknowledging gang membership can have profound negative implications. National gang databases, annual gang surveys, and federally sponsored gang prevention programs are operational. Many cities have detailed anti-gang police units and many states have enhancement laws for crimes committed by members. Gangs are now a major concentration of the justice system.

This chapter is about the evolution of gangs as a topic of study, from media-based accounts to formal investigations. The first part of the chapter examines early research and perspectives, starting with journalistic accounts in 18th- and 19th-century America. Next, the work of Thrasher is reviewed. A near-chronological overview of research from the 1950s until the early 1970s follows. This includes the work of A. K. Cohen and that of Cloward and Ohlin regarding delinquent subcultures. From here, W. B. Miller's "focal concerns" and Yablonsky's "near-group" are examined. Next, a review of Short and Strodtbeck's work on group processes and gang delinquency is provided. Then Keiser outlines various roles occupied by members. The chapter concludes with a discussion of the early work of Klein and his findings about gang intervention services.

18TH- AND 19TH-CENTURY GANGS

Remember, remember the 5th of November! These words are from a chant about Guy Fawkes's gunpowder plot, a failed attempt to blow up Parliament—the home of the British government—on November 5, 1605. A tradition emerged, and November 5 every year is known as Guy Fawkes Night. In addition to copious amounts of fireworks, part of this tradition includes setting alight an effigy of Fawkes.

B. Miller (2010) provides an overview of archival material on pre-Revolutionary War Boston, 1745. He notes how, over many years, two gangs, the North End and South End, prepared for the festivities on November 5. Each gang had rankings, such as officers, captains, and lieutenants. They had lavish costumes and spent hours constructing elaborately decorated effigies. They were also armed with all sorts of deadly weapons, including clubs, cutlasses, and staves. Every Guy Fawkes Night, they marched to a Common located near the borders of their respective territories. Following tradition, they burned effigies in celebration. After this, they battled one another. B. Miller (2010) offers an excerpt from a newspaper and a witness about the attack:

> [The gangs fell] upon each other with the utmost Rage and Fury. Several were sorely wounded and bruised, some left for dead, and rendered incapable of any business for a long time to the great Loss and Damage of their respective Masters.

> What a scandal and Infamy . . . to fall upon one another with Clubs and Cutlashes in a Rage and Fury which only Hell could inspire or the Devil broke loose from chains there could represent! . . . What madness must seize the two mobs, united Brethren . . . to fall upon each other, break one another's Bones or dash one another's Brains out?[1]

---

1   From B. Miller (2010). *Gang Warfare in 18th Century Boston.* Available at http://outofthiscentury.wordpress
   .com/2010/02/16/18th-century-gang-warfare-in-boston/.

B. Miller (2010) notes that by 1770, the North End and South End each had approximately 2,000 members. The members were not always uneducated ruffians. The leader of the North End was a 50-year-old, Harvard-educated male who studied both law and the clergy and had friends who were members of the Loyal Nine, an embryonic version of the Sons of Liberty. Each also had juvenile factions that fought with one another. B. Miller (2010) quotes one of the members of the South End gang reflecting on his time as a youth:

> Around this pole I have fought battles, as a South End boy, against the boys of the North End of town; and bloody ones, too, with slings and stones very skillfully and earnestly used. In what a state of semi-barbarism did the rising generations of those days exist! From the time immemorial these hostilities were carried on by the juvenile part of the community . . . nothing could check it. Was it a remnant of the pugilistic propensities of our British ancestors; or was it an untamed felling arising from our sequestered and colonial situation?

The November 5 battles went on for decades. They began to dwindle as more British soldiers arrived in the 1760s, and then they focused on attacking a common enemy (B. Miller, 2010). Their battles with soldiers became a frequent occurrence in Boston prior to the Revolutionary War (B. Miller, 2010).

Postrevolutionary gangs were youth groups fighting over local territory, not serious criminal organizations (Howell, 2012; Howell and Moore, 2010; Spergel, 1995). Around 1820, things began to change with an uptick in immigration (Howell, 2012; Spergel, 1995). Wave after wave of people from various European countries arrived, with different languages, cultures, and styles and little money or prospects, and they were forced to live in poor areas. For economic and protective reasons, they lived together, forming small communities that would later be referred to as the Irish, Italian, or Polish areas of the city. Youth gangs emerged to exercise power and control with what little resources were available (Howell, 2012). Many of their members were employed in the services of the speakeasies—vegetable stores that served as fronts to sell alcohol at lower rates (Ashbury, 1927). In 1826, one of the first gangs with an identifiable leadership was called the Forty Thieves, a collection of tough guys, robbers, and pickpockets (Howell, 2012; Shelden et al., 2001).

New York City was a focus in the early to mid-19th century, particularly within the Five Points area, when more serious gangs were considered to have emerged (Sante, 1991). Ashbury (1927) studied the Dead Rabbits, Bowery Boys, Plug Uglies, Shirt Tails, and other gangs and cataloged the origin and significance of their uniforms. Like contemporary gangs, they could be identified by symbols that connected them: the Plug Uglies wore large Plug hats; the Shirt Tails wore their shirts untucked outside their trousers; and the Dead Rabbits had a rabbit impaled on a pike (Ashbury, 1927; Haskins, 1974). They largely fought with one another and had vicious rivalries (Ashbury, 1927). One of the most famous rivalries was between the Bowery Boys and the Dead Rabbits. These were two megagangs—conglomerations of many smaller gangs that lived in close proximity—that fought on a weekly basis between the 1830s and the 1860s (Ashbury, 1927; Spergel, 1995). These battles would last for days and each gang incurred their share of death, maiming, and beatings (Spergel, 1995).

In late-19th-century New York City, poor, young, uneducated Irish and Italian immigrants who could not find work formed gangs for social and practical reasons (Decker and Van Winkle, 1996; Spergel, 1995). They served additional purposes in the community. Haskins (1974) notes how politicians tapped into their intimidation potential in Five Points by leveraging gangs' meeting places—saloons and dance halls. If gang members did favors for the politicos, like frightening unsupportive citizens to keep them from voting and assaulting political opponents, then they would be allowed to continue to use these meeting places. Haskins (1974) reports that most local politicians had gangs working for them. They also helped law enforcement during this time, although in a different fashion. Sante (1991) notes how the police allowed members to kill one another or kill themselves with alcohol to help eliminate difficult people in slum areas. The idea was to let the chaos in the inner city run rampant so the troublemakers wiped each other out.

THRASHER: THE FIRST GANG RESEARCHER

Thrasher is the godfather of gang research and his work is part of the tradition of criminology's Chicago School. Gangs have been around much longer than Thrasher, but reports that emerged prior to his research were journalistic. Thrasher's book is considered the first academic study of the topic. He studied many gangs in Chicago as well, mapping out troubled areas. The subtitle of his 1927 publication, *The Gang: A Study of 1,313 Gangs in Chicago* (2000), is an inside joke among colleagues: 1,313 was apparently the address of a local brothel (Howell, 2012; J. Katz and Jackson-Jacobs, 2007). Regardless of the actual numbers, Thrasher's study remains a landmark contribution. He notes that gang culture in Chicago can be traced back to feudal and medieval times and even to a tribal ethos of codes related to glory, honor, and respect. Some of his insights, particularly on how he defines gangs, have been echoed in contemporary discussions (Brotherton, 2008a; Dimitriadis, 2006; Hagedorn, 1998).

Thrasher's work is a contribution to social disorganization theory (see Box 1.1). His map of the location of all of Chicago's gangs fits nicely with Park and Burgess's (1925) transitional zones in their concentric map of Chicago. Thrasher said that gangs were found in Chicago's "interstitial" areas, those "spaces that intervene between one thing and another . . . fissures and breaks in the structure of social organization" (2000, p. 6). These areas were considered part of Chicago's poverty belt, characterized by deteriorating neighborhoods, populations in flux, poor employment opportunities, slums, and general isolation—geographic, moral, and cultural—from the areas of business, industry, and residence. These aspects were interwoven with other conditions that gave rise to gangs, including poor schooling and ineffective parenting, lack of recreational activities for youth, and interactions with negative peers. The overall result was weak and ineffective institutions that led to a lack of social control. This and the overall tumult in the community are reasons that gangs emerged. Thrasher provides a definition using the word interstitial again:

> The gang is an interstitial group originally formed spontaneously, and then integrated through conflict. It is characterized by the following types of behavior: meeting face to face, milling, movement through space as a unit, conflict, and planning. The result of this

---

BOX 1.1: SOCIAL DISORGANIZATION THEORY

Social disorganization theory has been perceived as beneficial in helping to explain why gangs first arose. Spergel (1995) provides a definition:

> Social disorganization refers to the ineffective articulation of elements of social structure, and even the personality system, at various levels of value, action, and relationship. At societal and community levels, social disorganization is often associated with, or a consequence of, large and rapid population movements of minority low-income or working-class groups; social, political, economic changes or political disruption, for example, the influx of a minority population from another country, or from central city to smaller cities, towns, or the suburbs; war or revolution; rapid industrialization or urbanization; a radical shift in the labor market; or the failure of key socializing and control institutions, such as schools, law enforcement, employers, and youth agencies to understand and develop policy and programs to appropriately meet the needs of a different, new or changing

population. These social structural elements may be distinct yet interacting. (p. 152)

Although its origins are older, the theory was formally developed by Shaw and McKay (1942) and is part of the Chicago School, a strong body of criminological research focusing on ecological contributions to crime and disorder. Many researchers have related social disorganization to the emergence and proliferation of gangs (see Decker and Van Winkle, 1996; Hagedorn, 1988, 1998; Pyrooz et al., 2010; Sullivan, 1989; C. S. Taylor, 1990; C. Taylor, 1993; see also Klein, 1995; Howell, 2012; J. W. Moore, 1991; Shelden et al., 2001; Spergel, 1995). A related concept is called collective efficacy (Sampson et al., 1997), which relates to the extent of disorganization within communities (Howell, 2012). Social disorganization and collective efficacy have been used to explain gang homicide (Curry and Spergel, 1988; Mares, 2010; Papachristos and Kirk, 2006; see also Costanza and Helms, 2012; Pyrooz, 2012). Social disorganization theory cannot explain why gangs emerge in stable lower-class communities and ignores other considerations that give rise to gangs (Howell, 2012).

> collective behavior is the development of tradition, unreflective internal structure, *esprit de corps*, solidarity, morale, group awareness, and attachment to a local territory. (2000, pp. 18–19, emphasis in original)

Interstitial refers to a period of time between childhood and adulthood, wherein gangs were something that boys did prior to becoming men. All potential playgroups could be gangs, and they morph into gangs when they come into conflict with other, similar playgroups. Without conflict, they simply remain groups. Thrasher's definition does not include offending as a characteristic. Among the 1,313 gangs, more than half either were nondelinquent or the delinquency within them remained uncertain.

Gangs formed in stages. The first is the most tender, and loose leadership and a lack of cohesion result in an early death of the collective. If or when the gang progresses to the next stage, it becomes more solid. Conflict with other similar groups leads to cohesion among members and strengthens group boundaries. Violence creates solidarity.

Boys often leave during this period, and most go on to lead conventional lifestyles. Those who remain move on to the final stage: a commitment to delinquency. Their lack of conventional lifestyles means that the gang becomes their only economic option.

Thrasher noted differences between gangs. They were largely European immigrants and were predominantly formed around nationality (e.g., Irish gangs, Polish gangs, Italian gangs). White gangs were involved in serious offending, such as murder, extortion, and bootlegging. Black gangs were fewer in number, and they were primarily involved in petty theft and gambling (e.g., shooting craps). Thrasher described groups within groups, or subgroups. These subgroups included the core members, such as the leader and his lieutenants, the main body—rank-and-file members—and then those on the fringes, the marginal members. The small cliques that consisted of two to three youth were more co-hesive and more important to an individual youth than the overall gang. If conflict emerged between the gang's desires and those of the clique, a youth would always go along with his closest mates.

GANGS AS DELINQUENT SUBCULTURES

During the 1950s and 1960s, the term delinquent subculture was synonymous with gangs. Subcultures were a common focus during this time, and several attempts were made to help capture and contextualize why they formed and the functions they served the youth. What is important about this phase of research is the effort to construct theories. Prior to the work on delinquent subcultures, gang studies were largely atheoretical.

A. K. Cohen (1955) explained the origin of the delinquent subculture and reasons that its participants committed certain offenses. According to Cohen, the delinquent subculture was the solution to the working-class boys' problem of attaining status. He drew the first part of his theory—Why are there delinquent subcultures?—from Merton's (1938) strain theory (see Box 1.2). Like everyone else, working-class boys want to obtain conventional goals, such as money, property, and respect, because they confer status. The boys experience more strains toward achieving these goals legitimately. As a result, they suffer what A. K. Cohen refers to as "status frustration"—the inability to achieve status in the eyes of peers.

A. K. Cohen (1955) noted that juveniles are more likely to commit their crimes in groups. He said that the crimes juveniles committed seemed to serve no tangible purpose and were mean-spirited and what he called negativistic because they rejected middle-class values. Juveniles stole things they did not need, vandalized property for no apparent reason, and attacked others out of cruelty. These were not the types of crimes that adults

---

BOX 1.2:   STRAIN THEORY

Merton originally developed strain theory in 1938. The theory provides an explanation of the concentration of crime among lower-class urban areas. Merton borrowed Durkheim's (1897) concept of anomie—or state of normlessness—to describe the condition of modern America. Merton saw U.S. society as a balance between culturally approved goals (e.g., financial success, material goods, respect) and society's culturally approved means (e.g., hard work, thrift, diligence). Anomie occurred when dissociation existed between the approved goals and the approved means to obtain them. This dissociation could result in an individual circumventing the approved means (e.g., committing crime) to obtain such goals. Individuals did so, according to Merton, because they felt pressures or strains toward obtaining those goals.

Merton argued that the existence of a disjuncture between American goals and means explained crime among the poor. He said that the United States places a strong cultural emphasis on success (the goal), but that this emphasis is not matched by an equally strong focus on obtaining it (the means). Everyone, including the poor, is socialized to aspire to success and is constantly bombarded with it via schools and the media, creating a tremendous amount of pressure. Disadvantaged communities—largely poor and minority ones—do not have equal access to legitimate opportunities to be successful and, as such, are more likely to resort to illegitimate means to obtain success.

Agnew (1992) later expanded on this to create general strain theory, which includes other stressful life events that are not economic based (e.g., divorce, abuse). Some researchers have found support for strain theory when explaining why youth join gangs (Brownfield et al., 1997; Eitle et al., 2004). Strain theory has been criticized as being overpredictive of delinquency and of ignoring the fact that much crime is a group activity, not an individual one.

BOX 1.3:   DIFFERENTIAL ASSOCIATION THEORY

Sutherland developed differential association theory in 1939. The theory states that crime is like any other behavior in that it must be learned from others, particularly intimates (e.g., friends and family). Two specific things are taught: how to commit the crime and the attitudes, drives, motives, and rationalizations related to it. Individuals learn that certain crimes at certain times are deemed acceptable by friends and family and then behave accordingly. Specifically, crime occurs when definitions favorable to law violation [outweigh] definitions unfavorable to violation of the law. People are more prone to commit crime if others around them also believe that committing crime is acceptable. Additional considerations, such as social class, race/ethnicity, and family life, influence the likelihood of associating with individuals who find circumstances favorable to crime.

Sutherland's work has had a significant impact on the field of criminology. It spurred other major contributions that continue to receive wide empirical support. One such contribution is Sykes and Matza's (1957) techniques of neutralization, which argue that when people break the law, they know they are doing something wrong and feel guilty about it. They learn that committing particular offenses is justifiable and offer statements that neutralize such guilt (e.g., nobody got hurt, everyone is doing it). Another example is social learning theory, developed by R. L. Akers (1985). His work essentially fleshes out the initial learning process, including the mechanisms by which crime is learned, how it continues, and how other variables shape the process. A third is Thornberry's (1987) interactional theory, which argues that crime can be explained by the interaction of social control and social learning variables.

Several researchers have found support for social learning theory and gangs (Battin-Pearson et al., 1998; Brownfield et al., 1997; Deschenes and Esbensen, 1999; Kissner and Pyrooz, 2009; Roman et al., 2012; Winfree et al., 1994).

committed and could not be explained by Merton's theory. A. K. Cohen argued that boys committed these types of crimes to achieve status: not status in the conventional sense of the term, but in the eyes of their peers. In this respect, Sutherland heavily influenced Cohen's work. Sutherland (1939) developed differential association theory, which argues that crime is learned, like any other behavior (see Box 1.3). A. K. Cohen surmised that the types of offenses must be committed to impress others within that subculture. The answer to the second part of Cohen's theory—What purpose do these crimes serve the working-class boys?—draws on the importance of peers. By circumventing the rules and committing particular types of crime, youth could overcome status frustration.

Delinquent subcultures were formed in a process A. K. Cohen (1955) called "reaction formation": the delinquent boys were never going to attain status in the eyes of the dominant culture, so they rejected the rejecters and flipped these values on their head. The boys were good at being mean and destroying things, so by championing these behaviors, they attained status within their world.

A. K. Cohen and Short (1958) later expanded on this work by describing a variety of subcultures, each with a focus on a different type of offense. The delinquent subculture was renamed the parent male subculture, which remained nonutilitarian, malicious, and negativistic. This was the most common type of subculture and was small and informal. Another was the conflict-oriented subculture, which was large and relatively organized, with subgroupings and outside alliances. A third is the drug addict subculture. Delinquency in this subculture was utilitarian in that offenses were committed to generate money for drugs. A fourth is the semiprofessional theft subculture. These youth committed systematic, economically oriented offenses, which took up much of their time. They were older—around 16 or 17—and had once been a part of a parent male subculture. A fifth is the middle-class subculture, which emerged because of problems adjusting to middle-class lifestyles. These boys' mothers mollycoddled them, and participation in a delinquent subculture allowed them the opportunity to be masculine. A. K. Cohen and Short (1958) also reported on girls who participated in a female delinquent subculture. They committed delinquency and deviance because of a lack of education in virtuous behaviors and feelings of status frustration. Sexual promiscuity was theorized as a way for girls to overcome these issues.

DIFFERENTIAL OPPORTUNITY THEORY

Cloward and Ohlin's (1960) differential opportunity theory influenced policy— among the most profound impacts that a theory on youth gangs would ever have on approaches toward reducing delinquency (Klein, 1995; Spergel, 1995). Cloward and Ohlin borrowed the concept of the delinquent subculture from A. K. Cohen and

strain theory from Merton to develop what they coined differential opportunity theory. Deviant opportunities were seized by young men not simply to be malicious, as Cohen argues, but rather because these opportunities allowed them to circumvent the lack of legitimate opportunities for success.

Like A. K. Cohen and Short, Cloward and Ohlin (1960) reported on different types of subcultures. All were concentrated in poor, inner-city areas and consisted of delinquent boys. The type of subculture that emerged was dependent on the opportunities within the area to participate in certain types of delinquency. One of these subcultures had what was referred to as the presence of legitimate activities (i.e., everyday shops and businesses) alongside illegitimate ones (i.e., organized criminal syndicates). Organized crime feeds off legitimate businesses and can only exist in areas where such businesses operate. Youth within these areas were able to form what Cloward and Ohlin referred to as the criminal subculture. These youth committed money-generating crimes like extortion and theft. They were able to commit these crimes because adults in the criminal syndicates taught them how. The adults policed youth in terms of appropriate dress, demeanor, and behavior in public. They molded them, teaching them the benefits of maintaining a low profile so as to not attract attention. The criminal subculture was important to these adults because it served as a pool of juveniles from which future members of organized crime were drawn. Youth in this type of subculture were similar to Merton's innovator, who circumvented the laws to attain the goal of success.

Not all working-class areas have organized crime. Some are socially disorganized and do not have the legitimate businesses that organized crime needs to survive. Youth growing up in these environments do not have the opportunities to become part of criminal subcultures because no adults are around to teach them how to commit money-generating crimes. Facing this void and still wanting success, youth form what Cloward and Ohlin (1960) call conflict subcultures. Violence is prized, and the most vicious are the most respected. These youth are still illegitimately successful, but in this case it is because of their capacity for violence. Youth residing in areas with the presence of legitimate and illegitimate opportunities but who did not have the wherewithal to commit economically oriented crimes also joined conflict subcultures.

Cloward and Ohlin (1960) note that some youth in areas that were socially disorganized were not good at fighting. These youth were considered double failures: they were unable to be successful legitimately or through fighting or money-making crimes. As a result, they gave up and withdrew into substance use, homelessness, and the like. Much of their time was spent in various stages of intoxication and eluding the police. Cloward and Ohlin called these youth part of a retreatist subculture.

Cloward and Ohlin's theory of differential opportunity helped shape one of the largest delinquency prevention programs in the United States. The policies and programs that emerged with the Johnson administration's Committee on Juvenile Delinquency and Youth Crime of the 1960s were based largely on their theory (Spergel, 1995). One of these programs was called Mobilization for Youth (Krisberg, 2005). Rather than individual pathology, an emphasis was placed on increasing opportunities for youth in inner-city areas to decrease delinquency. This emphasis became a major part of the reform movements referred to as the Great Society, or War on Poverty.

Spergel (1964), a student of Cloward and Ohlin, examined their theory in three unknown areas on the East Coast he called Racketville, Slumtown, and Haulberg. His data were based on firsthand ethnographic fieldwork. Spergel offered support for the theory, and the type of offending that youth participated in was dependent on access to criminal and conventional opportunities. Each town Spergel studied was named after its most common type of delinquency. In Racketville, where organized criminal activities were prevalent, he found evidence of criminal subcultures. All sorts of opportunities were available in this area, including prostitution, drugs, and gambling. These opportunities were well integrated with other, conventional opportunities and run in a smooth, businesslike fashion. Youth in the criminal subcultures would eventually graduate into organized crime in Racketville.

Slumtown was socially disorganized. Youth had few chances at either legitimate or illegitimate economic success, so they turned to violence to gain status. Spergel (1995) found evidence for the conflict subculture, where reputations built on heart, toughness, and courage were paramount. Gangs waged organized battles to test reputations that needed to be consistently proven. The glory of the successful fighter was short lived.

Another area was called Haulberg. Spergel (1995) found limited criminal and conventional opportunities here, but they were both stable. Theft was the most common form of delinquency, and the youth coalesced into subcultures. Thievery centered on burglary, forgery, shoplifting, and theft of and from motor vehicles. The best thieves were the ones with the most status, although youth in Haulberg were involved in gangs for a short period of time. Spergel noted that each of the delinquent subcultures had its own cohorts of drug users, as opposed to finding a specific retreatist subculture.

Spergel (1995) also examined an intervention program, focusing particularly on the role of detached youth workers. Since at least the advent of the Chicago Area Project in the 1930s, many gang and delinquency intervention programs have relied on these individuals (Krisberg, 2005). Detached youth workers generally engage gang and delinquent youth within their environments, as opposed to having youth attend functions at particular community-based organizations. Most, if not all, detached youth workers have personal experiences with gangs and/or delinquency. These experiences helped them to work with current gang youth. Spergel indicated that the practice of gang and delinquency intervention must be theoretically informed and that those operating the program should know how and why gangs emerge in the first place. Successful programs required an appreciation and understanding of interrelated components. These included the workings of the delinquent subculture and their norms and values, the individual youth who operated within them, and the detached youth workers' ability to engage both the group and its individuals. Many suggestions on how to properly operationalize community-wide gang intervention programs emerged in this study and have now become incorporated into a program referred to as the Spergel model.

The subcultural perspectives on gang delinquency were popular for a time because they contextualized its group nature. Other theories to this point focused on individual rather than collective reasons. Much delinquency occurred in groups, and the concept of the delinquent subculture fits with this finding. But the subcultural conceptualizations did not explain other crimes that were primarily performed individually, such as rape or murder. These types of crimes could be compulsive and are not explained well vis-à-vis delinquent subcultures. Matza (1964) provided the most crucial blow to the subcultural perspectives by indicating that they overpredicted delinquency. If working-class boys rejected middle-class values, as A. K. Cohen (1955) argued, or formed different types of delinquent subcultures, as Cloward and Ohlin (1960) noted, then more of them would be apparent. Matza famously quipped about the existence of a subculture of delinquency, but not a delinquent subculture. Matza emphasized free will and freedom of choice, but the delinquent subculture thesis did not entertain these traits. Instead, committing certain delinquent acts within the delinquent subcultures was mandatory, and this aspect did not stand up to empirical findings. Youth committed delinquency and they committed it in groups, but these groups were rarely delinquent subcultures as outlined.

LOWER-CLASS CULTURE AND ADOLESCENCE

The prior theories largely focus on structure to explain gang behaviors. Cultural theorists saw gangs as a natural phenomenon of the lower-class youth that boys eventually grew out of. Based on years of research with many gangs or corner groups, W. B. Miller (1958) devised a cultural deviance theory or lower-class theory about gangs (Spergel, 1995). The subcultural perspective viewed gangs as a major delinquent product. W. B. Miller argues that gang boys did not reject middle-class norms and values inasmuch as they embraced lower-class ones. He says that lower-class culture has a set of focal concerns, particularly emphasized by male youths, which guide their beliefs and actions. In this context, gang delinquency was viewed as a way of life. Youth who faced the biggest gap between their aspirations and their realizations were most likely to heavily focus on these concerns and be more prone to delinquency. W. B. Miller outlined six focal concerns:

- Toughness: Defined as strength, grit, courage, and manliness. Tattoos and the sexual objectifications of women were signs of toughness, but sentimentality and appreciation for the arts were not. Squaring off with others, no matter what the circumstance, was also an indicator of toughness.
- Trouble: Getting into trouble in relation to fighting or females was valued, but so too was knowing how to avoid trouble with law enforcement. Savvy around avoiding detection in the course of delinquency was prized.
- Fate: Fate referred to the idea that an individual's life path has already been carved out for them. They were simply destined to follow it. "Life's just like that for us; we can't do anything about it" captures the sentiment.
- Excitement: Excitement referred to the pursuit of thrills as a worthy goal, and adrenaline-seeking behaviors were applauded. All sorts of gambling were sources of excitement. So, too, were chases (e.g., by law enforcement or other gangs or adults).
- Smartness: Today, this could be described as "street smarts," or the physical and psychological ability to negotiate, maneuver around, and/or foresee difficult life situations or beneficial ones within urban environments. Smartness also includes the ability to dupe others, but not be duped.
- Autonomy: Being self-governed and not letting others determine individual behavior. This focal concern was reflected in a general resentment of authority figures and those who made the rules.

W. B. Miller (1958) noted a lack of adult male role models and reported that female-run households were common within the lower classes. Boys and young men, as a result, sought to develop and test masculine traits on the streets with youth going through similar experiences. Youth gangs, according to Miller, did not engage in serious intergang conflict, but fought among themselves—a finding that would ring true more than half a century later.[2] The types of delinquency gangs committed were serious, but were viewed as standard reactions to growing up within a lower-class environment. The gang boys would eventually become men and assume adult responsibilities related to work and marriage.

Bloch and Niederhoffer's (1958) conclusions about gangs are similar to those of W. B. Miller. The gang can be found in all cultures as a way for boys to achieve adulthood, but is more pronounced in cultures that delay the onset of adult responsibilities. Bloch and Niederhoffer looked at different cultures in several countries and noted that all youth strive for adult status. Some societies, such as the United States, do not adequately prepare the youth for this transition. As a result, boys establish their own culture as a way of preparing for entry into manhood, creating gangs. Bloch and Niederhoffer's anthropological study indicates that the rites found within American street gangs mimic those of manhood

---

2   W. B. Miller later revised his view of gangs and found them to be extremely violent (W. B. Miller, 1975).

among boys in other cultures. They are found in tribal and native cultures on various continents and surround puberty, including circumcision and decorations that distinguish boys from men. They provide status. Gangs in the United States are similar in that they engage in various forms of delinquency that serve as rites of passage to manhood. Power and control are important within gang culture, and manipulation and domination of other people and events are ways to prove manhood. A gang provides an outlet for boys to develop ego, courage, and power—qualities associated with being a man.

Bordua (1961) leveled two critiques at the perspective of W. B. Miller. He panned it for being tautological, essentially explaining a way of life as a way of life (see also Wooten, 1978). Bordua noted all lower classes are *not* isolated from mainstream society. The idea that lower-class individuals have their own set of values ignores the fact that most are law abiding. Many have what were perceived as middle-class values and participate in middle class–dominated institutions, such as school. A similar critique can be charged against Bloch and Niederhoffer's work: most boys from lower/working-class communities do not commit crime—and even fewer will join gangs. Nonetheless, the impact of the research of W. B. Miller and Bloch and Niederhoffer was profound. The focus on cultural determinants to explain gang behaviors was a fresh and novel approach.

GANGS AS NEAR-GROUP

Yablonsky (1959, 1962) focused on gang violence. Similar to Thrasher, he found different types: delinquent, violent, and social. The violent gang was the most problematic. It emerged in relation to external threats and served to protect its members from victimization. These gangs were loosely structured but, like Thrasher, Yablonsky noted that the small cliques within them were much more cohesive and important to individual members than the gang in its entirety. Leaders in violent gangs simply arose, and they were psychologically disturbed. Violence became a way of life and would arise in relation to the smallest provocation. The gang provided an outlet for the boys to express violence.

Yablonsky argued that the violent gang was a "near-group" in terms of its levels of organization. He notes three general social collectives: social groups, mobs/crowds, and his term—near-groups. A standard group is identifiable, with a specific range of participants, and involves some form of self-recognition to delineate in-group from out-group members. Those within groups have clearly defined roles and expectations as well as norms and values, which align with the values of the broader society. Mobs spontaneously form around a specific event and then disperse. Contact within these groups is limited and roles and membership are confusing, if present. Near-groups fall between these two extremes. Values, membership statuses, and behavioral norms within violent gangs, Yablonsky argues, are less clear compared to those in groups, but more clear compared to those in mobs. The violent gang as a near-group has several characteristics (Yablonsky, 1962, 1997), including the following:

- Individuals within near-groups are sociopathic and more so tend to hold leadership and core positions. They cannot function within other social groups because of these personality traits. Violence is random and sporadic, against both outsiders and in-group members.

BOX 1.4:   MEDIA CHECK!

80 Blocks from Tiffany's

What do a documentary about gangs in New York City in the late 1970s and the music videos for Paul Simon's "Call Me Al" and the Bangles' "Walk Like an Egyptian" in the 1980s have in common? The director, Gary Weis. His *80 Blocks from Tiffany's* focuses on two gangs in the South Bronx, the Savage Nomads and Savage Skulls, as well as how different people in the community interact with and respond to them. Weis provides interview footage he collected from current and ex-gang members, community and business owners, successful older hustlers, juveniles who might join a gang, and professionals who work with them, including clergy and law enforcement. The documentary emerged in 1979, the same year as a famous Hollywood movie about gangs—*The Warriors*. Whereas *The Warriors* is a comic caricature of gangs in New York City in the late 1970s, *80 Blocks from Tiffany's* is gritty reality.

Violence among gang youth is endemic and casual. One youth recalls all the violent crimes he has committed—shootings, stabbings, beatings—but that these events do not mean he is a bad person or immune from success. Violence was a way of life in the South Bronx. A hustler reflects on the violence by telling a story of a shootout in the middle of the street. He says that during this incident, others in the immediate vicinity—girls skipping rope, older gentlemen reading or playing dominoes, two youth throwing a football—hardly looked up to see what was happening. The type of weaponry available was incredible. One gang member, Fly, says, "I've seen 357s, I've seen 12 gauge shotguns. . . . I've seen 45 military specials with clip. I've seen fucking Thompsons. . . . I've seen hand grenades. I've seen big beer can bazookas made. Damn things hit you it's just as getting hit with a gun. I've seen 22s zip gun. I've seen 38 zip gun. . . . I've seen dynamite . . . on the street."

Weis also interviews female members, one after being hit in the face when she got caught between a fight among two gang males. Gang girls use the same language surrounding respect, violence, and street life as guys. The sexist attitude of male gang members is glaringly apparent. So, too, are the double standards: a gang male demands a classy female who can intellectually stimulate him (if one should exist, he notes). One of the girls, India, talks about how her gang gets along with the Savage Nomads. But, she continues, her gang tries to not prevent her from wanting to go back to school. "School is more important," she says.

A theme of moving on and getting by emerges within the documentary. Older members desire more in life and want to leave their childhood in the gang behind. One member talks about how he had a tattoo that said "Born to Lose" removed because now he feels differently. He has a message for the younger members: "You better wake up before you never wake up again. . . . It's not nice to be hard." Another is afraid of dying and wants to live, asking, "What's life, huh?" A blog on the website that shows the documentary says that some of the gang members interviewed are currently doing all right. Several others were murdered or died from a drug overdose many years ago.

One interesting aspect is how the community views the gangs. Several people, including shopkeepers, value the members. Community members mention some important functions gangs perform, such as neighborhood policing. A shopkeeper tells the story of how when riots erupted and buildings were on fire, members protected his business from being destroyed. A community resident indicates how Fly, although he is a rascal, helps keep the peace. Evidence that some gangs serve prosocial purposes is clearly presented.

The last 10 minutes of the film are more upbeat and cover a block party. During this time, a disco beat plays and India toasts the community on the microphone, saying "Yes, yes, ya'll. Freaken to the beat, ya'll." This is significant because it reflects a new form of music that emerged in the South Bronx around this time: hip-hop. A sister documentary, *Rubble Kings*, discusses the role the South Bronx gangs had in the development of hip-hop music and culture, including the Savage Nomads and Savage Skulls. As another aside, the stogie-smoking Father Louis Gigante is interviewed about his work with South Bronx gangs. He is the brother of the former leading members of he Genovese mafia, including Vincent "The Chin" Gigante, who was considered the most powerful organized-crime boss in the United States.

Please visit YouTube to watch 80 Blocks from Tiffany's.

- The gang fulfills individual and emotional needs related to masculinity, but demands little in terms of individual requirements. No consensus on acceptable behaviors is evident.
- Membership is fluid, and members drift in and out of core and peripheral positions. Leadership fluctuates depending on the particular behavior at the moment.
- Norms and values are generally deviant/delinquent, but no clear goals exist.

Few researchers have found support for Yablonsky's sociopathic gang members (Cummings, 1993; J. Patrick, 1973). Others, however, have argued that gangs are not amoral and rarely exhibit psychotic tendencies (Decker, 1996; Hagedorn, 1998; W. B. Sanders, 1994). Violence is a common feature, but deadly violence is much less so. If members were sociopathic, then deadly violence would be common. Few gangs commit deadly violence and some gangs are deadlier than others. Research after Yablonsky has reported that members are not psychologically disturbed, but have values similar to the general population (W. B. Sanders, 1994, 1997). Also, gangs talk about violence more than they commit it, giving the impression that battles are fought on a near-daily basis (Decker, 1996; Decker and Van Winkle, 1996; Klein, 1995).

GROUP PROCESS AND GANG DELINQUENCY

An important legacy of research was its focus on the group influences toward delinquency. The less ephemeral groups are considered gangs. But what motivates youth to commit delinquency? Something about the collective must be related to individual criminal behavior. Short and Strodtbeck's (1965) research entitled *Group Process and Gang Delinquency* is a landmark study that addresses this point. What is remarkable about this study is its methodology. The authors studied white and black and poor and middle-class gangs using qualitative and quantitative data from multiple sources, including police records, self-report data from gang and non-gang youth, and reports from detached youth workers about individual members. Their research included an evaluation of a gang intervention program. Among contemporary standards on the study of street gangs, the methods of Short and Strodtbeck's research remain exemplary.

Short and Strodtbeck's (1965) work was theoretically informed in that they sought to test theories on gangs and delinquency. However, they found little support for these theories. A key problem pertained to how theories depicted gang youth as being committed to delinquency. The authors reported that most of the time youth were involved in nondelinquent activities, such as hanging out, a point that remains true today (Klein, 1995; Spergel, 1995). Delinquency was a relatively small part of their lives, and youth were not nearly as devoted to it as other perspectives suggested. The authors noted five characteristics of gangs: conflict; having sex, hanging out, drinking, and selling drugs/alcohol; having illegitimate children; violence; and auto-related thefts. Short and Strodtbeck (1965) noted that these same behaviors were common among non-gang youth. Like Yablonsky, the authors found that gangs had shifting membership and leadership, and their overall structures and group norms were nebulous. Youth would drift in and out, with members not being seen or noticed for days or even weeks at a time. Gang cohesion and commitment were relatively weak.

Status was important to members, and any threats were taken seriously and held great significance. Status threats were a major source of conflict and "status management" was paramount for boys (Short and Strodtbeck, 1965, p. 215). Threat is the reason gangs emerge. This threat comes from three areas. One is adult institutions, such as school, work, and law enforcement. Gang boys did not do well at school and had poor relations with the police and limited job prospects, which have no chance of providing status. Threats also come from the culture of the community, such as organized recreational and athletic clubs. The boys lacked athletic skills and were barely organized. However, they ranked high in notoriety and fighting skills. A final threat to boys' status related to the culture of street gangs in the surrounding neighborhood. Different gangs in various locations throughout lower-class communities were a constant threat. These gangs were actively seeking status by venturing into neighboring communities, looking for fights. Boys also needed an audience in which to act out, and gangs provided it.

Short and Strodtbeck's (1965) most important contribution from this research was also the most overlooked: the centrality of group processes (Klein, 1995; Short, 2006). The authors developed what they refer to as the group process perspective, which indicates how interactions among members help develop their culture. Opportunities to become involved in delinquency emerged impromptu: criminal and violent events were less planned and more dependent on the right elements serendipitously coming together at the right time with the right people. The way in which the individual members interacted with one another in the presence of these opportunities helped explain much of gang crime.

Short and Strodtbeck (1965) argued that most gang youth generally seek out and approve conventional goals, but are not taught the skills and values that will allow them to obtain stable employment. School is not for them and they have no other educational alternatives. Their families have been torn apart by fear, economic stress, and helplessness. Gang boys rely on themselves and the streets to provide gratification and socialization. They have bleak prospects, so instead they focus on how they dance, dress, and fight, all short-term consequences. These cultural aspects mean nothing to the outside world, but through interactions within the gang—group processes—they are of paramount importance. As the authors note, "the process of interaction within a group transforms culture" (Short and Strodtbeck, 1965, p. 273). Several of W. B. Miller's focal concerns, including toughness, smartness, and fate, were evident within this culture. Delinquency, violence, and substance use were culturally acceptable ways for gang boys to join the action, achieve something, and obtain instant gratification.

ROLES WITHIN GANGS: KEISER AND THE VICE LORDS

The research examined to this point focused almost exclusively on gangs in terms of their relationship with the community and society. The main questions research sought to answer were: Why did gangs exist? and Why did gang boys commit delinquency? Keiser's (1969) research with the Vice Lords was different in that it sought to detail the social organization and cultural systems of the gang. He chose to study the Vice Lords because they were one of the largest and better-organized gangs in Chicago, and, perhaps more important, because he was able to befriend current members. Keiser approached the leaders of a faction of the gang known as the City Lords. Keiser told the leaders he wanted to write a book and that he would share any royalties generated from it. The gang held a meeting in which they voted about Keiser's plan and the vote passed. The Vice Lords would later emerge to become a nationally known gang under the umbrella People Nation with thousands of members (Knox and Papachristos, 2002; Short, 2006).

Like other street gangs, Keiser indicates that the Vice Lords began as a social club, but later morphed into a fighting gang because of tumult in the community surrounding other,

BOX 1.5: ON TRIAL

This case involves a young man who self-identifies as a gang member. He has the name of the gang tattooed across his forehead, accompanied by tattoos of a series of horns on the crown of his head. The gang he is part of is well known, so much so that they have appeared in numerous movies. Both the fact that he is a gang member and the fact that the group is a bona fide gang are not in question. The extent to which the crime was gang related is.

The offense is murder. The prosecution argued the crime was committed "for the benefit of" and "in association with" the gang, but not "at the direction of" it. The defense argued that none of these things was applicable and instead that the offense was strongly related to the intoxicated status of the youths at the time. Had copious amounts of drugs not been present, this murder likely would not have happened.

Several youths are hanging out smoking crack. They are binge-using crack—smoking it nonstop—and have not slept in at least three days. Their crack use is also punctuated by alcohol and marijuana use. Most of these guys are gang members, although not from the same gang. For a couple of days, everyone is enjoying themselves. On the third day, the crack runs out and they seek more. A non-gang member in the group says that he knows where to get some and makes a phone call. He then tells the group that he is going to go retrieve more crack and will return soon. One of the gang members says that he will keep this guy company, and the two proceed on foot to a house to buy crack. The sun is beginning to set on the third day, and night has fallen by the time the guys approach the house. The youths are about 100 yards from the house when several police cars turn up and raid the place. The two youths freak out and run in opposite directions. They did not realize that the police were not after them; in fact, the police did not even notice them.

Later that evening, both youth return to the house in a heightened state of anxiety. The gang youth accuses the non-gang youth of setting him up, knowing that the house was under police surveillance. The non-gang youth proclaims his innocence, having no idea of what just happened or why. The gang youth begins to attack, and other gang members join in the beating, thinking the youth is a snitch. The youth is then threatened, saying that he now "owes" money to the gang youth for setting him up. He says he has no money and takes another beating. They eventually leave him alone and proceed to get more crack from someone else. Although a bit dazed from the beating, the non-gang youth eventually cleans himself up and rejoins everyone. They all have a meal together. More crack arrives later and the partying continues. "I'm still gonna get you for setting me up," one of the gang youth says to the non-gang youth. All the while, they continue to party, smoking crack and marijuana and drinking alcohol. The other gang youth seem to have forgotten the incident. Another day passes, and everyone continues to party through the night. On the morning of the fifth day, no one has slept at all. The gang youth orders the non-gang youth into a car, drives him out to a remote place, and shoots him multiple times, killing him. The killing occurs outside of the gang's territory and no one witnesses the act.

The prosecution argued that the homicide benefitted the gang as a result of increasing its reputation as a violent organization within the community. The killing helped generate fear of the gang, which in turn allows them to operate with impunity and commit more offenses within their territory. The homicide was also done in association with the gang because several gang members were present at the home prior to the incident. Several gang members did beat and threaten the non-gang youth, and the murder was the inevitable outcome of the threats.

The defense argued that not all homicides committed by gang members benefit the whole gang. They argued that the killing of someone addicted to crack is not necessarily something that would glorify the gang. In fact, the defense argued that crack use is highly stigmatized within gang culture and that the killing of a crack user might potentially highlight the fact that the gang youth himself also used. This would bring shame to the gang. The defense argued that the homicide was not committed in association with the gang because the shooter was alone and the killing occurred many miles away from the gang's territory. The threats the gang youth made together also did not appear credible. Saying "I'm gonna kill you" is one thing, but actually carrying out homicide is another. On a day-to-day basis, many people say bad things they have no intention of doing. Also, the defense argued that after the threats were made, all of the youth continued to hang out and party. A couple of days had passed since the threats were made and the murder occurred, suggesting that they were not genuine. The defense argued that most murders are not planned, but spontaneous. The prolonged use of crack and other drugs by the defendants suggests they were not in a mental state to plan a homicide and that it appeared to have been committed at a whim.

already existing gangs. Boys who were not affiliated were approached and recruited by the Vice Lords, and smaller existing gangs were also incorporated, at times through violence. Had the threat of these larger groups not been present, the coming together of these disparate individuals and gangs into the Vice Lords would not have occurred. The concept of threat more generally has relevance for gang violence (Decker, 1996). The Vice Lords became a large organization known as the Vice Lord Nation and eventually split into various branches

or cliques with their own territory, name, and type of offences. These branches included the Maniac Lords, the War Lords, and the Sacramento Lords. At times, they fought with one another, but the battles ceased if a larger, external threat emerged. The Vice Ladies were their female counterparts and they associated with various branches. The Lords did not necessarily control the Ladies, many of whom dated members of rival gangs.

As the Vice Lords grew, members adopted certain roles. At the top was the president, who made all major decisions involving the Vice Lord Nation. Each of the branches had its own president, but leadership fluctuated and depended on the context, as members emerged as natural leaders. Even within these branches, subcliques were apparent and had their own unofficial leaders. They were often age graded, with the oldest being considered the Seniors, followed by the Juniors, the Midgets, and the youngest the Pee Wees. Physical attributes, such as size and fighting prowess, also differentiated them. Like Thrasher, Keiser noted that the camaraderie and the strength of friendship ties within these smaller groups were more important to individual members than was the gang itself. Even within the different branches of the Vice Lord Nation, subcliques competed with each other for various positions and clout.

Leadership had a quick turnover as the police or rivals targeted them, within either the Nation or the individual branches. This gave rise to the role of vice president, who would take over if the president was killed or arrested, decreasing the chances of a power vacuum emerging. Other roles included war counselors, who were responsible for organizing and directing violence. Keiser could not get an accurate number of how large the Vice Lords were, with sizes ranging from 600 to 3,000 members. A problem with precisely gauging their size had to do with how membership was perceived. The groups were loosely structured and leaders did not feel comfortable discussing the size of the organization. Who was and was not a bona fide member of the Vice Lords figured into this uncertainty.

The Vice Lords were a fighting gang to whom territory and defending turf were paramount. Displays of bravery, heart, and soul were ways by which members evaluated one another, and prowess at fighting was how they proved and displayed these traits. Heart was courage in the face of adversity and being able to stand ground. Soul referred to how committed an individual was to his actions, the extent to which someone put all he had into any given situation. Rivals entering Vice Lord territory were susceptible to being attacked, but so were strangers who accidentally wandered into it. Vice Lords were seldom attacked in their own neighborhoods, but they were fair game in areas controlled by rivals or in communities where no gang dominated. The Vice Lords fought with other gangs for revenge and retaliation, leading to an endless display of tit-for-tat battles. When these battles were forming, members mobilized depending on the nature and severity of the previous clash. Different branches were responsible for defending their own territory within Vice Lord City. One described the context of the gangbang or fight between gangs (Keiser, 1979, p. 51):

> Now a fight like this really look funny when it starts, but it turns out to be terrifying. When it's just coming night is when most of the fighting occurs so if the Man come, then everybody can get away.
>
> You get a stick, or maybe a knife, or a chain. And some fools got shotguns. What you really do, you stand there and the [war] counselors are the first ones up. You stand back and you wait and see if they come to an agreement and talk. Now everybody standing there watching everybody else to see what's going to happen. And all of a sudden maybe a blow will be passed, and if it is, a fight start right there. . . . You just standing there and you're looking—you're watching the counselor. And if a blow pass, automatically the first thing you do is hit the man closest to you. After that if things get too tight for you then you get out of there. If it look like you getting whupped, you get out. It's all according to your nerve. The first who runs, that's it right there. Naturally if you're standing there and you're fighting, and you see half the club starting to run, you know the other half going to run soon. All it takes is one to run and the whole crowd breaks up. That's how a club gets it rep—by not running, by standing its ground.

The concept of brotherhood was also important to the Vice Lords. These individuals spent most of their time hanging around in each other's company. Much of this time was focused on "pulling jive"—drinking wine or trying to obtain enough money to buy it through begging or robbing. The Vice Lords would pour some of the liquor out on the street in remembrance of fallen or incarcerated members. Drinking was a social lubricant that helped celebrate camaraderie, pass time, remember friends, prepare for battles, and ease the pain associated with violence. Singing and dancing while drinking were daily activities of the Vice Lords. The concept of brotherhood had its limits and, economically speaking, each gang member was out for his own. The idea that members share the proceeds from criminal endeavors with others who were not involved was as mythical then as it is now. *Whupping the game* referred to cleverly benefitting economically or materially, often in relation to committing offenses. Part of this included shortchanging co-offenders on the proceeds from their offending.

STREET GANGS AND STREET WORKERS

Klein's (1971) early research, *Street Gangs and Street Workers*, evaluated theoretically informed intervention programs in Los Angeles: the Group Guidance Project and the Ladino Hills Project. The first was the Group Guidance Project, and Klein reported on the unintended consequence of this program in that it *increased* delinquency. Ironically, gangs who received the most services, including more interactions with detached youth workers, reported more delinquency. The reason, Klein argued, is that these services and workers increased the solidarity of the gang and, consequently, the youth's commitment to violence. External forces and pressures, as opposed to internal norms and regulations, are related to increases in gang cohesion, which, in turn, are related to escalations in delinquency. The program backfired, and instead of drawing youth away from gangs and limiting their appeal, it attracted more youth.

Klein (1971) applied the lessons learned in this program toward the Ladino Hills Project. In this project, efforts were made to avoid increasing the external pressures that contributed to gang solidarity and cohesion. Law enforcement, schools, and detached workers were encouraged to give less attention to gangs during this intervention. Competitive events, like sporting events, were also avoided. If less attention were given to gangs, perhaps they would simply disappear—a point issued by Thrasher decades prior. Although gang cohesiveness and overall delinquency declined during the Ladino Hill Project, serious delinquency increased.

Outside of evaluating these programs, Klein (1971) also examined the organizational character of the gang and the overall behaviors of its members. The gang consisted of youth who were rejected by the community. Members were immature and lacked self-confidence. The gang as an entity was a clustering of incompetent young males who had no common interests or goals. Delinquency was not something they were committed to; it happened as a result of acting out and trying to impress others. The gangs were not miniature organized criminal syndicates, but disorganized and spontaneous groups that focused on immediate gratification. Offending patterns were "cafeteria style" (Klein, 1971, p. 125)—not specialized or purposeful, but picked and chosen at a whim, as if they were selecting food options at a cafeteria. Like others, Klein found that gang members spent most of their time hanging out and doing nothing. When violence did emerge, it occurred among other members.

Klein (1971) found that leadership varied in youth gangs, and different leaders emerged in relation to various activities. Some held leadership roles when it came to fighting and others dominated in sports and romantic pursuits. The leaders were not easy to ascertain by an outsider and age played an important role. Boys behaved in excess and overstated their roles. Overall, Klein found that the structure of the gang was hard to distinguish from the culture of non-gang youth in the area.

Another important contribution of Klein's research is the development of a definition of gangs. Klein (1971, p. 58) defined a gang as

> any denotable group of youngsters who (a) are generally perceived as a distinct aggregation by others in their neighborhood, (b) recognized themselves as a denotable group (almost invariably with a group name) and (c) have been involved in a sufficient number

of delinquent incidents to call forth a consistent negative response from neighborhood resident and/or enforcement agencies.

If the group had these qualities, they were a gang. If not, they remained a group. This was a widely accepted definition and served as a jumping-off point for empirical research. It helped other researchers determine whether gangs were present in their neighborhoods. Klein's definition was among the first to specify delinquency as a characteristic.

SUMMARY

For hundreds of years, urban areas have given rise to groups of youth involved in delinquency and mischief. These groups consist of mostly boys and men. They often claim to be from a specific area and have symbols or insignias that denote membership. These groups have been called ruffians, hooligans, rowdies, riff-raff, thugs, hoods, goons, punks, and tough guys. They are also known as gangs.

Gangs have been considered an inevitable outcome of living in poor, inner-city areas. European immigrants throughout the 19th century fought for and defended what little resources they had, the result of which was the formation of different gangs from various ethnic or religious enclaves in the city. These gangs fought with one another, but they were also known to be helpful within their communities. In the mid- to late 19th century in places like New York City, gangs became more seriously involved in delinquency and were equated with social unrest and community unease.

Many early reports were journalistic. Proper academic research emerged in the first part of the 20th century. Early research was atheoretical, but later investigators drew on and helped further develop general theories on delinquency that are still taught in classrooms today. Some of these theories contributed to major policy initiatives on reducing delinquency that were implemented on a national level. Gang researchers also examined delinquency reduction interventions that targeted members, including the roles of the interventionist—a figure who retains an important yet contentious role in these programs. Some of the findings from these early studies continue to inform gang policy used across the United States.

Early research examined organizational and cultural aspects of gangs. In some cases, they were tightly organized and had chains of command, such as a president, war counselor, and treasurer. Evidence suggests that most were loosely organized, with leadership roles naturally emerging and dependent on the context. Researchers also worked on developing specific definitions of the term gang.

CHAPTER REVIEW QUESTIONS

1. How did some of the 18th- and 19th-century gangs in England and the United States distinguish themselves in terms of style and activities?
2. What were some of the names of the 18th- and 19th-century gangs? What was significant about these names?
3. How did the police and politicians interact with gangs in the Five Points area in New York City in the 19th century?
4. What were the different ways Thrasher used the term interstitial in his description of gangs?

5. Outline A. K. Cohen's theory of the delinquent subculture.
6. Outline Cloward and Ohlin's differential opportunity theory.
7. Explain the group process perspective as outlined by Short and Strodtbeck.
8. Describe the organization of the Vice Lords.
9. What was ironic about Klein's findings?
10. Compare and contrast Klein's and W. B. Miller's definitions of gang.

LINKS TO ARTICLES ON EARLY GANG RESEARCH AND PERSPECTIVES

Gang warfare in 18th century Boston
By B. Miller
http://outofthiscentury.wordpress.com/2010/02/16/18th-century-gang-warfare-in-boston/

The growth of youth gang problems in the United States: 1970–1998
By W. B. Miller
https://www.ncjrs.gov/html/ojjdp/ojjdprpt_yth_gng_prob_2001/contents.html/

History of street gangs in the United States
By J. C. Howell and J. P. Moore
http://www.nationalgangcenter.gov/content/documents/history-of-street-gangs.pdf/

City gangs
By W. B. Miller (with an introduction by S. H. Decker)
http://gangresearch.asu.edu/walter_miller_library/walter-b.-miller-book/city-gangs-book/

CHAPTER 2

DEFINITIONS, DAILY LIFE, DYNAMICS, AND RISK FACTORS

KEY WORDS

Causes and Correlates studies: A series of longitudinal studies on the initiation, persistence, and desistance from delinquency and crime. Findings began to emerge from these studies in the 1990s. They are conducted in five North American cities: Rochester, New York; Pittsburg, Pennsylvania; Denver, Colorado; Seattle, Washington; and Montreal, Canada. The risk factor approach or variables paradigm emerged from these studies.

Eurogang definition: Defines gang as "any durable, street oriented youth group whose involvement in illegal activity is part of its group identity." This is the most common definition of the term gang in that it is used by more academics than any other.

Intensity: Also referred to as embeddedness. This refers to the various levels of involvement in the gang and participation in crime and violence. Core gang members are more centrally involved in gang activities, whereas fringe members are less so.

Membership: Commonly indicated by self-identification, whereby youth admit to belonging to a particular gang. Membership may not be straightforward, with youth entering and exiting gang participation whimsically. Also, youth may not always perceive themselves to be members of a gang, but could nonetheless be identified as such by others, such as researchers or law enforcement.

Organization: Aspects that indicate gangs are organized include a vertical chain of command, rules guiding appropriate conduct, sanctions for violating such roles, clear goals, strong cohesion, regular meetings, and membership dues. Most gangs do not have these qualities. Rather, they are a loose collection of subgroups, with limited cohesion, a high turnover rate, no clear leadership, and a horizontal chain of command.

Protective factor: A condition that buffers or negates against risk factors for gang membership. Things such as prosocial peers, community involvement, and religiosity have been found to protect youth from the influences of gang members. Protective factors are less understood in comparison to risk factors.

Risk factor: A condition that increases an individual's likelihood to join a gang. Risk factors are cumulative and overlapping, meaning that they happen at different stages of a person's life and build on one another. Risk factors for gang membership are in five general domains: community, individual, family, peer, and school.

Subgroups: Also referred to as cliques or sets. These are gangs within gangs and are particularly found in larger (>100 members) gangs. Subgroups are often more important to individual gang members when compared to the overall gang. Individuals within subgroups may even have their own roles, symbols, and ideals.

Chapter Learning Objectives

- Recognize the various types and definitions of gangs.
- Identify common gang activities and benefits of membership.
- Understand interrelated organizational qualities of gangs.
- Distinguish variables positively correlated with gang membership.

INTRODUCTION

In the 1980s and 1990s, the number of gangs and members, the amount of media attention to them, the quantity of research, and the focus from law enforcement increased dramatically. The mid-1980s to the early-1990s were among the most violent within 20th century U.S. history. Firearms and crack cocaine became ubiquitous within the inner city, and gangs were believed to be responsible. A series of popular violent movies and the ascendance of gangsta rap helped cement in the minds of the public and law enforcement the interrelationship among gangs, drugs, and deadly violence. Gangs were suddenly everywhere—big and small cities, suburban sprawls, and rural locales. They reemerged as Public Enemy Number One and have since retained this label. Research became sophisticated and included a series of ethnographic studies and several longitudinal investigations. Despite these advancements, debate remains as to the most basic question: how to define a gang.

The chapter begins by reviewing sociological and legal definitions of the term gang. From here, it discusses how various other collectives are *not* gangs (e.g., motorcycle clubs). Next, a structured typology is provided that captures different types of gangs. Data are then offered on the daily activities of gang members and the positive and negative aspects of life in the gang. The chapter then examines interrelated gang dynamics, including the concept of membership, the extent gangs are organized, the importance of subgroups or cliques, and the intensity or embeddedness of gang involvement. The Causes and Correlates studies are then discussed, which provide important data on the risk factor or variables approach toward understanding who joins a gang and who does not.

SOCIOLOGICAL DEFINITIONS

Various sociological definitions of the term gang have been developed (Delaney, 2013; Greene and Pranis, 2007; Klein and Maxson, 2006; Matsuda et al., 2012).[1] This has been a concern for decades (Ball and Curry, 1995; Bursik and Grasmick, 1993; Coughlin and Venkatesh, 2003; Esbensen et al., 2001; Fleisher, 1998; Hagedorn, 1998; Horowitz, 1990; W. B. Miller, 1975; Spergel, 1995). Social scientists know what gangs are, but not how to define them. The main crux of the problem is the inclusion of illegal behaviors as a feature (Bursik and Grasmick, 1993). Some have used delinquency/violence as a defining character of gangs (e.g., Miller, Klein, Sanders, Spergel), although others have avoided this characterization (e.g., Thrasher, Short, Hagedorn, Brotherton). Others still argue that the search for a uniform definition is certain to end poorly (Bursik and Grasmick, 1993; Sullivan, 2006).

A common definition of gang is the Eurogang. Of all the definitions, more researchers, policy makers, and practitioners appear to use this one (Klein and Maxson, 2006). The Eurogang definition has outshouted the others. This definition has helped facilitate transnational research and determine whether street gangs are solely an American product (Klein et al., 2001). The Eurogang definition of gang is as follows:

> Any durable, street-oriented youth group whose involvement in illegal activity is part of its group identity.

Klein and Maxson (2006) take apart this definition to illustrate the profound differences between street gangs and the more common phenomena of groups of youth who get in trouble together. They note that durable in this context refers to the longevity of the group and means that it exists despite a turnover in members. The length of time a gang must be in existence to be considered durable may only be several months. Groups of youth that disperse after a couple of months would not qualify, but those still around after several months would. Street-oriented refers to spending a considerable amount of time away from home, school, or work, and instead outdoors. A group of youth who spend most of their time inside playing video games would not qualify. Youth means that the group does not consist solely of adults, but is a combination of juveniles, young adults in their early 20s, and some older individuals. Without the juvenile element, the gang would be a group or an adult criminal syndicate. Klein and Maxson (2006) note that illegal activity refers to how the group focuses on crimes beyond drug use or rowdy behavior. A bunch of guys hanging out smoking weed would not constitute a gang. The authors conclude these behaviors are also linked to group identity—not that of the individual.

---

1   Terms such as gang, youth gang, street gang, and criminal street gang are generally used interchangeably within the literature. They all refer to the same phenomenon. However, researchers have previously developed distinct definitions on variations of the term gang, such as gang, street gang, and traditional youth gang (Spergel and Curry, 1990).

Not all researchers and practitioners define gangs in terms of their illegal behaviors. Hagedorn (1998) highlights Joan Moore, who defines gangs as,

> unsupervised peer groups who are socialized by the streets rather than by conventional institutions. They define themselves as a gang or "set" or some such term, and have the capacity to reproduce themselves, usually within a specific neighborhood.[2]

Hagedorn (n.d.) offers his own definition of gangs:

> Organizations of the street composed of either 1. The social excluded or 2. Alienated, demoralized, or bigoted elements of a dominant racial, ethnic, or religious group.

> The gang is not a stable form, but can, and has, changed its shape and functions over time. While most gangs begin as unsupervised adolescent peer groups and remain so, some institutionalize in barrios, favelas, ghettoes, and prisons. Often these institutionalized gangs become business enterprises within the informal economy and a few are linked to international criminal cartels. Others institutionalize as violent supporters of dominant groups and may devolve from political or conventional organizations. Most gangs are characterized by a racialized or ethno-religious identity as well as being influenced by global culture. Gangs have variable ties to conventional institutions and, in given conditions, assume social, economic, political, cultural, religious, or military roles.[3]

Short (1996, p. 1) notes that the inclusion of delinquency in defining gangs has been so problematic that other researchers have avoided this term and instead refer to them as "co-offenders," "bands of teenagers congregating on street corners," "unsupervised peer groups," "networks of juveniles who violate the law," and "delinquent groups." J. Katz (1988), too, does not say gang members but "barrio homeboys" and "street elites." Brotherton (2008c) views gangs in a radically different way as a "street organization." Short (1996), to "avoid the logical circularity of including in the definition the behavior that is to be explained" (p. 4), defines gangs as

> groups whose members meet together with some regularity, over time, on the basis of group-defined criteria of membership and group-defined organizational characteristics; that is, gangs are non–adult sponsored, self-determining groups that demonstrate continuity over time. (p. 3)

Klein and Maxson (2006) reject the circularity argument for two reasons. First, gangs differ from one another in terms of the context, frequency, and types of criminal and violent behaviors. Including delinquency as a characteristic of gangs still means that these aspects of their involvement in it can be predicted. Second, crime remains one of many aspects examined. Other important considerations include organization and leadership structure, gender and ethnic makeup, subgrouping, and cohesiveness. How these relate to individual and collective forms of crime and violence are important (Hughes, 2006).

---

2   Moore's definition of gangs can be found here: http://gangresearch.net/GangResearch/Seminars/definitions/mooredef.html/.

3   Hagedorn's definition can be found here: https://www.uic.edu/orgs/kbc/Definitions/hagdef.html

An alternative is to stop searching for a uniform definition and instead focus on how various forms of behavior contribute to individual and group processes that result in delinquency (Short, 2006; Sullivan, 2006).

Sullivan (2006) offers a partial solution to the question of delinquency and violence in sociological definitions (see also Short, 2006). Sullivan focuses on the importance of youth violence and how such violence can take different collective forms based on how its participants associate with one another, the extent to which they identify as a group, and their illegal behaviors. Sullivan refers to these as the action-set, clique, or named gang and defines them as follows (2006, p. 20):

- **Action-set**: a group of individuals who come together for a specific purpose and then disperse as a collective. They may not identify themselves as a group, nor be seen by others as such. They do not necessarily have any plans to get together down the line for the purposes of additional activities, but they might.
- **Clique**: a group that has some degree of solidarity and engages in a variety of activities with one another with some degree of regularity. They do not necessarily have a group name, a group leader, or any symbols that identify that as being part of a particular group.
- **Named gang**: a group that has the same properties as the clique, but with more defined boundaries of group membership. They are also more likely to have leaders, rules/codes, rituals and symbols that all convey a sense of membership, but not necessarily all of these traits.

Sullivan (2006) highlights an important point in relation to gangs and youth violence. Youth gangs increased in the 1990s at the same time that youth violence decreased significantly. If gangs are so strongly related to violence, then the expectation is that membership and overall violence would increase. However, this was not the case.

LEGAL DEFINITIONS

The extent to which offending is a defining feature of gangs is a sociological question that academics will argue about for generations. One way to skirt this issue is to examine the legal definition (see Ball and Curry, 1995; Bursik and Grasmick, 1993; Morash, 1983). For instance, the California Penal Code 186.22, which was enacted in relation to legislation known as the STEP Act—the Street Terrorism Enforcement and Protection Act of 1993.[4] It defines criminal street gang as follows:

> Any ongoing organization, association or group of three of more persons, whether formal or informal, having as one of its primary activities the commission of one or more of the criminal acts . . . which has a common name or common identifying sign or symbol, whose members individually or collectively engage in or have engaged in a pattern of criminal gang activity.

---

4   For a list of how different states define the term gang, see *Gang-Related Legislation by State* here: http:// www.nationalgangcenter.gov/Legislation/.

Under this definition, a group is a gang if at least three people are present. From there, the law indicates that the primary activities must be one or more of the criminal acts. These acts can be referred to as predicate offenses and include a range of serious offenses. Personal drug use and petty theft are often not considered predicate offenses. Similar to the socio-logical definitions, a group of three guys hanging out smoking pot would not constitute a gang. Offending must also be a primary activity of that group for it to be a gang. If a guy in a group of three were to commit a drive-by shooting—a predicate offense—that would not make the group a gang because only one of its members has committed an offense. Primary activities by definition assumes that more than half of the individuals commit predicate offenses for the group to be a gang. If that group has three people, then at least two of those three would have to have committed offenses for the group to be a gang. The term primary activities indicates the *frequency* of offending. If three guys all commit a felony burglary together—a predicate offense—but that is the only burglary they have committed, is it a gang-related offense? Can the committal of one predicate offense be translated into the primary activities of this collective to define it as a gang? These are legal inquiries. Like the sociological definition of gangs, the legal one raises numerous questions.

WHAT GANGS ARE NOT

Greek organizations (e.g., fraternities or sororities), motorcycle clubs, taggers, terrorists, skinheads, stoners, co-offenders, and organized criminal adult syndicates are not gangs. Bursik and Grasmick (1993) note that Greek organizations do not qualify because of their lack of commitment to delinquency. They are formed for social purposes. The *raison d'etre* of these organizations is not offending, which makes them different from gangs.

The same thing can be said about motorcycle clubs: they are formed for noncriminal purposes. More than anything else, the members want to ride their motorcycles (Klein, 1995). They spend a considerable amount of time working on, talking about, and focusing on motorcycles. As the website for the Hells Angels indicates,

> The key words are Motorcycle Club, which means they are true motorcycle enthusiasts and their motorcycle is their primary means of transportation. On the average a club member will ride 20,000 mile plus a year, and this means rain, snow or sunshine.[5]

Individuals of specific motorcycle clubs have a history of criminal involvement. Some clubs are similar to gangs in that they have generated negative attention from law en-forcement (e.g., Hells Angels, Mongols, Vagos).[6] Most motorcycle clubs are not like this,

---

5   This quote is taken from the Hells Angels website here: http://www.hells-angels.com/?HA=faq/. The website also indicates the correct spelling is "Hells" without the possessive apostrophe, to acknowledge the existence of multiple Hells.

6   Motorcycle clubs like the Hells Angels and Vagos have many ganglike qualities, including meaningful colors and symbols, roles, and initiation ceremonies (as do fraternities and sororities). Evidence has emerged that some chapters of motorcycle clubs are criminally inclined and, in such cases, might meet the criteria for the definition of a criminal street gang. (For more on the daily life of chapters of these motorcycle clubs, see Rowe, 2013; H. S. Thompson, 1966). Some motorcycle clubs have chapters all across the United States and a few have chapters around the world.

however. Determining whether motorcycle clubs like the Hells Angels are a gang is far from simple because of the uncertainty of their commitment to illegal behaviors.[7] Another reason motorcycle clubs are not gangs is that they are composed solely of adults. Without the juvenile element, they are not what social scientists define as gangs (Klein, 1995). Terrorist groups and organized criminal syndicates are also not considered gangs because they are adults.

For the most part, skinheads are not considered gangs. They lack street orientation and spend most of their time indoors (Klein, 1995; Klein and Maxson, 2006). Co-offenders are not a group in the sociological sense, so they cannot be considered gangs (Bursik and Grasmick, 1993). The members are just in the same place participating in the offense and may go their separate ways after it finishes; they are not durable.

Stoners use many drugs, not just marijuana (Shelden et al., 2001). They would not be a gang in either the sociological or the legal sense. Legally, drug use is not a predicate offense. Sociologically, illegal activity as a characteristic of gangs refers to behaviors outside of substance use. The delinquency of stoner groups also extends to graffiti, often of musical groups (e.g., *Black Sabbath Rules!*)—which makes its character distinct from that of gang graffiti (R. Jackson and McBride, 1992).

Taggers are a different story. They are not considered gangs, but have in some cases engaged in ganglike behaviors. Tagging graffiti is not done to mark territory (Wooden, 1995) and is different from gang graffiti. The purposes of tagging are to say *I was here* and express an appreciation for hip-hop culture (Coffield, 1991; Sanders, 2005a). Wooden (1995) sees taggers as middle-class, white, suburban youths who attempt to emulate the gangsta culture of inner-city, working-class minority youth. The term tag-bangers are those who take on more ganglike characteristics, such as rivalries with other crews that include violence with weapons (Shelden et al., 2001). These rivalries are for no other reason than to see who can tag their name in more places. Other rivalries between tagging crews can be similar to conflict among criminal street gangs. The chief sociological and legal difference between taggers and gangs is their level of involvement in crime and violence. Taggers also lack gang characteristics, such as initiation ceremonies, organization, and definitive membership status (Wooden, 1995).

A STRUCTURED TYPOLOGY

Gangs vary in terms of their size, ethnicity, leadership, organization, age range, patterns of criminality, origins, drug usage, and whether they are territorial. This variation led to the development of typologies (Fagan, 1989; Huff, 1989; Klein and Maxson, 2006; Taylor, 1990; Valdez, 2003, 2007). Some focus specifically on Mexican American gangs (e.g., Valdez) and

---

7   Examples exist of motorcycle club members being charged with gang enhancement statutes. However, it cannot be claimed that all chapters of such motorcycle clubs or their members are committed to crime and violence. Some are more ganglike than others. See, for example, http://www.agingrebel.com/2313/; http://www.foxnews.com/us/2013/10/03/life-for-parole-for-ex-vagos-leader-in-2011-killing-rival-hells-angel-at-nevada/; http://www.sltrib.com/sltrib/news/56230002-78/curtis-gang-members-roy.html.csp/.

others describe them based on their commitment to violence, crime, or partying (e.g., Huff, Fagan, Taylor).

Klein and Maxson (2006) argue that many of the previously developed typologies were based on behavioral differences (e.g., the party gang; the violent gang; the drug-selling gang) and were problematic on two accounts. First, the different typologies reflected different methods and locales of data locations, as well as the perception of the researchers. Second, there was a strict focus on behavior to distinguish gangs, because most (and delinquents more generally) do not focus on one type of crime, but instead commit several different types. Klein and Maxson (2006) also comment on how structural typologies—or those based on the organizational structure of the gang—are tricky because they give rise to exceptions and do not focus on other important aspects that distinguish different types.

To remedy this, Klein and Maxson (2006) developed their own typology using data from police gang experts in cities across the United States. These experts or gang cops were chosen because they work with gangs up close and personal and are often not limited to one specific area of a city. After a review of reports from hundreds of gang cops in different cities, Klein and Maxson (2006) then sent out detailed questions about the size, age range, crime patterns, territory issues, duration, and existence of subgroups. Based on their responses, the authors developed a five-tiered typology: traditional; neotraditional; compressed; collective; and specialty.

- **The traditional gang**: This is the largest gang type, consisting of at least 100 members. In some cases, membership reaches the thousands. They have been around for 20 years or more and are able to continue to exist by recruiting new, younger members. As such, this gang regenerates from below to help ensure longevity. The traditional gang contains subgroupings of youth that are distinguished by age or neighborhood. They have the widest age range, with the youngest members around 9 or 10 and the oldest ones in their 30s. They are territorial and claim a specific area as their own. They engage in the "cafeteria style" pattern of offending in that they commit a variety of crimes.
- **The neotraditional gang**: This gang is similar to the traditional type. The chief differences are the length of its existence and its overall size. The neotraditional gang has been around 10 years or less and has between 50 and 100 members. Like a traditional gang, subgroupings are evident in most cases, they have a pattern of criminal versatility, and they are territorial or becoming increasingly so. Over time, the neotraditional gang is on course to become a traditional gang.
- **The compressed gang**: As the same sounds, this is a smaller gang, consisting of no more than 50 members. Because of their relatively small size, subgroups do not emerge. The age range is small, with no more than 10 years between the oldest and youngest members. They are also relatively new, being around for 10 years or less. They commit a variety of crimes. They may or may not be territorial. Given their small size and duration, it remains uncertain whether this gang will morph into one of the larger ones, remain the same, or die out altogether.

- **The collective gang**: This type of gang is a larger version of the compressed gang. This gang is medium large, with more than 50 members but less than 100. Despite the size, subgroups are not evident. The age range is medium wide, with about 10 or so years between the youngest and oldest members. The gangs have been in existence a medium length of time, between 10 and 15 years. They may be territorial. They are criminally versatile.
- **The specialty gang:** As the name suggests, this gang specializes in one type of offense and is specifically formed for this purpose. They have fewer than 50 members and no subgroups. The age range is narrow—less than 10 years—and their duration is about the same. They are territorial only to the extent that it impacts the crime they specialize in. If they focus on selling drugs, they establish and defend territory to secure sales. Others selling drugs in their area would be targeted for victimization.[8]

Klein and Maxson (2006) then sought to determine the accuracy and extent of these types of gangs across the United States by questioning gang cops in numerous cities. They found that all but a few recognized these types of gangs in their community. Klein and Maxson also looked at the prevalence and predominance of the gang types and reported that the compressed version was the most common and the collective one the least.

An important conclusion drawn was the changing face of gang structures. No longer did evidence support the notion that gangs were limited to the classic vision of the large collective with identifiable subgroups and a transgenerational establishment in the community. White and Asian members also had a much larger presence in these new gangs, accounting for a quarter or slightly more of all members in the collective, specialty, and compressed versions. Multiethnic gangs were found to account for about a quarter of all neotraditional types and about one-fifth of all specialty ones. Members of traditional and neotraditional gangs had the most arrests, but this was because they had the highest number of members. Those in specialty gangs, although smaller in overall numbers, were much more likely to get arrested. Klein and Maxson (2006) argued this was because of police units that focus on specific offenses being drawn to youth who commit them (e.g., narcotics).

Youth in the Los Angeles Study[9] were asked how many people were in their gang. The least amount ($n = 6$) indicated 50 or less members, suggesting they were either compressed or specialty under the Klein/Maxson typology. About the same amount ($n = 7$) said they had 50 to 100 members, suggesting they were collective or neotraditional. The remainder of the sample mentioned 100 or more members, which by definition in the typology indicates they are members of traditional gangs. Several youth in the Los Angeles Study, when asked about the amount of people, responded in the hundreds or thousands or provided an exact number, such as 450, 850, or 900. A few gave ranges such as 200–300 or 350–450.

---

8   To be clear, drug selling was the most common form of crime focused on by specialty gangs, closely followed by graffiti and then fighting (Klein and Maxson, 2006, p. 181).

9   For more information on data from the Los Angeles Study, see the Appendix.

This is not surprising to the extent that cities like Los Angeles have a longer history of activity are home to more traditional gangs (Klein and Maxson, 2006).

DAILY LIFE

Most of the time, gang members hang out and do nothing (Klein, 1995; Spergel, 1995). This finding is decades old. Youth in the Los Angeles Study were asked what they did on an average day and read a list of 22 possibilities of both delinquent and nondelinquent activities. Table 2.1 shows their responses.

The most commonly reported daily activity among gang youth was nondelinquent: hang out with the homies—a tradition within gang life. Talking to the opposite sex and going to school were the next most commonly reported activities—also nondelinquent. About half the sample (52–55%) said that delinquency in the form of smoking weed, fighting (both in-group and out-group members), and gangbanging/putting in work happened daily. The terms gangbanging and putting in work are synonyms and refer to a range of delinquent behaviors committed on behalf of the gang (B. Sanders et al., 2010). An infrequent form of this among the Los Angeles sample was selling drugs, and a common behavior was venturing into rival neighborhoods or seeing rivals in the course of everyday events and then antagonizing them with words and gestures (e.g., displaying gang signs; shouting out the name of a gang; cursing the name of rival gangs). The point of this type of gangbanging was to provoke violence. About the same amount (55–50%) reported that other nondelinquent activities like hanging out with family, playing sports (e.g., handball,

TABLE 2.1   DAILY ACTIVITIES OF GANG YOUTH FROM THE LOS ANGELES STUDY

Nondelinquent Activities	N/%	Delinquent Activities	N/%
Hang out with the homies	53/88	Smoke weed	33/55
Talk to the opposite sex	45/75	Fight	32/53
School	37/62	Gangbang/put in work	31/52
Hang out with the family	33/55	Drink beer	22/37
Play sports	32/53	Do graffiti	20/33
Make out	30/50	Drink liquor	15/25
Work out	28/47	Steal things	9/15
Chores	27/45	Fire guns	7/12
Have sex	27/45	Use hard drugs	7/12
Study	22/37		
Play video games	20/33		
Work	12/20		
Nothing	11/18		

*Responses rounded to nearest 1. Responses exceed 100% because of multiple possibilities.

basketball, baseball, football), and making out (i.e., kissing and fondling the opposite sex) occurred daily. Few committed petty theft or relatively serious delinquency, like firing guns or using hard drugs.

An important point reflected in these findings is often neglected: that of gangs' involvement in nondelinquent, routine, day-to-day activities (Brotherton and Barrios, 2004; Greene and Pranis, 2007; Hughes, 2006; J. Katz and Jackson-Jacobs, 2007; Short and Strodtbeck, 1965). Delinquent activities have long been argued to be a small fraction of what gang members spent their time doing, and select researchers focus on this aspect. The fact that this information is often not addressed is a contentious point in sociological arguments about the definition of the term gang. The focus on the criminality of gangs has led to many myths. Greene and Pranis (2007, p. 51) list several of these myths, including the following:

- Most gang members are hardened criminals.
- Gang members spend most of their time planning or committing crimes.
- Gang members are responsible for the bulk of violent crime.

The notion of hardened criminals might evoke visions of individuals who kill at will and are committed to delinquency. However, the reality is that few gang members are actually like this. One report indicated that perhaps as much as 10% of all members perpetrate deadly violence (Advancement Project, 2007). National data concur. The FBI states that of all homicides, gang members are responsible for between 6 and 10%, depending on whether a firearm was used (Harrell, 2005). This statistic indicates that most homicides across the nation have nothing to do with gangs and that most members do not commit homicide. Many youth want to live conventional lifestyles. They do not see themselves involved in crime and violence their whole lives. In fact, very few do (cf. Sanders, 2005a). Many crimes are unplanned, opportunistic events (Conklin, 1972; Gibbons, 1973; Shover, 1972). Crimes committed by gang members are no different. None of these qualities is suggestive of the life course of a hardened criminal.

POSITIVE AND NEGATIVE ASPECTS

Rather than asking *Why did you join?*, youth in the Los Angeles Study were asked what they liked about life in the gang. The various responses fit into five distinct themes: socialization, family, and action were the most common answers, and protection and nothing were the least common themes. Youth offered multiple reasons that reflected more than one of these themes, and others have reported similar reasons (Klein, 1995; Spergel, 1995; Weisel, 2006).

Family refers to a sense of belonging, provision, support, and brotherhood. Youth said the gang "was there for me," they "accept me," and they "are like me."

Now, what do you like about the gang?

I don't have to worry about nobody turning on me because it's like basically all my family. We grew up since we were in diapers, everybody in my age group from, if they are like 13 to 22, I grew up with them. I rolled dice with them, learned how to skateboard with them, played on the basketball team with them. So I know everybody in and out, I know what would make them mad and all that.

So you like them because you are really close with these guys, is that right?

Yeah, I could not be from nowhere else 'cause I don't love no other neighborhood like I love my neighborhood that I was born and raised in.

Now, what do you like about the gang?

I like everything. The only fact that most people don't understand that we actually become a family when we are a gang. Most of the reason why you join the gang is because of another person that is obviously close to you. Once you join you become closer to that person then you start hanging around a certain amount of people all the time, all the time, all the time, every day, every week, every night and they become more of a family. It becomes more real, more your people. It's like, for instance, if something went down they would be the ones to respond maybe if they start shooting at your mom, your dad, you know what I am saying? Or something like that.

Now, what do you like about the gang?

I like the fact that when I needed the brotherhood, the love that I was searching for, they were there, you know? They accepted me with all my faults, flaws, and failures. They were never like, "You should be like that." No man. They were like, "If you are fucked up, we are fucked up, too. Just come on, dog."

Another theme is socialization, which refers to hanging out. Hanging out with the homies was the most common activity of gang youth from the Los Angeles Study. Being with friends was the second most common activity.

What do you like about being in the gang?

Kick it with the homies.

What else do you like about it?

Just like partying with them.

Hanging out with them?

Yeah.

Anything else?

No.

What do you like about it? Tell me what you like, what are the good things?

I like my friends, the homies. I like being with them, just hanging out.

Now, what do you like about the gang?

More like friends, like you become closer with people.

Anything else?

That is it.

A third theme to emerge was action—excitement, partying, adventure, power, respect, girls, crime, and money. The gang served as a way for members to increase their likelihood of having fun.

Now, what do you like about being in the gang?

What attracted me and caught my attention was, was the fact that you do whatever you want, you know? Pretty much. You get a sense of like, you get all kinds of illusions, you know what I mean? Being out there, the adrenaline rush, running from the cops, trying to make your own little money on the side. Well, not going to school, parties, you know fucken liquor, drinking, girls, you know? Someday having so much money that you are able to buy you a car you know, at a young age maybe. You know, stuff like that.

What do you like about being in the gang?

Position of power, respect and then it's not just that but it's the lifestyle, doing what you want to do, knowing that you're part of something and it's like something that we just grew up. . . . Other than that there's so much money to be made. You have, like I said, the position of power meaning that you could tax anybody you want. Nobody can sell drugs in your neighborhood unless they give money to you. The ice cream man, you can take his money and he can't do a thing about it. Anybody, you can take their money and they can't do nothing about it. Pretty much, you're being the bully and ain't nobody going to tell you nothing. . . . What I like, that's how I exist. It's kind of like life is an adventure, when you're out there you're a soldier. It's like the army. Why do people like the army? Action, adventure, shooting guns: You're running around making targets and this and that, same thing in the neighborhood. You got your people, different people in different positions. You got guys that are good at making the money, selling the drugs. You got the guys that are top gunners, you got the guys that are good drivers, you got the guys that keep point, by saying keeping point I mean they keep watch—the cops, enemies, you got all your men set up. It's like a game of chess or a game of war or whatever you want to call it. You got soldiers, you're trying to build something up. At the same time, not get caught. Our worst enemies are the cops. Those are the army guys that can really break us down. Now with the way technology is building up, it gets harder. They got . . . heat motion detectors, and the helicopters and all that shit. Now, my trip is trying to get above them, trying to get better than them.

What do you like about the gang?

> Like I said, it all goes back to the money. I needed money and the only way I knew to get money was selling drugs. In my neighborhood you couldn't sell drugs unless you were part of the gang and also too, you have enemy rival gangs who want that territory also and I needed the protection also. . . . We get to hang out, drink, use, party, you know, hang out all the time, go places and you know even have serious talks with one another. And it's fun. And I don't know, for some reason, man, that type of lifestyle attracts me. I like it. It's like it runs through my blood almost. Anytime I get around my friends I get that feeling like yeah that's where I belong and this is what I like to do, I like to, up to no good.

Action, family, and socialization were ranked equally high. Two other themes, in contrast, were mentioned relatively few times. One was protection: the youth said that the best thing about the gang was having others watch their backs.

Now, what do you like about the gang?

> Your homeboys having your back. About if you need somebody you know where to go, you know? Like, if somebody is bugging you, bugging your family, you call a couple of homeboys and they will be right there. They will get your back on anything, you know? Especially when they are rivals or just a gang that we don't know, that we really don't get along.

Now, what do you like about the gang?

> The protection.

Protection from who?

> I feel protected.

Now, what do you like about the gang?

> Just people. Just knowing people all around your community and like feel like I am protected, like all day.

Some responded "Nothing" or "I don't know," meaning that the gang served no purpose or that they did not know what they liked about it.

So tell me, what do you like about being in it?

> Nothing really to like.

What do you mean?

> You don't get shit out of it like they say.

You don't get anything out of it?

> No.

What do you like about being in the gang, what are the good things?

> There's not really that many good things about it.

Now, what do you like about the gang?

> I don't know, really.

Not too sure?

> Not too sure.

The sample was also asked what they disliked. In some cases, the things members liked were similar to the things they disliked. These and other ironies of membership have been highlighted previously (Klein, 1995). The sample liked that the gang offered them protection, but the most common dislike was violence, victimization, and fear.

Now tell me what do you dislike about it?

> Bad things can happen to you.

What do you mean like bad things?

> People could die, get hurt, you know?

What do you dislike about it?

> Having to watch my back.

Is that something that happens all the time?

> Yeah, it's all the time.

> Okay, I know that we fight territory right? And we fight amongst our self, and sometime we have to do it but I mean it hurts, when I see on the news that somebody got killed, and they are Mexican. I think about it and I put myself in their place. What if it was my brother and I can truly feel and hear, like how their mom must be feeling because one of my homies got killed last week too. . . . Yeah, like I felt it. Like a tear ran down my eye. And I was like, "Fuck!" You know? I saw his mom, and she looked like a mess.

Although they felt the gang provided a sense of family, they did not like the infighting and backstabbing. Members said that the others were not there for them when they were needed. This was a common dislike of the sample.

> Things I hate, how many snakes there is, you know? Backstabbers.

Within your crew, in your gang?

> Yeah, how drugs just took over the whole union, pretty much destroyed everything, friendships and everything.

Now, what do you dislike about the gang?

> Like, homies are dumb. Like, they will be trying to fight with each other sometimes.

You are fighting with each other?

> Well, not me but the other homies.

The other homies fighting with each other, you don't like that?

> Yeah.

Do they fist fight each other?

> Yeah, sometimes.

What do you dislike about the gang?

> Like, when somebody is trying to do something to me and they leave me right there, they don't help me out.

They don't help you?

> Yeah.

So they run away? So who are you talking about, your friends your homies?

> No, like sometimes they are not there, like when I am getting in a problem.

So your homies are not around when you are getting in trouble?

> Yeah. Like, when someone is trying to beat me up or something.

Another irony of the family aspect of membership is when they are ordered by others to commit violence against their homeboys.

What do you dislike about the gang?

> Sometimes, not always, you have to turn your back on relatives or family members or close friends that, they do something. And it's either you do something about it to them or they're going to come at you. It's like saying you and me are close friends in the gang and you do something and now everybody wants you. And since they know that you and me are close they like, "Why don't you just do him?" I don't think that's right, but if I don't do him they going to do me.

When you say "do him" do you mean punch and beat him up or shoot them?

> Yeah.

Shoot them?

> Yeah.

Sometimes the guys in the gang tell you to go shoot somebody and you don't want to do that?

> It's never happened to me personally, but I seen it happen.

So you've seen other people, other guys in the gang tell other gang members that they want someone shot and if they say no they don't want to do that? . . .

> . . . You've heard of something called the green light?

You mean when someone gets the green light, meaning that it's okay to go ahead and "do them"?

> Yes. . . . So he gets the green light . . . and if it's not done, the whole neighborhood gets the green light which means all the neighborhoods come at us. So it's either him or more of us. And that's happened several times that I've seen and I was like, "No."

The sample also said they like the respect they get from membership, but do not like being disrespected by community members and the police.

What do you dislike about the gang?

> That people, you know, look at you wrong.

Look at you wrong?

> Yeah. They think you are a killer, a fuck up and shit.

So when you say "other people" do you mean other people in your neighborhood?

> Yeah. Like, other people, people that live in the neighborhood. Yeah, or call the cops or something. They dislike us.

What do you dislike about the gang?

> I don't like being harassed by law enforcement because I am being judged because I am part of a gang, I don't like the fact that gangs are being labeled as terrible. I don't like that. Just because I am part of a gang it separates me from the community and the society because it takes away my privileges and things and places I can't go. I don't like that I can't go to every city and state to state. That is all I can tell you that I don't like about it.

So you said you like the family aspect of it. Now tell me, what do you dislike about it?

> I could say that, what everybody puts on it, like it's the most horrible thing in the world, I can't believe, "If you see these guys stay away from them cause they are all gang members." You know? Just the fear of other people towards you. Like, if I am walking out in the street and it's two of my homies and we are walking down the street, people are hugging their babies and grabbing their purses. Like, we are not trying to bother you guys.

The other things they liked least included jail, drugs, and committing crime and violence. Finally, just as some said "nothing" in terms of what they liked, others said the same thing about what they disliked.

What do you dislike, what don't you like about it?

> Nothing.

You don't like anything but you don't dislike anything?

> Yeah, it's normal for me, probably because I started out younger so I had no problems with it, probably that, cause nothing really bothers me.

What do you dislike about the gang?

> It's pretty good.

Is there anything that you don't like about it?

> It's pretty good. They don't pressure you to do stuff. Like, it's not that bad, you know?

So everything is cool then?

> Yeah.

What do you dislike about the gang?

> Nothing.

Nothing bother you?

> No, not really.

BOX 2.1: MEDIA CHECK!

Colors, Boyz N the Hood, South Central, Menace II Society

In the late 1980s and early 1990s, a quartet of violent movies about gang life in Los Angeles emerged: *Colors* (1988), *Boyz N the Hood* (1991), *South Central* (1992), and *Menace II Society* (1993). They came out during a period of heightened gang violence and the crack epidemic and served to advertise to all Americans a snapshot of life and drugs in the inner cities. With the exception of *Colors*, the focus of the movies is black communities.

"In the heart of our cities people die everyday for wearing the wrong colors." This is the tagline on the movie poster for *Colors*, directed by Dennis Hopper. Hopper has played a drug-addled, motorcycle-riding hippie (*Easy Rider*), a ranting, lost-in-the-jungle photojournalist (*Apocalypse Now*), and a nitrous oxide–sucking, psychotic mobster (*Blue Velvet*). *Colors* is different because it attempts to contextualize how gloomy and desolate gang life is. Youth in the movie discuss the gang as their family—the first real one they have ever had—and how it serves as a way to obtain power and respect. But life in the gang is reckless. Drug use is rampant and innocent people are randomly shot and killed at parties. The tragedy is fully exposed. So, too, is the helplessness the police face when attempting to bring about any real change. The rapper Ice-T introduced a single of the same name that became the de facto song about gangs in Los Angeles, delivering this prophetic message: "The gangs of LA will never die, just multiply." *Colors* contains some of the early performances of then unknowns Don Cheadle, Damon Wayans, and Mario Lopez.

"One out of every twenty-one Black American males will be murdered in their lifetime. Most will die at the hands of another Black male": over the sound of automatic weapon fire and cars peeling out, these words are displayed in the trailer for *Boyz N the Hood*. The movie takes its name from a song of the same name by the band NWA. True to form, one of the rappers of NWA, Ice Cube, plays a main character, Doughboy—a childhood friend of two other main characters—Tre and Ricky. The film illustrates how these three friends had different trajectories growing up in South Los Angeles (née South Central Los Angeles). Tre is the smart one, but also has a habit of acting up. As a result, his mom sends him to live with his disciplinarian

father. Ricky is the All-American football player attending Crenshaw High School with dreams of going to the University of Southern California (USC) on a scholarship. Doughboy is a crack-selling gangster, a role Ice Cube was born to play. The story focuses on Tre's dilemma: he wants to live up to his father's expectations because of his talent and college aspirations, but is simultaneously attracted to the gangster lifestyle that Doughboy and his friends have. Tre is smart but he is also angry. *Boyz N the Hood* was nominated for an Oscar: not bad for first-time director John Singleton, who grew up in South Central and attended USC.

South Central is a film about intergenerational strife and gang life. The film exposes the prison-to-gangs-and-back-to-prison cycle many members face. Once out of prison, Bobby revisits his old neighborhood and finds that his friend Ray-Ray is now an active member of the Hoover Deuce Crips, Ray-Ray's girlfriend has given birth to their son, and she is getting hooked on crack. Ray-Ray talks Bobby into killing a member of a rival gang. Bobby does this, gets caught, and is then sent back to prison, this time for 10 years. Inside, he becomes a Muslim and educates himself. When he gets out, South Central has deteriorated. Bobby finds out that Ray-Ray is grooming his now 10-year-old son for membership in the Crips. *South Central* is based on a book written by a high school teacher in South Central Los Angeles and was directed by an ex-convict.

These movies are all violent, but *Menace II Society* is the most graphic. The film exposes the tension with Korean shop owners and black patrons in Los Angeles. The riots of April 1992 were still fresh when this film came out, and during this time Korean shop owners were seen armed and defending their properties from gangs of youth. Other real life–inspired tragic incidents involving Korean shop owners are also played out in the movie. Violence—both perpetration and victimization—runs throughout. The main protagonist, Caine, seeks a chance to get out of the hood and start a new life with a new love. Rappers MC Eiht and Too $hort make appearances in the film, as do Samuel L. Jackson (a year before his major role in *Pulp Fiction*) and Jada Pinkett (years before marrying Will Smith). Apparently, the gangsta rapper par excellence, Tupac Shakur, was originally going to play Caine's ultraviolent homeboy, O-Dog.

Please visit YouTube for the opportunity to watch trailers for Boyz N the Hood, Colors, South Central, *and* Menace II Society.

INTERRELATED DYNAMICS

Membership, organization, subgroups, and intensity are interrelated dynamics. Membership is not always clear-cut. Youth can weave in and out, and the meaning of membership is cloudy even to the so-called members. Another dynamic is organization, which is interesting because most gangs are not organized. The importance of subgroups or cliques—smaller groups within groups—to individual behavior has been noted for nearly 100 years. The interaction of these subgroups is related to the gangs' organization. Membership, organization, and subgroups are linked to individual members' *intensity* of gang involvement—the centrality of it within their lives. From wannabes to core members and everything in between, individuals report varying levels.

MEMBERSHIP

Individual youth are identified as members through their affiliation with a particular street gang. One way this occurs is through self-nomination—saying "I am a gang member." This self-nomination is taken at face value by both researchers and law enforcement. A common way youth establish membership is through initiation ceremonies. These ceremonies often entail a violent ritual known as getting jumped in—beaten for a period of time by current members. Through this ritual, the youth is acknowledged by others as a bona fide member and can officially recognize him/herself as a member.

In some instances, what are perceived as gangs could be nothing more than a collective of individuals who have grown up together, spend a lot of time outdoors hanging out, and occasionally offend with each other. They might not have in-group/out-group boundaries or view themselves as a gang (e.g., Fleisher, 1998; Joe-Laidler and Hunt, 2001; cf. B. Sanders, 2005a). With regard to the legal and sociological definitions, their group matches the criteria. Youth can be part of a collective that they may not interpret to be a gang, but that is officially considered one.

Chapter Three of Fleisher's (1998) book *Dead End Kids* highlights this point. He presents data on the lack of clarity surrounding membership among a gang in Kansas City—the Fremont Hustlers. To them, "membership . . . is a peculiar idea" (Fleisher, 1998, p. 39). When asked directly, individuals could list who they thought were Fremont Hustlers, but Fleisher notes that these youth did not "see themselves as having joined a gang, nor do they view each other as members. "'Member,' 'membership,' 'join,' and 'gang' are static notions which fit neither the natural flow of Fremont social life nor the perceptions of Fremont kids" (Fleisher, 1998, p. 39). These were concepts imposed by law enforcement and researchers. The Fremont Hustlers had no written rules and, as a result, no punishments for rule violations. Nothing established membership in the Fremont Hustlers, and they had no initiation rituals, leadership structure, or hierarchical organization. The Fremont Hustlers were a group of kids who had known each other a long time. As Fleisher (1998, p. 40) notes,

> To these kids, Fremont is defined by the interaction of social histories of families; current and former love relationships; boy–boy, girl–girl, and boy–girl hostilities; envy and bitterness over possessions; current and past crime partnerships; arrests and imprisonment in jails, detention centers, and juvenile treatment facilities; histories of prior gang affiliations; and length of interpersonal affiliation.

The Fremont Hustlers utilized the concepts of "time" and "tightness" to describe group dynamics. Time in this context refers to how often the youth hang out on Fremont; those who do so often have closer ties than others. Their concept of time was divided into four categories based on the frequency of visits. On one end were the youth who were "here all the time," six to seven days a week. This was followed by those who were "here a lot"—three to five days a week. Next were those who "come around" a couple of times a week. A final category was those who "will be here if we need them" and visited several times a month. Fleisher also notes that dead or imprisoned youth were still considered Fremont Hustlers.

Tightness referred to similarities in the youths' personal biographies. Most Hustlers were once members of other gangs and also knew one another from time shared together in correctional facilities. In other instances, youth became tight relatively quickly with one another. Tightness between different members of the Fremont Hustlers was temperamental. Youth at one moment would swear allegiance to one another for eternity and the next moment be bitter enemies.

Spergel (1995, p. 85) highlights some of the complexities surrounding the meaning of membership, which can be "vague and shifting." Members are unlikely to know who is in their gang, especially in larger gangs. They might not know who their rivals are. Spergel (1995) says that those who hang around the gang might also be considered members. Individuals might be members for a matter of days or weeks.

ORGANIZATION

Keiser (1979) outlined a federation of gangs organized under one banner—the Vice Lord Nation—and how each branch related to one another. The overall picture was of a large, structured organization. Decker et al. (2008) refer to this as the instrumental-rational view. Media and law enforcement portrayals of gangs tend to indicate they are all this way and, in doing so, exaggerate the levels of organization (Decker et al., 2008; Klein and Maxson, 2006; Spergel, 1995). This portrayal leads to stereotypical depictions that are far removed from reality. Few gangs are organized this way. Those that have a pyramidlike hierarchical structure whereby a couple of leaders sit at the top, followed by lieutenants and then foot soldiers, as well as other roles, rules of appropriate conduct, and tight relations between members are the exception (Decker, 2001; Decker and Curry, 2002; Decker et al., 1998, 2008; Spergel, 1995; Weisel, 2006). Most are a loose collection of cliques or subgroups, with a high turnover rate of membership, horizontal organizational structure, limited cohesion, and no clear leadership or roles (Decker et al., 1998, 2008; Fleisher, 1998; Hagedorn, 1988, 1998; Klein, 1971, 1995; Klein and Maxson, 2006; Spergel, 1995). Gangs in this respect are like amoebas: they have no definitive shape (Klein, 1995; Spergel, 1995).

Weisel (2006) focused on how the organization of various gangs in different cities changed over time, as well as the extent to which they could be described as organized. The research team focused on the most organized gangs in San Diego and Chicago to help answer this question. In doing so, they sought insight about the organizational levels of other, less-organized gangs. Gangs in Chicago had thousands of members and had been around since the 1960s and 1970s, and those in San Diego had hundreds and had been around since the 1940s, 1970s, and 1980s. What is important about this work are the details that come from the police and gang members, as well as how both offered similar portraits. The most common type of gang reported by the police were those characterized by partying, vandalism, and other forms of delinquency, followed by violent and drug-selling gangs. Officers largely noted that gangs in their jurisdictions were mainly loose collections of youth with no formal structure that were territorial and geared toward crime.

From the members' perspective, important differences emerged between the two cities. Gangs in Chicago had roles, leadership, meetings, rules and punishments for violating them, and membership dues. One was integrated firmly with legitimate businesses in the area, operating similar to criminal syndicates. Gangs in San Diego were not like this. The structure of their leadership was informal and their main goals were to socialize—hang out and party. Chicago gangs did enjoy these activities, but they were secondary to criminal enterprise. Gangs in Chicago reported evolving from other, smaller gangs that had once existed in the area, but those in San Diego indicated how gangs splintered off into other, independent groups. Regarding organization, Weisel (2006, pp. 96–97) concluded,

> Gangs . . . represent a fundamentally different form of organization, one that can be described as adaptive or organic rather than bureaucratic . . . [with] an emphasis on individual goals concurrent with organizational ones, diffuse leadership, the active role of subgroups, a generalist orientation, persistence in a volatile environment, and continuity despite the absence of hierarchy. . . . These gangs have [not] evolved into formal organizations mirroring traditional organized crime.

Decker et al. (2008) note that the structure and organization is a "black box": something about which little is known. The authors were interested in the extent that the organizational character was related to crime and victimization. They created an index to gauge organization using seven characteristics: presence of a leader, regular meetings, rules, punishment for breaking rules, use of symbols, roles and responsibilities, and whether members gave money to the gang. They asked current and former members to indicate the presence of these characteristics. The most common characteristics reported were symbols (e.g., gang colors, signs, clothing) and punishments for rule violations. The least common were members giving money to the gang, roles and responsibilities, leaders, and regular meetings.

Decker et al. (2008) reported that the level of gang organization was related to patterns of victimization and crime among individual members. Individuals who were part of gangs that were more organized indicated higher levels of victimization, sales of a variety of drugs, and greater violence compared with those who were part of less-organized gangs (see also Peterson et al., 2001). Decker et al. (2008) hypothesize that shifts in the structure of the gang, although they are not well organized in the first place, resulted in changes in their criminal behavior patterns.

SUBGROUPS

Researchers since Thrasher have noted the importance of the smaller grouping of youth within gangs. Spergel (1995, p. 81) refers to these subgroups as "the basic building block of the gang." As indicated in the Klein/Maxson (2006) typology, subgroups are common features of larger gangs (see also Klein, 1995). These subgroups are referred to as cliques (*klikas*), sets, factions, crews, or gang clusters (Alonso, 1998; Klein, 1971, 1995; Shelden et al., 2001; Spergel, 1995; Spergel and Curry, 1990). Among age-graded cliques, the oldest subgroups might be considered Original Gangstas or *veteranos* (veterans) and the youngest ones Babies, Pee-Wees, or Midgets (Alonso, 1998; Klein, 1995; J. W. Moore, 1978, 1991; Shelden et al., 2001; Spergel, 1995). Female cliques are associated with a larger male gang (Klein, 1995; Spergel, 1995). Outside of cliques, pairs and lone gang members are also part of the overall structure (Klein, 1995).

Subgroups may also emerge by location, such as a geographic area. The Bloods and the Crips are in numerous cities and within different areas across them. Crips can be found in Los Angeles and San Diego, but also in different areas of these cities (e.g., Crips in Watts; Crips in Venice). Within specific Crip and Blood gangs, subgroups are apparent. Take, for example, Crip and Blood gangs that have the word "Rollin" in their names, like the Rollin 60s. This geographic reference comes from the fact that members from this gang live on 61st, 62nd, 63rd Streets, and so on. They have thousands of members and have been around for generations, and they consist of a federation of smaller cliques that live in different areas. Each clique is likely to have its own leadership structure (Klein, 1995). The Rollin 60s are also part of a larger umbrella gang called the Neighborhood Crips. Gangs under the Neighborhood Crips are rivals with those under another umbrella called the Eight Tray Gangster Crips.[10]

These types of groupings are evident in other types of gangs. Mexican American gangs in the Southwest are similar. Many will have the number 13 (or *trece*) after their name, meaning they are linked with/controlled by the Mexican Mafia. These gangs are often bitter rivals with one another. Within any *trece* gang, various subgroups are likely to exist.

Spergel (1995) notes how these cliques are likely to have their own goals, organizational character, and specific symbols. Subgroups are likely to be part of a larger gang, operating either outside of its influences or in accordance with them. Spergel says that some cliques may specialize in types of offending and identify with a particular gang. Those cliques may consist of members of other gangs who come together to commit certain offenses. This goes against the stereotypical portrayal of members from different gangs being at constant war with one another. Spergel indicates the importance of these subgroups in that their behaviors and activities can have a significant impact on the focus and organization of the overall gang.

INTENSITY

Position within the gang and commitment to delinquency are other important aspects. The terms core and fringe or peripheral members have emerged to describe youth with

---

10   From http://www.streetgangs.com/crips/losangeles/r60scrips/ (see also Alonso, 1998).

varying degrees of intensity or embeddedness (Decker and Pyrooz, 2011; Hagedorn, 1998; Horowitz, 1983; Klein, 1995; Knox, 1997; Pyrooz, Sweeten et al., 2013; Sweeten et al., 2013). Klein (1995, p. 103) noted that law enforcement employed additional terms to describe various levels of involvement: "core," "hard-core," "actives," "rostered," "confirmed," "certified," "associates," and "wannabes." Spergel (1995, p. 84) indicates these and other terms like "floaters, "peripheral members," "recruits," and "old gangsters." Fleisher (1998) said that the "here all the time" youth in his study correspond to the core and regular intensity of membership, whereas those "there if we need them" are more marginal members. Whatever the term, a spectrum of intensity of membership is evident.

At one end of the spectrum are the core or hard-core members—those who are known to put in work, often violence in the name of their gang (Klein, 1995; B. Sanders et al., 2010). The gang means a great deal to them. Core members spend substantial time with the gang, strongly identify with it, and are heavily involved in serious criminal activities (Klein, 1995; Spergel, 1995). On the other end of the spectrum are the fringe members. These youth do not spend much time with the gang and weakly identify with it. Fringe members are involved in relatively minor forms of delinquency, much of it having nothing to do with the gang (e.g., substance use; petty theft). Fleisher (1998) also noted that those members who spent less time hanging out were less involved in selling drugs.

Outside of core and fringe, other levels of involvement are evident. Spergel (1995) mentions floaters. These individuals might not be identified members of a gang, but rather float between different gangs, having special talents or resources beneficial to some more than others. They may serve as liaisons between warring gangs or arrange certain business transactions involving drugs, guns, or stolen property for individual members. According to Spergel (1995, p. 84) floaters "tend to be entrepreneurial, well respected, and articulate, with many community connections, legitimate and illegitimate." Spergel (1995) also discusses those individuals who desire to be members—wannabes or recruits—as well as those in the twilight of their careers—veterans or old gangsters.

Intensity is linked to differential probabilities of being involved in criminal activity. Core members are more likely to commit crime than those on the fringe, but the versatility in their patterns of offending are similar (Klein, 1995). Esbensen and Huizinga (1993) found no differences in self-reported delinquency or in their levels of involvement between core and peripheral members. Likewise, Fagan (1989) reported that leaders had similar levels of drug use and participation in delinquency compared to others.

Given the unique ways in which youth experience the gang, youth might have varying risk profiles for membership. Core members should have more risk factors in their lives—things contributing to their membership—when compared with fringe members. Klein (1995) found no differences between core and fringe youth based on their sociodemographic backgrounds. He did report that the core had lower intelligence, higher rates of impulsivity, fewer social skills, and higher dependence on their peers than the fringe (see also Vigil, 1988a). Yablonsky (1962) found core members were much more likely to be psychologically disturbed, but fringe members were similar to everyday youth. Others

reported the exact opposite: core members were intelligent and sociable and the fringe members were not (Horowitz, 1983; Klein, 1971; Short and Strodtbeck, 1965).

Core members were in the middle age range (e.g., 15–19 years old) compared to younger (e.g., 11–13 years old) and older (e.g., 20 years and older) gang members, who were much more likely to be fringe members (Klein, 1995). This means that, throughout their lives, youth can weave in and out of core and fringe statuses—and everything in between (Spergel, 1995). As Spergel (1995, p. 85) says, "Gang members may 'graduate' from lower- to higher-status gang positions, particularly as they age. However, they may also shift from core to peripheral or associates positions and back again."

THE CAUSES AND CORRELATES STUDIES

In the 1990s, findings began to emerge from a series of large-scale longitudinal studies on youth development. These studies sought to examine the onset, persistence, and desistance of delinquency (Krisberg, 2005) and were conducted in five cities in North America: Seattle (Battin et al., 1998; Hill et al., 1999, 2001; Seattle Social Development Study), Rochester (Rochester Youth Development Study; Thornberry et al., 1993, 2003), Denver (Denver Youth Study; Esbensen and Huizinga, 1993; Esbensen et al., 1993), Pittsburg (Lahey et al., 1999; Loeber et al., 1998; Pittsburg Youth Study), and Montreal (Gatti, Tremblay et al., 2005; Lacourse et al., 2003; Montreal Longitudinal Experimental Study). Together, the Causes and Correlates studies (as most of them have been referred to: Krisberg, 2005; Thornberry et al., 2004), have further established the variables paradigm. Members, compared to non-gang young offenders and non-gang nonoffenders, have particular risk backgrounds according to this model.

The studies were developed utilizing a public health method toward studying crime and delinquency using a "risk factor" approach (Hawkins and Catalano, 1992). As Krisberg (2005) notes, heart disease can be predicted in part by participation in certain behaviors that place individuals at risk for the condition, such as poor diet, lack of exercise, and smoking. Heart disease can be prevented by avoiding these behaviors. Participation in crime and violence was perceived to be predicted in similar ways, meaning that if youth had certain characteristics within their lives, they would be more likely to commit crime and violence. These are considered risk factors.[11]

The risk factor approach (also called the "variables approach" [Hughes (2006)]) indicates five different domains: individual, family, school, peer group, and community. Compared to non-gang youth, gang youth are more likely to report risks across all five domains (Howell and Egley, 2005). These factors are cumulative and overlapping. This means that over the life course, risks build on and influence each another at different stages of youths' lives. Howell and Egley (2005) detail the five risk domains and the specific risk factors in each:

Individual risks:
Violence and aggression
Delinquency
Conduct disorders and externalizing behaviors (disruptive, antisocial)
Early involvement with the opposite sex (e.g., dating; promiscuity)
Antisocial/delinquent beliefs
Hyperactivity
Early substance use (alcohol, tobacco, illicit drugs)
Depression
Life stressors
Poor refusal skills

Family risk factors:
Poverty and transitions (e.g., loss of family member)
Family financial stress
Antisocial behavior
Low attachment to parents or family
Abuse (sexual, physical, mental)
Low parental education level
Parent prosocial attitudes toward violence
Family management issues
Teenage fatherhood

School risk factors:
Low achievement in school
Negatively labeled by teachers

---

11 The risk factor approach also utilized within major policy initiatives aimed at reducing delinquency (e.g., Title V of the Juvenile Justice Act [see Krisberg (2005)]).

Low academic aspirations and school attachment; low school commitment
Low attachment to teachers
Low parent educational expectations for child
Learning disabilities

Peer group risk factors:
Association with peers who engage in delinquency, aggression, or other problems

Community risk factors:
Availability of drugs and guns
High community arrest rate
Feeling unsafe in the neighborhood
Low neighborhood attachment
Poverty
Social disorganization

PROTECTIVE FACTORS

Just as certain conditions place youth more at risk of joining, others are protective in that they help insulate youth (Howell and Egley, 2005; Krisberg, 2005; McDaniel, 2012; Vigil, 2007). These conditions include positive beliefs about life and healthy living and participating in prosocial activities (e.g., sporting teams; attending religious services; helping in the community). Another condition is being around individuals with prosocial views. Recognition is as important as participation, and youth must be publicly congratulated for their achievements, obtain a sense of belonging, and be given the opportunity to use their newly acquired skills (Krisberg, 2005). Through this combination, the impact of risk factors can be blunted (Hawkins and Catalano, 1992).

More is known about the influence of risk factors compared to that of protective ones. Evidence has suggested that the same factor may have a risk or a protective effect, and that a factor that protects in one instance may contribute to risk in another (Howell and Egley, 2005). Protective factors are those defined as negatively related to membership (McDaniel, 2012). Whereas weak family relations are positively related to membership, strong family relationships are negatively related. Under this definition, family relationships are a protective factor. Using a similar definition, others have found that solid social skills and religiosity (e.g., strong connections to religion) are protective factors (Li et al., 2002; Maxson et al., 1998). Other factors negatively related to joining include strong coping skills and peer support (McDaniel, 2012). McDaniel's (2012) point helps illustrate how protective factors can outweigh and outinfluence risk factors. Even among youth who have many of the risk factors, joining a gang is far from inevitable, and families, schools and youth can play active roles in reducing their allure (Vigil, 2007).

SUMMARY

No consensus on the definition of a gang exists. As with early perspectives, including delinquency in this definition remains a sensitive issue. On one side is the argument that delinquency cannot be both included in a definition and then examined as a product of membership. This would be tautological. However, including delinquency in the definition is paramount because it distinguishes gangs from other groups. The circulatory argument of including delinquency in the definition of gangs has also been rejected because other aspects—their size, organizational character, longevity—can be measured as they relate to individual and/or group involvement in crime and violence. Many types have been found and criminal patterns are distinguishing characteristics. Other qualities that separate the types include their longevity, territoriality, presence of subgroups, size, and age range of members.

One way around these arguments about sociological definitions is to employ legal definitions. These definitions present a unique set of problems, however. First, they often differ by state, as do the conditions necessary to convict someone of a gang-related offense. The terminology used to define gang, gang member, or gang related can be unclear. The police might consider a group of individuals a gang regardless of whether they or third-party researchers see themselves as such. Other gray areas include groups that are not considered gangs, such as motorcycle clubs, taggers, and skinheads, but that have been called gangs under legal statutes by law enforcement and prosecuting attorneys. Despite the progress on narrowing definitions, problems of accuracy remain.

The daily activities of members and the pros and cons of membership were examined. The Los Angeles Study reported that gangs hang out and do nothing more than anything else—a finding that emerged among some of the earliest studies. Many ironies are present in what youth say they get out of a gang. Interrelated subtleties were also discussed, including the extent to which gangs were organized, what membership means and how to ascertain it, the presence and importance of subgroups, and the intensity of a youth's involvement. Researchers and law enforcement have differing views as to the levels of organization. Intensity is important to understand because of its link with youth participation in crime and violence. Finally, the risk factor approach was reviewed, which argues that a series of conditions within youths' lives increases their likelihood of gang membership. This approach also revealed that certain conditions protect youth from gangs, although less is known about how and why this happens.

CHAPTER REVIEW QUESTIONS

1. What is the Eurogang definition of gang? Explain what each part means.
2. Discuss the tautology of using delinquency as a defining characteristic of gangs. How has this argument been rejected by Klein and Maxson?
3. What are some of the problems with legal definitions of gangs regarding the clarity of terms used?
4. Why are groups like Greek organizations, motorcycle clubs, stoners, and taggers *not* considered gangs?
5. Describe the different gangs within the Klein/Maxson typology.
6. What are some problems with the concept of membership?
7. What are the conclusions from Weisel and Decker et al. on gang organization?
8. What is the intensity or embeddedness of gang involvement?
9. List each risk domain and some of the specific risk factors under each one.
10. What are some examples of protective factors?

HYPERLINKS TO ARTICLES ABOUT DEFINITIONS AND RISK FACTORS

Gang-related legislation by state and subject
http://www.nationalgangcenter.gov/Legislation/

The Causes and Correlates studies: Findings and policy implications
By T. P. Thornberry, D. Huizinga, and R. Loeber
https://www.ncjrs.gov/html/ojjdp/203555/jj2.html/

Modern-day youth gangs
By J. C. Howell, A. Egley Jr., and D. K. Gleason
https://www.ncjrs.gov/html/ojjdp/jjbul2002_06_1/contents.html/

CHAPTER 3

RACE, MIGRATION, AND IMMIGRATION

Acculturation: A process of acquiring, modifying, or adapting to a culture.

COINTELPRO: A counterintelligence program operated by the FBI that targeted the activities of black militant groups such as the Black Panther Party and the U.S. Organization.

Critical race theory: An argument that racism is deep seated within American culture and history and that such racism has impacted and continues to negatively impact non-whites on various levels.

Diaspora: The scattering or movement of people from their country of origin to another.

Emigrate: To leave and resettle in another country; leaving a country of origin; to emigrate from.

Ethnicity: A sociological construct that refers to culture, nationality, language, ancestry, and beliefs. Often used interchangeably with race.

The Great Migration: The movement of millions of African Americans during the 20th century from the South to other areas of the United States, particularly the West (e.g., Los Angeles), Northeast (e.g., New York City), and Midwest (e.g., Chicago).

Jim Crow laws: Legal forms of discrimination within Southern states that restricted housing, education, employment, and other opportunities for nonwhites, particularly African Americans.

Immigrate: To settle in another country; arriving in a new country; to immigrate to.

Race: A biological construct about physical appearance, such as skin, hair and eye color, and bone structure. Often used interchangeably with ethnicity.

Race relations: In the United States, this concerns the relationship among whites, African Americans, Latinos, Asians, and Native Americans.

Racism: The combination of prejudice and power. The ability of one group's prejudice to impact shape, limit, and/or control the behaviors, options, and/or outcomes of other groups. Racism can be overt, such as violence, or it can be institutional, such as discriminatory hiring and promotion practices.

Refugee: A person who has left their country of origin because of persecution, the fear of persecution, or natural disaster.

Segregation: Either a voluntary or an enforced separation or isolation of a particular class of people based on race, class, nationality, or other considerations that often restricts their options in relation to education, employment, and housing.

SHARPs/SARs: Acronyms for "Skin Heads against Racial Prejudice" and "Skinheads against Racism."

Tong: Chinese word for gathering place, hall, or social club. Some tongs have been considered criminal organizations.

Triad: Chinese word that refers to the triangle of heaven, earth, and mankind. Triads are secret societies that once focused on political revolution, but later evolved and now refer to organized crime.

TTTT: Or the four "T's"; Vietnamese symbol that stands for "thoung, tien, tu, toi," which translates to "love, money, prison, crime."

Chapter Learning Objectives

- Describe migration and immigration patterns of minority gangs.
- Explain how discrimination contributed to gangs in minority communities.
- Understand the impact of culture on gangs and gang activity.
- Clarify the character of white gangs or white youth in gangs.

INTRODUCTION

Race relations have deeply impacted American society. For most of the history of gang research, the importance of race has been downplayed. Within recent years, however, race has emerged as a critical variable in understanding the etiology and control of gangs. Within poor black and Latino communities, other risk factors are more important to acknowledge in determining who joins and the consequences of membership. When explanations are sought about which communities have gangs and which do not, ignoring race is difficult. A comparison of poor white with poor black and Latino communities suggests that gangs are significantly more likely to be found within the latter areas. This phenomenon is related to the impact of generations of blocked opportunities and limitations they and other minorities have suffered as a result of white prejudice. Immigration and migration are key issues to address when looking at race and the emergence of gangs.

The chapter begins by offering a brief history of race relations in America with an intent to underscore how employment, housing, education, and other restrictions have negatively impacted minorities and contributed to the rise of gangs in their communities. African Americans are discussed first, including how racism and segregation eventually led to supergangs like the Crips and Bloods. Next, Latinos are examined, with a particular focus on different types of Mexican American gangs and the People and Folk Nations—two different conglomerations. From here, the focus turns to Chinese, Southeast Asian, and Filipino gangs, the most common being Asian and Asian Pacific Islanders. Native American gangs are then reviewed. Finally, the chapter explores gangs, including skinheads, in white neighborhoods.

A BRIEF NOTE ON RACE RELATIONS IN AMERICAN HISTORY

Race and ethnicity are used interchangeably within the research literature, but they are distinct.[1] Race refers to biological concerns such as physical appearance (e.g., skin, hair and eye color, bone structure), and ethnicity refers to sociological concerns, such as culture, nationality, language, ancestry, and beliefs. Within any race, various ethnicities exist. For example, Asian is a race and Chinese, Vietnamese, and Japanese are ethnicities within that race. In the United States, race relations (as opposed to ethnic relations) refers to relationships among five categories of people: white, black, Asian, Native American/American Indian, and Hispanic/Latino. These relations have deeply impacted various domains of U.S. society.

Individuals whose family heritage stems from European countries would today consider themselves white. But in late 19th- and early 20th-century America, European immigrants had distinct identities that shaped housing patterns and employment opportunities. Conflict occurred among waves of immigrants and prejudices helped fuel hostilities (Olzak, 1989). Those from northern European countries who had come to America earlier and were more established helped design and pass laws that restricted the amount of southern and eastern Europeans allowed to enter the country on an annual basis (i.e., the Immigration Act of 1924; Olzak, 1989). The act also targeted Jews. In the mid 19th to early 20th centuries, race relations largely concerned conflict between people from different European nationalities and origins.

Throughout the 20th century, people from different ethnic European backgrounds assimilated and the definition of race relations in America shifted. Immigration and migration patterns among nonwhites were the catalyst for this shift. Conflict emerged between the dominant white culture and people from different races. These struggles were in the form of overt and institutionalized racism that deeply impacted the lives of nonwhites in terms of housing, education, employment opportunities, civil rights, and the meeting of basic needs. This occurred for generations. One result is income disparities between whites

---

1   This chapter utilizes the term race instead of ethnicity and the following terms to describe five races: white, black (or African American), Latino, Asian/Asian Pacific Islander, and Native American.

and minorities, particularly Latinos and African Americans. Nowadays, blacks earn about three-fourths of what whites do and their unemployment rate has remained twice that of whites (Rodgers, 2008). Latino men earn less—about two-thirds that of white men.[2] Gender further impacts differentials. Black women earn 70% and Latino women earn 60% that of white men.[3] Income disparities have contributed to the concentration of Latinos and blacks within poor, socially disorganized communities—those linked to higher rates of crime, violence, and victimization.

The introductory chapter of this book reported that groups of inner-city youth who get in trouble together have been around for hundreds of years and the image of a delinquent has long been one of the young urban male (Pearson, 1983). In the latter half of the 20th century, this criminal Other became racialized, whereby the image of the delinquent became the young urban *minority* male (Jefferson, 1993). In the United States, this minority male is predominately either black or Latino. The disproportionality of Latinos and blacks within the criminal and juvenile justice system is staggering (Sampson and Lauritsen, 1997). The war on drugs has devastated their communities (Banks, 2003; Fellner, 2009; B. Sanders, in press; Wacquant, 2001). Between 1999 and 2005, blacks and Latinos each constituted 12% of the overall U.S. population, but among prisoners incarcerated on state drug charges, about 58% were black and 20% were Latino; inside federal facilities, 44% of prisoners on drug charges are black and 33% are Latino (Mauer, 2009). To compare, whites comprised about 70% of the population between 1999 and 2005, but only about a quarter of state drug prisoners and federal drug prisoners were white (Mauer, 2009). The United States has five times as many white drug users as black ones, but blacks are about 10 times more likely to be sent to prison on a drug-related charge (Mauer, 2009; National Association for the Advancement of Colored People, n.d.; Wacquant, 2001). One in three black men in their twenties is incarcerated, on probation, or on parole (Donziger, 1996; Wacquant, 2001). The prisons have become ghettos (Wacquant, 2001).

Incarceration makes reentry and immersion back into conventional lifestyles difficult. The impact of incarceration among minorities has been likened to the new Jim Crow laws—legalized forms of discrimination (Alexander, 2010; Wacquant, 2001). Criminal convictions restrict housing, employment, and voting rights, which is what the old Jim Crow laws did (Alexander, 2010). Limitations on employment and housing contribute to recidivism and returning to jail or prison. These are monumental issues within the justice systems, and they have distressed Latino and black communities for decades.

Race relations genuinely divide America. Latinos and blacks in particular continue to experience employment, educational, and housing limitations compared with whites. Even criminal justice policies, such as stop and search, have unfairly targeted blacks and Latinos (Geller and Fagan, 2010; Rudovsky and Rosenthal, 2013). The phrases driving

---

2   See U.S. Current Population Survey and the National Committee on Pay Equity; also Bureau of Labor Statistics: Weekly and Hourly Earnings Data from the Current Population Survey, retrieved from http://www.infoplease.com/ipa/A0882775.html/.

3   See *op. cit.*

while black and driving while brown have emerged as modern-day colloquialisms that capture the increased likelihood that Latinos and African Americans face in relation to being pulled over by the police. The struggles that African American and Latino families have had to contend with have shaped numerous aspects of their lives, including gangs in their communities.

BLACK GANGS

About one-third of all gang members in the United States are African American (National Gang Center, n.d.). Racial discrimination against African Americans is linked to the emergence of gangs within their communities (Adamson, 2000; Alonso, 2004; G. C. Brown et al., 2012; Davis, 2006; Hagedorn, 2006a; see Box 3.1). Hagedorn (2006a, p. 194) refers to the focus on structural determinants and the ignorance of race in the etiology of gangs in black communities in Chicago as "sociological shibboleth." He presents a revisionist history whereby overt and institutionalized racism and white supremacy are the chief reasons for megagangs, such as the People and Folk Nations. G. C. Brown et al. (2012) draw on critical race theory, which argues that racism is intrinsic within American society, and contend that it significantly contributed to the cause of black gangs. Alonso (2004) posits that "racialized identities" are important to acknowledge when explaining the structural disadvantage blacks suffered, which resulted in gangs in Los Angeles. He argues that gangs are a result of a combination of institutionalized and overt racism in the forms of intimidation, police brutality, educational and residential segregation, workplace exclusion, and extreme marginalization.

During the Great Migration, many blacks left the South to escape Jim Crow laws and blatant, often violent discrimination (G. C. Brown et al., 2012). When they arrived, local statutes limited the residential areas where they could purchase land, eventually resulting in overcrowded and substandard conditions (Alonso, 2004; Hagedorn, 2006a). G. C. Brown et al. (2012) note that the experience within Los Angeles was shaped not by a desire of racial groups to live among themselves, but by being legally excluded from other areas for no reason other than being black. Watts and South Los Angeles (formerly South Central) were once thriving white, middle-class communities. Over time, they turned into ghettos, complete with junkyards, abandoned warehouses, and few safe public recreational spaces. This transition led G. C. Brown et al. (2012, p. 215) to conclude, "it is clear how restrictive covenants and other racist real estate practices can take a neighborhood and turn it into an impoverished slum by forcing the underclass to become trapped within it" (see also Alonso, 2004).

When blacks fought for greater rights, whites reacted with hostility. Part of this reaction included the formation of gangs that terrorized black communities with violence and intimidation (Adamson, 2000; Alonso, 2004; G. C. Brown et al., 2012; Davis, 2006; Hagedorn, 2006a; Keiser, 1969; Suttles, 1968). In Los Angeles, one group was called the Spookhunters (Alonso, 2004); Chicago had the Murderers (Hagedorn, 2006a). These and other groups of white thugs were committed to harming the black community through fire bombing homes, assassinations, kidnappings, harassment, and mob violence. Black gangs

BOX 3.1: A THEORY ON RACE, CLASS, AND URBAN INEQUALITY

Sampson and Wilson's (1995) theory of race, class, and urban inequality is specifically about impoverished inner-city African American communities and how structural conditions have given rise to a culture of tolerance in relation to violence, gangs, and crime. The authors discuss race candidly. The theory borrows heavily from W. J. Wilson's (1987) underclass perspective and the tenets of social disorganization theory (Shaw and McKay, 1942). In brief, underclass theory argues that high rates of violent crime in black communities are a result of the impact of economic deprivation and the high rate of black men without jobs on the structure and harmony of African American families. Many theories on crime often emphasize structure, whereas others elaborate on culture. Sampson and Wilson's theory uses these concepts in combination. The theory posits that "macro-social patterns of residential inequality give rise to the social isolation and ecological concentration of the truly disadvantaged, which in turn leads to structural barriers and cultural adaptations that undermine social organization and hence the control of crime" (Sampson and Wilson, 1995, p. 38).

Sampson and Wilson (1995) indicate that blacks and whites live in distinct ecological conditions across the United States. Urban poverty and family disruption are clearly concentrated by race. The authors report that the worst urban area in terms of economic deprivation and family disruption for whites is much better than the average context in which blacks reside. Criminogenic conditions—lack of jobs, poor schools, family disruption, and no positive role models—are concentrated in black inner-city communities. Poor blacks are more likely to live in areas characterized by structural social disorganization.

Why is this the case? The freeway system, which helped blacks begin to leave the South decades earlier, was expanded in the 1950s. New developments meant the freeways would now be going through the heart of many black communities. These freeways, along with other forms of urban renewal, were responsible for displacing and dispersing black residents. Deindustrialization in the 1960s and 1970s, although it had a wide negative impact on many communities, particularly devastated black ones. Sampson and Wilson also comment on the policy decisions to concentrate blacks and other poor minorities within public housing. These decisions included a toleration of the segregation of black families within urban housing markets, opposition from organized community groups toward the development of public housing in particular areas, and a lack of investment within poor, black inner-city communities. Race plays a significant factor in these policies. The combination of racial segregation, structural economic change, the migration of the black affluent classes, a lack of jobs for black men, and housing discrimination led to the concentration of poverty and family disruption in black inner-city communities.

Sampson and Wilson (1995) continue to note that the characteristics related to structural social disorganization spawned cultural social isolation. Poverty, anonymity, instability, and distrust have resulted in a lack of communication between community members, which, in turn, has led to a paucity of information about different ideas on acceptable values, including those related to delinquency. This lack of consensus of appropriate behaviors has resulted in the emergence of a culture that either legitimizes or tolerates crime and violence. Disorder, crime, drugs, and violence have all become somewhat expected, routine aspects of everyday life within black ghettos. These values are maintained by the isolation of such communities from mainstream society.

Over generations, violence has become a way of life—an unavoidable reality whereby youth are disproportionately exposed to individuals who preach violence and who themselves witness and become victims of violence. Black inner-city youth know violence because they interact disproportionately with people who value it. The "cognitive landscapes" that emerge in structurally disorganized neighborhoods "influence the probability of criminal outcomes and harmful deviant behavior" (Sampson and Wilson, 1995, p. 45).

Sampson and Wilson's (1995) theory of race, class, and inequality can be applied to understanding the emergence and persistence of gangs. Many of the structural risk factors that are related to gang involvement are illustrated within the theory. So, too, are many of the cultural attributes commonly reported among gang members. Sampson and Wilson (1995) acknowledge many qualitative studies within the inner city that support their argument that structurally disorganized communities give rise to the emergence of cultural value systems that tolerate or legitimize crime and violence (e.g., E. Anderson, 1990; Horowitz, 1983; Kornhauser, 1978).

first emerged as a form of protection. Over time, the attacks from whites decreased in frequency and they moved out *en masse*. As white people left communities like South Los Angeles and Southside Chicago, the white-on-black violence declined. Hagedorn (2006a) makes the point that the Irish and Italian gangs in Chicago—who once terrorized black communities—were referred to not as gangs but as social athletic clubs whose members eventually became the city's police, firemen, and, in some cases, politicians.[4]

Racism not only resulted in segregation within the housing market, but also excluded blacks from major industries (Adamson, 2000; Hagedorn, 2006a). Blacks were largely conscribed to jobs within the service sector, where they worked in substandard conditions with little job protection (G. C. Brown et al., 2012). They were limited in opportunities for participating in illicit enterprise (Hagedorn, 2006a). Young people faced the worst job prospects. Legitimate and illegitimate jobs were limited, and drugs, gambling, and pent up frustration were everywhere, leading to unprecedented levels of black-on-black violence (Alonso, 2004; G. C. Brown et al., 2012).

Black youth infighting continued until the riots in the mid 1960s and the period that followed in major U.S. cities. Then, black youths in communities in places like South Los Angeles and Southside Chicago became more politicized and united through the assistance of the Black Panthers and the U.S. Organization—semimilitarized political movements. The result was a reduction of black-on-black gang violence and a more cohesive front against the external threat of police brutality that impacted the entire black community. This type of control waned over time as the FBI weakened these organizations. With the increasing social influence of the Black Panthers, the FBI monitored their activities and targeted their members via a counterintelligence program known as COINTEL-PRO (Alonso, 2004; G. C. Brown et al., 2012; Davis, 2006; Hagedorn, 2006a). In a short period of time, many members of the Black Panthers and other militant organizations were assassinated or imprisoned, and the groups soon ceased to exist. Evidence suggests that the FBI, then led by J. Edgar Hoover, engaged in espionage and subterfuge to combat and eliminate black militant groups (Alonso, 2004; G. C. Brown et al., 2012; Davis, 2006; Hagedorn, 2006a).

After witnessing leaders in their community killed or jailed, as well as assassinations of national black figures like Martin Luther King, Jr. and Malcolm X, poor urban black youth lacked effective role models. A type of anomic order set in where goals became unclear, and youth resorted to forming gangs, similar to their forefathers in the late 1940s, who protected themselves from white racist thugs (Alonso, 2004; G. C. Brown et al., 2012; Davis, 2006). Lacking a political conscience and searching for a fresh identity, these newly formed gangs resorted to petty crime and violence, preying on one another. The increase in these behaviors brought about more media attention, which attracted more police. The media's reportage, although largely negative, had the unintended consequences of advertising to poor, disenfranchised urban black male youth that gangs were tough and exuded masculinity (Alonso, 2004). As a result, more black youth were attracted to gangs during the late 1960s and early 1970s, and membership soared in South Los Angeles.

---

4   Hagedorn (2006a) notes that Richard J. Daley, who was the mayor of Chicago from 1955 to 1976, was once a member of the Hamburg gang in 1919. Allegedly, the Hamburg gang was one of the leading white gangs responsible for initiating and participating in the Chicago race riots of 1919.

THE CRIPS AND BLOODS

Two major black gangs are the Crips and Bloods. They first emerged in Los Angeles and "migrated" to other parts of the nation (see Maxson, 1998). The Crips, like the Bloods, are not one large unified gang, but are composed of various sets based on specific residential locations (see *Media Check!*). In Los Angeles, these include the 107 Hoover Street Crips, one of the oldest Crip sets (G. C. Brown et al., 2012), as well as the Inglewood Crips, Compton Crips, Westside Crips, and many others. Blood sets, also known as Pirus, named after a tiny street in Compton, are similar in that they are also from certain areas (e.g., Athens Park Bloods; East Compton Bloods). Not all Crip sets get along, nor do all Blood sets. A collective of Crip sets known as the Neighborhood Crips, which include the Rollin 60s, are rivals with another set known as the Gangsta Crips, which include the Eight Tray.

Several accounts explain the origins of the Crips and Bloods. One position has it that Crips is an acronym that stands for "Continuous Revolution in Progress," but this occurred *ex post facto* (G. C. Brown et al., 2012; Davis, 2006). Researchers note that, in 1969, after the Black Panther Party was wiped out, Raymond Washington, a 15-year-old Fremont High School student, started a gang that would later be known as the Crips (Alonso, 2004; G. C. Brown et al., 2012). Having admired an older gang from the 1960s called the Avenues, Washington started a gang called the Baby Avenues, also known as the Avenue Cribs, indicating that they were a younger version. The Cribs had a distinct style that included wearing an earring in their left earlobe and leather jackets and using walking canes (G. C. Brown et al., 2012). Crips is a mispronunciation of Cribs. According to G. C. Brown et al. (2012), the name change happened after several members of the Cribs robbed an elderly woman, and witnesses reported that the assailants were carrying canes, assuming they were crippled. Based on these accounts, the media reported that the robbery was from a gang called the Crips, and the name stuck.[5] Washington and several other tough and respected youth within the surrounding neighborhoods, including Stanley "Tookie" Williams,[6] helped coalesce other gangs into various Crip sets. Today in Los Angeles, more than 100 Crip sets operate, with many more in cities across the United States.

The Bloods formed as a reaction to the Crips. Several gangs outside of the immediate area of Watts and South Central felt pressure from the other gangs that united under the banner of the Crips (G. C. Brown et al., 2012). Black youth from other residential areas who were not Crips found themselves attacked and intimidated. These youth were often members of other independent gangs within the area, like the Brims, Compton Pirus, Bounty Hunters, and the Bishops (G. C. Brown et al., 2012). A turning point was when the Crips murdered a member of the Brims (G. C. Brown et al., 2012). To combat the external threat of the Crips, various other gangs federated under the banner of the Bloods (G. C. Brown et al., 2012). Bloods are

---

5 Another interpretation has it that Crips is a combination of "Crib" and RIP (rest in peace; Martinez and Ramos, 2008). This interpretation was mentioned in the documentary *Bastards of the Party*.

6 Stanley Williams is notable for at least two reasons. First, during his long stint in prison, he wrote children's books preaching nonviolence and, as a result, was nominated for a Nobel Peace Prize. This is depicted in the biopic about his life, *Redemption* (2004). Second, he is one of about a dozen people executed by the state of California since the mid-1970s.

also referred to as Damus, which comes from the Swahili word for blood. Currently, dozens of Blood sets are active in Los Angeles, with many more throughout the United States.

LATINO GANGS

A rich body of ethnographic research conducted in several cities is available on gangs whose families immigrated to the United States from Latin countries (e.g., Puerto Rico, Mexico, El Salvador; see Brotherton and Barrios, 2004; Horowitz, 1983; J. W. Moore, 1978, 1991; Padilla, 1992; Vigil, 1988a, 1988b, 2002; Ward, 2012; Zatz and Portillos, 2000). Latinos are the largest ethnic minority in the United States. Approximately one-sixth of all Latino Americans are gang members, although that figure is much higher in particular neighborhoods (Krohn et al., 2011; National Gang Center, n.d.).

Latino and African American communities share similar histories in terms of the etiology of gangs. Researchers have argued that what occurred in black communities also occurred in Latino ones; Latino *barrios* are the same as black ghettos (G. C. Brown et al., 2012; Valdez, 2003; Vigil, 1988a, 1988b). Mexican American communities in large cities witnessed an increase in criminogenic conditions in the mid- to late 20th century, including rises in male joblessness, single-parent families, and those claiming welfare dependency, as well as decreases in public-sector funding and services. Similar to African American communities, race played a critical role in the emergence of Latino gangs (Brotherton and Barrios, 2004; Vigil, 1988a, 1988b, 2002). Latinos experienced racism on a systematic level that limited educational and economic opportunities and shaped residential patterns. These factors impacted family and school controls and encouraged a process of street socialization and gangs (J. W. Moore, 1978; Padilla, 1992; Vigil, 1988a, 1988b, 2002).

Latino youth growing up under these conditions are at a heightened risk for membership because of acculturation (Krohn et al., 2011). Acculturation refers to a state of being caught between two cultures: the traditional culture of the home country (e.g., Mexico, El Salvador) and that of the United States. The differences Latino youth juggle, what Vigil (2008, p. 55), refers to as "the tensions of cultural dissonance," are additional stressors and strains that exacerbate poverty, social marginalization, and racism. Acculturation can contribute to both the emergence and the persistence of gangs.

Latino parents' traditional and conservative expectations of their children living in a liberal and pluralistic American society are often the chief source of this tension. Immigrant parents attempting to adapt to the culture of the United States can also undermine their control, which contributes to the risk of membership (Vigil, 2008). Several studies have found that Latino members were less likely to be acculturated compared to nonmembers (Horowitz, 1983; Lopez and Brummett, 2003; J. W. Moore, 1978; Vigil, 1988a, 1988b). In these cases, Latino gang youth rejected mainstream white, American society and embraced the *cholo* culture. Low levels of acculturation and marginality feed off one another. The lack of acculturation leads to further marginality, which impacts the acculturation process, contributing to Latino youth becoming further enmeshed in the gang lifestyle (H. V. Miller et al., 2011).

Valdez (2003) indicates three unique populations of Latino gangs: Puerto Rican American, Central American, and Mexican American. Puerto Rican American gangs are primarily located within urban areas in northeastern and midwestern states and focus on drug selling as a primary criminal activity (see also Brotherton and Barrios, 2004; Padilla, 1992). Central American gangs consist mainly of relatively recent immigrants, particularly from Guatemala and El Salvador, who have moved to Southern California's multiracial urban areas (Valdez, 2003). One of the more infamous gangs originally from El Salvador is *Mara-Salvatrucha 13*, also known as MS-13 (Ward, 2012). Specific areas within Los Angeles are known for large percentages of Guatemalan and El Salvadorian immigrants (Vigil, 2002). These gangs, in contrast to the Puerto Rican ones, are more territorial based, and their criminal activities are limited to fighting other rival ethnic gangs (Valdez, 2003). Most Latino gang members are Mexican American (Spergel, 1995; Valdez, 2003).

THE PEOPLE NATION AND THE FOLKS NATION

The People Nation and the Folks Nation are two large umbrella gangs under which numerous others claim affiliation. These "nations" are conglomerations from different cities concentrated in the Midwest (e.g., Chicago, Milwaukee). The People and Folks Nations consist largely of Latinos, but African Americans are also represented (Spergel, 1995). The People Nation originated as an assortment of some of the oldest gangs in Chicago, including the Black P Stones (aka, the El Rukns), the Almighty Latin King and Queen Nation, and the Vice Lords. The Folks Nation was also formed by some of the oldest gangs in Chicago, including the Gangster Disciples, Maniac Latin Disciples, and the Black Disciples. The People Nation are aligned with the Bloods, as the Folk Nation are with the Crips. Like the Crips and the Bloods, the People and Folk Nations do not get along.

These nations have all sorts of cultural minutiae loaded with significance and meaning, such as wearing clothing on the right or left side of the body. The Folk Nation prefer the right; they tilt their hat and wear earrings or their colors on that side (e.g., a blue bandana in the back pocket).

Those affiliated with the People Nation prefer the left side. Many of their members are Muslims and, because the number 5 is important to them, the People Nation identify with this number. Other symbols include the 21-brick pyramid, the 5-point crown, the cane, the cross, the colors red, gold, and black, and the playboy bunny. Symbols of the Folk Nation include the colors blue and black, the 6-point star, a pitchfork, and dice.

A TYPOLOGY OF MEXICAN AMERICAN GANGS

Mexican American gangs were similar to the multigenerational European gangs studied by early researchers (Valdez, 2003). These multigenerational ties curbed extreme behaviors of members through informal controls, such as the presence of long-standing neighbors and extended family networks (Valdez, 2003; Zatz and Portillos, 2000). These generational links deteriorated after years of urban strife and economic hardships in the barrios, a result of which was the breakdown of informal controls and the emergence of a diversity of gang types (Valdez, 2003). Mexican American gangs now vary considerably in terms of their organization and patterns of criminal activity.

Valdez (2003, 2007) developed a typology of Mexican American gangs based on research in San Antonio that provides a structural framework from which to analyze and identify their diversity. Four types were reported: criminal-adult dependent, criminal nonadult-dependent, barrio-territorial, and transitional. Five variables distinguished them: illegal activities, organization, drug use patterns (i.e., whether they had rules on hard drug use), adult influences (i.e., the extent that adults shaped the nature of the gangs' delinquency), and violence (i.e., expressive [or purposeful] versus personal [or random] acts of violence).

For the criminal-adult dependent gangs, adults provided drugs, firearms, the opportunity to sell drugs, and a national and international market for distributing stolen goods. Selling drugs, particularly heroin, was the principal source of income. This type of gang was tightly organized, with a pyramid-like leadership structure. Violence was instrumental and centered around the business of selling heroin. Although heroin use was discouraged, several members became addicted after they began to sell. Two different types of adults were involved in these gangs. One consisted of relatives and extended family members, which was referred to as "adult-criminal gang dependent." These include the Gangsters, who were focused on making money:

> You're not going to be a Gangster unless you got some sense. You ain't gonna just be a thug. I mean there is no such thing as a thug (in the Gangsters). If you ain't making money, bringing something to the boys that's profitable for everyone, then we don't need you. If you don't want to be productive for yourself, then you won't be a Gangster. (Valdez, 2007, p. 29)

The other type was "prison gang dependent." Prison members recruited youth to sell heroin. The Nine-Ball Crew, a street gang, was controlled by the Chicano Brotherhood, a prison gang in the Texas system. The group was tightly organized, with strict rules surrounding how drugs are sold, as one of them said:

> There is one guy in charge of selling. Yeah, he's the main guy that controls the drugs. He says who is going to sell and who ain't going to sell. If you're selling without permission and don't bring money to him your going to get in trouble, get a v [violation]. (Valdez, 2007, p. 27)

Within the criminal nonadult-dependent gangs, adults have less influence. Gang crimes reflect more of the cafeteria pattern, and members commit crimes more for themselves than to benefit the gang. The gang does offer individual members protection to carry out crimes. Rates of alcohol and drug use are high, including heroin. Infighting is common, as is fighting with rivals for personal reasons. Some violence revolves around drug selling. This type of gang is also territorial and has two subtypes based on varying levels of organization and leadership. One consists of loosely knit members with flexible leadership. The Chicano Boyz were one of the most violent gangs on the west side of San Antonio and the following excerpt captures their brutality:

> This dude was a Nine-Ball. We had already kicked his ass I don't know how many times. We were saying fuck Nine-Ball and all this shit. We started laughing. We let him get up. He took off and started running. . . . My homeboy took out an AK from the truck, my other

homeboy took out a 9mm. My homeboy got on his knee, aiming at him. He shot him in the head. My other homeboy just ran up and shot him in the back too. (Valdez, 2007, p. 32)

The other type is highly structured, with a vertical hierarchy and strong membership, often having ongoing battles with other gangs.

Most gangs that Valdez studied were barrio territorial gangs. Their members use a variety of drugs, but have comparably lower rates of heroin use. Members act independent from adult influences and commit a wide variety of crimes for individual purposes that are often unplanned and disorganized. These gangs have rituals and symbols, but are less organized. Violence was territorial based, but often random, emerging from interpersonal conflict.

Transitional gangs were smaller and loosely organized, with no clear leadership or structure, often having one enigmatic person who served as an informal leader. Residential proximity binds youth in these gangs together and partying and substance use are their principal activities. A wide variety of crimes are committed for individual purposes by members. They have links to adults—often relatives—who provide them with firearms and drugs. Geographically, they are more spread out, because members might not live in close proximity to one another. Fighting centers around romantic and personal disputes, and most gang activities concern school friends. In one instance, a transitional gang was only around when school was in session. Although this gang declined during Valdez's research, others emerged. Up and Above (UAA) evolved into a gang because of external threats from others. One of Valdez's (2007) respondents, a UAA member, said he was mistaken for being from another gang (pp. 39–40):

We were cruising in our van with the rims. We cruised in it all the time before it got stolen. Some black Crips pulled up next to us. They thought we were Crowns because we were dressed in black. They were talking shit and threw their fucking beer bottles at the van. We were like "fuck," you meet us over there . . . we both parked and all started getting out. And one of them looked like he was going to reach for a gun. We were like, "ah damn man!" So, I was in the back. I hooked one of the UAAs with a Tech 9 that my uncle got for me. So we fired on the whole car and they took off. We only shot a couple of rounds, just enough to scare them.

Another type of transitional gang discovered was the Killing Crew, who were known for their ability to supply marijuana and firearms. One of them talked about relatively sophisticated weaponry:

We do a lot of gun smuggling. We get many different arms, like grenades and armor piecing bullets and guns like "cop killer" and AK-47's. A lot of these guns we use ourselves. Once we get busted, they start taking away the guns. Guys start fucking up. By the time I know it, I look into the case and there is nothing there no more. (Valdez, 2007, p. 41)

ASIAN AND ASIAN PACIFIC ISLANDER GANGS

Under the National Youth Gang Survey, Asian and Asian Pacific Islander (API) gangs fall under the Other category, with the lowest numbers of members in the United States. Asian youth are often underrepresented in juvenile delinquency statistics (Krisberg, 2005). During the Great American Crime Drop of the 1990s and early 2000s, although arrest rates of whites, blacks, and Latinos decreased, those for Asian and API youth soared (Lam, 2012). Vietnamese youth had some of the highest rates of institutionalization in the 1990s (Vigil, 2002).

The United States has dozens of different Asian and API communities that have gangs, including Korean, Japanese, Hawaiian, and Samoan. The most common of these gangs are Chinese, Southeast Asian (e.g., Vietnamese, Cambodian), and Filipino (Shelden et al., 2001). Asian gangs can be grouped among ethnic lines, although some consist of youth from a variety of Asian and API backgrounds. Asian and API gangs focus largely on property crimes, and their violence is primarily instrumental rather than expressive (Klein, 1995; Shelden et al., 2001). They have been known to be secretive, smaller, cohesive, and more likely to have links to organized crime and/or adult criminals compared to other gangs (Klein, 1995; Shelden et al., 2001; Spergel, 1995; Toy, 1992a, 1992b; Valdez, 2007). They are also heterogenous and significant differences exist in their etiologies and criminal patterns (Klein, 1995; Spergel, 1995).

Immigration and racism have played key roles in the origin of Asian and API gangs. In the aftermath of the conflict in Vietnam, the United States offered South Vietnamese the opportunity to immigrate to provide a safe haven. Many Vietnamese fled their war-torn nation, landing in the United States with no skills and language and culture barriers (Du Phuoc Long and Richard, 1996; Lam, 2012; Needham and Quintiliani, 2007; Shelden et al., 2001; Vigil, 2002; Vigil and Yun, 1990; S. X. Zhang, 2001). The Hmong and Lao fled Laos when their country fell to the communists (W. B. Sanders, 1994). The killing fields of the Khmer Rouge in the 1970s, where more than a million Khmer people were murdered, led to a massive diaspora of Cambodians (aka Khmers) into the United States. Today, Long Beach has the largest concentration of Cambodians outside Cambodia (Needham and Quintiliani, 2007). The passage of the 1965 Immigration and Naturalization Bill brought Chinese immigrants to the United States by the thousands (Chin, 1990; Shelden et al., 2001; Toy, 1992a, 1992b; S. X. Zhang, 2001). Political upheaval in the Philippines influenced the flight of Filipinos away from their homeland and into the United States (Kim et al., 2009; W. B. Sanders, 1994; Shelden et al., 2001). Many Filipinos fought in U.S.-led wars, particularly Vietnam, which helped pave their way to the United States (W. B. Sanders, 1994).

Rather than being welcomed into American's melting pot, many Asian and API immigrant and refugees faced obstacles, including social and economic marginality (Du Phuoc Long and Richard, 1996; Toy, 1992a, 1992b). Language difficulties and significant cultural differences were evident, and the communities within which they settled in the United States were ill-prepared to accommodate them (Spergel, 1995; Toy, 1992a, 1992b; Vigil, 2002). The Asian and API newcomers experienced violence and terrorism, not only from whites, but also from Latinos, blacks, and locally born Asians and APIs (Kim et al., 2009; Spergel, 1995; Toy, 1992a, 1992b). Asian and API gangs first formed as a way to protect themselves from victimization (Chin, 1990; Du Phuoc Long and Richard, 1996; Kim et al., 2009; Needham and Quintiliani, 2007; W. B. Sanders, 1994; Shelden et al., 2001). Youth from Vietnamese and Cambodian communities were also picked on at school because of their small stature and foreignness. These are relatively unique risk factors that contributed to the gang membership of Asians and APIs (Chhuon, 2014; Du Phuoc Long and Richard, 1996; Lam, 2012; Vigil, 2002; Vigil and Yun, 1990).

BOX 3.2: MEDIA CHECK!

Crips and Bloods: Made in America

Most documentaries on gangs are not worth watching. They glamorize life in the gang, focus on cultural minutiae, provide biased accounts, or depict graphic violence and use shock tactics. *Crips and Bloods: Made in America* is different. It provides an honest and direct explanation of the emergence of Crip and Blood gang sets in Los Angeles.

The film focuses on the Crips in South Los Angeles (formerly South Central) and the Bloods in Compton. Within Compton is a small street called Piru. This is important because Bloods refer to themselves as Pirus and their hand sign is the letter "P" made with the index finger touching the tip of the thumb and the remaining fingers pointed down. The documentary provides a historical overview of the various structural concerns and cultural aspects that led to the emergence of these gangs. Former and current members offer personal experiences within different neighborhoods to explain how and why they joined, including details of their daily lives. Some of these guys are interventionists who work closely with law enforcement and community stakeholders.

A few clips within the documentary are heavy. Images of bloody dead bodies filled with bullet holes and knife wounds— one with the knife still embedded in the corpse—are shown toward the beginning. Images of young black men with military-grade hardware, one who is able to hide what looks like an M-16 rifle down his trousers, are also peppered throughout. Such images quickly flash by. One of the most sobering sequences comprises the shots of crying mothers holding pictures of their young dead sons lost to gang violence. How did things ever get so bad within particular black communities? No punches are pulled in the documentary's pursuit to answer this question.

The film focuses on how the Parker-led Los Angeles Police Department and the Hoover-led FBI targeted black political organizations like the Black Panther Party and U.S. Organization that emerged in the aftermath of the Watts uprising in the 1960s. Local and federal law enforcement agents attempted to destroy these groups because they emulated and promoted Black Power. The FBI infiltrated the U.S. Organization and assassinated two major players in the Black Panthers on UCLA's campus. Later, the Los Angeles Police Department's SWAT unit descended on the Black Panther Party's headquarters in South Central, resulting in a day-long siege and eventually the decimation of the Panthers. These incidents were major turning points that contributed to the emergence of deadly gang violence. While the Black Panthers and U.S. Organization were active, gangs were quiet. But as these groups became depowered through intimidation, incarceration, and assassination, a leadership vacuum emerged in black communities and youth lacked effective role models. As a result, gang activity dramatically increased to levels never seen before. Black-on-black youth violence soared.

An interesting aspect of *Crips and Bloods* is the director, Stacy Peralta. His two prior movies were about surfing massive waves (*Riding Giants*) and the modernization of skateboarding (*Dog Town and Z Boys*). Stacy is a former world-champion professional skateboarder from the 1970s and half of the legendary skateboard manufacturing company Powell & Peralta that dominated the scene throughout the 1980s. Back then, Stacy put together a group of world-class skaters known as the Bones Brigade. One of them was Tony Hawk, who would eventually become the world's most successful and recognizable skateboarder.

Visit YouTube for clips of Bloods and Crips: Made in America.

CHINESE GANGS

With few exceptions, prior to 1965—and the arrival of Chinese immigrants *en masse*—Chinese living in America were generally law-abiding, hard-working individuals, with delinquency being uncommon among youth (Chin, 1996, 2006; S. X. Zhang, 2001). Their massive influx from 1965 threatened the stability of the already-established Chinese communities and impacted the abilities of families and "district associations" to effectively cope with the newcomers (Chin, 2006, p. 176). This breakdown led to an increase in crime (Chin, 1996, 2006). Although few gang members existed prior to 1990—Chin estimates that their numbers were no more than 2,000—federal authorities predicted that Chinese gangs would come to dominate heroin sales and other criminal rackets (Chin, 1996, 2006). This prediction proved inaccurate. What occurred, similar to Vietnamese gangs in Southern California (W. B. Sanders, 1994), is that a few high-profile incidents—in San Francisco's and New York City's Chinatowns—fueled by media hype led to the misperception that Asian gangs were a novel and dangerous entity (S. X. Zhang, 2001). The evidence suggests that, in terms of criminality, Chinese gangs are remarkably similar to other gangs (Chin, 1996, 2006).

Chin (1996, 2006) described the dynamics of two Chinese gangs in New York City: the Ghost Shadows and the Flying Dragons. Many of the Ghost Shadows were from Hong Kong. With the exception of a few Koreans and Chinese Vietnamese, Chinese gangs in New York City have consisted of youth exclusively from Chinese backgrounds where Cantonese is the principal dialect (Chin, 1996, 2006). The Ghost Shadows had a top-down organizational structure. At the top were four or five leaders, known as the *tai lou* (big brothers). They were in command of the lieutenants, who commanded the street soldiers. These soldiers were known as the *ma jai* (little horses) and committed most of the criminal activities. The leaders maintained contact with older Tong members and received payment for guarding the gambling houses. The Ghost Shadows had chapters in other cities, including Boston, Chicago, and Houston.

Prior to 1970, most Chinese youth voluntarily joined gangs, enjoying each other's friendship (Chin, 1996, 2006). Later, many joined from fear of victimization—not from white thugs, but from their own community (Chin, 1996, 2006). Newcomers were targeted, given their loose connections and poor command of English. Secret rituals similar to those conducted by Triads centuries before were part of the initiation ceremony. As Chin (2006, p. 178) notes, to join a gang, a "youth takes his oaths, burns yellow paper, and drinks wine mixed with blood in front of the gang leaders and the altar of General Kwan, a heroic figure of the secret societies." Infighting is common among Chinese gangs, with members reportedly more likely to be killed by one of their fellow members than by a rival (Chin, 1996, 2006). Membership is fluid, and members may switch from one gang to another, at times without any violent retaliation (Chin, 1996, 2006).

Despite many similarities, Chinese gangs are distinct in several ways. They are often closely linked to powerful community businesses or organizations and are not the products of poor and depressed neighborhoods (Chin, 1996, 2006). They invest in legitimate business and spend a lot of their time with these efforts, enmeshed within daily economic life (Chin, 2006). Klein (1995) noted that Chinese gangs appear to be located between street gangs and organized crime. Many members have connections across the United States and abroad (Klein, 1995). They are also influenced by secret societies in China, such as the Triads and Tongs,[7] and control vast amounts of money (Chin, 2006; Toy, 1992a, 1992b). Rather than cafeteria-style crime patterns, Chinese gangs focus on property crimes, largely against local businesses with profit as the driving motivation (Chin, 2006; Toy, 1992a, 1992b). Crimes often lack the expressive character of offending from their Latino, black, and white counterparts.

Drug use is discouraged, although this seems to be more the case with Chinese gangs prior to the 1980s (Chin, 1996, 2006; Toy, 1992a, 1992b). The gangs are organized similar to criminal syndicates and youth may be a pool from which future Triad and Tong members are pulled (Shelden et al., 2001; Spergel, 1995). Many battles between different Tong factions in San Francisco's Chinatown were fought by youth who were affiliated with them (Toy, 1992a, 1992b). In San Francisco, the *Wah Ching* (Chinese youth) were a street gang linked to the Hop Sing Tong (Toy, 1992a, 1992b). Unlike most street gangs, Chinese gangs are likely to have members in their thirties and forties (Toy, 1992a, 1992b). Like others, Chinese members largely target and attack one another, as opposed to fighting with those from other races or ethnicities (Chin, 1990).

After a hard day of work, many Chinese immigrant laborers in the United States enjoyed gambling and using opium as a way to wind down (Toy, 1992a, 1992b), which gave rise to the emergence of clandestine gambling halls in Chinatown (Chin, 1996, 2006). Because of gambling's illegality, the halls needed security to keep an eye out for the police, as well as would-be robbers (Chin, 2006). Gangs provided this security. One of Toy's (1992a, pp. 655–656) respondents said that gangs were necessary in the community:

> What do you do, hire the cops to protect your gambling parlor? If you find Chinese people, you find gambling. There's no fucking doubt. What are they going to do, go to the police and say, "Can you check my gambling joint after 2:00 in the morning?" There's no way. And when they gamble, they don't gamble like the old people with $2 or $5. The real gamblers, they gamble big stakes, so you need protection. Along with gambling, there's always

---

7   The word "tong" translated to English refers to a gathering place or a hall (Chin, 1996, 2006; Toy, 1992a, 1992b). In the United States, tongs were established in cities such as San Francisco by some of the first waves of Chinese immigrants in the 1880s (Chin, 1996, 2006; Toy, 1992a, 1992b). Prior to the emergence of tongs, the family and "direct associations" (Toy, 1992a, 1992b, p. 649) were the foremost forms of control within Chinese communities. Chinese immigrants who were not welcomed into these associations instead joined together and formed tongs (Toy, 1992a, 1992b). A central purpose of the original tongs was to assist recent immigrants from China with the difficulties inherent in settling in a new country with a different culture and different language (Toy, 1992a, 1992b). Tongs were later viewed as criminal organizations in the early 1970s and mid 1980s by the U.S. Attorney General and were believed to be involved in heroin trafficking, prostitution, and extortion (see Chin, 1990, 1996, 2006). Many tongs, however, are also viewed as "social clubs" and have nothing to do with crime (Toy, 1992a, 1992b). In a similar vein, Chin (1990) explains that Triads first emerged in 17th-century China as secret societies for political and revolutionary purposes, but then later evolved into criminal syndicates that focused on the heroin/opium markets. Triad means a "triangle of heaven, earth, and man" (Chin, 2006, p. 183).

the drinking. You don't find gambling without Hennessy or Courvoisier. You would never survive. So along with the drinking, you always find the quaaludes, the downers, and on and on. 'Cause where there's gambling there's drinking, where there's drinking there's drugs, where there's drugs there's women, where there's women, there's prostitution, and it goes on and on, and there's a business. So you can't believe that there will never be gangs in Chinatown.

Extortion is a major crime committed by Chinese gangs in New York City's Chinatown (Chin, 1996, 2006). For those unwilling to pay, the gang will destroy the business and/or harm or kill the owners. In some cases, several gangs extort the same businesses because these different gangs claim territory within that geographic area (Chin, 1996, 2006). According to Chin (1996, 2006), extortion of businesses by gangs in Chinatown has occurred in several ways. One method is to explicitly ask for money from emerging businesses. Gangs ask for a loan or to assist fellow Chinese who have been arrested or are in trouble. The second method is more implicit: the gang would sell items to a Chinese business—for example, firecrackers at inflated prices. The process of extortion starts when several members enter an establishment and stay there for many hours, intimidating customers, causing destruction, and generating fear. They cause problems until the business owner realizes it is economically wise to simply pay them off. In other methods, gangs order large amounts of expensive food without paying and leave their calling card (e.g., "The Dragons were here"; Chin, 1996, 2006). Another method was referred to as *hei bai lian* (black and white faces): the gang orders food, but refuses to pay. While this is happening, other members come in and side with the restaurant manager by chastising the offending youth. They then inform the manager that if another incident occurs, they will protect the restaurant (Chin, 1996, 2006). A fourth method, *tai jian tsi* (carrying a sedan chair), is when members nominate a businessman as a Big Brother, acting as if they are loyal followers. If the businessman then associates with the gang, it becomes too late to ditch the Big Brother title, and he ends up paying. Another method is *wo di* (undercover), which happens when a member becomes an employee of the business and then provides sensitive information about the business to his gang. Chin (1996, 2006) says that although extortion is primarily committed for monetary gain, other motivations include power, control, revenge, and intimidation.

SOUTHEAST ASIAN GANGS

Southeast Asian gangs can be distinguished as youth from Vietnamese, Cambodian, Laotian, Hmong, and Chinese Vietnamese backgrounds. Within this category are a group called *Amerasians*, children who were fathered by American soldiers during the Vietnam War (Du Phuoc Long and Richard, 1996; W. B. Sanders, 1994). Amerasians have been particularly marginalized, being rejected by their Southeast Asian country of origin and having no reference group or family ties in the United States (Du Phuoc Long and Richard, 1996; W. B. Sanders, 1994). Some gangs have a mixture of youth from different Asian backgrounds. Confusion remains as to which racial group such youths belong to. In San Diego, many who are from specific Southeast Asian countries use the term Oriental in their name

(W. B. Sanders, 1994). On the surface, this masks the fact that these gangs represent distinct nationalities. The Tiny Oriental Crips and the Oriental Killer Boys are mainly Lao, with a few Hmong and Vietnamese youths, but the Oriental Boy Soldiers are Khmer with some Vietnamese and white youths (W. B. Sanders, 1994).

An important point to keep in mind is the difference between being an immigrant and being a refugee to the United States (Du Phuoc Long and Richard, 1996; W. B. Sanders, 1994). Refugees do not have the option of leaving their country on their own accord, as immigrants do. Refugees are usually made to leave their country, either through persecution or through the constant threat of death. They are ill-prepared to enter the United States and likely to experience poverty once they arrive (Lam, 2012; W. B. Sanders, 1994). Waves of refugees from Southeast Asian countries had access to resources and, consequently, unique experiences on arriving in the United States. The first Southeast Asian refugees who arrived between 1975 and 1979 had greater resources and more education and became better adjusted to life in the United States (Lam, 2012; W. B. Sanders, 1994; Vigil, 2002). The second wave—the "boat people"—landed between 1979 and 1982 (Vigil, 2002; Vigil and Yun, 1990). They were not as educated, more rural, and less likely to speak English (Du Phuoc Long and Richard, 1996; W. B. Sanders, 1994; Vigil, 2002). The third wave of Southeast Asians were immigrants rather than refugees, facilitated in part by an agreement between the United States and the Vietnamese government. They contained a large proportion of boat people who were poorer, more rural, and less educated than those in the second wave (Du Phuoc Long and Richard, 1996; Lam, 2012; W. B. Sanders, 1994; Vigil, 2002).

Most research on Southeast Asian gang members is concentrated in Southern California, but they can also be found in cities across the United States (Du Phuoc Long and Richard, 1996; Kent and Felkenes, 1998; Klein, 1995; Lam, 2012; W. B. Sanders, 1994; Shelden et al., 2001; Vigil, 2002; Vigil and Yun, 1990). Southeast Asian members are stereotyped as being experts in martial arts, knowledgeable about automatic weapons, and involved in vicious acts of violence (Klein, 1995; W. B. Sanders, 1994). Below are two interviews on the perception of Asian gang members as experts with sophisticated weaponry (W. B. Sanders, 1994, p. 162):

> [African American Crip] The Orientals are known for having real heavy equipment like nine-millimeter Uzis and stuff. They have the high-powered guns. The Long Beach 20 are really known for it. It's just a known fact that you don't mess with them.

> [Mexican American East Side Brown Angels] The Oriental gangs are more aggressive. They have more guns. My gang thinks they are wannabes, and they are trying to prove themselves.

These are myths. Empirical data suggest that with regard to experiences of fighting, weapons use and availability, and deadly violence, Southeast Asian gangs are no different than others (W. B. Sanders, 1994). A unique aspect is *inter*ethnic violence. Most violence is *intra*ethnic—within the same ethnicity. However, W. B. Sanders (1994) reports that Southeast Asian members in San Diego were attacked by and retaliated against members of Latino and black gangs (see also Lam, 2012). Likewise, Needham and Quintiliani (2007) found that Cambodian gangs in Long Beach often fought with Latino gangs.

Of all Southeast Asian gangs, most research has focused on Vietnamese gangs. They are not territorial based and operate in secret, avoiding ganglike attributes: dress, group names, hand signs, and tattoos (Du Phuoc Long and Richard, 1996; Klein, 1995; Shelden et al., 2001; Vigil, 2002). A tattoo linked with Vietnamese gangs is the four "T's"—T T T T—which stands for "thoung, tien, tu, toi" and translates to "love, money, prison, crime." Organization is loose and membership fluid, with no role differentiation (Chin, 1990; Vigil, 2002; Vigil and Yun, 1990). Vietnamese gangs focus on burglary, extortion, and home invasion robberies (Du Phuoc Long and Richard, 1996; Klein, 1995; Shelden et al., 2001).[8] A cultural habit of the Vietnamese is keeping large amounts of money and valuables within the home and being unfamiliar with the U.S. banking system, making their residences attractive to the gangs (Vigil, 2002; Vigil and Yun, 1990). Violence is instrumental rather than expressive, which distinguishes Vietnamese gangs from others (Klein, 1995; Shelden et al., 2001). They are also reportedly mobile and known to commit crimes many miles from where they live (Lam, 2012; Spergel, 1995). Members emulate the style of Latino gangs, including pressed khaki trousers and Nike Cortez shoes (Lam, 2012; Vigil, 2002).

Vigil and colleagues have discussed the role of culture in the emergence and persistence of Vietnamese gangs (Vigil, 2002; Vigil and Yun, 1990). The authors note that, as the children of refugees, American-born Vietnamese youth have less connection to their homeland than their parents and are more Americanized. Being caught between two cultures confuses the development of their identity, leading to family strains and personal exposure to bigotry. The youth are more American than Vietnamese. The gang offers an opportunity for Vietnamese youth to delve further into their culture because new members learn the language and customs from current members. The gang has become a "culture carrier" of traditions and ways, a preservation of Vietnamese ways of life (Vigil, 2002, p. 105; see also Du Phuoc Long and Richard, 1996). Similarities in cultural and racial differences, the development of a particular ethnic identity, and other aspects of marginalization helped bind youth together into gangs. The formation of gangs was inevitable given the socioeconomic marginalization, cultural differences, and language barriers of the refugees (Vigil, 2002). Racism also contributed to gangs. As two of Vigil's (2002, p. 109) respondents said,

> That's what it started out as, and what happened was that the Asian kids were banding together for protection, much like the Hispanic kids banded together, and that's basically how [Vietnamese gangs] got started [law enforcement agent].

> It's just that I was thinkin' I'm Vietnamese, so I should be hanging with other Vietnamese better. . . . I knew that white people were prejudiced. . . . They hated me and I hated them.

FILIPINO GANGS

Filipino Americans are the second largest Asian population in America. Filipinos immigrated to the United States in the 1970s and 1980s during the wake of political unrest in

---

8   However, as W. B. Sanders (1994) indicates, the media portrayals of high-profile home invasion robberies involving several Vietnamese perpetrators and victims in San Diego contributed to the misperception that the incident was gang related. None of the perpetrators was a gang member (see also Vigil, 2002).

the Philippines (Kim et al., 2009; Shelden et al., 2001). Gangs are concentrated in the Western states, as well as Hawaii, Nevada, and Alaska (Kim et al., 2009; Shelden et al., 2001).

Filipino gangs can be found throughout San Diego, including in less affluent areas, such as Paradise Hills. They adopt the names of African American gangs (i.e., Crips, Bloods), dress like black or Mexican American members, and do what most do: hang out and do nothing (Klein, 1995; W. B. Sanders, 1994; Spergel, 1995). Many Filipino gang members from San Diego do not come from poor and undereducated backgrounds. A member of the Bahala Na-Barkada[9] gang (W. B. Sanders, 1994, p. 155) said this in an interview:

> Our rivals are the Be Down Boys [Bloods]. We fight against them [gangbang]. The only time we fight is when we run into each other. Or we may look for revenge against them. . . . A lot of our members have normal jobs or we get money from our parents. About a quarter of us dropped out of school. The rest of us attend school on a regular basis.

> On an average day I would leave my house as if I was going to school, but I would end up at a friend's house instead. . . . We would kick it, or go to a girl's house—someone that also ditched or had already graduated—and whatever. Sometimes we would drink or smoke weed. We would drive around . . . sometimes we would run into guys from other gangs. Most of the time we had guns in the car. Our gang is known for having a lot of guns.

> They consider us like the Crips. We fight Bloods, yet we dress more like a Mexican gang [member], similar to the *cholo* style. Some dress like a black gang member. We dress however we feel like. There is no absolute certain way to dress.

Hawaii has a large Filipino American population and about two in five of all members are Filipino (Kim et al., 2009). Unlike in San Diego, Filipino Americans in Hawaii have the lowest median household income compared to other minority groups (Kim et al., 2009). Many work in the agricultural industry and few are in the professional field (Kim et al., 2009). Filipino Americans have suffered from many years of degradation and discrimination, particularly at school, which has contributed to their marginalization (Kim et al., 2009; see also W. B. Sanders, 1994). The main source of discrimination was not from whites, but other API youth, particularly native Hawaiians and Samoans and even local-born Filipinos (Kim et al., 2009). Such victimization is the main reason why Filipino youth in Hawaii initially formed gangs (Kim et al., 2009). Others have found that gangs first emerged because youth wanted to party (Alsaybar, 2002).

NATIVE AMERICAN GANGS

Gang activity in Native American[10] communities increased in the 1990s, with nearly a quarter of all tribal lands reporting gangs by the beginning of the 21st century (Major et al., 2004). Hundreds of gangs have been reported within Native American communities (Joseph and Taylor, 2003; Major et al., 2004). Some indicate that up to 15% of all Native

---

9   Bahala Na means "come what may."
10   Also referred to within the research literature and government publications as American Indian.

American youth are part of gangs (Joseph and Taylor, 2003); others indicate that more than a third have associated with gangs (Whitbeck et al., 2002). Earlier reports noted that 5% of males and less than 1% of females reported gang membership (Donnermeyer et al., 1996). Gang migration patterns have been attributed as a partial cause of this increase (Armstrong et al., 1999; Major et al., 2004; Maxson, 1998). More centrally, Native American gangs have emerged for the same reasons as others. Poverty, social, economic, family dysfunction, geographic marginalization, and cultural conflicts between parent and host cultures in concert have contributed to their emergence and persistence of gangs (Donnermeyer et al., 1996; Freng et al., 2012; Joseph and Taylor, 2003; Major et al., 2004; L. Martinez, 2005; Whitbeck et al., 2002).

Native American gangs are similar to other gangs in several ways, including their cafeteria-style offending patterns, loose organizational structure, and focus on partying and hanging out (Freng et al., 2012). Native Americans join gangs for similar reasons as most youth, such as a sense of belonging (Grant and Feimer, 2007). They report higher levels of drug use and crime than nonmembers (Donnermeyer et al., 1996; Freng et al., 2012), but they differ in that they contain more female members, have more mixed-gender gangs, and are less violent (Freng et al., 2012; Major et al., 2004). Most are part of gangs that are predominately Latino or black and not indigenous gangs from tribal lands (Joseph and Taylor, 2003). Some youth believe that had they been more involved within their traditional culture, they would have been less likely to join gangs (Grant and Feimer, 2007). Policing gangs on Native American land poses unique challenges. One is the limited number of police officers covering a large territory. Joseph and Taylor (2003) reported that about six police officers were responsible for patrolling an area the size of Connecticut (see also L. Martinez, 2005).

Studies of Native American gangs are based on data from community members and law enforcement, not the youth, and are mostly on Navajo youth (Freng et al., 2012; Major et al., 2004). One exception is a study by Freng and colleagues (2012). The authors surveyed about 100 youth in junior high and high school, most of whom were Native American. About 25% of the sample reported membership and 40% of the members were female. The gang youth had traditional risk factors similar to other gang youth, such as having a family member who was also in a gang. The sample was unique in that almost all came from families who held jobs and had completed high school. The sample was doing well in school compared to youth not in gangs. Gang youth reported more drug use, violence, and property crime. They joined for similar reasons as other youth (e.g., for fun, protection, respect). Most gangs were organized, with leaders and symbols, and many had rules or codes of conduct and specific roles for members. They were, on average, much larger, often exceeding 30 members. They were also more likely to report some victimization compared to non-gang youth, which is consistent with the research literature.

WHITE GANGS

European Americans from lower-class backgrounds have the longest recorded history of street gang activity (Spergel, 1995). Most of the 1,313 gangs that Thrasher (2000 [1927]) studied were from immigrant Europeans, including Irish, German, Polish, and Italian. Nowadays, these youth would be considered white. Few contemporary gang members are white. As Klein (1995, p. 106) noted, "the white gang problem, although present, is not in any sense comparable to the size of the minority gang problem." Between 1996 and 2008, white gang membership hovered around 10%, ranging from a high of 13.4% in 1999 to a low of 7.9% in 2004 (National Gang Center, n.d.).

The percentage of white youth that constitute the overall gang population varies by area. Between 2005 and 2008, rural counties had the highest proportion of whites within youth gangs (18.9%) and urban areas had the lowest (9.3%; National Gang Center, n.d.). Mortality data report that cities with longer histories of ganging, such as Los Angeles, Long Beach, and Oakland, have a much higher percentage of white victims of gang homicides (Centers for Disease Control and Prevention, 2012). In the Los Angeles site, being white was significantly correlated with gang homicide victims, but being black was not (Centers for Disease Control and Prevention, 2012). White youth in the Los Angeles Study were difficult to come by, and the one individual introduced to the study refused to participate (B. Sanders et al., 2010). Decker and Van Winkle (1996), while acknowledging that white youth were present in the areas they studied, also noted the difficulty of recruiting members to their study.

A reason for this paucity of data is sampling techniques. Most studies report on older samples—individuals who are in their mid- to late teens. Studies that have enrolled younger youth—those in middle or junior high schools—report more whites. Data derived from the Gang Resistance Education and Training studies have reported significant numbers of white gang youth (Esbensen and Winfree, 1998; Peterson et al., 2001). Membership for all races can be a fleeting experience, perhaps a year or so, and middle school/junior high is a peak age period for both joining and leaving gangs (Thornberry et al., 2003). High numbers of whites in gang studies conducted in these schools reflect the fact that they were conducted during a time when youth in general are more likely to report membership. Few researchers have studied residential areas dominated by whites, which contributes to a lack of data on gangs in those communities. As Esbensen and Lynskey (2001) note, the racial composition of youth gangs often reflects the sociodemographics of a community (see also Esbensen et al., 2008).

Another reason for the lack of data is that white gang youth express delinquency in other ways. Delinquent groups have been defined as punks, freaks, stoners, heavy metal enthusiasts, wannabes, and Satan worshipers (Shelden et al., 2001; Spergel, 1995). White gang members are also better integrated into their communities, have greater access to legitimate opportunities, are exposed to more adult social controls, and are less violent (Spergel, 1995; Sullivan, 1989). Other labels include skaters, straightedge (for non–substance using hardcore music fans), Goths (for gothic style and music), surfers, dopers, EMO (for emotional hardcore style and music), ravers/clubbers, and more distinguished by musical preference, substance use patterns, and/or style (see Borden, 2001; Greenberg, 2007; Hodkinson, 2002; Muggleton, 2000; W. B. Sanders, 1994; B. Sanders, 2006a, 2006b; R. T. Wood, 2006).[11] The delinquency of these white groups is often limited to substance use, and they have higher economic and educational statuses (R. K. Jackson and McBride, 1996).

Whites are often part of Latino, African American, or racially mixed gangs (Decker and Van Winkle, 1996; Fleisher, 1998; W. B. Sanders, 1994; Shelden et al., 2001; Spergel, 1995). Decker and Van Winkle (1996) reported that whites played important roles in African American gangs. Many in the People and Folks Nations are white (Spergel, 1995). The concept of multiple marginalization, although largely applied to nonwhite youth in Latino and Vietnamese gangs, has been used to help explain gang membership among whites (Freng and Esbensen, 2007). Freng and Esbensen (2007) reported that marginalization occurred differently for whites than it did for blacks or Latinos, who experienced it regardless of gang involvement. White youth had fewer risk factors than blacks or Latinos prior to joining, but membership itself further marginalized them in ways similar to blacks and Latinos. Freng and Esbensen (2007) also found that ecological and economic factors were more salient in understanding membership among whites compared with blacks and Latinos. Additional studies on white gangs are needed, especially among those in their late teens and early twenties.

SKINHEADS

The closest white delinquency groups to gangs are skinheads. They have ganglike characteristics such as a group name, specific tattoos and symbols that signify membership, a distinct style, significant substance use patterns, and criminal behavior (R. K. Jackson and McBride, 1996; Spergel, 1995). Skinheads are portrayed not as gangs, but as hate

---

11 Although based largely on research from the United Kingdom, the works of Borden, Hodkinson, and Muggleton resonate in the United States.

groups that target racial and sexual minorities (Klein, 1995; Schneider, 1999; Simi, 2006, 2008). Some skinheads are organized against this type of hatred, such as the SHARPs—Skin Heads against Racial Prejudice—or the SARs—Skinheads against Racism (Dichiara, 2008a). Skinheads are more ideological than gangs (although see Brotherton and Barrios, 2004; Brotherton, 2008c). Black and Latino gangs emerged as a result of an external threat of groups of white youth who wanted to cause them harm. Skinheads formed in relation to threats that were already in their community—other white, largely noncriminal youth—jocks, cowboys, and rockers (Simi, 2006). Age and gender also differ between skinheads and street gangs. Females comprise around 30–40% of all skinheads (Dichiara, 2008b; Simi, 2008), whereas that number is around 10% for gang females. The skinhead lifestyle is often short lived, with few maintaining it into their thirties (Dichiara, 2008b).

Skinheads do not have many common attributes of criminal street gangs, such as a specific area or territory, spending lots of time hanging out on the street, and a broad range of criminal activities (Klein, 1995). Youth have been attracted to the style of the skinheads—the Doc Marten boots, shaved head, suspenders, and Ben Sherman and Fred Perry shirts—and wear such clothing as a form of resistance to distinguish themselves from conventional lifestyles (Brake, 1985; Hebdige, 1979; see also S. Hall and Jefferson, 1976). Within skinhead culture, style is paramount; being a skinhead goes hand in glove with looking like a skinhead (Simi, 2006). Youth who identify as skinheads may also come from different geographical locations, whereas members of street gangs are likely to live in close proximity to one another.

SKINHEADS AS GANGS

Evidence suggests skinheads may share more in common with street gangs than is thought. Simi (2006, 2008) reports that skinheads in the early 1980s would be described as non-political social gangs that fought other similar groups of white youth (e.g., punks, other skinheads). They were like Cloward and Ohlin's (1960) conflict subculture. Early skinheads were similar to other spectacular subcultures, such as the punks or mods or New Wave, that organized around style and engaged in substance use and petty delinquency (Brake, 1985; Hebdige, 1979; B. Sanders, 2006b). They were less hierarchical in their organization and did not have age-graded cliques.

Simi's (2006) qualitative study on racist skinheads in Southern California concluded that skinheads had many qualities like street gangs, including territory, participation in a broad range of criminal activities, and a coherent, organized structure. They had initiation rituals to distinguish members from nonmembers. Their emergence was related to the threat of victimization from nonwhite street gangs. Racial conflict played a significant role in the emergence of skinheads, just as it did for black and Latino gangs (see Spergel, 1995). As one of Simi's (2006, p. 154) respondents indicated,

> I grew up in a pretty dark neighborhood and most of my homeboys did too. . . . . We were
> surrounded by mostly spic gangs and all we had was each other and if we didn't want to

get punked all the time then we needed to have some reinforcements to fight back . . . so yeah that [racial conflict] played a big role in how we got started and I think that was true for other skinhead gangs as well you know maybe not so much for some of the ones down in OC [Orange County] but even they were started to get invaded by all these nonwhite gangs trying to take over neighborhood and all that bullshit. (Norwalk Skinhead interview, March 16, 2001)

Most of the gangs in Simi's (2006) study were territorial. This was evident in their names, which linked them to a specific area (e.g., Huntington Beach Skins), tagging them throughout and/or approaching youth not from this area and hassling them. Their violence was racially motivated. Similar to the intraethnic nature of street gangs, the skinheads attacked groups of white youths, such as the punks. Simi (2006) notes that the racially motivated violence was territorial; the skinheads did not seek to do violence against nonwhites outside of their territory, only to those who entered it.

NAZI LOW RIDERS

The Nazi Low Riders (NLR) are a white gang based in prison and on the streets (Anti-Defamation League [ADL], 2005; C. Jackson, 2004; Valdez, 1999). They are a neo-Nazi group who originated in the California Youth Authority in the 1970s and have the strongest presence in California, but are also found in Nevada, Arizona, Florida, New Mexico, and other states (ADL, 2005; C. Jackson, 2004). Their strength is their affiliation with the Aryan Brotherhood (AB) and NLR is a younger offshoot of the AB; most are in their teens or early twenties (ADL, 2005; C. Jackson, 2004). Despite its racist ideology, NLR has allowed Latinos in, some of who have at least one white parent (ADL, 2005; C. Jackson, 2004). The relationship between NLR and Latinos parallels that of the AB and La Eme: despite the racist ideologies, AB and NLR members interact with some nonwhites.

NLR members commit violent, racist attacks, primarily against African Americans, but have also been involved in drug selling (primarily methamphetamine), murder, robbery, and home invasions (ADL, 2005; C. Jackson, 2004; Simi, 2006). They have been targeted by federal law enforcement and indicated on violations of the Racketeer Influenced and Corrupt Organizations Act designed to target organized crime (C. Jackson, 2004). NLR do not appear to be territorial based, nor is their structure clear (ADL, 2005).

SUMMARY

Race is a critical variable in explaining why gangs emerged within minority communities. Overt and institutional racism has resulted in the concentration of minorities, particularly blacks and Latinos, living in some of the most dangerous inner-city areas in the United States. Over time, racism has produced deep levels of deprivation, hopelessness, and a tolerance of violence and crime. Although race has been ignored for many years within criminology in general and gang studies in particular, it plays a significant role in relation to contemporary gangs. Ignoring the connection between race and gangs is no longer feasible.

An understanding of black gangs starts with migration, when black people moved away from the southern states, seeking peace from racist policies and community norms. Once in the West and Midwest, they continued to face discrimination, being attacked by mobs of whites and hassled by police officers. They suffered institutionalized discrimination that limited their employment, educational, and residential opportunities. When black leaders emerged, they were targeted by the government and wiped out. Lacking leadership, black communities imploded, and youths began attacking one another. Gangs were the outcome.

Annexation and immigration set the backdrop for the understanding of Latino gang youth. Many Latinos from Mexico and Central America flocked to the United States to join family and find work that was unavailable in their home countries. Similar to African Americans, many Latino families faced obstacles in relation to jobs, schools, and housing. Language barriers and cultural differences exacerbated the situation. With school and families unable to provide a natural form of social control, youth spent time away from such institutions and hung out on the street. They faced harassment from law enforcement and violent victimization from gangs composed of white youth. These conditions are the reasons for the emergence of gangs. Today, most gangs across the United States are Latino, and most Latino members are Mexican American. Several types of Mexican American gangs have been found that vary by level of organization, influence from adults, criminal patterns, uses of violence, and relation to prison gangs.

Asian and API immigrants were welcomed to the United States. Many parallels can be found between their histories and those of Latinos and blacks in terms of segregation, discrimination, and limited opportunities. As with Latinos, language and cultural differences made things worse. Southeast Asian gangs are among the most common. A key difference between Southeast Asian gangs and other racial gangs is their refugee status. Rather than coming to the United States to seek work and find family members, most Southeast Asians fled their countries for fear of death. Millions had already been slaughtered by the time the United States offered asylum. Despite stereotypes, Asian and API members are no better at martial arts or handling sophisticated weaponry than other gang members. They appear to be slightly more discreet and less likely to use as many drugs.

Gangs are not really the province of white youth, despite the significance of immigrant Europeans in the history of gang research. To be clear, white gangs do exist and studies of middle school children often indicate sizeable proportions of white members. White group delinquency among youths often takes the form of musical subcultures. Some skinheads have been considered gangs. Researchers often do not target white communities, which feeds the perception that whites do not join gangs. Whites have joined predominately black, Latino, or Asian/API gangs, but pure-white gangs that are not skinheads are rare. Aside from immigration, language, and cultural differences, the research on contemporary white members suggests they have many of the same risk factors and join gangs for the same reasons as minority youth.

CHAPTER REVIEW QUESTIONS

1. How did the white community react when blacks sought greater rights in cities like Los Angeles and Chicago? How is this related to why black gangs first emerged?
2. What is the importance of black militant groups in both the deescalation and the escalation of violence between different black gangs?
3. Where do the terms "Crip" and "Piru" come from?
4. How does acculturation potentially contribute to gang membership among Latinos?
5. What are the similarities and differences between the different types of Mexican American gangs outlined by Valdez?
6. In what ways are Chinese gangs different from other gangs?
7. What are the methods of extortion among the Chinese gangs Chin discussed?
8. What are some of the stereotypes of Southeast Asian gangs?
9. For Vietnamese youth, the gang has been considered a "culture carrier." What does this mean?
10. In what ways are skinheads similar to street gangs? In what ways are they different?

LINKS TO ARTICLES ON RACE AND GANGS

Race not space: A revisionist history of gangs in Chicago
By J. M. Hagedorn
http://gangresearch.net/Archives/hagedorn/articles/racenotspace.pdf/

Race and gender difference between gang and nongang youths: Results from a multisite survey
By F-A. Esbensen and L. T. Winfree
http://citeseerx.ist.psu.edu/viewdoc/download?doi=10.1.1.511.5884&rep=rep1&type=pdf

Racialized identities and the formation of black gangs in Los Angeles
By A. A. Alonso
http://64.20.37.146/academic/2004ug_gangsla.pdf/

Defensive localism in white and black: A comparative history of European-American and African American youth gangs
By C. Adamson
http://www2.arnes.si/~srazpo1/TPTvSI2_2008_2009/Defensive_Localism_in_White_and_Black__A_Comparative_History_of_European-American_and_African-American_Youth_Gangs.pdf/

The new criminal conspiracy? Asian gangs and organized crime in San Francisco
By K. A. Joe
http://www.uk.sagepub.com/lippmanccl2e/study/articles/Joe.pdf/

Deadly symbiosis: When prison and ghetto mesh
By Loc Wacquant
http://loicwacquant.net/assets/Papers/DEADLYSYMBIOSISPRISONGHETTO.pdf/

CHAPTER 4

FEMALES

KEY WORDS

Autonomous gang: A female gang that is independent of any male gang.

Autonomy: To be self-governed; in control of self-action and self-thought.

Auxiliary gang: A female gang that is a smaller counterpart to a male gang.

Bootstrapping: When status offenses are treated as criminal offenses.

Empowerment: To supply with an ability; to enable; an investment in authority.

Femininity: Socially acceptable traits and behaviors of females.

Gender: A social construct that refers to the concepts of masculinity and femininity.

Masculinity: Socially acceptable traits and behaviors of males.

Mixed-gender gang: A gang that consists of males and females.

Respectability: The quality of being socially acceptable; to be held in high esteem.

Sex: A biological construct that refers to male and female.

Sex object: A term used to refer to a girl affiliated with a male gang who assumed a passive disposition and was romantically involved with gang males.

Sexual victimization: To make a victim of a sexual-based offense (e.g., rape, attempted rape, molestation).

Stereotype: A widely held, fixed, and often simplified idea about something.

Tomboy: A term used to refer to a girl affiliated with a male gang who assumed an aggressive disposition and participated in violent offenses and other masculine activities.

Traditional: Conventional; accepted standards; customary.

Chapter Learning Objectives

- Comprehend sexist and stereotypical portrayals of females in gangs.
- Explain the various relationships that females have in gangs or with members.
- Illustrate the unique backgrounds and experiences of females in or around gangs.
- Discuss traits particular to females as they shape their gang involvement.

INTRODUCTION

Most of the 20th-century information on girls in gangs was stereotypical and sexist, provided by journalists, social workers, or gang males. Female members were considered odd and unfeminine, sexual auxiliaries to their male counterparts who vicariously participated in crime and violence. They were bad girls who hung around male members for social and sexual reasons, antagonizing rivalries and assisting in gang fights. Few researchers examined females in gangs. However, things began to change toward the end of the millennium, and the study of female gangs, gang members, and those associated with gangs had become much more sophisticated. Data indicated that females joined gangs for similar reasons, had comparable risk backgrounds, and participated in crime and violence like males. In other ways, they are different. Gang females have gone from helping their boyfriends conceal drugs and guns and supporting bogus alibis to selling drugs on the corner, shooting firearms at enemies, and requiring alibis of their own.

The chapter begins by reviewing early sexist and stereotypical research on females in gangs. Next, it reports on the increases in female arrest and incarceration rates and advancements in research on female gang members. From there, differences and similarities between males and females are offered. Then, the overall numbers and the different types of female gangs and gang members are described. Female gang violence and sexual victimization are then discussed. The interrelated concepts of identity, femininity, sexuality, and respect among females in gangs are examined. The final parts of the chapter look at pregnancy and motherhood, prosocial functions, and post-gang lives.

EARLY STUDIES AND STEREOTYPES

For many years, law enforcement and researchers ignored gang females (Chesney-Lind et al., 1996; Curry, 1998; Sikes, 1997). Little was known about why girls joined gangs or what they did once in them. Some argued that not focusing on females as gang members was a matter of policy (Curry et al., 1994). The director of a multiagency gang task force told a gang researcher in the mid 1990s, "There aren't any female gang members" (Peterson, 2014, p. 271). Girls were not considered gang members or a threat (Sikes, 1997). One reason for this is that girls in gangs would challenge the established orthodoxy of the demonized gang member. As J. W. Moore (1991) notes, acknowledging females in gangs would distort the media and public perceptions and make them seem more humane.

Early studies of females were stereotypical. They downplayed their roles in offending and gang membership and focused on their relationships with the males, clothing, mental health, or promiscuity. Ashbury's (1927) description of 19th-century gangs in New York City notes that females made weapons handy when the males fought or they reported weaknesses in the opposition's line of defense. Among the thousand-plus gangs Thrasher (1927) studied in Chicago neighborhoods, only several were all-girl gangs; some revolved around sports, but others focused on stealing. Girlfriends of gang members in Thrasher's study were thought to weaken the group's commitment to fighting. The behaviors of bona fide girls in gangs chiefly concerned sexual activities, and Thrasher's discussions of them centered on immorality.

Social maladjustment and psychological dysfunction remained the focus of female gang members in the 1950s and 1960s (Cloward and Ohlin, 1961; A. K. Cohen, 1955; Short and Strodtbeck, 1965). An observer in Short and Strodtbeck's (1965, p. 242) seminal work highlights this:

> The sight of these girls was almost grotesque. They were dressed in a mannish manner; men's suit jackets, dirty sweaters and blouses, their hair was in disarray and their street-corner slouch was very much in evidence. Or I should say their toughness. Leading the prancing was a model-teacher who looked not like a model at all, although she was an attractive brown-skinned Negro woman who possessed some very unmodellish curves. The girls tried to imitate her, failed, and giggled.

W. B. Miller (1973) studied a gang of girls called the Molls. He reported that attracting males and looking tough were often the focus of their activity. These girls primarily committed status offenses, such as truancy and underage drinking, but also property damage and shoplifting. Assault by the Molls was uncommon. Likewise, W. B. Miller's (1975) nationwide survey confirmed that the delinquency of female members was far less serious and frequent than that of males.

Campbell (1984, 1992) discussed the history of girls' roles within gangs and notes how girls in the company of male members were considered either Tomboys or Sex Objects. She indicates that Sex Objects were passive girls who focused on sexual and romantic relationships with gang males. These girls provoked fights and revealed one boy's secrets to another. Their passivity encouraged deceitful gang males to lead them into prostitution and/or drug addiction. Tomboys were just as tough as the males, accompanying them to fights, participating in violent crimes, and priding themselves in the solidarity of the gang. Both types of gang girls used their femininity to benefit the gang, such as spying on other gangs, carrying weapons where they cannot be searched for on the street by male police officers, or luring males from rival gangs into uncompromising positions to be victimized by their own gang. Neither of these two roles was perceived as flattering: Sex Objects were rejected by their family and girlfriends and Tomboys were resented by gang boys and ridiculed by their friends and family. From early depictions of gang fighting in the 19th century in New York between the Five Points and Bowery gangs through details on gang fighting in the 20th century, girl gang roles as either Sex Object or Tomboy persisted (Campbell, 1984, 1992; Vigil, 2002).

INCREASES IN FEMALE ARRESTS AND INCARCERATION

Despite considerable drops in overall levels of crime in the latter years of the 20th century, female arrests began to surge. Over a 16-year period (1981–1997) the Violent Crime Index arrest rate rose 103% for females. In 1980, females made up less than 20% of serious crimes such as murder, robbery, and burglary and about 13% of drug crimes; by 2008 the number rose to about 30% of all serious crimes and almost 20% of all drug crimes (Frost et al., 2006). From 1977 to 2004, the rate of females incarcerated per 100,000 people in the United States increased from 10 to 64. This translates to 11,212 female prisoners in 1977 to 96,125 of them in 2004—a 757% increase (Frost et al., 2006). Females were arrested for relatively serious offenses. From 1981 to 1997, their arrest rate for firearm offenses tripled (Snyder and Sickmund, 1999). The story was similar for juvenile females. Between 1988 and 1997, their arrest rate increased by more than 80% (Krisberg, 2005).

The overall evidence suggests that females did not become more involved in offending. It indicates that sensitive measures to detect female offending and sophisticated prosecutorial techniques were deployed, resulting in an increase in their arrest and incarceration (Krisberg, 2005; Steffensmeier and Schwartz, 2004; Zahn et al., 2008). Changes that have been explained as contributing to these increases include the following:

- A practice called bootstrapping, which refers to how females guilty of committing status offenses are more likely to be incarcerated than males guilty of the same offenses if they violate the conditions of their sentence. Status offenses rarely result in jail time, but elevating them to the criminal level helped snare more females in the justice systems.
- Family disputes and/or conflicts were now considered "domestic violence." For instance, aggressive incidents between siblings and parents and children—including shoving and slapping—could now be classified as common assault. Mandatory arrest laws limited police discretion and served to arrest many females as a result.
- More schools nationwide enacted zero-tolerance policies toward violence. Police referrals about girls fighting in school increased, resulting in more arrests.
- The War on Drugs also intensified, which continued to detect female drug users.

Although more females were arrested and incarcerated over time, these arrests were for offenses they had traditionally committed, such as fraud and theft (Krisberg, 2005). Violent crimes among females did *not* increase during this time and, in fact, the trend showed significant reductions in the numbers of homicides committed by females (Greenfeld and Snell, 1999).

FURTHER DEVELOPMENTS IN FEMALE GANG RESEARCH

The overall rise in female arrests and incarcerations paralleled an increase in attention to female membership from journalists, researchers, and officials. Campbell's (1984, 1992) research in New York City was among the first to suggest that female participation was not related to immorality, sexual dysfunction, or significant mental health issues. Similar to males, the females were delinquents. Campbell's girls in the gang committed traditionally male offenses, such as substance use (alcohol and marijuana), fighting, and theft. They became involved in gangs by similar circumstances as boys. Campbell found that independent female gangs organized as a way to survive within a capitalist society, isolated from the mainstream. The gang provided the girls with potential answers to living a life of poverty and a bleak future outlook. Several themes emerged. The first was the dull prospect of a life of domestic labor with no hope of education or alternative occupations. Another theme was their subordination to males, something that was even more acute within Latino culture (see also Harris, 1988; J. W. Moore, 1978, 1991; Vigil, 1988a, 2002). Childrearing fell exclusively to them and kept them trapped within the house. A final pressure was living in a deprived environment with high levels of crime and the constant threat of victimization. For Campbell's girls, a gang provided them with excitement and the perception of acceptance and safety, despite the realities they faced.

J. W. Moore (1978, 1991) compared males and females in gangs in East Los Angeles at different points in time. She presents a picture of gang girls that is unique. Rather than being affiliated with a specific male gang, many gang girls socialized and partied with boys from different gangs. At times, this led to fights between two different gangs vying for the affection of a girl, but at other times, girl members were able to help cool things down and avoid violent confrontations. Moore's girls were not as "down for their neighborhood" as the male members. Moore also found that many of the girls were responsible for bringing up their children and that the fathers, who were often other gang members, had lost contact (see also Lauderback et al., 1992). Incarceration of boyfriends and husbands was often a cause for the collapse of relationships in Moore's study.

Additional research in the 1980s and 1990s indicated that female gang members were now participating in traditionally male-dominated gang-related activities, such as fighting, robbery, and drug selling (Esbensen and Huizinga, 1993; Fagan, 1990; Joe and Hunt, 1997; J. Miller, 2001b; C. Taylor, 1993). C. Taylor's (1993) ethnography in Detroit highlights female gang members' roles as drug sellers and in some cases leaders of drug-selling gangs, as well as some vicious stories about females perpetrating violence. Ignoring females in gangs and the central positions that they hold was no longer an option. The study of female gangs and members matured and became sophisticated, and theories emerged to help contextualize their behaviors.

DIFFERENCES AND SIMILARITIES BETWEEN GANG FEMALES AND MALES

Gang membership is similar between females and males in some respects and different in others. Girls often become members for the same reasons as boys (Brotherton and Salazar-Atias, 2003). They both have similar background characteristics, including poverty, marginalization, educational and employment limitations, family issues, victimization, and poor future outlooks (Harris, 1988; Joe and Chesney-Lind, 1995; J. Miller, 2001b; J. W. Moore, 1991; Sikes, 1997). The family backgrounds of female gang members can be much more troubled than those of males (J. Miller, 2001b; J. W. Moore, 1991). School risk factors may also vary for boys and girls in terms of gang membership. Esbensen and

Deschenes (1998) reported that school commitment and educational expectations were slightly different for girls than for boys. Risk seeking and commitment to deviant/ delinquent peers have been found to be stronger explanatory factors for gang involvement for females (Esbensen and Deschenes, 1998).

The way girls join gangs is often the same way boys do. In some cases, gang initiation includes a violent ritual (e.g., getting jumped in) and in others youth drift into gangs or a friendship group will simply coalesce into one. Sikes (1997) discusses how girlfriends of current gang members may find themselves joined to a gang through association. They may be perceived as members of the gang because they are in a romantic relationship with a known gang member (see also Cepeda and Valdez, 2003; Valdez, 2007).

Similar to boys, girls often realized that life in the gang did not accomplish their needs. Rather than being filled with excitement, most of the time girl gang members hang out and do nothing, and the idea that the gang provided a sense of family was more myth than reality (Campbell, 1992; Shelden et al., 2001). And although girls may have joined gangs because of a poor future outlook, membership did not increase their chances at legitimate success, but instead further embedded them within marginalized social and economic positions (Campbell, 1992; J. W. Moore, 1991). The gang often created new problems (Joe and Chesney-Lind, 1995).

As with boys, girls in gangs, compared with those who are not in gangs, are more likely to be involved in delinquency and violence (Bjerregaard and Smith, 1993; Cervantes et al., 2006; Deschenes and Esbensen, 1999; Esbensen and Huizinga, 1993; Harper and Robinson, 1999; Thornberry et al., 2003). Cervantes et al. (2006) reported that female adolescent violence propensity was the strongest distinguishing factors between girls with a gang affiliation. Wingood et al. (2002) found that gang females were more than three times more likely to report three or more fights in the previous six months compared with non-gang girls. The effects of gang membership can have a profound impact on females (Thornberry et al., 2003). In the Rochester study, Thornberry and colleagues (2003) found that female members reported more deviance than male nonmembers, and the disproportionate share of serious and violent crime attributed to members was greater for gang females than for males (see also Howell, 1998). Membership was linked to negative life experiences for both sexes in the Rochester study, and early pregnancy, parenthood, and employment problems were more pronounced among females.

Females generally commit less serious crimes than males (Bowker et al., 1980; Fagan, 1990; J. Miller, 2001b). Fagan (1990) reported no significant differences between boys and girls in terms of alcohol use, drug sales, property damage, or extortion, but males were significantly more involved in serious forms of offending. Most female members are arrested for committing status, property, and drug offenses—what female juveniles are arrested for more generally (Chesney-Lind et al., 1996; Esbensen et al., 1999; Klein, 1995). This is because males might exclude females from violent activities (Bowker et al., 1980; J. Miller, 2001b). Also, although female members did commit violence, its nature was less serious. Female members rarely perpetrated homicides. Reports indicated that fewer than 1% of homicide suspects were females (Klein, 1995; Shelden et al., 2001). Another study reported few female victims and no female perpetrators of homicide (J. Miller, 2001a). The overall character of female gang offending is similar to that of males in that they commit a variety of crimes—the cafeteria style (Klein, 1995).

The pattern of offending among gang females depends on the sex composition of their gang (J. Miller, 2001a, 2001b; Peterson et al., 2006). Primarily female gangs (independent or affiliated) and those with a large amount of females emphasized social and relationship aspects (Campbell, 1984, 1992; Joe and Chesney-Lind, 1995; Lauderback et al., 1992). Females in gangs that consisted largely of males were more likely to be thought of as "one of the guys" or equal in committing crime compared with males (J. Miller, 2001b).

Peterson et al. (2006), using a nationwide survey data set from middle school students, examined the sex composition of gangs. They reported that in sex-balanced gangs, or those that had roughly equal members of males and females, girls occupied more central roles. These gangs were oriented toward various types of crime. Males in gangs that were all or majority male were less likely to report that their gang was involved in various types of crime compared with males in the sex-balanced gangs. Females were significantly less likely to report involvement in crime when compared to males in the same gang. In the majority-male gangs, both sexes reported similar levels of offending. Gangs that had some females but mostly males had the highest rates of delinquency for both sexes. Peterson et al. (2006, p. 217) concluded that males in sex-balanced gangs feel a "gendered status threat" resulting from the presence of girls and respond by narrowing their opportunities to participate in traditionally "masculine" activities (J. Miller, 2001b).

THE NUMBER OF FEMALE GANGS AND GANG MEMBERS

The definitional issue surrounding gangs applies as much to females as to males. Confusion surrounds the actual number of female gangs or members. Accurate counts are difficult to ascertain, including whether female membership has changed or stabilized over time (Peterson, 2014). Some data report that 6–7% of all gang members are female (Chesney-Lind et al., 1996; Howell, 1998; National Gang Center, n.d.). The number of female members recorded varies by location. Whereas only about a quarter of gangs in large, urban cities report having female members, close to half of all gangs in suburban counties, smaller cities, and rural areas report female members (National Gang Center, n.d.). Other studies have reported that anywhere from a third to a quarter of *all* gangs are female (Esbensen and Huizinga, 1993; J. W. Moore, 1991). Survey data from middle school students also indicate similar levels, with 25–50% of the sample in gangs (Esbensen et al., 2012, 2014; Esbensen and Lynskey, 2001; Peterson, 2014; Thornberry et al., 2003). Some studies indicate that between 20 and 40% of younger female juveniles were in gangs (Klein and Maxson, 2006), but these numbers dwindle when looking at membership among older juveniles and young adults.

Research in middle schools has found many more female gang members than previously suspected (Peterson, 2014; Peterson et al., 2006). However, the middle school years are a period in the lives of young females where they are also more likely to leave the gangs (Thornberry et al., 2003). When attempting to determine "how many" females are in gangs, keeping this point in mind is important: sampling younger populations will likely reveal a *higher* percentage of female members than when sampling older ones because girls often leave the gang earlier than boys (Peterson, 2014).

DIFFERENT TYPES OF FEMALE GANGS

Klein (1995) notes how female gangs, like male gangs, come in all varieties of size, organization, age range, and levels of participation in crime. Some had clearly defined leadership, with dozens of members and a great capacity for crime, whereas others were leaderless, with only a few members who were disinclined to commit crime. W. B. Miller (1975) developed a three-tier typology of female gangs that continues to receive support from research findings. In the most common tier, female members are affiliated with a known male gang and are referred to as an auxiliary. The Tiny Locas in Harris's (1988) research were aligned with the male gang the Locos; Campbell's (1984) Sandman Ladies were counterparts to the Sandmen; the Latin Queens are aligned with the Latin Kings and together they form the Almighty Latin King and Queen Nation (Brotherton and Barrios, 2004); the Del Vikings are aligned with the Del Vi-Queens (Klein, 1995); and so on (Shelden et al., 2001).

Another tier is the autonomous gang that is exclusively female and completely independent (Hunt and Joe-Laidler, 2006; Lauderback et al., 1992; J. Miller, 2001b). W. B. Miller's (1975) survey revealed that independent female gangs amounted to less than 10% of all gangs. Nearly 20 years later, the Bureau of Justice Assistance (1998, p. 14) issued a report that females were no longer just auxiliaries to known male gangs, but that "female gang members manage their own affairs, make their own decisions, and often engage in a system of norms that is similar to that of male gangs." Lauderback et al. (1992) reported on one of these gangs in San Francisco that had its own drug-selling enterprise. This female gang formed because of previous dissatisfactions with their roles as drug sellers within the male gang, so instead formed their own drug-selling gang. The lack of oversight and interference from their male counterparts allowed for their success (Lauderback et al., 1992; see also C. Taylor, 1993). Although comparative data are limited, the evidence suggests that African Americans are more likely than Latinas and Asian Americans to form autonomous gangs (Joe-Laidler and Hunt, 1997; J. Miller, 2001b; Peterson, 2014).

A third tier is the mixed-gender gang. Mixed-gender gangs are majority male, but have a considerable amount of females. Fleisher (1998) provides a vivid portrait of a mixed-gender gang in Kansas City called the Fremont Hustlers. The prevalence of these gangs is relatively unknown, although researchers generally agree that autonomous female gangs are the exception and that those who are part of mixed-gender gangs are more common (J. Miller, 2001a, 2001b; Vigil, 2002). Vigil (2002) reports that most female gangs in Los Angeles were auxiliaries and that autonomous and mixed-gender gangs were ephemeral in nature.

Another addition to W. B. Miller's (1975) tier should be girls who hang around with male members and participate in many of their street-based activities, but who do not consider themselves members. There could be more of these types of gang girls than the others previously recognized, especially within Latino neighborhoods. Valdez (2007) studies these girls, whom he considers "beyond risk": already engaging in substance use, crime, violence, and unsafe sexual behaviors. Despite their lack of formal gang identification, these girls hang out with male members, some of whom are their boyfriends or relatives. These girls have not internalized conventional values, beliefs, and norms regarding appropriate behavior. They instead have adopted cultural norms within impoverished, marginalized communities, with weak social controls, lack of educational and employment opportunities, poor social support networks, high violent crime rates, and drugs, gambling, and prostitution. In addition, they are raised within a Mexican culture that places importance on male dominance. Against this background, females involved in gangs transgress traditional female gender roles and participate in high-risk behaviors, including crime and violence (Valdez, 2007).

Like males, females experience the gang in unique ways, including their participation in drug use, crime, violence, and risky sexual behaviors. Valdez (2007) developed a typology of classifications for females based on how they identified themselves, their relation to the gang, and their levels of crime, substance use, and risky sex (see also Cepeda and Valdez, 2003). One of these was the "girlfriend/wife" who had been in a steady relationship with males in gangs, some married with children. These females were respected, unlikely to be harassed and victimized, and least involved in gang activities. On the other end was the "hoodrat": heavy drug users who were sexually promiscuous, with unattached romantic relationships with the gang males. They spent the most time on the street and earned respect by participating in male-dominated forms of crime and violence. Another was the "good girl"—a childhood friend of the male members. They closely followed traditional gender roles, were less street smart, and did not participate in crime, violence, or substance use. A final category of gang girls was "relatives," such as sisters and cousins. These girls had special status, especially if they dated one of the male members. The relatives had minimal participation in crime, violence, and the gangs' street activities. Cepeda and Valdez (2003) note how positions that females held in gangs were not fixed and could move from one type to another over time.

FEMALE GANG VIOLENCE

Female gang violence can be similar to that of males. Vigil (2002) noted how some females became as aggressive and angry as some males. Autonomous girl gangs have been noted for their aggressiveness and participation in violence (Joe-Laidler and Hunt, 1997; Lauderback et al., 1992). C. Taylor's (1993) research details female members' violence and use of deadly weapons. One of his respondents, Vickie, a 20-year-old member of a mixed-gender gang, commented on being prepared:

> The streets is rough. . . . That's why I be with these fellas, if somebody fuck with girlfriend they gotta deal with these boys and trust me, this here crew got the shit for "anybody." Yo ass will be very dead, with a quickness. So it pays to belong to some kinda crew, it's smart to have somebody out here watching yo back, right? . . . I am hard, I ain't soft, I can get it on with fellas or whoever wants to try yo girl, I am ready, ready and gonna do it. (C. Taylor, 1993, p. 116)

Another one, Pamela, a 24-year-old former member of a corporate gang, talks about the necessity of firearms:

> Call it violence if you want, but I say it's just taking care of yourself. If everybody else is packing [carrying a firearm], you be dumb as fuck to not have some kinda protection. When all the gangsters, rapists, killers, crazy babes, boys, and little kids wouldn't have their heaters [firearms] maybe that's when I will stop having my gun . . . that ain't violence, that's just straight and staying alive. (C. Taylor, 1993, p. 100)

Hunt and Joe-Laidler (2006) cataloged various forms of violence among female members based on the type of gang they belonged to (see also Joe-Laidler and Hunt, 1997). They dichotomized the types into independent all-girl gangs and separate-but-equal mixed-gender gangs. They then reported how girls in the "separate-but-equal" gangs were much more likely to experience more varieties of violence and how this greater exposure was largely a result of their associations and activities with their male counterparts. Girls in independent gangs reported only two forms of violence: conflicts in relation to selling drugs and confrontations with females in other gangs. Many carried weapons while on the street to protect themselves from addicts and robbers who might perceive female drug sellers as easy targets. They also faced potential violence from other gang members over territory, as well as from female members in mixed-gender gangs over romantic disputes.

In comparison, girls in the mixed-gender gangs encountered five types of violence. One was being jumped in—an initiation ceremony where several current members assault the lone newcomer. The protagonists here could be females, males, or both. Below, two different young females in the Los Angeles Study[1] talk about being jumped in:

Did you have to join the gang?
> I got jumped in by guys.

---

1   See the Appendix for the methodology and objectives of this study.

How many guys did you fight?

I got down, well to get in to my gang, 13.

You had to fight 13 guys at the same time?

Well they just, I had to fight back, you know?

But what I am saying is, was it you versus 13 guys?

I was down for my hood you know what I am saying?

After you fought those 13 guys you were in?

I was in, I got that with my big home girl, cause I wanted to get into [name of gang] you know what I am saying? Cause . . . I was down and I got down with my home girls for 64 seconds.

When you joined, did you have to do anything to join the gang? Did you have to get jumped in?

I had to, I actually, around when I got put on, it was like, I had a lot of problems because I have a very disrespectful mouth so, I had to, really you are suppose to take two men, two people are suppose to but fade. Two people are supposed to put you on that spot. But I had to take a five man fade because and it was every, my homies and homegirls because. . . .

When you say "five man fade" you mean, like they are fighting? Is it like you and five dudes?

Five girls.

A second form of violence experienced by girls in the mixed-gender gang was with males from other gangs (Hunt and Joe-Laidler, 2006). In this context, when a female intervened in a fight where several rivals suddenly attacked a gang male she was with, she risked assault. A third form of violence, similar to that experienced by girls in independent gangs, was conflict with girls from other gangs. Sometimes this violence was instigated by males within the girl's own gang who enjoyed watching them fight. A fourth type was when girls fought girls within their same gang in relation to conflicts over the opposite sex, "talking shit," and being intoxicated. Similar to the context of violence among males from the same gang, these types of fights normally involve fists only; the goal is to redress insults—real or imagined—not to permanently injure or kill one another. A fifth form of violence experienced by girls in the mixed-gender gangs had to do with deflecting unwanted sexual advances and, in some cases, rape and other sexual victimization.

Girls get into gang fights for similar reasons as males: to represent their neighborhood. One way to do this is by gangbanging or committing violence against another gang (W. B. Sanders, 1994). Here, a couple of young gang females from the Los Angeles Study talk about being down for the hood and putting in work.

I was down for my hood you know what I am saying? . . . I am going to ride it for my hood, you know what I am saying? . . . I did missions. I did things that people were expecting me. . . . I put in work. I have respect for my hood, you know what I am saying? . . . When I go to my hood, I put in work. . . . The homies try to get it, they will be like, "What's up dog?" And I will be ready to run and rush them, you know? . . . If I see my enemies, I will say, "What's up dog?," and then I'll just rush them or whatever if I have something, you know what I am saying?

Like for instance the other day, like a couple of weeks ago I was at Jack in the Box in my hood. . . . It was a guy and I had gotten into it with him in the hood because he was Crip in my hood, you know what I am saying? And I just feel like really disrespected, and I am like this is going to go down out here and we got into it. . . . Me and him was really like about to go at it, like have a shoot out at Jack in the Box because I am not understanding what is going on out in these streets. Like, it's cool for Crips to come in our hood now? You know what I am saying?

In relation to being "down for the hood," female members experience the full range of violent victimization, including getting jumped, beatings, and shootings. Here, several females from the Los Angeles Study discuss their injuries:

I have two bullets still in me. . . . I got shot two days after my birthday. . . . They can't take them out. . . . When it's cold like, you know, it hurts. Yeah because they are in the bones, you know what I am saying? So, it's the bullet, you know? When you see my x-ray, you can see the bullet going through my bone and it hurts.

About how many people jumped you?

About six of them.

What happened?

I bit the fuck out of his hand. I bit that fool. If there are six of them, you don't care, any damn fool, you know?

Did they leave any marks where they hit you?

Oh, yeah. My head was all big and bumps and shit, my forehead, my eyes too.

They [jumped me]. I got 18 stitches. I got pistol whooped. And I got shot, one inside of my head.

Yeah, I had a black eye, busted lip. I just had a big knot on my head. They cracked me. They sliced me.

Gang females shoot firearms, as opposed to simply carrying them for their male counterparts. Here, two young female gang members in the Los Angeles Study discussed how easy it would be to obtain serious firearms:

Have you ever fired a gun?

Yeah.

What kind of guns have you fired?

9s, AK-47, 357, 45s, 38s, 22s.

Where did you fire them?

> Enemies.

Do you know how they got the guns?

> You know, personal business.

Right now in your experience, how easy would it be to get a gun?

> For me it's easy, I can call my homeboy right now.

How many people do you know that have guns?

> Everybody I know.

How many people would that be?

> Like, 60 or 70 people.

And you said you fired a gun. What kind of guns have you fired?

> SKS, 45, 38, shotgun, 22s, 25s, 357 magnums, 9s, 38 revolvers.

BOX 4.1: MEDIA CHECK!

Mi Vida Loca (1993)

Mi Vida Loca, which translates to *My Crazy Life*, is set in the Echo Park area of Los Angeles, an area with a strong history of Latino gangs. The phrase extends generations and is often represented by a tattoo of three dots that form a triangle. Each dot represents the words Mi Vida Loca. This tattoo is commonly placed near the webbing on the hand between the index finger and thumb, but also next to the outside corner of the eye.

Although many of the people in the movie are members, the movie is not necessarily about gangs per se—not even girl gangs. One focus is on two girls who are in a gang (the Locas) and also in a relationship with the same guy who is a member of the male counterpart (the Locos). One of these girls is called Mousie, and the guy she is with is called Ernesto (aka Bullet). Ernesto has a nice truck called Sauvecito. When the weight of motherhood causes Mousie to become shy, Ernesto's attention is increasingly drawn to her best friend, Sad Girl. As one thing leads to another, Sad Girl becomes pregnant with Ernesto's child. This infidelity causes drama between Mousie and Sad Girl, who have been best friends since childhood.

Ernesto starts selling drugs to cover the costs of supporting his two baby mommas. He also has to watch his back from El Duran, the leader of another gang—River Valley. Mousie and Sad Girl's anger with one another reaches a climax and just as the two girls are about to throw down, the plot thickens. Shots ring out and Ernesto gets plugged while selling drugs to a white girl. This shakes Mousie and Sad Girl into the reality that they must now forge for themselves if they want to feed their children and make ends meet. They learn to forget their differences and focus on how they are going to make it, including plans to locate Ernesto's truck, Sauvecito, so they can sell it and live off the proceeds. The thing with the truck leads to drama throughout the movie, including one stereotype often associated with gang violence.

The film weaves in and out of life narratives from other girls in the neighborhood. Whisper, is a chola who apprentices under Ernesto in how to sell drugs. (Note: The film does a good job getting the chola make-up, hairstyle, and style right. Even the names are spot-on; "Sad Girl" is not an uncommon moniker for gang girls in Los Angeles and elsewhere.) Whisper survives the attack that took Ernesto's life, although he takes a bullet in the leg. La Blue Eyes, Sad Girl's sister, is a college student who has been sending and receiving love letters from a prisoner who turns out to be El Duran. She later meets him at a party thrown by River Valley—prior to the big drama of the movie. Giggles, an older-generation Loca, is first seen coming out of jail for a crime she did not commit—she covered for her husband, who had since died. Giggles tries to reconnect with the homeboys and girls from her past, and, when first offered a chance at living a more conventional lifestyle, continues on the path of fierce independence. The movie ends with Giggles reconsidering.

Mi Vida Loca is less about girls in the gang and more about the lives of Latinas and their own families in a marginalized inner-city community. Whereas Mousie and Sad Girl are girls who are in romantic relationships with guys in gangs, Whisper and Giggles are involved in proper gang activities. Some will find the movie an actual portrayal of life in the gang for females and others will find it way off base. Current residents of Echo Park, some of whom own million-dollar homes, will be able to use the film as solid evidence of the community's gentrification and wild heyday.

Visit YouTube to view a trailer for Mi Vida Loca.

Despite their access to weapons, gang females have expressed a reluctance to engage in behaviors that may lead to deadly violence. Similar to boys, not all girls come across as committed to deadly violence. Although camaraderie and representing the neighborhood were seen as positive aspects of membership, female members in the Los Angeles Study have reported that one downside was deadly violence in terms of perpetration and victimization:

What did you dislike about [the gang]?

> Cause sometimes you don't want to go do a mission, you know and you have to did, cause then you are a punk.

And when you say a mission, you mean put in work?

> Yeah, to go shooting and stuff.

> I lost my homies, you know what I am saying? They really died and they are not coming back, you know what I am saying?

Girls in gangs have been instrumental in promoting the opportunity for violence committed by gang males. This can happen by luring rivals into compromising positions. Harris (1988, pp. 142–143) provides an account from Reselda, who discussed this.

> The homegirls will see guys from another barrio and set them up. Say there's another gang that we don't get along with and we want to get them back for something they did. There's some girls that could go off and bring them back and say there's a party or something and they could have them already set up, and tell our homeboys where they're going to be at. Some girls do that. . . . I knew a guy that happened to. There was two guys I knew. . . . These other girls set them up with these other guys who wanted to get those two guys in a parking lot. They were partying and all of a sudden these guys came and shot them up.

SEXUAL VICTIMIZATION

Sexual victimization is both a cause and a consequence of female gang membership. Females have reported histories of sexual abuse by family members prior to joining a gang (Joe and Chesney-Lind, 1995; J. Miller, 2001b; J. W. Moore, 1991). J. W. Moore (1991) found that about one in three girls said that they had been sexually abused in the home, but that few reported it to the police. Similarly, Joe and Chesney-Lind (1995) found that close to two-thirds of the girls in their study were sexually victimized—either abuse or assault. Gang boys have reported histories of abuse in the home, but few have mentioned sexual abuse (J. W. Moore and Hagedorn, 1996; Schalet et al., 2003). Seeking refuge from sexual victimization is a key reason why females join (J. W. Moore and Hagedorn, 1996). Following Chesney-Lind's (2013) perspective on female offending more generally, girls escaping from sexual victimization in the home end up spending more time on the street, where they seek solace and security in the gang (Harris, 1994; J. W. Moore, 1991; Sikes, 1997).

Once in the gang, males subject females to more sexual victimization and/or sexual exploitation (Harris, 1994; Joe-Laidler and Hunt, 2001; J. Miller, 2001b; J. W. Moore, 1991).

Yablonsky (1997) highlights the case of Tonya, whose "relationship to the gang was typical. Most gangs have females counterparts like Tonya" (p. 114). According to Yablonsky (1997), Tonya fought alongside the males and helped them sell drugs, but was also sexually active with many of them, at times exchanging favors for cocaine. Harris (1988, p. 143) noted that homegirls might set up others for sexual victimization, as experienced by Maryann:

> The guys [from the other gang] in the park had beer and I started drinking beer, and then I started drinking tequila. I was messed up. My friend was messed up too. But she went into the car, and I couldn't get out. She wasn't raped. That's what pissed me off. She must have set me up or something.

One reason for females' heightened risk of victimization may be related to status threat (J. Miller, 1998, 2001b). Gang males have not found it appropriate that females spend a lot of time with them on the streets (Joe-Laidler and Hunt, 1997). They feel that violent and serious offending are not proper behaviors for females and that if females behave this way, it will threaten their status within the gang (J. Miller, 1998). As such, males limit females' participation in gangs. By not participating in such behaviors, females are viewed as not deserving the same levels of respect as males (J. Miller, 1998). Gang males do not respect female gang members and they are treated as lesser individuals, which leads to their mistreatment (J. Miller, 1998).

Another reason for females' heightened risk of sexual victimization is sexism. J. W. Moore (1991), in her study of Latino gangs, reported that about half of the males viewed female members as sexual "possessions," which contributed to their victimization and exploitation. Many of the males reported that the gang was their domain and that anything negative that happened to the homegirls was just desserts. Male members in Moore's study also displayed hostile and chauvinistic attitudes toward females and treated them "like a piece of ass" (J. W. Moore, 1991, p. 55). Although gang girls did date gang boys, many of the males in Moore's study had a preference for dating non-gang girls, who they believed would be their future wives (see also Cepeda and Valdez, 2003; Valdez, 2007).

One form of sexual exploitation experienced by some girls is an initiation ceremony referred to as being sexed in. Rather than fighting several active gang members for a period of time, some evidence has emerged that females have the option of having sex with a number of the gang males to gain membership (J. Miller, 2001b; Miranda, 2003; Shelden et al., 2001; Sikes, 1997; Vigil, 2002).[2] A youth female in the Los Angeles Study who was jumped into her gang through violence mentioned this:

> There are two ways to get into the hood you know, what I am saying?

Can I ask you, what is the other way?
> You get fucked in by 13 guys.

---

2   Miranda (2003) says that sexed in can also refer to when a girl has a boyfriend who is a gang member or when a girl has had several boyfriends all within the same gang. These girls would be sexed in to the gang because of previous or ongoing sexual relationships with males from that gang. In such cases, being sexed in is not a specific ritual associated with becoming a member.

Okay, so have sex with them, so you say, "I am going to go in the gang this way?"

> Yeah, yeah, have sex with them. Cause my homeboys were like, I have a lot of home girls right, and they get fucked in, you know?

At times, male and female members from the same gang have disagreed about initiating a female through sexual activity (Decker and Van Winkle, 1996). Entering by being sexed in generates suspicion centered on the belief that perhaps all females joined this way. Females can and do join by being sexed in, but it can damage the respect they receive from other members (W. B. Miller, 2001; Schalet et al., 2003; Shelden et al., 2001). As one of J. Miller's (2001b, p. 170) respondents, Tonya, said,

> When you a girl, you don't get no respect when you get sexed in, you don't get no respect.

The few female members who do join by being sexed in are often regarded as whores and not bona fide members (J. Miller, 2001b; Schalet et al., 2003). Another one of J. Miller's (2001b, p. 173) respondents, Chantell, expressed concern about girls who were sexed in because it failed to demonstrate heart and toughness, values that were tested when initiated through violence:

> [Being sexed in]'s just showin' how good you can fuck. But if it's just us, we have to have each other's back. You don't know how good she can fight, because you never seen her fight, you've just seen how good she can fuck. Like, just say there was three girls that had sex in, and there was one girl that fought in. And if we went to the mall, we seen all these Slobs, and they came to us. We don't know, and I'm just by myself, I don't know how good they could fight. They prob'ly can't fight and I get beat down, because of them.

Sexual exploitation and victimization is apparent in other research on female gangs (Brotherton and Salazar-Atias, 2003; Hagedorn, 1998; Lauderback et al., 1992; J. Miller, 1998). These experiences may lead to teenage pregnancy and motherhood, as well as marrying a gang member, which in turn helps trap females within marginalized social and economic positions (Harris, 1988; J. W. Moore, 1991; Thornberry et al., 2003). The husbands of gang females, being members themselves, are often incarcerated, leading to the females having to raising their children alone in gang communities—perpetuating the risk factors that lead to initial involvement (Sanders, Lankenau et al., 2009). The sexual objectification and exploitation of females contributes to the vicious cycle by producing children who are at a substantial risk of joining gangs in the future.

Another form of sexual victimization experienced by females is group sexual activities, which is defined as sex involving multiple partners concurrently. One or two gang females may be partying and having sex with several gang males. This has been referred to as the train or pulling a train or simply training (J. Miller, 2001b; J. W. Moore et al., 1995; Sanders, Lankenau et al., 2009). One male from the Los Angeles Study mentioned this.

> Training them, like gang banging, like one after the other: three guys in one room with a girl naked right there. One goes, and when he is done, the next [guy] just jumps right in. (Sanders, Lankenau et al., 2009, p. 67)

Among the males who participated in this behavior in the Los Angeles Study, all of them indicated that such sex was consensual. However, none of the females interviewed participated in such behaviors, and data about their perspectives on this were not collected. Other researchers have indicated that females who participated in group sex clearly did not wish to (J. W. Moore et al., 1995). The amount of drugs and alcohol involved in such episodes further complicates matters of consent. In the Los Angeles Study, about three-quarters of the youth mentioned using alcohol in combination with drugs such as cocaine, PCP, marijuana, and crystal methamphetamine prior to group sex.

IDENTITY, FEMININITY, SEXUALITY, AND RESPECT

Identity, femininity, sexuality, and respect have been themes within the research on female gang members since Campbell's early work. Campbell (1984, 1992) noted how gang girls rejected traditional female roles of the passive, stoic, loyal housewife adhered to by their mothers. Instead, the gang represented independence, autonomy, freedom, and emancipation. By joining, girls were able to embody these traits. Symbolically, the gang released them from their marginalized status and served as a form of resistance (Brotherton, 1996; Brotherton and Salazar-Atias, 2003; M. Brown, 2002; Mendoza-Denton, 2008; J. W. Moore, 1991).[3] As M. Brown (2002, p. 83) argues, the gang provides youth with the illusion that they are "restructuring their relationship" with society. In this regard, the gang has served similar purposes as working/lower-class youth cultures have for disenfranchised youth for decades in various countries—a fantastical representation of liberation and conventionality (Brake, 1985; P. Cohen, 1972; Hall and Jefferson, 1976; Hebdige, 1979; Willis, 1978).

Despite the ideals of empowerment and liberation that the gang may provide, girls still faced sexism and double standards. Vigil (2002) reported how in some cases, male members were indifferent toward females. Brotherton and Salazar-Atias (2003) noted that females in the Almighty Latin King and Queen Nation in New York City were not on par with the boys in terms of decision making, and the fact that different rules applied demoralized the Latin Queens. Also, the Latin Queens were not unified in their beliefs about womanhood, with some favoring more traditional models and others more radical ones. Many girls face risks and disadvantages in relation to gender inequality within the gang (M. Brown, 2002; Campbell, 1984; Fleisher, 1998; J. Miller, 2001a, 2001b). J. Miller (2001a, 2001b) indicates that females are typically in gangs that are predominately male and that male members often exclude females from serious and violent offenses that confer status. Although the girls might realize the gender inequality and the double standards regarding acceptable behaviors for men and women they experienced prior to joining, membership did not alleviate these concerns, but reinforced them (Fleisher, 1998; Horowitz, 1983; J. Miller, 2001a, 2001b; J. W. Moore, 1991).

---

3 Others have also discussed how gangs are symbolic representations. Mendoza-Denton (2008) coined the term *hemispheric localism* to argue how *Norteno* and *Sureno* street gang members are political actors and analysts and that their gang affiliations are ways in which they interpret global power realities.

The idea of balancing traditional models of identity and femininity with modern models is another theme. Gang girls are conventional in that they strongly identify with their race and care for and raise their children (Brotherton and Salazar-Atias, 2003; Harris, 1988; Nurge, 2003). Help with aspects of motherhood, such as clothes and furniture for the baby and babysitting, have also been reported as key economic benefits of life in the gang (Brotherton and Salazar-Atias, 2003). Other researchers have reported girls performing more gender-specific activities, like preparing meals (Messerschmidt, 1997). Notions of identity and femininity for girls may vary by race. J. W. Moore and Hagedorn (1996) reported that female members from Mexican American families were subjected to more traditional expectations of femininity, such as exclusivity, virginity, and lack of sexual pleasure, compared with females from African American households (see also Valdez, 2007). African American members have a longer custom of economic and familial independence (J. W. Moore and Hagedorn, 1996; Portillos, 1999; Vigil, 2002). The link between femininity and identity is dependent on how the concept of femininity is perceived and practiced within the parent communities.

Other research on girls in gangs centers around issues of respect. Messerschimdt (1993) indicates that masculinity and respect are often two sides of the same coin and that males engage in violence as a way to "do gender"—display to others their masculinity. Respect and masculinity are vital on the streets. Messerschmidt (1997) says the female gang violence is a particular form of femininity: the bad girl. By acting tough and engaging in violence, female members are practicing a more traditional male behavior. Several researchers have reported that female members have now adopted similar masculine codes (Harris, 1988; J. Miller, 2001a, 2001b; J. W. Moore et al., 1995; Sikes, 1997). By participating in violence, including instigating fights at the slightest provocation, females can earn respect. These are not stereotypical catfights, but vicious and ruthless (Sikes, 1997; Vigil, 2002). Although females may not engage in violence at the same frequency as males, reports indicate they have the capacity to act with the same intensity. Female gang members on the street are exposed to a patriarchal power structure, and only through adopting such masculine traits can they gain currency with respect and reputation (J. Miller, 2001b).

Gang colors, symbols, and signs are prideful indications of identity and community, and male members wear them with subtle and blatant indicators of their membership. Females do the same. They use their style to enhance their current status as members and to achieve a sense of power (Vigil, 2002). The *cholas* of Harris's (1988) study adopted a macho homegirl demeanor and dressed like the homeboys (e.g., white t-shirt, flannel shirts buttoned only at the top, chino trousers)—and rejected traditional Latina roles as housewife and mother. Miranda (2003) notes how some homegirls wore oversized shirts and baggy pants that hid their female body and accentuated a masculine, street-tough demeanor. Miranda's (2003) homegirls consciously dressed like this so as not to be perceived as sexual property. Style is a way that females "do gang membership"—display to others that they are members.

J. Miller (2001a, 2001b) argues that females balance issues of traditional femininity and street masculinity. She reports that they mimic masculine gender norms in relation to violence, toughness, and independence to be "one of the guys." These females are critical of those who get sexed in and others who are promiscuous. When the males began to speak of females in derogatory ways because of their sexual promiscuity, many females were able to join in. This gave females the belief that they were on equal pairing with the males in terms of respect, which is what they desired. Membership served as a resistance to traditional forms of femininity (see also Joe-Laidler and Hunt, 2001).

J. Miller (2001a, 2001b) notes that females must balance being "different" from outsiders, but not so much to offend the males who have expectations about females' sexual relations, childrearing, drug use, and violence. Female members transgress socially approved norms of behavior because their gang involvement is a type of proclamation of their rejection of communal expectations of them (J. Miller, 2001a). They see themselves different from their peers—the good girls (Harris, 1988). The *chola* look not only served to publicly display female members' differences from the good girls, but also made them less attractive to males. Although the *chola* style may have found acceptance within the male gangs, most males do not wish to marry or have children with the *cholas*. They prefer the good girls, the ones the *cholas* try so hard not to be (Cepeda and Valdez, 2004; J. Miller, 2001a; J. W. Moore, 1991).

Joe-Laidler and colleagues suggest that the concept of respect among girls in the gang is highly gendered and must be understood in a distinct context from the concept of the dominant form of masculinity of the streets (Hunt, Moloney, Joe-Laidler and MacKenzie, 2011; Joe-Laidler and Hunt, 2001; Schalet et al., 2003). For these authors, the concept of femininity is centrally connected to respectability, in which autonomy and sexual reputation are paramount. These authors examined the different ways that homegirls talked and thought about sexuality and its relationship to autonomy, loyalty, and control (Schalet et al., 2003). Homegirls who maintain sexual responsibility fear being labeled as sexually promiscuous "hos" because it could damage their loyalty and affiliation with the gang. Most of the homegirls in the study behaved this way. They were battling the widespread (mis)perception of the whoring female. They attempted to maintain a balance between being a true gang member and a respectable female. They disassociated with those who were promiscuous to reduce being perceived in the same way.

Some of the homegirls practiced sexual autonomy. They were less concerned about their own purity and loyalty to the gang and stressed their own desires, needs, and preferences. The authors highlight sexual subjectivities, which were gang girls' experiences as sexual beings and agents competent to achieve their own interests (Schalet et al., 2003). Homegirls' sexual subjectivities helped resolve tensions between maintaining independence from others while navigating and adopting to the restricting norms of femininity. The authors noted the interrelationships between the ways homegirls talked, practiced, and negotiated their sexuality (Schalet et al., 2003). They must construct their discourses of sexuality not only within the confines of gender norms, but also within the context of being members of a gang. And although gangs may provide them with the opportunity to adhere to behavioral norms of femininity outside of those that dominate their traditional institutions (e.g., home, family, school, church), membership may also serve to oppress them.

PREGNANCY AND MOTHERHOOD

Pregnancy and motherhood are not uncommon among gang females. Schalet et al. (2003) reported that 40% of their sample were either pregnant or had children. Early motherhood has often been associated with several negative health outcomes, including a lack of pre-natal care, poor school performance, unemployment, child abuse and neglect, and poor parent–child relations (H. Wilson and Huntington, 2006). Young mothers are at risk for a variety of health-related problems, including substance use and risky sexual behaviors (Koniak-Griffin et al., 2003). Teenage mothers are considered a "vulnerable population" because of their marginal economic and social positions and increased likelihood for mor-bidity and mortality—both for them and for their children (Lesser and Escoto-Lloyd, 1999). Teen mothers are highly stigmatized (Yardley, 2008). Membership makes all these issues worse. Gang communities are not conducive to healthy development and may help transmit values supportive of crime and delinquency. Young people growing up in gang communities with a mother who is a member have some of the strongest risk factors that predict membership (Hill et al., 1999; Thornberry et al., 1993, 2003).

Additional aspects of becoming a mother while in the gang may have prosocial quali-ties. When talking about gangs and risky sexual behaviors, an interventionist in Los Ange-les who works with young males and females argued that she does not discourage girls in gangs from getting pregnant. She specified that she does not promote pregnancy and en-courages safe sexual practices among all youth. She was well aware of the risks and conse-quences of teenage pregnancies. However, she did *not* discourage pregnancy among the girls because motherhood offered a safe passage out of the gang. She continued by describ-ing teen pregnancy among gang girls as the lesser of two bad situations. She said that al-though teen pregnancy and young motherhood are problematic, they paled in comparison to the problems of continued membership. Leaving the gang is a tricky subject, but motherhood is a distinct pathway out.

Hunt et al. (2011) examined motherhood among members. Their team gathered quantitative and qualitative data from 65 females who were also mothers in the San Francisco Bay Area. The women came from a variety of different types of gangs, from those whose existence spanned generations to smaller, more flexible gangs. Some were all female and others were mixed gender. Although all reported engaging in a variety of risk behaviors, such as crime, violence, and substance use, many decreased or stopped once they became mothers. In contrast to being promiscuous, about 20% of the sample had become pregnant after their first sexual experience. About a third had discontinued contact with their child's father because many were either unwilling or lacking in resources to help.

Early motherhood in some cases was a partial result of gang membership and, ironically, served as a way to distance mothers from the gang. Hunt and colleagues (2011) indicated that a sense of family and bonding attracted many to the gang. Once in, they felt pressured to have sex, and in some cases the male members compelled them to have their children. The idea of being a good mother helped encourage them to spend less time with the gang (see also Giordano et al., 2002). Most also improved relationships with their real families after becoming parents, used drugs and alcohol less, if at all, and spent more time indoors with their children. They began to do different things and their self-perceptions changed. All of these considerations in concert helped steer many away from the violence and victimization. Graciela, one of their respondents, said this:

> [Becoming a mother] kind of made me grow up faster than I should have because now it's like I think about my baby first before I think about myself. . . . Before, I don't care about nothing and, you know, I'm going to do what I want to do. And then when I had my baby, I thought of him first and I changed my way of thinking . . . and I don't want to take my baby out with me and hang around my friends, and drink and hang out on the corner or whatever. . . . I don't want my baby there. (Hunt et al., 2011, p. 153)

PROSOCIAL FUNCTIONS AND POST-GANG LIVES

Most of what has been written about females in gangs suggests that they come from at-risk backgrounds, participate in heightened levels of high-risk behaviors, are subjected to further victimization by rivals and members of their own gang, and lead poorer lives after leaving the gang. In these regards, membership is similar for males and females. Within the literature are indications that the gang provides prosocial functions for females and that membership is slightly beneficial for them. Some leave without much fanfare and move on to lead productive and fulfilled lives. If gangs are "way stations" for females, then clearly they interpret membership as something temporarily beneficial for them (Brotherton and Salazar-Atias, 2003, p. 195; see also Miranda, 2003). The first part of the title of Nurge's (2003) article on females in gangs—"liberating yet limiting"—captures this perceived benefit.

What was missing in their lives females said they found in gangs. One such benefit is a sense of family (Brotherton and Salazar-Atias, 2003; Joe and Chesney-Lind, 1995;

W. B. Miller, 2001; Miranda, 2003; Nurge, 2003; Peterson, 2014; Quicker, 1999). Life with their biological families is troublesome, and girls have described fellow gang members as family that provides emotional support and a sense of sisterhood. Miranda (2003) notes that many of the Latina homegirls around Oakland have a lot of fun just hanging out. To them, the gang was their main peer group consisting of good friends. The homegirls in Miranda's (2003) study discussed taking precautions about becoming pregnant because pregnancies would mean they would have to leave and miss out on the good times (see also Hagedorn and Devitt, 1999). As she notes, the girls described pregnancy as "getting old' and . . . drawing away from the intimacy and solidarity of gang life" (Miranda, 2003, p. 152).

Data on desistance from the gang among females are limited. Although violence can and does accompany leaving, this is not always the case and in fact may only occur in a minority of instances. Hagedorn and Devitt (1999), in their study in Milwaukee, found that close to half of the girls left the gang simply by walking away. Quicker's (1999) focus on Latinas in East Los Angeles also noted that the "passive" departure was the most common, whereby girls drifted away from the gang with no ceremony (see also Harris, 1988). School students from the GREAT II program also found that the most common process for girls was walking away without consequence (Peterson, 2014). In other cases, the gang dissolves and the girls go in their own directions (Miranda, 2003; Valdez, 2007). Miranda (2003) says that maturing out of gangs for males means accepting more responsibility, but for females it can be socially isolating. She argues that the concept of maturing out of gangs for females is a misnomer given the strong bonds formed among members.

Girls have led productive lives after leaving. Nurge (2003) found that all of the female members studied went on to lead positive, healthy lives. Miranda (2003) says that some of the homegirls in her study returned to school, went to job training, and/or had families after leaving the gang. Quicker (1999) notes that the main reasons for passive departures were positive accomplishments or opportunities, such as graduating from high school or a new job. These girls were viewed as emeriti and given the honorific status of *vetrana* (Quicker, 1999). The gang interventionist mentioned earlier in this chapter is another example. Although she is in her fifties, she says she is still a member of the same gang she was as a youth, but does not commit offenses anymore and is not active. When she was active, she committed some serious and violent offenses and was a hard-core member. For decades now, she has helped other at-risk and beyond-risk boys and girls from gang communities and has been a vital local resource.

SUMMARY

Females in gangs were ignored for a long time by researchers, law enforcement, and policy makers. Early depictions of girls were stereotypical in that they focused on their relationship with males and immorality. Girls in gangs were considered either sexually promiscuous sex objects or overtly masculine tomboys. Although girls within gangs continue to occupy such statuses, contemporary portraits indicate this simple dichotomy is no longer accurate. Girls nowadays hold various roles and positions, including hard-core shot callers, and all-girl gangs are participating in levels of crime and violence on par with their male counterparts.

Despite the growth in the attention to female members, it remains uncertain how many exist. The responses vary depending on the methods used and the population studied. Surveys from middle schools reported substantial proportions of members. Girls enter and exit gangs earlier than boys, and such data may overestimate the number of gang females. Studies on adult female members noted that girls comprise a small fraction of the overall gang population. What is unclear is the extent to which girls identify themselves as members, as opposed to girlfriends or relatives of members or those who simply hang out. Regardless of actual numbers, the attention toward females has grown. This could be because of the increase in attention in female gangs among researchers and law enforcement, a growth in the socioeconomic conditions that give rise to gangs, changes in policies, or a combination of these considerations.

The study of female members has become more sophisticated and the quality of research has improved. Girls join for similar reasons as boys: excitement, protection, and a sense of family and belonging. The risk factors that predict membership for males and females are similar: chaotic, violent, and socially and economically marginalized communities. A history of sexual abuse is a unique risk factor for girls in terms of membership.

The ironies and impact of membership hold true for females. They realize that gangs are not really exciting, but boring, because days are filled with hanging out and doing nothing. Rather than protection, gang membership places girls at an increased risk of violent victimization. Instead of experiencing a feeling of belonging, females in gangs are often not respected by males. Gang females are much more likely to commit crime and violence than their non-gang counterparts. Females find that membership negatively impacts short- and long-term goals. Regarding why they join and how membership influences crime, violence, and long-term health outcomes and occupational goals, females and males report similar results.

In some respects, membership is worse for girls than for boys. Females face a wider array of violence, including sexual victimization, particularly from male members. Girls in gangs also question traditional roles of femininity. Females balance notions of femininity with being down for their gang, in a sense juggling between being masculine and feminine behaviors to occupy an appropriate gang status. Males do not face this obstacle because being a gang member and masculinity go hand in glove. Pregnancy and motherhood are much more significant in the lives of females and are an honorable way for girls to leave. Mothers are expected to hang out less with the gang and stay off the streets and take care of the children in the home.

The gang experience for females does have some benefits, and not all female gang members are destined for bleak futures. Like they do for males, gangs provide females with prosocial functions, such as a sense of autonomy, identity, and family. They also provide females with the opportunity to gain and demonstrate respect. And, like many gang males, females are able to leave gangs without much ceremony and go on to lead productive, law-abiding lives.

CHAPTER REVIEW QUESTIONS

1. Explain why early accounts of female gang members were sexist and stereotypical.
2. What are the reasons for the increases in female arrests toward the end of the 20th century?
3. What are some differences and similarities in reasons that males and females join gangs?
4. What are some differences and similarities in the effects of gang membership for males and females?
5. Explain how the sex composition of a gang shapes patterns of offending for males and females.
6. What are the contexts of sexual victimization among females both prior to and during gang membership? What shapes such victimization?
7. Describe the different types of female gangs.
8. What are the various forms of violence experienced by gang females? How does the sex composition of a gang shape such violence?
9. How are gender, respect, and identity shaped by gang membership among females? How do female gang members balance these qualities?
10. What is the impact of pregnancy and motherhood on females in gangs? How does this differ from the impact on gang males?

HYPERLINKS TO ARTICLES ON FEMALE DELINQUENCY AND GANG INVOLVEMENT

The Girls Study Group: Charting the way to delinquency prevention for girls (2008)
By Margaret A. Zahn, Stephanie R. Hawkins, Janet Chiancone, and Ariel Whitworth
https://www.ncjrs.gov/pdffiles1/ojjdp/223434.pdf/

Violence by teenage girls: Trends and context (2008)
By Margaret A. Zahn, Susan Brumbaugh, Darrell Steffensmeier, Barry C. Feld, Merry Morash, Meda Chesney-Lind, Jody Miller, Allison Ann Payne, Denise C. Gottfredson, and Candace Kruttschnitt
https://www.ncjrs.gov/pdffiles1/ojjdp/218905.pdf/

Resilient girls: Factors that protect against delinquency (2009)
By Stephanie R. Hawkins, Phillip W. Graham, Jason Williams, and Margaret A. Zahn
https://www.ncjrs.gov/pdffiles1/ojjdp/220124.pdf/

Causes and correlates of girls' delinquency (2010)
By Margaret A. Zahn, Robert Agnew, Diana Fishbein, Shari Miller, Donna-Marie Winn, Gayle Dakoff, Candace Kruttschnitt, Peggy Giordano, Denise C. Gottfredson, Allison A. Payne, Barry C. Feld, and Meda Chesney-Lind
https://www.ncjrs.gov/pdffiles1/ojjdp/226358.pdf/

Young women and gang violence: Gender, street offending, and violent victimization in gangs
By J. Miller and S. H. Decker
http://www.michelepolak.com/200fall11/Weekly_Schedule_files/Miller.pdf/

Gender and victimization risk among young women in gangs
By J. Miller
http://64.20.37.146/academic/miller_genervivt.pdf/

Life-course events, social networks, and the emergence of violence among female gang members
By M. S. Fleisher and J. L. Krienert
http://eblackcu.net/portal/archive/files/fleisher_krienert_2004_7136b93533.pdf/

Accomplishing femininity among the girls in the gang
By K. J. Laidler and G. Hunt
http://troublesofyouth.pbworks.com/f/Laidler+-+Accompany+Feminity+in+the+Gang.pdf

Female gangs: A focus on research
By J. W. Moore and J. M. Hagedorn
https://www.ncjrs.gov/pdffiles1/ojjdp/186159.pdf/

Risk behaviors among young Mexican American gang-associated females: Sexual relations, partying, substance use, and crime
By A. Cepeda and A. Valdez
http://www.ncbi.nlm.nih.gov/pmc/articles/PMC3016046/

CHAPTER 5

DRUG USE AND SALES

KEY WORDS

Addiction: Persistent and compulsive dependence on a substance.

Benzodiazepine: A prescription drug that alleviates anxiety and helps induce calm or sleep. Examples include Xanax and Valium.

Crack cocaine: A rocklike combination of powder cocaine with baking soda or ammonia. Street slang for crack includes "cavi," "rock," and *piedra* ("rock" in Spanish).

Negative health outcomes: Things that impact physical health, such as death, addiction, overdose, abscesses, injury, disability, trauma, and sexually transmitted infections, such as HIV and hepatitis C virus (HCV).

Opiate: A drug derived from morphine that induces sleep and alleviates pain. Opiates include heroin and prescription drugs such as oxycodone and hydrocodone (e.g., Vicodin and Oxycontin).

PCP: Short for phencyclidine, a dissociative anesthetic in the same family as ketamine. PCP usually comes in a liquid form and is administered by dipping a cigarette or joint into the liquid and then smoking it when it dries. Street slang for PCP includes "sherm," "wet," "water," "H2O," and "angel dust."

Polydrug use: The use of more than one drug over a period of time. This can include the simultaneous use of drugs (e.g., injecting a mixture of heroin and cocaine; ingesting ecstasy and LSD at the same time) or the sequential use of drugs (e.g., drinking beer, then later smoking a marijuana joint and then later sniffing cocaine). Polydrug use may also be classified as having ever used more than one drug.

Prescription drug misuse: The misuse of prescription drugs usually can refer to noncompliance for individuals who are legitimately prescribed the drug (e.g., using more than the recommended dosage, administering the drug in ways not intended, such as snorting or injecting, or using the drug without a prescription for recreational purposes).

Stimulant: A drug that makes the user feel more alert, energetic, and enthusiastic. Stimulants include cocaine and crystal methamphetamine and prescription drugs like Adderall and Ritalin.

Tar heroin: A relatively newer form of heroin that emerged in the early to mid-1990s. The purity within tar heroin allowed the drug to be smoked rather than injected. This shift in administrations invited new waves of users, and overall rates of use and Drug Enforcement Administration seizures have radically increased since. In the United States, the drug is largely imported from Mexico.

Tecato: A criminally inclined heroin addict within impoverished Latino communities, particularly Mexican American and Dominican American.

Chapter Learning Objectives

- Describe patterns of substance use among gang members.
- Explain attitudes and consequences of use among members.
- Differentiate between myth and reality in relation to drug sales and gangs.
- Comprehend the nature of drug sales and violence among gangs.

INTRODUCTION

Gang membership is an indicator of chronic substance use. Alcohol and marijuana feature prominently in common, daily activities, such as partying, hanging out, and doing nothing. Substance use provides a variety of symbolic and tangible purposes, including lamenting the loss of dead homies, easing the pain associated with violence, welcoming new members into the gang, and gathering courage to commit violence. Drug selling and gangs are tightly interwoven in the minds of law enforcement and the general public. Few gangs are organized around distribution and few members will become wealthy. Most will end up incarcerated or in the morgue. Open-market drug selling within urban environments with long histories of crime and violence is usually a short-lived, dangerous, and difficult operation.

This chapter begins by offering data on the differing rates of substance use between gang and non-gang youth. Next, it examines the significance of alcohol and marijuana within gang culture. It then looks at rates of other illicit drugs and members' ambivalent attitudes toward them. Explanations about the inconsistent feelings about hard drugs are offered. Drug addiction among members is discussed next. The second half of the chapter addresses drug selling among gangs. Particular attention is given to the emergence of the crack cocaine market and its impact on inner-city communities. The organization of drug selling in gangs and the different relationships between members and drug sales is explored. Myths about the wealth gang members accumulate from drug sales are then exposed. The final section provides data on the association among violence, drug sales, and gangs and drugs, with a focus on the heightened level of risk involved compared with the returns generated.

SUBSTANCE USE PATTERNS

Delinquent subcultures—a phrase that was synonymous with the word gang in the 1950s and 1960s—were linked to substance use. Youth in Cloward and Ohlin's (1960) retreatist subculture were committed to substance use. Youth who either did not have the opportunity or required a skill set to be illegitimately successful through economic means or violent prowess fell into drunkenness and retreated from society. These youth were double failures—they could not make it in the legitimate sector or in the illegitimate one—and instead opted for a persistent state of intoxication. Researchers in the 1960s and 1970s also noted high frequencies of substance use among gang members (Keiser, 1969; Klein, 1971; J. W. Moore, 1978; Spergel, 1964).

The Causes and Correlates studies found that youth who report membership are much more likely to use illicit drugs compared with youth who are not in gangs (Esbensen and Huizinga, 1993; Gatti et al., 2005; Gordon et al., 2004; G. P. Hall et al., 2006; Hill et al., 1999; Loeber and Farrington, 2000). Gang status itself helped predict the use of substances above and beyond the influence of delinquent peers (Battin et al., 1998; Hill et al., 1999). Other comparative studies have found that gang youth were more likely to report early alcohol and substance use with greater frequency than non-gang youth (Swahn et al., 2010) or greater current and lifetime rates of overall substance use (Lanier et al., 2010). Studies specifically on gang members have indicated relatively high rates of use, early use, and the use of a variety of illicit substances (De La Rosa et al., 2006; Hagedorn et al., 1998; Hunt et al., 2002; Mata et al., 2002; B. Sanders, 2012; B. Sanders, Valdez et al., 2013; Valdez et al., 2006).

In some cases, drug use begins or rises only after youth join, suggesting that something about the gang increases youths' likelihood to use drugs (Bjerregaard, 2010; Hagedorn et al., 1998; Lanier et al., 2010; L. Zhang et al., 1999). Alternatively, drug experimentation and membership might happen around the same time. The socioeconomic profiles that predispose youth to join are the same that place them at higher risk for use. Here, the relationship between gang membership and substance use is spurious, explained by family conflict, peer influence, and/or social disorganization (Bjerregaard, 2010). Other researchers have noted that gang youth were exposed to alcohol and illicit drug use at much earlier ages than the general population (see also De La Rosa et al., 2006; D. G. Stewart et al., 1997). Hagedorn et al. (1998) found that males who had family members in gangs and who used drugs were more likely to report frequent cocaine use. They reported that "marijuana and alcohol use coincided with our respondents' initial gang involvement" (Hagedorn et al., 1988, p. 128). They also reported that "cocaine use for Latinos and Latinas occurred almost entirely after joining the gang" (Hagedorn et al.,

1988, p. 128; see also Lanier et al., 2010). Hagedorn et al. (1998) found that major theories of delinquency such as social control theory and differential association theory did not help explain the variation in substance use among their sample of gang members (see also B. Sanders, 2012).

Substance use and gang membership are tightly interwoven. Research indicates that gang members have differential rates of use and attitudes toward various substances—the use of some substance is ongoing, whereas the use of others is more limited (Decker, 2000; MacKenzie et al., 2005; J. W. Moore, 1978; B. Sanders, 2012; C. S. Taylor, 1990; Waldorf, 1993a). Alcohol and marijuana have a special relationship within gang cultures, whereas other drugs are less so. Hard drugs such as cocaine (powder and crack), heroin, and crystal methamphetamine have been stigmatized (Decker, 2000; Hagedorn et al., 1998; B. Sanders, 2012; Waldorf, 1993a; cf. Bourgois, 1995; Jacobs, 1999). Substance use can be broken down into three general categories: alcohol, marijuana, and other drugs.

ALCOHOL

Alcohol is the most popular, has the longest history of use, and is used with greater frequency and quantity (Fagan, 1993). When hanging out and doing nothing, alcohol use is the norm (Hagedorn, 1988; Hunt et al., 2000; Hunt and Joe-Laidler, 2001; Padilla, 1992). Alcohol has many functions. Drinking is something to do and helps facilitate social interactions. Alcohol plays a key role in establishing group cohesion and solidarity (Hunt et al., 2000; Hunt and Joe-Laidler, 2001; J. W. Moore, 1991; Vigil and Long, 1990). Hanging out morphs into partying when members consume even larger quantities of alcohol, which further contributes to group togetherness (Hunt et al., 2000; J. W. Moore, 1991; Vigil, 1988a). Consumption can also lead to conflict within a gang (Valdez et al., 2006). One of Hunt et al.'s (2000, p. 346) female members said,

> when we are drunk, we are more violent . . . towards each other. . . . For no reason. It is just the alcohol. Alcohol does that to a person.

Members from various races have differential patterns and attitudes toward alcohol use. The Chinese view drunkenness as inappropriate behavior (Chin, 1990). Studies on other Asian and Pacific Islanders has revealed widespread, but not heavy use (Toy, 1992a; Waldorf et al., 1994). Hunt and Joe-Laidler (2001) found that African Americans have higher rates of use than Asians and other racial groups. De La Rosa and Soriano (1992) reported that whites had higher rates than Hispanics and African Americans.

Alcohol has symbolic roles. Gang members may pour liquor on the ground for the deceased (Campbell, 1992; Hunt et al., 2000; Hunt and Joe-Laidler, 2001). This type of ritual stems back millennia in other cultures, such as wakes or toasts for the dead. Gangs visit the graves of dead homeboys and leave bottles next to the site and/or pour liquor over the gravestone to show respect (Hunt and Joe-Laidler, 2001). This further contributes to social cohesion and bonding within gang cultures.

Alcohol helps youth to commit criminal behaviors that they might otherwise not have the mettle for (Hunt et al., 2000; Hunt and Joe-Laidler, 2001; Vigil, 1988a; Vigil and Long,

1990; cf. B. Sanders et al., 2010). It acts as an "enabling mechanism" (Hunt and Joe-Laidler, 2001, p. 70). One of the female members in the study by Hunt et al. (2000) mentioned how alcohol helped her prepare for a fight:

> Usually I drink before I fight because it pumps me up. Like I said, I am not the type of person, I am not a violent person. But if you mess with me then you know what I am saying, all hell is going to break loose. So I usually drink, say just to get my blood warm. Just to get me pumped. (p. 340)

Vigil said that substance use helps induce *locura*, which is "A state of mind in which various quasi-controlled actions denoting a type of craziness or wildness occur" and that "only a very few can play *loco* without the use of liquor and drugs" (Vigil, 1988a, p. 440). Alcohol is one of several drugs that acts as an enabler. Youth in the Los Angeles Study said that they used alcohol and other substances to help them gain courage and relax their nerves to commit violence. One former member, who now works as a counselor and gang interventionist, talked about how heavy alcohol and PCP use allowed her and her home-boys to commit drive-by shootings with shotguns and rifles. While sober, some might not have the mind-set to commit deadly violence, but alcohol and/or other drugs helps them to attain it. Substance use and violence both contribute to solidarity within the gang (Hunt and Joe-Laidler, 2001; W. B. Sanders, 1994; Vigil, 1988a, 1988b).

Alcohol accompanies postviolent situations, such as getting jumped in as a form of initiation. After the new recruit has gone through the ritual, the gang celebrates the member's new status, and drinking plays a key role (Hunt et al., 2000; Hunt and Joe-Laidler, 2001). Alcohol is used to numb the pain from victimization, and habitual intoxication helps buffer the burden of a difficult existence and a bleak future (Hunt et al., 2000; Hunt and Joe-Laidler, 2001; Sikes, 1997). It allows members to temporarily forget about their problems (Hunt et al., 2000). As Sikes (1997, p. 27) noted in her study of gang girls, "Drugs helped protect them from things that would, if fully perceived, drive them crazy."

MARIJUANA

Marijuana is the most commonly reported illicit drug used and that used with the greatest frequency (Hunt et al., 2002; Mata et al., 2002; B. Sanders, 2012; Valdez et al., 2006). More than 90% of gang members have reported lifetime rates of marijuana use, with more than half using it in the past 30 days (Hunt et al., 2002; Mata et al., 2002; B. Sanders, 2012; Valdez et al., 2006). As one fieldworker in Valdez's (2005, p. 851) research said,

> These guys smoke marijuana while walking to school, cruising, and even during pick-up basketball games at neighborhood playgrounds. It's just common behavior.

Marijuana has enjoyed a significant degree of acceptability within gang culture (MacKenzie et al., 2005; Moloney et al., 2008; B. Sanders, 2012). The drug is widely available, and some members sell it. Attitudes toward harder drugs, such as crack cocaine, crystal methamphetamine, and heroin, are more critical and in sharp contrast to how gang members feel about marijuana (B. Sanders, 2012; C. S. Taylor, 1990; Waldorf, 1993a).

Marijuana features prominently within gangsta rap. Some songs, including *Hits from the Bong* and *Getting High in My Cadillac*, and some albums, such as *The Chronic*, are dedicated to marijuana. Gangsta rappers Cypress Hill and Snoop Doggy Dogg have made a living making music about marijuana. Others have assumed stage names that suggest use, like Cannabis. Few rappers, however, celebrate the use of hard drugs. Marijuana holds a special place in the repertoire of use and is culturally significant among gang members.

OTHER ILLICIT DRUGS

Although the use of other illicit drugs is lower than that of marijuana, members have high rates of using cocaine (crack and powder), heroin, PCP, crystal methamphetamine, and other drugs. Hagedorn et al. (1998) found that 69% of their sample had ever used cocaine. Mata et al. (2002) noted that 29% had used LSD (acid) and 48% had used inhalants (e.g., glue, paint, air freshener). About a quarter of Valdez's (2005) sample reported using heroin (*chiva*) in the previous month, and about half of them had injected the drug. Crystal methamphetamine (speed, crank) has been used as well (Robinson, 2001). PCP and/or formaldehyde has a strong history within gang cultures, where PCP has been referred to as wet, sherm,[1] water, and/or H20 (Fagan, 1989; Fleisher, 1998; W. B. Moore, 1978; B. Sanders, 2012).

Twenty years of studies funded by the National Institute on Drug Abuse (1990–2010) on gang youth from San Antonio, San Francisco, and Los Angeles have reported high rates

---

1   PCP is often in liquid form, hence the water references. "Sherm" is a slang term for PCP that emerged from the practice of dipping Sherman-brand cigarettes in liquid PCP to facilitate its use.

TABLE 5.1 LIFETIME AND 30-DAY ILLICIT SUBSTANCE USE FREQUENCIES* (% SAMPLED; B. SANDERS, VALDEZ ET AL., 2013)

Drug/site (Lifetime/30-Day)	San Antonio (%)	San Francisco (%)	Los Angeles** (%)
Marijuana	98/75	96/77	98/56
Methamphetamine	29/7	17/3	35
Heroin	57/26	9/3	7
Powder cocaine	90/53	36/3	32
Crack cocaine	26/6	14/3	33
Speedball***	44/14	NA	2
Ecstasy	NA	30/0	35
LSD	NA	21/1	10
Phencyclidine	NA	12/0	25
Psilocybin	NA	NA	22
Glue/inhalants	35/4	10/0	22
Prescription drugs	74/28	10/3	33

*Frequencies are rounded to the nearest tenth.
**Thirty-day substance use data not recorded except for marijuana.
*** Simultaneous use of heroin and cocaine.

of hard drug use (see Table 5.1; B. Sanders, Valdez et al., 2013). National sentinel data from Monitoring the Future and the National Survey on Drug Use and Health indicate that few people in the general population have ever tried meth, heroin, PCP, crack, or coke (Johnston et al., 2012; Substance Abuse and Mental Health Services Administration, 2011; see Table 5.2).

Prescription drug misuse has been reported among gang members (Hunt et al., 2002; Mata et al., 2002; B. Sanders, 2012; B. Sanders, Valdez et al., 2013; Valdez et al., 2006).

TABLE 5.2 LIFETIME RATES OF SUBSTANCE USE (% SAMPLED)

Drug Type	10th Graders (15 or 16 Years Old)* (%)	12th Graders (17 or 18 Years Old)* (%)	Youth 16 or 17 Years Old** (%)	Youth 18 to 20 Years Old** (%)
Crack cocaine	1.6	1.9	0.5	1.4
Powder cocaine	3.3	5.2	3.1	8.5
Methamphetamine	2.1	2.1	1.0	2.4
Ecstasy	6.6	8.0	5.1	9.9
PCP	NA	2.3	0.4	0.9
Heroin	1.2	1.4	0.3	1.6
LSD	2.8	4.0	1.4	4.5

*Data are from Monitoring the Future in 2011 (Johnston et al., 2012).
**Data are from the National Survey on Drug Use and Health in 2010 (Substance Abuse and Mental Health Services Administration, 2011).

Valdez and colleagues reported that 74% of their San Antonio sample reported lifetime use of prescription drugs. Earlier research has noted the use of opiates and barbiturates or pills (Decker, 2000; Fagan, 1989; Mata et al., 2002). Researchers more recently have provided data on the specific types of prescription substances used, including opiates (e.g., Vicodon, Oxycontin), stimulants (e.g., Ritalin, Adderall), and benzodiazepines (e.g., Rohypnol, Xanax; B. Sanders, 2012; B. Sanders, Valdez et al., 2013; Valdez, 2007).

Crack cocaine has long been linked with African Americans, but studies have reported that they are less likely to use crack compared to those from other races (Robinson, 2001; Waldorf, 1993a).[2] Crystal methamphetamine has historically been a drug used by whites, but Robinson (2001) found that Hispanics had the highest rates of use compared to white and black members. PCP use occurs in Mexican American barrios of East Los Angeles (J. W. Moore, 1991; Vigil, 1988a), but its use has also been reported elsewhere and from different races. Fleisher (1998) reported that the Fremont Hustlers, a multiracial gang, used dank—cigarettes dipped in formaldehyde.[3] The overall rates of use may vary by race. Esbensen and Winfree (1998) found that African Americans were less likely to report use.

Marijuana and alcohol are used daily, but hard drug use is limited. Valdez (2005) found that snorting cocaine was viewed as acceptable only during special occasions, such as a concert, sporting event, or when a member acquired a large amount of cash. In the Los Angeles Study, crystal, crack, and ecstasy were used only on occasion. Some said they binge used cocaine or crystal along with alcohol and marijuana for several days.

Males and females may have different patterns of use. Hunt, Joe-Laidler and colleagues (Hunt and Joe-Laidler, 2001; Hunt et al., 2000, 2002, 2005; MacKenzie et al., 2005; Moloney et al., 2008, 2010; Schalet et al., 2003) reported that gang males and females in the San Francisco Bay area had the same reported levels of marijuana use, but females reported *higher* lifetime rates of methamphetamine, powder cocaine, crack, LSD, PCP, and heroin (B. Sanders, Valdez et al., 2013; see Table 5.3). Robinson (2001) noted that females were significantly more likely to use crystal methamphetamine than males. Conversely, Esbensen and Winfree (1998) found no significant differences in

---

2 This finding aligns with sentinel data on substance use among youth more generally. A 30-year review of data from Monitoring the Future revealed that white juveniles (i.e., 8th, 10th, and 12th graders) had higher rates of use for every major drug of abuse except heroin compared with Latinos and blacks (Terry-McElrath et al., 2009). Among the U.S. population more generally, the National Survey on Drug Use and Health reported significantly more whites used crack and other drugs compared with Latinos and blacks, and the number of problematic white substance users is more than double the number of problematic black and Latino users combined (Substance Abuse and Mental Health Services Administration, 2012; see B. Sanders, in press). The overall evidence suggests that nonwhites do not use more drugs, but are rather more likely to be apprehended, arrested, adjudicated, sentenced, and incarcerated on drug-related charges (see B. Sanders, in press).

3 In the drug research literature, uncertainty exists as to whether youth seek to use PCP, formaldehyde, or both. These drugs are administered the same way, have a similar odor, and produce a similar effect. "Embalming fluid" is another reference, which may or may not also be PCP and/or formaldehyde (Singer et al., 2005). Some researchers argue that all of these drugs are likely various preparations of PCP (Erowid, 2009). In sum, this means that what gang youth believe to be PCP could well be embalming fluid and vice versa.

TABLE 5.3 FEMALE AND MALE GANG MEMBER LIFETIME RATES OF SELECT ILLICIT DRUGS (HUNT AND COLLEAGUES)[4]

Drug	Female (%)	Male (%)
Methamphetamine	38	17
Powder cocaine	57	36
Crack cocaine	32	14
LSD	57	21
PCP	48	12
Heroin	13	9

self-reported drug use among males and females. Bjerregaard and Smith (1993) also found few distinctions, such that females smoked marijuana somewhat more frequently than males.

Gang members mix drugs. This is referred to as polydrug use (Decker, 2000; B. Sanders, 2012; Valdez, 2005; Vigil, 1988a). Common polydrug combinations include the sequential use of alcohol and marijuana and the simultaneous use of heroin and cocaine (aka speedball). Other combinations include marijuana joints dipped in liquid PCP, called lovelies and primos, and marijuana joints containing crack cocaine, known as p-dogs, woolas, and primos. Different types of drugs are mixed, mainly within marijuana joints. In the Los Angeles Study, youth reported 21 polydrug combinations, including 14 with two drugs (B. Sanders, 2012; see Table 5.4).[5] One youth used six different substances in what he referred to as a ghost buster joint:

> You know what you should put on there?

What?

> Ghost buster.

What is that?

> It's a [marijuana] joint, with glass [meth], heroin, coke, some cavi [crack], roll it up and dipped in sherm [PCP].

How was that?

> [Rolling eyes] Whew, man, ya know?

---

4   Please see Hunt et al., 2002, 2005; Joe and Hunt, 1997; MacKenzie et al., 2005; Schalet et al., 2003; Moloney et al., 2009, 2010; see also B. Sanders, Valdez et al., 2013).

5   Polydrug uses pose many challenges for epidemiologists (and gang researchers) because of all of the possible combinations. Other polydrug combinations include goofballs (heroin and crystal methamphetamine), candy flipping (ecstasy and LSD), hippy flipping (ecstasy and psilocybin mushrooms), CK1 (cocaine and ketamine), and trail mix (a variety of powdered drugs, such as cocaine, heroin, methamphetamine, and/or ketamine; see B. Sanders, 2006a, 2006b; B. Sanders et al., 2008).

TABLE 5.4 POLYDRUG COMBINATIONS AMONG GANG MEMBERS (B. SANDERS, 2012)

Ever-Used Combinations with Two Substances	Ever-Used Combinations with Three Substances
1. Alcohol/marijuana	1. Marijuana/alcohol/crystal
2. Marijuana/crack	2. Marijuana/alcohol/crack
3. Marijuana/crystal	3. Marijuana/alcohol/cocaine
4. Marijuana/PCP	4. Marijuana/alcohol/PCP
5. Alcohol/crystal	
6. Crystal/crack	
7. Alcohol/RX opiate*	
8. Alcohol/ecstasy	
9. Alcohol/cocaine	
10. Alcohol/crack	
11. Marijuana/LSD	
12. Marijuana/ecstasy	
13. Marijuana/psilocybin	
14. Marijuana/cocaine	

*RX, prescription drug.

ATTITUDES ABOUT HARD DRUG USE

Hard drug use is stigmatized within gang cultures. Crack is one of these drugs. Members reject crack use because of its harmful effects and how being intoxicated on it limits their ability to make money selling drugs (Decker, 2000). Crack selling is fine, but usage violates gang norms (Decker, 2000). Waldorf (1993a) reported that crack use among members was viewed as the opposite of being down for the hood. Some participants in the Los Angeles Study[6] were ashamed to report using it:

Have you ever used crack?

No.

Have you ever smoked a p-dog?

No, I smoked sherm [PCP] sticks. . . . Okay. P-dogs. Yeah, I smoked a p-dog.

Did you smoke a p-dog?

Yeah, I did not mean to. But, ya know?[7] (B. Sanders, 2012)

---

6   See the Appendix for more on the methodology and objectives of this study.

7   Although speculative, crack cocaine use may have been underreported in the Los Angeles Study because of the way the drug was administered. Smoking "p-dogs"—marijuana joints that contain crack—was more commonly admitted to than smoking crack cocaine by itself. Perhaps when asked whether they had ever used crack, youth may have had a tendency to answer in the negative because they failed to perceive smoking p-dogs as equivalent to crack cocaine use. Had the questions about smoking marijuana joints specifically also asked about other drugs (e.g., crack, heroin, PCP), the overall reported usage rates for them likely would have been much higher.

W. B. Sanders (1994) noted that heavy intoxication could make members, in Goffman's terms, "cow-like, slow to be mobilized" (p. 68) and "easy targets" for victimization.

Other evidence suggests hard drug use is not censured by members given their high rates of the use of cocaine (powder or crack), crystal methamphetamine, PCP, and, especially for Latinos, heroin. Studies show high levels of use of these drugs (B. Sanders, Valdez et al., 2013).

The evidence on members having rules against hard drugs is conflicting. Several researchers have found no evidence to support the notion that gangs had such rules (Decker, 2000; Decker and Van Winkle, 1996; Klein, 1971; Vigil, 1988a, 1988b). Gangs are often unable to obtain money generated from the crimes committed by their members or organize their members for specific criminal activity, so the finding that they do not have rules against certain drug usage is no surprise (Decker, 2000). Other researchers, however, have offered evidence of rules related to hard drug use that, if violated, invited punishment (B. Sanders, 2012; Valdez, 2005). One of the youth in the Los Angeles Study mentioned how his gang had "a little code" that if anyone used crystal, "you get your ass beat" (B. Sanders, 2012). Valdez's (2005, p. 7) gang youth talked about policies about heroin use:

> The rules were just something everybody knew. It was just understood that heroin was not allowed. If a person was known to have done heroin and the gang leadership found out about it then a violation would be given to the gang member who was accused of doing heroin. The punishment depended on how bad the violation was.

W. B. Sanders (1994) found that, although Hispanic gangs did not have rules against any hard drug use, African Americans did have rules about using crack cocaine, a violation of which could lead to violence. A Piru said that if he used crack, "The big dudes will beat you up" (W. B. Sanders, 1994, p. 70). A Neighborhood Crip said something similar:

> There is no way we can use when selling. I just smoke a little weed. You would get your ass kicked if you use. The big guys will get you. (W. B. Sanders, 1994, p. 70)

The confusion about whether gangs have rules against the use of certain drugs may be related to the way the data were collected. A possibility within research on substance use among gang members is the provision of what are referred to as socially desirable responses (B. Sanders et al., 2010; see also Hagedorn et al., 1998). In such cases, participants do not report to researchers behaviors that they believe will cause them embarrassment, stigmatization, or censure. They only report those behaviors they think are acceptable. The provision of socially desirable answers can be found in all types of research (e.g., surveys, interviews), and evidence has suggested this is more common in data collection where someone other than the participant is present (e.g., the researcher or a parent or friend; Aquilino et al., 2000). If gang members provide socially desirable responses in relation to their substance use, evidence suggests that they do so no more than youth not in gangs. V. J. Webb and colleagues (2006), relying on self-report data and urinalysis, found that arrestees who were in gangs and those who were not differed little in terms of their disclosure of hard drug use (see also C. M. Katz et al., 2005).

Sometimes members do not report hard drug use. Decker (2000) argues that members do this to give the impression that they are above such behaviors and to shield themselves from the stigmatization that hard drug use carries in their communities.

Another possible explanation has to do with where the gang members were sampled. B. Sanders et al. (2010, p. 747) reported that "both the type of community-based organization [CBO] and its geographical location are associated with the level of drug use-related risk history of the gang youth that were recruited." Sampling from CBOs in South and East Los Angeles, where youth were court-ordered to attend, indicated that enrolled gang members had much higher levels of substance use than those recruited from CBOs in West Los Angeles, where the youth attended voluntarily (B. Sanders et al., 2010). Recruiting older versus younger members or those from different locales—schools, on the streets, or in jail or prison—will result in unique and conflicting patterns and attitudes toward substance use (B. Sanders et al., 2010; see also Decker, 2000).

Gang members' ambivalence helps explain the differences between what they say and what they do (see also Hagedorn et al., 1998). Perhaps their attitudes about hard drugs change. Valdez (2007, p. 33) provided a comment from a youth that captures this ambiguity:

> You can do cocaine and weed. Heroin is something that is up and down with us. Sometimes we say nah, you can't use it. But, they use it anyway. What can you do. *Les gusta* [they like it]. They can't stop, so that's something we live with. You just try not to let the "juniors" get involved.

Attitudes toward hard drug use may change with age. Valdez (2005) found that heroin use among the older gangsters, although frowned on, did not invoke any retaliatory actions. As the last excerpt suggested, however, juniors were dissuaded from using heroin. Among the general population, as adolescents become young adults, their substance use increases. Given this pattern, critical attitudes toward hard drugs among gang members may soften with age.

The change in attitude could result from reasons external to the gang. Valdez (2005) notes that when one prison gang, Pura Vida, moved into the heroin trade, Mexican American street gang members who were affiliated with them began to use. This occurred because Pura Vida pushed the drug by making it more accessible to them, lowering the price, increasing the purity, and employing both members and their peers to sell the drug.

Changing attitudes are also related to administration—moving from a drug once injected, but now snorted. As Valdez (2005, p. 10) noted, "[The] attitudes about heroin users changed as gang members began to increase their noninjecting use of [it]."

Other reasons include the type of gang that the youth belongs to and the youth's overall position in the gang. Some gangs are focused on partying and substance use and others on defending territory or criminal enterprise (Fagan, 1989; Huff, 1989; Klein, 1995; Shelden et al., 2001; C. S. Taylor, 1990). A gang's organizational character and *raison d'être* will impact members' attitudes and rates of use. Hedonistic/social gangs, party gangs, predatory gangs, and organized/corporate gangs use various drugs compared to

drug-selling and serious delinquent gangs who use little if any (Shelden et al., 2001). Other gangs are committed to substance use. Wooden (1995) reports on white stoner gangs who like heavy metal music, practice Satanism, and use amphetamine, inhalants, PCP, LSD, and marijuana.

Members experience the gang in unique ways, including their levels of substance use (Shelden et al., 2001; Vigil, 1988a, 1988b). C. S. Taylor (1990) cataloged a five-tier typology of members based on their distance from the gang: corporates, scavengers, emulators, auxiliaries, and adjuncts. Hagedorn (1994) reports on what he refers to as hard-core versus peripheral members or wannabes. Other researchers have reported on fringe and core gang members. Fringe members report less involvement in the gang, as well as lower involvement in crimes and risk behaviors, including substance use, and core members report a higher level of involvement in such behaviors (Horowitz, 1983; Klein, 1995; Vigil, 1988a). The youths' *intensity* of gang membership—their degree of attachment to and involvement in the gang—may link somewhat to their substance use patterns, with more involved members reporting higher rates of use (Decker and Van Winkle, 1995; Hagedorn et al., 1998; B. Sanders, 2012).

DRUG ADDICTION

High rates of drug use place members at significant risk of related negative health outcomes, such as addiction. Waldorf (1993b) indicated that more than half of Mexican American and Salvadorian gang members felt addicted to a drug at one point. De La Rosa et al. (2006) found that gang members reported many transitions of drug use—moving from the use of one drug to that of another—and that these transitions greatly increased their risk for problematic drug use, such as addiction. One-third of the Los Angeles study reported that their substance use had "caused them problems" and half said that they had a family member who had a "problem" with substance use.

Hagedorn (1994) reported on dope fiends—members who were addicted to cocaine (see also Waldorf, 1993a). Most of them smoked cocaine rocks daily, although others sniffed it or smoked it in joints and some injected it. African Americans had the lowest rates of cocaine use and whites and Latinos had the highest (see also Robinson, 2001; Waldorf, 1993a). Contrary to the perception of the dazed and incapacitated junkie, many of Hagedorn's dope fiends were legitimately employed and involved in some degree within the drug business. Hagedorn notes that these individuals are the opposite of Cloward and Ohlin's (1960) double failures within retreatist subcultures. Similar to long-time heroin users, the dope fiends were ripping and running—working for, locating, using, and selling cocaine (Johnson et al., 1985; Preble and Casey, 1969; see also Ruggiero, 1993, 2000; Ruggiero and South, 1995). Sometimes the dope fiends were trusted and valued and other times they were ostracized.

Mexican American gangs have a history of heroin addiction (J. W. Moore, 1978; Valdez, 2005; Vigil, 1988a, 2002). Since the end of World War II, Mexican Americans dominated the heroin trade in the United States, facilitated, in part, by similarities between their language and ethnicity of the Mexican heroin suppliers (J. W. Moore, 1985; Valdez, 2005). Within poor Mexican American communities, injecting is common (Valdez, 2005). Heroin addiction has given rise to a unique subculture, *tecatos*. *Tecatos*, or heroin addicts, often have a street identity, a history of criminal involvement, and ongoing interactions with the criminal justice system (Valdez, Kaplan, and Cepeda, 2000; Valdez, 2005; see also J. W. Moore, 1978, 1991; Vigil, 1988a, 2002). They occupy an interesting position in that, like Hagedorn's (1994) dope fiends, they are at one point considered worthless and at another highly valued. One respondent in Valdez's (2005, p. 10) study described them as "dirty, sick, and always scratching themselves." *Tecatos* are also a regular part of the urban landscape. Some are in gangs and others are related to those who are. *Tecatos* may also help members who sell heroin by linking them to other users and buying heroin from them for personal use. Although gangs might not like *tecatos*, they are happy to sell to them.

A few members in Valdez's (2005) study became *tecatos* over time. Snorting heroin led to injecting it, and they then became addicted. They started committing fewer gang-related offenses and focused on compulsive drug seeking. Petty burglary and shoplifting paid for the heroin. Addiction became so widespread within one Mexican American gang that others began to refer to them as "a bunch of *tecatos*" (Valdez, 2005, p. 12).

Heroin was not limited to males. J. W. Moore (1978, 1991) reported that about a quarter of the Latinas in their sample were using by the age of 20. Although a greater percentage of males used, females did so for longer periods of time. Many of the girls grew up with a heroin user (J. W. Moore, 1978, 1991; see also J. W. Moore and Devitt, 1989; Vigil, 1988a, 2002). J. W. Moore and Devitt (1989) report on addiction among Chicana members who were mothers. Half of the women in their study had used drugs during pregnancy, and heroin was the most popular. Of these women, one-third gave birth to babies addicted to heroin. The heaviest users in J. W. Moore and Devitt's (1989) sample were more likely to

BOX 5.1: MEDIA CHECK!

Dark Alliance: The CIA, the Contras, and the Crack Cocaine Explosion by *Gary Webb*

In what sounds like an action-packed summer blockbuster movie, Gary Webb's *Dark Alliance* (1998) reports on the links among the Central Intelligence Agency (CIA), Nicaraguan revolutionaries, the spread of crack cocaine, and drug sellers in gang neighborhoods. The story was made into a movie called *Kill the Messenger* (2014), with Academy Award–nominated Jeremy Renner playing Webb. The abridged version goes something like this.

The Reagan administration, via the CIA, secretly supported a wing of the Contras, a disparate group of pro-democratic rebel fighters wishing to overthrow the Sandinista regime in control of Nicaragua. The CIA took interest for fear that communism might spread throughout the region, destabilizing U.S. interests. By supporting the Contras, Nicaragua became a Cold War proxy between the United States and the Soviet Union. Congress prevented the Reagan administration from sending dollars to support the Contras, but someone thought of a way around this. Rather than giving money to the Contras, they could support their revolutionary activities by selling one of its chief exports, cocaine, to its biggest consumer—America. Essentially, the CIA helped establish a cocaine link between Nicaragua and inner cities across America.

During the early 1980s, the price of cocaine nationwide began to drop and a surplus accumulated. Drug distributors needed to find a way to shift this glut of product. Cocaine was a drug used by the rich. How could sellers maintain their high profits and offer it to those who were less affluent? Enter Freeway Rick Ross. Mr. Ross is credited with being one of the pioneers of the crack cocaine trade. He had the specialized ability to turn powder cocaine into cocaine rocks that could be smoked through a mixture of baking soda or ammonia. Crack was sold in greater quantities and to a broader range of people, including those in the lower classes. The drug was an overnight success. Its addictive properties bred return customers, which was excellent for those wishing to make money. The crack market has been posited as being partially responsible for some of the most violent times in the second half of the 20th century.

Dark Alliance at once received tremendous praise, but also vicious attacks. The backlash against Webb's reporting that first appeared in the *San Jose Mercury News* caused him to lose his job. Several others who have looked into Webb's findings believe overall that he got most things right. Even Congress vetted his report in 2002 and conceded his accuracy. Freeway Rick Ross was convicted in 1996 and paroled in 2009, and he tells his story on YouTube, in television shows, and in the movie *How to Make Money Selling Drugs* (2012). An overall implication within *Dark Alliance* is that the U.S. government had a significant role in facilitating the crack cocaine epidemic that swept the nation. Webb was found dead in 2004 from gunshot wounds to the head—two of them. His death was ruled a suicide.

Visit YouTube for videos on "Freeway" Rick Ross, the CIA, Nicaragua, and crack cocaine.

---

have given up children to family members. Those who used drugs during pregnancy were more likely to come from *cholo* families, which were defined as having at least one nuclear family member who was also in a gang (J. W. Moore and Devitt, 1989). Some of the Chicanas felt that heroin complemented routine parenting, allowing them as the mother to take care of the house and children. As one explained,

> Well, you know what you're doing with the kids, and you know you can do your housework, and other drugs you can't—you don't know what you're doing. (J. W. Moore and Devitt, 1989, p. 64)

DRUG SELLING

Drug selling and gangs have a long history (Decker and Van Winkle, 1996; Fagan, 1989; Hagedorn, 1988; J. W. Moore, 1978, 1991; Padilla, 1992; Short and Strodtbeck, 1965; C. S. Taylor, 1990; C. Taylor, 1993; Vigil, 1988a; Williams, 1989; Yablonsky, 1962). This relationship is not straightforward. In the 1960s, reports emerged of gang members riding drug sellers out of their communities (Short and Strodtbeck, 1965; Spergel, 1964). In the 1970s and 1980s, evidence emerged to suggest that gang youth were more involved in drug sales than other adolescents (Fagan, 1989; J. W. Moore, 1978; Skolnick, 1990). However, during this time drug selling was a relatively minor gang-related activity, with marijuana being the primary drug sold (Fagan, 1989; Hagedorn, 1994; Klein, 1995).

Things began to change in the mid- to late 1980s and gangs became more involved in drug sales (Decker, 2000; Klein, 1995; Spergel, 1995; although see Inciardi, 1990; Inciardi et al., 1992). Two reasons are offered for this: the widespread loss of jobs and the emergence of crack cocaine (Decker and Van Winkle, 1996; Hagedorn, 1988; Howell and Decker, 1999; Klein, 1995; Spergel, 1995; Vigil, 1988a).

Deindustrialization occurred in cities across the United States and manufacturing plummeted. Work began to disappear for the working class. Factory jobs had formed the backbone of many inner-city communities, often populated with high percentages of African Americans and Latinos. Without the money generated by this workforce, community resources disappeared and many did not have the means to leave. Whole communities became socially and culturally isolated and traditional informal social controls disappeared (Decker and Van Winkle, 1996; Hagedorn, 1988; see also Sampson and Wilson, 1995; W. J. Wilson, 1987).

A radical shift in the drug market occurred. In the 1980s, a glut of cocaine emerged in the United States. Attempts to sell as much of it as possible led to the discovery of novel ways to introduce the drug to a broader, less affluent clientele. Enter crack: a combination of cocaine, baking soda, and ammonia. The drug was an overnight success, leading to a crack epidemic. The government's complicity in this situation was disturbing (see *Media Check!*). The Central Intelligence Agency (CIA) helped funnel cocaine from Nicaragua to America's inner cities, and the money generated from selling crack was sent back to Nicaragua to fund pro-democratic counterrevolutionaries (G. Webb, 1998). One of the main individuals on the receiving end of the cocaine was Freeway Rick Ross, who is credited as being one of the few people who had the know-how to make crack.

Crack devastated black communities and was linked to increased sexual risks, including HIV exposure, and prostitution (Golub et al., 2010; Hendricks and Wilson, 2013). Crack babies—children born to mothers addicted to the drug—became a nationwide phenomenon and were thought of as "a different kind of child" because the attention to drug use among pregnant women was unprecedented (E. Logan, 1999, p. 152). The crack market was believed to be driving the homicide rate in major cities (Goldstein, 1985; Zimring, 2006). The media created a moral panic (Decker, 2000; Decker and Van Winkle, 1995; Hartman and Golub, 1999; Klein, 1995; Reinarman and Levine, 1997). Gangsta rap was introduced in the mid-1980s, cementing the relationship among crack cocaine, gangs, and homicide in the minds of the public. People were terrified. The government responded by enacting harsh penalties for crack cocaine, including the Anti–Drug Abuse Acts of 1986 and 1988 (Mauer, 2009; Reinarman and Levine, 1997). The police linked the African American community with crack, ignoring its use and sales in white communities (see Beckett et al., 2006; Fellner, 2009). The results were devastating. Across the United States, about five times as many whites use drugs compared to blacks, but blacks are 10 times more likely to be sent to prison on a drug-related charge (Mauer, 2009). Approximately 80% of federal prisoners of crack-related convictions are African American (Mauer, 2009).

Crack cocaine emerged in impoverished black communities as a viable employment option or work for disenfranchised youth (Howell and Decker, 1999). Howell and Decker (1999) point out that a government report indicated that, by the late 1980s, the Crips and Bloods controlled nearly one-third of the crack/cocaine distribution in the United States and that the National Drug Intelligence Center "concluded that most street gangs are involved in drug trafficking to some extent, generally in a street-level distribution network" (p. 3). Howell and Decker (1999) also note that the crack market and Chicago's Vice Lords both expanded at the same time in the mid-1980s. Evidence from the NYGS concurred, indicating that the law enforcement departments surveyed reported that 43% of the drug sales in their jurisdiction involved gang members. Data from the Causes and Correlates studies also indicated that gang members were more likely to report selling drugs compared to non-gang youth (Esbensen and Huizinga, 1993; Thornberry et al., 1993).

The business-minded aspects of gangs that sell drugs have been well documented (Hagedorn, 1994, 1998; Levitt and Venkatesh, 2000; Padilla, 1992; Skolnick, 1990; C. S. Taylor, 1990; C. Taylor, 1993; Valdez, 2005; Venkatesh, 2008). C. S. Taylor (1990) reported on "corporate gangs" in Detroit that had leadership, were well organized, and focused tightly on crack cocaine distribution. Mieczkowski's (1986) Young Boys Incorporated sold heroin in a similar way in the same city. Members of Skolnick's (1990) "entrepreneurial" gangs in Northern California joined the gang for the purpose of selling drugs on the street and were committed to the job. Hagedorn's (1994) "New Jacks" in Milwaukee enjoyed selling cocaine:

> I love selling dope. I know there's other niggers out here love the money just like I do. And ain't no motherfucker gonna stop a nigger from selling dope. . . . I'd sell to my own mother if she had the money. (Hagedorn, 1994, p. 214)

Females are involved in sales. NYGS data suggest that females are significantly less likely than males to be members of gangs that focused on drug distribution (Howell and Gleason, 1999). Smaller datasets have indicated females may be *more* involved in drug sales than males. Robinson (2001) reported that females were much more likely to have reported selling crystal methamphetamine than males. C. Taylor (1993) found that female members involved in selling drugs who were just as hardcore as the males. Some of these females were gang leaders (see also J. Miller, 2001b). C. Taylor (1993) provided the following excerpt from Pat in an area the field researcher referred to as Crack City:

> I am in business, making monay is hard these days. . . . Oh, it's like crazy some days, but they make more monay with me than with their old crew. . . . When I took over, this here clique was making ho paper [an insignificant amount of profit]. . . . I had worked in this thing since I was fifteen. I was in school working twelve hours everyday. My people didn't know I was working one of the big houses for the X organization. That was like school, they taught me how to cook the shit [crack]. . . . When I was sixteen, my boyfriend started to move up in the X. I just learned more things, this was my education. This is a career. . . . Me and this big fella started to kick it when I was twenty-two, he had the juice, big juice. I met all the real players

with this fella, it was sweet. Plus, I was getting it on, 'cause my man let me get some of his products directly from his source. Soon, I was crushing and had my own serious crew. . . . See, I am running a enterprise, okay? This is serious shit and I am gonna make all the dope monay I can; why not, it's 'bout time girls get some money that's real. (pp. 117–118)

Despite these statistics, most research suggests that few gangs are organized around selling drugs (Block and Block, 1993; Curtis, 2003; Decker and Van Winkle, 1995; Decker et al., 1998; Esbensen and Huizinga, 1993; Fagan, 1989, 1996; Klein, 1995; J. W. Moore, 1991; B. Sanders, 1994; Spergel, 1995; Valdez, 2005). Data from national law enforcement surveys conducted in the 1990s indicate that police officers, many of whom worked gang details, estimated that 16% of all gangs were "specialty drug gangs" (Klein, 1995). Evidence from gang members themselves has concurred with these findings, expressing that drug selling is something controlled by other people (Huff, 1996). Of all the gangs Fagan (1989) studied, drug gangs were the exception and most were not organized to sell drugs (see also Klein, 1995; Klein and Maxson, 2006). Decker and Van Winkle (1995) reported that few gang members said they joined a gang to make money selling drugs and that only a couple of gangs had expectations that members sell a certain amount. Among the gangs that did sell, Decker and Van Winkle (1995) noted a lack of formal roles and poor organization. Decker and Van Winkle (1995, p. 597) provide interview excerpts that illustrate the lack of organized drug selling:

Int: What kinds of different jobs do they do? Watchers?

005: No, everybody just out to make their money. They run out there like idiots instead of having a plan. They run out there try to be fools.

Int: Do people who sell them have different jobs? Do they organize it as a group?

011: They have jobs. Most of them have McDonald's or something like that.

Evidence suggests that members sell drugs as individuals, independent of the gang's authority or central interests (Decker, 2000; Klein, 1995). Decker and Van Winkle (1995) reported on gangs in St. Louis that were "constellations"—composed of many subgroups—and were below the organizational requirements needed for effective drug selling. Klein (1995, p. 42) lists four things required for a successful drug-selling operation: (1) a clear, hierarchical leadership; (2) strong group cohesiveness; (3) a code of loyalty and secrecy; and (4) a narrow focusing of efforts on the mechanics of drug sales and the avoidance of independent or non–sales related criminal involvement. These are *not* the hallmarks of typical street gangs.

Some gangs use the drugs they sell and others do not. This depends on whether the gang is specifically focused on selling drugs. Valdez and Sifaneck's (2004) typology helps untangle this relationship (see also Hagedorn, 1994). Valdez and Sifaneck (2004) interviewed 160 American Mexican members in San Antonio. They developed a four-tier typology based on being a street gang or a drug gang and whether the individual was a user/ seller or a seller who did not use. A street gang was one that had a common pattern of criminal activities, such as the cafeteria style—the committal of various types of crimes. A drug gang almost exclusively sold drugs.

One type of youth in the Valdez/Sifaneck typology was the homeboy. Homeboys were users/sellers who belonged to a street gang. They buy enough drugs to get high and sell small amounts to cover their costs. Homeboys do not sell to generate profits. Drug selling occurs independently and is unrelated to the gang. The proceeds are not shared among other members. The Valdez/Sifaneck typology indicates hustlers in street gangs. They sell drugs for profit, rather than to support personal use. Like the homeboys, selling for hustlers is independent of the gang, and proceeds are not shared. Both hustlers and homeboys may benefit from participation in the gang because membership offers them a level of protection while conducting business.

Another type of youth in the Valdez/Sifaneck typology was members of drug gangs. These youth were the mirror images of guys in the street gangs. A slanger (like the homeboy) is a user/seller and is not part of the higher levels of the drug-selling enterprise. Rather, slangers are excluded because of drug use. Slangers sell small amounts of drugs to cover their costs—getting by to get high—as the authors put it. Slangers were street-level dealers who were fronted drugs by the gang leader(s) and given protection. Their profits were shared among other members. The last tier in the Valdez/Sifaneck typology is the baller. Ballers are drug sellers who control the distribution. These members sit at the top of the pyramid. Although the ballers discourage drug use, some still use. They are less visible and unlikely to engage in publicized behaviors (e.g., drive-by shootings).

Valdez and Sifaneck (2004) drew several conclusions. First, members' involvement in selling was dependent on contacts within the criminal underworld. Many of the youth had family members who were in prison gangs involved in drug selling, which helped secure a supplier. Second, their work illuminates debate around "do gangs or don't gangs" sell drugs. Some gangs are focused on selling. Some members sell, but it is not a focus of the gang. Finally, the perception of all members as serious sellers may lead to increased attention from law enforcement. Youth who look like gang members are more likely to be approached by the police, and possessing a personal amount of drugs could be interpreted as selling. The authors call for more training in the criminal justice system to recognize that not every drug-using gang member is a baller.

Whether gangs sell drugs and the type of drugs they sell can vary by race. Klein (1995) and Spergel (1995) found that African American gangs were more likely to be involved in drug sales than Hispanic gangs. NYGS data support this, indicating that the more black members in a jurisdiction, the greater the amount of drug sales are operated by gangs and the larger the extent of members in control in overall sales (Howell and Gleason, 1999). Howell and Gleason (1999) reported that when the jurisdictions contained more Hispanic, Caucasian, or Asian gangs, a lesser amount of drug sales were controlled by members.

Media and popular opinion have linked African American gangs to crack sales despite the lack of supporting evidence (Klein, 1995).[8] Robinson (2001) noted that African American members were significantly more likely to report that their gang sold crack than

---

8 This parallels a more widely held belief that crack sales occur mainly in African American communities. Crack sales also happen in white and other communities, but crack is heavily policed in black ones (see B. Sanders, in press).

members from other racial/ethnic backgrounds. However, Robinson reports that no one gang had a monopoly on the crack trade, and rates of sales among Latino, white, and Asian/Chinese gangs were substantial. Historically, heroin sales have been linked to Mexican American gangs (J. W. Moore, 1978; Valdez, 2005, 2007), but Asian gangs have also been involved in this trade (Chin, 1990). Robinson (2001) examined crystal and crack sales by race/ethnicity and found that Latinos had the highest rates of reporting having sold crystal, followed by Asian/Chinese members and then whites. Robinson (2001) also reported more African American members had sold crystal than had used the drug. According to J. W. Moore's (1978) study of the Happy Valley Gang in Los Angeles to the many gangs in San Antonio, prescription drug sales have been specifically linked to Mexican American gangs (J. W. Moore, 1978; Valdez, 2005).

MYTHS ABOUT DRUG SELLING

One myth about drug sales is the high return. Of all street-based criminal activities, drug selling is one of the most lucrative. Reported annual returns have ranged from $20,000 to $30,000, but others investigations have shown that these estimates are overblown (Levitt and Venkatesh, 2000; see also Fleisher, 1998; Hagedorn, 1994; Jacobs, 1996). With unparalleled insight into the drug selling of a gang, Levitt and Venkatesh (2000) offer solid evidence that few gang members make real money selling illegal drugs (see also Venkatesh, 2008). One piece of data Venkatesh serendipitously obtained during his study of drug-selling members in Chicago was a detailed log tracking the financial activities of one gang. A leader compiled this log, which included costs and revenues, organizational details, the distribution of profits, price, quantity, and hours worked. According to Venkatesh, he was made gang leader for a day and obtained access to the log (Venkatesh, 2008). Interviews and observations of the members, as well as their deaths, injuries, and arrests, supplemented the financial data.

Levitt and Venkatesh (2000) provided profound insights after analyzing their data. One of the most significant is that street-level dealers—the foot soldiers, those who occupied the bottom level in the drug-selling organization—earned no more than $200 a month for most of the years studied. The dealers one step up from them, the soldiers, earned roughly $1,000 per month. Given the time and effort involved and the standard of living achieved, the job provided them with about as much money as full-time minimum wage employment. Other research has noted that, for all the hours put into selling, individuals could earn comparable money flipping burgers (Fleisher, 1998; Padilla, 1992; B. Sanders, 2005a). Levitt and Venkatesh (2000) note that those dealers higher up the distribution ladder made significantly more money than they could at a legitimate job. Gang leaders reportedly made $50,000 to $130,000. This fact, Levitt and Venkatesh (2000) argue, is why those at the bottom of the distribution continue to work: the belief of making it big one day through selling drugs. However, this rarely happened. After tabulating the earning of all of those selling drugs, Levitt and Venkatesh (2000, pp. 757–758) noted that "the average wage in the gang . . . is perhaps somewhat above the available legitimate market alternatives, but not appreciably higher." The risks faced by these youth hardly seem worth it.

Fleisher (1998), in his study of the Fremont Hustlers in Kansas City, questioned the amount of money being made from sales. Although the Fremont Hustlers who sold talked about "big money," Fleisher, who spent months hanging out with the gang, never saw any of it. As he explains, "Talk of earning big money is simply talk. . . . No one could tell me exactly how much he or she earned, although they talked about earning a lot. . . . I didn't see evidence of big drug earnings" (Fleisher, 1998, p. 76). Hagedorn (1994, pp. 202–203) reported similar findings in his study in Milwaukee: "About one-third of those who sold reported that they made no more than they would have earned if they worked for minimum wage. Another one-third made the equivalent of $13 to $25 an hour. Only three of the 73 sellers ever made 'crazy money,' or more than $10,000 per month, at any time during their drug-selling careers."

Drug selling does not allow for greater autonomy or income than working at a fast-food restaurant. Padilla (1992) made this point in his research. He studied the Diamonds, a group that eventually became a specialty gang that focused on drug selling. Because members were undereducated, the only jobs available were labor intense, with long hours, low pay, and no room for upward mobility. Because they did not find these jobs attractive, the Diamonds believed they could find success through selling drugs. As one of them said, "We can't get jobs, but we can certainly get our hands on as much [marijuana] and cocaine that we want" (Padilla, 1992, p. 54). They believed selling drugs would provide a greater sense of independence and further distance them from being exploited: they were no longer working for the man, but for themselves.

The irony is that, for most of the Diamonds, drug selling was no different than the legitimate jobs available. Most of the Diamonds never advanced through the ranks, remaining at the bottom (and most dangerous) level of the organization. The members at the top, who controlled the supply, wanted to remain in those positions and did not invite competition by promoting the sellers. Drug selling is dangerous and the street-level dealers have the most exposure to the risk of victimization, death, and arrest. Selling among the Diamonds was just as exploitive as the legitimate occupations that they shunned.

"Don't get high on your own supply" is a line in many gangsta rap songs, conveying the idea that gang members do not use the drugs they sell. This idea is more of an urban legend than a practice among gangs. This decree might have been adhered to with more conviction in generations of past members, but evidence suggests that many members now do use the drugs they sell—even hard drugs such as crack and powder cocaine, crystal, and heroin (Fagan, 1989; Hagedorn, 1994, 1998; Robinson, 2001; B. Sanders, 2012; B. Sanders, Valdez et al., 2013; Valdez, 2005; Valdez and Sifaneck, 2004; Waldorf, 1993a). Hagedorn (1998) noted that gangs in the 1980s used and sold cocaine, but cut back on using the drug as selling it began to bring in good money. Fagan (1989) reported that of gangs in major U.S. cities, those who sold more also used more, including cocaine, heroin, and PCP. Waldorf (1993a) found many gangs that used and sold drugs, such as powder cocaine and marijuana, but not crack. Drug selling allows some members to cover the

costs associated with their use (Hagedorn, 1994; Valdez and Sifaneck, 2004; Waldorf, 1993a; cf. B. Sanders, 2005a). Given the dangers involved in selling, members might also use drugs to help negotiate the fear of police detection and/or the threat of violence from drug customers, drug-selling rivals, or other criminals (cf. B. Sanders, Schneiderman et al., 2009).

Some gang members who sell have a hands-off policy because intoxication can hinder business or just run counter to acceptable substance use in their gang (Decker, 2000; Shelden et al., 2001). Gangs in New York City's Chinatown who sold heroin frowned on using drugs (Chin, 1996). The gangs were tightly organized and had strict rules about using hard drugs that were violently enforced. Waldorf (1993a) reported that less than one in five of the members selling crack in his study reported also using. Hagedorn et al. (1998) also noted that crack use was stigmatized among gang members who sold. Crack usage is more generally censured among young people who sell it (Jacobs, 1999; B. Sanders, 2005a).

DRUG SALES AND VIOLENCE

Crack sales and violence are interrelated in multiple ways. Violence is the outcome of competition within a limited area, territorial disputes, managing employees, the habitual desire to use crack, and the effects of the drug (Fagan, 1996; Howell and Decker, 1999). Erica, a 19-year-old cocaine distributor from C. Taylor's (1993, p. 111) study, commented on the violence associated with crack:

> It's tight, it's killing lots of people out in the life. Dope is real dangerous business, you know, it's bad everywhere.

Members who sell drugs must watch for law enforcement, rivals, drug-selling competition, and agitated drug users (cf. Jacobs, 1999). Drug sellers are ideal robbery targets. They carry more money than the average person or convenience store. The likelihood of reporting their victimization is low because they fear self-incrimination or because they abide by a normative code that they do not cooperate with law enforcement (e.g., the code of the streets; Jacobs, 1999; see also Lauritsen et al., 1991; Sampson and Lauritsen, 1994).

Violent flare-ups or wars between rival drug-selling gangs increase the odds of violent victimization. Levitt and Venkatesh (2000) revealed ongoing battles between different gangs, reporting that 7% of their sample died each year. Overall, Levitt and Venkatesh (2000) argued that the danger associated with violence was above and beyond the level of acceptable risk in relation to the potential payout. For some members, selling does not seem worth it. Levitt and Venkatesh offer the following conclusions about the risk-to-benefit ratio of selling drugs in relation to deadly violence:

> Given the relatively low economic returns to drug selling . . . the implied willingness to accept risk on the part of the participants is orders of magnitude higher than is typically observed in value of life calculations . . . we conclude that even in this gang—one of the most economically sophisticated and successful gangs—the decision making of members is difficult . . . to reconcile with that of optimizing economic agents. (Levitt and Venkatesh, 2000, p. 758)

Levitt and Venkatesh (2000) reported that leaders did earn significantly less when gangs warred with one another and had to endure other costs associated with violence: buying guns and ammunition, hiring mercenaries, and paying street-level sellers more to operate in a violent environment. The sellers received about 70% more when gangs were warring with one another. One of them said,

> Would you stand around here when all this . . . [shooting] is going on? No, right? So if I gonna be asked to put my life on the line, then front me the cash, man. Pay me more 'cause it ain't worth my time to be here when [the gangs are] warring. (Levitt and Venkatesh, 2000, p. 778)

The homicide–gang–drug selling interrelationship is not straightforward. Klein and Maxson (2006) examined the relationship among gangs, crack sales, and murder. Their study collected data from police stations in South Central Los Angeles—an area with a long history of the variables the authors sought to examine. During the late 1980s, homicides in Los Angeles were near epidemic proportions, with almost 1,000 murders annually, half of which were gang related. The authors examined gang and non-gang homicides involving drugs (mainly cocaine) or drug selling (any type of drug). These homicides were considered spurred by drug motives. Maxson and Klein found that such motives were more likely to be reported in non-gang homicides than in gang homicides. Their data offered little support for a strong gang–drugs–violence connection. Homicides involving drug use or sales in South Central Los Angeles were more likely to involve nonmembers. Howell (1999) noted that similar findings have been reported in Boston, Chicago, Miami, and St. Louis. Other researchers have also indicated that the connection among gang members, drug sales, and violence is weak (Block and Block, 1993; Centers for Disease Control and Prevention, 2012; Decker and Van Winkle, 1996; Inciardi, 1990; Inciardi et al., 1992; J. W. Moore, 1991).

An increase in members' involvement in drug distribution has led to more violence (Padilla, 1992; W. B. Sanders, 1994; C. Taylor, 1990; Venkatesh, 1996; see Howell and Decker, 1999, for a review). As W. B. Sanders (1994, p. 83) notes in his research in San Diego, "by 1988, many of the gang-related drive-by shootings . . . did appear to be connected to the sale and distribution of crack cocaine. . . . The increase in drive-by shootings in 1988 makes it clear that *something* occurred that year to make the number increase so dramatically. Since crack cocaine was introduced to the neighborhood . . . sales competition is hypothesized to be a primary cause" (emphasis in original).

Venkatesh (1996), in his study of a housing project in Chicago, noted that violence was once limited to specific types of people in certain areas and often was not deadly. When crack was introduced, a change occurred in both the frequency and the severity of violence. The picture that emerges in Venkatesh's research is one of warfare, with several gangs fighting for control to sell crack within a confined area and innocent bystanders getting caught in the crossfire. Decker and Van Winkle (1996) found that many in their sample were involved in sales, especially cocaine, and that one source of violence was drug related. The relationship between gang and drug market violence may also be more indirect. Howell and Decker (1999) note that illegal gun use has been correlated with both drug sales and gang membership independent of one another. The Causes and Correlates studies indicated that members are more likely to sell drugs and be involved in violent crime (Howell, 1998; Thornberry et al., 1993). Although drug trafficking is related to violence, the evidence has not established that selling by members causes *more* violence. Howell and Decker (1999, p. 8) suggest that further research should examine "the extent to which gang membership facilitates gun use in drug trafficking—possibly resulting in higher levels of violence—in the same way that the gang facilitates overall violent offending."

SUMMARY

Substance use has been linked to gangs for decades. Modern research indicates that gang youth report lifetime use of a variety of substances at significantly higher rates than do nonmembers. They also use a wider variety of drugs and use them in greater quantities and frequencies. Membership is an indicator of substance use. Alcohol has long been a staple of gang cultures and serves a variety of practical and symbolic purposes. Marijuana is used in large quantities and with recurring frequencies in gang cultures across the United States. When hanging out and doing nothing, alcohol and marijuana use feature prominently. Hard drug use, such as heroin, cocaine, PCP, and crystal, is also associated with members, but their use is much less frequent.

Marijuana is celebrated, but the use of hard drugs has been stigmatized. Gang members' attitudes toward illicit drugs are similar to the attitudes of many non-gang youth who are also substance users. Some discrepancy exists between what illicit drugs members say they use and what drugs they actually use. A number of suggestions have been put forward to help explain this discrepancy, including whether the gang has rules against the use of some drugs, issues related to sampling methodology (e.g., younger versus older gang youth; recruiting in schools versus "on the streets"), and members changing their views of drug use as they age.

Studies on addiction are surprisingly scant. Nonetheless, some examples of addiction have been offered, including heroin-abusing *tecatos* in Mexican American neighborhoods and crack cocaine–using dope fiends in African American communities. Closer attention to other drugs and their combinations will likely reveal newer patterns of addiction. As prescription drug misuse, addiction, and overdose have dramatically increased within the general youth population, so too are they likely to increase among gang members.

This chapter examined the relationship between gangs and drug sales. The most commonly reported pattern was of youth who sold drugs and were gang members, but that distribution was not a central, organizing feature of the gang. The only members who economically benefit from selling are those who are directly involved. Contrary to popular perceptions, a member who sells is unlikely to then distribute the proceeds evenly to other members. Few gangs specialize in selling drugs, and researchers have consistently indicated that most gangs are simply not organized to distribute drugs. Nonetheless, media and police projections and gangsta rap have helped fuel the perception that gangs and drug selling are tightly interwoven.

Violence in drug distribution is bad for business. Death and violent victimization are realities of drug-selling gangs, particularly during periods of war over territories. Despite the media hype about getting rich quick, the reality is different. Evidence of lucrative drug selling is limited, and gang members could make comparable money flipping burgers in a safer environment. Gang members who do sell drugs must keep an eye out for law enforcement, drug users who want to rob them, and rivals who wish to eliminate them. Most of the violence associated with the drug game appears non–gang related, despite perceptions to the contrary. Most drug-related murders do not involve gang members.

CHAPTER REVIEW QUESTIONS

1. Why has it been hypothesized that gang members use more drugs than non–gang members?
2. Discuss the purposes of alcohol within gang cultures.
3. What qualities might help explain the discrepancies in reporting the illicit use of drugs other than marijuana among gang youth?
4. What is polydrug use? What is challenging and problematic about it?
5. What are *tecatos*? Why are they stigmatized? What role do they serve within gang communities?
6. What does the evidence support more: that most gangs sell drugs or that gang members who do sell drugs often operate independent of the gang? Explain.
7. Why did crack selling among gang members increase?
8. What does the Valdez/Sifaneck typology say about gang members, drug use, and drug sales?
9. What are some of the ironies about gang members and drug selling that are revealed in Padilla's study?
10. Explain Levitt and Venkatesh's analysis of drug selling by gang members.

LINKS TO ARTICLES ON DRUG USE AND SALES AMONG GANGS

The youth gangs, drugs, violence connection
By James C. Howell and Scott H. Decker
https://www.ncjrs.gov/pdffiles1/93920.pdf/

Youth gang drug trafficking
By James C. Howell and Debra Gleason
https://www.ncjrs.gov/pdffiles1/ojjdp/178282.pdf/

Drugs and gangs: Fast facts
By the National Drug Intelligence Center
http://www.justice.gov/archive/ndic/pubs11/13157/13157p.pdf/

Youth gang drug trafficking and homicide: Policy and program implication
By James C. Howell
http://www.ojjdp.gov/jjjournal/jjjournal1297/gang.html/

Alcohol and violence in the lives of gang members
By Geoffrey P. Hunt and Karen Joe-Laidler
http://pubs.niaaa.nih.gov/publications/arh25-1/66-71.htm/

Youth gangs, delinquency and drug use: A test of the selection, facilitation, and enhancement hypotheses
By Umberto Gatti, Richard E. Tremblay, Frank Vitaro, and Pierre McDuff
http://www.researchgate.net/publication/7527197_Youth_gangs_delinquency_and_drug_use_a_
    test_of_the_selection_facilitation_and_enhancement_hypotheses/file/504635268d969b7ccc
    .pdf/

Risk and protective factors for alcohol and other drug problems in adolescence and early adulthood: Implica-tions for substance abuse prevention
By J. David Hawkins, Richard F. Catalano, and Janet Y. Miller
http://adai.washington.edu/confederation/2008readings/Catalano_86.pdf/

Gang youth, substance use, and drug normalization
By Bill Sanders
http://www.ncbi.nlm.nih.gov/pmc/articles/PMC4160842/

CHAPTER 6

VIOLENCE AND VICTIMIZATION

KEY WORDS

Candy shop: An apartment unit in a housing project that is transformed into a convenience store that sells snacks and drinks to local people so that they do not have to venture outside of their immediate area, where they could be subject to victimization.

Caught slipping: Being detected by rival gang members that often leads to violent encounters.

Gang-affiliated violence: An act of violence committed by a gang member for self-serving purposes. This is also referred to as the "Los Angeles definition."

Gang-motivated violence: An act of violence committed by a gang member to benefit the gang. This is also referred to as the "Chicago definition."

Getting jumped: A surprise attack involving one or two victims and multiple attackers.

Jumped in: A common way for youth to enter gangs whereby the new recruit is beaten for several minutes by current members of the gang to prove courage and toughness.

Jumped out/rolled out: A way youth exit gangs whereby they are beaten for a period of time by current members in a ceremony that establishes their new identities as non–gang members.

Mad dogged: A prolonged, hard stare meant to intimidate and threaten, often as a precursor to a violent confrontation.

National Crime Victimization Surveys (NCVS): Annual surveys that provide the primary source of criminal victimization in the United States. These surveys ask whether the victim believed or knew that his or her attacker was a gang member.

Rumble/riot: A collective form of fighting with at least two opposing gangs, each with multiple members, simultaneously attacking each other.

Violence victimization: To have been made a victim of violence, includes witnessing or hearing violence and knowing others who have been victims of violence.

Chapter Learning Objectives

- Clarify the definition of gang-related violence.
- Describe the prevalence and contexts of gang violence.
- Comprehend the relationship between gangs and firearms.
- Explain the nature of victimization among gang members.

INTRODUCTION

Violence is a hallmark of gang life. Youth enter gangs through a violent initiation ritual where they are pummeled to prove heart and toughness. They may also exit through violence. Between joining and leaving, youth can expect many violent episodes with rivals (and even members of their own gang) and must constantly watch their backs for fear of victimization. Rivals often live in adjacent neighborhoods and the threat of deadly violence is a daily reality. Gangs encourage members to participate in violence and expose them to it. This fact underscores an irony about membership: youth say they join gangs for protection, but end up being more victimized. The threat of violence limits members' exposure to public places and participation in average activities. Although innocent people have been harmed in gang-related violence, more than anything else, members target and harm one another. Those who are not killed have received devastating injuries.

The chapter begins by examining the various definitions of gang-related violence and their differences and similarities. From here, the prevalence of gang violence is explored, as well as witness intimidation. Next, an issue that has received relatively little attention in the research literature is discussed: fighting. Various contexts of gang fights are offered, including individual fights, getting jumped, jumping others, and group rumbles. Firearms are then reviewed, with a focus on the sophisticated weaponry and the utility of guns within members' day-to-day lives. The topic then shifts to the most commonly written about, yet atypical behaviors among gangs: homicides. Prevalence rates are provided, as is an explanation of which members are most at risk. The chapter concludes with a discussion of victimization.

THE DEFINITION OF GANG-RELATED VIOLENCE

Gang-related violence can mean different things (Howell and Decker, 1999; Maxson et al., 1985; Maxson and Klein, 1990, 1996; Rosenfeld et al., 1999). In some cities, gang-related violence refers only to that committed by a gang member. This is referred to as the "Los Angeles definition" or "gang-affiliated" version (Rosenfeld et al., 1999). Shelden et al. (2001, p. 111) note that this is the most common type of gang violence, but that "much of what is officially labeled as gang violence is not gang violence per se. A great deal of violence is committed by gang members acting on their own and is not part of the gang's objectives" (see also Hagedorn, 1998). Other cities define gang-related violence as violence committed specifically to benefit the gang, which is referred to as the "Chicago definition"—or "gang-motivated" violence (Rosenfeld et al., 1999). When members target and kill rival gang members, it qualifies as gang-related violence under this definition. The homicide in this example directly benefits the entire gang (e.g., by increasing their reputation for violence or eliminating enemies). If two drug-selling gangs were fighting over territory in relation to drug distribution and several were killed, this event would also fit the definition.

The importance of these different definitions has been studied (Decker and Curry, 2002; Maxson et al., 1985; Maxson and Klein, 1990, 1996; Rosenfeld et al., 1999). These authors examined different gang homicides, as well as non-gang homicides, with regard to the presence of firearms or drugs; witnesses; use of vehicles; public or private locations; age of victim; gender; race; and the relationship of the victim to the offender. Maxson et al. (1985) found that gang murders were more likely to be committed with firearms and to happen in public areas. Gang homicide participants (victim and offender) were younger overall and less likely to know one another. Later, Maxson and Klein (1990) examined the various ways that police departments defined "gang related homicide"—motivated versus affiliated—and found few differences between them. A later analysis yielded similar results (Maxson and Klein, 1996). Rosenfeld et al. (1999), in contrast, found important differences and similarities between these types of homicides. Gang-motivated homicides were more likely to occur in public and less likely to involve drugs, and participants were more likely to be closer in age.

The variations in definitions of gang-related violence are profound in terms of the size and extent of a city's gang problem, as well as the monies allocated for gang intervention and suppression services to control that problem (Maxson et al., 1985; Maxson and Klein, 1990, 1996; Rosenfeld et al., 1999). Violence is a way to stoke fear in the public. When a city has a gang problem, an effective way to garner attention and allocate resources is to highlight violence, particularly in rare instances when innocents are harmed. If cities like Los Angeles that use the broader definition of gang-related murder instead adopted Chicago's narrower definition, the city would have fewer gang-related homicides (Maxson and Klein, 2006). Using different definitions of gang-related violence is like comparing apples with oranges: if no consensus exists, the scope of the problem cannot be accurately compared (Rosenfeld et al., 1999). Keeping in mind the various definitions of gang-related violence is critical for researchers, law enforcement, policy makers, and students.

THE PREVALENCE OF GANG VIOLENCE

One way to examine the prevalence of violence is through the National Crime Victimization Surveys (NCVS), which report on whether victims of crime believe the perpetrator was a gang member.[1] Between 1993 and 2003, NCVS data reported that members have been responsible for between 6 and 10% of all nonfatal violent offenses, such as rape/sexual assault, robbery, and aggravated and common assault (Harrell, 2005). Victimization peaked in 1996, decreased to about 6% a couple of years later, and then remained mostly

---

1   For a review of the utility of NCVS data to capture gang violence, see Rennison and Melde (2009).

unchanged until 2003 (Harrell, 2005). Victimization by gang members then increased slightly between 2003 and 2005, but by 2008 had decreased to about 5%.

The NCVS found violent victimization is higher among males than among females, among Hispanics than non-Hispanics (and African Americans at a higher rate than whites), among younger people than older people, and in urban areas compared to rural communities (Harrell, 2005). These statistics reflect trends of gang victimization more generally (see Block and Block, 1993; Cooper and Smith, 2011). The NCVS also reports that members committed other types of violence: 12% of all aggravated assaults; 10% of all robberies; 6% of all simple/common assaults; and 4% of rapes. Data from the FBI's Supplementary Homicide Reports indicate that from 1993 to 2003, members committed 5–7% of all homicides, although 8–10% of those committed with firearms (Harrell, 2005). Cooper and Smith (2011) note that every year between 1980 and 2008, the highest percentages of homicides committed with firearms involved gangs.

Comparative data between gang and non-gang at-risk youth show that violent acts were more likely to be committed by members. Huff (1996) found that individuals in gangs were more likely to assault rivals, assault victims or witnesses, commit drive-by shootings, carry guns or knives to school, commit homicide, assault their own members (or friends), commit assault in the streets, assault shoppers, and commit robbery. Huff (1996) also reported that membership accelerated youths' involvement from less serious nonviolent offenses to serious, violent ones.

Gang violence is concentrated in impoverished, inner-city areas with high concentrations of minorities, but it is not evenly distributed. Ecological models suggest that some communities are more at risk. Kyriacou and colleagues (1999) examined the relationship between socioeconomic factors and gang violence in Los Angeles. They reported that per capita income and proportion employed, as well as the interaction of these variables, were significantly associated with gang homicides. Their data indicate that issues related to deprivation are important to consider when addressing the likelihood of such violence. Spatial models show that firearms are concentrated in a few inner-city areas. Researchers examined firearm and homicide data in parts of Boston and reported that, over a 28-year period (between 1980 and 2008), 5% of city blocks experienced about 75% of gun assaults and 50% of homicides and about 75% of gun assaults were committed by less than 1% of the youth population— mainly gang members and serious young offenders (Braga et al., 2008, 2010).

Block and Block (1993) found that gang violence was concentrated in specific inner-city areas. Their data link different types of violence to lethal and nonlethal outcomes. Some gang members engaged in expressive forms of violence, such as defending turf, and others in instrumental forms, such as in relation to selling drugs. They may specialize in one form over another. In a review of the homicide data, the Blocks reported that the most prevalent type was expressive, not instrumental; only 8 homicides of the 288 gang-related homicides involved drugs. Their findings support those from Los Angeles and elsewhere that indicated most drug-related homicides did not involve members or that gang-related homicides often do not involve drugs (Centers for Disease Control and Prevention, 2012; Klein and Maxson, 1989). The Blocks also reported that instrumental violence was concentrated in neighborhoods in decline, whereas expressive violence was most likely to occur in areas that were prospering and becoming more populated. Block and Block (1993) noted that most of the areas studied with high rates of lethal and nonlethal gang violence also had relatively low rates of other types of lethal violence.

WITNESS INTIMIDATION

Gang members participate in witness intimidation (Finn and Healey, 1996). A National Institute of Justice report in 1996 said that the extent of witness intimidation by gang members was unknown, but noted a perceived increase (Finn and Healey, 1996). The 2000 NYGS asked about witness intimidation by gangs, and about 80% of the police jurisdictions reported that they were responding to it (Egley and Arjunan, 2002). J. Anderson (2007, p. 1) noted that "witness intimidation was a frequent activity of gangs and remains a sizeable problem in all regions of the United States." Anderson (2007) reported that district attorneys have testified before a Senate judiciary committee about witness intimidation being a major obstacle in successful gang prosecution across the nation.

Intimidation can take two forms: overt and implicit (Anderson, 2007; Finn and Healey, 1996). In overt intimidation, witnesses are threatened, such as during the crime, in or around the courtroom, or in their neighborhood. This form of intimidation may include property damage or refer to actual victimization, including murder. Numerous examples exist of witnesses to gang crimes being killed (Anderson, 2007; McDonough, 2013).

Another form of intimidation is implicit. One common form is the stop-snitching sentiment (McDonough, 2013). Community members who are seen to be helping law enforcement are viewed as snitches and might be subjected to threats or other forms of victimization. Stop-snitching and other forms of witness intimidation is also immortalized within the music that gang members listen to, such as gangsta rap (McDonough, 2013).

FIGHTING

Fighting is a common and universal form of violence, but also one of the least studied. As Klein and Maxson (2006, p. 79) note, "despite its rarity within the full continuum of gang violence, we may know more about gang homicide than any other form of gang violence." Fighting takes several forms, including initiation or exiting rituals; one-on-one fighting, which can be with rivals, fellow members, or whomever; and collective forms, such as getting jumped (i.e., a surprise attack involving several attackers and one or two defenders) and jumping others. Another form of collective fighting is rumbles or riots that involve dozens of individuals from at least two gangs.

One of the most commonly reported methods by which youth join gangs is through being jumped in or beaten in (Decker, 1996; Huff, 1989; J. W. Moore, 1978; Vigil, 1988a, 2002). The new prospect is punched and/or kicked for a period of time. By enduring this ritual, the recruit shows toughness and heart, indicating that he or she is ready to fight on behalf of the gang and demonstrating competence in having other members' backs. In the Los Angeles Study,[2] 90% of the youth said they joined this way.

---

2   See the Appendix for more on the methodology and objectives of this study.

Did you have to do anything to join the gang?

> Yeah, I got jumped in. Everybody has to be jumped in.

How many people jumped you in?

> About 5 of them.

You had to do that and you were in?

> Yeah and I was in. "Welcome in!," they will say and shit. They will give you a pistol and start drinking. They give you a 40 [ounce bottle of beer].

Did you have to join the gang?

> Yes.

What did you have to do?

> Fight.

How many people?

> Five.

Five guys? Anything else?

> It was not just five guys, OK? I fought the first guy and I got over that fight and the other guy jumped in and beat me. I got up from doing that and we kept going on, on.

So in the end you were defending yourself against five people?

> Yeah.

Did you have to do anything to join the gang?

> Yeah, I got jumped in.

How many people did you have to fight?

> Just one. . . . This fool was big. He just got out of the pen [prison]. He was built up. Me? I was just like 12 years old, you know? I did not need a lot of people, you know? It was just one on one.

So after you fought him you were in, is that right?

> Yeah. . . . That happened to be my brother in law.

The guy who jumped you in?

> Yeah, but he died. They killed him. Just right around when he jumped me in.

Prospects may have to commit violence against a rival to join. A few youth in the Los Angeles Study talked about going on missions as part of their initiation. Decker (1996, p. 255) offered an example from a St. Louis member on a mission:

> To be a Crip, you have to put your blue rag on your head and wear all blue and go in a Blood neighborhood—that is the hardest of all of them—and walk through the Blood neighborhood and fight Bloods. If you come out without getting killed, that's the way you get initiated.

Within gang culture, the phrase "Where are you from?" (or "*¿De donde?*" in Spanish) is a way for members to challenge others and claim or identify as being part of a gang.[3] This antagonistic declaration is often accompanied by a prolonged hard stare, referred to as being mad dogged (Vigil, 2002, 2003; see also J. Katz, 1988; W. B. Sanders, 1994). These stares and questions are the precursors to fights.

Why do you get into fights?

Like some fool is dogging you, like give you a look and then like, "What the fuck?" and then like, "Fucking claim something or not. You claim something? Fuck your shit!" and then that's it. That's how it starts.

He was like, "Where are you from?"

And that kind of starts it off?

Yeah, cause I was with my girlfriend and he goes, "Where are you from?" And she was like, "Nowhere," she was like, "Nowhere." And she was trying to push me away. I was like, "Alright. Whatever." So I just kept walking and I did not say nothing. So then he came across the street and he was like, "where are you from?" and then I said, "Where are you from?" And he said "[name of gang]." And then we just like this and that.

What was the [last] fight about?

I'm walking down my neighborhood. . . . I'm taking my lady to get ice cream, you know what I mean? And on the other side of the street, I see some gang bang out fools, in my neighborhood. I was like "What's up?" I am still affiliated with it. You know what I mean? So I told him, "What's up? Where the fuck are you from?" That fool named the neighborhood, and I said, "This is my neighborhood." . . . And he just stood quiet and shit. I am not going to let no bald headed fool through our neighborhood and shit if they are from a different neighborhood and shit. . . . And its gang related. So yeah, he did not know who I was, you know what I mean? "You're a bitch, you aint from my neighborhood." . . . And I fucken cracked him. . . . And a tall fool came out the car and I cracked him cause I thought he was going to crack me first. And his uncle jumped out and I started to get down on him but he did not really do shit. Yeah, you can see he did not do shit.

Gang members come across as if they rarely provoke fights (Decker, 1996; W. B. Sanders, 1994; B. Sanders et al., 2010; cf. B. Sanders, 2005a). Someone is always doing something to them, and members simply respond to perceived threats or challenges to their respect. The likelihood is that they are as much instigators of this type of violence as they are responders.

The motivation for violence might be ever present, but the opportunity is not. Collective forms, such as getting jumped and jumping others, have a random nature. Being

---

3   See Garot (2010) for more on claiming and the use of the phrases akin to *Where you from?*

caught slipping describes events when an individual, alone or with friends, encounters a larger number of rivals by chance (Valdez et al., 2009). These incidents lead to violence.

> Ten other fools just jumped me.

Wow! Were they from a rival gang?
> Yeah, they were rival gang members. I was on my way walking, so when they heard where I was from. I had to go from my enemies' neighborhood to get to my neighborhood. And I fucked up cause I was walking by the riverbed, and I found the spot where they kick it at. And they fucken mopped [beat] me up.

How old were you the first time you got jumped?
> About 15.

Fifteen, okay. Who did you fight? How many people?
> There were about 4 or 5 kids.

Were they from a rival gang?
> Rival gang.

Tell me about it, what happened?
> I was walking through the wrong street, so somebody's enemy and in my enemies' neighborhood cause I had to go to school through there, in order for me to get to school a faster way. I passed and they see me and they chased me and they caught up to me and they were jumping me and kicking me and I had to fight back which ever way I could fight back. After that, run.

So those aren't gang related fights or . . . ?
> No. . . . I have enemy gang members going to the same school, getting in fights at school, or on the streets, you know? Walking out of the liquor store, being jumped, three of my enemies waiting for me. I guess they were rolling past and I went in the store and they seen me going in the store and as I was coming out. One was in front of me and two were on the side and they just attacked me.

How many people jumped you?
> At least 7 people.

Rival gang?
> Yeah.

Where did that happened?
> School.

Did you hit the guys?
> Hell yeah! I knocked out like two of them. . . .

And the other guys?
> No after that, I just hit the floor.

So you got two of them out and they started to jump you?

Like, they started jumping me. I got caught. I see them. They were coming up to me. I was trying to get them and more of them started coming and that was when I started to lose my advantage and I fell to the floor and they started kicking me and shit. . . . I was really hurt.

How old were you the first time you got jumped?

This was around my late teens, like 16, 17.

Who did you fight? How many people jumped you?

I don't know how many people were they because I got my ass whooped pretty good. They jumped out of a van. I know for sure it was a good four, but after that I don't know. I was on the floor. I was out.

A chief difference between being a victim or a perpetrator of this type of violence depends on the number of rivals an individual encounters and the number of fellow members with them. The youth who provided the above examples from the Los Angeles Study could have easily been on the receiving end (Horowitz and Schwartz, 1974).

Retaliatory violence is common (Decker, 1996; Hagedorn, 1988; Klein and Maxson, 1989; J. W. Moore, 1978; W. B. Sanders, 1994; Vigil, 1988a).

When you get into fights, what are they about?

Other people, you have to get back at them for doing something they did to you, so you just jump them back. It's like revenge.

Why did you fight those guys?

They are the ones that jumped me like that. I tell the homies, "They got me so we had to get them."

In some cases, it takes the form of group rumbles or riots.

Have you ever been in a rumble or riot—anything like that?

Oh yeah. . . . We went to a different neighborhood. They jumped my homeboy and so that's how it started, they jumped my homeboy. So then the thing is that one of my home-boys, his brother was from that neighborhood, that rival neighborhood or whatever. So what he did was talk to his brother and say set it up, "I'm going to take my homeboys over there. You have your homeboys in your neighborhood. And we're just going to, you know?" We separated, we all go into our sides and then it just basically, whoever wanted to get in first. . . . We're a good 50 of us, they're the same thing: a bunch of motherfuckers, guns, baldheaded, everywhere. It was a trip, in the middle of the street.

Retaliatory violence can be directed at those in the same gang, who will attack their fellow members over issues of disrespect, drug use, or failing to provide backup support during a gang fight.

What do you dislike about the gang?

Like, sometimes the homies kill other homies. Like, I can't pick sides cause I love them both. So I got to stand to the side, stay in the sideline. But I don't want to do that because in the end somebody is going to lose out.

By you standing on the sidelines?

Yeah.

So what would you do instead of that?

Like, I try to talk to them one on one. Sometimes it works and sometimes it don't. Sometimes it will just be a fight, but they will be cool though. It's getting to be like, sometimes they, like the fight don't end at the fight. It's like when we use to fight that is it. You shake hands and smoke a blunt or whatever you do and then you all chill and talk about it. But that was like if you got an argument, but now people are like, I don't know.

Who do you fight, in general?

All for my neighborhood, and really, I wouldn't like my neighborhood to have a bad name for being tweakers [crystal methamphetamine users] and shit. You can't trust those fools. I don't tweak, not anymore. But my homies put up bad names. I fucken mop [beat] them up real quick and shit. Like, "Cut your shit out, fool! You are putting a bad name for the neighborhood" [gang]. Mop up a couple of homies real quick.

What was [your last fight] about?

Because I got jumped two days before. Before me and her we got into a conflict. I had gotten jumped and she did not do anything about it. She did not even jump in for me.

Gang fighting can occur while members are intoxicated. In the Los Angeles Study, about 17% of the sample reported using drugs or alcohol prior to their more recent fight. The relationship between substance use and violence is complex and suggesting that the former leads to the latter is simplistic. Alcohol alone or in combination with other drugs has been related to violence, but the use of some drugs has not (see H. R. White and Gorman, 2000, for a review; see also Valdez et al., 2006). Other variables outside of intoxication might be stronger predictors. Drug use and violence are the merging of two common behaviors among gang youth, but how they interact is not clear.

Research by Valdez and colleagues (2006) helps untangle the drugs–violence nexus. The authors examined causal connections between substance use and violence among male Mexican American gang youth in South Texas. They looked at violent outcomes, including the frequency, intensity (i.e., weapons used or not), and severity (i.e., injuries sustained) of fighting, and the relationship between the parties involved, location, motivation, whether the fight was gang-related, and how many people were present. Background characteristics examined included violence risk—self-reported history and feelings of violence and other variables, such as frequency of fighting in school, history of suicide ideation, and physical neglect. Substance use was broken down into types (e.g., marijuana, heroin, and cocaine) and combinations of drugs, as well as whether both parties were intoxicated during the fight. Findings indicate that about two-thirds of fighting (61%) was gang-related, with more than half against rivals (58%). Over a third of all fighting (37%) occurred when a participant was intoxicated. Close to a third of gang members (29%) reported fighting with friends, family, and fellow members. The authors found no relationship between the number, intensity, and severity of fighting and violence risk (i.e., feelings and history of violent acts).

Valdez et al. (2006) found supporting evidence that types of substance use moderated the relationship with violence. Cocaine and marijuana use were related to fighting: the more of these drugs the youth used, the more fights they reported in the previous three months. Among cocaine users, those with a higher violence risk score reported the most number of fights compared with the other groups. Heroin use interacted with violence risk to moderate the intensity and number of fights. Whether the rival was intoxicated also moderated the effect of risk on the severity of the fight. Severity and intensity were higher if the fight was gang related and if other people were present. More fighting was common among those with a higher risk and among those who fought an intoxicated rival. Intense fighting was reported among those with a history of childhood physical neglect and those who used marijuana. Fighting was more severe if the rival was drunk, but not if he or she was high on other drugs. Among participants who scored high on risk and when the rival was intoxicated, the fight was more severe. Although Valdez et al. (2006) acknowledged that much gang fighting occurs while individuals are intoxicated, other variables are important to understand when examining frequency, intensity, and severity of such fighting.

Collins's (2008) microsociological analysis indicates that violent actors engage in a great deal of posturing. The purpose of this posturing is to give the impression to others (including the antagonist) that the individual is tough and ready. In truth, the individual does *not* really want to fight and will only do so as a last resort to save face. Fighting, according to Collins, is not something that people are particularly good at and generally fear. Some evidence has emerged to indicate that members attempt to avoid fighting. Garot's (2010) work highlights how gang and other youth negotiate their environments to avoid fights. His research reveals that youth have interactional, relational, and emotional resources at their disposal—various identities related to gangs and street culture—that they employ to avoid violence. The question *Where you from?* (or its equivalent) is often a precursor to fighting, but Garot's (2010) research shows how youth can use these types of phrases to avoid altercations. This is an extension of research on street culture more generally with regard to the importance of identity management, such as saving face (J. Katz, 1988; Luckenbill, 1977; see also Garot, 2007). Fighting among gang members is something they talk about, such as reminiscing about past events or planning future ones, much more than they actually commit (Klein, 1995).

FIREARMS

Gangs became more violent over time (Bjerregaard and Lizotte, 1995; Hagedorn, 1998; Klein and Maxson, 1989; W. B. Miller, 1975; J. W. Moore, 1991). They once used fists, knives, bats, chains, and other handheld weapons, but this gave way to gunfights and drive-by shootings (Bjerregaard and Lizotte, 1995). The days of fair fighting where combatants shake hands and avoid cheap shots are long gone. Hagedorn (1998) provides an interview excerpt from a gang member from Milwaukee on the increase in violence over time.

> I come from three generations of gangs. . . . We're in a new generation now. Back then . . . everything was like fistfights. . . . It's gotten worse, it's like shoot-outs all the time. . . . It's scary walking down the street and knowing that you're on the opposition's turf. Nowadays you're afraid to get shot at. You know, before, you didn't even worry about that! (Hagedorn, 1998, pp. 365–366)

A youth from the Los Angeles Study said how common guns were.

> Everybody can get a gun now. So you can get shot over anything and not even gang banging. You can just bump into somebody and they feel like you are disrespect and now they want to shoot you.

Significant increases in youth violence occurred across the United States in the 1980s and 1990s. Researchers focused on the role of gang members in such high levels of deadly violence (Block and Block, 1993; Hagedorn, 1998; Klein and Maxson, 1989; Rosenfeld et al., 1999). Between the early 1980s and early 1990s, nationwide gang homicides increased significantly. In Los Angeles County, such homicides grew from 205 in 1982 to 803 in 1992 (Song et al., 1996). From 1987 to 1994, the number of homicides doubled in

Los Angeles and increased fivefold in Chicago (Hagedorn, 1998). About 25,000 gang members were killed across the United States since 1980 (T. Hayden, 2004).

Researchers have proposed various ideas to help explain the increase of deadly violence (Hagedorn, 1998). The effects of deindustrialization across the United States created pockets of extreme deprivation within inner-city areas that were largely populated by ethnic minorities (Hagedorn, 1998; Sampson and Wilson, 1995; Wilson, 1987). Members were staying in the gang longer and socioeconomic conditions that give rise to gangs increased (Hagedorn, 1988; J. W. Moore, 1991). Both factors helped swell the overall number of gangs. Legitimate work became hard to find and the informal economy opened doors. A glut of cocaine in the 1980s inspired new ways to sell the drug more quickly, leading to the emergence of crack. Crack sales offered an attractive way to earn money. The increase in crack cocaine markets created a need to protect these investments through deadly violence (Blumstein and Wallman, 2000; Fagan, 1996; Zimring, 2006).

Crack cocaine expansion, increases in firearms, and an overall rise in homicides paralleled one another. The diffusion of gun culture within the inner city more generally was related to the rise in the number of people selling crack and using firearms (Blumstein and Wallman, 2000). The increase in deadly gang violence is directly related to the expansion of the crack cocaine markets (Hagedorn, 1998; W. B. Sanders, 1994; Waldorf and Lauderback, 1993). Another reason for the escalation of deadly violence is the influence of prison gangs. Hagedorn (1998) noted "the effect of mainstream cultural values of money and success" (p. 370) and provides a few interview excerpts from a couple of gang members with "dollar signs in their eyes" (p. 401):

Q: "Why did you start selling dope?"

A: "Shit, fast money man. Don't you want a big car too? Don't you want cash? Don't you want a house on Lake Drive?"
(Latino gang member)

A: "Why? For the money. For the profits, you know, make money, have everything that I can get—'cause the more I got the more I want, know what I'm saying?"
(African American gang member)

This escalation has also been viewed as a type of one-upmanship, with younger members trying to outdo the older ones by committing more violent acts (Decker, 1996; J. W. Moore, 1991). As J. W. Moore (1991, p. 60) says, "younger members often want to match or outdo the reputation of their predecessors. Respondents from the more violent cliques were significantly more likely to believe that their clique was more violent than its immediate predecessor." As generations of gangs attempt to surpass one another, the ubiquity of firearms usage across the United States is the eventual logical outcome.

The availability of firearms increased substantially in the postindustrial era. From 1970 to 1990, about 120 million firearms were available in the United States (Reiss and Roth, 1993). The escalation in the severity of gang violence is related to increases in the availability and lethality of firearms (Bjerregaard and Lizotte, 1995; Block and Block, 1993; Hagedorn, 1998; Klein and Maxson, 1989; W. B. Miller, 1982; J. W. Moore, 1991; Shelden et al., 2001;

Vigil, 2003). The types of firearms available to gang members were once limited to firearms they obtained through theft (Shelden et al., 2001). Nowadays, gang members can purchase a variety of firearms on the street. Firearms used to be limited to Saturday night specials or zip guns—homemade, one-shot gizmos that needed to be fired at close range to do damage (Bjerregaard and Lizotte, 1995; Hagedorn, 1998). Today, gang members have access to sophisticated hardware, some military grade. Huff (1996) found that nearly 75% of all the youth interviewed said they could get firearms and that 90% preferred powerful weapons to lower-caliber handguns (see also Bjerregaard and Lizotte, 1995; Block and Bock, 1993). Data from Chicago indicate that the use of larger-caliber firearms increased threefold from the late 1980s to the early 1990s (Block and Block, 1993).

Anywhere between 50 and 70% of samples reported that they owned firearms (Hagedorn, 1988; Lizotte et al., 1994; C. S. Taylor, 1990). Guns were pervasive within the Los Angeles Study. Almost all participants (96.6%) said they knew at least one person who owned a firearm, and on average they knew 30 such people. About half (54.2%) of the youths' family members owned guns. About three in four (72.9%) reported firing a gun and, when asked about obtaining them, 88.1% said it would be "very easy" or "easy" to do.

The Los Angeles Study reported a wide range of high-caliber, semiautomatic and automatic weaponry, as listed in Table 6.1. They discussed sophisticated hardware, both modern (e.g., AK-47, SKS, M-16) and dated (e.g., M1, Thompson machine gun or Tommy gun). One youth said he could obtain a rocket launcher:

TABLE 6.1 TYPES OF FIREARMS AVAILABLE TO GANG YOUTH (*N* = 60)

Firearm	Percentage Who Could Obtain
.22 (a)	53.3
.38 (a), 9mm (a)	51.6
"Shotguns"	43.3
AK-47 (b)	41.6
.45 (a)	40
.357 (a)	23.3
M16 (b), .25 (a)	18.3
"Rifles," M1 (b)	15
.380 (a), SKS (c)	11.7
UZI, (d), TEC-9 (a), .40 (a)	8.3
.44 (a),	6.7
.30-30 (f)	5
M14 (f), .32 (a), MAC-11 (e), Thompson (d)	3.3
. 325 (f), .270 (f), Mini-M14 (c), M4 (c), MAC-10 (e), Calico 9mm (c), AR-15 (c), .41 (a), .270 (f), .50 (a)	1.7

a = handgun; b = assault rifle; c = semiautomatic rifle/carbine; d = submachine gun; e = machine pistol; f = rifle. Percentages are rounded to the nearest tenth. Percentages exceed 100% because of multiple nominations.

What kind of guns can you get your hands on?

> I could get like a mini rocket launcher.

Like how much would that cost?

> 1,500.

What would you do with that?

> Blow up a car. Blow up a house. Like, if you wanted someone done. . . . You can just drive calmly and hit the corner, and, just like, you know, aint no one going to know. . . . If you know how to use it, you can take out an entire house.

Assault rifles and larger firearms were used less frequently because they were not as easily concealed.

What kinds of guns could you get?

> You can get pretty much everything . . . you'll get from an AK, from an M1, to an SKS. . . . You can get them, but the thing is, a lot of homeboys have guns like that but you can't really bring them out, you know? . . . Usually, you want to fuck around with a 9, a 45, something that is carry-able, that you can carry.

The increases in firearms led to the ubiquity of drive-by shootings beginning in the 1980s in cities with long gang histories. W. B. Sanders (1994, pp. 65–66, 68) studied drive-by shootings in San Diego and provided the following examples:

> The victims, some members of Da Boys, were at home. Some Be Down Boys drove up, got out of the car, and shot at the victims, their car, and dog. After firing several shots, they got back in their car and drove away.

> Members of Eastside Piru were hanging out in front of a liquor store when a car drove by. Some Crips in the car said, "What's up, blood?" The Pirus ignored them and walked away. After a Piru member refused to come over to their car, the Crips began firing, hitting the victim three times. Then the Crips drove away.

> Some VELs were standing in front of their house when two 70s on a motorcycle drove by and shot a pistol at the house and car, hitting the car.

> The victim, a Syndo Mob member, was working inside his car on the back window. He saw a white van back down the alley. When the van's passenger side door came in front of his car, a Piru pointed an Uzi machine gun at him and fired eighteen rounds, hitting his car several times but missing him.

A youth in the Los Angeles Study recalled how he was injured during a drive-by shooting:

What happened to you when you were shot?

> I was walking down to the liquor store. A car pulls out, guy jumps out and shoots me on the arm, my left arm, left elbow, exit out here, right through here [pointing to where the bullet went through his arm]. Really, I just thought it was a 38 special. On my leg.

You got shot there, too?

    Yeah.

How gang members obtain sophisticated hardware is difficult to answer (Decker, 1996; Hagedorn, 1998). Some researchers have indicated that gangs could get guns as if they were ordering fast food at a restaurant (Cook et al., 2007). This parallels what most youth in the Los Angeles Study said: getting guns was easy. The involvement of gang members in the illicit firearm trafficking market is unclear. Gangs have increased their presence within the armed services and have been responsible for diverting military weapons into their communities (Eyler, 2009; National Gang Intelligence Center, 2007). Other evidence suggests gangs are not involved in selling guns. Cook et al. (2007) found that gangs in Chicago avoided selling guns for two reasons. One, selling drugs was much more lucrative. Two, the police had prioritized antifirearm efforts, which could bring unnecessary attention and jeopardize drug profits. Members bought guns, but did not sell them (Cook et al., 2007). One reason provided by an older member in the study by Cook et al. (2007, p. 14) is that members did not travel far out of their own neighborhoods:

> Most of us, we never been outside these four or five blocks, our neighborhood. Now, how can you bring the guns here if you don't even know how to get to other places?

A lack of mobility of gang youth was found in the Los Angeles Study. A few youth mentioned candy shops within housing projects. Candy shops are apartments that have been transformed into convenience stores that sell candy, chips, sodas, snacks, and other treats. These shops allow members and others living in or adjacent to the housing projects to buy items without having to leave the safety of their immediate environment. Another youth in this study was interviewed in a restaurant a few blocks from where he lived, but he had never visited there because it was outside of his gang's territory (B. Sanders et al., 2010).

Given the severe legal repercussions linked to membership and firearm possession, exercising caution with guns is a prudent maneuver. A youth from the Los Angeles Study discussed how he was caught with firearms after being pulled over by the police for smoking marijuana:

Have you ever been arrested for an offense involving a gun?

    Yes.

What was that?

    I was riding in a car . . . and [the police] stopped us and I was kind of tripping because I had weed on me and [my friends] were smoking [marijuana]. And then I was like "Damn, we're going to get arrested and shit." And then [the police] come and they see the whole smoke come out [of the car] and shit. Then they get us out and they start checking us and they find the weed. They find three of the blunts in other people's pockets and they start searching the car. They found a .357 Special, a .38, a .22, and a Tech 9, too. They locked us up, but since they checked who had used it they didn't find nothing on me so they let us go but they didn't give us our guns back. (B. Sanders et al., 2010, p. 746)

As opposed to being ardent firearm enthusiasts, the Los Angeles Study had ambiguous and conflicting opinions. Only one voiced an opinion of firearms in positive terms. Over half of the sample (51.6%) offered negative views, using words such as "bad," "shit," "stupid," and "cowardly" to describe firearms, and some (8.3%) had no or unclear opinions (see also Stretesky and Pogrebin, 2007). The remainder (38.3%) was ambivalent, saying things like "that's just how it is" or they are used "as a last resort" or "only if necessary."

> It's just the way it is right now. I can't really say nothing, I can't judge them, you know? Right now everybody is living by the gun and dying by the gun, you know?

> I feel if you don't need to use one, don't use it. The only time you feel fit to need to use one is if you feel your life is really at stake. If someone pulls out a gun on you and you have one, then it's only natural you're going to pull yours out if he pulls his out, you know? But I don't think you should ever just pull one out. I was raised, "Don't pull one out if you're not going to use it," so I don't pull a gun unless I know I'm going to use it.

> I think, my opinion of using guns is like, its purposeless unless your life is in, unless your life is threatened, threaten my life or threaten my family. That would be a purpose for me to use a pistol and a purpose for me to use the gun. If it was not like a desperate situation or a terrorist threat or a threat towards me and my family then there is no purpose to use a gun.

Bjerregaard and Lizotte (1995) asked some important questions in their research that sought to untangle the relationship between gang membership and firearm possession. Drawing on data from the Rochester Causes and Correlates study, they reported that members were much more likely than non–gang members to own guns for protective reasons but no more likely than non-gang youth to own guns for sporting purposes (see also Thornberry et al., 2003). As members age, ownership of guns for both sport and defense increased. Members were more likely than non-gang youth to carry guns and to report friends who owned guns for protection. Bjerregaard and Lizotte (1995) found that membership enhances gun ownership for protection, but that gangs are likely to select people who already have guns for protection prior to joining. When youth leave, they also leave the gun subculture. In their multivariate analysis, Bjerregaard and Lizotte (1995) offer support for the selection hypothesis in that gang members were more likely to recruit youth who already owned guns for defense purposes. Owning a gun for protection was more likely to precede gang membership (see also Thornberry et al., 2003).

Stretesky and Pogrebin (2007) examined the interplay among gang-related gun violence, street socialization, and self-identity. The authors argue that members used guns for both symbolic and tangible purposes. Many carried them in order to provide a sense of protection, mostly from other members who also had guns (see J. Katz, 1988). Guns among gang members also played more emblematic roles, allowing them to project a violent identity, intimidate, and ward off potential danger, as the following excerpt suggests (Stretesky and Pogrebin, 2007, p. 101):

> The intimidation factor with a gun is amazing. Everybody knows what a gun can do. If you have a certain type of personality, that only increases their fear of you. When it came

to certain individuals who I felt were a threat, I would lift my shirt up so they would know I had one on me.

Gang members threaten one another with firearm violence more than they perpetrate it. Gun ownership allowed them to project a *willingness* to engage in deadly violence (Cook et al., 2007; W. B. Sanders, 1994; Stretesky and Pogrebin, 2007). Stretesky and Pogrebin (2007) note that by having guns, members were able to maintain a reputation for deadly violence, which decreased their likelihood of victimization, especially because most of them spent a considerable amount of time engaging in street activities (e.g., violent crime, drug selling). By carrying a firearm, members project the image of "someone not to be

---

BOX 6.1: MEDIA CHECK!

When Gangsta Rap Became Gangster

Gangsta rap emerged in Los Angeles with artists such as NWA (Niggaz with Attitude) who dubbed themselves "the world's most dangerous group." NWA consisted of Eazy-E, Yella, MC Ren, Ice Cube, and Dr. Dre, who claimed to be from Compton, California. Compton houses a tiny street called Piru, which is where the Blood gang supposedly originated. (The hand sign of the Bloods is like an OK sign but with the middle, ring, and pinky fingers pointing straight down so the hand forms a P when looking at it straight. The P refers to Piru Street.) NWA's songs included the hits "Fuck tha Police," "Dopeman," and "Gangsta gangsta," which leave little to the imagination as to their lyrical content. These guys even looked like gang members, with the jheri-curl hairstyles, Loc sunglasses, khaki trousers, flannel shirts, beanies, and baseball hats with Compton written in Old English—the gangster typeface par excellence. Their music, appearance, and general response from the streets suggested that the members of NWA were real-life gangsters. They were not. Outside of Eazy-E, a former crack seller from Compton who later succumbed to HIV, the history of crime and violence among the other members of the band prior to forming NWA is relatively unknown. Dr. Dre and Yella were once part of an electro-pop group called the World Class Wreckin Cru, wearing sparkling clothing reminiscent of Earth, Wind, and Fire in the 1970s.

Over time, the distinction between being a studio gangsta rapper (i.e., someone who just rapped about gang life) and a bona fide gang member from the streets began to blur. Perhaps the most famous of these episodes involves the artists Tupac Shakur (2Pac), from Los Angeles, and the Notorious BIG (Biggie Smalls), from Brooklyn. Like other gangsta rappers, these guys often rapped about drug dealing, murder, gang-banging, and other aspects of street culture. Although they were once apparently friends, something happened between the two and they became bitter enemies. They dissed each other in their songs, fueling the perception of a beef between East Coast and West Coast artists. Arguments like these have been a staple of hip-hop since its inception, but what made the feud between 2Pac and Biggie so profound is the fact that they were both assassinated, within a relatively close time of one another. 2Pac was gunned down in Las Vegas in September of 1996 and Biggie Smalls was shot and killed in Los Angeles in March of 1997. Both of the murders were drive-by shootings and both remain unsolved.

Examples of gangsta rappers being involved in gang life after the Biggie/2Pac incident became more common. Curtis Jackson (aka 50 cent) is a former drug dealer from New York. One time, an assailant shot him point blank nine times, including once in the face to finish him off. He did not succeed. Despite his past, 50 Cent would continue to lead a successful career as a musician. Even Oprah invited him on her show. Other stories about rappers-who-are-actually-gangsters do not end so well. Twenty-two-year-old M-Bone, from the group Cali Swag Group, was killed in a drive-by shooting in Inglewood, California. Freaky Tah, a 28-year-old member of the Lost Boyz, was shot and killed in Jamaica Queens, NYC. Two members of Eminem's group D-12, Bugz (age 21) and Proof (age 32), were both shot and killed. Big L, a 24-year-old member of the Diggin in the Crates Crew, was shot and killed outside his home in New York City.

On the other end are gangsta rappers who have killed people. These include Big Lurch, who killed his girlfriend. C-Murder is in prison for life for second-degree murder. Steady B is in prison for life for his role in the murder of a police officer in Philadelphia. The Mac is serving a 30-year sentence for manslaughter. X-Raider was sentenced to 31 years for his involvement in a deadly gang shooting. And what about those gangsta rap artists who have been arrested on other charges? Dozens of them, including some women, have been collectively sentenced to decades in prison for their involvement in weapons offenses, battery, assault, rape, and sexual assault. Even Dr. Dre, who became one of gangsta rap's most successful artists, was arrested for assault for kicking and punching a female television personality. In 2013, Dr. Dre sold his Beats headphones to Apple for billions of dollars.

messed with," a form of impression management that occasionally works. Cook et al. (2007, pp. 9–10) provided some interview excerpts from gang youth that captured this sentiment:

> You have to let [other people] see it without letting them see it. See, it's all about them not messing with you.

> Thing is, see, it ain't really about fighting or nothing, because even if you have a group of guys and you see a group of guys, lot of times, it's just you show 'em you got one, they show you they got one, and you just be on your way. It's just like signifying that you prepared.

HOMICIDE

In large cities, gangs are responsible for a disproportionate amount of homicides. Los Angeles is an example. One reason the city has been called the gang capital of the nation—if not the world—is the annual high number of gang-related murders. For several years, half of all murders in Los Angeles were gang related, tying Chicago for the city with the highest amount (Egley and Ruiz, 2006). Gang homicides steadily decreased in the mid-1990s. Toward the end of the first decade of the 21st century, national survey data noted a slight uptick in gang homicides in cities with more than 100,000 people (Egley and Howell, 2011).

Tita and Abrahamse (2004) found that gang homicides in Los Angeles are responsible for a disproportionate amount of both gang and overall homicide in all of California. Over a 21-year period between 1981 and 2001, 75% of the 10,000 gang homicides in California occurred in Los Angeles County (Tita and Abrahamse, 2004). Such victimization is about seven times greater in Los Angeles County compared with the rest of California, but other types are about twice as high (Tita and Abrahamse, 2004). When controlling for demographics, non-gang homicides were just as likely to occur in Los Angeles as in the rest of the state, with certain types less common in Los Angeles (Tita and Abrahamse, 2004). The statewide increases at the turn of the century were driven by gang-related homicides in Los Angeles County (Tita and Abrahamse, 2004). The authors conclude that "what truly sets Los Angeles apart from the remainder of California is . . . *the existence of a specific milieu that has fostered the development of a violent gang culture unlike any other gang culture in the state*" (Tita and Abrahamse, 2004, p. 16, emphasis added).

Tita and Abramhase's (2004) work highlights those most at risk. California has the youngest victims compared with victims of other types of homicide (mean age = 22 years old) and the highest rate of male victims (95%), with those between 15 and 35 years old at greatest risk (Tita and Abramhase, 2004). African American males have the highest rate of gang killings (14.7/100,000), followed by Hispanic males (6.5/100,000) and then other males (0.3/100,000). In contrast, the rate of such victimization for non-Hispanic, non–African American females in California is zero.

Gang violence occurs between people of the same race (Curry and Decker, 1998; J. Katz, 1988; J. Miller, 1998; J. Miller and Decker, 2001; W. B. Sanders, 1994; Tita and

Abrahamse, 2004; Valdez et al., 2009). Some reports of *inter*racial gang violence (between different races) have emerged, which are concentrated in Los Angeles. The federal government targeted one Latino gang in the city that had specifically attacked African Americans over a 20-year period to drive them out (Stoltze, 2011). Also, a predominately Latino gang, 18th Street, has an ongoing battle with the Rollin' 20s, an African American blood set.[4] The Southern Poverty Law Center issued a report that indicated Latino gang members were terrorizing and killing African Americans across Southern California in what was tantamount to ethnic cleansing (Mock, 2006). One report that examined hate crimes in Los Angeles County concluded, "there is strong evidence of race-bias hate crime among racial minority group-based gangs in which the major motive is not the defense of territorial boundaries against other gangs, but hatred towards a group defined by racial identification regardless of any gang-related territorial threat" (Umemoto and Mikami, 2000, p. 1).

In Los Angeles in 2006, a series of shootings between African Americans and Latinos occurred. These interethnic gang-related killings kicked off a moral panic regarding the rise in black versus brown gang shootings (Leovy, 2007). Youth in the Los Angeles Study also mentioned this:

Who do you generally fight?
> Blacks.

What are these about?
> I just have tension, you know?

Racial tensions?
> Yeah, jail time and where I grew up at, you know?

So is it kind of where are you from, down in [city] and do you live next to a black community?
> Yeah, you know? It's kind of equal, Mexicans and Blacks so we bump fucking heads so much.

Does your gang have anything to do with them?
> Yeah, it's all about the gang.

Do you know anybody who has been shot by a gun?
> Yes, me, my brother. They shot us at [name of cross streets]. That is my brother right here [name of brother tattooed on arm]. He is 20 years old, they killed him December 27, 2006, right there on [name of cross streets]. They dumped him in the night. They shot him in the back of the head. He had lived in the house with me since he was 14 years old. You know, that is why I hate Mexicans.

---

4   The feud between 18th Street and the Rollin' 20s was highlighted in the 2008 slaying of a high school student with no gang connections. The student was murdered by an 18th Street gang member who suspected him to be a member of the Rollin' 20s because of the red in his backpack (S. Wilson, 2012).

Have you ever been in group rumbles? How many times has that happened?

Hell yeah! With the blacks.

How often do those happen?

A lot of times, cause we don't get along with black people. My neighborhood does not get along with black people.

Who do you generally fight?

Rivals, or kids at school. And it came a time when I was in juvenile hall, we were fighting blacks. When I was in Sylmar, it was like the racial riots, so it would be like on and off.

Have you ever been in like a group rumble or a riot?

Yeah.

How often do they happen?

Racial riots, all the time. Shit.

How often do they happen?

At school it happens a lot. In school, like in school is like every day, like couple of days thing. That shit happens a lot.

What do you dislike about the gang?

I don't like that, deal with other issues or other people's problems. I don't like the racism in the gang, as far as Hispanics against Blacks, I don't really like that too much.

Of all the homicides within Los Angeles in 2007, the total number of interethnic homicides between African Americans and Latinos accounted for about 13% and some concerned the killing of African Americans in Latino gangs (Leovy, 2007). This statistic suggests that the moral panic was unfounded and that members were still more likely to shoot and kill others of the same race. Research on the topic of interracial violence is in its infancy, and more is required to obtain a clear picture.

Valdez and colleagues (2009) provide a situational analysis of homicide among Mexican American street gangs. Valdez developed a typology of gang types that varied with regard to whether they were related to a prison gang, whether they were juvenile or adult, and the extent to which they were territorial or transitional (Valdez, 2003). Using this typology, Valdez et al. (2009) reported that the frequency varied by gang type, with the "criminal non-adult dependent" gangs responsible for almost half of all gang homicides recorded in their study. The authors suggest that the lack of adult influence on these types of gang may contribute to their higher number of homicides. In contrast, those gangs that had ties to prison gangs involved in illegal drug distribution were responsible for fewer homicides. Valdez et al. (2009) suggest this is because individuals in the prison gang discouraged street members from committing homicides because it could attract attention from law enforcement and potentially interfere with drug profits.

Many of the gang homicides occurred between rivals who lived in close proximity of one another and in relation to territory and honor. What is interesting is the random nature of being a victim: youth get caught slipping. Valdez et al. (2009, pp. 9–10) offer an interview excerpt of one account:

> Me and RadioMan were walking over by the wall and didn't notice we went into their neighborhood. It was around Christmastime. At first I thought they were firecrackers, but they were shooting at us from the alley. I got shot in the stomach. When I turned around, RadioMan got shot too. All I remember was seeing him lying there, and he died in the ambulance.

A member in W. B. Sanders's (1994, p. 131) research offered a similar account:

> One day when we were coming back from school our worst enemies drove by our neighborhood. They were looking for guys to shoot. They saw us and said "Big bad East Side," so we told them, "Fuck East Side. It's all about big bad Casa Blanca Los Devilwolves gang." So they took out their guns and started shooting at us. So all of us ran and jumps the wall but they shoot my homeboy and killed him. My homeboy was real close to me.

Valdez et al. (2009) found that the gang homicides could be broken down based on circumstance and motive. Five distinct disputes associated with gang homicides included drugs (e.g., argument over a drug transaction), personal, gang, assault (i.e., surprise attack), and rolling (i.e., exiting ceremony). Six distinct motives of homicide included personal vendetta, revenge, rivalry, territorial trespassing, solidarity, and spontaneous retaliation. The majority were revenge or rivalry, most of which involved firearms. For the majority of the cases, the victim was intoxicated and the primary substance used was alcohol.

Decker and Curry (2002) examined homicides between Crips and Bloods in St. Louis and found that they killed their own members. More Bloods were killed than Crips, and

the Bloods were more likely to be murdered by non–gang members. The Crips were more likely to be killed by other Crips. Overall, Decker and Curry (2002) conclude that these gang organizations are not effective at controlling the behaviors of their members, and loyalty did not control who was a victim of homicide. Non-gang individuals killed most members. When members murdered other members, mostly they were from the same gang.

VICTIMIZATION

Innocent bystanders occasionally become victims. Hutson and colleagues, in their study in Los Angeles County from 1979 through 1994, found that close to one-third of those killed were not gang members or criminals (Hutson et al., 1995). Song et al. (1996) found that within the same area between 1982 and 1992 about a quarter of all gang-related homicide victims were nonmembers. Hutson et al. (1994) reported that, in 1991 in the city of Los Angeles, more than a quarter of all juveniles injured in gang-related shootings were non–gang members. These studies suggest that gang members victimize a considerable amount of people unrelated to gangs and their activity.

Media reports emerge from time to time of innocents caught in the crossfire. These reports generate huge debate and garner significant attention. Numbers of how many innocent people are killed by members on a city-by-city or national basis are not available. A youth from the Los Angeles Study acknowledged that innocent people do get killed, but that these instances are rare:

Tell me your opinion on people using guns.

> Mistakes [are] made by dumb people and people that don't think. But at the same time people that I hang around, I can at least say, the people that I hang around at least know okay when, it's time to use a gun, how to use a gun, how to not get innocent people not involved, you know? Like, how to do things. It's like everybody makes it seem like "Oh, well," like your typical movie set . . . and all that. Driving down the street, kids are outside playing, there is one rival member in the house. They are not going to shoot up the whole house and to kill their family and kids. It does not go like that. I mean it's possible, it could happen . . . [but] everybody makes it seem like it's the typical aspect of gang members.

W. B. Sanders (1994) reported that gang members had strict rules about shooting innocents; women, children, and those not in the gang were off limits. Others note that gang members have expressed indifference to random people getting mistakenly shot. As one of Vigil's (1988a, p. 440) respondents, Psycho, said after wounding a 5-year-old girl in a gang shooting, "I don't give a fuck. Why do you think they call me Psycho?"

The odds of average people getting caught in the crossfire of shootings or other gang-related violence are low. This risk increases among those who live in gang communities and those in close proximity to members. Valdez et al. (2009) report that the mother of a member was killed when rivals shot at the house, and a man was killed when members attempted to retrieve a gun they had thrown on his roof. The risk of being a victim of such violence increases among those who associate with gangs, as well as among those who have been romantically involved with them. One of the youth from the Los Angeles Study discussed how rivals went looking for him, but shot his girlfriend instead:

What happened with your girlfriend?

> She got shot in the leg with a .22. They went looking for me but they could not find me . . . they shot up her house. But she's doing all right cause she can walk still though.

Comparing innocent bystanders killed by gang versus non-gang homicides reveals another interesting portrait. The Centers for Disease Control and Prevention (2012) provided a five-city comparison of the characteristics associated with gang and non-gang homicides that occurred between 2003 and 2008. Long Beach reported no innocent bystanders in either type, and the rest of the cities had a *greater* number of innocents killed in *non*-gang homicides. Despite these numbers, innocents were slightly more likely to be killed in gang homicides than in non-gang homicides, but this likelihood was only statistically significant in Newark. Overall, the Centers for Disease Control report indicates that more innocents *in total* were killed in non-gang than in gang homicides, but that the *likelihood* of innocents getting killed was slightly greater for gang homicides (and only significantly more likely in one city).

Although members are often portrayed as perpetrators of violence, they are also victims. Los Angeles is a city of about 4 million people, and approximately 40,000 are gang members (Advancement Project, 2007). This translates to gangs comprising about 1% of the overall population of the city. Approximately half of all murders in Los Angeles have been considered gang related (Egley and Ruiz, 2006). Research suggests that gangs largely target and kill one another (Block and Block, 1993; Decker, 2001; J. Katz, 1988; W. B. Sanders, 1994). If these findings are accurate, then 1% of the Los Angeles population have been the victims and perpetrators of 50% of all homicides. That places the odds of violent death among members significantly higher than that of non-gang youth. Howell (1998) has indicated that gang youth are about 60 times more likely to be violently killed than non-gang youth. Papachristos et al. (2012) report that members occupy positions within their social networks that greatly increase their chances of future victimization. The fact that youth report joining for protection, but then ultimately place themselves at risk for violence is, as Klein and Maxson (2006, p. 83) note, "an unfortunate irony." Violence is the worst part of being in a gang. Its threat is an ongoing reality for members, as the following excerpts from the Los Angeles Study suggest:

> I can't take the bus. I never take the bus because I don't like sitting at a bus stop. That's the one way you can get shot. If you're sitting at a bus stop, someone is going to drive by, they're going to see you waiting at the bus stop and what happens? You're a sitting duck. They're going to run up on you. . . . You have no idea, they ain't going to tell you nothing. They probably already know who you are because you put yourself out there, you've been to jail. So they just be like *boom*, smooth run up and that's it. You're dead.

> Gangbanging and shit. . . . Getting jumped and all that shit. Like, for instance, I can walk out right now and walk to the corner and I get jumped or something like that. . . . I am used to that. It's not like a probability for me; it's highly possible. I know that every day I walk around, every day I do anything, it's highly possible and I accept it.

The fact that any given day anybody can come and take your life away. The fact that at any given day you could be in the situation where you took somebody's life away.

You get caught slipping by another motherfucker that you're not supposed to be caught by then you're gone for life.

If I go to the wrong neighborhood or a neighborhood around here that's one of my enemies then I better be strapped. If not, I'm going to get it. You can sit there and fight but chances are you're going to get it. You're going to get hit. And seeing as I've been hit already I don't want to get hit again.

Members are more likely to be victims of other forms of violent and criminal victimization than non-gang youth. Survey data from various middle schools across the United States found that gang youth were much more likely to report victimization than their non-gang peers (Peterson et al., 2004; T. J. Taylor et al., 2007, 2008). Peterson et al. (2004) found that, compared with nonmembers, gang youth were more likely and more frequently to be victimized and that this likelihood peaked during the year they were initiated. T. J. Taylor et al. (2007) expanded on this and indicated that members compared to nonmembers reported more victimization in the previous year as well as more types of victimization (e.g., simple assault, robbery, aggravated assault). The authors then said that members are exposed to more risk factors and fewer protective factors than non-gang youth and that the gang youth most likely to be victims are those who report the most exposure to risk factors and the least exposure to protective ones. T. J. Taylor et al. (2007) found that membership was associated with a decrease in the chances of general victimization, but an increase in the odds of a serious victimization. When important risk and protective factors were taken into consideration, the differences between gang members and nonmembers in terms of victimization were negligible. In another examination of their data, T. J. Taylor et al. (2008) examined whether the lifestyle or routine activities of gangs contributed to an understanding of their victimization. Such behaviors were measured by positive and negative peer involvement and commitment, drug use, delinquency, and hanging out with adults. T. J. Taylor et al. (2008) noted that involvement in delinquency and the availability of drugs significantly mediated the relationship between gang membership and serious victimization.

Melde et al. (2009) looked at the unfortunate irony of membership in more detail. They were interested in untangling the paradox that youth members join for protection but ultimately experience more victimization. Melde et al. discussed the acceptability of risk using a psychometric paradigm that examines fear (i.e., dread) and controllable and uncontrollable risk (Slovic, 1987). This paradigm indicates that fear and perceived risk interact when making judgments. When risks are unknown and produce a high level of fear, they are considered unacceptable. When risks are known, they produce less fear and are viewed as more acceptable. This paradigm, according to the authors, adds clarity to the acceptability of gang membership in the face of an actual increase in risk. The authors examined victimization and fear among gang and non-gang youth and their results were "not indicative of a purely rational depiction of fear" (Melde et al., 2009, p. 585). Consistent with some of their other research (Peterson et al., 2004; T. J. Taylor et al., 2007), the authors found that members were much more likely to report actual victimization. The fear of victimization among gang members was substantially *lower* when compared with that of nonmembers. Although membership does not reduce victimization from an objective standpoint, it serves an emotive function. Whether the gang offers protection depends on how protection is measured. Melde et al. (2009) suggest that additional research should examine the extent to which perceptions of fear and risk and experiences of victimization differ across gang structures, as well as across youth differentially involved.

SUMMARY

The definition of gang-related violence is not clear-cut, and jurisdictions across the United States use different versions. Whether members commit violence for their own purposes (i.e., the gang-affiliated Los Angeles definition) or whether the violence is committed to benefit the gang (i.e., the gang-motivated Chicago definition), similarities and differences have been found. Gang violence is not everywhere, but is concentrated within impoverished, inner-city areas. Within these areas, such violence is limited in its distribution.

Violence has many forms. Youth enter and exit the gang through violence and experience numerous incidents between these ceremonies. Violence includes being jumped in, jumped out, getting jumped, jumping others, group rumbles, and homicide. One form of violence may quickly escalate into another, whereby a fight can lead to a homicide. A small amount of all violence is homicide and only a fraction of all homicides involve members. Of all the forms of violence, fighting is the most common. Gang members must watch their backs constantly so as not to get jumped by rivals or attacked by members of their own gang. Much of this violence is retaliatory, leading to never-ending tit-for-tat battles. The increase in the ubiquity of firearms has led to an increase in deadly violence. Firearms nowadays are high-powered, large-caliber weaponry that can inflict serious damage. Gang membership and gun ownership are intractably linked.

Innocent people have been caught in the crossfire, but the overall odds of being killed by a gang member are low, particularly among individuals who do not hang out with gangs or live in their communities. The victims of such violence tend to be other members, including those from the same gang. Gangs largely target and kill those of their own race, but evidence has emerged about interethnic violence, particularly in Los Angeles. Members are much more likely than non-gang youth to be victimized. This stands to reason given the overall victim–offender relationship, in that perpetrators of violence are also likely to be victims.

CHAPTER REVIEW QUESTIONS

1. What does NCVS say about gang members?
2. Describe the Los Angeles and Chicago definitions of gang-related violence. What are the key differences and why are they important?
3. Describe the prevalence of gang violence. What are the types of violence that gang members are responsible for? Where is such violence concentrated?

4. What are the symbolic and tangible reasons why youth are jumped in and beaten out of gangs?
5. Some gang members are more likely to engage in violence than others. What helps explain this?
6. What happens when someone is caught slipping? What determines whether a youth will be a victim or an aggressor in such a situation?
7. What did Valdez and colleagues indicate about the drugs/violence nexus among gang youth?
8. Why has it been argued that gangs became more violent in the 1980s and 1990s?
9. How common is gang homicide? What are the characteristics of gang homicide and how do they differ from other types of homicide?
10. Who are primarily the victims of gang violence? Why is this ironic?

HYPERLINKS TO ARTICLES ON GANG VIOLENCE AND VICTIMIZATION

The drugs–violence nexus among Mexican American gang members
By Avelardo Valdez, Charles D. Kaplan, and Alice Cepeda
http://www.ncbi.nlm.nih.gov/pmc/articles/PMC3015236/

Homicidal events among Mexican American street gangs
By Avelardo Valdez, Alice Cepeda, and Charles D. Kaplan
http://www.ncbi.nlm.nih.gov/pmc/articles/PMC3016850/

Collective and normative features of gang violence
By Scott H. Decker
http://faculty.cua.edu/sullins/SOC371/Decker%20-%20Gang%20Violence.pdf

Honor, normative ambiguity, and gang violence
By Ruth Horowitz and Gary Schwartz
http://tm.ermarian.net/Academic%20Junk/Sociology/Horowitz,%20R.,%20Schwartz,%20G.%20(1974)%20-%20Honor,%20Normative%20Ambiguity%20and%20Gang%20Violence.pdf

Gang membership and violent victimization
By Dana Peterson, Terrence J. Taylor, and Finn Aage-Esbensen
http://www.antoniocasella.eu/restorative/Peterson_2004.pdf

Fact sheet: Gang violence
By the Violence Prevention Coalition of Los Angeles
http://www.ph.ucla.edu/sciprc/pdf/GANG_VIOLENCE.pdf/

Fighting gang violence
By the Federal Bureau of Investigation
http://www.fbi.gov/about-us/investigate/vc_majorthefts/gangs/recent-statistics/

Violence by gang members, 1993–2003
By Erika Harrell
http://bjs.ojp.usdoj.gov/content/pub/pdf/vgm03.pdf/

CHAPTER 7

STYLE AND MEDIA

KEY WORDS

Blog: An electronic forum on a website to offer opinions and points of view.

Birmingham School: A collective of scholars from the United Kingdom from the Center for Contemporary Cultural Studies at the University of Birmingham who focused on spectacular youth subcultures.

Bricolage: In relation to clothing and popular culture, a term used to indicate how signs or symbols with well-established meaning are given new, coded meaning.

Cultural criminology: A wing of criminology that views crime and its control from a variety of viewpoints that derive insight from labeling theory, critical criminology, and cultural and media studies, as well as the roles of emotion and leisure.

Fearmongering: The use of scare tactics to influence actions and opinions, involving repeated and exaggerated claims.

Hegemony: Refers to the economic, political, and social influence and practice of the dominant group within society.

Homology: In relation to youth culture, a sameness or similarity among attitude, behavior, and style.

Magical resistance thesis: Developed by Phil Cohen to help explain the emergence of postwar spectacular youth subcultures in Great Britain. The thesis indicates that through the adaptation of a radical style, youth are able to subvert and resist the dominant culture. This resistance is perceived as "magical" because of its symbolism; youths' positions remained unchanged.

Moral panic: A negative societal reaction and fear toward a particular group, behavior, or issue that emerges from hype, fearmongering, and overreaction by the mass media.

Placas: In reference to gangs, graffiti by Latino gang members that has the name of the gang, a list of its members, and messages constructed in a unique style referred to as "barrio calligraphy."

Sagging: Deliberately wearing clothing sizes that are too large.

Tagging: Tag is short for "name tag" and tagging is writing a street name or nickname on various places in the form of graffiti.

Verstehen: German word employed by the sociologist Max Weber that means "interpretive understanding" of social phenomena.

Chapter Learning Objectives

- Explain cultural criminology.
- Interpret the significance and meaning of gang style.
- Discuss moral panics as they pertain to gangs and policy.
- Understand gang presence and function on the Internet.

INTRODUCTION

Style includes clothing, tattoos, symbols, graffiti, music, and overall presentation of self in everyday life. Style is pregnant with significance, with common signs assuming dual meanings. Style is important to consider because it offers visible clues about individual behavior. A reflexive relationship between style and behavior is apparent: gang youth commit crime and violence and adopt a style that radiates a deviant aesthetic. The mass media has a perennial interest with gangs because the topic provides entertainment. The media give the imprint that gang communities are war zones and that violence is an imminent threat, everywhere and at all times. This view blows things out of proportion and has fueled moral panics that generate fear and lead to the engineering of public policy that negatively and disproportionally impacts minority youth and communities.

The chapter begins by offering an overview of cultural criminology, which is the theoretical framework that fits the themes of style and media in relation to gangs. From there, the importance of style is examined, with a focus on how gangs repurpose recognizable symbols to declare membership. Next, the meaning and significance of graffiti and gangsta rap are explored. The following section addresses a homology or sameness between gang members and their style and how this style has been diffused into the mainstream and criminalized. The second half of the chapter looks at the mass media's fascination with gangs. The concept of moral panic is defined, and examples of moral panics as they concern gangs are then illustrated. The chapter concludes with a discussion of the gang presence on the Internet.

CULTURAL CRIMINOLOGY

Cultural criminology is the theoretical framework that fits the themes of style and media in relation to gangs. The roots of this field can be traced back to the work of British scholars in the 1970s. Many were at the Center for Contemporary Cultural Studies at the University of Birmingham and represent a train of thought collectively known as the Birmingham School. Their focus is couched within a neo-Marxist perspective. One of the more famous early works to emerge was *Resistance through Rituals* (S. Hall and Jefferson, 1976). This book focused on postwar spectacular youth subcultures of the British working class, such as the Teddy Boys, Skinheads, Mods, Rastas, and Rude Boys.

Phil Cohen's (1972) magical resistance thesis was central in these discussions. The theory argues that the subcultures were not only another wave of youth going through the latest trend, but also manifestations of resistance and rebellion. Youth rejected the dominant values of society through the adaptation of a particular style. This was "magical" in the sense that the youth did not change their situation at all; the resistance was symbolic (S. Cohen, 1972; Willis, 1977). Willis (1977) later illustrated that this rejection of the dominant values expressed by a lack of faith in the school system was how working-class kids got working-class jobs.

Antonio Gramsci's (1971) term hegemony is a focal point within the Birmingham School. Hegemony is the dominant social order and way of doing things. The Birmingham School examined the significance that youth in the spectacular subcultures attributed to various aspects of fashion and style and how style allowed them to subvert the community's expectations. The Birmingham School also borrowed the term *bricolage* from the French anthropologist Claude Levi-Strauss to capture the processes by which youth obtained common objects and then assigned them new identities and uses (Clarke, 1976). Hebdige (1979) highlighted the dual meaning youth from various subcultures held in relation to their style. Small things held large importance and hidden meanings were everywhere. The appearance of youth from these subcultures was not haphazardly thrown together, but constructed to convey meaning and consequence (see also Brake, 1985; Willis, 1978).

The Birmingham School focused on how the media demonized young people. They borrowed the term moral panic from Stan Cohen, who had just completed his seminal work on youth subcultures, the media, and constructions of deviance, to help capture the public reaction to youth delinquency (S. Cohen, 1971, 1972; S. Cohen and Young, 1973; Young, 1971). Another book produced by the School, *Policing the Crisis*, on the reportage of black youth, street robbery, and the media, proved S. Cohen's point (S. Hall et al., 1978).

Other influences of cultural criminology were the authors of the new criminology in the United Kingdom (I. Taylor et al., 1973). These theorists espoused a Marxist criminology and rejected biologically based explanations of crime. The new criminologists argued that the powerful institutions in society constructed what was determined "crime." The media plays a major role in this construction.

Although its origins were in the United Kingdom, modern-day cultural criminology emerged in the United States, largely brought about by the efforts of Jeff Ferrell (Ferrell,

1996, 1999; Ferrell and Sanders, 1995a, 1995b; Ferrell and Websdale, 1999; Ferrell et al., 2004, 2008). Cultural criminology is a "hybrid orientation" (Ferrell, 1999, p. 396) of traditional sociology and cultural studies within a postmodern context. The field examines culture and media as it relates to constructions of crime and its control. It draws from labeling theory, critical criminology, and postmodernism. Under the cultural criminological gaze, "form is content, that style is substance, that meaning thus resides in presentation and re-presentation" and the study of crime must investigate the extent to which "images created and consumed by criminals, criminal subcultures, control agents, media institutions, and audiences bounce endlessly one off the other" (Ferrell, 1999, p. 397). The discipline explores the ways in which the public are both consumers and producers of images associated with crime and deviance.

Cultural criminology favors the symbolic interactionist perspective that focuses on the meaning of words and behaviors in relation to crime. Ethnography and media and textual analyses are the preferred methods, aiming to obtain criminological *verstehen*—a Weberian term meaning interpretive understanding (Ferrell, 1999; Ferrell and Sanders, 1995b). J. Katz's (1988) concept of transgressive theory, which examines the role of emotions in relation to crime, is drawn on by cultural criminologists, as are the aesthetic and leisure associated with criminal conduct (Ferrell, 1996; O'Malley and Mugford, 1994; Presdee, 1994, 2000; Rojek, 2000).

THE IMPORTANCE OF STYLE

Style has been a vital part of the study of deviant behaviors for decades (e.g., Finestone, 1957; Lerman, 1967; see also W. B. Miller, 1958). Clothing, monikers, gait, signs, symbols, hairstyles, music, and presentation of self are part of what constitute style. Style serves as a way for individuals to develop their own identity (Burke and Sunley, 1998; Clarke, 1976; Hebdige, 1979). Style can also be used as a general indicator of potential behaviors and attitudes and is relevant to young people.

J. Katz (1988) writes about the style of "the badass" and "street elites" in inner-city environments, and gang members fit this description.[1] The badass aims to look tough, mean, and alien (J. Katz, 1988; W. B. Miller, 1958). Gang members can achieve this look through the appropriation of various stylistic indicators that ooze masculinity, sexuality, and menace: dark sunglasses, bandanas, baseball hats, and hoodies (J. Katz, 1988; J. A. Miller, 1995). Below is a description of Hispanic gang members from the Los Angeles Police Department (LAPD) website:

> The uniform of Hispanic gangs is standard and easily recognizable. Most gang members adopt a basic style that includes white T-shirts, thin belts, baggy pants with split cuffs, a black or blue knit cap (beanie) or a bandana tied around the forehead similar to a sweat band.[2]

---

1   J. Katz (1988) avoids the term gang and instead prefers "street soldiers" and "barrio homeboys."
2   Visit http://www.lapdonline.org/get_informed/content_basic_view/23468/.

Tattoos are another way gangs express dread and distinguish themselves from wannabes (Curry and Decker, 2003). They also wear oversized clothing with trousers that sag below the backside and tops that extend below the waist.[3] This clothing helps conceal weapons (J. A. Miller, 1995). Inmates also wear oversized clothing, and street gang members prefer the sagging look to emulate prison culture (J. A. Miller, 1995). This is one way that prison gang culture has been argued to influence street gang culture.

Hairstyle is a way gangs project menace and dread (J. Katz, 1988; J. A. Miller, 1995). Shaved or closely cropped hair is popular. As one of J. A. Miller's (1995, p. 222) probation officers noted, Hispanic gangs wear their hair this way to "give them the look like as if they're in state prison—that hardcore look."

The way gang members walk aims to project menace. They engage in a slow saunter full of braggadocio, with the chest puffed up and out, the arms flailing on either side, and head tilted up in a defiant manner (J. Katz, 1988; J. A. Miller, 1995; B. Sanders, 2005a). This has been referred to as the barrio stroll or ghetto bop (J. Katz, 1988). For gang youth, getting from place to place assumes "a deviant esthetic statement" that indicates they live within "a morally deviant place" that is "outside and antagonistically related to the morally respectable center of society" (J. Katz, 1988, p. 88). A probation officer in J. A. Miller's (1995, p. 222) research commented on the walk:

> He's trying to express himself in a certain way, maybe he feels he's tough, strong, bad, insane, and they'll try to incorporate those feelings into a physical walk or gait, or the way they stand sometimes.

Gang members often have a neat appearance (J. Katz, 1988). Style is a way for them to appear affluent. *Cholos*, J. Katz (1988) notes, will assume a squatting position, whereby they are looking up at others, but down their noses—similar to how the aristocracy views the peasants. This allows them to transcend and embrace their marginalized status. The names of gangs are another way they promote themselves as larger than life. Themes that emerge include religion (e.g., the Bishops, the Chaplains), nobility (e.g., Duke, Viceroys, various forms of Lords, and various forms of Kings), medieval times (e.g., Cavaliers, Bishops, and various forms of Knights), predators (e.g., Hawks, Falcons, Cobras), and the supernatural (e.g., Satan's Disciples, Vampires; J. Katz, 1988; Schneider, 1999).

Colors are important because they help identify a youth as a member of a particular gang. What is confusing is that *all* colors are related to gangs. The LAPD describes gang colors on their website:

> The "Crips" identify themselves with the colors of blue or black or a combination of the two. "Blood" gangs generally use red accessories, such as caps or bandanas, to identify themselves. . . . Green can either mean the gang member is declaring neutrality for the

---

3 Having said this, from around 2006 until at least the early 2010s, slim-fit or skinny jeans were fashionable for males and females. According to an interventionist, teenage African American gang members in the southern parts of Los Angeles have been known to wear such clothing. As such, gang youth wear clothing that reflects a general youth style but also wear and adopt clothing so as to also influence this general style. Sagging clothing might have first emerged within gang culture, but has been a part of mainstream youth culture for decades.

moment or is a drug dealer. Black is worn by some Hispanic gangs and Heavy Metal Anglo gangs. Other common gang colors include brown or purple.[4]

Symbols are ways in which marginalized gang youth reinvent forms of communication (Ferrell, 1999). Hand signs are used as a way to communicate with one another or disrespect other gang members.[5] Hand signs also appear in graffiti (Alonso, 1998).

Bricolage within gang culture relates to wearing professional sports teams' clothing, but using the team's logos, symbols, or colors for gang purposes (Booth, 2008; Castanon, 2008; J. A. Miller, 1995; W. B. Sanders, 1994). Many gangs in different parts of the United States wear San Francisco 49er hats and shirts. This may suggest the individuals are fans, but within gang culture there could also be different meanings. The main colors of the 49ers are red and gold. Red is also the color worn by Latino street gangs in Northern California that are affiliated with Nuestra Familia, a prison gang. By wearing 49er gear with red in it, the gang youth could be showing their allegiance to Nuestra Familia while cloaking it in loyalty to an NFL team based in the region. Another aspect of both 49er gear and that of the city's baseball club, the Giants, is their logo, SF. Gangs that have these initials in their name, such as San Fernando or Santa Fe, will also appropriate 49er or Giants baseball hats to display their allegiance to their gang.

Numerous other examples are evident across the United States. Baseball hats that have a G, such as for the Green Bay Packers or Georgetown Hoyas, could be used to convey allegiance to the Gangster Disciples or gangs from areas that begin with the letter G, such as Gardena in Los Angeles. Los Angeles Kings clothing may reflect membership in the Latin Kings, the People, or the Folks.

One of the more famous sports teams in relation to gangs is the Los Angeles Raiders. The team has black and silver colors and a one-eyed mascot in front of crossed sabers. Because Los Angeles is home to some of the largest and most notorious gangs, as well as some of the most expensive riots in U.S. history, Raider clothing is a good fit with gangs in the city (Burke and Sunley, 1998). The members of NWA—one of the first major gangsta rap groups—also cemented the association of gangs and the Raiders by wearing baseball hats with the team's names and logos.

African American gangs were among the first to use recognizable symbols from well-known companies (Alonso, 1998) such as Calvin Klein, whose initials, CK, are worn by members of blood sets to indicate they are Crip Killers. British Knights shoes and Burger King restaurants have the initials BK and Crips wear clothing advertising these businesses to suggest they are Blood Killers (J. A. Miller, 1995). The Vice Lords wear Louis Vuitton apparel because the LV logo in reverse represents them. Gangs within the People Nation use Starter brand merchandise, whose logo is a five-point star, because this has significance for them.[6] The Warner Brothers iconic symbol, WB, has been used by the West Boulevard

---

4   Visit http://www.lapdonline.org/get_informed/content_basic_view/23468/.

5   To see the hand signs of numerous gangs, visit http://members.tripod.com/westside_crip/id18.htm/ and http://www.chicagogangs.org/index.php?pr=HAND_MAIN/.

6   For websites that provide lists of gangs that use sports team logos as a way to display their gang affiliation, please visit the following: http://www.ncgangcops.org/archives/Team%20Logos.pdf/ and http://www.corrections.com/news/article/23317-gang-clothing-your-favorite-sports-team/.

Crips in their graffiti (Alonso, 1998). White racist gang members also use this symbol to represent White Boy.

INTERPRETING GRAFFITI

Most graffiti is not gang related (Alonso, 1998; Ferrell, 2008; Shelden et al., 2001). Some graffiti is artistic, and it captivates a large global audience (Coffield, 1991; N. MacDonald, 2001; Phillips, 1999; Shelden et al., 2001). Much of graffiti is tagging—the writing of names (the word tagging is short for name tag). The purpose of tagging is to say "Here I am" and to express a love for hip-hop culture (Alonso, 1998; Coffield, 1991; Ferrell, 1996, 2008; N. MacDonald, 2001; Phillips, 1999; B. Sanders, 2005a).

Graffiti has been important in gang culture for many years. Padilla (1992, p. 2) noted that graffiti on walls and garages within the neighborhood served as "the most prominent method for communicating or displaying . . . symbols of gang cultural identification." Graffiti has various purposes, including defining territory or turf, issuing warnings or challenges, stating membership, reporting an event (e.g., the death of a member), or saying "Here we are" (Alonso, 1998; Ferrell, 2008; Klein, 1995; W. B. Sanders, 1994; Schneider, 1999; Shelden et al., 2001; Spergel, 1995; Vigil, 1988a; Weide, 2008). Graffiti by racist skinheads is directly related to violence in that its principal aim is to cause terror and intimidate racial and sexual minorities (Ferrell, 2008).

Gang graffiti is linked to danger and threat by law enforcement. The LAPD website notes, "Why gang graffiti is dangerous":

> The purpose of gang graffiti is to glorify the gang. Gang graffiti is meant to create a sense of intimidation and may increase the sense of fear within a neighborhood. . . .

> Of greater concern is the inherent violence associated with gang graffiti. When a neighborhood is marked with graffiti indicating territorial dominance, the entire area and its inhabitants become targets for violence. Anyone in the street or in their home is fair game for drive-by attacks by rival gang members. A rival gang identifies *everyone* in a neighborhood as a potential threat. Consequently, innocent residents are often subjected to gang violence by the mere presence of graffiti in their neighborhood.[7]

Gang graffiti can record and instigate violent events. It can also be used as a way to avoid such events, whereby symbolic violence (e.g., writing threats on the wall) displaces the need to commit actual violence (Ferrell, 2008). The violent and criminal rhetoric surrounding such graffiti has served to generate support for campaigns against it more broadly, whereby *all* graffiti is viewed as gang graffiti and criminalized (Ferrell, 2008). Such graffiti has also been used by commercial artists and has been copied by many youth (Hutchinson, 1993; Shelden et al., 2001).

Latino gang graffiti may contain slang terms. *Rifa* (or *Rifan* or *Rifamos*) translates to "we/ they rule" or "we/they are the best." *Con Safos* translates to "with respect" and serves as a symbolic protection from future insults.[8] For instance, graffiti that says *Lomas Rifa Con*

---

7   Emphasis in original. Retrieved from http://www.lapdonline.org/get_informed/content_basic_view/23471/.

8   *Con safos* can also be abbreviated as CSX (Shelden et al., 2001).

Safos translates to "The gang Lomas is the best and you cannot say otherwise." In other instances, the initials "LCSR" will appear near the name of the gang, which means *Locos Con Safos Rifan.* Translated, this means "The guys in this gang are crazy, they are number one, and nothing you say or do will change either of these things." Other Spanish words used within Latino gang graffiti include *Puro* (pure), *Total, Tol,* or *To* (united), and *Controlla* (controls) (Shelden et al., 2001).

Gang members cross out certain letters of graffiti that they have written. This is to show disrespect and/or issue a challenge. Bloods will cross out the letter C, just as Crips will cross out the letters B or P.[9] Blood sets that live in the city of Compton refer to it as "Bompton" as a way to signify their gang affiliation and issue a sign of disrespect to Crip sets. Crossing out the graffiti of another gang name is a sign of disrespect. The photo above shows that Eastlake has been crossed out by those from Lincoln Heights.[10]

Numbers, subgroups, and locations are represented as abbreviations, symbols, or words that have dual meaning (Shelden et al., 2001). Gangs use Roman numerals. XL identifies the Rollin 40s and XVIII represents 18th Street. Latino gangs with XIII after their name are affiliated with the Mexican Mafia (aka La Eme) because 13 is significant to them; gangs with XIV after their name are affiliated with Nuestra Familia because 14 is significant to them. Slang replaces numbers, particularly in African American graffiti. The word deuce refers to the number 2, and the Nine-Deuce Hoover are the 92nd Street Hoovers. The word trey (or tray) replaces the number 3, and the Eight Tray Gangster Crips are the 83rd Street Gangster Crips.

Many gangs are made up of subgroups that are referred to as sets or cliques. Sometimes gang graffiti will have the name of the subgroup. Members of the Rollin 60s might put up a tag with the numbers 61, 63, and 65. This tag represents members of the subgroups (or

9   Bloods are also referred to as Pirus, which is why Crips also cross out the letter P.
10   The L and H for Lincoln Heights are meshed together, where the bottom of the L forms the bridge of the H.

sets) from 61st Street, 63rd Street, and 65th Street. The subgroups could be females associated with the gang (e.g., the Locas affiliated with the larger gang the Locos) or the younger affiliates (e.g., the Tiny Locos, Midget Locos, or Pee-Wee Locos; Shelden et al., 2001). The tag might also indicate a location, with abbreviations like W/S (for Westside), N/S (for Northside), and so on (Shelden et al., 2001).

Conquergood (1997) in Chicago and Phillips (1999) in Los Angeles focused on the construction of gang graffiti and its messages. Many were clever and increasingly inventive ways of disrespecting rivals gangs through the manipulation of images. Conquergood (1997) believed that the graffiti, outside of its literal interpretation, also serves as a symbolic resistance to the degradation minority youth suffer at the hands of a society that has marginalized them (see also Alonso, 1998).

Although graffiti holds similar purposes for gangs regardless of race, Phillips (1999) draws general distinctions between Latinos and blacks. Latinos—*placas*—are more elaborate and follow a close form that has been around for decades. This style and form has been called "barrio calligraphy" (Ferrell, 2008, p. 57). The *placas*, although relaying messages for and about the gang, are similar to murals that have long been a source of ethnic pride and community solidarity in inner-city Latino neighborhoods (Ferrell, 2008; Vigil, 1988a; see the photos on this page and the next).

Phillips (1999) indicates that Latino gang graffiti in Los Angeles rarely uses symbols, as both she and Conquergood (1997) have found in Chicago. According to Phillips (1999), graffiti tends to be more of a source of pride for Latinos than for African Americans. Both Latino and African American graffiti share much in common. They cross out the names of rivals, write the names of members, and provide geographical references and symbolic representations. Phillips's findings echo the earlier work of Hutchinson (1993), who examined differences in graffiti between Los Angeles and Chicago. In Chicago, Hutchinson (1993) found, gangs use more symbols (e.g., the five-point star to represent the Latin

Kings), whereas in Los Angeles such graffiti was often *placas*. Alonso (1998) notes that African American graffiti is usually constructed in block or square writing and is referred to as "hit ups."

Some graffiti has hidden connotations. Take, for instance, a 2012 image located in Jefferson Park in Chicago.[11] The image is the head of a king with a five-point crown. This likely means that the gang is the Latin Kings, who are also part of a larger conglomeration of gangs called the Peoples Nation (the five-point crown has significance because the number 5 is important for this collective). What is uncertain is the meaning of the tear on the king's face. Tears in gang culture usually represent death, but in this piece, no consensus has been reached as to the exact meaning. Some believe the tear means a member has been killed, and when the tear is filled in, it means the gang has avenged the death. Others claim that the tear does not mean a death, but that someone in the gang has committed murder. Still others posit that the tear only means that someone close to the person who drew the graffiti has died, and the death may have nothing to do with the gang.

The meaning of arrows within Latino graffiti is uncertain. Sometimes the arrows are pointing down (see the photo on the next page), which carries multiple interpretations. In one interpretation, the arrow is believed to be pointing south, suggesting that the gang is affiliated with La Eme (*surenos*). Others believe the arrow is a geographical indicator of the beginning of that gang's territory or is simply used to say "We are here."[12]

---

11 For the image, visit http://news.medill.northwestern.edu/chicago/news.aspx?id=200952/ or http://www .graffitizen.com/g/latin-kings-graffiti-symbols/deciphering-gang-graffiti-isn-39-t-easy-as-experts-disagree -on-2870/.

12 For more on this discussion of the meaning of arrows, visit http://www.corrections.com/news/article/ 29911-sureno-gang-graffiti-understanding-the-art-of-war/ and http://www.oncentral.org/news/2012/03/07/ know-your-graffiti-disses-threats-and-mexican-mafi/.

GANGSTA RAP

Many youth listen to gangsta rap music, as do real gangsters. The themes of violence, sex, misogyny, drugs, and antiauthority, as well as the look of the artists, help criminalize gang members. Artists, producers, record company executives, and/or retailers of this music have been persecuted by the criminal justice system for obscenity (Deflem, 1993; Ferrell and Sanders, 1995a; Southgate, 2008). Gangsta rap has been at the center of political and public protest, with accusations that the music promotes and causes youth crime (Hamm and Ferrell, 1994). Public outrage about the music young people listen to is not new, and gangsta rap is just one in a long line of musical types outlawed by the parent culture.

According to Lyddane (2009), gangsta rap offers insight into the mentality of gang members. *Rather* than reflecting a general lifestyle, Lyddane contends that real-life gangsters' rap reveals their criminal behaviors. Their talk about making large amounts of money selling drugs is real. The profits from making music serve as a way to launder money from drug sales. At times, the song lyrics offer law enforcement clues that form the basis of successful investigative leads and have been used as evidence in court. Lyddane suggests that law enforcement might watch local radio stations that attract gang members because some of these members could be aspiring rappers providing coded messages.[13]

---

13 In 2014, a San Diego–based rapper, Tiny Doo, with no criminal convictions was charged with a gang allegation because he rapped about murders that were committed by gang members. Visit http://www.nbcsandiego.com/news/local/Rapper-Tiny-Doo-to-Stand-Trial-on-Gang-Conspiracy-Charges-for-Lyrics-284829561.html/.

Hagedorn (2008) views hip-hop music as a way for those involved in gangs to give meaning to their lives and to empower themselves (see also Fernando, 1995; George, 1998; Rose, 1994). Hagedorn argues that as society understands the music members listen to, they will have a better understanding of those individuals. Hip-hop music serves as an emotional outlet after years of subjugation of a white racist society, following blues and reggae before it. "Gangsta rap is the power of the negativity to keep on living in the awareness of ghetto conditions that are unlikely to be improved by government, business, or liberal whites" (Hagedorn, 2008, p. 88).

An irony about this hype is that publically condemning gangsta rap serves to attract more young people to it (see G. C. Brown et al., 2012). Controversy makes money, which record industries are aware of (see *Media Check!*). Most of the youth that listen to gangsta rap are law abiding. Even fewer are actual gang members. History suggests that gangsta rappers rarely participate in the behaviors they rap about. The artists want to give the impression that they are criminals or gangsters because that image sells albums and makes people rich (Hagedorn, 2008).

Southgate (2008) discusses the impact that the Parents' Music Resource Center (PMRC) had on the music industry and how gangsta rap was a principal source of important change. The PMRC's original members consisted of politician's wives, including the wife of former vice president Al Gore, but their core was fundamental religious groups and parents. They sought to warn parents about material that mentioned sex, drugs, and violence—staples of gangsta rap and rock 'n' roll. PMRC pressured the Recording Industry Association of America to place a sticker on recordings containing these themes that said "Parental Advisory—Explicit Lyrics." Southgate (2008) notes many claims of bias against black artists then began to emerge. Country and bluegrass music, which is sung largely by white artists and also contains messages about sex, violence, and drugs, did not require the sticker. This double standard emerged as racist and asymmetrical (Southgate, 2008).

HOMOLOGY, DIFFUSION, AND CRIMINALIZATION

Gang style reflects behavior. Willis (1978) calls this a homology—a sameness between the action and culture of young people. Homologies are when "items parallel and reflect the structure, style, typical concerns, attitudes and feelings" of a group whereby there exists a "continuous play between the group and a particular item which produces specific styles, meanings, contents and forms of consciousness" (Willis, 1978, p. 191).

Youth who want to become gang members can stylize themselves in this way. This helps crystallize their identities, as well as how others *react* to them. Their style of sagging clothes, bandanas, and tattoos helps construct a hard image. Gangsta rap, with its themes of violence, drugs, and antiauthority, radiates danger. Drug use, hanging out, and delinquency are aspects of their lives and the music they listen to reflects them. This is part of the reflexive nature between their culture and their actions (B. Sanders, 2005a, 2012). The various aspects that constitute gang style—the tough look, aggressive music, strut—illuminates members' "structure of feeling and characteristic concerns" (Willis, 1978, p. 4). Style is an indicator of behavior.

Gang style has been diffused into the mainstream and is now popular. The mass media are responsible for its spread throughout Middle America (Lyddane, 2009). Music videos were a primary culprit:

> Those in rap videos who falsely posture as gang members are responsible for the proliferation and bastardization of gang culture. This in turn has led to there being copycat gangs across the country that try to fit their frame of reference into contours of L.A. gangs like the Crips/Bloods. In turn, you have a crop of gangs popping up that have no structure, unity, loyalty and knowledge of the particular set they are claiming. (George, 2007, as quoted in Hagedorn, 2008, p. 84)

This diffusion is partially responsible for youth identifying as gang members (Klein, 1995; J. A. Miller, 1995). Gangs were not really a hot media topic until the mid- to late 1980s, around the same time crack cocaine emerged (J. Katz, 2000). Crack, gangsta rap, and violent movies about gangs (e.g., *Colors, Boyz n the Hood, Menace II Society*) all aided in the construction of gang members being a new, modern folk devil.

White, middle-class youth are the largest consumers of gangsta rap music, and many talk, walk, and dress the part (McCorkle and Miethe, 1998). This diffusion can have at least two negative ramifications. First, youth who do not have the risk backgrounds of gang members or are not associated with them may be unnecessarily stopped and questioned by the police (McCorkle and Miethe, 1998). Second, youth could further mimic the gang lifestyle by committing crimes. As McCorkle and Miethe (1998, p. 58) note, "today's celebration of the gang culture by middle-class youths is blurring moral boundaries and fostering 'in-group' deviance even in the best-ordered communities."

An example of this diffusion is how the *cholo* look has been advertised. This look is a conglomeration of fashions worn by some gang members. One is freshly pressed khaki trousers, a t-shirt under a flannel shirt (especially Pendleton-brand flannels) buttoned only at the top, Nike Cortez shoes, and hair shaved short and/or slicked back with a hair net (J. Katz, 1988). Another style is wearing shorts that extend below the knee, socks hiked up as far as they go, and a white cotton tank top, colloquially referred to as a wife beater. These styles have been advertised as popular fashion and have been around for decades.

Gang style has been criminalized. Looking like a gangster can get someone in trouble because distinguishing between people who look like gang members and those who are bona fide members is difficult. When gangs go looking to do harm, they attack based on attire (J. A. Miller, 1995). Most colors represent gangs, and sagging clothing is a popular fashion. The LAPD website provides the following description of gang attire:

> Gang clothing styles can be easily detected because of the specific way gang members wear their clothing. Examples are preferences for wearing baggy or "sagging" pants or having baseball caps turned at an angle. Gang members . . . like to wear plaid shirts in either blue, brown, black or red. These shirts are worn loosely and untucked. . . . Excessive amounts of dark clothing or a predominance of one-color outfits, white T-shirts and Levis with up-turned cuffs are also indicators of possible gang involvement. . . . Other signs that

BOX 7.1: ON TRIAL

A young woman was tagging (i.e., spray painting) the name of a well-known African American gang in an alley on a building, along with other signs and symbols indicating the gang is the baddest. She was doing this tagging in an area with dozens of different gangs in part of the city with a long tradition of gang activity. Unfortunately for the young lady (and something that happens with amazing regularity), the police drove by while she was tagging. She was arrested and charged with felony vandalism—a predicate offense—to which the gang enhancement was added. The police said that the gang graffiti serves to act as a territory marker and to cause fear among other gangs and average community members.

This incident might seem like a case of a member tagging the name of their gang. But here is the catch: the young woman has no history of gang involvement, no previous gang-related offending, and no official record that she is a gang member. She does not self-admit to being in a gang and the police have no field interview (or FI) card that indicates gang involvement. The young woman has never even been arrested before. She does have a history of tagging and self-admits to being part of a "tagging crew," the name of which is tattooed on her. She has an FI card that says she is a member of this tagging crew. The question is, why would she tag the name of a gang she is not a part of? The prosecution believed that members of this gang provided her with spray paint cans and additional incentive to go out and tag their name and symbols in various places. They said that this tagging helps create terror in the community and helps the gang reassert its dominance. The defense argued that dozens of gangs existed in the area and that this young lady tagged the name of the particular gang on her own to provoke the other gangs into action. She was caught writing this graffiti in an area that serves as the intersection of at least three territories from different gangs. By tagging the name of one of these gangs, the defense continued, she and her friends were trying to stir intergang rivalries. The young woman has a shallow history of offending and no history of gang involvement. The only thing that has ever linked her to this gang at all is the fact that she was caught tagging its name. For the prosecution, this was enough evidence to suggest membership.

Outside of questioning her gang membership simply based on tagging its name, the defense argued that the graffiti itself does not constitute a predicate offense. Enhancements can only be applied to felony vandalism, the threshold for which is $400 worth of damage. If it costs less than $400 to clean up, the vandalism would only reach the level of a misdemeanor and the enhancements could not be applied. So how is the cost of the damage ascertained? The city uses a formula that provides exact costs to remove different types of graffiti based on where the graffiti is (e.g., curb, light, sidewalk) and the type of removal needed (e.g., chemicals, pressure washing). Administrative costs such as staffing, gasoline, travel time, and insurance are also included. Taken together, about two dozen different costs emerge for the removal of various types of graffiti. Of these costs, one-third are less than $400—meaning they are not felonies. In other words, the city's costs associated with removing two-thirds of all graffiti bring such graffiti to the felony level. Given this, gang enhancements can be applied to most graffiti cases.

The defense provided alternative methods to remove the graffiti, all of which were at a substantially lower cost than those indicated by the city and none of which would result in a felony charge. One method was to use the cost of graffiti removal as indicated by another community-based organization that specifically provides gang graffiti removal services (and is subcontracted by the city to remove gang graffiti). The estimate provided by that organization was half the estimate of the city and would not reach $400. If it were not for the administrative fees added by the city to the costs of graffiti removal, such graffiti would not reach the level of felony vandalism. A second calculation was the cost to hire day laborers given the right amount of paint, brushes, and time to do the job. Through this method, the cost to clean up the graffiti would have been about $150.

The defense concluded with two important points. First, they argued that allowing gang enhancements in this case would set a dangerous precedent in that all it would take to establish gang membership is writing a name on a wall. The only evidence presented that this young woman was in a gang was her tagging. The second point concerned the way in which felony vandalism was established. If the graffiti were cleaned up using methods alternative to the city's formula, fewer felony vandalism would be recorded, making enhancements more difficult to apply.

youngsters may have joined gangs include . . . females wearing heavy eye make-up and dark lipstick, fingernails painted a certain color, certain undergarments, gang-colored shoelaces in their athletic shoes and specific hairstyles (such as shaving their heads bald, hair nets, rollers or braids).[14]

---

14 Visit http://www.lapdonline.org/get_informed/content_basic_view/23468/.

J. A. Miller (1995) found that law enforcement determine youths' levels of gang involvement, how dangerous they are, and the levels of disrespect they are willing to achieve through their style. Those members whose tag was visible and/or had gang tattoos were considered more involved (J. A. Miller, 1995). The style itself has become criminalized and, in the minds of law enforcement, justifies punitive responses (J. A. Miller, 1995). J. A. Miller (1995) notes that gang clothing has been outlawed by the Los Angeles County Probation Department, and youth on probation were forbidden to wear baggy clothing, certain hats, and colors. Photographs or drawings that could be interpreted as gang related could be used in court as evidence of violating the terms of probation (J. A. Miller, 1995). Community members' interpretations of gang style limit members' mobility. Tattoos, colors, and other insignia that associate them as members compromise their safety the moment they step out of their own territory (J. A. Miller, 1995).

THE MASS MEDIA

The mass media have a perennial fascination with gangs. Gang crimes captivate the public's attention and attract advertisers to television, websites, and the print media. News about gang crimes leads to the misperception that everyone is at risk when the actual threat is slim, if at all.

Gangs largely commit their offenses within their own community, and violence is targeted at other members. Media portrayals help generate fear among the general population, particularly when innocents are mistakenly killed. These incidents—although incredibly rare—are depicted as commonplace and on the increase, leading to demands that the police take action. More resources for gang suppression tactics and policies are then requested. Such incidents have led to multimillion-dollar approaches toward gangs—some of which have been massive wastes of money (Klein and Maxson, 2006; J. Lane and Meeker, 2000). Time passes and the public forgets, although the overall threat has not changed. This pattern repeats itself: gang crimes captivate the public's attention, followed by a phase of reaction and then a period of indifference until another captivating incident occurs, *ad infinitum*. Media portraits of gangs fit a pattern of fearmongering and overreaction referred to as a moral panic (Brotherton, 2008b; Esbensen and Tusinski, 2007; Ferrell, 2008; J. Katz, 2000; McCorkle and Miethe, 1998; J. A. Miller, 1995; cf. Chibnall, 1977; S. Cohen, 1972; Critcher, 2008; Ericson et al., 1987; Goode and Ben-Yehuda, 1994; Sparks, 1992).

Researchers have examined gang crime within the print media (Esbensen and Tusinski, 2007; J. Katz, 2000; Lane and Meeker, 2000; P. Perrone and Chesney-Lind, 1997; C. Y. Thompson et al., 2000). C. Y. Thompson et al. (2000) found that over a six-year period, the media averaged two gang stories a day. Gang rape was used to describe rape committed by several individuals, but only in some cases were the rapists actual gang members. A common message was that everyone was at risk from gang violence, that innocent bystanders were often victims, that get-tough policies were the only rational response, and that gangs have international connections. The authors found more stories about community responses to gangs than to stories of gang crimes, leading them to conclude that reporting on gangs was "perhaps a bigger part than actual gang activity" (C. Y. Thompson et al., 2000, p. 425; see also J. Katz, 2000; P. Perrone and Chesney-Lind, 1997).

BOX 7.2: MEDIA CHECK!

CB4

Style, media, moral panic, and gangsta rap: the spoof documentary *CB4* offers a wonderful parody and reflection. *CB4* is to gangsta rap what *This Is Spinal Tap* is to heavy metal—a satirical take on a musical genre (with a few hidden truths). *CB4* lampoons numerous aspects about gangsta rap that emerged in the late 1980s and early 1990s and the overall hysteria surrounding gangsta rap.

The movie centers on the efforts of three middle-class black guys who want to be hip-hop artists. Noting the popularity of gangsta rap, they embark on a mission to reinvent themselves. But, being middle class, they are far removed from the inner-city street life that gave birth to hip-hop. They meet with a criminal, Gusto, who declines to help them. By happenstance during this meeting, the cops rush in and arrest Gusto. Gusto thinks the guys set him up, which leads to all sorts of hilarity. The lead rapper, played by Chris Rock, takes the name MC Gusto. He is inspired by the location where the real Gusto is incarcerated—cell block number four—and calls his band CB4. The other guys also reinvent themselves, one as Dead Mike and the other as Stab Master Arson. They claim to be from a rough inner-city area, Locash.

CB4 eventually get a recording deal by promising that they will cuss, glorify violence, and defile women with their lyrics. They are over the top throughout the movie; the more controversy they create, the larger the paychecks. CB4 mold their style and sound on the real-life gangsta rap band Niggaz with Attitude (NWA). One indication of this is the jheri-curl hairstyles worn by CB4; the band's lead rappers Ice Cube and Eazy-E, who wore this fashion back then, both have cameos in the film, and Eazy tells CB4 that they need to get a good haircut. Even more directly, CB4 has a song called *Straight outta Locash*, which is set to a similar rhythm as NWA's classic *Straight outta Compton*. In their video, CB4 tear through a giant map of Locash just as NWA tore through a map of Compton.

The late comedian Phil Hartman does a hilarious job as the politician Virgil Robinson, who takes up the cause against gangsta rap and the eminent threat it posed to American values. He slanders their style: "Any person who defiles America's pastime by wearing a baseball hat backwards. Well, that's an evil that speaks for itself!" CB4 is his main target. Later, Hartman's character notices that his son is a fan of this new musical genre and, enraged, decides to take the law into his own hands and hunt down the lead rapper, MC Gusto.

Despite its parody format, many truisms were evident. The movie depicts the main characters—middle-class suburbanites—who want to become hard-core gangsta rappers. Although some gangsta rappers have criminal records, many come from relatively well-to-do families. The movie takes an early jab at gangsta rap's hypocrisy: they champion authenticity but are themselves unauthentic, rapping about behaviors that they have not performed or urban environments in which they have never lived. The director of the documentary is white and, to underscore this point, his last name is White and the title of the movie within a movie is *A Rapumentary by A. White*. This terminology reflects the fact that the largest consumers of gangsta rap are middle-class white youth, as well as how a record label that produced gangsta rap in the early years was cofounded by a white man. The moral decay allegedly caused by gangsta rap and proselytized by Hartman's character as well as the criminalization of fashion worn by gang members reflect real events. So, too, does the obscenity trial parodied in the film. When the film was released, gangsta rap was one of the latest controversies to emerge from pop culture. A final truism, perhaps even a message of the film, was that acting like a gangster can have real-life negative repercussions. MC Gusto's whole facade caused him problems and he learns the best way to avoid such problems is to keep it real.

See YouTube for links to the trailer for CB4 *and the music video for their song,* Straight outta Locash.

Reporting on gangs creates fear among those least likely to be victimized. This happened in Orange County, California. Despite the megawealthy, beachfront communities, small pockets of poverty exist and within them are gangs. Lane and Meeker (2000) reviewed public attitudes within Orange County newspapers. They found that the reportage made the "concern about gangs more universal" (Lane and Meeker, 2000, p. 514). The authors note that the majority of those sampled were white, but most of the gangs were Latino. As a result, "many [white] people in the area avoid those areas that are primarily Latino because they are afraid of . . . gangs" (p. 516).

The false impression that gang violence is everywhere has been perpetuated across the United States. The "big three" weekly magazines, *Time*, *Newsweek*, and *U.S. News & World*

Report, have exaggerated the threat of gangs (Esbensen and Tusinski, 2007). Esbensen and Tusinski (2007) reviewed close to three decades' worth of reportage and found inaccurate information. None of the articles examined defined what gangs meant, but portrayed all of them as organized, profit oriented, and violent. Esbensen and Tusinski (2007) said that reporters used brutal terminology to describe gang murders, many of which were tied to drug selling. Most of the reports portrayed gangs as highly organized and tightly disciplined. These erroneous depictions skewed public perceptions about the actual threat gangs posed and helped generate fear (see also P. Perrone and Chesney-Lind, 1997). One of these weeklies said that the majority of victims of gang violence were innocent bystanders (Shelden et al., 2001). Sentinel data on mortality statistics associated with gang homicides indicate that innocent bystanders are rarely killed and that they are about as likely to be killed in non-gang homicides (Centers for Disease Control and Prevention, 2012).

The mass media hype the gang threat because it serves as a proxy for larger issues. C. Y. Thompson et al. (2000) reported that race and school policies are tied to discussions about how to respond to gangs (see also Hagedorn, 1998). C. Y. Thompson et al. (2000) argued that the newspapers simultaneously viewed gangs as a "symptom and as a consequence" (p. 427) of the threat to public safety. Lane and Meeker (2000) note that gang crime is a code language for larger issues of race and class. Gangs constitute a large part of the public's general fear of crime. By suggesting that gang members kill innocent bystanders, the mass media help fuel the idea of such violence as random, whereby everyone is at risk. This, in turn, helps generate support for additional anti-gang or crime policies (J. Katz, 2000; McCorkle and Miethe, 1998).

MORAL PANICS, POLICY, AND OTHER OUTCOMES

Moral panic is a sociological construction that helps "expose the processes involved in creating concern about a social problem; concern that bore little relationship to the reality of the problem, but nevertheless provided the basis for a shift in social or legal codes" (Rohloff and Wright, 2010, p. 404). The origin of the phrase moral panic to capture these processes is generally attributed to Stan Cohen (1972). His work focuses on an incident involving the Mods and Rockers in the 1960s in a British seaside resort town. These groups were spectacular youth subcultures that many identified with (Brake, 1985; S. Hall and Jefferson, 1976). S. Cohen illustrates how media attention to a few isolated events led to the perception that violence was amplified between youth. The media called these small altercations "riots" and "battles" that culminated in an "orgy of destruction" (S. Cohen, 1972, p. 26). A result was the call for more law and order across the United Kingdom, and significant legislation was passed. Additional attention to the problem of delinquency led to more police actions, which in turn led to significant increases in the numbers of young people arrested. Moral panics were sequential and occurred in different stages among principal actors: the mass media and the public and what Cohen called moral entrepreneurs and the control culture.

The inventory stage is where the media play an important role in producing a social reaction to images of deviance. Processes of exaggeration and distortion of what actually happened occur, and the real event is blown out of proportion. *Symbolization* happens when the images of the event and those involved are equated with threat. These reports and images are shown repeatedly, and the event and those associated become the new folk devil. This allows the public to direct its concern to an archetype: someone or something tangible and easily identifiable. Next, the moral brigade emerges—politicians, clergy, editors—who, in combination with so-called experts (academics?), come in to explain the nature and scope of the folk devil. They want to tell people why this is happening and make gloomy predictions if immediate action is not taken.

The stage has now been set for panic. Enter the moral entrepreneurs: individuals who have designed effective and meaningful methods, programs, or interventions. Whether these methods work is irrelevant because the entrepreneurs are being sold as the answer. They influence the control culture—those with institutional power, such as the justice systems and politicians. The control culture is now sensitized to this folk devil, often noting it now has national, as opposed to local, ramifications. It advocates for new measures aimed at curtailing the folk devil, what S. Cohen refers to as innovation. The main audience is the public and their opinion, because the primary consequence of the moral panic is a real or imagined change in the law or its enforcement. Whether the folk devil has been tackled is irrelevant; all that matters is the *perception* of the appropriateness of the response in the public mind (see also Critcher, 2008; Goode and Ben-Yehuda, 1994).

Moral panics happen because society needs a boogeyman—something that it can condemn (S. Cohen, 1972; Critcher, 2008). They "fulfill a function of reaffirming society's moral values" (Critcher, 2008, p. 1130). In some cases, the moral panic is genuine: people really are afraid of something, a source Goode and Ben-Yehuda (1994) call the grass-roots model. Reasons for moral panics are *not* authentic. Moral panics generate money or support for a cause because of the fear they cause. Glassner (2002) notes the "immense power and money that await individuals who can tap into Americans' moral insecurities for their own benefit" (p. 819) and that fearmongering may be created to sell a candidate or an approach to a problem. Major policy initiatives are at stake, as well as millions of dollars (Glassner, 2000, 2002). Money is related to institutional legacy—the establishment of new laws, agencies, and jobs—and normative transformations—the acceptability of new behaviors that "redraw society's moral boundaries" (Critcher, 2008, p. 1133; Goode and Ben-Yehuda, 1994).

Moral panics can be used to create a diversion and serve as "the transposition of fear" (Young, 2008, p. 176). Glassner (2000, 2002) indicates that a key feature of fearmongering is misdirection: helping focus community resources at targets and removing attention from critical concerns. Glassner uses the analogy of a magician attempting to steer the view of the audience away from the trick. When mass shootings happen, rather than argue against the widespread availability of firearms or the lack of stringent background checks to obtain them, the focus instead is on the influence of violent video games or alternative music (Glassner, 2002; see also Killingbeck, 2001). Goode and Ben-Yehuda (1994) refer to this as the elite-engineered model, when an organization run by the rich and powerful creates and/or exaggerates a threat to divert attention away from something embarrassing or toward something lucrative.

Crime is routinely presented as a moral panic (Glassner, 2000; S. Hall et al., 1978; Lane and Meeker, 2000; Sparks, 1992; Surette, 1992; C. Y. Thompson et al., 2000). Crime rates are believed to be skyrocketing or soaring when in fact they have been declining. This belief is not surprising given how skewed such data appear in the media. As Glassner (2002) found, between 1990 and 1998 the number of stories about murder on network newscasts increased by 600% although the murder rate dropped about 20% (see also P. Perrone and Chesney-Lind, 1997). Stories on crime are the staple of news shows. Some crimes receive more attention, particularly school shootings (Critcher, 2008; Glassner, 2000). These incidents are rare and isolated, but they are portrayed as being on the rise (Glassner, 2000, 2002; Killingbeck, 2001). Drugs are another example. From crack cocaine to ecstasy to crystal methamphetamine to medical marijuana, a pattern of hype is evident and the supposed threat does not match empirical reality (see Omori, 2013; B. Sanders, 2006b).

Gangs have been discussed in relation to moral panics (Brotherton, 2008b; Ferrell, 2008; P. Jackson and Rudman, 1993; J. Katz, 2000; McCorkle and Miethe, 1998; P. Perrone and Chesney-Lind, 1997; C. Y. Thompson et al., 2000; Zatz, 1987). Zatz (1987) argues that the Phoenix police in the 1970s exaggerated the role gangs played in crimes and sensationalized the few crimes that were committed. She found evidence that police inflated the number of members and the overall size of gangs and offered warnings of grave consequences if immediate action was not taken. The focus was on Chicano youth. Zatz revealed juvenile court records that indicated Chicano youth gang members were mostly arrested for fighting and relatively small property crimes—not the brutally violent or drug-involved crimes that law enforcement believed they committed. Zatz concluded that Chicano gang youth posed no more of a threat to society than non-gang youth.

McCorkle and Miethe (1998) note that, before the mid-1980s, Las Vegas did not have a gang problem. A wave of interest in gangs began to emerge; whereas in 1985 the city had 1,000 members, in 1986 that number skyrocketed to 4,000. This was accompanied by an increase in the news stories; in 1983, a couple of stories were reported, but by the end of the decade well over a hundred emerged. Law enforcement began focusing more on gangs. New laws targeting activity materialized, and policies faced little obstruction and passed with relative ease. By the early 1990s, the wave had rolled by. The police had significantly disrupted gang activity in Las Vegas, with hard-core members now serving lengthy prison sentences. The newspapers printed fewer stories and focused on a new menace: radioactive waste. McCorkle and Miethe (1998) argued that the official response to gangs in Las Vegas was overblown given the actual number of members and their contribution to overall crime. They were responsible for a fraction of all violent crimes, and drug offenses among them were nearly nonexistent. This conflicted with the message from law enforcement about the inexorable link among gangs, violence, and drugs. McCorkle and Miethe (1998) reported that many of those convicted under anti-gang laws were *not* members and most (~90%) of the gang enhancement charges were dismissed.

The media are not inventing stories about gangs. They obtain their information from the police (J. Katz, 2000; McCorkle and Miethe, 1998; Zatz, 1987; see also Chibnall, 1977; Ericson et al., 1987; S. Hall et al., 1978). An important question to ask is, Who benefits from the media hype about gangs? The answer is the police. What we see with gangs is that the police feed the media exaggerated stories to scare the public, which in turn drums up support for legislation that provides more money and resources to the police. Media stories influence policy. Decker and Kempf-Leonard (1991) report that gang policy makers receive their knowledge from the media. Other researchers have argued that lawmakers are influenced by media stereotypes of gangs as uberviolent, drug-selling masterminds, with knowledge in advanced weaponry (McCorkle and Miethe, 1998). By inflating the threat, law enforcement and other agencies stand to benefit economically (J. Katz, 2000; McCorkle and Miethe, 1998; Zatz, 1987). Zatz (1987) argued that law enforcement in Phoenix in the late 1970s hyped the Chicano gang problem to obtain funds for a new gang unit. Likewise, McCorkle and Miethe (1998) note that the Las Vegas Police Department (LVPD) were deeply impacted by a recession in the 1980s that led to hiring freezes and reduced budgets that impacted services. Gangs also serve as a distraction. The LVPD in the 1980s were facing a crisis of legitimacy because of an increase in citizen complaints, including brutality, harassment, and illegal searches (McCorkle and Miethe, 1998). The media began reporting more on gangs, and fewer reports emerged about police misconduct in the city. McCorkle and Miethe (1998, p. 57) conclude that the LVPD "created and sustained a moral panic to obtain needed resources and to repair a badly tarnished image."

Although the police help fuel moral panics for their own benefit, additional outcomes impact other aspects of society. McCorkle and Miethe (1998) point out the rise in the number of wannabe or marginal gang youth who were placed in databases kept by law enforcement in relation to how they dressed. The authors noted significant increases in the number of minority males labeled as members, which underscores the argument that policies serve as a proxy to further restrict the movements of young minority males. McCorkle and Miethe (1998) also note that the monies allocated to gangs are disproportionately high compared to the actual threat they pose.

In Los Angeles, J. Katz (2000) notes that gangs were not common news in the city until the 1980s. His point is that gangs are not as responsible for significant levels of violence in cities across the United States, particularly Los Angeles. He argues that the belief that street gangs are responsible for large amounts of violence has been generated and perpetuated to steer policy prioritizations. To support his point, Katz compares gang data between New York City and Los Angeles. Controlling for variations in demography between the two cities, if gangs do cause violence, then the criminogenic forces at work would operate differently between them. If gangs cause violence, then they should do so at equal levels, regardless of location, but this is not the case. Gangs are responsible for a significant number of violent crimes in Los Angeles—up to half of all homicides—but not in New York City. How can this be explained? One explanation is media coverage: Los Angeles prints hundreds of stories on gangs, whereas New York City produces a couple of dozen (J. Katz, 2000). Gang mythology in Los Angeles is "especially dangerous because of the relative lack of constraints that the local legal community can place on the police department" (J. Katz, 2000, p. 186).

Gangs are portrayed as immoral, indecent, lazy individuals that stand against hard work, family, and community. People like to read about how society is winning the "war on gangs" and need high-profile stories about successful law enforcement gang busts. The more threatened people feel about gangs, the better they will feel when stories about their demise are published (J. Katz, 2000; C. Y. Thompson et al., 2000). By escalating the gang threat, the feel-good factor can be achieved. And feeling good—being entertained—is a major function of the mass media.

THE INTERNET

Gangs are on the Internet.[15] Their presence includes web pages devoted to their gang, blogs, and the use of social media websites like MySpace and Facebook, as well as social networking applications like Twitter. Gang websites display the gang's colors, hand signs, and symbols, with pictures of members or cartoon images. Gangsta rap soundtracks play, and hyperlinks are provided to other rap songs or videos posted on YouTube, often by rappers from that gang. Many have images of and links to pornography. Blogs are dedicated to opinions and information, and gang members (or those posing as them) use them to brag or issue threats with derogatory statements and profanity (see *Streetgangs.com* and the links at the end of the chapter).

Gang members use the Internet for similar reasons as other young people—to socialize, organize parties, make new friends, and post videos (Decker and Pyrooz, 2011; King et al., 2007; National Gang Intelligence Center, 2009). They might use the Internet *more* than non-gang youth (Pyrooz, Decker et al., 2013). Other researchers suggest that gangs use the Internet to help enable criminal behaviors, such as arranging drug sales or coordinating violence (National Gang Intelligence Center, 2009). The extent to which this occurs is not clear, and research has indicated that gangs rarely use the Internet for such purposes (Pyrooz, Decker et al., 2013). Members have used texts and Twitter to organize fights and insult rivals, which allows them to organize violence and issue threats much more quickly than traditional word of mouth.[16] Statements made on social media have been used against gang members as evidence in court (Holt and San Pedro, 2014; W. L. Patrick, 2012). Bragging about a gang, declaring allegiance to it, or advertising and celebrating an offense can be used to establish whether an individual is a bona fide member and whether an offense is gang related.[17]

One concern was whether gangs were using the Internet to recruit new members (Patton et al., 2013). Research has revealed that few do this (Decker and Pyrooz, 2011). One variable that helped explain whether gangs used the Internet for recruiting was the level of gang organization. Moule et al. (2014) found that gangs that were better organized were also more likely to seek new recruits online. This is counterintuitive in that gangs with higher levels of organization might be more focused on illicit enterprise and less

---

15 Gangs here refer to criminal street gangs that use the Internet. Others have referred to "online gangs" of youth who engage in a behavior known as "happy slapping": attacking strangers in public while digitally recording such events and then uploading them onto the Internet (King et al., 2007). Whether these online gangs are criminal street gangs is unclear, as is whether criminal street gangs participate in happy slapping.

16 This has been reported in New York and Chicago (see Austen, 2013; Main, 2012; Weichselbaum, 2009).

17 This is based on personal experience in two different criminal cases, one where a social media website helped establish that the individual was a gang member and another whereby a series of texts between two parties assured the credibility that the criminal threats that culminated in a homicide were gang related.

likely to advertise to law enforcement and others online (Pyrooz, Decker et al., 2013). Nonetheless, because most gangs do not appear to be organized, the likelihood is that most do not seek to recruit youths online. As with music and movies, the Internet helps spread gang culture, which has been argued as influencing the development of gangs outside of the United States and attracting youth to gangs in the first place (Decker et al., 2009; Densley, 2013; Moule et al., 2014; Sela-Shayovitz, 2012).

More than anything, gangs' main presence on the Internet is their use of blogs. Insults toward rivals and aggrandizements of their own gang are common themes (Decker and Pyrooz, 2011; National Gang Intelligence Center, 2009; Patton et al., 2013). Blogging has been argued to be the main benefit of the Internet for them because it helps further demonstrate and hone their reputations for violent prowess and skills at disrespect (Decker and Pyrooz, 2011; Densley, 2013). Bragging and disrespecting are referred to as Internet banging and cyber banging (Patton et al., 2013). In some cases, insults have directly led to violence. Decker and Pyrooz (2011) reported that about a quarter of their sample had attacked someone because of an insult and about one in five said that those they insulted online had attacked them (see also Densley, 2013; Pyrooz et al., 2013). Gang-related offending via the Internet is limited to the occasional real-life violent incident. In terms of members committing crime more generally on the Internet, downloading music illegally is the most common and is not gang related (Decker and Pyrooz, 2011). Compared to non-gang youth, gang youth have been found to commit more of this and other Internet-based crime (Pyrooz et al., 2013).

SUMMARY

This chapter contributes to the cultural criminology of gangs, which has examined style and the mass media in relation to gangs. Style is the overall look of the gang member, from their clothing, to their demeanor, to their way of moving about, to the music they listen to. Style is important because it offers clues about potential behaviors. Being a gang member means acting tough, and their style projects toughness. The names of the gangs resonate dread. Style is how youth do gang membership. What they wear and how they present themselves confirm their identity as a gang member and helps them establish it as their own identity. Gangsta rap serves a similar purpose. Youth listen to this music because it reflects behaviors they have participated in and environments and situations they have experienced.

Gang culture is loaded with code. Youth wear clothing with images of everyday signs and symbols, but give them new significance. Barrio calligraphy and other forms of graffiti contain minutiae that provide information and tell stories. Colors, hand signs, and lettering on clothing have more than one meaning. These are ways that gangs communicate with one another, with the community, and with rivals. Through close attention, greater interpretation of the significance of gang culture emerges.

The media likes gangs because they provide entertainment and make money. Middle-class and other youth have flocked to gang culture, absorbing the music and style. They look like gang members, act like them, and listen to music about things that gangs do. This creates confusion as to who is a true member. Noncriminal youth dressed like gang members might be stopped by the police or attacked by real gangsters. They might also be encouraged to participate in the gang lifestyle and commit crime. Non-gang minority youth from inner-city areas wear gang clothing because of its popularity. This provides law enforcement with further incentive to stop and question them about their gang status. One outcome of this is much unnecessary questioning and detainment of minority youths.

The media distort information on gangs. Isolated events are sensationalized and create terror. Moral panics lead to the misperception that everyone, everywhere is in danger, despite the reality that their threat is marginal. Society needs its bad guy and gangs play this role. Policy makers respond to the news by passing harsh legislation to combat gangs. This response puts gang communities under an additional spotlight from law enforcement, who benefit by having annual budgets increased to help tackle the threat. The disproportional amount of media coverage on gangs results in other, more pressing concerns that affect many people being ignored. Gangs are like rodeo clowns who jump into the arena to distract the bull (society) when he throws the rider (the true antagonist). When the bull focuses on the clowns, the rider is allowed to get to safety.

CHAPTER REVIEW QUESTIONS

1. Define cultural criminology. What are some of the main concepts that emerged from this field?
2. How do gang members achieve the "badass" look?
3. What are some common themes found within gang names?
4. What are some examples of gang symbols and *bricolage*? Are there any others you are aware of?
5. What is the purpose of gang graffiti? What are some differences in gang graffiti between Latino and African American gangs?
6. Discuss the diffusion and criminalization of gang culture.
7. What are some common themes found in media coverage of gangs?
8. Discuss how and why moral panics are created.
9. What are the reasons for and outcomes of moral panics about gangs?
10. Why do gang members use the Internet? How are these reasons similar and different from use of the Internet by non-gang youth?

LINKS TO GANG GRAFFITI, HAND SIGNS, TATTOOS, AND STYLE

The golden age of gang graffiti
http://www.flickr.com/photos/80643375@N00/sets/72157594333288415/

Gang graffiti, art and culture
http://hoodart.blogspot.com/

Into the abyss: Gang graffiti and other identifiers
http://people.missouristate.edu/MichaelCarlie/what_i_learned_about/gangs/graffiti_and_other_identifiers.htm/

See YouTube for videos of gang hand signs, walking patterns, and tattoos.

CHAPTER 8

THEORIES ON GANGS
AND GANG BEHAVIORS

KEY WORDS

Code of the streets: Informal rule governing interpersonal behaviors in public, particularly violence; centers around the concept of respect and how violence emerges in relation to respect.

Drug normalization thesis: An observation of substance use within a specific regional area, a research study sample, or a semipublic environment that is premised on the following characteristics: availability, acceptability, high rates of overall use, intention to use, cultural attributes (e.g., clothing, music) supportive of use, and being knowledgeable about the effects of various drugs beyond personal use.

Enhancement perspective: Argues that youth are involved in high levels of delinquency prior to joining a gang, commit more crime while part of the gang, and then decrease their involvement in crime after leaving the gang.

Facilitation perspective: Argues that youth have low levels of delinquency prior to joining a gang and after leaving it, but increase their involvement in delinquency while part of a gang.

Grounded culture theory: A theory that argues that behaviors are grounded in their meaning and can only be understood from the culture in which they arise. The theory argues that when gang members commit violence, they are expressing conventional values, not malicious, unconventional ones.

Kingism: A moral and political way of life that argues that America is a deeply racist society, that so-called Latino leaders have been planted by the dominant society to cause subterfuge and as a resistance to colonial social control.

Locura: As defined by Vigil (2003, p. 230), *locura* refers to "a state of mind . . . defined as a spectrum of behavior reflected in a type of quasi-controlled insanity." *Locura* is valued by gang members and a way to display *locura* is through violence.

Moral transcendence: Argues that violence provides gang members with excitement and seductive glory because, without it, their lives would be mundane, boring, and insignificant.

Multiple marginalization: A theory that argues that various considerations, including immigration, racism, substandard living and working conditions, family and school stresses, and negative interactions with law enforcement, have all contributed to the emergence and persistence of Latino street gangs.

Routine activities theory: A theory on criminal behaviors that focuses on the opportunity to commit crime; changes in crime rates may be related to increases or decreases in such opportunities.

Selection perspective: Argues that gang members commit more crime and violence than non-gang youth because these youth were already involved in relatively high levels of such behaviors prior to joining a gang.

Social injury hypothesis: A perspective that indicates that gang membership for females is much more violent than for males. Gang membership itself causes more violent victimization in the lives of females and worsens their overall negative experiences in the gang.

Street organization: A collective of marginalized youth that provides a source of identity, resistance, and opportunity to challenge the dominant culture, escape daily pressures, and fulfill spiritual needs.

Subculture of violence: A perspective that indicates that lower/working-class communities have a tendency to use violence as a legitimate way to solve problems. Violence is culturally acceptable and individuals do not feel guilty about committing it.

Threat: As defined by Decker (1996, p. 244) in relation to gang violence, threat is "the potential for transgressions against or physical harm to the gang, represented by the acts or presence of a rival group" that "plays a role in the origin and growth of gangs, their daily activities, and their belief systems" and "helps to define them to rival gangs, to the community, and to social institutions."

Women's liberation thesis: A perspective that suggests that women's increase in gang membership and serious gang offenses has allowed females to achiever a greater sense of liberation, empowerment, autonomy, and freedom.

Chapter Learning Objectives

- Compare perspectives on why youth join gangs and why gangs emerge.
- Discuss how theories on crime and drug use have been applied to gangs.
- Explain gender-specific perspectives on gangs.
- Differentiate among the various perspectives on gang violence.

INTRODUCTION

Gang research has shaped criminological theory. Thrasher's pioneering study contributed to the development of social disorganization theory. The theories of delinquent subcultures were essentially theories of street gangs. Many studies have examined the power of major criminological insights (e.g., strain, social disorganization, social learning) to explain gangs. These theories attempt to account for: (1) why gangs emerged, (2) why individuals join or leave gangs, or (3) a specific gang-related behavior—crime, violence, or substance use. Perspectives that have been developed to specifically explain gang phenomena are less common. A few theories outside the field of criminology have been applied to gangs. This chapter largely focuses on the insights from these latter groups of theories.

First, the chapter provides an overview of a perspective developed to help understand Latino gangs: Vigil's multiple marginalization. Next, the enhancement, selection, and facilitation perspectives are examined. Brotherton and colleagues' concept of gangs as a street organization is discussed. The extent to which gangs are liberating, harmful, or both among female gangs is then reviewed. Following, the sociological concept of drug normalization is applied to marijuana use among gang youth. Theoretical miscellanea are then offered. The second half of the chapter is about violence. Various perspectives are defined, including the concepts of threat, *locura*, the subculture of violence, masculinity, transcendence, and grounded culture. The chapter concludes by introducing a theory about fighting. It argues that normative codes supportive of violence provide motivation and routine activities provide opportunity and that, taken together, these considerations help explain a large amount of gang-related fighting.

MULTIPLE MARGINALIZATION

The connection between racial inequality and the emergence of criminal street gangs has largely been ignored (Spergel, 1995; although see Adamson, 2000; Alonso, 2004; G. C. Brown et al., 2012; Davis, 2006; Freng and Esbensen, 2007; Hagedorn, 2006a; Pyrooz et al., 2010). Pyrooz and colleagues, in a macrolevel study of U.S. cities with gang problems, reported that race was a key variable toward understanding the extent of membership, leading the authors to conclude that "those ignoring [race/ethnicity] in the gang context may be missing a key piece of the gang formation/gang membership puzzle" (Pyrooz et al., 2010, p. 884). The absence of race in the etiology of gangs is perplexing given the significant overrepresentation of blacks and Latinos within the justice system, as well as the history and impact of gangs within their communities. Vigil's (1988a, 1988b) concept of multiple marginalization focuses on race and is important for understanding the emergence and persistence of gangs.

Multiple marginalization was developed to explain gangs. It incorporates elements of social disorganization, strain, control, social learning, and subcultural theories. Vigil was a student of Joan Moore, who conducted research in East Los Angeles in the 1970s and 1980s (J. W. Moore, 1978, 1985, 1991; J. W. Moore and Devitt, 1989). Vigil examined various considerations that together explain the formation and persistence of street gangs. The research is among Latinos, but he draws parallels with how the same conditions contributed to the emergence of black and Southeast Asian gangs. The focus is on males. Vigil notes that females had the same risk factors as males, but also unique ones, including sexism, conflicting gender norms, and physical and sexual assault.

A key part of the theory concerns immigration patterns of Mexicans and Central Americans into the southwestern United States. In Los Angeles, many of these Latinos were concentrated in poor areas because of discrimination, racial steering,[1] and lack of economic resources.

Los Angeles has several large swaths of Latino neighborhoods. These include areas with a high concentration of people whose family heritage stems from El Salvador or families from specific states of Mexico (e.g., Oaxaca, Sinaloa, Michoacán). Immigration and housing patterns among Latinos were similar to those experienced by waves of Europeans coming to the United States around the turn of the 20th century. They lived in overcrowded situations, with several families housed together in units built for one family.

Overcrowding was compounded by poverty. Employment was limited to low-paying and hard-working jobs that were semiskilled or unskilled. Other Latinos were blocked because of racial discrimination, a lack of required and necessary skills, and language barriers and communication difficulties. Housing and employment did not improve for decades. Second- and third-generation Los Angeles–born Latinos faced similar blocked opportunities and limited mobility as their parents and grandparents.

Poverty, overworked parents, and a general hostility toward Latinos by the dominant society impacted two major sources of informal social control: family and school. Latino parents working long hours in low-paying jobs had little time to supervise their children. The disruptions in parenting and lack of discipline impacted the children's ability to develop self-control. Hence, youth became involved in delinquency.

School is another important institution for socialization. Vigil (1988a) notes that low-income minority youth in the United States experience a gap between what they want to be (aspirations) and what they will be (expectations). He says that minorities suffer negative and damaging experiences not only in terms of racism and prejudice, but also in terms of how Latino communities are more likely to contain inferior classrooms with little money and poor teachers with little regard for the Latino culture (see also Zatz and Portillos, 2000). Vigil argues that the school system indirectly informs low-income, Latino

---

1 Racial steering is an illegal practice whereby realtors show potential buyers houses for sale only in areas where other people from that buyer's race/ethnicity reside.

youth that they will never attain their dreams (e.g., financial success) because of the menial jobs available to them. Cultural differences exacerbate the problem. Vigil notes that Latinos viewed the U.S. school system as foreign because they were wary of their children being supervised every day by non–family members.

Multiple marginalization suggests that because family and school are not controlling some young Latinos, they drift into offending. One result of their involvement in petty crime is contact with law enforcement. This is a critical point because the justice system has become a formal source of control that has replaced informal sources.

The theory continues with the argument that Latino youth who are not at school or around family and are in trouble with the law hang around outdoors. They then come into contact with others who have gone through similar experiences. These youth then are socialized on the streets and coalesce into groups that provide friendship, protection, emotional support, and nurturing. This new group becomes their primary reference group, and the youth begin to identify strongly with it.

Over time, the gang becomes its own institution, providing a strong alternative to school and family. Latino youth for generations have experienced similar problems in family and school and the job market. As a result, they are attracted to gangs. This is how they have persisted. Vigil (2002, p. 13) defines multiple marginalization as follows:

> The persistent pattern of inferior living situations and substandard working conditions that [individuals] confront results in major family stresses and strains, deep-rooted schooling barriers and difficulties, and hostile and negative relations and interactions with law enforcement personnel. From this context, the street culture and sub-society [gang] has emerged.

The concept of multiple marginalization has received support in other studies conducted by Vigil (G. C. Brown et al., 2012; Vigil, 2008; Vigil and Yun, 1990) and others (Alonso, 2004; Covey et al., 1992; Freng and Esbensen, 2007; Krohn et al., 2011; see also Zatz and Portillos, 2000). Multiple marginalization remains an important perspective from which to understand the emergence and persistence of minority criminal street gangs. The theory has been applied to explain membership among youth from black, Salvadorian, Vietnamese, and Filipino and white communities (Freng and Esbensen, 2007; Kim et al., 2009; Vigil, 2002).

ENHANCEMENT, SELECTION, AND FACILITATION HYPOTHESES

From the Rochester Youth Developmental Study, one of the Causes and Correlates studies, three perspectives emerged to help explain why youth joined gangs and why they commit more crime and violence than nonmembers. They are called the selection, facilitation, and enhancement models (Thornberry et al., 1993, 2003, 2004).

Selection refers to the affiliation process that youths go through prior to joining. It argues that gangs recruit potential members who are like them—already involved in crime and violence or displaying a willingness to engage in such behaviors. This process reflects the "birds of a feather flock together" thesis (Lahey et al., 1999). Once part of the gang and after they leave, such youth continue to commit crime and violence. The selection model argues that the reason gang youth are more criminally involved than non-gang youth is that they were already predisposed to these behaviors. Delinquency here is related to the youth's background.

Facilitation argues that the gang contributes to the youth's participation in crime and violence. In this model, delinquency is relatively low in youths' lives prior to joining, but once members, they become involved in delinquency because of the influences of the lifestyle. After they leave the gang, they decrease their involvement to levels similar to that prior to joining. Something about gang involvement contributes to youths' overall involvement in delinquency.

Enhancement is a combination of the selection and facilitation models. Enhancement argues that youth participate in relatively high levels of crime and delinquency prior to joining, increase their involvement in such behaviors once they are part of the gang, and then decrease involvement after they leave. Gang youth commit more crime and violence than non-gang youth during all three stages, but more so during membership.

The facilitation and enhancement models have received empirical support (Bendixen et al., 2006; Esbensen and Huizinga, 1993; Gatti, Tremblay et al., 2005; Hill et al., 1999; Lacourse et al., 2003; Thornberry et al., 1993, 2003), but the selection model has not (with a few exceptions, e.g., Bendixen et al., 2006).

GANGS AS RESISTANCE

The work of Dave Brotherton and colleagues has focused on the gang as a form of resistance and represents a radical departure from the majority of discourse (Barrios, 2003, 2008; Brotherton, 2008a, 2008c; Brotherton and Barrios, 2004; Kontos, 2008). Brotherton argues that gangs have been demonized and that this perspective is cemented in the minds of academics, policy makers, and the public. The gang is a byword for societal malaise and had been linked with terrorists, organized crime, drug trafficking, prison disorder, school decay, super predators, and harm (Brotherton, 2008a).

Brotherton says that the gang "may constitute counter-hegemonic forms of both individual and collective resistance" (Brotherton, 2008a, p. 55). He utilizes a more "resistance-based theoretical orientation" (p. 56) to contextualize behaviors. The term gang is problematic and loaded with negative connotations and Brotherton and colleagues prefer street organization, which is defined as follows:

> a group formed largely by youth and adults of a marginalized social class which aims to provide its members with a resistant identity, an opportunity to be individually and collectively empowered, a voice to speak back to and challenge the dominant culture, a refuge from the stresses and strains of barrio or ghetto life and a spiritual enclave within which its own sacred rituals can be generated and practiced. (Brotherton, 2008c, p. 234; Brotherton and Barrios, 2004, p. 23)

Brotherton focused on research of the Almighty Latin King and Queen Nation (ALKQN) in New York City. He argues that the ALKQN provides its members with the opportunity to defy authority. These "oppositional gestures" increase over time and develop into behaviors that are "transformative both in terms of the self and the life worlds of actors" and serve as "conscious and/or unconscious opposition . . . to structural constraint" (Brotherton, 2008a, p. 54). The outcome of resistance is uncertain and depends on the culture of the gang and the context of their actions.

Brotherton (2008c) compares and contrasts the street organizational model to those studies in the United States (U.S. Model) and studies on youth subcultures of the Birmingham School (UK Model). All three focus on lower-class/underclass youth and the importance of symbols in culture. The street organization model goes further by incorporating racial and ethnic-based experiences, as well as the performance of gang symbols and identity (see also Garot, 2007, 2010). Unlike the other models, the street organization provides "transformative agency" (Brotherton, 2008c, p. 237) for its participants. This agency is based on three considerations: (1) youth subcultures in late modernity have become more autonomous in relation to the global corporatization; (2) youth subcultures emerge as a "hybridization of street and prison cultures" (Brotherton, 2008c, p. 237), particularly in relation to the mass incarceration of minorities; and (3) the politicalization of radical ex-inmates who bring these ideas back to their communities. History is another area whereby the street organization model differs. Although history is important within the UK models and some of the U.S. ones, within the street organization model, history is central. Here, the epochs when organizations emerged (e.g., modern to postmodern) and under which political–economic situations the emergence occurred (e.g., capitalist to postindustrial) are critical variables.

A reason that distinguishes ALKQN as a street organization as opposed to a "gang" is their culturally religious concept referred to as Kingism (Barrios, 2003, 2008; Brotheron and Barrios, 2004; Kontos, 2008). Kingism is a moral and political way of life that is distinct from other gangs and noncriminal groups. It revolves around the belief that America is a racist society and that so-called leaders in the Latino community have been planted by the dominant society to engage in subterfuge and cause distractions. In response to this, ALKQN claim be to the true ambassadors of inner-city Latino neighborhoods in terms of "socio-cultural resistance" (Barrios, 2008, p. 143). ALKQN rejected stigmatizing labels about their organization and attempted to be visible in their community, shouting out slogans such as *Amor de Rey* (Love from the King). These are ways in which they were "dedicated to resisting and ending processes of social–psychological subjugation that is the modus operandi of colonial social control" (Barrios, 2008, p. 143). One member of the ALKQN, King Crazy Dino, defined Kingism:

> Kingism as a belief, as a way of giving our blessing to the Almighty and as a way of showing love and respect to ourselves as a Latin nation did not take form or was revealed . . . that the trials and tribulations, we as Kings were having was the work of our creator to test those of us who were chosen . . . Kingism shall be a religion unto itself. It shall be a cry unto itself. It shall be a cry of unity, love, and respect to the lost Latino Nation. . . . We are the sun People of the Lion Tribe, the strong tribes that were lost and now found. (Kontos, 2008, p. 155)

Barrios (2008) indicates that ALKQN members desire conventional lifestyles. They want to complete their education, move out of the housing projects, and send their children to decent schools. Through the practice of Kingism, ALKQN were able to give meaning to their lives within a society that was becoming increasingly fragmented, competitive, and devoid of meaning. Kingism is an optimistic, positive, and forward-thinking way of dealing with life among marginalized youth experiencing poverty, unemployment, racism, and police brutality. Kingism is a form of spirituality that allows members to entertain "alternative consciousness" (Barrios, 2008, p. 145), provide them the tools to resist the current social order, and address marginalization.

WOMEN'S LIBERATION AND SOCIAL INJURY HYPOTHESES

Two hypotheses on females' participation in gangs are the women's liberation thesis and the social injury hypothesis (Curry, 1998; J. W. Moore, 1991; Nurge, 2003; C. Taylor, 1993).

The women's liberation thesis is borrowed from Adler (1975). She focused on women's increased inclusion in society vis-à-vis the women's movement in the 1960s and argued that inclusion was related to increases in female crime. The theory says that as women's opportunities for legitimate work increased, so too would their opportunities for involvement in illegal activity. Traditional gender norms were changing, allowing more women to participate in male-dominated areas—including crime. Under this perspective, the increase in female gang activity is viewed as women taking advantage of opportunities to become involved in gangs, violence, drug selling, and other offenses. By doing so, they were allowed to achieve a greater sense of freedom, autonomy, empowerment, and liberation (Curry, 1998). Nurge (2003) further extends the thesis to understand women's achievement of these qualities *within* gang cultures. By moving into the previously traditional forms of male-dominated crime, females increased their respect and social capital. Behaviors analogous to crime, such as getting crazy, were other ways to gain status and respect from other females (Harris, 1988, 1994; Vigil, 2002).

Themes of liberation and autonomy are reflected in the work of Brotherton and colleagues on the ALKQN in New York City. Brotherton and Salazar-Atias (2003) report that the gang acts as a surrogate family for females who grow up in violent and traumatic households. They join to escape the daily abuse from their biological family and learn to trust others (see also Joe and Chesney-Lind, 1995). The gang acts as a support network when a girl has problems with her real family and needs time to recuperate. For Brotherton and Salazar-Atias's girls, the gang provides key family functions such as security, safety, and support. One of their respondents talked about this:

Interviewer: What does family mean to you?

Respondent: All my Latin King/Queen nation . . . Beautiful. Love, respect, I'm treated like gold, you know, like I should've been treated, you know? That's my life. You know, if I fall, they're there to pick me up. They raised me, you know? (Brotherton and Salazar-Atias, 2003, p. 198)

Freedom and liberation via gang membership are echoed by Vigil (2002). He says that the strong history of sisterhood among African American women is also apparent within their gang culture, whereby those in gangs often support and rely on one another—similar to the interreliance shown among males. The gang offers the perception of both freedom and security.

In contrast, the social injury hypothesis says that membership is much more harmful and damaging for females than for males (Curry, 1998; Joe-Laidler and Hunt, 1997; J. W. Moore, 1991). Females face a broader array of violent victimization. Not only do they have to endure similar problems as males, such as confrontations with rivals and law enforcement, but also females are at a heightened risk for exploitation, sexual victimization, and stigmatization. Harris (1988) portrays the grim reality of females in the San Fernando Valley, including rape from males of the same gangs.

The primary targets of violence are other members (Block and Block, 1993; Decker, 1996; J. Katz, 1988; W. B. Sanders, 1994). As more females engage in violence, they are likely to experience retaliation. Like boys, girls who join gangs seeking protection find out that membership increases their likelihood of future violent victimization (Klein and Maxson, 2006). The social injury hypothesis suggests that membership for females can further marginalize their social and economic positions, as well as narrow their future prospects for conventional standards of living (Curry, 1998; Joe and Chesney-Lind, 1995; Joe-Laidler and Hunt, 2001; J. W. Moore, 1991; Nurge, 2003). J. W. Moore (1991) reports on the bleak futures common among many of Latina members in East Los Angeles.

The social injury and women's liberation theses may complement one another. The evidence suggests that both perspectives can be applied to females—that they can empower and increase victimization. Nurge (2003), in her study in Boston, set out to test both perspectives and reported on evidence to support the liberation, but not the social injury thesis. For some of the girls, membership provided them with means to different ends, such as a way to defend themselves, make money, and get out of violent relationships. Membership was positive, but drawbacks were also evident. Despite victimization, the social injury model was not seen as applicable because most girls were in violent situations *prior* to joining—many of which were more severe than those related to the gang. Others indicated that females are likely to suffer immediate and long-term negative health consequences related to their involvement, including victimization and drug addiction (J. W. Moore, 1991).

Images of both the social injury hypothesis and the liberation thesis are apparent in Vigil's (1988a, 2002) concept of multiple marginalization. He argues that the conditions that lead boys to join also apply to girls. He indicates that multiple marginalization is exacerbated by several conditions for females, including sexism, family conflict of traditional versus modern attitudes, motherhood, childrearing, and sexual victimization. Latinas have tensions because of a clash of values and norms between traditional and modern culture. The street socialization process that females must contend with is more complex because of conflicts in gender identifications and the need to be aggressive. In addition to the negative experiences that have contributed to their membership, girls must negotiate degradation and victimization. Sexual victimization in the home and further traumas on the street may lead to a "convoluted mindset" (Vigil, 2002, p. 24), someone who is attempting to live up to the reputation of a crazy person. The concept of *locura*—craziness—was valued among Latino members, and by acting this way females can gain credibility and respect (Harris, 1988; Sikes, 1997; Vigil, 1988a, 1988b). Vigil (2002) notes that females have engaged in crazy activities, becoming more involved in street culture and committing crimes alongside the men. Being seen as crazy serves as a defense mechanism. Females project the image of a crazy person to ward off potential attackers (Campbell, 1992; Harris, 1988; Sikes, 1997).

MARIJUANA NORMALIZATION

The availability, acceptability, overall number of users, and supportive cultural references of marijuana, as well as the fact that members have critical attitudes toward hard drugs and are drug wise, indicate marijuana's normalized character (MacKenzie et al., 2005; Moloney et al., 2008; B. Sanders, 2012; B. Sanders, Valdez et al., 2013). Drug normalization is considered the most influential perspective within the sociology of substance use in the 21st century (Measham and Shiner, 2009). Drug normalization has been applied to help contextualize use patterns and attitudes among regions of youth (e.g., the northwest of England; Aldridge et al., 2011; Measham et al., 2001; Parker et al., 1995, 1998, 2002), certain settings (e.g., nightclubs; B. Sanders, 2005b, 2006b), or particular groups (e.g., injection drug users; B. Sanders et al., 2008). The concept has been applied to gang members (MacKenzie et al., 2005; Moloney et al., 2008; B. Sanders, 2012). Drug normalization does not suggest that the use of all drugs is normal for all youth. It argues that the use of certain drugs—particularly marijuana—has become common behavior. The concept of normalization rejects explanations of substance use as delinquency or deviance. It focuses instead on the use of drugs within the context of pleasure and common leisure activities (Blackman, 2004; Presdee, 2000; Young, 1971, 1999). The normalization thesis offers flexibility in terms of understanding patterns of drug use among high-risk youth.

Evidence suggests marijuana normalization among members (MacKenzie et al., 2005; B. Sanders, 2012). In the Los Angeles Study,[2] most (98.3%) had ever used the drug (overall use) and more than 90% of the sample knew where to obtain it (availability). In terms of cultural supports, all youth favored hip-hop music, and some had tattoos of marijuana-related imagery (e.g., characters smoking joints). In terms of acceptability, more than half (56.7%) reported that marijuana was their drug of choice, and many offered positive views of the drug (B. Sanders, 2012):

It's cool. . . . It's healthy.

It really does help me out.

Personally, I don't really think weed is a drug. It's just like drinking beer.

I like the smell, I like the look, I like how you feel.

Honestly, if I did not smoke weed, I would probably be in jail.

I don't think it's nothing major.

---

2 See the Appendix for more on the methodology of the Los Angeles Study.

Marijuana is really not a drug . . . they are giving [it] away to people now [at] the doctor. [Marijuana] don't do nothing to you.

Like marijuana, it's like whatever, it's just a plant, you can dry it out.

Similar comments were not forthcoming about other illicit drugs used by the sample. Many members had negative views about hard drugs that stemmed from direct (i.e., their own use) and indirect experiences (i.e., friends' and families' use). These critical attitudes have been expressed elsewhere (Hunt and Joe-Laidler, 2001; J. W. Moore, 1978; C. S. Taylor, 1990; Waldorf, 1993a). Gang youth are drug wise about the use and effects of various illicit drugs beyond their own use, which is an additional aspect of marijuana normalization. The following are some responses from youth in the Los Angeles Study when asked about their opinions on crystal methamphetamine, crack cocaine, heroin, and PCP:

Cuz that's the drug my mom died over, so it was very personal. I just won't fuck with [heroin].

Wow, well, meth, I mean, will eat the shit out of your body . . . [it will] make you an ugly person.

I have a lot of older friends that I remember, that immediate family, like my grandparents, brother, sister, mom, my mom's friends—they are all on crack. Honestly, I don't like the way it works. I know what people do for crack. I know what they do. People get addicted to it. I am too scared.

[PCP's] like embalming fluid, so it's like you're basically killing yourself.

[Meth is] just something I hate. . . . It killed a friend of mine. He had a heart attack. His heart popped. . . . Then his cousin and then his brother . . . my gang team.

I am scared. My homeboy died of [heroin].

I see people do [heroin]. They wake up all crazy . . . mad, depressed. They look all funny.

I live downtown. I see what they can do. . . . I am not messing with [heroin].

They overdose on [heroin]. Some people die from the first time they take it.

Cause I used to see people that do [heroin]. They would just be in the streets, laying down and being stupid, you know?

The youth in this study have similar differential attitudes toward illicit substance as do youth across the United States. Sentinel data from Monitoring the Future and the National Survey on Drug Use and Health consistently indicate that the attitudes youth have toward illicit drugs vary. In particular, marijuana ranks higher in overall acceptability and lower in perceived health risks than drugs like heroin, cocaine (crack or powder), and crystal methamphetamine. The viewpoints of hyperoffenders (e.g., gang youth) are like those of nonoffenders (e.g., the general youth population). It becomes problematic to characterize illicit substance use among gang youth in pathological terms because the values they have about use are similar to the values of everyday youth in general who use drugs (B. Sanders, 2012).

Gang members shun hard drugs because of personal experiences with their negative social and health outcomes. Members receive real-life drug prevention messages on the streets, not hypothetical ones from teachers (or law enforcement). Hard drug use is the antithesis of how members believe they are required to behave (B. Sanders, 2012). Honor and loyalty are important values within gang culture (W. B. Miller, 1958; W. B. Sanders, 1994, 1997). Hard drug use impairs the ability to activate these values when needed (B. Sanders, 2012).

Considerations of gang culture have championed marijuana use and stigmatized the use of hard drugs. This is particularly prominent within gangsta rap—the soundtrack to gang members' lives (B. Sanders, 2005a). By emulating the rappers, members behave how they believe gang members should. A message within gangsta rap is that hard drug use goes against the grain of what it means to "do gang membership," and many avoid hard drug use as a result (B. Sanders, 2012). This is an example of the reflexive relationship between the actions of members and their culture, whereby each reinforces and supports the other. Willis (1978) referred to this as a homology—a sameness between action and culture found within different youth groups.

Given the high rates of the use of other drugs reported from different studies, the use of illicit substances other than marijuana might be normalized among *subgroups* of members (B. Sanders, 2012). This suggests that illicit drug use generally is "differentially normalized" (Pilkington, 2007; Shildrick, 2002).

THEORETICAL MISCELLANEA

Major criminological perspectives have been applied to understand gangs and their behaviors, including control and labeling theories, as well biosocial insights. Below, each of these is discussed.

CONTROL THEORY

Surprisingly few gang studies have examined control theory (Kissner and Pyrooz, 2009). This theory argues that offending is a result of low self-control (M. R. Gottfredson and Hirschi, 1990; Hirschi, 1969). The development of self-control is related to parental affection, monitoring, and discipline. Parents who love and care for their children, ensure that they are supervised, and use appropriate and consistent measures to punish bad behaviors are less likely to raise children with low self-control. Low self-control is characterized by a clustering of traits, including impulsivity, sensation seeking, insensitivity, and a lack of foresight. Offending is one manifestation of low self-control; accidents, injuries, trouble keeping relationships, addiction, and early death are others.

Researchers have offered support for control theory in relation to why youth join gangs. Lynskey et al.'s (2000) analysis of data from eighth graders found that students with lower levels of self-control were more involved. The authors reported that females had more self-control than males and blacks and Asians had more self-control than whites. Hope and Damphousse (2002) examined gang membership in rural Arkansas. They noted that low self-control was a significant predictor of both current and previous membership. Kissner and Pyrooz (2009), in contrast, found that low self-control predicted current but not former gang membership. Fox et al. (2013) said that gang members had a range of self-control.

Flexon et al. (2012) investigated the link among low self-control, gang membership, and other variables. Rather than being a dependent (outcome) variable, the authors utilized it as an independent one. They found that gang membership predicted low self-control (not the other way around). They reported that affiliation and low self-control also predicted police contact. But their findings differed by race. Low self-control was related to membership among Latinos, but not among African Americans. Fox et al. (2013) also found a link among low self-control, gang membership, and increased likelihood of victimization.

LABELING

Labeling theory argues that the criminal justice system responses make matters worse and further embed people in a life of crime (Becker, 1963; Lemert, 1967; Tannenbaum, 1938). The theory is premised on the belief of self-fulfilling prophecy: youth are repeatedly called offenders and act accordingly. Former offenders are stigmatized, which limits their employment opportunities and exposes them to more serious offenders. Labels such as "offender" trap them in a never-ending cycle of crime and incarceration.

Bernburg et al. (2006) are among the few to examine the labeling theory and gangs. They were interested in the impact of official labeling and interaction with deviant social networks. They collected baseline data from 1,000 middle school students in Rochester, New York, and then gathered follow-up data in several waves. Labeling was measured by contact with the juvenile justice system (i.e., juvenile intervention) and deviant social networks were gangs. Gang members were more likely to commit more crime and violence than nonmembers. The authors reported that those who experienced juvenile intervention

BOX 8.1: MEDIA CHECK!

A Clockwork Orange

Anthony Burges, the author of *A Clockwork Orange*, says he heard the phrase "As queer as a clockwork orange" in a London pub prior to World War II. This is Cockney rhyming slang for extreme madness. Madness is at the center of this story. The movie was both praised and doomed. The original rating in the United States was X, the movie was banned in the United Kingdom, and the National Catholic Office for Motion Pictures rated it C for Condemned, forbidding Roman Catholics from seeing it. The film was nominated for several Oscars, BAFTAs (the British equivalent of the Oscars), Golden Globes, and many other awards. The book is considered one of the best written in the 20th century.

The story centers around Alex, the leader of the Droogs. They have their own style that distinguishes them from other gangs, as well as their own language: Nadsat, a hybrid of Russian, Cockney rhyming slang, and words Burgess made up himself. Alex's narration of the story is peppered with this tongue, and the book offers an appendix translating Nadsat to English. Alex and his Droogs have a wonderful time committing random and senseless acts of violence. These events do not quell the Droog's bloodlust, and the next day they take pleasure in more mischief. This time Alex gets arrested, tried, and convicted, and sentenced to many years.

In come the State and its Ludovico Technique, a type of aversion therapy. The book and movie vary as to exactly why Alex becomes a guinea pig for the Ludovico, but the process and outcome are generally the same in each. The Technique involves an injection of drugs and the witnessing of violent images—with Alex's eyes pried wide open so that he cannot shut them. Whereas violence previously titillated Alex, the Ludovico Technique alters this reaction. After the procedure, the mere thought of violence causes him to react poorly. The State demonstrates the effectiveness of their intervention to stakeholders. When a bully hits and taunts Alex, he cowers and cannot raise a fist to him. The Technique has stunted Alex's previously voracious sexual appetite and even his appreciation of

"Lovely Ludwig Van" Beethoven, whose Ninth Symphony is part of the film's soundtrack. During this demonstration, the prison chaplain notes that Alex has lost his capacity for free will. The doctor indicates that this point is not of consequence and that the only thing that matters is the reduction of violent crime (and overcrowded prisons).

A Clockwork Orange touches on a point that criminologists will find uncomfortable: perhaps no reason exists as to why individuals break the law. As Alex himself says, "This biting of their toe-nails over what is the cause of badness is what turns me into a fine laughing malchick [boy]. . . . But what I do I do because I like to do." Alex does not come from a high-risk background, nor can it be claimed that he is a sociopath [the last bit of the American version of the book is about Alex's redemption (sort of)]. Alex is not maladjusted, but rather seems to engage in crime and violence whimsically, just for the hell of it. If people commit crimes for such reasons, then what can be done about it?

Burgess's original concept for the book was about curing juvenile delinquency. In *The New Yorker* article, he mentions that the idea of aversion therapy was ludicrous. He was unimpressed with the insights of behavioral psychologists at the time, particularly about any notions of interfering with human will—no matter how deprived. He concluded that, between a desire to harm others born of free will and a desire to control the impulses to harm, the former was the lesser of two evils. The capacity of an individual for self-determination, regardless of the outcome, cannot be impaired. Burgess asked, "Is it better for a man to have chosen evil than to have good imposed upon him?"

Visit YouTube to watch the trailer for A Clockwork Orange.

Link to Nadsat dictionary:
http://www.mattiavaccari.net/mis/nadsat.html/
"The Clockwork Condition," by Anthony Burgess. *The New Yorker*, June 4, 2012.
http://www.newyorker.com/magazine/2012/06/04/the-clockwork-condition/

were more likely to offend again at later ages. These two variables were also related: juvenile intervention triggered involvement in the gang, which then led to more offending. The authors explain that after youth come in contact with juvenile intervention, they are stigmatized. Gangs provide a harbor from this humiliation. Once in, youth become more criminally involved because of peer influence. The authors conclude that gangs provide a critical role in the labeling process. The deviant self-image of the individual is solidified in the gang, and membership embeds them within a criminal lifestyle and pushes them farther away from conventional society.

BIOSOCIAL

Biosocial perspectives on crime and delinquency have remerged as important consider-ations. They focus on genetic makeups that are prone to problematic behaviors. The gene examined is "the low-activity alleles of a functional polymorphism in the promoter region of the monoamine oxidase A (MAOA) gene" (Beaver et al., 2010, p. 1).

Data from the National Longitudinal Study of Adolescent Health allowed for this in-vestigation because it collected biological specimens (i.e., saliva) and also queried about gangs. Of more than 1,000 youth, only 3.5% were members. No relationship emerged between the MAOA gene and membership or weapons used in fights for females. Beaver et al. (2010) found that boys and young men with low MAOA activity genes were more at risk for membership and more likely to use weapons in a fight than those with the high-activity gene. Beaver et al. (2010) note that gene research is beneficial in identifying subgroups of gang members who are more or less likely to use weapons.

PERSPECTIVES ON GANG VIOLENCE

Perspectives on gang violence can be broken down into three general categories. One per-spective borrows from major theories on crime and delinquency (e.g., the subculture of violence; Messerschmidt's point on masculinity; Katz's theory of transcendence). A second set notes the role of central concepts related to violence (e.g., Decker on the role of threat; Vigil's note on *locura*). A third perspective has been developed to understand gang violence (e.g., Sanders' grounded culture).

THREAT

Several researchers have observed that young men hanging out on street corners eventu-ally result in formalized gang structures because of external threats (Decker, 1996; Hagedorn, 1988, 1998; J. Katz, 1988; Klein, 1971; W. B. Sanders, 1994; Sullivan, 1989; Thrasher, 1927; Vigil, 1988a, 2002). Thrasher's (1927) work is among the earliest studies on gangs, and he argues that their primary function was conflict from groups of immi-grants. The gangs in Thrasher's time were oriented around nationality (e.g., German gangs, Irish gangs, Polish gangs) living in close proximity. Hagedorn (1988) indicates that conflict between groups of young men and the police led to proper gangs in Milwaukee. Sullivan (1989) in New York City and Klein (1971) in Los Angeles make similar points, arguing that what started off as groups of youth evolved into violent street gangs because of the percep-tion of threat from outside groups, either law enforcement or like groups of youth from other areas. Decker (1996) and W. B. Sanders (1994) discuss how external threats from other, similar groups of youth lead to violent clashes. Many African American and Latino gangs began as groups of young men who defended themselves and their communities from mobs of prejudiced white youths in the 1940s and 1950s (Alonso, 1998).

Threats external to the gang help build cohesiveness, which increases their capacity and willingness to engage in violence, which leads to the escalation of violence between different gangs (Decker, 1996; Decker and Van Winkle, 1996; Hagedorn, 1988; Klein,

1971; Maxson, 1998; Padilla, 1992; W. B. Sanders, 1994). Threat is "the potential for transgressions against or physical harm to the gang, represented by the acts or presence of a rival group," which "plays a role in the origin and growth of gangs, their daily activities, and their belief systems" and "helps to define them to rival gangs, to the community, and to social institutions" (Decker, 1996, p. 244). The bigger the external threat, the greater the increase in group cohesion, the more likely the group will engage in violence (Decker, 1996). This increase of cohesion can help attract more youth to join the gang (Vigil, 1988a, 1988b). A violent act is met with retaliatory violence, which is then met with an even more serious retaliation, *ad infinitum* (J. Katz, 1988). This is the "escalation hypothesis" (Klein and Maxson, 1987, p. 219).

Decker (1996) suggests that the collective violence of gangs in his research fits McPhail's conceptual model. McPhail (1991) argued that violence can be viewed as a type of collective behavior that arises because of group processes that involve common, purposeful actions. Gangs are loosely organized groups that lack goals, leadership, and structure. The identification of a threat, Decker (1996) says, unites members and increases cohesion because they are responding to a common enemy. The threat can be real or imagined and "mythic violence" acts as the principal catalyst toward group solidarity, increasing members' willingness to engage in violence (Klein, 1971). Some sort of "mobilizing event" occurs—a rumor, an insult, or a violent act—"that pushes a ready and willing group beyond the constraints against violence" (Decker, 1996, p. 262). Interactions then occur leading to the violent event—a drive-by, group rumble, getting jumped—followed by a quick decrease in interaction. Within this situation, youth on both sides are the victims, perpetrators, and/or witnesses. Because one or both sides suffer, retaliation is likely, which in turn leads to ongoing tit-for-tat violence. The origin of the conflict starts off as the perception of threat, but the continuation is retaliation.

LOCURA

Vigil (1988a, 1988b, 2002, 2003) reports on the concept of *locura*, which he defines as "a state of mind . . . defined as a spectrum of behavior reflected in a type of quasi-controlled insanity" (Vigil, 2003, p. 230). Vigil (2003) uses *locura* to define the mind-set among Mexican American gang members and the phrase "crazy niggah" (p. 230) to define the mind-set among African Americans. *Locura* (or crazy niggah) is a "gang ideal" (Vigil, 1988a, p. 439), and youths display this with violence. Through *locura*, they gain respect and approval. The most violent individual is considered the most *loco* and vice versa (see also Decker, 1996). The degree to which each member can display *locura* varies. Vigil says that the most loco gang youth come from traumatized households with severe family and economic stress that have brought about emotional duress, self-hatred, and worthlessness—a "psychosocial death" (Vigil, 1988a, p. 439).

Not all gang youth have traumatic backgrounds, and acting crazy does not come easy. Acting crazy can also make youth apprehensive and anxious. One way to combat the apprehension is with substance use. Vigil (2002) says that drugs and alcohol assists in obtaining the *locura* mind-set, which helps facilitate the gang's expectations of members to commit violence. Substance use helps violent behaviors by supporting the short-term development of a mind-set that allows for those behaviors. *Locura* is the "psychosocial mindset [that] has become a requisite for street survival and a behavioral standard for identification and emulation . . . it helps [gang members] assuage fear and the anxiety associated with the fight-flight . . . dilemma that street realities impose on a person" (Vigil, 2003, p. 230).

SUBCULTURE OF VIOLENCE

Subcultural perspectives indicate that young males in inner-city, working-class areas use violence as a way to obtain status. Delinquent subcultures argue that because youth are not able to achieve middle-class status because of blocked legitimate opportunities, violence becomes a way for them to be illegitimately successful (Cloward and Ohlin, 1960; A. K. Cohen, 1955; Cohen and Short, 1958; Spergel, 1964). The delinquent subculture that was the most violent was also the most respected; so, too, was the most violent individual within any subculture (Short and Strodtbeck, 1965). This theme continued in research that suggests a subculture of violence in the inner cities more generally. Wolfgang and Ferracuti (1967) argue that one thing that distinguishes lower-class/working-class communities from their affluent counterparts is the willingness to engage in violence. This subculture is marked by its commitment to violence as a legitimate way to solve problems. Individuals are ready for violence, have weapons handy, and have no remorse for their violent actions.

The subculture of violence is reflected in a street code revolving around respect found in poor, inner-city communities (E. Anderson, 1990, 1999; Horowitz, 1983; Horowitz and Schwartz, 1974). Horowitz and Schwartz (1974, p. 240) noted that:

> gang members subscribe to a code of personal honor that stresses the inviolability of one's manhood and defines breaches of interpersonal etiquette in an adversarial idiom. . . . For these youth, honor revolves around a person's capacity to command deferential treatment (i.e., "respect") from others who are, in other respects, like themselves.

E. Anderson (1990, 1999) reported on these findings. Based on data within disadvantaged inner-city communities in Philadelphia and New York City, Anderson argues that the code of the streets is an unspoken, informal rule that governs interpersonal behaviors in public, especially violence. The code centers around respect and how being tough and fearless can command it. The ultimate indiscretion within this code is to be disrespected, and the only acceptable response is violence. Given the importance of maintaining respect, disrespect could be the tiniest provocation (Fagan, 1989; Horowitz and Schwartz, 1974). Fagan (1989) described these provocations as "the smallest impersonal slight" and Horowitz and Schwartz (1974) noted how individuals in honor-based subcultures, like gangs, are "always searching for insults that lurk behind seemingly innocent statements or actions" (pp. 240–241).

MASCULINITY

Respect is closely linked to masculinity. Messerschmidt (1993, 2000, 2004) applies his theory on crime and masculinity to violence among street gangs. Violent terms such as smash, grab, punch, fight, kill, and maim are verbs with masculine overtones. Even in lay terms, violence can be viewed as boys being boys—engaging in routine behaviors that are expected masculine displays. When youth leave their childhood and take up adult responsibilities, they are able to display masculinity in more conventional terms, being "the man of the house" by going to work, paying the rent and bills, and providing for the family.

Messerschmidt (1993, 1997, 2000, 2004) says that as young males in poor inner-city areas age, they may continue to have blocked opportunities to display masculinity in conventional ways. They commit offenses as a way to "do gender" within the realm of hegemonic masculinity on the streets—showing others and proving to themselves that they are masculine. Hegemonic masculinity refers to autonomy, independence, heterosexuality, and the dominance of women—values and behaviors demanded on the streets. One of W. B. Miller's (1958) focal concerns, toughness, could be included here. Masculinity and respect are two sides of the same coin, and any perceived slight may damage it, which leads to violence. Hagedorn (1998, p. 368) summed this up properly when he suggested gang violence is "boys or men acting like 'tough guys,' picking a fight with other boys or men also acting like tough guys." Gang violence is a ritual that allows young people to display masculinity (see also Hagedorn, 1998; J. Miller and Decker, 2001; Stretesky and Pogrebin, 2007; Vigil, 2003).

Violence may be proactive as opposed to reactive. Another way for gang youth to display masculinity is to be the violent aggressor without provocation, such as robbing others, instigating fights, or selling drugs. Gang violence has characteristics of "aggressive notions of masculinity" and, when combined with substance use, hanging out, doing nothing, and firearms, "increased violence is a predictable outcome" (Hagedorn, 1998, pp. 398–399). This form of masculinity works for young females as well. By engaging in traditional aggressive masculine street crimes, female members were able to earn respect (J. Miller and Decker, 2001).

VIOLENCE AS TRANSCENDENCE

J. Katz (1988) applies his theory of crime as moral transcendence to violence among street gangs.[3] He suggests that individual members are street elites who attempt to project dread, wishing for others in the community to see them as ready and willing to engage in violence. Echoing the work of the British critical cultural theorists from the Birmingham School (e.g., P. Cohen, 1972; S. Cohen, 1972; Hall and Jefferson, 1976; Hebdige, 1979), Katz views violence among youth in gangs as a way to transcend everyday reality: "For without the violence, would-be street elites would appear to be bound to the social world of childhood" (J. Katz, 1988, p. 129). Violence within gangs "is essentially so that membership may have a seductively glorious, rather than a mundane, indifferent, significance" (p. 128). Life in the gang is boring. To counter this plain existence, Katz notes how the prospect of violence—the preparation, the posturing, the perception of eminent threat—add a

---

3   J. Katz prefers terms like street fighting groups, barrio homeboys, ghetto fighting groups, and the like instead of gang. The word gang, Katz argues, is a term sociologists have applied to groups of youth from inner-city areas who may not necessarily view themselves as a gang. The term is readily applied to groups of poor minority youth, but not to affluent white youth who commit violence.

touch of excitement and give meaning to youths' lives. Rivals "collectively sustain antago-nistic relations in which each effectively cause the other's existence" (p. 128). The imminent threat that members project when residing in a warzone is really from other youth just like them. The fact that most violence, particularly homicides, occur because of areas related to territory and disrespect between rival, neighboring gangs adds strength to this claim. Gang members' violence toward one another assists in the development of a world that is much more exciting for them than one where such retaliatory violence does not exist.

GROUNDED CULTURE

W. B. Sanders's (1994) perspective was developed specifically to explain gang violence. His theory of grounded culture is based on 10 years of ethnographic research and police data in San Diego. The theory borrows heavily from Goffman's (1967) symbolic interac-tion perspective on interpreting behaviors and partially from Garfinkel's (1967) ethnomethodology—a method that focuses on minutiae in relation to the interpretation of data. Ethnomethodologists are interested in how individuals make sense of their be-haviors. W. B. Sanders begins to explain his theory by indicating that behaviors are an expression of values. The ability to make sense of these values does not occur in a vacuum; it requires a process of grounding in actions that verify their meaning. The meaning of words or actions is unknowable without details about the context in which their use oc-curred; they can assume one meaning in one context and another meaning in another. The word "bad" can be used as a positive affirmation of a behavior (e.g., "Do you see that guy jump over all those cars on his motorcycle? That was bad!") or as way to admonish a negative one (e.g., "I can't believe you broke the television. That was bad!"). Behaviors, including violence, can be understood in a similar way.

According to W. B. Sanders, strain, low self-control, social disorganization, and other major criminological theories are inaccurate in explaining gang violence. Sanders claims that when members fight, they are expressing conventional values. The difference is that members have limited ways to express these values in a legitimate way. Instead, they use violence to show others that honor and loyalty are important to them. Other people might express these values by rooting for a home team or supporting a colleague at work, but gang members use violence.

Take the following example. A young male member from Gang A walks by another male from Gang B. The guy from Gang A says something negative about Gang B. The guy from Gang B then attacks the guy from Gang A. According to W. B. Sanders's theory, the youth from Gang A is attacking the guy from Gang B to show loyalty—he expresses loyalty to his gang by fighting someone who disrespects it. Loyalty is a middle-class value, not a countercultural one. W. B. Sanders argues that when members commit violent acts (largely against other gang members), they are expressing conventional values, countering the claims that gang members are sociopathic (like Yablonsky), or reject middle-class values (like A. K. Cohen and Short or Cloward and Ohlin). W. B. Sanders's findings challenge the demonization of immoral gang members heard from the media, police, and academia. Such data offer hope that gang youth are not irredeemable and appear to have a lot in common with average citizens.

W. B. Sanders (1997) later tested his theory. He examined how gang youth and non-gang college students rated a series of values. A total of 17 values were reviewed, some of which were conventional (e.g., education, family, hard work) and others were nonconventional (e.g., coolness, courage, respect others). Youth responded on a weighted Likert scale about the importance of each value to them (e.g., very important, not important at all). Both samples of youth were similar in terms of age, ethnicity (Mexican American), and gender.

According to W. B. Sanders (1997), gang members were significantly more likely to rank the nonconventional values higher than the college students. Gang members placed a higher value on things like coolness and respect. Sanders also reported that gang youth graded the conventional values relatively high, and few distinctions could be made between the college students and the gang youth. This finding provided additional support that gang members do not reject conventional values. Outside of his own support, researchers have not sought to test Sanders's theory.

TOWARD A THEORY ON GANG FIGHTING

Using data from the Los Angeles Study[4] and existing findings, an overview of a perspective that attempts to explain why gang members fight is provided. This perspective explains the opportunity for fighting in relation to routine activities theory and the motivation for violence in relation to cultural norms supportive of violence (see Vigil, 2003). Although the motivation to fight is always present, the opportunity is not. A proportion of gang fighting can be explained by being in the wrong place at the wrong time. Fighting refers to both individual and group contexts (i.e., getting jumped, jumping others).

Research on the offender/victim relationship reveals that lifestyle and culture are important characteristics (L. W. Kennedy and Baron, 1993; Lauritsen et al., 1991; Sampson and Lauritsen, 1990; Schreck et al., 2008; E. A. Stewart, Schreck, and Simons, 2006). With regard to lifestyle, offending and victimization are related to daily, routine activities (Cohen and Felson, 1979; Hindelang et al., 1978). Young offenders in urban environments spend much of their time away from school and work and instead find themselves on the streets. Through the principle of homogamy (Sampson and Lauritsen, 1990), different groups of youth leading risky lifestyles and spending considerable time on the streets increase their odds of conflicting with one another. This convergence of space and time creates opportunities to be a perpetrator and a victim. Offender victims are ideal targets because they are unlikely to report their victimization for fear

---

4   See the Appendix for the methodology of this study.

of implicating themselves (L. W. Kennedy and Baron, 1993). Street crime—both from the perspective of the victim and from that of the perpetrator—is the outcome of opportunity that arises in the course of common, ongoing activities of life on the streets.

Cultural perspectives argue that behavioral norms supportive of violence help explain its occurrence, particularly among young males within impoverished, inner-city areas (Anderson, 1990, 1999; Cloward and Ohlin, 1960; A. K. Cohen, 1955; A. K. Cohen and Short, 1958; Horowitz, 1983; W. B. Miller, 1958; Sampson and Wilson, 1995; W. B. Sanders, 1994; Spergel, 1964; Wolfgang and Ferracuti, 1967). With limited opportunities and a bleak outlook, a culture emerges where values such as honor, loyalty, and respect become paramount. Young men engage in violence when their commitment to these values is challenged. Youth are tuned and alert, and being disrespected can arise from the slightest provocation, such as a "wrong" look (Fagan, 1996). Young males engage in violence as an aggressive way to demonstrate respect, loyalty, or honor. Rather than redressing a perceived wrong (e.g., being disrespected), youth are the instigators (e.g., doing the disrespecting), actively showing others the importance they place on such values (J. Katz, 1988; W. B. Sanders, 1994).

Understanding the lifestyle and culture of gang members helps explain why they are both perpetrators and victims of gang fighting. Culture explains the motivation. Research on gang youth suggests they have traditional normative codes of violence that center around respect, honor, and loyalty. Violence is the outcome of defending or displaying these values (Horowitz, 1983; W. B. Miller, 1958; W. B. Sanders, 1994). Fighting in the Los Angeles Study was about being disrespected. Fights erupted as a result of disrespect directed either at the individual or their gang. Forms of disrespect included hard stares or mad dogging or negative comments about members, their girlfriends, their families, or being owed money.

Why do you get into fights?

It actually, it can be the stupidest shit. It could just be from, just the wrong look, from somebody looking at your lady, saying some stupid remark. Just little stupid things. . . . It's just basic shit like that, you know?

What are your fights all about?

Out here, small shit, as to where you owe me a dollar to where you're pointing a gun at me to where you are disrespecting my girl. . . . I mean, you don't disrespect me. You know you can't be doing that. . . . You let him disrespect you and fuck your reputation or are you gonna fuck him up?

By equalizing this disrespect through fighting, gang youth are able to maintain or defend self-respect in the face of their peers (Anderson, 1990, 1999). Youth demonstrate honor and loyalty toward their gang by redressing those who show contempt toward it (W. B. Miller, 1958; W. B. Sanders, 1994). Within gang culture, violent retaliation is an accepted response of victimization (Anderson, 1999; Baskin and Sommers, 1997; Decker, 1996). Respect traps members in a never-ending cycle of fighting perpetration and victimization (Decker, 1996; Decker and Van Winkle, 1996; Klein, 1995; W. B. Sanders, 1994).

Lifestyle helps explain the opportunity for fighting. A consistent finding in research is that gang life is chiefly spent hanging out and doing nothing. Youth in the Los Angeles Study were asked details about what these behaviors entailed. They mentioned conversing, going to the store, walking around, relaxing, using alcohol, cigarettes, and/or marijuana, and listening to music. "Doing nothing," as it turns out, is full of activities (see Corrigan, 1979). While behaving in these ways, many bumped into rivals. One talked how common this was:

How many times has something like that happened where you've been jumped?
At school, coming out the store or if I'm visiting one of my girlfriends and she lives in the wrong neighborhood and I go over there and they see me or they hear about me being over there, they probably wait for me outside or catch me at the bus stop on the way home, then I'll have to get into a couple of fights.[5]

Another youth said that when rivals see one another, the outcome is fighting:

If it's like a group of us and a group of them and we see each other, we obviously are enemies so we got to get at it.

Vigil (2003, p. 233) says, "Is it an accident that most gang violence . . . occur[s] between gangs from similar marginal areas?" Getting caught slipping describes how youth were jumped or when they jumped others. Fighting was not really planned, but just happened. On occasion, these haphazard situations become homicides (Valdez et al., 2009). A youth from Los Angeles talked about how a random incident almost killed him:

One night I was walking behind my neighborhood and walking down the creek and two guys just ran up. I don't know who they were. I don't know what they looked like. I don't know nothing like that. And we didn't know who they were so we yelled at them, "Who are you guys? Identify yourselves" this and that and then as soon as we did that they started letting off on me and my other friend.

You mean letting off you mean firing rounds?
Yeah firing at us. One had an AK and the other had a 9mm. The guy with the AK hit me and the guy with the 9mm hit my homie. He hit me six times and my homie got hit four times.

Gang youth come into contact rivals who have similar normative codes regarding violence that mandate on-sight violence. When the groups meet, the one with the lesser amount of individuals gets caught slipping, whereas the one with the greater amount does the jumping. When equal numbers meet, the result could be a rumble or a riot. If weapons are handy, murder could be the outcome. The opportunities for various contexts of gang fighting are guided by their lifestyles. Although fighting is at times random, the frequency

---

5   See additional examples in Chapter 6.

of hanging out and other routine activities greatly increases the probability of individuals being perpetrators and victims. Although innocuous, hanging out is centrally related to the opportunity for fighting.

SUMMARY

Few theories focus on why gangs exist. Vigil's multiple marginalization theory explains the development and persistence of gangs in Latino communities. Multiple marginalization begins by addressing the history of experiences of immigrants from Mexico and Central America and incorporates insights from major theories on crime—social disorganization, social learning, social bonding/control, and subculture—into a coherent explanation. It interweaves political, structural, cultural, economic, and social reasons related to why young Latinos join gangs. Empirical support has been found for the theory to explain gang membership in African American, Southeast Asian, Native American, and white communities.

The work of Brotherton and colleagues views gangs as a form of resistance. They bring a Marxist discourse to the literature whereby the gang serves as a form of struggle against a racist, oppressive society. Gangs are multigenerational in some cities. Youth in parts of Los Angeles and Chicago can say they are part of the same gang as their great-great grandfather, showing the importance and permanence of gang culture within certain communities. This tradition suggests some degrees of resistance.

The social injury hypothesis and women's liberation thesis have been examined to help explain female gang membership. The research indicates that gangs can be led to liberation, victimization, or both. Gangs have been argued as providing a sense of autonomy, freedom, and respect for females. But they also lead to further physical and sexual violence, particularly from male members in the same gang.

Marijuana use is normalized among gang members. This normalization is based on the drug's availability, acceptability, number of overall uses, intent to use in the future, cultural attributes supportive of use, critical attitudes toward hard drug use, and being drug wise beyond personal experiences. The normalization thesis has been considered one of the most important developments in the sociology of drug use within the past 20 years. It offers more flexibility in understanding drug use among youth than do theories of deviance and delinquency. The idea that gang members have similar differential attitudes toward illicit drug use compared with the general youth population suggests comparable values.

Several researchers have examined the extent to which major criminological theories, such as control and labeling, as well as recent insights from a biosocial perspective, help explain gangs or their behaviors. Many researchers have focused on gang violence. Decker applied a model of threat and collective behavior to help explain it. Vigil focused on the development of a crazy mind-set to engage in it. Such violence has been found to epitomize the code of the street/subculture of violence ethos. Messerschimdt and J. Katz used it as ways to support their general perspectives on violence using the concepts of masculinity or moral transcendence, respectively. W.B. Sanders developed the theory of grounded culture to explain it as an expression of conventional—not deviant—values. Following this tradition, another Sanders argued that routine activities explained the opportunity and subculture of violence, the motivation and that, together, these activities explained much of the incidence of gang fighting.

CHAPTER REVIEW QUESTIONS

1. What are the major theories of crime that are reflected in the theory of multiple marginalization? Explain how each crime theory is incorporated into the multiple marginalization theory.
2. Outline the selection, enhancement, and facilitation hypotheses.
3. Discuss the concept of gangs as a form of resistance.
4. What are the social injury and women's liberation perspectives? What did Nurge report on these two theories among her sample?
5. What is drug normalization? What are the characteristics of normalization? What does the normalization of certain drugs among gang members mean?
6. Describe how the concept of threat leads to gang violence according to Decker.
7. Compare the subculture of violence to the idea of "doing gender" to explain gang violence.
8. J. Katz believes that gang members transcend their everyday lives through violence. Explain this.
9. What is the theory of grounded culture? How does it make sense of gang violence?
10. Outline B. Sanders's theory on gang fighting.

CHAPTER 9

PRISON GANGS

KEY WORDS

Aryan Brotherhood: Also known as the Brand, the largest white prison gang in state and federal penitentiaries.

Black Guerilla Family: Also known as the Black Family, the largest African American prison gang in state and federal penitentiaries.

Clavos: Spanish prison slang for illegal drugs.

Importation theory: Argues that prison gangs are the result of a culture imported from the streets.

Indigenous formation theory: Argues that prison gangs formed as a reaction to the deprivation and pain associated in incarceration as a form of self-protection. Also referred to as the *adaptation/deprivation perspective*.

Institutionalization: A process whereby a person within an institution (e.g., prison) is reprogrammed to acknowledge and agree with the controls that allow that institution to operate. The individual self is destroyed and strict obedience is enacted. Individuals' ability to be self-governed is limited by processes whereby they are told when and how to perform basic human needs, such as eat, sleep, and use the facilities.

Judas: Spanish prison slang for correctional officer.

Mexican Mafia: Also known as La Eme, the largest Latino prison gang in state and federal penitentiaries. Latino street gangs throughout the Southwest use the number 13 to acknowledge affiliation to La Eme.

Nortenos: Street and prison gang members affiliated with Nuestra Familia.

Nuestra Familia: A Latino prison gang based in Northern California that emerged in opposition to the Mexican Mafia. They are referred to as "Farmers" and use the United Farm

Workers symbol as their own. Latino street gangs throughout Northern California use the number 14 to acknowledge affiliation to Nuestra Familia.

Radicalization: Occurs when individuals take on extremely different views in relation to social, economic, political, or religious ideals. Such ideals often attempt to undermine society in general or particular aspects about society. An example of radicalization includes profound right-wing views that espouse racism and hatred of all non–group members. Another example would be developing antigovernment or anti-American sentiments whereby the objective is to instill a new world order.

Supermax prison: Short for super–maximum security prison. These prisons within prisons offer the most secure level of custody. They normally house the most dangerous prisoners, the so-called "worst of the worst," by providing long-term segregated housing units. In such units, inmates are normally confined 23 hours a day within a single cell (i.e., solitary confinement) and held there an indefinite amount of time. Few activities or interventions are provided, and prison authorities often have absolute authority to punish and manage prisoners without oversight.

Surenos: Street and prison gang members affiliated with the Mexican Mafia.

Verdes: Or "green light"; Spanish prison gang slang referring to those on a list for assassination.

Chapter Learning Objectives

- Understand how and why prison gangs emerged.
- Highlight general and specific characteristics of prison gangs.
- Underscore differences and relationships between prison and street gangs.
- Discuss the impact of prison gangs within correctional systems.

INTRODUCTION

In the latter half of the 20th century, significant changes occurred within America's correctional institutions. The population increased dramatically. By the dawn of the millennium, approximately one in four of the world's prisoners were housed in the United States, yet the country has about 5% of the global population. The racial composition of prisons also shifted. The majority of prisoners in the 1950s were white, but by the 2000s most were African American or Latino. Overcrowding became a major issue, with prisoners bunking in gymnasiums and closets. Another significant change was the emergence and ascension of prison gangs, called security threat groups by administrators. These gangs arose on the West Coast, but are now nationwide as well as in federal penitentiaries. Data on prison gangs are clouded; members operate in silence and administrators are not forthcoming about the nature and scope of the problem.

The chapter begins by offering the definition of a prison gang and theories about why they emerged. From here, the number of prison gang members is reviewed, as well as the difficult nature of obtaining accurate counts. Next, the chapter describes the three largest prison gangs divided by race: the Aryan Brotherhood, the Mexican Mafia, and the Black Guerilla Family. The differences and similarities between street and prison gangs, as well as the relationships between the two, are discussed. The chapter then focuses on radicalization among prison gang members, including anti-American and antigovernment actions and beliefs. Misconduct by prison gangs and the extent to which guards are in some way facilitating such behaviors is then considered. Leaving prison gangs is mentioned, followed by the extent to which recidivism is related to membership. The chapter concludes with an overview of responses to prison gangs.

THE EMERGENCE OF PRISON GANGS

Prison gangs emerged on the West Coast in the 1950s and 1960s. One of the first known prison gangs was the Gypsy Jokers in Washington (Fleisher and Decker, 2001; Pyrooz et al., 2011). The definition of prison gang has not received nearly as much focus as that of street gangs (Pyrooz et al., 2011). Lyman's (1989, p. 48) definition is one that has been repeated within the literature:

> An organization which operates within the prison system as a self-perpetuating criminally oriented entity, consisting of a select group of inmates who have established an organized chain of command and are governed by an established code of conduct.

Three major contemporary prison gangs are the Mexican Mafia (La Eme), the Aryan Brotherhood (The Brand), and the Black Guerilla Family (Black Family). They originated in California penitentiaries, but are found throughout the nation and in some provinces in Canada (Fleisher and Decker, 2001; Schoville, 2008). Many smaller gangs are found in other facilities, including Special Needs Yards.

Prison gangs have been theorized to form for one of two reasons (Hunt et al., 1993; Knox, 2000a; Pyrooz et al., 2011). One theory suggests that prisoners developed the culture as a reaction to the deprivation and pain associated with incarceration. Gangs are part of prisoner culture shaped by inmates' need for self-protection (Fleisher and Decker, 2001; Fong et al., 1992; Schlosser, 1998). This is the indigenous formation theory (Knox, 2000a) or the adaptation/deprivation perspective (Pyrooz et al., 2011). Loners, or those who are not affiliated, are more vulnerable to victimization (Ross, 2008).

Another viewpoint suggests that they are the result of a culture inmates bring with them from the outside (Byrne and Hummer, 2007; Drury and DeLisi, 2011; Ross, 2008). This is the importation theory (Knox, 2000a; Pyrooz et al., 2011). As Byrne and Hummer (2007, p. 81) say, "it would be a mistake to ignore the potential influence of gang culture in . . . institutional . . . settings." Long-term criminals, including street members, are attracted to prison gangs while they are incarcerated to further benefit from illicit enterprise.

Hunt et al.'s (1993) research indicates that the indigenous formation and importation models do not fully capture the reasons for dramatic changes within prisons. The authors note that an increase in disorder within the system brought about three interrelated circumstances: changes in policy, a shift in demographics, and newly formed street gangs. These actions undid previous loyalties and allegiances and altered the landscape of prison culture. Hunt et al. (1993) based their findings on interview data from ex-prisoners who had been incarcerated in California. Overcrowding was viewed as a major contributor to the formation of prison gangs. Instead of prisoners aligning along racial divisions (e.g., white, black, and Latino gangs), many subdivisions emerged.

The two major Latino gangs inside California's prisons are La Eme and Nuestra Familia. Members from each of these gangs each have branched off to form different gangs (Hunt et al., 1993). Black inmates from the San Francisco Bay Area formed a prison gang called the 415s—a reference to the city's area code (Fleisher and Decker, 2001; Hunt et al., 1993). All of the new prison gangs disrupted old friendships and alliances and the patterns of interethnic violence (Hunt et al., 1993). The influx of younger inmates led to generational clashes. Older inmates valued codes related to respect, honor, and looking out for one another. Younger prisoners lacked these qualities and were perceived as being quick to snitch (Hunt et al., 1993). The growth of gangs, Hunt et al. (1993) contend, went hand in glove with the growth of a chaotic and violent prison culture. Tradition and safety were compromised.

Hunt et al.'s (1993) findings echo some of the earlier work of Pelz et al. (1991). Pelz et al. (1991) argued that three factors have contributed to the growth of prison gangs: segregation and racial conflict, informants, and policy changes. The authors indicate that enforced policies that segregated inmates based on racial lines helped create hostility because of a lack of communication. Racial violence has long been a problem within the system, and racial tension is the reason for the formation of gangs (R. K. Jackson and McBride, 1996).

Prison officials once used what they called "building tenders"—inmates who were supposed to inform administrators of other inmates' activities (Pelz et al., 1991). Rather than doing this, they acted as agent provocateurs by providing misinformation and fueling rumors that spurred hostilities (Pelz et al., 1991). Judicial interventions led to the removal of these building tenders, replacing them with prison guards. Pelz et al. (1991) report that this rapid change created an anomic order within the culture of the guards, who were uncertain of their authority. This allowed gangs to act without oversight from officials; no one seemed to be clear as to whose job it was to combat them. The Prisons Rights Reform Movement also resulted in inmates being transferred, allowing them to inform others throughout the system of new alliances and power structures (R. K. Jackson and McBride, 1996). Changes resulting from the Reform Movement allowed prisoners from different settings to communicate. They ordered beatings and assassinations and conveyed to others changes in the dynamics and leadership (R. K. Jackson and McBride, 1996).

THE NUMBER OF PRISON GANGS

Data on the number of prison gangs and their members are difficult to obtain (Fleisher and Decker, 2001; Pyrooz et al., 2011). Like the study of street gangs, true accounts of prison members vary based on when and where the study was conducted and how data were collected.

Multistate studies offer one perspective. A survey sponsored by the U.S. government in the early 1980s found that, in 29 state correctional facilities, 114 different gangs with more than 13,000 members were reported (Camp and Camp, 1985). The American Correctional Association said that between the mid-1980s and early 1990s, the number of members quadrupled (Baugh, 1993). Knox and Tromanhauser (1991) note that the figure hovered around 100,000 nationally. About 20 years later, Knox recalculated and his report to the National Gang Crime Research Center indicated that, in a survey of 193 state correctional facilities within all but one state, on average one in four prisoners was a gang member (Knox, 2005). Knox's later study indicated that some facilities reported up to 90% as members, with an average of about 30% of inmates in all facilities surveyed believed to be members (Knox, 2012). The number of gangs has increased just as the number of overall prisoners has.

Female correctional facilities also have gangs. In 1995, a survey found that the average rate of female prison gang members within facilities nationwide was around 3%; by 1999, this number more than doubled, to 7.5%, and by 2012, it had climbed to 8.8% (Knox, 2000b, 2012). Knox (2000b) reported that, for both males and females, as the security levels of the facilities increased, so too did the percentage of those facilities that contained members. Maximum-security prisons have more gang members than minimum-security ones.

Whether inmates are street gang members in prison or bona fide prison gang members is unclear. M. Lane (1989) found that 80–90% of inmates were in gangs, but whether they were in gangs that originated on the streets was not identified. Another report said that the extent of gangs is overexaggerated and that less than 5% of inmates are either in a street or in a prison gang (Trulson et al., 2006). Other figures are based on the type of facility. Jails have noted that members are about 13% of all inmates (Ruddell et al., 2006). This statistic matches the number of members within state correctional facilities, with reports ranging from 12 to 17% (Griffin and Hepburn, 2006; Krienert and Fleisher, 2001). Just under 10% of all inmates in federal prisons are members (Gaes et al., 2002).

Fong and Buentello (1991) indicate three factors related to the lack of clarity about gangs: missing documentation, the reluctance of administrators to allow researchers into their facilities, and the fact that members are reluctant to talk to outsiders. Pyrooz and colleagues (2011) echo these concerns and underscore the administrative difficulties inherent in this type of research. Correctional agencies screen all research proposals and only allow those that directly contribute to the operations and programs within such facilities (Pyrooz et al., 2011). The way gangs are defined and the way administrators collect data vary, with subjective interpretations of what defines a "prison gang" and "prison gang member" clouding the data (Fleisher and Decker, 2001; Gaes et al., 2002; Pyrooz et al., 2011).

PRISON GANGS BASED ON RACE

The largest gangs in the United States are broken up along lines of race. The big three are the Aryan Brotherhood, the Mexican Mafia, and the Black Guerilla Family. Other gangs exist inside correctional facilities across the United States, including Special Needs Yards. These three gangs have amassed considerable power and influence in many state and federal facilities across the United States, which extends to the streets.

ARYAN BROTHERHOOD

The largest white prison gang is the Aryan Brotherhood (AB), also known as The Brand. Motorcycle and racist Nazi inmates in San Quentin, California, formed the AB in 1968 (Fleisher and Decker, 2001; Pelz et al., 1991). In the 1950s and 1960s, San Quentin had a group of white inmates known as the Blue Bird Gang (FBI, 1982). As Latino and African American inmates formed gangs, white inmates realized they needed the strength of numbers to protect themselves. The result was the AB. At first, members of the AB had to claim Irish ancestry to join (FBI, 1982), which helps explain their use of Celtic imagery in tattoos and affiliation (e.g., the shamrock is the gang's official symbol). They later abandoned this rule and welcomed any strong whites who were willing to fight.

The AB espouses a racist ideology of white supremacy and many members have tattoos that reflect this, including Nazi insignias, like swastikas, war birds, and the *Schutz Staffeinel* (or SS, often represented as twin lightning bolts). Other tattoos include the number 666 and ancient Celtic runes. ABs can be found in prisons and jails in most states, particularly California and Texas, as well as federal penitentiaries. Members are linked to prostitution, drug trafficking, gambling, and murder—all while incarcerated. Reasons for murder include being a suspected informant, failure to pay drug debt, or simply making disrespectful remarks about the AB (FBI, 1982). Many of the murder victims are members of AB.

> I will stand by my brother
> My brother will come before all others
> My life is forfeit should I fail my brothers
> I will honor my brother in peace as in war
> *(Aryan Brotherhood creed; FBI, 1982)*

Despite their racist ideology, not all members of AB are white. Michael Thompson, one of the former higher ranking members within the AB, is part Native American. Also, AB members have in the past formed an alliance with Latino inmates part of the Mexican Mafia to team up against other Latino inmates who are part of Nuestra Familia (FBI, 1982). The central purpose of the AB is to gain power, not pursue racist beliefs (FBI, 1982). The AB has established links with Asians (e.g., Chinese, Thai) related to drug trafficking. AB has a history of partnering with members of mob syndicates, such as La Cosa Nostra, whereby AB members protect mob members while incarcerated and, in return, are introduced to some rackets on the streets (FBI, 1982).

ABs are known for their brutality. An FBI report (1982, pp. 49–50) describes stabbing incidents in the early 1980s that helped establish this within the federal prison system:

> A Correctional Officer, was stabbed to death by . . . crime partner. AB member . . . stabbed [the officer] between 35–40 times, another correctional officer 6 times, and another correctional officer 2 times. The purpose of the murder is known, and . . . had said earlier that day if anyone laid a hand on . . . for the murder, he would take care of business.

Correctional Officer . . . was stabbed in the throat and killed by. . . . Information developed after the murder indicates that . . . has had an AB tattoo. . . . After the murder, he sent word to . . . that he had taken care of business.

. . . advised that he feels that the killings of the correctional officers was to set an example to the other correctional officers that they are not to mess with AB members or they will be killed. The ABs know there is not death penalty for killing a correctional officer, so they are utilizing members who are doing a lot of time to kill correctional officers.

. . . feeling . . . is that they will continue to kill in the Federal System. . . . They know that they cannot win, but by killing they can set an example of honor in winning favor and support in the eyes of the inmate population. The more they establish themselves in this concept, the more they become established as a true organized crime organization in the prisons and streets. The ABs feels that the Federal System has been abrasive to them so the killing of the correctional officers is retaliatory in nature and an attempt to establish a base on fear which affects both correctional officers and other inmates.

THE MEXICAN MAFIA

The first prison gang in California was the Mexican Mafia, known as La Eme (Hunt et al., 1993; see *Media Check!*). La Eme translates to The M, and M is the 13th letter in the alphabet. Street gangs affiliated with La Eme have the number 13 after their name (which can be written as X3 or XIII). La Eme's symbol is a black hand with an M in the middle. They are known as The Black Hand (Blatchford, 2009).

La Eme formed in 1957 at the Deuel Vocational Institution near Tracy, California. Street gang members affiliated to La Eme are referred to as *surenos* (southerners), which is shortened to *sur.* They are enemies with the *nortenos* (northerners) who are linked to Nuestra Familia. Translating to "our family," Nuestra Familia is based in Northern California. Originally known as Blooming Flower, northern California laborers who were tired of being pushed around by inmates from La Eme formed Nuestra Familia (Hunt et al., 1993). Whereas La Eme use 13 as a symbol, Nuestra Familia use the number 14 (because N—for Nuestra—is the 14th letter of the alphabet).[1] Nuestra Familia, in acknowledging the agricultural background of many of its members and family, uses the United Farm Workers symbol. They are nicknamed Farmers (R. K. Jackson and McBride, 1996). Delano, Fresno, Bakersfield, or somewhere near Kern County serves as the dividing line between the two prison gangs, with those north of these cities claiming to be *nortenos* and affiliating with Nuestra Familia (Hunt et al., 1993; Schoville, 2008). The Texas Syndicate is another gang that emerged in defiance of both of these gangs, believing they were too Americanized (Hunt et al., 1993).

La Eme are linked to narcotics trafficking inside and out of prisons, as well as racketeering, providing protection, and loan sharking (R. K. Jackson and McBride, 1996). Although

---

1   An exception to this is Clanton 14, which is one of the older gangs in Los Angeles, formed before La Eme gained influence on the streets. Clanton 14 is linked to La Eme.

their stronghold is in California, La Eme members are found throughout prisons in the southwest in Arizona, Nevada, New Mexico, and Texas. They have also been reported in Canadian provinces and states bordering Canada, such as Idaho and Wyoming (Schoville, 2008). La Eme has rules for behaviors of other incarcerated *surenos*. Schoville (2008, pp. 41–42) provided a list from Los Angeles County Jail about them, which included the following:

> No getting in the *judas'* (correctional officer) face. Stay off the nurse, store clerk, etc. Show Respect.

> No mad-dogging the Homies in the high power cages. (Don't provoke the older, established members from the other Security Threat Groups.)

> All *clavos* (drugs) are to come to me; I will cut the third (the author—or shotcaller—explains drug transactions go through him and that he will take one third off the top of any drug exchange).

> Mandatory workout your choice, minimum of one hour.

> If one of the Homies feels disrespected and takes off (attacks) on the *judas* (correctional officers), all Homies will follow (back him up).

> Gang Module Homies (shotcallers) blast (assault) all *verdes* ["green light" list of people for assassination], *varrios*, and personals (gang or individual green lights).

A youth in the Los Angeles Study who was a member of a street gang with ties to La Eme discussed what a green lighter was:

> Green lighters is when they don't pay dues. . . . They don't pay up to the mob or they are northsiders or they basically want to make their own business . . . for them own self . . . instead of getting drugs from other people, they make their own drugs . . . and sell them among each other. . . . In their little click they will be doing the drug business and they don't pay dues and they don't pay to the mob. That is basically what a green lighter is. They don't really like the sound. They don't like the 13.

Some gangs in the Los Angeles area, like the Maravilla cliques in East Los Angeles, became disillusioned with the leadership and direction of La Eme and ceased affiliation (Schoville, 2008). They became *verdes* in the eyes of La Eme, who still control many Latino gangs throughout Southern California and other parts of the United States.

BLACK GUERILLA FAMILY

The largest African American gang is the Black Guerilla Family (BGF). The BGF was formed in San Quentin Penitentiary in the mid-1960s and held similar ideological and political views as the Black Liberation Army and the Black Panther Party (Fleisher and Decker, 2001; Hunt et al., 1993; Zohrabi, 2012). One of the main originators of the BGF was George L. Jackson, who was also a Panther and the author of *Soledad Brother*. Jackson studied law and politics during long stints in solitary confinement. He later held meetings to inform other black inmates about what he had learned, and from these meetings the BGF was born (Zohrabi, 2012). Jackson and others were murdered during tit-for-tat violence between guards and inmates. The BGF emerged to counter what inmates felt was their oppression and improper treatment and conditions (Zohrabi, 2012). Over time, an ideological social movement morphed into a gang that focused on criminal activity. Zoharbi (2012) makes an important case with regard to how the policies of the California Department of Corrections and Rehabilitation confused behaviors that could be considered part of this movement.

The BGF is active on the East and West Coasts and has links to several street gangs, including those that originated in Los Angeles, like the Bloods and Crips, and those that initially emerged in Chicago, like the Vice Lords and Gangster Disciples. The BGF is enemies with both the AB and La Eme and espouses antiwhite sentiments (FBI, n.d.). What follows are excerpts from "The Oath" of BGF members derived from FBI files (FBI, n.d., pp. 10–19):

THE OATH

Those of us under this pledge are not at liberty to discuss the contents with any person except those directly involved, at any risk for any purpose, at any time or place, without the consent of all. This pledge is primarily concerned with mature guerrillas, those who know what must be done and have dedicated their lives to securing this end. Those under this pledge have chosen to carry out the necessary actions (duty) with courage and sincerity to the best of our abilities to the bitter or otherwise. We are not at liberty to trust anyone. Therefore, everyone is to be considered as enemies or guilty until proven innocent. . . .

It is not our duty to trust people. Our duty is to rid humanity of the many institutions that deprive the ignorant masses who serve these institutions blindly, yet in good faith. We shall only believe in the dead (i.e., trust only ourselves). No one else can be trusted or believed in, no matter how trustworthy they seem by act, appearance, or talk, trust them not. . . .

We, as black revolutionaries, cannot become bogged down in or by any form of racism, but because whites are devious by nature and will give their daughters to put a cease to our endeavors, none can ever be trusted even if they're known to be revolutionaries. . . .

If you want such things as fame, glory, recognition, wealth, voting privileges, fair education, equal employment opportunities, then you want equalities and not liberation; pacifiers are your wants along with compromises and pity. There are no grounds for anyone to hold these views on the battlefield unless they desire six feet of dirt stained with their own blood. . . .

We must never forget that there is no cure for the evils of the western world other than through uncompromising destruction. . . .

Since this society's destruction is our ultimate goal—we must be twice as cruel, three times as dirty, a thousand times as merciless, and we must strike first and swiftly with precision. . . .

Two points to remember: First, before the new can live the old must die; second, none can live forever. So destroy and worry not for the new, and lady death is on our side. . . .

Power to the revolution and death to all dissenters. . . .

DIFFERENCES AND SIMILARITIES BETWEEN STREET AND PRISON GANGS

Prison and street gangs are similar. Both have signs, symbols, and mottos, as well as rules (written and unwritten) and punishments for violations (Fleisher and Decker, 2001; Pyrooz et al., 2011). Prison gangs are different in that they have a pyramid-like organizational structure, similar to criminal syndicates (Fleisher and Decker, 2001; Pyrooz et al., 2011). Several leaders sit at the top, each with his or her own set of lieutenants. Under these lieutenants are the foot soldiers, or those that do most of the work. And below them are potential recruits and others who are down for the cause to receive protection. About one in five members are hard core and/or have leadership positions (U.S. Department of Justice, 1992). Most street gangs are organized horizontally, with several cliques having equal say and power.

Another way in which both differ is secrecy (Fong and Buentello, 1991; Pyrooz et al., 2011). Letters to and from AB members containing secret messages have been seized. In one case, a letter written on yellow legal pad in ball-point ink also had another, invisible message written in urine that was legible only after applying a hot iron to it (FBI, 1982). AB members may also communicate through secret codes, where words have dual meanings. Street gangs are overt in their behaviors and have a tendency to let others know they are in a gang. Examples include asking other youth "Where you from?" and shouting out their gang name.

Race, age, and patterns of offending are additional ways in which the gangs differ (Pyrooz et al., 2011). Prison gangs are drawn strictly along lines of race. Street gangs are less rigid and have been known to have members from a mix of races. Street gang members are much younger than those in prison gangs. The average age for a street member is usually in the mid- to late teens, compared to prison members who are mostly in their twenties, with some in their thirties and forties. The types of crimes committed by street gangs are considered cafeteria style: they focus on a range of crimes (Klein, 1995). Prison gangs commit instrumental forms of violence and concentrate on profit-oriented crimes, of which drug trafficking is a big one (Pyrooz et al., 2011).

THE RELATIONSHIP BETWEEN PRISON AND STREET GANGS

The growing numbers of street gangs shaped the culture and dynamics of prison gangs. Many prison members previously belonged to street or biker gangs (R. K. Jackson and McBride, 1996). The reverse is also true: street members were influenced by prison dynamics. As one of Montgomery's (2009, p. 91) respondents reported, "The NF [Nuestra Familia] isn't a street gang that's gone to prison. It's a prison gang that's hit the streets." Cultural attributes more generally of prisoners—tattoos, slang, customs—have become the standards of street culture (Schlosser, 1998). Some prison gangs have produced gangsta rap music (Montgomery, 2009).

In some instances, prison gangs directly control the behaviors of street members (Schlosser, 1998). La Eme is considered the principal supplier of drugs to Latino gangs in southwestern states. In exchange, the gangs pay La Eme a percentage of the overall take, called a tax (Valdez, 2005; Valdez and Sifaneck, 2004). Other prison gangs do this as well. Montgomery (2009) reports that Nuestra Familia demanded a quarter of the profits generated from drug sales by street gangs in their jurisdictions.

Some gangs that started in prison morphed into criminal syndicates. Pura Vida, which originated in San Antonio, is one such gang (Valdez, 2005). When released, extortion, fencing, and drug selling were some of the crimes they committed. The leadership of Pura Vida remained incarcerated although they took over much of the heroin and cocaine markets on the streets. Anyone selling drugs within areas under the control of Pura Vida was required to pay 10% of the profits, referred to as *el diez por ciento*, or risk victimization.

Valdez (2005) reports that Pura Vida transformed these drug markets, organizing them similar to retail markets and adopting a paramilitary-like vertical hierarchy.

Pura Vida members pushed heroin on to other gangs by offering purer dope for lower prices. This brought about changes in the way the drug was perceived by youth. The stigmatization of heroin use began to dissolve as rates of use increased among gang youth. This led to more heroin addiction among Latino gangs and, consequently, more arrest and incarceration. Valdez (2005) notes that this increase in heroin use resulted in members being less able to fulfill their obligations to the gang; they were morphing into *tecatos*—heroin addicts. Pura Vida recruited other members to be independent drug sellers or associates. They approached Latino members when they were sent to a Texas correctional facility, who then became part of this prison gang. On release, youth were no longer members of their original gang, but *soldados* (foot soldiers) of Pura Vida. As they grew, they absorbed members from other gangs. Valdez (2005) notes similar processes to those which occurred in San Antonio may be happening across the United States. Young gang-involved adults come out of prison with stronger ties to organized criminal syndicates, which increases their capacity to commit more crime and violence on release (see also Schlosser, 1998).

Prison gangs influence norms related to violence on the streets. Street gang violence is primarily intraethnic—within the same ethnicity. Evidence suggests that interethnic violence among gangs is directly related to the hostilities held between prison gangs. La Eme has a long-standing animosity with the Black Guerilla Family. Gangs linked to La Eme in the Los Angeles area have been involved in intimidating and victimizing African American families. Federal authorities have focused on one gang in particular, Azusa-13, a Latino

BOX 9.1: MEDIA CHECK!

American Me

American Me is a fictionalized story of the emergence of the Mexican Mafia (La Eme) in California prisons from the 1950s through the 1980s. Beginning with the zoot suit riots, the movie captures the hardships faced by Latino families, mostly Mexican immigrants, in relation to their lived experience in East Los Angeles. Edward James Olmos, who directed the movie, stars as Santana, the embryonic leader of La Eme. Olmos's character is based on Rodolfo Cadena, a founding member of La Eme. Interestingly, another of the founding members is a guy named Pegleg Morgan, who has an Eastern European family background. William Forsythe, who plays the fictional character JD based on Morgan, does a fantastic job of nailing the prison gang slang, accent, and demeanor. A white guy is one of the originators of the Mexican Mafia.

Young Santana is sent to a correctional facility, where he is sodomized. Santana murders the youth, commencing his lengthy stay in prison. The youth Santana killed had terrorized other inmates, and Santana realizes that through his act of deadly violence, he has now gained respect. Violence in prison, he learns, is an effective way to demonstrate power. Flash forward 20 years and Santana is the leader of La Eme inside Folsom Prison. Narcotics and their control is a central theme within the film, which depicts minutiae of how drugs are supplied and the rules surrounding the trade. The movie shows how drugs are smuggled into prison in graphic detail and depicts how and why inmates are murdered for stealing and adulterating them. The film is violent, with brutal stabbing and rape scenes.

Santana is eventually released, albeit temporarily, and while he is back on the streets he finds that things have changed, particularly in the drug trade. Heroin has devastated parts of the barrio he grew up in, and Santana realizes that he has been partially responsible for that, given his control of La Eme. Santana has also never really been with a woman, only men, and the film depicts his awkwardness with his first female date outside of prison. He has been incarcerated for most of his life, and Santana comes across as a complete stranger in his own neighborhood.

A film about a dangerous and vicious prison gang based on what was considered insider information might not sit well with prison gang members. Members of La Eme were apparently furious for the way the film depicted one of its revered leaders, Cadena (the Santana character played by Olmos), especially because the film showed him being raped as a youth and then later murdered by his own members. In real life, Cadena was killed by La Eme's rivals, Nuestra Familia. In retaliation for the way La Eme were depicted in the film, three consultants—all of whom were previously or currently involved in La Eme—were murdered within a year of the film's release. One of these murders happened less than two weeks after the film was first shown. Olmos was also a victim of extortion by members of La Eme, including Pegleg Morgan.

Olmos spoke about the film at the University of California, Riverside, in the early 1990s. He took questions from the audience. One individual, who looked like he could be part of a gang given his tattoos and facial hair, called Olmos out. He told Olmos something along the lines of, "You need to go talk to so and so about setting things straight" in a tone inflected with slang. Olmos stood his ground and indicated that he had already "talked to so and so" and made good. Things were tense in the room for several moments and it seemed clear that Olmos's movie had upset people.

Visit YouTube to see the trailer for American Me.

---

gang within Los Angeles that has been accused of systematically targeting blacks (Quinones, 2013; Tokumatsu and Bernstein, 2013). Raids captured many of the key players, who are now serving lengthy sentences in federal prisons.

RADICALIZATION AND PRISON GANGS

Radicalization in prisons refers to two things: right-wing extremist groups with a racist ideology and religious zealots with antigovernment, anti-American beliefs. The former are hate groups, such as the AB. Pelz et al. (1991) studied the Texas branch of the AB. They used Lipset and Raab's (1978) five-point theoretical model to contextualize the emergence of extremism. The first point relates to the historical dynamics, referring to the desegregation of the Texas Department of Corrections (TDC). White inmates felt threatened by the influx of blacks and believed that their status had declined. One of their respondents said,

> Young black inmates started coming into TDC thinking they could push white inmates around just because they had civil rights now. They were rude and disrespectful to white inmates and in prison all you have is your respect. (Pelz et al., 1991, p. 6)

In response, whites coalesced into a group, and many were part of racist ideological collectives on the outside, like the Ku Klux Klan and Aryan Nations. Black inmates responded similarly, forming their own group, which led to further cohesion of the whites and eventually tit-for-tat violence between black and white inmates.

A second tier of the Lipset and Raab model is a change in population dynamics. In response to desegregation, white inmates utilized extreme violence against nonwhites in an attempt to reestablish segregation. White inmates developed a reputation as violent and ruthless, committing deadly violence in plain view of the guards and other inmates. Some of these acts were captured on closed-circuit television. The only way that white inmates would regain the upper hand socially within the TDC was to eliminate or subjugate all nonwhites, including Jewish people. The AB's reputation for violence within the TDC attracted new recruits. Violence—at times unprovoked—became a staple of the culture of the AB in Texas. One of Pelz et al.'s (1991, p. 11) interviewees commented on this:

> Simply stand your own ground and make it known that anyone who disrespects you, a brother or a member of your family will be killed, his family will be killed and their house burned to the ground, along with every blade of grass on their property.

The third tier is political dynamics. Pelz et al. (1991) relate these dynamics to the norms, behavioral lifestyle, and symbolism adopted by the AB. The AB began to view themselves as the last bastion of defense of pure white men against the influx of inferior races. The tattoos of the AB—the shamrock, the swastika, the numbers 666, lightning bolts—were used to advertise the AB's ideology of white supremacy. The AB believed they were on a mission from God to defend humanity, and the killing of nonwhites was part of a holy war. As one of their respondents said, "killing is like having sex. The first time is not so rewarding, but it gets better and better with practice, especially when one remembers that it's a holy cause" (Pelz et al., 1991, p. 9). Such idealism leads to the fourth tier: political baggage. The AB believe that the prison system is illegitimate because it catered to minorities and to non-AB whites who are sympathetic to them. The system was set up to enslave whites so minorities could victimize them. Because the AB see the legal and the correctional systems as dishonest, they feel justified to go beyond the law.

The fifth and final tier of the model is politicalization. The AB in Texas rallied others to their cause, including true believers. These individuals were part of Aryan organizations prior to incarceration, such as the National White People's Party and the National Association for the Advancement of White People. The AB provided a legitimate platform for inmates to express their views. Others joined for protection because they believed an increase in sexual assaults by blacks was occurring. The Texas branch of the AB splintered into different factions under the weight of increased pressure from prison officials, which weakened the group. Some were committed to white supremacy and others to criminal activities. This type of internal conflict that leads radical groups to dissolve was also predicted in the Lipset and Raab model.

BOX 9.2: ON TRIAL

What amount of evidence is needed to indicate a former prison gang member's status? The individual in question is on the verge of his 60th birthday. He has about a dozen grandchildren. During a random police sweep of parolees, he was busted for a weapons violation. The prosecution added a gang enhancement to the charge because of his history in a prison gang. However, he has not been in a prison gang for several years and has evidence to document this.

As a teenager in the 1970s, the individual formed his own gang. This gang was multiracial, with whites, Asians, Latinos, and a few Filipino youths. By the time he turned 19, he was beginning the first year in a 20-year stretch for attempted murder. He did about 14 years for that offense, was paroled, was out for about a week, and was then rearrested on a burglary. He was then sentenced to 10 more years. During his time in prison, being white, he became part of the Aryan Brotherhood. He rose in rank and became a relatively prolific member, being allowed to tattoo a shamrock across his chest and stomach (the shamrock is a symbol used by the Aryan Brotherhood), as well as numerous other neo-Nazi tattoos, such as swastikas and lightning bolts. He was a committed, full-fledged member of the Aryan Brotherhood. Some of his family members who were not incarcerated also became affiliated with the gang and were involved in drug sales on the streets and in prison. This man took orders from some of the top members—the lifers. He admits "putting the hurt" onto people who owed money, but celebrates the fact that he never killed anyone. He lived a comfortable life in prison. The Aryan Brotherhood looked after him.

Over time, however, he became disillusioned with the lifestyle. He noticed people getting seriously hurt and sometimes killed for the smallest infractions. Other instances occur whereby the Aryan Brotherhood kill people he knew and loved. He began to question their rules and their direction. Eventually, he decided to distance himself from the Aryan Brotherhood and contacted prison officials. He "rolled over" on the Aryan Brotherhood by cooperating with prison officials and telling them everything he knows about the gang. Both for his protection and to help ensure his intentions are bona fide, he was housed in a separate unit filled with other prisoners who now want to leave prison gangs, all going through a "debriefing

process." This process could last up to several years, during which times the veracity of his statements and knowledge about the Aryan Brotherhood were checked, and his visitors were screened (including all mail and telephone calls). Finally, his probation officer, who officially documented this process, confirmed his new status: "drop out of a prison gang—Aryan Brotherhood." The individual was then released from prison, having both served his sentence and completed the debriefing process.

On being released, he returned to the family home in the same community he grew up in. He could not afford to move, and everyone in the community was aware of who he is and his newfound status as an ex-member of the Aryan Brotherhood. The Aryan Brotherhood issued him a "kite"—an indication that the individual is now targeted for assassination—and he received several death threats. Even his family was threatened. Several individuals visited his families' homes on behalf of the Aryan Brotherhood. One time they vandalized the home of a family member. The man informed the police, but no action was taken. Another time he was shot when he randomly came across an affiliate of the Aryan Brotherhood while out shopping. He did not have health insurance, so he patched himself up and was grateful the bullet went straight through. The police still offered no help. As a result, he bought a gun for protection. The man spent most of his time at home.

The man had the tattoo of the shamrock removed from across his chest and belly. This removal was done with lasers and was described as being more painful than having the tattoo completed in the first place. The stomach area is also known for being a particularly sensitive area for laser tattoo removal. He then had a giant cross tattooed in the same spot. The man became a devout Catholic.

In this case, the man's ex-prison gang status was confirmed officially by his probation officer, as well as by his experience of going through the debriefing process while incarcerated. The attempts on his life by those affiliated with the Aryan Brotherhood also suggest their dissatisfaction with him, which could arguably be the result of his participation with prison officials. Even the man's own efforts of having his prison gang–related tattoo removed suggests his ex-gang status. If such experiences do not convey the status of an ex-prison gang member, then what does?

Terrorism is another form of prisoner radicalism. The terrorist attacks of September 11, 2001, had significant implications for gangs. They have been successfully prosecuted under terrorist clauses, the first being the St. James Gangs in New York City in 2004 (Garcia, 2005).[2] Gangs "terrorized" local communities through violence and intimidation. But do

---

2   Although convicted in 2007, New York's Court of Appeals later overturned this decision, stating that the Bronx District Attorney erred in attempts to prosecute a criminal street gang with state terrorism charges (see Buettner, 2012).

gangs or members actually set out to commit mass destruction in the name of ideology like terrorist organizations? Hamm (2008) examined radicalization among inmates and reported a direct link to gangs. He found that many individuals in his study were in prison gangs, and most were also members of criminal street gangs prior to incarceration. Each had converted to some sort of religion while incarcerated, including Christianity, Islam, and Buddhism, as well as Odinism, Wicca, and Jam'iyyat Ul-Islam Is-Shaheed (JIS), a fringe group of Sunni Muslims with proterrorist views.

Spirituality was beneficial for most of the prisoners who converted. A few, particularly those affiliated with JIS, became more ideological, which spurred new forms of criminality. They were likely to be in maximum-security prisons with little rehabilitation services. Hamm (2008) reported that JIS acted as a prison gang, with its own organizational hierarchy, secret codes, behavioral norms, and shared identity. Rather than other gangs, JIS's main target was the U.S. government. Charismatic leaders radicalized individual prisoners serving long sentences who had little family contact through intense personal sessions. Antigovernment sentiments were stoked within these sessions. Officials noted a significant increase in these attitudes within the past 10–20 years. Hamm (2008) reported that few prisoners who develop radical beliefs—whether they are ideologically racist or anti-American—will violently act upon them. The main threat, Hamm concludes, lies with the small number of radical prisoners who, on release, may band into terrorist cells.

PRISON GANG MISCONDUCT

What constitutes prison misconduct and the accuracy of reporting such actions is debated (Byrne and Hummer, 2007). Much of this misconduct is attributed to members, including disproportional amounts of violence, drug sales, and other illegal behaviors (Byrne and Hummer, 2007; Fleisher and Decker, 2001). Similar to street gangs, the selection, facilitation, and/or enhancement models proposed by Thornberry and colleagues (1993) are also applicable to prison gang members (Pyrooz et al., 2011).

Gangs commit more violence while incarcerated than inmates with no affiliations. Support for this finding has emerged from various studies. On one level, facilities that have higher percentages of members also have higher rates of homicide (Reisig, 2002). Gaes et al. (2002) reported that short-term inmates who were members were more likely to be involved in a range of violent behaviors. Likewise, Fischer (2002) found that adults in gangs were two to three times more likely to commit serious incidents of misconduct, especially violence. In Florida, membership predicted violent behaviors among inmates (Cunningham and Sorensen, 2007). In the early 1980s in the TDC, prison gangs were responsible for between about one-quarter and one-third of homicides (Pelz et al., 1991). Griffin and Hepburn (2006) noted that in the Arizona Department of Corrections, individuals in gangs were more likely to commit assaults and issue threats (see also Krienert and Fleisher, 2001). In a multistate investigation, Huebner (2003) reported that members were more likely to assault staff.

Nonviolent behaviors are also common (Gaes et al., 2002; Shelden, 1991). Shelden (1991) reported that, compared to non-gang members, inmates who were part of street gangs violated drug use regulations and did not receive treatment options. Krienert and Fleisher (2001), in their report from Nebraska, found that members used drugs.

Drury and DeLisi (2011) were interested in the relationship between street gangs and prison misconduct. Using data from more than 1,000 inmates in southwestern correctional facilities, the authors sought to test whether members who were incarcerated on homicide charges also committed institutional infractions. The authors created a variable called gangkill—the risk of membership combined with a conviction of different types of homicide (e.g., first- or second-degree homicide, manslaughter). Their analyses revealed that the individuals most at risk for membership who were convicted of homicide were much more likely to report infractions for major violations while incarcerated. These infractions included carrying a weapon, disobeying officers, damaging property, and carrying contraband (e.g., drugs).

The gangkill variable also predicted inmates who committed several minor violations. Consistent with other research, those convicted of homicide without risks of gang membership were unlikely to have committed all forms of misconduct. Only when the gang variable was added did the correlations between behavioral infractions arise. The authors suggest that members convicted for homicide pose a significant threat to prison authorities. Gang murders are distinct from other homicides because other homicides are often crimes of passion involving intimates or accidents. Gang-related homicides are related to interpersonal issues such as disrespect, revenge, or loyalty. When members who have been convicted of homicide enter the prison system, they bring these values with them. These values are related to the reason that inmates are more likely to report misconduct (Drury and DeLisi, 2011).

PRISON GUARD MISCONDUCT AND GANGS

The relationships between the guards and the gangs are multifaceted. Hunt et al. (1993) noted ways in which gangs financially benefitted the guards. Gangs were perceived as a threat that required proper staffing. Acknowledging their ever-present danger, annual budgets allowed for additional security and overtime pay. The guards also encouraged division among the inmates, particularly the main rival gangs, to instigate violence. This helped the guards because if the gangs were fighting each other, they were less likely to fight the guards.

Hunt et al. (1993) reported that prison guards sold gangs drugs, weapons, and other items. As one of the inmates said,

> You'd be surprised who the guards affiliated with. Guards have friends that's in there. They have their friends outside, you know. Guards'll bring drugs in. Sell 'em. Guards will bring knives in, weapons, food. The guards play a major role. (p. 401)

Schlosser (1998, p. 17) noted the contraband that prisoners have been caught with, including "a leader of the Gangster Disciples [who] had . . . kept cellular phones, a color television, a stereo, a Nintendo Game Boy, a portable washing machine, and up to a hundred pounds of marijuana in his cell." The constant reports of prisoners obtaining these goods suggest one of two things: either the guards are ignorant of the problem of contraband or they are involved in it. The underground economy within prisons and the officers' role within it are difficult to ignore and combat.

Drugs in prison are a lucrative business, with prices ranging from 10 to 30 times higher than on the streets (Riveland, 1999). The massive amounts of money circulating inside jails and prisons in relation to the illicit drug trade makes prison staff vulnerable to being coopted into participation (Fleisher and Decker, 2001; Riveland, 1999). Like on the streets, control for the market leads to violence with competing gangs. The drug trade in prisons has been considered one of its greatest challenges (Riveland, 1999). The fact that so many prisoners report substance abuse issues prior to incarceration helps ensure an endless supply of customers. Drugs find their way into the hands of gang members in various ways, including visitors bringing drugs during visiting hours and delivering them to inmates, drugs being thrown over the prison wall, and airplanes flying over and dropping drugs into yards at night (Ross, 2008).

Inmates may recruit or coerce guards to bring drugs. They can do this through blackmail or threats to report observed illegal behaviors, such as drinking or using drugs on the job or having sex with an inmate (Ross, 2008). A study on Illinois correctional officers reported that, compared to inmates, the officers were *more* likely to test positive for substance use (Knox, 2000a). Inmates may also threaten a guard's family to get drugs. Knox (2000a, pp. 433–434) mentions a report from the Illinois Department of Corrections that says if officers do not allow inmates' visitors to bring in contraband, "the correctional officers are shown that the prisoners possess photographs of their homes, their wives, and children." In other cases, the guards may have been gang members to begin with. Prison gangs have been known to get an associate on the outside without a criminal record to apply for a job with the correctional facility, who would then act as a liaison between the gang and the outside world, bringing in whatever they need (Hagedorn, 1988).

Evidence has emerged about guards having sex with gang members. Toobin (2014) writes about the intimate relationships that several female guards had with a member of the Black Guerilla Family in the Baltimore City Detention Center. The gang member reportedly had five children with four different guards, two of whom had his name tattooed on them. Another gang member was sexually involved with five other guards in the same facility. Toobin (2014) discussed how gang members preyed on vulnerable guards who were characterized as young, with low self-esteem and insecurities, and who were easily manipulated. These relationships were reported as being mostly consensual and often initiated by the inmates. Toobin (2014) highlights a report whereby the guards said the relationship offered them protection, that the inmates were physically and emotionally available, and that the guards felt in control of the relationship. Some financially benefitted by participating in drug selling.

LEAVING PRISON GANGS

Little is known about how and why people leave prison gangs. Fong et al. (1995), using data from 48 former members of prison gangs who had left, asked what motivated the change. Losing interest was commonly reported, as was refusal to carry out a gang-ordered assassination on a nonmember. Other reasons included violating a rule and fearing retaliation, outgrowing a sense of belonging, becoming an informant, disagreement with leadership, and failing to commit a gang-related crime when ordered.

RECIDIVISM

One of the greatest predictors of being incarcerated in the future is having been previously incarcerated. This phenomenon has been referred to as the revolving-door cycle of arrest–incarceration–release–rearrest–reincarceration. Having been punished for a crime is a specific deterrence, which is ineffective for three reasons: (1) offenders are not rational and instead are likely to display negative emotionality (e.g., anger); (2) the strains pressuring people to commit crime (e.g., poverty, peer influence) are stronger than the threat of punishment; and (3) punishment itself is ineffective; if the chance of getting caught is low, then the chance of subsequent apprehensions must be even lower (Cullen et al., 2013).

Gang membership is another predictor of recidivism and has been shown in studies not about prison members, but about street members who have been incarcerated. Inmates with active gang affiliations are more likely to be rearrested than others (Olson and Dooley, 2006). Huebner et al. (2007) reported that of young males recently released from state prison, about one-third were members. These individuals were twice as likely to recidivate and to do so more quickly than other types of inmates, particularly drug offenders. Both studies indicate that although recidivism is a problem among prisoners returning home, it also remains a concern for gang-involved inmates returning home (Pyrooz et al., 2011).

G. S. Scott (2004) offers some important insight, based on research in Chicago, into how the revolving-door policy of inmates impacts gang members. Members have more risk factors in their lives than nonmembers and most are nonwhite. The members in Scott's study were from African American inner-city communities in Chicago. On release, those who entered as gang members returned to their same communities. Scott (2004) indicates that herein lies a major problem: these individuals were already sidelined prior to being incarcerated, but now, with a criminal record, they are further marginalized. Former inmates still have ties to their old gang. Their community provides them with emotional and social support, as well as a way to make a living selling drugs. Legitimate employment is something members recently released from prison are cut off from, and selling drugs becomes a rational choice (see Fleisher and Krienert, 2004). The fact that they are ex-convicts with current gang ties who are also involved in selling brings significant attention from law enforcement. Membership, with its premium on loyalty and making money, traps them in this cycle. Richard, one of Scott's respondents (2004, pp. 118–119), said this:

> I get out and I need me some money, man. I know what I'm gonna go. Shit. Damn. Where's G. G. at, man? Them niggahs still sellin' dope over there? Man, hook me up with G. G. I'm gonna call G. G. . . . So now you running with them, and now you might be carrying a pistol or something, and after a while you showin' your loyalty, and that you're comin' every day, you know. They gonna give you some shit [drugs] to work with. . . . So he gives you this little package here, and you make four Gs off of it [Four thousand dollars]. . . . You rollin'. It's good for me. . . . Shit, I got a car outside now, got my woman dressin' clever, and my kids are wearing Michael Jordan gym shoes, the rent's paid. I'm starting to see some progress. I've been out of the joint for what, eight months now? I'm doing all right . . . [the

gang] looked out for me, I'm gonna look out for them. I know where my bread is buttered at. The loyalty is with the money, man. And when you got loyalty working with money, and you're in the gang structure and everything, too, then you got a double hold on a guy. That gangs have that double hold. They got the loyalty workin', and the money workin'. You know, I'm loyal to my guys. It puts food on my table. Protects me and my kids.

RESPONDING TO PRISON GANGS

Responses to prison gangs vary. Dramatic actions have been taken, such as segregating members in different buildings, locking away leaders in solitary confinement in maximum-security prisons, intercepting communications, creating task forces, and placing entire facilities on lockdown (Fleisher and Decker, 2001; Hunt et al., 1993; Kassel, 2003; Pyrooz et al., 2011). Other reactions have included interrupting members' communication, both inside and outside the prison, case-by-case examinations, and the robust prosecution of gang crimes (Fleisher and Decker, 2001). In some cases, the problem of gangs is completely ignored (Knox and Tromanhauser, 1991).

Jacketing, or having a dirty jacket, is an administrative tool for identifying a prisoner as a suspected member (Fleisher and Decker, 2001; Hunt et al., 1993; Pyrooz et al., 2011). Jacketing helps facilitate a transfer to a Supermax—a maximum-security facility that offers limited mobility and contact (Riveland, 1999). At times, as Hunt et al. (1993) note, it might not matter whether a prisoner is a member; it is simply how the situation is perceived by officials. Individuals who hang around known members may be jacketed for doing so. The word of a confidential informant, who may have both financial and other reasons to falsely label someone, may also come into play (Hunt et al., 1993).

Stop-snitching is something heard on the streets, although members in prison or street gangs have a history of it. In prison, this method works by squeezing information out of individuals in solitary confinement or other high-security, low-mobility units. Inmates know that if they provide information, they stand a chance of improving their situation (Hunt et al., 1993). The problem is that such information, although not coerced, is dubious in nature because of the reasons surrounding its *quid pro quo* motivation.

One of the most common approaches to gangs is to send their leaders to different facilities (Riveland, 1999). This is referred to as bus therapy, or diesel treatment, and is the most common approach taken by officials (Knox, 2000a; Knox and Tromanhauser, 1991).

Another approach is placing them away from the general population (Riveland, 1999). Individuals sent to a Supermax can expect this isolation, as well as having all of their services (e.g., food, laundry) performed in their cells, further restricting their movement and communications (Pyrooz et al., 2011; Riveland, 1999). Whether isolation is effective is unclear (Kassel, 2003; Pyrooz et al., 2011). The constitutionality of sending inmates to secure housing units because they are members has been challenged in federal courts (Pyrooz et al., 2011; see also Kassel, 2003). If gang members are not violating the rules, then they should not be sent to secure housing units (Kassel, 2003; Pyrooz et al., 2011).

Kassel (2003) argues that isolation is counterproductive because it leads to prisoners identifying as members, most of which are minorities. Kassel (2003) says this approach contributes to gang solidarity and cohesiveness and increases the capacity of prisoners who are labeled as members to commit crime, which undermines the security within the prison and public safety. This echoes Knox's (2000b) observation that prison officials do not believe that segregation is effective because members are still able to commit crimes (see also Spergel, 1995). Instead of isolation, Kassel (2003) recommends evenhanded policies that focus on misconduct, the training of guards and officials, and educational programs targeting suspected members. In other cases, evidence suggests that isolating members has worked. Ralph and Marquart (1991) report that when Texas put all known members into segregation, violence in the general population decreased.

Alternative programming, such as getting members to rethink their lives and behaviors, is another response. The evidence on this approach suggests that members do not embrace these types of interventions (Fleisher and Decker, 2001). One study reported that cognitive behavioral therapies for gang and non-gang members resulted in lower recidivism rates for both groups (DiPlacido et al., 2006).

Holvey (2009) describes a three-part program to combat prison gangs. On intake, inmates are questioned about their status and checked for any tattoos, clothing, or paraphernalia that could be considered gang related. Problematic gang-affiliated inmates and leaders are then isolated from the general population within a security threat group management unit. While in these units, inmates are required to participate in programs that focus on reducing violence and improving cognitive skills. Prior to completing these programs, they must renounce their links to gangs. Holvey (2009) reports that, as a result, staff assaults decreased by more than 40%, organized violence declined by more than 80%, and the recidivism rate was about half that of the national average. Approaches similar to the one outlined by Holvey have been reported elsewhere (Ross, 2008). Other researchers have found these programs to be problematic because they force prisoners who feel that they have been mislabeled to renounce membership, leading to false claims (Kassel, 2003).

SUMMARY

Prison gangs emerged in the middle of the 20th century in western states. Three large prison gangs aligned by race are the Aryan Brotherhood for whites, the Mexican Mafia for Latinos, and the Black Guerilla Family for African Americans. Gangs are theorized to have emerged for two reasons. The indigenous formation theory suggests that prisoners formed gangs because of deprivation and victimization. The second theory suggests that gangs are the outcome of a culture imported from the streets. Street members, once incarcerated, bring their culture inside and form gangs. Evidence to support and refute both models has emerged. Inmate segregation and policy changes that impact the dynamics of prison life are also important considerations when discussing the emergence of gangs.

The number of prison gang members is unclear. Various methods surveying different types of facilities (e.g., state, local, federal) have produced inconsistent results. The reluctance of inmates and administrators to be open about the extent of gangs is a major obstacle to accurately tabulating their numbers. Regardless, gangs are responsible for a disproportionate amount of violence and other behavioral infractions. Some gangs have involved guards, who have been known to facilitate the criminal activities of members.

Prison and street gangs have many similarities, one of which is the use of signs, symbols, and imagery with dual meaning and significance. Prison gangs differ from those on the street, particularly with regard to organization. Prison gangs are like a regular business, with a pyramid structure with a few leaders sitting at the top and lieutenants below them controlling the foot soldiers, who do most of the work. Few street gangs are organized this way. Prison gangs are secretive and closed, but those on the street are blatant and open. Prison members are also often in their thirties and forties, but on the streets members are largely in their teens and twenties. Offending patterns also differ, with street gangs being involved largely in intraethnic violence and a broad pattern of criminal behaviors, whereas prison gangs commit interethnic violence and focus on profit-generating criminality. In some cases, prison gangs exert a degree of influence and authority over street gangs, such as with La Eme and *sureno* members. In other cases, the relationship between prison and street gangs is less understood, as with the Aryan Brotherhood.

Responses vary from doing nothing, to bus therapy, to segregation, to behavioral modification programs. Some of these approaches have received support, but, similar to many street gang programs, others either have not been evaluated or have provided mixed results. Incarceration settings offer ideal opportunities to reach out and intervene in the lives of inmates to help reduce the likelihood of committing institutional infractions, as well as to help prevent inmates from returning to prison. Membership further increases the chance of reincarceration.

CHAPTER REVIEW QUESTIONS

1. What are the reasons that gangs formed? How do these reasons compare to one another?
2. How many members are there? What are some potential problems with obtaining accurate counts?
3. Describe the three major gangs.
4. How are prison and street gangs similar? How are they different?
5. Explain how misconduct is related to members.
6. What is the radicalization of prisoners referring to? What are the main points that Lipsett and Raab outline in relation to radicalization of the AB? How does this radicalization differ from what Hamm discussed?
7. Provide some examples of guards involved in the illegal activities of gang members.
8. What do we know about leaving gangs?
9. What do we know about recidivism and being a member?
10. What are some official responses? What are some pros and cons of each approach?

CHAPTER 10

DESISTANCE AND LEAVING THE GANG

KEY WORDS

Age–crime distribution: Refers to the age of individuals who commit crime within a population. The distribution indicates that participation in crime peaks between 16 and 20 years old and then declines rapidly. This distribution has been consistent over time.

Age–drug distribution: Refers to the ages of individuals who use illicit substances within a population. The distribution indicates that such use peaks between 18 and 20 years old and then declines gradually. This distribution has been consistent over time.

Agency: A concept that refers to the ability of individuals to determine and choose their own actions, free will, and beliefs; the capacity and awareness that humans have to act and govern their own behaviors and futures.

Crystallization of discontent: When an offender realizes that his or her criminal regimes are the cause of poor social and economic standing and results in actively seeking new, noncriminal lifestyles.

Desistance: The process by which people stop offending. Desistance can come about naturally, whereby people simply stop because of a variety of reasons. Criminal justice and public health–related interventions also initiate or assist the desistance process.

Displacement: Shifting from one crime to another. Someone who committed violent and property crimes at one point in life, but then was only involved in drugs later in life would be an example of displacement. Criminal displacement can also refer to the shifting of criminal activity from one geographic area to another.

Future selves: A concept that helps guide individuals toward identity change, whereby they take actions to ensure their positive "other" self and avoid their negative "feared" self.

Identity: The distinct personality of an individual; a set of behavioral and personal characteristics; all of the attributes of a person, such as physical, social, emotional, and psychological.

Life-course perspective: A multidisciplinary approach that examines socioeconomic context, parent–child relations, and changes in social bonds over the period of individuals' lives. This perspective focuses on the initiation, persistence, and desistance of criminal behaviors as being related to important and powerful events.

Making good: A narrative about redemption, cessation of offending, and contributing positively to society that helps former offenders desist from further crimes.

Pull factors: In the context of desistance, these are agents external to the gang, such as new family or employment obligations that help pull youth out of gangs.

Push factors: In the context of desistance, these are agents internal to the gang, such as experiences of violent victimization, that help push youth out of gangs.

Trajectories: A long-term pattern of behavior, including crime or conformity.

Transitions: Major life events, such as getting married, having a child, becoming employed, or joining the military.

Turning points: A shift away from crime and toward conformity that is usually preceded by transitions.

Chapter Learning Objectives

- Outline key points on the process of desistance from crime and delinquency.
- Understand characteristics that shape how and why people leave gangs.
- Underscore the outcomes of leaving gangs.
- Discuss how youth from high-risk communities avoid gangs.

INTRODUCTION

Gang membership is often a temporary part of an individual's life. Most youth eventually walk away without much ceremony. How they leave the gang is not well understood. Despite decades of research, only a handful of studies have examined why members decide to leave. Even fewer studies have examined this process in relation to gender. Understanding why and how people leave gangs and move on with their lives is important on a number of levels. First, it would assist law enforcement in developing qualifications to establish ex-membership and improve the ability to distinguish between current and former members. Second, such information would help intervention practices better target their services and the specific services different types of gang members are likely to need. Finally, it would provide current gang members something to aim for, a plan of action of accomplishments they must achieve to earn their status as ex-gang members.

The first half of the chapter examines desistance from crime more generally. This is further broken down into three areas of focus: the life-course perspective, identity and agency, and displacement and drug use. Desistance miscellanea are then provided. The second part of the chapter focuses on leaving the gang. Getting beaten out is explored, as is the extent to which leaving parallels a reduction in risk behaviors and victimization. Next, the intensity of youths' participation, the overall organizational level of their gang, and shifts in peer network affiliations are discussed. How leaving the gang links with life-course events and job expectations and aspirations are then discussed. The chapter concludes by looking at the extent to which youth have truly left gangs, as well as how to resist gangs in the first place.

DESISTANCE FROM CRIME AND DELINQUENCY

Reviewing desistance from crime is important if we are to understand why people leave gangs. Desistance is broken down into three different areas of focus: the life-course perspective, identity and agency, and displacement and drug use.

THE LIFE-COURSE PERSPECTIVE

Most juvenile offenders do not mature into adult criminals, but instead "age out" of crime, usually between 16 and 20 years old (Farrington, 1986). This phenomenon is consistent across Western nations. Something happens around this age that pulls individuals out of crime. This age-graded theory of social control is referred to as the life-course perspective (Laub and Sampson, 2001, 2003; Sampson and Laub, 1993, 2005).

In an attempt to understand the processes underlying desistance and the role of social context in shaping its dynamics, Sampson and Laub argue that changes in social relations over the life course can affect future involvement in crime despite earlier criminal propensities. They employ three concepts: trajectories, transitions, and turning points. A trajectory is a long-term pattern of behavior, including levels of involvement in offending. Transitions are major life events, such as marriage, employment, parenthood, or military service. These transitions may result in turning points: a change in an individual's trajectory away from crime. Strong empirical support for the life-course perspective has emerged (Moffitt, 1993; Nagin and Paternoster, 2000; O'Connell, 2003; Paternoster and Brame, 1997).

Laub and Sampson (2003) discussed desistance as a process involving four stages. In the first step, a transition occurs, such as a new relationship, having a child, getting a job, or joining the military. The individual now has responsibilities. He or she has an increase in informal social control and behaviors are monitored more closely. Now that the individual is situated and involved in conventional lifestyles, he or she may decide that committing crime is no longer necessary. Coinciding with these new responsibilities is a change in daily activities. Criminals often lead unstructured lifestyles, where they are free to associate with whomever, whenever. Their new involvement in everyday life means that they now must be in certain places at certain times. When they begin to enmesh themselves into routines, they associate more with prosocial peers and less with antisocial ones. The next step is a commitment to this new, noncriminal lifestyle. At this point crime has become too risky because the individual jeopardizes all of the hard work he or she has accomplished.

Laub and Sampson note that this process is neither inevitable nor possible for all offenders. Transitions can be fortuitous and situations change for no apparent reason. Not all individuals are savvy enough to recognize life-altering opportunities or to capitalize on them. This is where human agency plays an important role.

IDENTITY AND AGENCY

What comes first: the opportunity or the desire to become more involved in conventional lifestyles?[1] Theories of desistance often recognize that conventional institutions like marriages, jobs, and noncriminal social networks are important. Less agreement exists as to how offenders come on these opportunities. Prosocial relations and legitimate employment prospects are not evenly distributed in society. What could emerge first is the desire for self-change, which is then strengthened by subsequent involvement in conventional institutions (Artesti et al., 2010; Giordano et al., 2002; Maruna, 2001; Paternoster and Bushway, 2009; Sommers et al., 1994). In this scenario, desistance comes about when people are dissatisfied with their current identity and lifestyle as an offender and actively do something about it. When the decision to change the individual self is prepared, people then seek out conventional institutions, such as legitimate jobs, marriages, and social networks. Agency plays a fundamental role in desistance.

Maruna (2001) suggests that internalized factors surrounding the narratives that offenders create for themselves are more important than externalized conditions. He discusses how those who develop a redemption narrative about "making good," where they make a conscious decision to stop committing crimes and contribute positively to society, are more likely to desist. A key focal point here is the ability to separate past histories of offending from current self-perceptions. Maruna talks about two different selves: the core and the other self. The core is the law-abiding person that the individual sees himself or herself becoming. The other is the law-breaking person that the individual was. Maruna argues that those who were successful in distancing themselves from the other and creating and embracing the core were able to quit crime. He focused on the internalized self as an important consideration toward desistance, but also notes the centrality of external influences. Most individuals who desisted talked about the intervention of a central person who believed they had the ability to change. Maruna says that one of the biggest obstacles desisters face is their new self being accepted by society. This highlights a contradictory nature of the justice system: community penalties are a way offenders pay their debt to society, but offenders continue to face stigmatization and extreme difficulties on reentry.

Other researchers have discussed possible or future selves and the balance of new identities with the other or feared self in terms of desistance (see Oyserman and Fryberg, 2006; Oyserman and Markus, 1990a, 1990b). These concepts have been utilized in gang intervention strategies (see Clark and Humphries, 2013). Criminologists have taken an interest in these concepts. Pasternoster and Bushway (2009) present a theory of desistance that focuses on the feared self and the importance of identity. Similar to Oyserman, the authors make a distinction between the current self or working identity and the possible

---

1   For research that directly examines this question, see LeBel et al. (2008).

(future) self. And, like Oyserman and colleagues, Pasternoster and Bushway say that the possible self is a balance between hopes and fears.

What drives individuals is a desire for the good and a fear of the bad. Without these, the ultimate goal of desired change will not be met. Similar to Maruna's (2001) ex-convicts who developed an internal narrative to make good, the positive possible self serves as a blueprint for change. An avoidant motive, such as unhappiness related to a current life-style, is the spark that starts the self-change to increase the likelihood of a positive possible self. When an offender realizes that unhappiness is directly linked to his or her lifestyle—constantly having to be on the lookout for police, the low returns from offending, the in-crease in the likelihood of detection over time, the fatigue associated with crime[2]—this realization is the crystallization of discontent and leads to change internally and inten-tionally (Baumeister, 1991; Paternoster and Bushway, 2009).

According to Paternoster and Bushway (2009), the desire for a change in self-identity serves as an impetus for the switch of daily activities and peer associations. In breaking away from crime, individuals play with their new identities and lead safer prosocial lives. They begin affiliating with individuals who do not break the law. Friends involved in crime become less important and romantic partners take on greater significance as the individu-als begin to spend more time with them. Success means severing ties with former friends. Mixing with pro- and antisocial networks may cause a relapse into crime. Desistance can be accidental—falling in love, a lucky break finding work—leading to an increase in social control, but identity and human agency play a significant role.

HOOKS FOR CHANGE

Giordano et al. (2002) examine how offenders change their self-conceptualization. They contrast the theory of cognitive transformation with the life-course perspective and stress the importance of the actors' own roles within desistance. Their research, based on qualita-tive and quantitative data, focuses on males, females, whites, and nonwhites, noting that studies on desistance have focused only on white males using cross-sectional data. Giordano et al.'s findings indicated that neither job stability nor attachment (to spouse, to children) was a significant indicator of ceasing criminal behavior. Adult social control variables were in the direction of Sampson and Laub's life-course perspective, but they were not significant variables in predicting desistance.

The authors referred to specific "hooks" as "catalysts for lasting change when they en-ergize fundamental shifts in identity and changes in the meaning and desirability of deviant/criminal behavior itself" (Giordano et al., 2002, p. 992). One such hook was prison and treatment. These were not sources of lasting change, although some focused on these experiences. Another hook was spirituality. Many respondents, particularly women, felt that religion put them on the right path. Having children was another hook, but this was only slightly associated with behavioral change. The sample did not express childrear-ing as a major source of desistance. Some viewed children as more of a burden and others were involved with child endangerment cases. Childrearing was more likely a catalyst for

---

2 See work by Shover (1983) and Shover and Thompson (1992).

lasting change among females. Some individuals discussed a good-parent role, but disassociated themselves from that title because of their delinquent ways, whereas others expressed that they had changed or were trying to change for their kids. The final hook was marriage, whereby partners had a large influence on the individual. Some individuals did not believe in the effects of change brought about by having a partner. Some were happily married, but remained involved with criminal activities. Others had low-quality marriages, but reported a move away from offending. Others still did not have any romantic ties, but utilized their single status to their advantage in reaching for positive change.

The authors conclude by arguing that desistance comes down to personal responsibility and internal and external forms of control. They suggest that future studies should examine concepts of determination and responsibility, especially how behaviors can be taught and learned. They underscore the importance of cognitive openness—being ready for change—as one of the most important precursors of desistance.

DISPLACEMENT AND DRUG USE

Displacement is a shift in offending patterns over time.[3] If an individual had a history of committing violent crimes in adolescence but by adulthood was focused on property offenses, this would be a form of displacement. In this example, offending has not completely stopped, but the type of offense has changed to one that is less serious. Drug use is an important issue in relation to displacement. Over time, youth may stop committing violent and property crimes, but increase their use of drugs and alcohol (Hammersley, 2011; Massoglia, 2006).

Massoglia (2006) examined displacement using longitudinal data from the National Survey of Youth. Delinquent patterns among youth ages 11 and 17 were later reviewed against their criminal patterns as young adults. The sample was grouped into four categories based on offense type. The first group, called the normative class, contained about half of the sample (55%) and was characterized by a low to moderate probability of being involved in violence and general deviance. In adulthood, the normative class represented about half of the sample (48%). Another group was called the predatory class and constituted about a quarter (27%) of the youth. Compared with the normative group, the predatory class was six times more likely to be involved in vandalism, 11 times more likely to be involved in theft, and 3 times more likely to commit violent acts. The predatory group comprised 25% of the population as young adults. About 1 in 10 of the adolescents (11%) reported significant drug use, but also committed more vandalism, theft, and violence than youth in the predatory class. In adulthood, the number of individuals in the drug class doubled. The last group, the pervasive class, was represented by 7% of the population and was characterized as being involved with all types of illegal behavior. As adults, 6% were in the pervasive class. This research suggests that during adolescence, offenses like

---

3 Displacement can also refer to a shift in criminal activity from one geographic area to another. If police target a hot spot for crime in one area and then, as a result, crime goes down in that area but rises in another adjacent area, this is also displacement.

violence, theft, and vandalism play a significant role. As adults, these offenses become less apparent, although the incidence of substance use rises.

The age–crime distribution indicates that crime peaks around 16 to 20 years of age and then declines rapidly. When looking at the age–drug distribution, drug use peaks later—around 18 to 21 years of age (Substance Abuse and Mental Health Services Administration, 2011). Social bonds and/or changes in identity and/or hooks for change might have differential impacts on drug use and offending patterns. Substance use increases with age because of youths' newfound freedoms and exposure to different lifestyles as they assume adult responsibilities (Massoglia, 2006). Hammersley (2011) is critical when addressing surveys on delinquency and desistance because they often include substance use as a form. Collecting data this way makes it difficult to tell which youth in these surveys are only using drugs. Hammersley (2011) notes that most delinquents eventually desist and that substance use is problematic (i.e., addictive) among a small proportion of the population. Delinquency, in contrast, is a common pattern of behavior among youth, and normative patterns of drug use among noncriminal adults are also evident (Hammersley, 2011). Given these considerations and the confusion around recording involvement in delinquency outside of substance use, Hammersley (2011, p. 269) notes, "What happens to . . . substance use as [young people] desist from crime is much less clear" (see also Hser et al., 2007).

DESISTANCE MISCELLANEA

A few studies have examined the extent to which strains or pressures that cause negative emotionality (e.g., anger) are related to desistance (Eitle, 2010; Gunnison and Mazerolle, 2007). Gunnison and Mazerolle (2007), using data from the National Youth Study, examined desistance and persistence in relation to general strain theory (GST) and other theories. Strains examined included employment, negative life events, poor interactions with adults, and neighborhood stressors. The authors found differences between individuals who continued to offend and those who did not in the levels of strain they experienced, particularly in terms of neighborhood stressors and poor interactions with adults. Eitle (2010) conducted a longitudinal study among middle school students to determine the extent to which GST helped shape desistance. He found that the "core GST relationship between strain and crime was also found to be an important predictor of desistance" (Eitle, 2010, p. 1119). This held true after controlling for other variables in the youths' lives, such as their parents' levels of education, marriage history, and employment. Eitle found that anger was the key variable in explaining desistance, and youth with an angry disposition were much more likely to report sustained involvement in criminal activity.

Other researchers have focused on personality traits in explaining desistance. Blonigen (2010) examined the age–crime relationship and linked it to natural changes in personality. Rather than just an increase in social bonds, Blonigen (2010) theorizes that declines in delinquent and antisocial behavior are the result of normative changes in individuals' personalities. Desistance usually happens from late adolescence to early adulthood. Blonigen's (2010) argument is that the natural process of maturation of key personality traits during this time undergirds biological and sociological processes.

BOX 10.1: ON TRIAL

The young man involved in this case is a self-admitted gang member of a well-known and notorious gang that has several hundred members. The gang is so well known that various chapters of the organization are present in a couple of cities across the United States.

He has a history of arrests for grand theft auto, so much so that after he attends court for his (alleged) involvement in stealing one car, he then proceeds to (allegedly) steal another one in the vicinity of the courthouse he just left. He drives to a residential area in a middle-class neighborhood in the suburbs. Uncharacteristic of gang-related offenses, this one happens many miles from the inner-city area in which he resides. The young man is alone and is not wearing anything that can be considered gang attire—no specific colors or symbols. What he does not know is that, given the suspicion he aroused from law enforcement for his participation in a string of thefts and being the prime suspect in an ongoing case—he has been followed by an unmarked police car since he left the courthouse. The undercover officer observes him breaking into two different cars: one he cannot seem to enter and the other he enters, but the owner of the car returns when the young man is in it. The officer sees the young man flee from the second car, follows him, and then has a marked police car containing uniformed police officers pull over and arrest him.

The prosecution claims that the car theft was gang related. The theft, they say, benefits the reputation of the gang and that of the young man. The young man, they argue, is putting in work—crime on behalf of the gang—by stealing the car to increase his repute within the gang. The prosecution claims that grand theft auto benefits the gang because the car could be used in a drive-by shooting, to transport drugs or guns on behalf of the gang, or sold, with the proceeds going to a kitty—a specific account held by the gang that individual members could draw on when in need. Such needs, the prosecution says, include buying guns or drugs so members can continue their criminal organization and expand their empire. The gang has national connections, as evidenced from the different chapters in various cities across the United States, and also has a strict hierarchy of command, with the so-called shot callers—those making the important decisions—serving life sentences in prison. This chain of command dictates the overall operational-ization of the gang, including day-to-day activities, appropriate use of the funds in the kitty, and who is targeted for assassination and why. The car thefts were committed at the direction of the gang in this manner. The prosecution claims to know these things about this particular gang based on the testimony of a gang cop who has worked with the gang for a couple of years. The gang cop indicates he knows these things about this specific gang because members have told him directly. He said they volunteered such information. The prosecution also claims that the car thefts were done in association with a gang because the young man used his reputation as a gang member to create fear and intimidation within the community in which he attempted to steal cars.

The defense claims that no evidence has been presented to indicate that the attempted car thefts were committed for the benefit of, at the direction of, or in association with a gang. Stories whereby gang members distribute their ill-gotten funds evenly among their fellow gang members not involved in the offense are based more on myth than on reality. It does not stand to reason that a gang member would distribute these funds to those not participating in the offense any more than it would for average citizens to distribute their paychecks evenly to their neighbors. Moreover, no evidence was presented in this case that the young man had any intention of giving money generated from his (alleged) participation in the car thefts to his fellow gang members. When asked directly, the young man responded that he had never heard of gang members doing such things before or of gang members placing money into a kitty. As a result, the defense noted no evidence had been presented to indicate the thefts were committed for the benefit of a gang.

Also, no evidence was presented that the crime was committed at the direction of the gang. This is akin to saying that the gang ordered the young man to commit grand theft auto. Generally speaking, gangs are not organized in this way and, for the most part, individual members have autonomy—they make their own decisions about their behavior. Specifically in this case, the prosecution could not offer any evidence that anyone from the gang had told the young man to commit grand theft auto.

Finally, no evidence was presented that the thefts were committed in association with a gang. The young man was alone when he committed the offense and no others were arrested alongside him. He was not wearing gang attire and did not shout out the name of his gang during the committal of the offense. He also committed the offense well outside the territory of his gang. Despite the relative notoriety of the gang, the fact that he committed the crime many miles away from where he lived—in a different county, in fact—means that the idea that people in the relatively affluent suburb would know and thus fear this gang is suspect.

Beaver et al. (2008) note that environmental considerations that contribute to desistance, such as marriage, employment, and a shift in peer network affiliations, might also be shaped by genetic polymorphisms. The authors used data from the National Longitudinal Study of Adolescent Health. They were interested in dopamine and serotonin transporter genes, dopamine receptor genes, and a gene that has been linked to aggression. As predicted, the authors found that marriage increased the likelihood of desistance. Second, they noted that the dopamine receptor and transporter genes, as well as the gene related to aggression, significantly predicted desistance independent of other environmental variables for males. Third, they found that some genes interacted with marital status to predict desistance for males. This was the first study to offer evidence that genes and the environment interact in relation to desistance.

Maruna et al. (2004) borrow from labeling theory and the concept of "the looking-glass self" to better understand desistance. Society is skeptical of ex-offenders given their past histories of bad behavior. As the authors note, this is a major obstacle toward rehabilitative efforts because of the self-fulfilling prophecy: society treats ex-convicts as if they will reoffend; living up to this expectation, ex-convicts then reoffend. Going straight is a two-way street where not only must the ex-offender accept a conventional lifestyle, but also society must accept the ex-offender. As Lemert (1967) talked about primary and secondary deviance, Maruna et al. (2004) discuss primary and secondary desistance. Primary desistance refers to the discontinuance of criminal activity. Secondary desistance is "the movement from the behavior of non-offending to the assumption of the role or identity of a 'changed person'" (Maruna et al., 2004, p. 274). One way to do this is for others to recognize desistance in the ex-offender and to consider him or her rehabilitated. This is a process of relabeling the offender from negative to positive, and the looking-glass self plays an

BOX 10.2: MEDIA CHECK!

American History X

American History X is the first film directed by Tony Kaye, a Londoner better known as a Grammy award winner for music videos. The film is about white racist skinheads in Los Angeles. Kaye is well placed as a director, covering what is arguably a British export—skinheads—in the heart of movieland USA. A cropped-haired Edward Norton was nominated for an Academy Award for Best Actor for portraying the film's main protagonist, Derek Vinyard. Vinyard is an intelligent young man whose perception of blacks and Latinos is significantly impacted by the fate of his father—a firefighter who was killed by a black drug seller while responding to a call in South Los Angeles. Vinyard is athletic, and he, along with his neo-Nazi buddies, enjoys basketball at the public courts in Venice Beach. The irony here is also thick, with Vinyard excelling in a sport dominated by people he hates.

Vinyard's racist sentiments turn criminal when two black gang members he has had a previous run-in with attempt to steal the truck given to him by his father. Vinyard grabs his gun, sneaks up on the intruders, and kills them. The police arrive and Vinyard is arrested and sentenced to three years in prison for voluntary manslaughter.

Prison life starts out well for Vinyard, who fits right in with the Aryan Brotherhood. Later, he notices that the Brotherhood do not let their racist beliefs get in the way of doing business. When Vinyard sees one of his fellow racists involved in drug trafficking with a Latino, he becomes enraged and turns his back on the Brotherhood. The Aryans do not take kindly to this and exact their revenge by raping Vinyard in the shower. Vinyard then isolates himself and becomes a loner. Instead of continuing to victimize him, the gang leaves him alone to sulk.

Vinyard self-reflects about his racist beliefs and begins his transformation.

By the time Derek Vinyard is released, he has let go of his neo-Nazi identity and has a decent haircut. Rather than mixing it up with his old skinhead pals back home, he distances himself from anyone involved in the movement. He realizes that all his hatred has gotten him nowhere and that the racist ideology only has merit as long as it does not impact the bottom line: making money. His old friends are fools and his mentor—Stacy Keach, playing the patriarch of the young Aryans—is a false idol full of words. The only catch Vinyard has in leaving all of this neo-Nazi business in the past is his younger brother, Danny, who emulates Derek. While Derek was in prison, Danny grew up and became entrenched within the lifestyle and is now a full-fledged racist skinhead. Derek tries to save his brother from making the same mistakes he did.

Southern California has been a hotbed of anti-Semitic, racist, neo-Nazi hatemongering for years. This ugly part of white culture has been buried under avalanches of media coverage of gang violence, celebrity drug busts, and high-speed police chases. Tom Metzger, a former grand dragon of the KKK and original founder of the White Aryan Resistance, for many years lived in Fallbrook, an unincorporated area in northern San Diego County. The Southern Poverty Law Center acknowledges him after David Duke as the most notorious white supremacist alive in the United States. Racist attitudes among the young can be heard in some of the hard-core and punk bands throughout Southern California and seen in some of the gangs of youth, such as the Death Wish Kids in San Diego and the OC Skins and Public Enemy Number One in Orange County. The federal government has taken notice of these groups and Operation Stormfront netted dozens of hard-core white supremacists in Southern California for various crimes, many of which included gang enhancements.

---

important role. Successful integration back into conventional society "might involve the negotiation of a reformed identity through a process of prosocial labeling" (Maruna et al., 2004, p. 279). The authors conclude that the labeling process is an underappreciated aspect of desistance.

LEAVING THE GANG

Youth do leave gangs, some through violent death or lifelong incarceration. Others drift away. Most juveniles do not become adult members. Decker and Pyrooz (2011) note that the age–gang curve matches the age–crime curve, suggesting that age is a critical variable in understanding how and why youth leave (see also Bjorgo, 1999; Decker and Pyrooz, 2014; Melde and Esbensen, 2011, 2014; Pyrooz et al., 2014; Pyrooz and Decker, 2011). Desistance from gangs is so understudied that it clouds conceptualizations of an ex-gang member (Decker and Lauritsen, 2006; Decker and Pyrooz, 2011).

Leaving a gang has been reported in a handful of studies. From this evidence, the following themes have emerged: violent rituals; positions within the gang and gang organization; a shift in peer network affiliations; a reduction in risk behaviors and victimization; family and employment; and routine activities and disposition. Research on gender in relation to gang desistance is even more limited, but available evidence has reported few differences (Carson et al., 2013; O'Neal et al., 2014; Peterson, 2014; Pyrooz and Decker, 2011).

VIOLENT RITUALS

Most youth simply walk away from gangs (Bolden, 2012; Decker and Lauritsen, 2006; Decker and Pyrooz, 2011, 2014; Decker and Van Winkle, 1996; Hagedorn and Devitt, 1999; Peterson, 2014; Pyrooz and Decker, 2011; Quicker, 1999). Evidence has emerged that some youth leave through violence (Decker and Lauritsen, 2006; Harris, 1988; Peterson, 2014; Pyrooz and Decker, 2011; Valdez et al., 2009; Vigil, 1988a). Like getting jumped in, youth are jumped or rolled out of the gang. These incidents can be violent and, unlike getting jumped in, the aim is to do lasting harm (Harris, 1988). Valdez et al. (2009) offer a participant's description of someone who was rolled out of the gang:

> He was a homeboy, he wanted to get out. He told us that he wanted to get out because of his chick (girlfriend). We told him, all right, well, we are going to have to roll you out because you don't dis [disrespect] a homeboy for a ho [girl]. We were all drunk, and he was dissing us for just to go with his chick. So they kicked his ass. He was just laying there, then they just cracked his head open with a rock. They killed him. (Valdez et al., 2009, p. 12)

Shelden et al. (2001, p. 147) report that "It is not uncommon for female gangs to 'beat out' members, with other members taking turns beating each girl who has asked to quit the gang. In some instances, members kill those who want out or force the girl to kill a member of her family in order to leave the gang." Others have also noted this (Harris, 1988; Vigil, 2002). Harris (1988, p. 122) provides Vicky's example:

> You know those knuckle bracers and those machetes, you know those big knives. We would use those. Not kill them but just slice them a few times. We were all loaded. We never killed them, jumping them out, but they were like half-dead like. They're lucky they're alive.

Pyrooz and Decker (2011) note that violent exiting ceremonies were related to the reasons for leaving. Those who left the gang to start a new family or get a job were much less likely to report hostile departures. This is similar for females who leave the gang because of pregnancy, which is viewed as honorable. In contrast, Pyrooz and Decker (2011) report that those who left because they got tired of it or feared further trouble with the law and/or victimization were more likely to experience violence.

POSITIONS WITHIN THE GANG AND GANG ORGANIZATION

Youth vary in their intensity of membership, with implications that relate to desistance (Decker and Pyrooz, 2011; Pyrooz et al., 2013, 2014; Sweeten et al., 2013). Depending on their position, youth are likely to experience the process of leaving in distinct ways. Horowitz (1983) offers some evidence for this when noting that fringe and peripheral members, who committed few, less serious crimes and were not as active, had less difficulty leaving than core members, who committed serious offences and spent much of their time within the gang (see also Bolden, 2012; Caldwell and Altschuler, 2001; Vigil, 2007). An important point suggested here is that hard-core members can and do leave.

The intensity of membership is not limited to those most and least involved in the gang. A spectrum of intensity is evident and Pyrooz et al. (2013) explored how this is related to desistance (Sweeten et al., 2013). The authors borrow the term embeddedness from Hagan (1993) to describe the various levels of gang intensity. Embeddedness refers to both involvement in criminal behaviors and deviant networks and distance from prosocial activities and individuals. Frequency of contact, position, importance, proportion of friends in the gang, and frequency of gang-related violence measured embeddedness. It captures individual immersion into a criminal social network "reflecting varying degrees of involvement, identification, and status among gang members—the adhesion of the gang member to the gang" (Pyrooz et al., 2013, p. 243). The authors found that gang members with lower levels of embeddedness left quickly, whereas those who were more embedded stayed longer.

Gangs have varying levels of organization, which is related to desistance. Knox (1997) reported that youth with higher levels of organization report more difficulty in walking away than youth from gangs with lower levels of organization.

A SHIFT IN PEER NETWORK AFFILIATIONS

A key problem for an ex-member is hanging around old gang friends (Decker and Lauritsen, 2006). If youth do not perceive themselves as members, but continue to socialize with members, then that youth is unlikely to be thought of as a nonmember. Pyrooz et al. (2014) examined peer connections of ex-members and the extent to which they helped or hindered desistance. They found that as the length of desistance increased, youths' number of ties to their former network decreased. Many of these ties were school based, and leaving the gang was linked to leaving school (see also Pyrooz and Decker, 2011; Valdez, 2003, 2007).

Fleisher's (2006) study on females highlights social network findings. He collected data among former and current members from the same gang and asked them to rank people they knew on a scale of 1 to 5 in terms of their current involvement in violence and crime. Fleisher calculated the mean scores and compared the scores between the current and former gang females. He found that current members reported associating with others who engaged in crime and violence at higher levels than the associates of the females who were formerly in the gang. Leaving the gang also coincided with hanging out with fewer people involved in crime and violence (see also Fleisher and Krienert, 2004; Melde and Esbensen, 2011, 2014; Weerman et al., 2015).

BOX 10.3: ON TRIAL

This case involves a man in his mid-twenties. He was once a self-admitted gang member and has the tattoos to prove it. He has FI cards that indicate his gang membership. He committed a couple of crimes in his late teens and spent several months in a probation-operated detention facility as a result of one of them. When he emerged, he shaped up, indicating that the influence of a probation officer who befriended him while incarcerated had a tremendous impact on his worldview. The young man gets out of the gang and goes straight.

Seven years go by, and the young man is arrested for selling an ounce of weed to an undercover cop. He is not a drug dealer; rather, someone in his neighborhood gave him the weed as a form of reimbursement for borrowed money. The young man was selling it to recover that money. His one drug sale has the unfortunate result of being caught randomly by law enforcement: they were after a different individual. The young man has never sold—let alone really used—drugs (outside of smoking weed a few times). Gang enhancements are added to his charge of selling illegal narcotics. The prosecution asserts that the drug selling was done for the benefit and direction of a criminal street gang.

The young man swears that he stopped his gang involvement when he was released from detention years ago and supplies a number of points that support this declaration. One of the gang tattoos was located on the crown of his head, which was prominent when his head was shorn. But he says he deliberately grew his hair out to cover the tattoo. The other gang tattoo was not really obvious until he pointed it out in the crook of his arm, opposite his elbow. He says that he did not get these tattoos removed because they were easily hidden (and because he heard tattoo removal is very painful).

Other things the young man did to suggest distancing himself from the gang were becoming enrolled in vocational courses (masonry) at a local community college and holding employment in this and related work. He provided documentation that he had attended school and employers called in to vouch for the quality of his work, reliability, and overall good character.

One of the more interesting aspects of what this youth said about his ex–gang membership status was that he got jumped out—beaten for a period of time by current members. Although the opposite is common (i.e., getting jumped in), beatings out of gangs are reported less often. The young man said that he knew he had to get jumped out to leave the gang and that he had friends come with him to document this occasion—to make sure that there would be no question now as to his new status as an ex–gang member. Current members then beat him up. A friend confirms that he witnessed the young man being beaten out of the gang.

The prosecution highlights that members control drug sales and that such sales both contribute to the reputation of the gang and allow them the finances to purchase high-powered weaponry to continue their criminal operations. They argue that the gang influenced the day-to-day operations of the young man's drug-selling operation. The young man does not have a history of drug offenses, but has been convicted of a weapons charge—his prelude to deeper involvement in illicit business, the prosecution holds. They highlight his many FI cards generated over a six-year period. These cards indicate that law enforcement has documented through consistent interaction that the young man is a self-admitted member.

The defense argues that the young man has had to maneuver in his community with greater awareness and safety because of his status as an ex-member. The gang hangs out frequently near where he lives, and he consciously avoids certain areas at certain times for fear of running into members of the gang. This community is home to numerous other gangs, and police gangs units commonly operate on a visible basis (e.g., CRASH). Since getting out of prison and going straight—a five-year period—the young man says that he has been stopped by the police close to 100 different times. This translates to once or twice every month for five years.

When he was in the gang as a juvenile, the young man did admit to the police that he was a member and they recorded this on the FI card as self-admitted membership. Since he left the gang, he says he continues to be stopped and questioned by law enforcement, who often bring up his gang status, which they retrieve from their database. The young man replies that he is no longer in the gang and that he gave that lifestyle up many years ago. At times, the officers believe him and send him on his way. At other times, they do not believe him and instead provoke him with derogatory comments about the gang. They then document the encounter through an FI card. On the card, they write that he is a member of the gang and that they know this because he self-admits such status. This documentation occurs despite the fact that the young man has clearly indicated his former gang status.

In court, an FI card dated within weeks prior to him being involved in the drug sale was presented as evidence of the young man's current membership. The fact that the card read "self-admitted" was particularly damaging. The defense countered that the self-admitted part was drawn not from the officers' recent encounter, but from the previous string of FI cards that dated back to the original one issued when the client was a juvenile. In that first instance, the client did admit gang membership, which reflected his status at that time. Doubt is cast on the reliability of self-admitting membership on the numerous FI cards he has on file since his release from the detention center.

A REDUCTION IN RISK BEHAVIORS AND VICTIMIZATION

Research has found that membership length among teenagers was generally a year or less and that, as youth left, they desisted from offending and risk behaviors, such as substance use and violence (Battin-Pearson et al., 1998; Hill et al., 2001; Melde and Esbensen, 2011, 2014; Thornberry et al., 1993, 2003; see also Bendixen et al., 2006; Peterson, 2014; Weerman et al., 2015). Gangs are something that youth simply grow out of, with females doing so earlier than males (Decker and Pyrooz, 2011; Peterson, 2014; Thornberry et al., 2003; see also Harris, 1988). One female member in the Los Angeles Study[4] talked about joining a gang at the age of 12 as "dumb":

> I thought I was cool, for real. . . . Now that I think about, I was stupid, I was dumb, you know what I am saying, I did not know what was going on, I was 12 years old, I did not know, what was I doing, you know what I am saying? I was just being dumb. I think it's just ridiculous but I wish I can just go back and never be from a gang, whatever, I just really wish I could go back.

Victimization is common in gang life and has solidarity purposes; it has a contradictory effect of being a main impetus for youth leaving (see also Decker and Pyrooz, 2011, 2014; Peterson, 2014; Pyrooz and Decker, 2011). Many ex-members have reported leaving because of serious victimization (Decker and Lauritsen, 2006). These incidents were near misses when they, their friends, or their family members could have been or were killed. These events are "push factors" because they are a consequence of membership (Decker and Lauritsen, 2006; Decker and Pyrooz, 2011, 2014; Peterson, 2014). Other push factors are the threat of arrest, incarceration, and police harassment (Decker and Pyrooz, 2011). Former members believed to still be gang involved continued to be victimized by rivals (Decker and Pyrooz, 2011; Pyrooz and Decker, 2011). In general, though, studies have reported that youth who left gangs were much less likely to report victimization than those who currently identified as members (Decker and Pyrooz, 2011, 2014; Fleisher and Krienert, 2004; Pyrooz et al., 2014; see also T. J. Taylor et al., 2008).

FAMILY AND EMPLOYMENT

Decker and Lauritsen (2006) report on "pull factors" related to leaving a gang, including new employment, having a child, or starting a family (see also Bjorgo, 1999; Decker and Pyrooz, 2011; Fleisher and Krienert, 2004; Grant and Feimer, 2007; Moloney et al., 2009; Pyrooz and Decker, 2011, 2014; Vigil, 1988a, 2002). Employment is a major theme. The mottos of one gang intervention agency, Homeboy Industries, are *Jobs Not Jails* and *Nothing Stops a Bullet Like a Job*.

Current gang members want legitimate employment. Evidence of this desire emerged from the Los Angeles Study. Many gang members reported about jobs that were within reach and talked about plans to get them. Table 10.1 lists the types of jobs. The most

---

4   See the Appendix for more information on the methodology and objectives of this study.

TABLE 10.1   FUTURE EMPLOYMENT PROSPECTS OF GANG YOUTH (*N* = 60)

Job type	No. (%)
Criminal justice	18 (30)
Professional vocation	13 (21.6)
Arts and sports	13 (21.6)
Medical field	8 (13.3)
Unclear/no employment prospects	5 (8.3)
Own business	3 (5)

common job type, sought by 30% of members, was a career in criminal justice such as police or probation officer, lawyer, and youth counselor. One of the youth mentioned a college program that links students to criminal justice agencies, including probation:

Okay, so you can see yourself having a regular job and you want to be a probation officer. Have you made any plans to make that happen, have you taken any classes?

> The program I'm in at Cal State LA. . . . It's a six-week program. By the end of six weeks they're going to help us get into a job we want and they're going to help us reach our one goal of what we want to be. Get us started.

How likely do you think it is that you will get that job, probation officer, very likely, likely, not very likely, or not at all?

> Likely.

Another wanted to get a criminology degree at the University of Southern California (USC) prior to becoming a probation officer:

Like, what do you want to do when you get older?

> I am going to be a probation officer.

Okay, so that's what you want to do?

> Yeah.

And have you done any plans to make that happen?

> Yeah, I am. One of the things that I am doing is, first of all, is getting my diploma, which is more than anything, which is a self-fulfillment for me. I am doing that to make me feel good and to get it out of the way, for me. And also because I know it's going to be a little bit formal, once I go to junior college . . .

> I am going to go to ELAC which is you know, East LA junior college and take my general ed. there. Have a counselor set me up with you know my classes that I need to so I can transfer to USC and get a masters in criminal justice or criminology.

Another felt that his experiences in the gang would serve him well in a job as a youth counselor:

And you said you see yourself working with either young children or the elderly?
Yes.* (*nonverbal)

Would you like to work in a hospital setting or a school setting or . . . ?
To be honest, either or it does not really make a difference to me. Because, like I said, from my experience in the streets and gang banging and stuff like that, I know what younger kids are going through. 'Cause I have been through it and I want to help, you know what I am saying? And let them know that there are certain things that they are doing may not be the ropes because I have been out there in the streets so, you know? I might want to deal with battered kids or kids that are in foster homes or, you know, stuff like that.

The next most common occupation mentioned by 21.6% of the sample was working as electricians, construction, mechanics, and the like:

I want to be a constructor. Like do the houses and do roofs and yeah that kind of cached my attention since I was small.

Have you done any plans to make that happen?
I try to do some little works. "Oh you want to help me out and built this or his like that?" Not like a contract, contract just like helping people out.

Tied with these were arts and sports (21.6%). One of the more interesting of these responses was from a youth who wanted to become a lawyer, street fighter, rapper, or professional basketball player, football player, or boxer.

What do you want to do when you get older? What kind of job do you see yourself having?
I want to do like, I was thinking a lawyer, a street fighter, or rapper.

And if rap does not work out?
Like, sports basketball, football, and boxer.

Do you do all those sports?
Yes.* (*nonverbal)

Outside of the sports have you done anything to become like a lawyer or a street fighter?
I just take classes and stuff like that.

Out of all those which one would you like to be the most?
I don't know.

The next most common job interest was in the medical field, including dental and medical assistants, emergency medical technicians/paramedics, nurse, veterinary assistants, and coroners. One talked about a nursing career:

What do you want to do when you get older? You said you wanted to become a nurse, right?

> Yeah, I already finished half of my medical assistant class.

Well, that was the next question. Have you done any plans to make that happen? That is really good. How likely do you think you will get this job one day?

> You know, it's all up to you if you want to do it. If you want to do it you are going to do it. Or if you want to keep on the road that you keep on going towards, you know? I want to do it. I say like, Damn! It's going to take forever, but if it's up to you. If you keep on pushing it, it's going to go fast. It will go quickly.

Two important points emerge from these findings. For one, most youth in the Los Angeles Study saw themselves with proper jobs in their futures, suggesting that they consider membership a passing phase. None wished for a continued life of crime or for a life within the gang (see also B. Sanders, 2005a). The fact that so many of them wanted careers in criminal justice questions the way they perceive law enforcement. Second, the types of jobs the sample wanted—probation officer, electrician, emergency medical technician—were not out of their reach. Although criminal records might prevent some of them from working within the justice system, the sample mentioned the types of blue-collar jobs adults within their communities hold (Hagedorn, 1994; see also Downes, 1966).

With the presence of both push and pull factors, Decker and Lauritsen (2006, p. 66) argue that "gang experiences and social processes, rather than institutional commitments" were the main reasons for leaving. Similar to research on how ex-offenders "make good" or attempt to distance themselves from their criminal pasts (Maruna, 2001), Decker and Lauritsen (2006, p. 69) note that leaving the gang is not a solitary event, but occurs over time, and that informal social processes are more salient in understanding why youth leave in comparison to "institutional involvement or incentive." These and triggering events (e.g., violence victimization) are crucial to understanding how and why youth leave gangs (see also Decker and Pyrooz, 2011).

ROUTINE ACTIVITIES AND DISPOSITION

Several researchers have examined how Sampson and Laub's life-course perspective fits with leaving the gang (Melde and Esbensen, 2011, 2014; Sweeten et al., 2013). They found that, compared to individuals who remained in the gang, the desisters had a greater reduction in delinquency and associated less with negative peers. Desisters also reported a change in routine activities and disposition (e.g., anger; guilt). As they left the gang, they stopped hanging out and doing nothing and had structured lives. Those who left were less angry, felt more guilt, and/or were better able to control violent impulses.

HAVE THEY REALLY LEFT?

Bolden (2012) discussed the fluidity of membership, part of which concerned how members had switched allegiances. As one of his respondents said, "When I was younger I messed with more Crips and when I got older I started messing with Bloods" (Bolden, 2012, p. 219). This switching allegiance has been referred to as hood hopping. One reason for switching could be because the youth moved.

Over many years, youth cultivate the identity of a gang member, which they proudly display. When they leave a gang, the perception that they are still in the gang can linger. This has significant consequences. Decker and Pyrooz (2011) found that former members still suffered victimization and indignities from members and rivals. In terms of consequences, the police were the biggest issue. Most of the ex-members said that they felt that the police treated them like members and that they continued to stop and question them. Below are some excerpts from their interviews (Decker and Pyrooz, 2011, p. 15):

They [the police] are going to harass you regardless.

Cops still harass badly: "Once a gang member, always a gang member."

Harassed by the police all the time because of the gang; [leaving] doesn't make a difference.

Just as youth have varying intensities or embeddedness, so too do they appear to have different experiences with leaving (Sweeten et al., 2013). Pyrooz and Decker (2011) examined the extent to which youth have desisted from membership and crime—not one or the other (see also Fleisher and Krienert, 2004). Although aggregate data indicate that crime and violence decrease after youth leave gangs, not all former members stop committing crime. Youth may remain members, but desist from crime. This led Pyrooz and Decker (2011) to develop a four-tier typology on leaving a gang and desisting from crime. On one end of this typology are current members who commit crime, and on the other end are true desisters: former members who have completely stopped crime. Between these extremes are two other tiers: older members and youth who were socially tied. The older members are considered *veteranos*, or Original Gangsters, who still claim membership, but are not criminally involved. The last tier consists of former members who have emotional and social connections to their gang and are involved in criminal activities.

RESISTING GANGS

Most individuals who live in gang communities will not join. One study that has examined resisting gangs is Vigil's (2007) *The Projects.* The book focuses on Latino gang and non-gang families in East Los Angeles in the housing project of Pico Gardens. Some factors linked to avoiding gangs are the opposite of factors linked to joining them. Youth who do not join have high self-esteem and do not require approval from their peers. They engage in behaviors on their own behalf, not to impress friends or family. Vigil says this is an agent effect, whereby youths' own agency plays a critical role in refusing the allure of gangs.

Vigil (2007) mentions push and pull effects in relation to resisting gangs. A push effect is witnessing members bully others. Bullies are universally despised, and when youth see those engaged in bullying, it provides "negative reinforcement that results in an aversion to gang membership" (Vigil, 2007, p. 137). Strong and protective families are important. Being fearful of family members' retribution for joining is a powerful disincentive.

A pull effect attracts youth to more conventional lifestyles. Vigil (2007) notes that family and community are important. Positive family relations keep youth attracted to life at home. Having a family dinner together on a regular basis was noted as a key feature of non-gang families. Concepts such as respect for others and for the community were also mentioned as pull effects.

Parents who are active in their child's peer networks and who spend extra time at home provide interrupter effects (Vigil, 2007). Some parents went out of their way to help ensure that their children were not hanging around members by walking them to and from school or monitoring their outdoor play. Older siblings filled these roles when parents were unavailable. Having community connections who could inform parents about their children's whereabouts was helpful in interrupting interest in gangs. Non-gang families tended to be smaller, allowing for more interaction between parents and children and older and younger siblings.

Vigil (2007) reports that non-gang families face the same difficulties as gang families, but that the former develop creative ways to deal with marginality, including cooking, crafting, and automotive repair, which helped pay the bills. Family discipline and affection were other aspects that Vigil indicates stood out among non-gang families. Parenting was something they could control. Non-gang families were *authoritative*, less likely to use physical punishment and "to stress obedience to authority as a virtue in itself" (Vigil, 2007, p. 150). Discipline in gang families was lax or *authoritarian*, where the use of harsh punishments was routine. Non-gang families reasoned with their children and listened to their point of view, developing a reciprocal relationship. These parents set high standards, stressed the importance of independence and individualism, and gave their children affection and compassion.

Vigil (2007) notes that non-gang families kept their kids busy. With school and extracurricular activities, they had little time for gangs. They learned valuable and additional skills. Playing on sports teams and attending church helped instill a sense of responsibility and community pride. Non-gang families believed firmly in the American Dream—that rewards emerge through hard work and diligence. Education was stressed as the youth's only way to rise above and excel, and must be taken seriously. Vigil (2007) concludes that through various adaptations and practices, families in rough, inner-city areas can help their children resist gangs.

SUMMARY

An increase in social bonds, such as new family and employment obligations, and a desire to live a noncriminal lifestyle and become a law-abiding citizen are important. These considerations impact one another through a reciprocal relationship and it remains unclear which emerges first. Job opportunities are not evenly distributed throughout society and some individuals seeking change will have a difficult time. New family and job opportunities can be fortuitous events, and individual drive and determination are important. Those individuals who develop a mental script of what they hope and fear and have the drive to accomplish their goals are more likely to desist.

Displacement, defined as a shift between different types of offenses, is another important area in relation to desistance. A decrease in offending corresponds to an increase in substance use. Also, research has found that, when transitioning from juvenile to adult offenders, individuals are likely to progress away from property and violent crimes and toward substance use. The extent to which former offenders who use drugs can still be considered desisters has been called into question.

Aspects about desistance reflect major theories on delinquency. Personality traits, experiences of strain that produce negative emotionality, biosocial aspects, and labeling processes are all related. These factors act independent of one another and in concert. More research is needed to better understand how these variables are related to offending patterns. As many pathways into crime and delinquency are evident, desistance can be achieved through a combination of various considerations.

The scant evidence that exists on leaving a gang highlights several key points: (1) most youth walk away, but reports have emerged of violent exit ceremonies; (2) leaving parallels a reduction in risk behaviors and victimization; (3) desistance is linked to the youth's location within the gang (e.g., fringe or core member) and the organizational level; (4) leaving corresponds to a shift in the youth's peer network dynamics and affiliations; and (5) leaving is related to both push (i.e., consequences of gang membership) and pull (i.e., getting married; starting a family) triggers.

Leaving the gang and desistance from crime share many similarities. Both relate to changes in peer networks, new family obligations, and the burden of continued criminal participation. In other instances, leaving differs from desistance from crime. Members have cafeteria-style offending patterns, committing various types of crimes. How the types of crime they commit (i.e., property, drug, violent), as well as involvement in the gang—gang embeddedness—(e.g., core versus fringe) are related to both leaving and desistance from offending is unclear. The organizational level of the gang (e.g., territorial versus specialist) also shapes desistance.

Another question is why youth who come from impoverished communities do not become involved in gangs. What non-gang families practice and stress—affectionate and reflexive parenting, education, and prosocial activities (e.g., church; sports)—is the antithesis of some of the major causes of delinquency. Ineffective parenting, lack of faith in education and poor school performance, and an excessive amount of unsupervised time are all variables not only for gangs, but also for delinquency in general. Additional knowledge on how high-risk youth avoid the lure of membership will contribute to the development of more effective intervention techniques.

CHAPTER REVIEW QUESTIONS

1. What is the life-course perspective? What does it say about people leaving crime? What are the steps of desistance as outlined by Laub and Sampson?
2. How and why are identity and agency important in the process of desistance? What does "making good" mean? How does the conceptualization of the self assist in desistance?
3. What are some of the "hooks" for behavioral change? How do they differentially impact men and women?
4. What is displacement and how does it relate to substance use?
5. What are some of the key themes that researchers have found in terms of leaving the gang? What myths have been revealed?
6. In what ways are leaving gangs and desistance from crime more generally similar? In what ways are they unique?
7. How have peer network affiliations helped or hindered youth from leaving gangs?
8. What are some difficulties faced by ex-members?
9. Outline Pyrooz and Decker's (2011) typology of ex-members.
10. How can families resist gangs?

LINKS TO ARTICLES ON DESISTANCE

Highlights from pathways to desistance: A longitudinal study of serious adolescent offenders
By E. P. Mulvey (2011)
https://ncjrs.gov/pdffiles1/ojjdp/230971.pdf/

Substance use and delinquent behavior among serious adolescent offenders
By E. P. Mulvey, C. A. Schubert, and L. Chassin (2010)
https://www.ncjrs.gov/pdffiles1/ojjdp/232790.pdf/

CHAPTER 11

PUBLIC HEALTH ASPECTS

KEY WORDS

At-risk youth: Youth whose socioeconomic background and behaviors place them at an increased risk of negative health and social outcomes.

Epidemiology: A branch of public health that focuses on disease prevention and health promotion. It examines why people become unhealthy, but also how they can maintain or regain health. Behavioral epidemiology focuses on risk behaviors that incorporate traditional epidemiological concerns of host, agent, and environment, but also on context and motivation.

Epidemiology-criminology: An emergent field that employs traditional epidemiological principles toward criminal justice–related concerns, particularly substance use and violence.

Homelessness: A person experiences homelessness when he or she has inadequate access to secure and safe nighttime residence. Living in public or private places not designed for human habitation, as well as residing in cars, public buildings, emergency or transitional shelters, public transportation, and the like, is considered being homeless.

Negative health outcome: Includes outcomes related to risk behaviors, such as teen pregnancy, sexually transmitted infections, injury, disability, abscesses, addiction, overdose, and death.

Negative social outcome: Includes outcomes related to risk behaviors, such as school dropout, arrest, and incarceration.

Personality traits: In relation to crime and violence, the major ones are anger/irritability, impulsivity, risk/sensation seeking, and low empathy. These traits are established at an earlier age and do not change over the individual's lifetime. At times, these traits cluster together with others to form specific personality disorders, such as low self-control and antisocial personality disorder (and variants of these disorders).

Public health: A medical approach that is concerned with the health of entire communities as opposed to individual health. Key goals of public health include the assessment of the health of communities to identify health priorities and concerns; the formulation of policies designed to tackle such priorities and concerns; and assuring a community access to affordable health care, health promotion, and disease prevention.

Public health nurse: As opposed to individual patient care, public health nurses focus on entire populations. They educate people in the community about health care, improve community health and safety, and increase access to health care. Public health nurses also monitor unique trends or health risks within a community, advocate with authorities to improve health care and access, and implement health-care campaigns, such as immunizations.

Risk behaviors: Includes behaviors that increase the likelihood of negative health outcomes, such as unsafe sexual practices, violence, and substance use.

Sexually transmitted infection: Pathogens contracted through sexual behaviors, including chlamydia, gonorrhea, and HIV/AIDS.

Symptoms of mental health illness: Common ones include depression, anxiety, and stress. These illnesses can be treated and cured. They are distinct from less common mental health disorders, such as schizophrenia and bipolar disorder.

Unsafe sexual behavior: Includes sex initiation at early ages, sex while intoxicated or with someone intoxicated, lack of contraceptive use, sex with drug users, group sex (i.e., sex with multiple partners concurrently), sex while incarcerated, and survival sex (i.e., receiving money or goods in exchange for sex).

Vulnerable population: A term utilized by the nursing community to indicate marginalized individuals who are at an increased risk of negative health and social outcomes because of their overall socioeconomic background and current social position.

Chapter Learning Objectives

- Discuss why gang youth are a public health concern.
- Explain negative health and social outcomes related to gang membership.
- Outline specific public health–driven responses to gangs.
- Compare criminal justice to public health approaches to gangs.

INTRODUCTION

Violence, substance use, and the experiences of incarceration are issues that are important to the public health community. Minority young males from deprived inner-city areas are at an increased risk of these behaviors and outcomes. Gang members comprise a subgroup of this population who are at even greater jeopardy. The National Institutes of Health have prioritized risk behaviors (substance use, violence, and unsafe sexual behaviors) among gang-identified youth for these reasons. Gang members are more likely than non-gang youth to come from deprived socioeconomic backgrounds, use large amounts of substances, report high rates of unsafe sex, commit disproportional amounts of violence, be incarcerated, and experience significant levels of victimization. Gang members report these conditions at early ages and repeatedly over their life course. For such reasons, they are a public health concern.

The chapter begins by examining the at-risk backgrounds and high-risk behaviors of gangs and the common ground between criminology and epidemiology. From here, it explores various public health–related issues that affect gang members, the first of which is unsafe sexual practices and sexually transmitted infections (STIs). Next, it addresses the health risks of incarceration. Symptoms of mental health illness and psychiatric diagnoses are then discussed. A review of the extent to which gang members experience homelessness is then offered. Then, the injuries that gang youth receive from participating in violence are listed. Data on health miscellanea, including the diet, levels of exercise, weight, health concerns, and access to health care, are then provided. Nursing interventions that target gang members inside and outside of hospitals are then explored. The chapter concludes with a section that advocates a public health approach toward gangs.

GANG YOUTH AND PUBLIC HEALTH

Sociology and public health share common ground (Conrad and Leiter, 2003; Orcutt and Rudy, 2003; B. Sanders and Lankenau, 2006; B. Sanders, Deeds et al., 2013). One area is epidemiology and criminology (T. A. Akers and Lanier, 2009; Greifeinger, 2006; Lanier et al., 2010; B. Sanders, Deeds et al., 2013). Epidemiology is about health promotion and disease prevention. Criminology is the study of the nature, extent, cause, and control of crime.

One branch of epidemiology is behavioral epidemiology, which examines risk behaviors. Within this framework, traditional epidemiological concerns are addressed, such as the interaction of the host (i.e., the person), agent (e.g., drugs, violence), and the physical and social environment (Agar, 1996; Syme, 2000). Behavioral epidemiology also examines context, such as the how, why, and to what extent of the behavior. This is where the link with criminology is most apparent. This crossover is called "epidemiology-criminology" or "epi-crim" (Akers and Lanier, 2009). The terms at risk and high risk are used within the public health and criminological literature. Gang youth come from at-risk backgrounds that contribute to them participating in high-risk behaviors (see Figure 11.1).

Gang members have parallels with other groups of youth who are perceived from a public health viewpoint, such as homeless youth, pregnant teenagers, and drug users. The socioeconomic profile that exposes youth to gangs includes poverty and social deprivation; poor school performance; difficulties with conventional employment; familial alcohol and

At-Risk Background

High Risk Behaviors

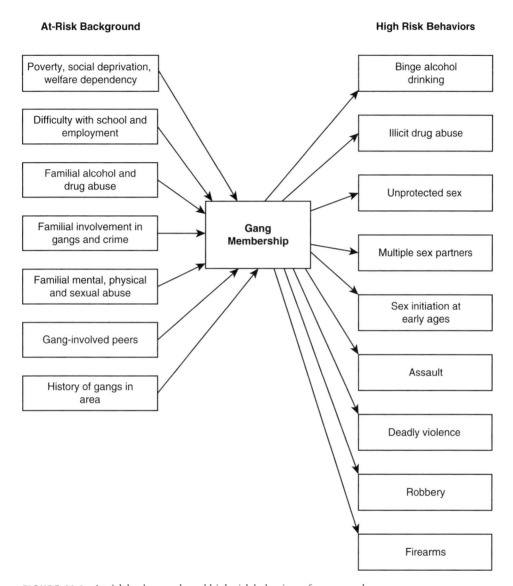

FIGURE 11.1 At-risk backgrounds and high-risk behaviors of gang members

drug abuse; familial mental, sexual, and physical abuse; and familial involvement in gangs and crime more generally (Esbensen and Lynskey, 2001; Hill et al., 2001; Thornberry et al., 1993). These same risk factors have been linked to drug users, homelessness, and teen pregnancy. Pregnant teenagers are a public health problem, whereas gang youth are a criminal justice problem. Drug use has been a major criminal justice concern, but has moved back in the direction of public health. Homelessness among youth straddles the intersection of criminal justice and public health. Homelessness has been criminalized, despite the public health–related reasons why individuals are homeless in the first place (e.g., substance abuse issues, mental health illness; see B. Sanders, Deeds et al., 2013).

Gang youth compared to non-gang youth are more likely to use drugs, binge drink alcohol, have sex at earlier ages, become teenage parents, have multiple sex partners, report an STI, become a victim and perpetrator of violence, including deadly violence, carry a firearm, and commit crime (Adimora and Schoenbach, 2005; Cepeda and Valdez, 2003; B. Sanders, Valdez et al., 2013; Thornberry et al., 2004; Voisin et al., 2004). High rates of participation suggest public health–related concerns. Gang youth interact with non-gang, low-risk youth, which is important for epidemiological research and social network data. When low-risk youth hang out with high-risk youth, their likelihood of using drugs, being the victims of violence, and participating in unsafe sexual behaviors increases (cf. Golembeski and Fullilove, 2005).

UNSAFE SEXUAL BEHAVIORS AND STIs

Young offenders are more likely to report risky sexual behaviors and STIs (Decker and Rosenfeld, 1995; Morris et al., 1995; see also Romero et al., 2013; Steinberg et al., 2013). In a study among low-income African American adolescent females living in a high-risk urban environment, gang involvement was found to be the strongest predictor of an STI, and members were more than four times as likely to have an infection (Salazar et al., 2007). Another report indicated that gang youth were more likely to report the STIs *trichomonas* and gonorrhea (Wingood et al., 2002). Social network data noted that young African American members were responsible for an outbreak of *Neisseria gonorrhoeae* and other STIs (*Morbidity and Mortality Weekly Report*, 1993).

Studies show higher rates of risky sexual behaviors among gang youth than among nonmembers. Voisin et al. (2004) found that, among detained 14- to 18-year-old males, those who were gang involved were more than five times as likely to have had sex and more than three times as likely to have gotten a girl pregnant. They also note that gang youth were almost four times as likely to have sex while intoxicated, have sex with someone intoxicated, and have group sex. Cepeda and Valdez (2003) noted that adolescent female members had earlier onsets of sexual behavior compared to the national average and that most had had an experience by their early teens, many had become pregnant, and nearly one in four had given birth. Harper and Robinson (1999) reported that former and current gang females were more likely to have a low frequency of condom use, to have sex at an earlier age, and to have a larger amount of sexual partners. Additional studies on Latina and African American female teenagers have documented a link between having a sexual partner who is a gang member and an increased likelihood of reporting an STI or pregnancy (Auerswald et al., 2006; Minnis et al., 2008).

The greatest threat of engaging in risky sexual behaviors is the exposure to HIV. One study exploring this risk among gang youth in the United States was conducted in Los Angeles. The researchers found that the attitudes of gang youth revealed high rates of inaccurate information about HIV and that many youth engaged in behaviors that put them at risk of exposure to the virus (Uman et al., 2006). Common risky sexual behaviors of the sample included having sex with someone they just met (65%) and having sex while intoxicated (49%). Most (90%) had inconsistent condom use, more than one-third (36%) engaged in survival sex (i.e., giving or receiving money or drugs in return for sex), and about 10% who had been in jail or prison reported having sex while incarcerated. Although none of the youth in the study was positive for HIV, only half of the overall sample was tested. Whether those with histories of participating in behaviors that exposed them to HIV were tested is uncertain.

Brooks and colleagues further analyzed these data (Brooks et al., 2009, 2011). Of 246 gang males aged 18 to 26 years old, only one-third had been tested for HIV. The majority of the sample (59%) had had unprotected vaginal intercourse (UVI) in the past year. These individuals were much more likely to have sex with someone they recently met, someone they believed or knew had an STI, and during incarceration than were members who did not report UVI. Gang members with a higher perceived vulnerability to HIV were less likely to have reported UVI in the previous 12 months. The authors also examined a subset of Latino males and asked about attitudes toward contraception (Brooks et al., 2009). They had negative attitudes about condoms and perceived themselves as vulnerable to HIV. About half (53%) reported having UVI in the past year and they were more likely than those who did not report having UVI to have sex with someone they just met and/or who they believed to have an STI and to have received money or drugs for sex.

Brooks et al. (2009, 2011) reported that many gang members expressed a willingness to participate in HIV screening and that their friends being tested was a reason for them to get tested. They found that members with a lower perceived vulnerability to HIV were the most likely to engage in unsafe sex. The authors believed that this was the case because most had never had a sexual experience with another male and, as a result, believed they were not exposed to HIV. Brooks et al. (2011) conclude by indicating that changing the perception of HIV risk among gangs poses challenges because gang culture itself may promote unsafe sex.

Risky sexual behaviors were common among the Los Angeles Study (see B. Sanders, Lankenau et al., 2009).[1] Youth had initiated sex between the ages of 9 and 21 with a mean age of 13½—several years below the national average and about a year younger than that reported in samples of racial minorities from urban areas (Ompad et al., 2006). Drugs and alcohol were not uncommon. At sexual initiation, about a quarter of respondents (23.3%) were intoxicated and during the most recent time they had sex, more than one-third (36.4%) were. Condom use was sporadic, with more than one-third (37.5%) reporting no condom use or other form of contraception during the first time and a similar amount (36.4%) not using anything the most recent time. One youth said that the first time he had sex was with a prostitute in an alley and that he used a plastic grocery bag as a condom. Over their lifetime, the sample reported

---

1   See the Appendix for the methodology and objectives of this study.

between zero and 50 incidences of unprotected sex, with 18 responding "too many times to count."

About a quarter reported group sex (23.3%). During these incidents, close to three in four (71.4%) were intoxicated.

Have you ever had group sex, either right before or after one of your homeboys had sex with her?
> Yeah.

How many times has that happened?
> About twice.

How old were you the first time it happened?
> 14.

Now that first time, where were you?
> My friend's house.

How many people had sex with that girl before you?
> It was like this man, the guy, the first one, he was in there first and then he got out and then three of us went back in there and we just did it to her.

So it was all three of you at once?
> Yeah.

The sample reported high numbers of sexual partners. Over the past month, they had zero to 9 different partners; within the past year, they reported between zero and 15 partners. Over their lifetimes, they reported having between 1 and 100 sexual partners, with a couple of youth mentioning "too many to count."

The fact that approximately one in six of the sample (16.7%) ever had an STI was not surprising. One of the youth indicated during the interview that he currently was suffering from an unknown STI.

Have you ever thought you had a sexually transmitted infection?
> Yeah.

Do you know what it was?
> No, I still don't know what it was.

Can you describe it for me?
> It was two things. One, I had some kind of a rash like little red bumps, right around my penis. You could see the color of my skin changes to a dark color or red and it itches.

Has it gone away?
> No.

You're talking about a rash that you currently have. Do you want to get that taken care of?

Yes.

I think that's a good idea. I'll call around and see what I can do.

[Interview stopped. Sexual health clinic contacted. Youth speaks with a counselor. Interview proceeds after the youth makes an appointment.]

I think about all of the girls that I fucked and I'm like damn if I gave it to them.

How long has that been going on?

It's been for a couple years now but it's like off and on.

Moving on, you haven't had any medical treatment, have you ever talked to anyone about this?

No, I've never told nobody.

About half of the youth (51.7%) have been tested for HIV and slightly more have been tested for HCV (61.7%). Some were uncertain what type of screening they received, particularly when it came to HCV.

Have you ever been tested for hepatitis C?

No, but I got the immunity. Like a little thing.

They don't immunize you for hepatitis C. There is no immunization, but you could get vaccinated from hepatitis A or B.

I got those then.

Have you ever been tested for hepatitis C?

I don't think so. I might have but I probably don't remember. I know I have had all my shots though.

You can't get a shot for hepatitis C.

Okay.

Have you ever been tested for hepatitis C?

Yeah, I think so when I was like a kid or something.

One time do you think, a couple times?

A couple times. That's when they put that thing right here, right? [indicates bottom of wrist] They give you that shot that's supposed to turn into a bubble or something like that?

No that's for TB, tuberculosis. No, the test is they pull out some blood and they test you for hepatitis C and HIV.

Yeah, that was in middle school, I think.

One in 10 of the sample had friends and family members with HIV/AIDS, with 6.7% having at least one friend or family member who had died from AIDS.

Do you have any friends or family members that have HIV or AIDS?
> Yes.

What is your relationship to them?
> My uncle.

How long has he had HIV?
> Since he was like 20.

Do you have any family members or friends who have died from AIDS?
> Yes.* (*nonverbal)

How many people do you know that have died from that?
> Three.

What is your relationship to them?
> Two of my aunts and one of my cousins.

> No, one of my homeboys had AIDS.

One of your friends has HIV? Did he have HIV or AIDS?
> He had AIDS.

Because HIV advances to AIDS.
> Yeah. AIDS. . . . Yeah and he is doing bad.

I'm sorry to hear that. Is he on medication?
> Yeah. He's on all kinds of shit.

Yeah. They usually put them on all kinds of things. Do you have any friend or family members who have died from HIV or AIDS?
> No, but I am pretty sure this fool is getting pretty close.

INCARCERATION AS HEALTH RISK

Individuals face numerous health hazards during incarceration, including exposure to HIV/HCV. In the United States in 2004, 1.8% of prison inmates were HIV positive, more than four times the estimated rate in the general population; confirmed AIDS cases among prison inmates are more than three times the estimated rate (Hammett, 2006; Maruschak, 2006; Okie, 2007). Annually, estimates indicated that approximately 25% of all HIV-infected persons, 33% of HCV-infected persons, and 40% of those with active tuberculosis in the United States spend time in a correctional facility (Okie, 2007). It remains unclear whether pathogens such as HIV are contracted while incarcerated or whether inmates become aware of the infection during their stay (Hammett, 2006). Between 2001 and 2010, both the overall rate of HIV among prisoners and that of prisoners who have died from AIDS decreased significantly and at levels that parallel the decrease in HIV infections/

AIDS deaths nationally (Maruschak, 2012). HIV transmission in prison is associated with men having sex with men or with sharing injection and tattooing paraphernalia (Okie, 2007).

Gang youth are at an increased risk for incarceration. A Department of Justice study that collected data from a random sample of U.S. detention facilities and juvenile training programs indicated that 88.5% contained gang-involved youth and that gang youth constituted between 5% and more than 50% of all youth (Curry et al., 2000). Gang participation has also been found to be a significant predictor of offender recidivism (Huebner et al., 2007).

While incarcerated, gang youth are more likely to engage in risk behaviors. Krebs (2006), in his study of incarcerated 18- to 29-year-olds, found a correlation between drug use and having sex while incarcerated and that both were associated with being in a gang. Karberg and James (2005) reported on risk behaviors among juveniles drawn from 39 correctional facilities and found an association among gang membership, substance use, and violence. Jenness et al. (2007) examined sexual assault inside the California prison system. In slightly more than half of all reports, the authors found that all of the perpetrators were gang members, and in about two-thirds of all sexual victimization, at least one was.

Youth in the Los Angeles Study were familiar with same-sex behaviors while incarcerated:

Has there ever been a time when you wanted to talk about your sexuality or your sex in general to somebody but were unable to?
> Yeah, there has.

Tell me about that.
> You know, when I was locked up, when I was in jail, I seen it happened a lot of times. Guys being with other dudes, you know what I am saying? Like I got tempted, but then at the last minute I was like, "Hell no! What the fuck am I doing, man? This is not me, man! This is, I am not cool with this shit!," you know what I am saying? I just didn't go along, but at that time I got scared with my own self, you know, like fucken man, "Am I turning gay here? What is going on, man?"

So you were kind of worried about it?
> Yeah, like what the fuck is going on here, man, you know?

So this was at jail and you wanted to talk to someone about it?
> Yeah, I just shined on. No, it was just curiosity. I was just like, "Everybody does it." I just wanted to join the club and it's cool. Within this fucked up little world it's something normal and shit, so you know? I am not fucked up. I just went along with the fucken flow. I caught my self, you know? I don't have to go with the flow. I could be different. And you know, I just didn't.

Unlike Australia, Canada, and several Western European countries, prisons and jails systems within the United States, with few exceptions, do not implement risk reduction strategies like providing condoms or clean drug injection paraphernalia to inmates. Coupled with the high rates of substance use and risky sexual behaviors, this greatly increases gang youths' risk of acquiring HIV, HCV, and other negative health conditions. Gang youth infected while incarcerated potentially expose others when they return to their communities. Examining the extent to which this occurs provides a more thorough understanding of the risk of exposure to community members with whom these youth have contact (cf. Golembeski and Fullilove, 2005).

Incarceration did have one unintended benefit to public health: it serves as a way station where youth are first screened for an STI. In the Los Angeles Study, youth who knew they had been tested for HCV/HIV had been screened while in jail or prison:

Have you ever been tested for hepatitis C?
Yeah.

In your life how many times have you been tested?
In my life I have been tested like every time I go to jail, I get tested.

Have you ever been tested for hepatitis C?
Yes.

How many times have you been tested for hepatitis C?
Every time I went to jail.

How many times is that?
About 10 times.

Have you ever been tested for HIV?
No, yeah, I have been tested.

So the same thing when you went to jail, like about 10 times?
Yeah.

Some might never be treated for their STIs if not for a prison screening:

Have you ever thought that you had a sexually transmitted infection?
I did. I had.

What did you have?
Gonorrhea and crabs.

How many times did you have gonorrhea?
One time.

How long did you have the gonorrhea problem for?
I didn't. I never even knew I had it. I didn't even know. I had it until I got locked up, when I was younger. When I got locked up they do a little test and they test you. And they were like, "You know, you got a little infection in your blood stream" and shit, you know? . . . Yeah. They gave me a shot, pills and it was all good.

And the crabs, how did you find out about that?

> The same thing, I did not know about it. I went to jail, I got locked up and did a test and they were like, "You got this bullshit," you know?

SYMPTOMS OF MENTAL HEALTH ILLNESS AND PSYCHIATRIC DIAGNOSES

Young offenders have disproportionate mental health care needs, although they often fail to be screened or treated for symptoms (Bailey and Tarbuck, 2006; Coalition for Juvenile Justice, 2000; Grisso and Underwood, 2004; Kessler, 2002; Lawson and Lawson, 2013; B. Sanders, Deeds et al., 2013). Research has focused largely on the criminology and sociology of gang involvement and less on its psychology (Wood and Alleyne, 2010). The psychology of gang involvement can be divided into three categories: personality traits conducive to crime (e.g., anger/irritability, low empathy, sensation/risk seeking, impulsivity, psychopathy) and low self-control, symptoms of mental health illness (e.g., depression, anxiety, post–traumatic stress disorder [PTSD]), and suicide ideation and attempts.

Studies have found that compared to non-gang youth, gang youth are more likely to report mental health illness. The Rochester Youth Study reported that gang youth were more likely to report depressive symptoms (Thornberry et al., 2003). A study on homeless adult males found that those who were currently or ever in a gang scored higher on a depression scale (Harper et al., 2008). J. Wood et al. (2002) reported that the incarcerated youth in their sample, many of whom were gang members, had symptomatology of depression (see also DuRant et al., 2000). This finding was examined briefly in the Los Angeles Study. More than one-third (36.7%) of participants said they currently felt "miserable" or "not very happy." Just over half (53.3%) had visited a mental health therapist and more than a quarter (28.3%) had been prescribed medication for a mental health illness. About a third (36.7%) mentioned attending family therapy at one point. Evans et al. (1999) discovered that emotional adjustment/instability, defined in part by feeling blue, was not uncommon among gang members.

Li et al. (2002) indicated that, among gang and non-gang youth aged 9–15 years old, those who were either currently or formerly part of a gang reported symptoms of PTSD. Wood and colleagues (2002) examined exposure to violence and PTSD among incarcerated boys and girls in Los Angeles. About three in four (76%) of the females and most (85%) of the males were gang members. Many reported numerous accounts of violence, such as physical and sexual abuse in the home, witnessing homicides of close friends on the street, and being threatened with weapons, including having guns held to their heads. Differences between gang and non-gang outcomes were not tabulated, but the authors note that many in the sample had high levels of psychological distress, including PTSD symptomatology—females more so than males (Wood et al., 2002). Symptoms of a related condition, acute stress disorder, have also been reported among gang youth. Hamrin et al. (2004) found that 75% of children who were gunshot victims were diagnosed as having symptoms of acute stress disorder and that being shot was strongly associated with gang involvement.

Personality traits conducive to crime have been found among gang youth. Esbensen and Deschenes (1998) reported that compared to non-gang youth, gang youth were more likely to be impulsive. Esbensen and Weerman's (2005) cross-national study found that members were more likely to be impulsive and to be risk/sensation seekers. Research from the United Kingdom found risk/sensation seeking to be related to gang membership (Dawson, 2008). Esbensen et al. (2009) found that gang members were significantly more likely to have low guilt. Other researchers have noted that gang members are more likely to use "moral disengagement strategies" than non-gang youth (Alleyne and Wood, 2010). Low self-esteem has also been linked to membership (Dukes et al., 1997; Esbensen and Deschenes, 1998; Maxson et al., 1998). Low self-control is characterized by impulsivity and sensation seeking, as well as by being short-sighted and insensitive (M. R. Gottfredson and Hirschi, 1990). The theory of low self-control, or control theory, enjoys widespread support. Few studies have examined low self-control among gang youth (Barnes et al., 2010; Esbensen and Weerman, 2005). Anger is also an understudied topic. What is surprising is that gang members have reported abusive households, and childhood maltreatment has been linked to anger (Caspi et al., 2006). Abuse, like low self-control, is a risk factor for membership (Evans and Mason, 1996; K. M. Thompson and Braaten-Antrim, 1998; Thornberry et al., 2003). Female members in particular have reported abuse in the home prior to joining gangs (Campbell, 1984; Joe and Chesney-Lind, 1995).

Psychopathy first emerged when Yablonsky (1962) discussed gangs as sociopathic "near-groups" with psychologically disturbed leaders. Conduct disorder is a condition with symptoms that include aggression, deceitfulness, and cruelty to animals and is often viewed as the precursor to antisocial personality disorder, which shares some behavioral characteristics with psychopathy. Studies have examined conduct disorder and psychopathy among gang members. Lahey et al. (1999) reported that conduct disorder helped predict gang youth in the Pittsburg Youth Study. Valdez, Kaplan, and Codina (2000) examined psychopathy among Mexican American gangs. They used the Hare Psychopathy Checklist screening version and compared gang members with violent non-gang individuals and samples of forensic and psychiatric patients and undergraduate students. The checklist examines personality traits such as superficiality, grandiosity, deceitfulness, lack of remorse, and impassivity. Valdez, Kaplan, and Codina (2000) reported that 44% of the gang sample scored moderately on the scale, suggesting that they were possible psychopaths. In addition, 4% scored high on the scale, suggesting that they were psychopaths. Gang youth scored higher on the total, affective, and behavioral scores of the psychopathy scale. They also scored twice as high on the lack-of-empathy scale.

Suicide among incarcerated youth is about four times higher than among youth in the general population (Roberts and Bender, 2006). Given their increased risk of incarceration, gang youth are more at risk for suicide. Evans et al. (1996) examined suicide ideation and sexual abuse among gang and non-gang incarcerated youth. The sample included 395 youth 12 to 18 years old from a variety of ethnic/racial backgrounds. Almost one in five (19%) of the sample reported sexual abuse. Female gang members had attempted suicide and were more likely to report sexual abuse than males. Sexually abused members reported higher levels of suicide attempts and ideation.

HOMELESSNESS

Homelessness has received scant attention in the gang research literature. In the Los Angeles Study, about a quarter of the sample (26.7%) reported ever being homeless. In other research on injection drug users, several homeless youth had histories of gang membership (B. Sanders et al., 2009).

A few studies have examined homelessness and gang membership. Yoder et al. (2003) collected data on homeless and runaway youth in the Midwest. About one-sixth of the youth (15.4%) were gang members and another third (32.2%) were involved in gangs. Overall, the gang youth and the youth who were gang involved reported worse background characteristics and more involvement in risk behaviors than those with no gang affiliation. Homeless youth who were members or who were gang involved reported more substance use, delinquent peers, school suspensions, and family legal problems and were more likely to run away at an earlier age. Current members fared even worse. Compared with non-gang youth, family abuse, street victimization, and deviant subsistent strategies (e.g., living on the streets via illegal means) were much more common among gang youth.

Harper et al. (2008) reported similar findings. The authors researched risk behaviors, mental health, and gang membership of homeless African American males. Their comparisons indicated that for general demographic and homelessness experiences, no significant differences were discovered. The homeless males were screened for negative affect, which was defined as depressive symptomatology, anxiety, and loneliness. Individuals in gangs were significantly more likely to report depression and anxiety. They were also more likely to report violence, graffiti, and substance use (alcohol and marijuana). The authors developed a scale to determine the intensity of involvement based on the number of times individuals participated in gang activities, including wearing gang colors and using gang signs.

BOX 11.1: MEDIA CHECK!

The Interrupters

Gang intervention is often a nebulous practice that includes terms like peace negotiation, conflict management, and rumor control. *The Interrupters* is a documentary about how gang intervention is practiced. Set in the South Side of Chicago, the movie takes its name from a group of outreach workers called violence interrupters, mainly former gang members who once held prestigious ranks. One of the interrupters is the offspring of a founding member of one of Chicago's largest and most notorious African American gangs. Many of the interrupters talked about coming from families involved in crime, drugs, and murder. All of them had served many years in prison—a total of more than 500 years combined is mentioned at one point. The violence interrupters see images of their formers selves reflected in the youth they work with.

One excellent aspect of the documentary is its job of capturing how violence interrupters talk and practice intervention. "Have there been any conflicts mediated on the front end?" a project manager asks during a meeting. A violence interrupter replies, "Two guys were arguing. One guy threatened to blow the other guy's wig back. I got the other guy to calm down, saying, 'He wasn't going to shoot you. He was just talking.' We stopped that one on the front end." The documentary also captures actual incidents of violence interruption in action, with one fight happening right outside their Englewood office. "I'm gonna pop him!," a youth yells after getting his teeth knocked out, as the interrupters whisk him away to cool down. One youth is hit in the face with a rock and another interrupter escorts him to a car and they drive away. The fact that violence was captured during the one-year filming of this documentary provides profound insight into the difficulties and dangers inherent in gang intervention.

The concept of violence interruption stems from an approach developed by Gary Slutkin at the University of Illinois at Chicago and is part of a wider violence reduction program called Ceasefire. Slutkin, an epidemiologist, developed Ceasefire based on his work with tuberculosis and HIV in Africa.

Violence was most seen as a disease in impoverished inner-city African American communities. Many young people living there figured that when they did die, violence would be the reason. Slutkin argues that violence is an infectious disease, and a public health approach could target efforts toward where violence is most likely to occur. The way forward was to intervene in the transmission of behaviors that lead to violence, mostly issues surrounding respect. A critical intervention point is when respect is challenged and there is a need to reach others before they retaliate.

The Interrupters also shines light on the difficult and dangerous nature of gang intervention. These individuals work in what one calls a "war zone" where violence is "epidemic," but they are paid little. Several have been shot at and one had been hit. The scenes of the violence interrupters at halfway houses, homes of concerned family members, and generally cruising around relatively well-known crime and violent hot spots in South Chicago underscore the perils inherent in such work. The crying mothers of dead sons contribute to its demanding aspects. The documentary captures several uplifting scenes where the interrupters were successful. The scenes of the many makeshift memorials in the city streets, however, are grim reminders of missed opportunities.

Why would anyone in his or her right mind do such work? The answer, although not explicit, seems clear: redemption. Several of the violence interrupters break down when discussing their own upbringings, including what they did wrong and the heartache they caused themselves and their families. Their pasts serve as a powerful incentive toward helping at-risk youth in the communities they once helped to destroy. "Why do you like fighting?" one of the interrupters asks a groups of youths. "That's just the way I was brought up," one youth responds. Exactly. Changing behavioral norms that lead to violence is an aim of Ceasefire, but the fact that these norms have been passed down from generation to generation for some time suggests the program's difficult struggle ahead. Ceasefire's claim to have interrupted 1,400 incidents and contributed to between a 40 and 45% drop in homicide is a wonderful start.

Visit PBS.org for the opportunity to watch The Interrupters.

They found that participants reporting higher levels of involvement were also significantly more likely to report substance use and violence. This finding suggests that the intensity of involvement is related to participation in substance use and violence. No differences emerged with regard to negative affect in relation to the intensity of membership.

INJURIES

Many gang members with gunshot wounds will not die on the street, but will be taken to hospitals with life-threatening injuries that will require surgery. Based on data from one

Los Angeles hospital, researchers found that from March 1992 through July 1994 almost one-third of all gunshot-wound victims were gang related (Song et al., 1996). Of these victims, the emergency department received about two in three with life-threatening injuries to parts of the head, neck, abdomen, and chest. Emergency surgery procedures, such as craniotomies (i.e., removal of part of the skull to access the brain), thoracotomies (i.e., an incision down the center of the chest to reach organs such as the heart or lungs), and laparotomies (i.e., large incisions through the abdominal wall to access the abdominal cavity), were performed on about 117 patients (Song et al., 1996). The authors reported that the price of these shootings, which included the costs of the emergency room, surgery, intensive care, and postsurgery convalescence in the hospital, was close to $5 million. More than half of the victims had no third-party reimbursement (i.e., health insurance).

Outside of homicide, the outcomes of gang violence are less well known. Youth in the Los Angeles Study were asked questions about their injuries. About a third (37.3%) had been hospitalized as a result of fighting. These hospitalizations were for deep cuts (6.8%), lacerations requiring stitches (27.1%), broken bones (11.9%), head injuries (16.9%), dislocated joints (5.1%), torn/sprained muscles (5.1%), and a variety of other injuries, such as gunshot wounds (10.2%). Youth did not always treat their gunshot wounds at a hospital. About one in six (16%) had been shot; more (79.7%) had been shot at. When asked about the likelihood of being shot in the future, 74.6% said that would be "very likely" or "likely." Below are some interview excerpts about being shot.

Is there something about your health or your body that you are currently worried about or not happy about right now?

My bullet.

How many bullets is that?

I just have one bullet in me right now.

Is it actually in you?

Yeah, it is.

It's in your chest?

Yeah, I have had two gunshots.

And that bullet is hurting you, you can feel it?

Yeah, you can feel it when I lay down. It will just be like popping out.

It pops out and you can feel it?

Yeah, it pops out and you put your hand like that and it's just like a bump and it's the bullet.

With an AK, you got hit with 6 rounds from an AK?

Yeah, I got shot through both of my arms, through my back, and then my leg right there. And they had to do a surgery on my ankle because they blew it out. This was just a big hole, so they had to put a muscle in here and got a skin graft from right here and covered that. As a result, pretty much I got shot and was in the hospital for a month. I had little operations and tubes all over the place, but I was still like, "Fuck it. Oh well."

One youth from the Los Angeles Study reported that he had died for several minutes after being shot.

> When I had got shot I was really bad and they did not want to mess with me. I had to fight it off on my own, if I wanted to live. Because I had lost a lot of blood and they put blood in me to revive me again 'cause I had died for four minutes and when I died for four minutes I had seen a gang of shit that I would have never seen, you know?

Like what?

> Just like tripped out shit. Like things you would not believe from someone if they tell you, like, like you would not believe it. . . . For four minutes I must have seen some tripping shit like everything, from my little dreams I went through déjà vu. I went through like quotes people used to tell me as I was growing up. I used to, like things, like that and things that would trip me out. Like see, "I told you, you were going to get shot one of these days." I actually had somebody talking to me. . . . I had Jesus like talking to me. . . . I was talking to Jesus. . . . I was telling him, "It's not my time, you know? I am too young, you know? It's not my time." And he was telling me, "You know what? I am going to give you one more chance." And he did.

Did you know that he was Jesus because of his look, like in your mind, or were you hearing his voice that you knew was his?

> I looked at him and it was a bright light, like he was just bright and everything around him and regular but he was bright and I was thinking like, "Wow."

The injuries the youth received from fighting depended on the context of the event. When they jumped other people, youth received a few minor injuries such as scratches and bruises, one got a bloody nose, and another broke his arm. At their most recent individual fight, they sustained slight injuries, like black eyes and broken noses and one who broke a bone. The most severe injuries were in collective forms of violence—such as group rumbles and getting jumped (see Table 11.1). One youth was kicked so hard that the shoe left an imprint of its logo on his back.

Like bruises on your back? Anything else?

> Yeah, and I had right here on the back of my neck like a Cortez mark.

What's that?

> Like a shoe, the Nike Cortez shoe.

You had an imprint of the shoe on your back?

> Yeah.

Victimization is also related to witnessing violence, including violence that has happened to loved ones. In total, 70% of the sample had had a family member murdered. The sample feared for their families' safety, with about two-thirds (67.8%) indicating they felt "very likely" or "likely" that a loved one would one day be shot and killed. About 62% of

TABLE 11.1 TYPE OF GANG FIGHT AND THE PERCENTAGE OF THE SAMPLE WHO REPORTED EVER RECEIVING INJURIES

	Jump Victim (%)	Rumbles/riots (%)
No injuries	6.8	16.9
Scratches	28.8	16.9
Bruises	44.1	35.6
Broken/bloodied nose	16.9	10.2
Black eye	27.1	27.1
Deep cuts needing stitches	6.8	13.6
Broken bones	1.7	5.1
Concussed	1.7	3.4
Left unconscious	3.4	5.1
Other	44.1	37.3

TABLE 11.2 FAMILY AND FRIENDS SHOT, KILLED, AND INJURED BY FIREARMS ($N = 60$)

	% (n)	Range	Mean
Friends/family shot	100 (60)	1–80	14.8
Friends/family killed	70 (42)	1–15	4.3
Friends/family, disabling injury	61.7 (37)	1–15	2.6
Friends/family, no disabling injury	40 (24)	1–20	2.5

the sample had friends and family who had been shot and survived, some with severe disabilities (see Table 11.2): 45.9% were in wheelchairs, 13.5% were in vegetative states, 10.8% were paralyzed from the neck down, 27% walk with a limp, 5.4% each lost an eye or could not talk, and 2.7% suffered from at least one of the following: blind, jaw disfigured, missing lung, lost leg, lost hand, hand disabled, arm disabled, colostomy bag, missing part of intestine, and bullet still in chest. Youth knew on average several individuals who had been killed or victimized with severe injuries. Violent victimization among gang youth extends well beyond what is inflicted directly on them. Examples provided by the youth follow.

And you said several homeboys died and the other people, did they survive?

   Like my homeboys?

Yeah, did they live?

   Yeah, there's a few. Hell yeah.

Anything happen to them, like are they disabled, in wheelchairs?

> [One] can't move his arm. He can only pick up like 30 or 40 pounds at the most that he can pick up. And one of them is on a wheelchair, some are like they can't talk and they have to carry a shit bag.

How many friends have died that you know?

> A few friends. Like 10 that I knew.

Before going into that, the other people that were shot and hit what happen to them?

> Like people that have died?

Yeah.

> I have six friends that have been shot by gunfire and have been killed. Six of my friends have been killed by gunfire.

What about your other homeboys, what happened to them?

> They just got shot and wounded a few times. They are okay.

What about relatives that were shot and hit?

> I have a brother who has been shot in the head twice.

Is he okay?

> He is a potato.

> I've seen a lot of my homies get shot before. I've seen a few die in front of me. . . . I never thought it would be one of us, the five of us. And when it finally did I was like damn. I been shot at. I been stabbed. I've been there when my homies died in front of me. And I knew, that's a part of gang banging. I knew it might happen to me one day. But when it happened to one of my closest friends, I never thought it would be one of us.

HEALTH MISCELLANEA

To obtain a fuller picture of the lives of gang youth, those in the Los Angeles Study were asked several questions about their overall health, including diet, exercise, weight, health concerns, and health care.

With regard to diet, they were asked whether in the past seven days they had consumed at least one soda pop and at least one serving of fruits or vegetables. They reported an average of 4.38 sodas and 4.50 servings of fruits or vegetables. They were also asked about how many times they ate at fast-food restaurants within that week. The reported average was just under four visits (mean = 3.93). To examine the extent to which the sample was overweight, they were asked for their height and weight to compile their mean body mass index (BMI). The average age was just over 18 (mean = 18.05), the average height was 67.82 inches (about five and a half feet), and the average weight was about 160 pounds. Given these figures, the average BMI was about 24.43. In relation to this, most (71.7%) felt "about right" in terms of how much they felt they weighed. A final question regarding diet concerned food insecurity, which refers to the lack of ability to obtain food. One of five (20%)

participants said that they had gone a day without food or had been concerned about where their next meal was coming from at least once in their lives. The sample was also asked about nondelinquent daily activities, including exercise. About half of the sample said that they worked out (45%) or played sports (51.7%).

The above findings were compared with national averages and the results indicate that individuals in the Los Angeles Study were relatively healthier than many Americans for some topics and less so for others. The consumption of sugary drinks in the United States has increased over the past 30 years and these drinks are linked to major health concerns, including poor diet, weight gain, obesity, and type 2 diabetes—the type caused in part by increased sugar consumption (Ogden et al., 2011). The first Gallup poll to query about average soda consumption across the United States found that about half of Americans (48%) drink soda daily and that the average consumption (including those surveyed who did not drink soda) was nearly one and a half sodas (1.3; Saad, 2012). Given these figures, the average American consumes 9.1 sodas in a week—about twice as much as youth in the Los Angeles Study. For fruit and vegetable consumption, the sample fared less well. The U.S. Department of Agriculture recommends three cups of vegetables every day for men but the sample did not average eating one fruit/vegetable.[2] This is also below the national average fruit/vegetable consumption of two cups per day from survey results (Produce for Better Health Foundation, 2010).

Fast-food consumption in the United States contributes to the twin pandemics of obesity and type 2 diabetes (Pereira et al., 2005). Comparing fast-food data from national surveys with that from the sample revealed that the sample ate out more than the general public. The sample averaged about four times a week eating at fast-food restaurants, whereas only 14% of Americans did so three or more times a week (DeSilva, 2014). This result could be a product of the sample's relatively low age (18 years) because data indicate that fast-food consumption decreases significantly with age (Fryar and Ervin, 2013).

The average BMI of the sample (24.43) was just within the healthy weight range (i.e., 18.5–24.9) and lower than the average BMI for both men (26.6) and women (26.5) across the United States.[3] This could be a result of the young age of the sample, as well as their overall high level of daily physical activity. Whereas 13.3% of the sample felt they were overweight, an average of more than a third (36.2%) of Americans surveyed said they were overweight (Xu et al., 2013). The sample perceived their weight to be healthier than that of many others. About 15% of Americans experienced food insecurity once during 2012, which is the highest ever since these statistics have been kept (Coleman-Jensen et al., 2013). The sample was not as bad off because their lifetime rates of food insecurity were not much higher than the annual national average.

The overall health of the sample was examined by the presence of any current health concern, health insurance, access to health care, and family health history. Again, the sample fared better in some areas and poorer in others compared with national averages.

---

2   Visit http://www.choosemyplate.gov/printpages/MyPlateFoodGroups/Vegetables/food-groups.vegetables -amount.pdf/.

3   Data from the National Health and Nutrition Examination Survey retrieved from http://www.cdc.gov/nchs/ data/nhanes/databriefs/adultweight.pdf/.

When asked about how they felt, one in five (20%) said "fair," a few said "poor" (1.7%), and the remainder said "excellent," "very good," or "good." In somewhat of a contradiction, 43.3% said that they had a "health worry." To compare, one survey of American adults reported that 22% felt their health was just "okay" (compared to "good" or "great") and 12% said their health was "not good" or "bad."[4] About a third of the sample (31.7%) had no health insurance and 41.7% had no dental insurance. Results from the National Health Interview Survey in 2013 show that 20.4% of all adults have no health insurance, and Gallup polls indicate that between 2008 and 2014, a low of 14.6% and a high of 18% of those surveyed had no health insurance (Centers for Disease Control and Prevention, 2014; Levy, 2014). About one in six (16.7%) individuals in the sample had ever been denied health care and slightly less (15%) had been denied care in the past year. The main reason was no insurance.

Finally, the sample was asked whether anyone in their immediate family had ever experienced one of a number of negative health conditions. Many of them had, including high cholesterol (38.3%), high blood pressure/hypertension (51.7%), stroke (26.7%), diabetes (53.3%), heart attack (21.7%), and obesity (20%). Nationally, about 25% of adults have high blood pressure, the national stroke prevalence rate is around 2.5%, about 8.3% of adults have diabetes, about a third (35.1%) of those age 20 years and older are obese, about 17% of adults have high cholesterol, and annually about a quarter of 1% have a heart attack.[5] The sample reported a pattern of serious health problems within their immediate families that was significantly higher than that experienced by average Americans.

NURSING INTERVENTION

Vulnerable population is a phrase used within the field of nursing to indicate a group of individuals who are susceptible to negative health outcomes. These include the elderly, prisoners, the developmentally disabled, the poor, racial and sexual minorities, and other marginalized groups. Gang youth are a vulnerable population (B. Sanders, Schneiderman et al., 2009). This is because of their at-risk background, participation in risk behaviors, and increased exposure to prison. The socioeconomic characteristics of youth before they join the gang and their involvement in risk behaviors once they become members will greatly vary. At the very least, given the cumulative and overlapping risk factors associated with membership, all gang youth can be found somewhere within the "intersections of vulnerability" (Delor and Hubert, 2000, p. 1563). Some are more vulnerable than others.

---

4 Visit http://www.phrma.org/sites/default/files/pdf/Second-Annual-PhRMA-Health-Short.pdf/.

5 For high blood pressure facts, visit http://www.stroke.org/site/PageServer?pagename=highbloodpressure/. For stroke prevalence rates, visit http://www.uhnj.org/stroke/stats.htm/. For diabetes prevalence rates, visit http://www.stopdiabetes.com/get-the-facts/diabetes-by-the-numbers.html/. For data on obesity, visit http://www.cdc.gov/nchs/fastats/obesity-overweight.htm/. For data on high cholesterol, visit http://www.cdc.gov/cholesterol/faqs.htm#6/. For data on heart attacks, visit http://www.cdc.gov/heartdisease/facts.htm/. The Centers for Disease Control indicate that about 720,000 Americans have a heart attack every year. The U.S. population is 313.9 million. Based on these figures and rounding up to the nearest hundredth, the percentage of Americans who have heart attacks annually is 0.23%.

Examples have emerged across the United States of the nursing community working directly with gang youth. Nurses in South Chicago noticed that the emergency room (ER) appeared to be gang members' primary source of health care (Burnette, 2006). They targeted gang members in an attempt to increase their access to health care and healthy living and reduce their number of ER visits. They offered recommendations to other nurses working with gang members, suggesting they partner with schools, law enforcement, and CBOs to offer preventive health care (see also B. Sanders, Schneiderman et al., 2009). Lee (1997) reported on the Gang Reduction Interagency Partnership, which involved criminal justice agencies, CBOs, and nurses. Nurses in the Gang Reduction Interagency Partnership served as a connection among the gang youths, their families, and other partners to provide a holistic approach that met their various needs.

The "Wraparound Project" in a San Francisco hospital is a program instigated by hospital staff toward gang members to reduce repeat visits to the ER (Stringer, 2007). This intervention targeted victims of penetration trauma, such as knife or gunshot wounds. Many were gang members. ER costs, much of which must be absorbed by taxpayers, are expensive (Song et al., 1996). To reduce the number of return visits to the ER (and lower overall costs), the Wraparound Project assigned patients with penetration trauma to case managers who connected them and their families with CBOs that focus on education and substance abuse. These efforts reduced the number of victims returning to the ER with penetration wounds.

A potential problem with hospital-based interventions is the fear they generate among the staff and patients. A concern expressed by nurses in East Los Angeles was that gang members might not come to the hospital because they knew that rivals would come looking for them there (Stringer, 2007). To negotiate this concern and to help develop a sense of calm in the hospital, gang patients were taken to a special part of the ER and treated by specially trained staff (Stringer, 2007). This practice assisted in reducing the fear felt by the nurses and allowed them to concentrate on treatment.

Public health nurses have provided violence prevention education within schools (Allender and Spradley, 2001). They often prioritize gang members because of their lack of access (Lee, 1997). Gangs are notoriously difficult to contact for research (B. Sanders et al., 2010). They may not attend mainstream schools that public health nurses often target. Nurses must be creative when trying to gain access to this population.

Public health nurses have partnered with the police to access gang youth and educate them about health care (Lee, 1997; B. Sanders, Schneiderman et al., 2009). The Culver City Police Department (CCPD) in Los Angeles did this (B. Sanders, Schneiderman et al., 2009). The partnership between the nursing community and the CCPD was fostered by the marriage between a public health nurse and one of the officers. CCPD offered a delinquency diversion/prevention program for juveniles arrested for nonviolent offenses. Many were already gang members or at risk for joining. The public health nurse was a guest speaker on three different occasions. During these times, no officers were present in the room to help build a sense of trust and rapport between the youth and the nurse. The nurse wanted the youth to feel comfortable talking about health-related concerns. The sessions were about morbidity and mortality, especially violence, major health issues among juveniles, like

obesity and sexual health, and risk prevention and health promotion. Only anecdotal evidence emerged about the program's success. About 70% of the youths' family members said that their children's attitudes had improved as a result of participating. Some of the youth also volunteered to tutor future rounds of youth in the program by assisting the nurse with her lectures. At the very least, the program allowed the nurse to interact with high-risk youth and provide information about their most pressing health concerns. The cost of such a program is low because most of the professionals involved volunteered their time. Given this and the potential for these types of programs to help redirect youth away from gangs and toward more positive lifestyle choices, such interventions involving nurses are important.

TOWARD A PUBLIC HEALTH AGENDA FOR GANG YOUTH

In the 1830s, cholera ravaged many British cities. Cholera patients were quarantined and isolated from the general population in special hospitals. People became fearful and enraged, and several riots broke out that largely originated around cholera patients and/or the doctors who attempted to cure them (Gill et al., 2001). Physicians were uncertain as to what exactly caused and transmitted cholera. Theories ranged from an act of God to a mist or miasma that swept through city streets. In London, such perspectives failed to explain the clustering of infected individuals within certain parts of the city. John Snow, recognized as one of the fathers of modern epidemiology, mapped the locations of the homes of some London cholera patients and eventually discovered that all of them obtained their drinking water from the same pump. By removing the pump's handle, rendering it useless, Snow stopped the cholera outbreak practically overnight. This discovery was so profound that the symbol of modern epidemiology is a 19th-century pump handle.

Criminal justice efforts aimed at reducing gangs are like pre-Snow approaches toward cholera: they quarantine and isolate the infected group (gang members) but pay little attention to the pump (community risk background factors). Spending on gang suppression led by criminal justice far outpaces funds for prevention and intervention (Greene and Pranis, 2007). But gang suppression is a notorious letdown. Leading gang researchers, who have spent decades studying gang youth and policies, have all noted the failure of criminal justice–oriented policies (Decker, 2003; Klein and Maxson, 2006). Los Angeles is called the gang capital of the nation, and successful prevention and intervention programs should have emerged from the city, but this is not the case. Despite the billions of dollars spent by city and state officials on policing, surveillance, increased sanctions, and reduced mobility applied to gang youth, more than six times the number of gangs and at least twice the amount of members are active in the Los Angeles region (Advancement Project, 2007;

Greene and Pranis, 2007). As one report said, "Los Angeles taxpayers have not seen a return on their massive investments over the past quarter century" (Greene and Pranis, 2007, p. 5).

The assertion that gang youth are a public health concern is based heavily on evidence from the general research literature that indicates that youth are at increased risk for incarceration and participation in risk behaviors and, consequently, are at an elevated risk of exposure to the many negative health and social outcomes. The importance on viewing gang youth as a public health concern lies within community responses to the phenomenon of ganging. Criminal justice efforts are a reactive approach; they serve to punish offenders, largely through incarceration or other community penalties. Public health approaches could be viewed as a defensive approach and should focus more efforts on preventing youth from becoming members (Haegerich et al., 2013; McDaniel et al., 2014). With a shift of efforts focusing primarily on gang prevention, the anticipation is that they can only achieve more positive results than what has been accomplished through gang suppression–heavy strategies.

One of the most salient outcomes of gang participation relates to deadly violence. In recent years, some public health–oriented approaches toward violence, particularly gangs, have either been implemented or encouraged (M. H. Moore, 1993, 1995; Sorenson, 2003; Welsh, 2005). The Ceasefire project in inner-city Chicago, which combines the efforts of various members of the community, has greatly reduced the number of firearm-related homicides since its inception (Skogan et al., 2009; see *Media Check!*). The Advancement Project (2007) called for similar actions in a report authored by civil rights attorney Connie Rice. Commissioned by the city of Los Angeles, Rice produced a report that requested the collaboration of various parts of the community—from the police to community members to social science and medical professionals—in what she dubbed a public health approach toward gang violence (Advancement Project, 2007). Rice considers gang violence an epidemic in the report and indicates that it should be treated similar to other diseases.

The public health agenda toward gangs encourages a shift in how they are studied, including the types of questions asked and a focus on the type of gang member; a shift in the perception as to why youth join gangs, participate in crime and risk behaviors, and the significance of gang life to them; and a shift in the overall response focusing more on prevention and treatment and less on punishment (B. Sanders and Lankenau, 2006; B. Sanders, Schneiderman et al., 2009; B. Sanders, Valdez et al., 2013).

Regarding methodology, criminological research focuses largely on crime and violence, but at the same time acknowledges that these behaviors are a small part of life in the gang. Little is known about the noncriminal and nonviolent aspects of gang life, although they form the overwhelming majority of how members spend their time. Other questions should center on victimization both prior to and after joining. Childhood abuse is discussed in the gang literature, but its outcomes are not. The development of personality traits conducive to crime is related to abuse. This lack of focus is a missed opportunity. Membership can be a fleeting experience, suggesting that many have legitimate plans they would like to seek when they become older. As discussed in the previous chapter, all but a few youth had conventional future plans that were not too far outside the jobs they could expect given their family and community backgrounds. By asking these types of questions, variability will likely emerge that links youths' risk backgrounds, participation in risk behaviors, extent of victimization, location in the gang, and likelihood of leaving and moving on to more prosocial lifestyles.

The public health agenda also calls for more qualitative research because the prior questions are difficult to gauge through precoded replies (B. Sanders et al., 2010). Many of these questions, particularly those regarding the significance of gang life and future plans, require open-ended questioning and probing. Serendipitous discoveries are also more likely with qualitative research because the youth might reveal information that is completely unexpected. "No one has ever asked me that before": several youth from the Los Angeles Study said this when asked about how they were feeling or whether they had any health concerns or what they wanted to do with their lives. Qualitative research is not easy, but the potential payoff is huge. During recruiting, qualitative research on gangs should look more closely at the type of gang member that is enrolled in the study, as well as his or her involvement in crime, violence, and other risk behaviors. For the Los Angeles Study, youths' involvement in the gang, crime, and violence could be reasonably predicted depending on where they were recruited (B. Sanders et al., 2010).

Theoretically, the public health agenda calls for the reason youth join gangs, commit crime, or participate in risk behaviors to move beyond explanations couched in pathology. A few reasons currently exist to explain why youth join gangs (Brotherton and Barrios, 2004), the meaning of violence (W. B. Sanders, 1994), or the role of marijuana (B. Sanders, 2012). The significance of the gang to youth varies, as does their participation in crime and other risk behaviors. Theories with strong explanatory power should be able to capture this, and looking outside the criminological literature might be fruitful. A closer look at the unfortunate irony about gangs, as well as the negative social and health outcomes that accompany membership, leads to this question: Why would someone join? In some cases, membership is the best option. In other cases, joining is whimsical. The theoretical underpinnings of this variability are less well examined. More information will better inform appropriate responses and approaches.

A shift in the approach toward gangs from suppression toward prevention is the third tier of the public health agenda. Prevention is the best cure: hospitals have known this for years. However, this is not what happens with gangs. Rather, we wait until they become sick (a gang member) and then attempt to cure (rehabilitation) them through incarceration. This approach is not working. To reduce the community costs of gangs, as well as the risk and vulnerability that members and their families face, more prevention efforts are needed. Such efforts should also be offered by those within the fields of public health, as opposed to criminal justice. Such educators should be drawn from the local population so as to better connect with the youth and highlight particular community risks.

Another shift should be the prevention message itself. One way to get a child to do something is to tell him or her, "Don't do it." Maybe something similar is happening to youth: they are only interested in gangs after they are told not to join. "Don't do it" is too simplistic a message. By highlighting the negative outcomes of membership, particularly victimization, youth could be more empowered and better informed to make decisions. A similar practice was used with a major public health concern: smoking. Experts have argued that the overall trend in the decline of smoking is directly attributable to the media campaigns that show graphic images related to long-term use (Egan, 2013). Showing youth similar images related to the long-term effects of gang membership (e.g., addiction, STIs, victimization) could have a similar impact.

A public health agenda geared toward youth in gangs cannot replace criminal justice efforts, but should compliment them. The police are needed to reduce gang violence, but this violence will continue unless more attention is given to prevention. Public health-related concerns are evident among gang youth across North America. Gang members should be viewed as youth in need of services and treatment, not fodder for the criminal justice system or morgue. New and radically different approaches to the gang situation are needed. The social science and public health communities should work toward removing the handle from the pump that consistently churns out youth likely to become involved in gangs.

SUMMARY

Gang youth share many characteristics with other groups of high-risk youth who are traditional public health concerns, including drug users, pregnant teenagers, and the homeless. Gang members come from an at-risk background characterized by poverty, conflict, and dysfunction. Once in a gang, youth engage in a variety of behaviors that place them at substantial risk for negative health and social outcomes. The nursing community has recognized the elevated levels of risk gang youth face and considers them a vulnerable population. Hospitals across the nation have developed specific intervention packages aimed not at reducing the number of gangs in the community, but at reducing the number of visits made to the ER.

Unsafe sexual behaviors are a major public health concern and are common among gang members. They initiate sex at early ages, have multiple partners, have sex while incarcerated, and report group and survival sex. These behaviors increase the risk of pregnancy and, in turn, the same conditions that give rise to gangs in the first place. Unsafe sexual behaviors place gang members at an increased risk of STIs, including HIV. Incarceration is linked to STIs and other health problems, and members are more likely to be incarcerated than their non-gang peers. If it were not for periods of incarceration, they might not know of any current STIs or treatment options available.

Mental health, homelessness, and injuries are areas common to the field of public health that have not been associated with gangs. Although the psychology of membership and organization is less studied, youth clearly have unaddressed mental health concerns that require further research. Homelessness has received scant attention in relation to gangs. Given their overall socioeconomic profiles, the fact that some gang members experience homelessness is not surprising, nor is the extent of their injuries. Violence is a common gang activity. A public health approach toward gangs that focuses on prevention will help alleviate the burden of membership.

CHAPTER REVIEW QUESTIONS

1. How are substance use and violence linked to both criminal justice and public health?
2. In what ways could gang youth be considered a public health concern?
3. How has the nursing community assisted gang members?
4. What are some of the risky sexual behaviors gang youth engage in? What are the related negative health outcomes?
5. How and to what extent are gang members exposed to HIV?
6. What are the health risks surrounding incarceration? Why are gang youth more likely to experience these risks?
7. What are the psychological characteristics of gang members?
8. What have researchers found in relation to gangs and homelessness?
9. What are some of the outcomes of violent victimization among gang youth?
10. What does the public health approach toward gangs advocate?

LINKS TO PUBLICATIONS ON PUBLIC HEALTH ASPECTS OF GANGS

Psychopathy among Mexican American gang members: A comparative study
By A. Valdez, C. D. Kaplan, and E. Codina
http://www.ncbi.nlm.nih.gov/pmc/articles/PMC3080033/pdf/nihms257995.pdf/

Risky sexual behaviors among a sample of gang-identified youth in Los Angeles
By B. Sanders, S. E. Lankenau, and J. Jackson-Bloom
http://www.ncbi.nlm.nih.gov/pmc/articles/PMC3178395/

Risk behaviors among young Mexican American gang-associated females: Sexual relations, partying, substance use and crime
By A. Cepeda and A. Valdez
http://www.ncbi.nlm.nih.gov/pmc/articles/PMC3016046/

The association between gang involvement and sexual behaviours among detained adolescent males
By D. R. Voisin, L. F. Salazar, R. Crosby, R. J. DiClomente, W. L. Yarber, and M. Staples-Horne
http://sti.bmj.com/content/80/6/440.full.pdf+html

Gang involvement and the health of African American female adolescents
By G. Wingood, R. J. DiClomente, R. Crosby, K. Harrington, S. L. Davies, and E. Hook III
http://pediatrics.aappublications.org/content/110/5/e57.full.pdf+html

Condom attitudes, perceived vulnerability, and sexual risk behaviors of young Latino male urban street gang members: Implications for HIV prevention
By R. A. Brooks, S-J. Lee, G. N. Stover, and T. W. Barkley, Jr.
http://www.ncbi.nlm.nih.gov/pmc/articles/PMC2819198/

Gang exposure and pregnancy incidence among female adolescent in San Francisco: Evidence for the need to integrate reproductive health with violence prevention efforts
By A. M. Minnis, J. G. Moore, I. A. Doherty, C. Rodas, C. Auerswald, S. Shiboski, and N. S. Padian
http://aje.oxfordjournals.org/content/167/9/1102.full/

HIV testing, perceived vulnerability and correlates of HIV sexual risk behaviors of Latino and African American young male gang members
By R. A. Brooks, S-J. Lee, G. N. Stover, and T. W. Barkley Jr.
http://www.ncbi.nlm.nih.gov/pmc/articles/PMC3244469/

Low school engagement and sexual behaviors among African American youth: Examining the influences of gender, peer norms, and gang involvement
By D. R. Voisin and T. B. Neilands
http://www.ncbi.nlm.nih.gov/pmc/articles/PMC2786183/

Fighting gangs the healthy way
By M. Burnette
http://www.minoritynurse.com/community-health/fighting-gangs-healthy-way/

Gang members in the ED
By V. Grossman and M. McNair
http://www.youthalive.org/storage/journal_of_nursing_0203.pdf/

Supporting gang violence prevention efforts: A public health approach for nurses
By D. D. McDaniel, J. E. Logan, and J. U. Schneiderman
http://www.nursingworld.org/MainMenuCategories/ANAMarketplace/ANAPeriodicals/OJIN/
TableofContents/Vol-19-2014/No1-Jan-2014/Gang-Violence-Prevention-Public-Health
-Approach.html/

What is the role of public health in gang-membership prevention?
By T. M. Haegerick, J. Mercy, and B. Weiss
http://nij.gov/publications/changing-course/Pages/public-health.aspx/

CHAPTER 12

GANGS OUTSIDE
OF THE UNITED STATES

KEY WORDS

18th Street: Also known as *Calle Dieciocho*; one of the *maras*—large, hierarchical gang allegedly involved in sophisticated crimes such as international drug, human, and weapons smuggling. The gang originated in Los Angeles, but 18 St. is also a *mara* allegedly responsible for a large amount of violence in various Central American countries.

Aussiedlers: German, refers to Russians of German descent.

Bang Pai: Chinese, roughly translates to gangs.

Bandes: French, refers to gangs.

Chavos bandas: Spanish, refers to gang youth in Mexico distinguished by a certain style.

El vacil: Spanish, refers to "the criminal lifestyle."

Eurogang definition: Defines a gang as any durable, street-oriented youth group whose own identity includes involvement in illegal activities.

Favela: Portuguese, refers to the ghettos/slums of major Brazilian cities, such as Rio de Janeiro and Sao Paulo.

Gopnik/gruppirovki: Russian, refers to gang members.

Jeugbendes: Dutch, refers to gangs.

Maras: Spanish, refers to large, multinational gangs, particularly 18th Street and Mara Salvatrucha 13 (MS-13), that are similar to organized crime in terms of structure and involvement in illegal activities. These gangs are particularly problematic in Central America and are believed to be responsible for a large amount of violence.

Mara-Salvatrucha 13 (MS-13): One of the *maras*—large, hierarchical gang allegedly involved in relatively sophisticated crimes such as international drug, human, and weapons smuggling. The gang originated in Los Angeles, and MS-13 has been considered responsible for a large amount of violence in various Central American countries. The name has been interpreted in different ways.

Mobbing: Australian, similar to "getting jumped" in the U.S. context, which is when one or two individuals are simultaneously attacked by numerous others.

NEW-ADAM: Refers to the New England and Wales Arrestee Drug Abuse Monitoring program in the United Kingdom.

Pandillas: Spanish, refers to small, locally based gangs in Central America or Spain involved in petty delinquency, drug sales, and territorial violence that are similar to street gangs found in the United States.

Swarming: Australian, similar to group "rumbles" or "riots" in the U.S. context, which is when two groups, each with numerous individuals, simultaneously attack one another.

Triadization: In Hong Kong, a process by which youth become socialized and assimilated into organized crime (aka the triads).

Chapter Learning Objectives

- Discuss the impact of the Eurogang research program.
- Compare and contrast characteristics of gangs from different countries.
- Recognize the role of immigration in the emergence of gangs outside the United States.
- Describe the influence of policies toward gangs in different countries.

INTRODUCTION

Groups of young offenders are evident around the world, but whether they are U.S.-style gangs has remained unclear for many years. Journalistic accounts or personal life histories in numerous countries have employed the term gang to describe youth committing crime and violence. In Kingston, Jamaica, gangs in public-sector housing estates have engaged in days-long firefights with the police and the military. A resurgence of skinhead gangs since the 1990s across Western Europe, Russia, Canada, Australia, and New Zealand has coincided with new waves of immigration and the rise of ultra–right wing politicians promoting a nationalist agenda. Evidence from Colombia depicts gangs of young men on motorcycles in rural areas committing drive-by shootings on behalf of the cartels. Armed drug gangs have controlled the *favelas* of Rio de Janeiro and Sao Paolo in Brazil for decades.

Organized crime in China and Japan has youth gang counterparts. Toward the end of the 20th century, researchers began to look more closely at the extent to which these and other gangs were similar to those found in America.

This chapter presents information on gangs outside of the United States. The first part looks at England, where a large amount of research has been conducted. From here, data from the Eurogang program are presented. The Eurogang Program is a collaboration of researchers from the United States and various European nations who developed a definition of gang for cross-national comparisons. This section provides overviews of these studies, as well as that of others who have utilized this definition in countries not in Europe. Next, the focus shifts to Latin America, including Mexico, El Salvador, Guatemala, the Caribbean, and Brazil. The concluding section examines gangs in Australia and China.

ENGLAND

England has been a focus of gang research. This is apt given the similarities with the United States and the special relationship between the nations. Both have a shared colonial history and are predominantly white, with English the main language. Both have similar religious, economic, and democratic systems. The United States and England even have a history of shared criminological insights (see Downes, 1966). If gangs are anywhere else in the world, they must be in England. Studies in England are broken down into three sections: early research, a study in South London from 1996 to 2002, and modern investigations.

EARLY RESEARCH

Over several decades, English researchers examined the context of group delinquency, and some set out to locate U.S.-style gangs (Corrigan, 1979; Downes, 1966; Foster, 1990; Mays, 1954; Parker, 1974; Robins, 1992; P. Scott, 1956; Willis, 1977; Willmott, 1966). None found gangs. Delinquency patterns and group contexts were different. Downes (1966) tested the delinquent subculture theories that were popular at the time (e.g., Cloward and Ohlin, 1960; A. K. Cohen, 1955; A. K. Cohen and Short, 1958). The newspapers had used terms like "gang warfare" to describe incidents of collective youth violence (see also S. Cohen, 1972). Downes (1966) found the character of delinquency distinct from the subcultures and couched these findings in significant differences in class and culture between the East End of London and America. Parker's (1974, p. 64) "Boys" in Liverpool were not described as a gang but as a "network of lads who've grown up together and are seen around together in various combinations . . . a loose knit social group." The Boys had some gang characteristics in that they valued toughness and smartness, two of W. B. Miller's (1958) focal concerns. Research in 1980s London revealed violent feuds between groups of youth and those involved in systematic theft, but they were not described as gangs, nor did they have many ganglike qualities (Foster, 1990; Robins, 1992).

J. Patrick's (1973) *A Glasgow Gang Observed* is unique because it is one of the only studies to find evidence of gangs in Great Britain[1] in the 20th century (see, however, W. B. Sanders, 1994). Patrick (a pseudonym) was a schoolteacher in his mid-twenties who, through the

---

1   Great Britain and the United Kingdom are synonymous and include four countries: England, Wales, Scotland, and Northern Ireland.

help of one of his students, began to hang around the Young Team—a gang from Glasgow. He did this as a participant, with the members having no idea that they were part of a study. The Young Team was violent, and Patrick witnessed vicious fighting. He considers the members sociopathic, especially the leaders, and draws parallels with Yablonsky's (1959, 1962) concept of the near-group. They had little structure and did not persist over time. Patrick felt threatened and waited a few years before publishing his findings. Glasgow is one of the more violent cities in the United Kingdom and its history and culture of violence may help explain why gangs were found there.[2]

SOUTH LONDON, 1996–2002

B. Sanders (2002, 2005a) conducted an ethnographic study in the South London borough of Lambeth in an attempt to determine the presence of gangs.[3] In-depth interviews and unobtrusive observations generated the data. Three different definitions of the term gang guided conceptualizations: W. B. Miller's (1958); Klein's (1971); and W. B. Sanders's (1994). Combining these definitions, gangs were thus

> named groups of youth that had territory, rivalries, meaningful symbols, and displayed a readiness to engage in deadly violence, and were known by others in the community, including law enforcement, for crime and violence.

Under this definition, the groups of young offenders in Lambeth possessed none of these qualities. Some interviewed had worked on delinquency programs in America and indicated that U.S.-style gangs were not present in the borough. As one said,

> I think because I've had experience working in America, I would define gang very differently in America from what I'd define gang here as. I don't think it's as organized or structured as it is in the States. . . . In England I would define the term gang as a group of people who hang out together and I think it's as simple as that.

A senior drugs squad officer from Brixton agreed:

> The gang situation here is a lot different to that in the States. . . . In London it is much more loose . . . there are loose groups that operate together, but they won't necessarily operate as a traditional gang. They will run for awhile then not exist anymore. . . . They're really more groups or associations of people rather than gangs.

Several of the young offenders interviewed said something along the lines of "this isn't America" when asked about gangs. The word gang itself was foreign to them. As one said,

> When you say gang, right, to me it means something different, like something organized, like people going out to do something.

---

2   The UK Peace Index (Institute for Economics and Peace, 2013) indicates that, in 2012, Glasgow was "the least peaceful major urban centre" in Scotland and the most violent in the United Kingdom. Moreover, the report indicates that violence in Glasgow had actually *decreased* over the previous decade. A 2011 report by the United Nations Office on Drugs and Crime, *Global Study on Homicide*, indicated the murder rate in Glasgow in 2009 was about twice as high as that in London (3.3 vs. 1.6).

3   See the Appendix for the methodology and objectives of this study.

The picture of young people with a history of offending in Lambeth was of small groups of between four and eight members who were the same sex and roughly the same age. These youth grew up together and shared similar interests. Offending was a small part of their lives, with the exception of the few who were heavily involved in crack or heroin sales. These youth did the same things as the young people who grew up before them and went through the same experiences (Foster, 1990; Willis, 1977).

Although the young offenders in Lambeth were not gangs, they were similar in some respects. Most of the time, they hung out and did nothing. Average days consisted of sitting around with others and "chatting," sports, video games, "checking" for girls, and smoking cigarettes and "bunning" marijuana. Below are responses from four youth to the question: *What do you and your friends do on an average day?*

Just typical day? Just like hanging around in the [housing] estate, walking up and down. Just looking for something to do really.

Sit down. Bun [smoke cannabis]. I don't know. We're just hanging.

Just hang around on the estate, listen to music.

Just hang out, smoke. . . . Cigarettes or sometimes weed, and just hang out, smoke, muck about, talk to girls. Just that stuff.

Three youth justice workers offered similar responses:

They hang out together . . . chat to girls. If they could go to a friend's house who was old enough to let them and listen to music. Just hang out mainly.

They would get together and listen to music at one of the parent's house where it was allowed. They would sit around in the house. They did used to go to youth clubs. . . . They would go along and play pool. They would stay for an hour and then move on. They would hang around outside of pubs. . . . Just hang around on corners.

They get up late, come together. Depends upon the funds available to go shopping. Or hang out and smoke, play computer games, watch television, listen to music until the evening time. . . . Go to some other houses, meet girls, get some drink maybe, then some [cannabis] would get used.

Like gangs, youth in Lambeth were criminally versatile. Even those who spent a lot of time selling crack and/or heroin participated in crimes such as burglary, robbery, vandalism, joyriding, and assault. Youth committed offenses with others who were in their same peer group. Both a youth probation officer and a community youth worker said this:

Generally, young people that we work with always will do most of the offences in groups. They don't do offences on their own. It's more unusual to come across someone who has committed an offence on their own, you know, a burglary or whatever on their own. It's usually in a group.

I know young people that commit crime and tend to do it in groups rather than individually.

Young offenders in Lambeth were perceived differently from gangs. Few of their groups had names, and the ones that did changed. None of the police officers, youth justice, or community workers could name any groups of young offenders. No one mentioned initiation ceremonies, symbols, colors, hand signs that held any significance, roles within the groups, territorial graffiti, or rivalries between neighboring youth. Deadly violence was rare—although Lambeth had a high homicide rate.

B. Sanders's (2002, 2005a) research was completed right around the same time as the Eurogang definition was constructed. In hindsight, the data indicate that groups of young offenders in Lambeth *still* fail to meet this definition. Below is the Eurogang definition:

> Any durable, street-oriented youth group whose involvement in illegal activity is part of their group identity.

A critical difference between this definition and the groups of young offenders in Lambeth is their durability. They were the exact opposite: ephemeral. As Klein and Maxson note, "durability refers to the *group*, which continues despite turnover of members" (2006, p. 4, original emphasis). No evidence of this surfaced.[4] These groups consisted of young people who have grown up and been arrested together. When they mature, the groups disperse, and the young people assume adult responsibilities. Most discussed legitimate aspirations that were well aligned with their expectations. The evidence suggests that over decades within Lambeth, groups of young offenders come from the same housing estates and go through similar experiences. Over time, no continuity exists between the most recent group and their predecessors. These groups did not regenerate from below.

Groups of young offenders in Lambeth were small—four to eight members, and the age range was narrow, about one to two years. In these respects, they are different from U.S.-style gangs. The Klein/Maxson typology says that compressed and specialty gangs have fewer than 50 members and have been in existence around for less than 10 years. Having fewer than 10 members and being in existence for a couple of years (at best) is far removed from qualifying definitions. Offending was occasional, even violence. The latter part of the Eurogang definition—"illegal activity is part of its group identity"—does not apply. Their main purpose was socializing. The exception to this was the few young people who were part of drug-selling collectives. They spent much of their time on the streets and participated in a variety of offenses.

Why were no gangs found in Lambeth? The conditions in the borough were right: high crime rates, presence of organized crime, social disorganization (e.g., poverty, ethnic/racial heterogeneity, rapid change—*toward* affluence, and transiency); drug use and sales, poor community–police relations, and a culture of violence. Their absence is attributed to several interrelated considerations.

Historical and cultural differences between the United States and England help account for the lack of gangs in Lambeth. Racial diversity and struggle in the United States is a significant basis for gang formation. Such diversity in England is a more recent

---

4   In a later Eurogang definition, durable referred to being in existence for at least three months (Medina et al., 2013). Under this definition, many of the groups of young offenders in Lambeth would be considered durable.

development. The lack of guns and lower rates of crack cocaine use and sales are also significant. The crack epidemic in the 1980s in the United States gave rise to street gangs. In England, that epidemic never materialized. England has a limited gun culture, whereas firearms are a substantial part of U.S. history. Guns in America allow members to apply territorial claims with deadly force, which increases the potential for tit-for-tat paybacks. Although the borough had one of the few ever gun amnesties in the country during the research period (i.e., 1997), the comparative lack of firearms has helped prevent the development of gangs.

B. Sanders's (2002, 2005a) conclusion about young offenders in Lambeth aligns with what Hallsworth and Young (2004, p. 12) mention in a brief article (see also Marshall et al., 2005):

> What happens in the US and what goes on in the streets of Britain are not the same. Nor is there any evidence to support the idea that the UK is home to US style gangs. . . . We must though be very careful to ensure that we don't generalise this US based tradition to describe all and every group caught "hanging around."

The findings in Lambeth are a contemporary anomaly. Nowadays, gangs are everywhere in Great Britain.

MODERN INVESTIGATIONS

Around the beginning of the 21st century, researchers began to find gangs in the United Kingdom. Survey data asked about gangs and members. One survey from police departments reported 71 different gangs (Stelfox, 1998). The *2004 Offending, Crime and Justice Survey* noted that 6% of all 10- to 19-year-olds reported belonging to a gang (Sharp et al., 2006). Sentinel data on drug use among arrestees (i.e., NEW-ADAM) also inquired about membership in 2000 (Bennett and Holloway, 2004); that year, 15% of all arrestees reported a history of membership.[5] Bennett and Holloway (2004) extrapolated their findings to suggest that of all those 18 years old and older who had been arrested in 2000/2001, about 20,000 were members. As of 2008, between 3 and 7% of all youth were believed to be in a gang (Hallsworth and Young, 2008). The Home Office launched a program for addressing this (e.g., *Tackling Gangs Action Program*), and major cities also have programs.[6] Manchester's integrated gang management unit aims to safeguard "young people, families, and communities from violent gang activity and supporting Gang Members exiting from the gang lifestyle."[7] The Policing and Crime Act of 2009 introduced gang injunctions, which are colloquially referred to as GANGBOs.[8] Pan-European reports on youth violence

---

5   ADAM is the Arrestee Drug Abuse Monitoring program in the United States. It provides data on drug usage among those arrested. The NEW-ADAM is the version used in the United Kingdom; NEW stands for New England and Wales.

6   http://webarchive.nationalarchives.gov.uk/20080804123613/http://crimereduction.homeoffice.gov.uk/test-bed/violentstreet011a.pdf/.

7   Visit   http://www.manchester.gov.uk/info/200030/crime_antisocial_behaviour_and_nuisance/6134/integrated_gang_management_unit/.

8   The name derives from the fact that such injunctions are a form of antisocial behavior orders.

in the United Kingdom also mention the role of gangs (Mills, 2013). Websites are also dedicated to gangs.[9]

Gangs have impacted major English and Scottish cities. In 2006, London's Metropolitan (Met) Police reported 169 different gangs (Metropolitan Police, 2006). Manchester has been referred to as Gunchester because of the amount of gang-related gun violence (Bullock and Tilley, 2002; Shropshire and McFarquhar, 2002). West Midland Police reported 42 gangs with more than 400 members, and Nottinghamshire had 15 gangs with up to 400 members (Mills, 2013). The Edinburgh Study of Youth Transitions and Crime, a longitudinal research following thousands of young people, is the largest of its type ever conducted in Scotland. The study found that constant membership over time was 5% between the ages of 13 and 17 (McVie, 2010; see also Bannister et al., 2010). Strayclyde had 170 gangs at one point and about 300 at another (Antrobus, 2009; Bannister et al., 2010), and Glasgow located 55 gangs with 600–700 members (Mills, 2013).

The United Kingdom has experienced the same problem as the United States: no uniform definition of gang exists (Antrobus, 2009; Bannister et al., 2010; Cox, 2011; Hallsworth and Young, 2008; C. Hayden, 2008; Mills, 2013; Pitts, 2007; Stelfox, 1998). The Met uses one definition, but it is different from that used within sentinel surveys (i.e., NEW-ADAM; Crime Survey of England and Wales), which is also distinct from the one used by the Home Office (Bennett and Holloway, 2004; Medina et al., 2013; Metropolitan Police, 2006; Mills, 2013). This definitional issue is not trivial. C. Hayden (2008) argues that what many young people considered a gang would not be defined as such by criminologists (see also Medina et al., 2013). The argument is not about their existence, but how to define them and the appropriate and effective response (Aldridge et al., 2008; Medina et al., 2013; Smithson et al., 2012).

Researchers have found evidence of gangs across Great Britain (Aldridge and Medina, 2008; Bannister et al., 2010; Bennett and Holloway, 2004; Bradshaw, 2005; Bullock and Tilley, 2002; Densley, 2013; Grund and Densley, 2012; Mares, 2001; McVie, 2010; Medina et al., 2013; Pitts, 2007, 2008).[10] As in the United States, gang youth in the United Kingdom are more involved in crime and violence than are nonmembers. According to the Home Office, they are more likely to carry guns and other weapons (Murphy, 2008; see also Bullock and Tilley, 2002). The Met indicated that the gangs in London were responsible for about 20% of all crime (Metropolitan Police, 2006). Across the nation, Stelfox (1998) reported that about 75% of gang members were involved in drug sales and that about 60% had firearms (see also Aldridge and Medina, 2008; Bullock and Tilley, 2002; Mares, 2001). NEW-ADAM data reported that members were much more likely to commit numerous types of property, violent, and weapons offenses, as well as to report cannabis use and drug injection (Bennett and Holloway, 2004). In London, half of all shootings and almost a quarter of all serious offenses involved gangs (Mills, 2013). In Scotland, Bradshaw (2005) reports that gang youth were more involved in crime than youth not in gangs.

---

9   For instance, visit http://londonstreetgangs.blogspot.com/.

10 The House of Commons has a clearinghouse of publications about gangs in the United Kingdom. Retrieved from http://www.google.com/search?client=safari&rls=en&q=youth+gangs+in+the+UK:+context,+evolution +and+violent&ie=UTF-8&oe=UTF-8/.

As in the United States, many researchers have stressed that because of the various ways that the term is constructed, accurately identifying the extent that gangs are responsible for disproportionate amounts of crime and violence is questionable (Bannister et al., 2010; Cox, 2011; Hayden, 2008; McVie, 2010). Another important parallel between the United States and the United Kingdom is that more than anything else, gangs hang out and do nothing (Aldridge and Medina, 2008; Bannister et al., 2010).

Like the Causes and Correlates studies, gang members in the United Kingdom have reported on similar risk factors as the United States (Aldridge and Medina, 2008; Bennett and Holloway, 2005; McVie, 2010). Youth get out of the gang for similar reasons and at about the same time in their lives. Youth have weaved in and out of gangs and reported leaving because of employment opportunities and relationships (Aldridge and Medina, 2008; Bannister et al., 2010; McVie, 2010). Longitudinal studies indicate members at age 13 left by time they reached 16 (McVie, 2010).

Other qualities of U.S. gangs have been found in the United Kingdom. Some have meaningful signs and symbols (Bannister et al., 2010; Bradshaw, 2005; Densley, 2012; Grund and Densley, 2013; McVie, 2010). Territory and rivalries are issues among some gangs. Densley (2013) notes that members in London have adopted a well-known American colloquialism when determining status: *Where are you from?* Named gangs have recruited younger members over decades and held rivalries lasting generations (Bannister et al., 2010). Graffiti is used to mark territory, as one respondent from a Scottish study said (Bannister et al., 2010, p. 20; see also Densley, 2013):

> The territorial thing is very much alive and well today . . . the width of a street can dictate whether you're going to get a scar for the rest of your life, because you have gone over to the other side of the street. You can walk 100 yards from this office and you will find territorial markers on the lampposts, on railings etc. and that's a warning, this is our area, and if you pitch up here and we either know or we either think you are from another gang . . . then there is the possibility that violence is going to result, simply on the basis of that.

Gang organization is not sophisticated and leaders were older, criminally seasoned youth (Aldridge and Medina, 2008; Bannister et al., 2010; Mares, 2001). Aldridge and Medina (2008, p. 17) noted that organization was "fluid, loose, messy" (p. 17), moderately cohesive, with a high turnover of leaders and members. Members are differentially involved in crime and violence, and some gangs are more involved in these behaviors than others (Bannister et al., 2010). Some had age-graded subgroupings (Densley, 2013; Pitts, 2007). A few had gang tattoos (Densley, 2013). They were also criminally versatile (Medina and Aldridge, 2008; Bannister et al., 2010).

In other respects, the gangs in the United Kingdom are different from those in the United States. Youth in Scotland resisted the term gangs and instead opted for team or group, and the amount of deadly violence is low (Bannister et al., 2010). The groups were smaller than gangs, about 10–20 members (although they could get bigger at times), and they had a relatively narrow age range, about 10 years (although in some cases it was wider; Bannister et al., 2010). Drug use varied, although use was higher than among non-gang youth (Medina and Aldridge, 2008). Drug use is diverse among U.S. members (B. Sanders,

2012). In the United Kingdom, drugs are limited to the frequent use of marijuana and the occasional use of ecstasy (Bannister et al., 2010). No initiation ceremonies were reported (Bannister et al., 2010; Medina and Aldridge, 2008).

Gangs in the United States are predominantly minorities, but this is not always the case in the United Kingdom. Studies in London and Manchester have indicated that a disproportionate amount of members are Afro-Caribbean youth, as well as West and East Africans (Densley, 2012; Mares, 2001). In Scotland, most are white (Bannister et al., 2010). Research in areas in England with high percentages of white residents also revealed large numbers of white members (Mares, 2001; Medina and Aldridge, 2008). Others studied have been ethnically mixed (Mares, 2001; Medina and Aldridge, 2008).

Female gangs have been found throughout the United Kingdom. Bennett and Holloway (2004) note that 5% of the gang members in the NEW-ADAM data were females. Others have reported that up to half are female (Sharp et al., 2006). In Scotland, Bannister and colleagues (2010) reported that most gangs were mixed gender, although females were less involved in crime and violence and viewed as associates.

EUROGANG RESEARCH

The Eurogang Program began as a collaboration between leading American gang researchers and criminologists from Western European countries in the late 1990s (see Decker and Weerman, 2005; Esbensen and Maxson, 2012; Klein et al., 2001; van Gemert et al., 2008). They converged to develop a uniform definition of gangs so as to allow comparison between various nations. Researchers from countries inside and outside of Europe have utilized this definition (Gatti et al., 2011; Haymoz and Gatti, 2010).

HOLLAND

Evidence for gangs has emerged from Holland (aka the Netherlands; de Jong, 2014; Esbensen and Weerman, 2005; van Gemert, 2001, 2005; van Gemert and Fleisher, 2005; van Gemert and Stuifbergen, 2008; Weerman, 2005; Weerman and Esbensen, 2005). Dutch media calls them *jeugbendes* (van Gemert and Fleisher, 2005; Weerman, 2005). A survey of about 2,000 secondary school[11] students showed that 6% belonged to gangs or "troublesome youth groups" and many were native Dutch (Weerman, 2005, p. 138). Weerman (2005) indicates that many gangs did not have names, but those that did borrowed heavily from American culture (e.g., the Bloods; the Crips; Westside Gangsters; see also van Gemert, 2001; van Gemert and Stuifbergen, 2008). Weerman and Esbensen (2005) compared this sample to school survey data in the United States and found that gang youth in Holland and the United States have the same risk factors. The authors noted that members in both countries were between four and six times more likely to be involved in various forms of delinquency (Weerman and Esbensen, 2005). Van Gemert (2005) surveyed police officers with intimate knowledge of young offenders from different neighborhoods in Amsterdam. They reported 85 youth groups, about half of which could be

---

11 Secondary school is the U.S. equivalent of the combination of middle/junior high and high schools (i.e., grades 7–12).

considered gangs. Many were of Moroccan descent.

Van Gemert and Fleisher (2005) focused on Moroccan youth in Amsterdam (see also van Gemert and Stuifbergen, 2008; de Jong, 2014). One was called the Windmill Square group after the area where they congregated. The police named them. They had known this group for several years and had compiled a changing list of members, suggesting durability.[12] The size of the group averaged about 25, and they had an age range of 16- to 20-year-old males. They listened to gangsta rap, but did not have the signs and symbols (e.g., colors, clothing, graffiti; see also van Gemert, 2001, 2005). They were not territorial and did not have fights with similar groups of youths (see also van Gemert, 2005). They had no leaders, no rules, and no subgroupings. They committed a variety of offenses, but did not specialize in any (see also Weerman and Esbensen, 2005). With the exception of rowdy behaviors, they committed offenses alone or in pairs—not as a group. But like U.S.-style gangs, most of the time they hung out and did nothing. Boredom occupied most of their days. Unlike U.S. gangs, some members in these gangs talked about politics and expressed anti-American and anti-Israel statements.

GERMANY

Research in Germany has focused on immigrant youth originally from Turkey, Russia, and Croatia (Bucerius, 2008; Kerner et al., 2008; Tertilt, 2001; Weitekamp et al., 2005). Tertilt (2001) studied the Turkish Power Boys in Frankfurt in the early 1990s—one of about 25 gangs in the city. Tertilt closely observed them, visited their families, and participated in recreational activities. They were a group of about 50 boys, ages 13 to 18 years old, with strong Turkish identities. They committed a variety of property, violent, and drug offenses, but most of their time was spent doing routine activities (e.g., school, recreation). The Boys expressed anger as a result of discrimination through theft, and in some instances they brutalized their victims, most of whom were German. The gang went from a structureless group of thieves to one that had a panel of leaders who focused on fighting other groups of youth. Over a short period of time, many of the Boys began using heroin and became addicted. By 1992, the gang had dissolved.

---

12 De Jong (2014) reported that durability was problematic among the gangs of Moroccan youth he focused on. He did note that the network of more than 100 Moroccan street boys he studied was durable, but that some from this network (in groups ranging from 3 to 6 "members") only came together periodically for the purposes of committing crime.

Weitekamp et al. (2005) researched *Aussiedlers*—Russians of German descent—and how they were likely to join gangs. Data were based on interviews with young incarcerated *Aussiedlers*. The authors found that many of the youth were in gangs that emerged in relation to survival in a violent atmosphere back in Russia. They were also discriminated against in Russia because they were seen as German fascists. When the Soviet Union crumbled in the early 1990s, Russians of German descent immigrated en masse to Germany and took advantage of laws that allowed individuals with German ancestry to obtain immediate citizenship. Life was not as bad for the *Aussiedlers* in Germany. Nonetheless, language and cultural barriers prevented them from properly integrating, and the education and training they received in Russia was subpar compared with German standards. They were also discriminated against in Germany, where they were called Russians. Weitekamp and colleagues concluded that having a history of ganging in their home country and feelings of rejection in their host country were the reasons why they formed violent gangs. Another study by Kerner and colleagues (2008) revealed that ethnic segregation was one of several reasons related to the emergence of troublesome youth groups and the disproportionate amount of violence among migrant youths in Germany (see also Bucerius, 2008).

Skinhead gangs have long been in Germany. Bucerius (2008) notes that they became a concern in the mid-2000s because of the increase in violent racist attacks. Bucerius indicates that skinheads are often from East Germany, where anti-immigration sentiments run high. She relates this to the frustration and unemployment the east suffered during the reunification of Germany. People here were underprepared for the new democratic, capitalist regime. Blame fell on immigrants. Most of the skinheads, Bucerius continues, are under 25 years old, and are largely males of loosely structured groups. They appropriate Nazi materials, but have differing opinions about the Third Reich: some use it to gain attention, whereas others are true believers. Most of the time they are hanging out, listening to skinhead music, but on occasion they have also been involved in assaulting and robbing foreigners.

FRANCE

Oualhaci (2008) reports on gangs or *bandes* in the French Republic. *Bandes* are recognizable collectives of youth found in the housing projects, known as *cites*. They are immigrants from the former French colonies in North Africa and the sub-Sahara, and others are various Europeans or French locals.

Ethnicity, delinquency, and gangs are sensitive topics in France and legal restrictions prevent reporting on their relationships (Debarbieux and Blaya, 2008; Fiori-Khayat, 2008). These restrictions have hindered more robust studies on gangs. Fiori-Khayat (2008) found evidence for gangs in some Parisian suburbs. They committed different types of offenses—property, violent, drug—but were also involved in politically motivated ones. In these cases, the youth—mostly minorities—lashed out in destructive ways. They felt their ethnicity was the reason their teachers failed them or why they could not find jobs. Drug selling was a way to make money. Fiorio-Khayat (2008) reports how a gang leader obtained a legitimate job and then forced the owner at gunpoint to hire fellow members. Many gang youth were angry at the French locals and at other immigrants. Relations between immigrants from West and North African countries were tense. Fiori-Khayat (2008) concludes that ethnicity was significant in the creation of street gangs (see also Debarbieux and Blaya, 2008).

SPAIN

In Spain, various groups of youth, including gangs, are referred to as *pandillas* (Feixa and Porzio, 2008) or *bandas* (Feixa et al., 2008). The end of the Franco regime in the mid-1970s ushered in a new era for Spain in terms of youth subcultures; various spectacular ones emerged, like the Teddy Boys, rockers, and hippies, but also Spanish-specific ones, such as *gamberros* and *Tribus Urbanas* (Feixa and Porzio, 2008). Evidence suggests that gangs, like the Ñetas and Latin Kings, began in the early 21st century in Barcelona in relation to massive increases of immigrants in the 1990s from former Spanish colonies in Latin America (Canelles and Feixa, 2008; Feixa et al., 2008; Feixa and Porzio, 2008). In 2005, the Catalan police reported that more than 20 different groups in Barcelona were Latin gangs with around 200 members (Feixa et al., 2008). The Spanish media created a moral panic about gang warfare involving the Latin Kings in 2003/2004 in relation to isolated and disparate events (Canelles and Feixa, 2008; Feixa and Porzio, 2008; Feixa et al., 2008). Gang members were depicted as wearing black bandannas, dressing in gold, black, and blue, and having tattoos of crowns (the symbol used by the Latin Kings; Feixa et al., 2008). They were highly organized and committed violence against everyone—rivals, the public, and their own members—and the number of gang members was increasing (Feixa et al., 2008).

Latin American youth immigrated to many Spanish cities in waves beginning in the late 1990s and these youth face problems in terms of properly integrating and seizing educational and employment opportunities (Canelles and Feixa, 2008; Feixa et al., 2008). They are primarily from Ecuador, Colombia, and the Dominican Republic. They are socially excluded and end up hanging out in public places; as Latinos they are ethnically and visibly distinct, contributing to stereotypes and fear (Canelles and Feixa, 2008). Other immigrants from North Africa also formed gangs in Barcelona, one of them called the Morro Boys, and Roma gypsies—long despised by many natives in European nations—formed a gang called the Gypsy Kings (Feixa and Porzio, 2008). Gangs of immigrant youth have battled with local working-class youth (Feixa and Porzio, 2008).

Feixa and colleagues conducted some of the first ethnographic studies in Spain (Feixa et al., 2008). The authors were careful to describe these collectives as "gangs-in-process . . . group-like networks and behaviors at an incipient phase" and not gangs under the Eurogang definition (p. 65). They noted that some members do engage in a variety of criminal behaviors and that such behaviors are linked to their identity. They had names like Latin Kings and *Mara Salvatrucha*, but they were not connected to these gangs in other countries. They were durable and male, with a significant amount of females. As in the United States, youth joined for identity, security, protection, and affection. They faced discrimination and blocked employment opportunities; immigrants were allowed to live in the country, but were not issued work permits. Young people had difficulties adapting to the new school system, and Latin families were living in overcrowded conditions. Cultural preferences, including style, demarcated them, and the media criminalized this style by associating it with gangs. It remains unclear whether these groups qualify as gangs under the Eurogang definition (Fexia et al., 2008).

ITALY

Gatti and colleagues conducted one of the earlier direct studies in Italy (Gatti, Angelini, et al., 2005; Haymoz and Gatti, 2010). Survey data indicated that about 16% of a sample of teenagers aged 13 to 16 years old self-reported membership (Haymoz and Gatti, 2010). A previous ethnographic study confirmed that the youth met the criteria of the Eurogang definition (Gatti, Angelini et al., 2005). They focused on a group of about 20 young people in Sperone in Genoa that consisted of two types: (1) the core—5 youth who have known each other about eight years; and (2) those loosely connected—15 youth who were girlfriends, acquaintances, and others who came and went within a short period of time. Leadership was informal. The youth did not battle with others and in many cases had friends or family in gangs in neighboring areas. The gang in Sperone was criminally versatile, with a history of involvement in a variety of crimes and seldom committed offenses outside of their group. Gatti, Angelini et al. (2005) note important differences between subgroups of gang members: those who were stable or transient. Stable members were more likely than the transients to have risk backgrounds for membership and to participate in crime and violence. They did not have any signs or symbols or a preference for gangsta rap. They listened to techno dance music and local Neapolitan songs. Associated females were girlfriends or former lovers.

NORTHERN COUNTRIES

Evidence for gangs has been found in the Northern Countries in Europe, such as Norway and Sweden (Bjork, 2008; Lien, 2005a, 2005b, 2008).

Bjork (2008) provided data on the perception of gangs in Gothenburg, Sweden's second largest city. The focus was on immigrant Muslims from the Balkans, Middle East, and North Africa and their cultural and ethnic differences compared to native Swedes. Bjork's data are based on police ride-alongs and interviews with those in custody. He indicates how within isolated pockets of Muslim communities, people benefitted from the criminal street gangs. In some cases, items were ordered and then later stolen and delivered by gang members. Rather than contacting law enforcement, community members sought to police these networks on their own. This desire, Bjork argues, is born of an ethnoreligious solidarity and honor code, as well as a desire for more autonomy. As a result, community members keep information about street gangs to themselves. They view the police as representative of the native Swedish outsiders. This process allows gangs to operate.

In Norway, Lien (2005a, 2005b, 2008) studied gangs within Pakistani immigrant communities in Oslo. Her ethnographic work stretches back decades (including work in Pakistan itself), and she was able to collect intimate knowledge from various community members. The A and B gangs—fierce rivals—had been around for decades. Kinship was of central importance because many of the members were either related to one another or

BOX 12.1: MEDIA CHECK!

Gangs in International Films

Romper Stomper (1992) is an Australian film that stars a young Russell Crowe as Hando, the leader of a gang of violent skinheads. The focus of their anger is Southeast Asian immigrants. Crowe does an excellent job portraying a frightening sociopath bent on destruction. The film is largely about their daily lives: partying and doing nothing, with the occasional bout of violence and disorder. They accurately reflect skinhead styles and behaviors around the world.

Once Were Warriors (1994) is a film from New Zealand about poverty and dysfunction in a Maori family. The story centers on the ultraviolent Jake the Muss—how he negotiates the world and how his family negotiates him. The movie highlights the desperation faced by modern-day Maori families living in isolation from mainstream society and coming to terms with their own identity. The film is about domestic violence, but the lure of gangs for Jake's son is a subplot. He eventually joins a gang of young Maoris.

Neds (2010; Non-Educated Delinquents) is about fighting gangs in Glasgow in the 1970s. The movie focuses on two gangs, the Young Car-D and the Krew, and John, a smart kid who ends up following his brother's violent footsteps. The movie exposes the pressures of being caught between academic aspirations and street culture. The thick Glaswegian accents from many of the actors will require close attention (or use the subtitles). The film's director, Peter Mullan, who also plays John's alcoholic father, grew up in the same environment and confronted similar problems.

A Prophet (2009) is a French film about warring factions of prison gangs between locals (Corsicans) and immigrants (Muslims). Malik, a French Algerian, is approached by a Corsican gang leader and asked to murder a Muslim who witnessed a crime. Malik does this reluctantly and is now with the Corsicans, who treat him with disdain because of his foreign status. Over time, the dynamics in the prison shift, with more Muslims and fewer Corsicans. Malik is called on to help the Corsicans, but at the same time is approached and befriended by other Muslims. With infighting among the Corsicans and the power of the Muslim inmates increasing, Malik becomes a double agent. His luck and propensity for deadly violence save him.

Sin Nombre (2009) means "without a name" and is about a Honduran family trying to illegally immigrate to the United States through Mexico and how one gang, Mara Salvatrucha, prey on them. (The movie poster has the letters S and M stylized, so as to represent MS.) Casper is an MS gang member with a girlfriend, but is afraid for her safety, so he keeps their relationship quiet. Casper's girlfriend follows him to a meeting, where she runs into another member, Lil Mago, who accidentally kills her during an attempted rape. Later, Lil Mago takes Casper to a location where they aim to rob illegal immigrants on a train on its way to America. When they rob a Honduran family, Lil Mago tries to rape the teenage girl, Sayra, but Casper intervenes and kills him. Casper then continues with the Honduran family as they head toward the U.S. border by train. The other MS gang members are enraged at Casper's disloyalty and pursue him relentlessly.

City of God (2002) is a Brazilian movie based on real-life events. It revolves around a journalist in a notorious favela in Rio de Janeiro—the City of God—and the armed gangs of youth that control it in the late 1960s through the 1980s. The movie focuses in part on the various factions of warring gangs over generations and the settling of old scores. One of these gangs, the Runts, consists of young children who have heavy military-grade weaponry. The Runts get shot, and one child, at the command of a teenage gang member, executes another child. Police corruption is exposed in the film. The movie was so popular that it gave rise to *City of Men* (2007). *Elite Squad* (2007) and its sequels are stories from the police point of view in controlling the drug gangs in a favela, specifically the Brazilian version of SWAT teams—the BOPE. Here, corruption and collusion with the gangs form the heart of the story.

*Visit YouTube to see trailers for **Romper Stomper, Once Were Warriors, A Prophet, Neds, Sin Nombre, City of God, City of Men,** and **Elite Squad.***

---

were able to join because of family ties. They had been criminally involved as teenagers and later morphed into more sophisticated enterprises focusing on drug sales. They had international ties and connections to other outlaw groups, including motorcycle gangs. The A and B gangs had a history of committing vicious offenses, including murder, drive-by shootings, and planning terrorism. Given this notoriety, the gangs' activities have attracted media coverage, and they have given many interviews to journalists. They regenerated from below, with the youngest members about 15 years old and the majority in their teens and early twenties. Some were in their early thirties or forties. They had a pyramid-like structure of organization, with subgroups based on age or through incorporating other, previously established gangs (e.g., the Young Guns in the A gang). Some became radical Islamic fundamentalists.

Similarities in the ethnic and religious identities of the members helped contribute to the gangs' solidarity: most speak Punjab, recognize and observe Muslim traditions, believe in separation of the sexes and male dominance, and place a premium on honor. In relation to honor, members of the A and B gangs viewed themselves as helping the community by correcting wrongs, replacing the role of the police who some viewed as competitors. Members of the A and B gangs have deep connections, both in the community welfare system and with politicians, and have been invited to speak about youth policy in public forums. In these and other respects, Lien's gangs are remarkably different than those in the United States.

RUSSIA

In Russia, *gopnik* and *gruppirovki* are derogatory terms used to describe young street people, at times gang members (Salagaev et al., 2005; Stephenson, 2012). Gangs, including skinheads, have been found in Russia (Salagaev et al., 2005; Shashkin, 2008; Stephenson, 2008, 2011, 2012). Groups of youth roaming the city streets are involved in delinquency and are not new (Stephenson, 2008, 2012). They have been described as durable and territorial, and some were linked to criminal syndicates involved in illegal enterprise (Stephenson, 2008, 2012).

The fall of the Soviet bloc and introduction of market reforms had far-reaching consequences. One was the emergence of new Mafia-like hierarchal gangs that were territorial and violent and committed serious crimes, including extortion, drug sales, and prostitution (Stephenson, 2008, 2011, 2012). They had subgroups stratified by age and rules, ceremonies and sometimes a central fund (Stephenson, 2008). They were predominately male, and the females occupied subordinate roles (Stephenson, 2008). Many have direct ties with organized crime and prison gangs (Stephenson, 2008). After the United States, Russia has the highest concentration of prisoners in the world, with one in four adult males who have been incarcerated (Stephenson, 2008, 2012). The culture of prison is highly influential, and a connection between prison and street gangs is evident (Salagaev et al., 2005; Stephenson, 2012).

Kazan has been a focus of research (Salagaev et al., 2005; Stephenson, 2008, 2011). In the early 1980s, the city had around 100 gangs, each with its own uniform, that fought similar groups; they also committed robbery and extorted local businesses (Stephenson, 2008, 2011). They had subgroups, leadership, symbols, regulations, and rituals (Stephenson, 2011). Gangs ruled different areas, and they had links to organized crime, law enforcement, and local institutions (Salagaev et al., 2005; Stephenson, 2011). Over time, these gangs "became a violent enterprise, a cohesive and disciplined unit, mobilized to extract economic value from territorial control" (Stephenson, 2011, p. 336). Violence was not wanton because it attracted negative attention (Stephenson, 2011). Many gangs were multiethnic, reflecting the assimilation in the city—Russians, Tartars, Armenians, Georgians, and others (Salagaev et al., 2005; Stephenson, 2011). Although gangs were feared, some served prosocial purposes, including resolving conflicts, locating stolen merchandise, and protecting businesses and individuals from victimization (Stephenson, 2011). Kazan citizens placed more faith in gangs than in the police (Stephenson, 2011). Gangs were institutionalized with Kazan, and youth from all social strata joined them until their mid-twenties, when they would then find a job and mature (Stephenson, 2011).

Stephenson (2012) discussed the culture of collective youth violence in Moscow. She researched groups of mostly males in their teens who had dropped out of school. They committed petty crime on occasion and used the money for arcade games, beer, and marijuana. They were territorial and would fight with other groups of youth from neighboring areas. Violence produced thrills and served as a way to toughen up. Stephenson notes that violence was an intergenerational way of life, with the adult generation serving as "overseers of violence" (Stephenson, 2012, p. 80). Stephenson (2012) noted that young people would have "arranged combat" as one of her respondents said (p. 85):

> It was like this in my area. A group of guys [from outside] challenged me and I said, let's arrange a group fight on our side of the river. They said, OK, how many? I said, collect about 40 people. I went home, got together with my mates, we saw three or four other guys we knew and asked them to come. I gathered the guys from our courtyard. There were about 30 of them. And the people who I talked to, they brought about 30 people more. The other guys came to the middle of the bridge, looked at us, saw that they were outnumbered and went back.

Since the 1990s, tens of thousands of violent skinhead gangs emerged in major Russian cities (Salagaev et al., 2005; Shashkin, 2008; Stephenson, 2008, 2012). They meet the Eurogang definition (Salagaev et al., 2005). They consist of young people in their twenties, they have been around for one to two years (i.e., they are durable), they are street oriented, and violence is part of their identity (Shashkin, 2008). They have attacked foreigners and immigrants—non-Russians—and have links to organized crime (Shashkin, 2008; Stephenson, 2008). Russian skinheads are racist neo-Nazis, although when they first emerged they were focused on the music and style (Shashkin, 2008). The economic crises in the 1990s had devastating consequences on informal parental, school, and community controls. Parents had to work several jobs, many schools closed, and programs that promoted arts and music were shuttered (Shashkin, 2008). Teenagers became disillusioned with communist thought and became attracted to fascist beliefs (Shaskin, 2008). Adding to this mix were a state-generated culture of violence and the influx of immigrants to Russia—giving the skinheads an easy, identifiable scapegoat (Shaskin, 2008).

CANADA

In Montreal, the Bloods and Crips are known more commonly as *les Rouges* and *les Bleus* (Descormiers and Morselli, 2011). Research in Canada is sparse. One of the Causes and Correlates studies is based on data from Montreal (Gatti, Tremblay et al., 2005; Lacourse et al., 2003). The study indicates that ganging has a similar impact on French Canadian youth as on Americans, increasing participation in delinquency and substance use (see also Bouchard and Spindler, 2010).

The profiles of Canadian and American youth who join and why they do so mirror one another: ethnic marginality, family dysfunction, peer support, and material gain (Gordon, 2000; Wortley and Tanner, 2006, 2008). Canadian researchers have developed a typology of gangs. Gordon (2000) details levels of involvement. On one end are adults in sophisticated "criminal business organizations" that focus on illicit enterprise. On the other end are juveniles who are "wanna-bes": loosely structured groups that spontaneously commit crime and violence for thrills. In between are "street gangs"—semistructured collectives that plan economic-oriented offenses and engage in violence against similar groups of youth. Canadian gangs have been linked to organized crime and prison gangs (Kelly and Caputo, 2005). Skinheads in Canada have been reported to be similar to gangs (Baron, 1997). A significant proportion of all gang members are Aboriginal (aka Native Canadian; Sinclair and Grekul, 2012; Totten and the Native Women's Association of Canada, 2010).

The definition in Canadian research has not been based on the Eurogang one (see Sinclair and Grekul, 2012). Wortley and Tanner (2008) conducted a study in Toronto that did employ this definition (see also Wortley and Tanner, 2006). The authors report that survey data from high school students indicated that members are more likely to be black or Hispanic, but less likely to be immigrants (Wortley and Tanner, 2008). This finding bucked media perceptions that linked immigration to the rise in gang activity. Like some American academics, Wortley and Tanner (2008) argue that racial discrimination from law enforcement, education, employment, and housing was directly related to why youth joined gangs. These gangs had between 10 and 30 members, most had names and symbols (e.g., colors, tattoos, graffiti tags), were territorial and durable (the average length of existence was 2.7 years), and committed different crimes. Their ethnic composition was similar to that in America: white members belonged to ethnically mixed gangs, and black and Hispanic youth belonged to ethnically homogenous ones. The authors indicate that, like gang youth in America, those in Toronto found similar benefits: money, respect, status, companionship, and protection. Racial injustice was another theme that emerged among nonwhite members as to why they joined. As one said,

> Canada does not care about me. Canada does not care about my family or about Black people. This country is for rich White people. They make the rules. They run shit here. They just want us to stay quiet and know our place. They want us to take the shit jobs and not complain about racism. I'm not being no White person's bitch. I'm not working no low-paying slave job. I will sell drugs in my crew and steal shit and not bow down to White people. At least that is some power. (Wortley and Tanner, 2008, p. 204)

ISRAEL

Of all the gang types, the presence of neo-Nazis in Israel is perhaps the least expected. Evidence has emerged to support that gangs exist under the Eurogang definition. Sela-Shayovitz (2012) argues that the twin impacts of migration and the influence of the Internet helped lead to their development. Sela-Shayovitz reports that neo-Nazi movements are a relatively recent development. The members were immigrants from the former Soviet Union, most of whom were non-Jewish. The youth came from poor, broken families, did not do well in school, and faced discrimination and harassment because they were immigrants who practiced Christianity in a Jewish country. Sela-Shayovitz finds support for Thornberry and colleagues' (1993) *enhancement model* that argues that members come from higher-risk backgrounds and become more involved in delinquency once they are members. Neo-Nazism was a form of resistance for these youth as a result of their victimization, isolation, and having limited opportunities in a foreign community. One of the youth mentions that becoming a neo-Nazi was his "solution." The Internet provided these youth with access to white power music and the musings of Hitler—hallmarks of neo-Nazis (see Hamm, 1993). Outside of drunken violence, they committed a variety of property offenses—the cafeteria style of offending.

LATIN AMERICA

Gangs in Latin America share things in common with U.S. and European versions, but their exposure to violence and involvement in crime are often much greater, and their socioeconomic backgrounds are grave. Religion, politics, the military, real estate, drug distribution, organized crime, and community relations are intertwined within the fabric of gangs in these countries (Hagedorn, 2006b). Hagedorn (2006b, pp. 162–163) offers a reason why gangs emerge in this context:

> groups of armed youth institutionalize in contested cities with high levels of racial, ethnic, or religious (rather than solely class) oppression, where demoralization and the defeat of political struggle have occurred, and in defensible spaces that provide natural protection opportunities for illegal economic activity.

MEXICO

Chavos bandas—gangs of youth distinguished by style—have been evident in Mexican cities for decades (Feixa, 2008; J. F. E. Martinez, 2008). They were not involved in serious and ongoing delinquency, nor were they related to the cartels. In the 2000s, drug-related violence cost tens of thousands of lives during the escalation of fighting between cartels; the border city of Juarez has been particularly impacted.[13] Distinguishing between autonomous street gangs and those linked to the cartels has been difficult (and researching these distinctions is dangerous).

Corcoran (2013) identifies three types of gangs involved in drug enterprise: cartels, subgroups of the cartels, and street gangs. The latter group is described as being closer to criminal street gangs found in the United States and elsewhere. Corcoran (2013) says that the Mexican government estimates 5,000 gangs exist throughout the country, 1,500 of them in the border town of Juarez. They have always been found in the country, but nowadays they are likely to be linked to the cartels or their subgroups. Gangs are an extension

---

13 The homicide rate in Juarez and the surrounding areas is among the highest in all of Mexico, ranging from around 600 to more than 1,500 homicides per 100,000 people (Diaz-Cayeros et al., 2011). In 2009 alone, more than 3,000 people were murdered in the city. The homicide rate in El Paso, the neighboring U.S. city, by comparison for that year did not reach double digits.

of these other collectives. Members benefit from collaborating with the cartels, but are at increased risk of violence. As Corcoran (2013) reports, when cartels wanted to send messages to rivals, they would target the street gang members for victimization. The cartels have expanded into other illicit money-making endeavors outside of drug sales, such as extortion, kidnapping, oil theft, pirating, and human smuggling, and street gangs are often involved.

THE CARIBBEAN

As in the United States, gang membership in the Caribbean increases youths' participation in crime, violence, substance use, and risky sexual behaviors. Ohene et al. (2005) conducted a pan-Caribbean study that enrolled more than 15,000 youth ages 10 to 18 in Antigua, Bahamas, Barbados, the British Virgin Islands, Dominica, Grenada, Guyana, Jamaica, and St. Lucia. About a quarter of all males ages 13 to 18 reported being in gangs, and more than 1 in 10 of all females in all age ranges reported membership. Gang involvement was correlated with early sexual experience, running away from home, weapon-related violence, or tobacco and alcohol use. The clustering of risk behaviors and attendant negative health outcomes led the authors to suggest that they may come from the same source. In addressing why youth join gangs, Ohene et al. (2005) highlight the relatively high rates of physical and sexual abuse of youth from other studies across the Caribbean.

Of all Caribbean countries, gangs pose more of a problem in Jamaica and have been believed to drive the national homicide rate (Moser and Holland, 1997). The 2010 Kingston Unrest that centered in Tivoli Gardens left 73 dead in a days-long gun battle involving the Shower Posse drug gang against the military and police. This incident made international news and was memorialized within Jamaican dance hall music.[14]

C. M. Katz and Fox (2010) focused on Trinidad and Tobago—among the richest of the Caribbean nations. They handed out surveys to more than 2,500 students in high-risk communities. About 20% of the sample reported being a gang associate or a former or current member. C. M. Katz and Fox concluded that membership is about as prevalent among youth in the United States, Canada, and Western Europe. Risk factors distinguished between youth who reported membership and those who did not; the more risk factors, the greater the likelihood of membership. These risk factors included the availability of firearms, delinquent peers, substance use intentions and friends who used drugs, lack of residential stability, parental attitudes favorable toward delinquency, and the early emergence of antisocial behaviors. Those who did not join had better social skills, prosocial friends, and a belief in the rule of law, order, and morality; the more protective factors existed, the less likely youth were to join.

---

14 The celebration of real-life gangsters within dance hall or reggae music has a long history. Christopher "Dudus" Coke, the apparent leader of the Shower Posse, is considered a Robin Hood–like figure and a hero within the housing projects and their surrounding areas. His father, Lester Coke, one of the apparent founders of the Shower Posse, enjoyed a similar status (see Peisner, 2010).

CENTRAL AMERICA

El Salvador, Guatemala, and Honduras are known as the northern triangle of violence because they have the highest murder rate in the world, with 53 homicides per 100,000 people (Bruneau, 2011; United Nations Office on Drugs and Crime [UNODC], 2010). The World Health Organization indicates that 5 homicides per 100,000 is "normal" and 10 or higher is "epidemic." These countries have poverty rates that hover around or above 50% (Bruneau, 2011). This, along with lax criminal justice administration, histories of conflict, victimization, and geographic proximity to the United States, makes for ideal conditions for drug and human smuggling operations (Bruneau, 2011). Youth living in humdrum existences could instead opt for *el vacil*—the criminal lifestyle (Bruneau, 2011; Ranum, 2011). El Salvador has approximately 17,000, Guatemala 32,000, and Honduras 24,000 gang members (Bruneau, 2011).

El Salvador and Guatemala share similar histories in terms of why they have gangs, including the combined effects of civil war; waves of refugees fleeing to the United States; their experiences of discrimination, poverty, and gang culture within the United States; mass deportations back to their home nations; importing this gang culture with them; and ripe political and socioeconomic conditions for gangs on their return. Honduras suffered from the effects of the Cold War that pitted democratic and communist social systems at great odds with one another, resulting in refugees who then had similar experiences as their Salvadoran and Guatemalan counterparts (Mateo, 2011). The end result was large gangs known as *maras*, 18th Street (*Calle Dieciocho*) and *Mara Salvatrucha* (MS-13), both of which originated in Los Angeles (Bruneau, 2011; Hagedorn, 2008; Mateo, 2011; Ranum, 2011; Rocha, 2011; Vigil, 1988a, 2002; Ward, 2012). The *maras* are different from the locally based *pandillas*—small gangs of loosely organized youth involved in drug sales, territorial battles, and petty crime that have been around much longer (Bruneau, 2011; Rubio, 2011; Wolf, 2011). The levels of violence and the sophistication of certain crimes (e.g., human smuggling) renders the *maras* like organized crime and the *pandillas* like U.S. street gangs (Bruneau, 2011).

Of all Central American countries, El Salvador has a relationship with gangs and civil war (Olate et al., 2012; Ward, 2012). The majority of Central Americans living in the United States are from El Salvador, and most of them live in Southern California; Los Angeles has the second highest concentration of El Salvadorans outside the capital city San Salvador (Vigil, 2002). About 1 million Salvadorans escaped the violence caused by the civil war, and many went to the United States, where the Reagan administration denied them refugee status (Wolf, 2011). The same thing happened to hundreds of thousands fleeing civil war in Guatemala or the effects of the Cold War in Honduras. Immigrants arrived in poor, gang-infested areas, where they experienced high unemployment and discrimination (Bruneau, 2011; Vigil, 2002). The lack of literacy, English language, medical care, and overcrowded living contributed to their underprivileged situation. Immigrants were exploited and in constant fear of deportation. Massive expulsions of illegal, undocumented immigrants occurred in the United States in the 1990s (e.g., the 1996 Illegal Immigration Reform and Immigrant Responsibility Act; see Vigil, 2002).

Those deported to their home nations were said to be responsible for importing the U.S. gang lifestyle, although the conditions in the communities were already ripe for producing gangs (Bruneau, 2011; Olate et al., 2010; Ranum, 2011; Wolf, 2011). A study in El Salvador indicated that about 10% of all members had a history of living in the United States, that about 95% of Salvadorans deported from the United States had no criminal records, and that less than 1% of those expelled from the United States were done so due to gang affiliations (Wolf, 2011). Ranum (2011) notes that gangs in Guatemala have been around since the 1950s, but that they were limited to major cities and only engaged in petty crime. Over time, they became violent and organized, and by 2006, the *maras* made up approximately 95% of all gangs in Guatemala and could be found everywhere (Ranum, 2011). The *maras* absorbed all of the local *pandillas* (Mateo, 2011; Ranum, 2011).

In El Salvador, Guatemala, and Honduras, the *maras* thrived because of interrelated social, political, and cultural issues (e.g., social exclusion, a culture of violence, endemic poverty, rapid growth, migration, social disorganization and family dysfunction) (Mateo, 2011; Ranum, 2011). Organized crime was rife, and many of the politicians, businessmen, military officers, and public officials were involved. This has hindered the development of a civilian police force, leading to the rule of law being absent in many areas (Mateo, 2011; Ranum, 2011). Hundreds of thousands of people have been killed in relation to the civil wars, and millions have been displaced. These countries have a history of militarization and became new routes from which the Mexican cartels smuggled drugs destined for the United States (Mateo, 2011; Ranum, 2011; Wolf, 2011).

The governmental response was fierce. *Mano dura* (strong arm) anti-*mara* policies have swelled prison populations. Gangs influence the daily operations in prison and those of the street gangs, making prisons staging grounds for executions between rivals (Ranum, 2011). The amount of vigilantism by average community members increased, leading to extrajudicial killings. The police and local citizens, fed up with gang-related violence, have been involved in a "social cleansing" of the "undesirables" (Ranum, 2011, p. 85; see also Mateo, 2011). In Honduras, the security system is too weak to effectively police the *maras*: the police and military are outnumbered, outfunded, and outgunned (Mateo, 2011).

The *maras* are believed to be responsible for a large percentage of the violence, although this has been questioned by academics (Mateo, 2011; Wolf, 2011). Wolf (2011) notes that the context of gangs in El Salvador began to change with the introduction of the *maras*. The gangs in the early 1990s were similar to U.S.-style gangs in terms of organization, offending, and background risk factors (see also Olate et al., 2010). The *maras* were different because they were organized and violent, with access to sophisticated weaponry and heavily involved in drug sales. Membership was taken seriously, and initiation rituals became violent to weed out the weak. Hard drug use was discouraged and stigmatized. Different areas within the cities had *clicas*—autonomous subgroups that claimed affiliation to and adhered to the principles of their respective *maras* (see also Ranum, 2011).

Wolf (2011) notes how the *maras* eclipsed other local gangs. One thing they both had in common was that they attract youth from marginalized backgrounds.[15] *Maras* perpetrate a significant amount of violence, but the extent to which they are involved in homicides is not clear; the data offer a confusing picture, and Wolf indicates that the number of these types of homicides is far lower than government estimates. Wolf (2011) argues that violence is so bad in El Salvador because of state-level responses to the Civil War, a culture of violence (approximately 25% of adult males own a firearm), and the Mexican cartels.

Another myth Wolf (2011) uncovers is the transnational relationships that *maras* enjoy. She highlights survey research from members indicating that although some had occasionally contacted their counterparts in other countries, no evidence emerged "of systematic and institutionalized links between the structures [of MS-13 and 18th St.] in North and Central America, let alone the existence of cross-border gang networks" (Wolf, 2011, p. 65). The *maras* are unlike organized crime in many ways, largely because of a lack of organization, which makes them poor vehicles as drug distributors.

Nicaragua is different in that it contains *pandillas*, but not *maras*. Rocha (2011) argues that Nicaragua was spared the *mara* problem because gang culture was not imported back into the country. Tens of thousands of Guatemalans, Hondurans, and Salvadorans were deported from the United States, but only about 3,000 Nicaraguans were. Nicaraguans who had come to the United States were more likely to settle in Miami as opposed to Los Angeles, where 18th Street and MS-13 originated. Nicaraguans enjoyed political refugee status and were more affluent, allowing them to better assimilate. Other immigrants from Central America had a traumatic experience in the United States. Rocha (2011) indicates that the democratization and demilitarization of Nicaragua in the wake of its civil war (1978–1990) was smoother and more complete compared to that of other Central

---

15 Rubio (2011) notes that although this remains largely the case, survey data from several Central American nations indicates that between 5 and 16% of youth from the upper classes had connections to either *pandillas* or *maras*.

American nations. This hindered the development of the *maras*. Another reason was the governmental response. The *mano dura* policies of other Central American countries actually backfired and led to the *maras* becoming more violent. The Nicaraguan government enacted civil policies that focused on employment, involving marginalized youth in local politics, and rehabilitation. They launched a relatively successful campaign to destroy the firearms that remained after the civil war.

What does *Mara Salvatrucha* mean? No consensus has emerged. Vigil (2002, p. 142) says the following:

> The name of *Mara Salvatrucha* gangs is derived from *mara*, a local street-Spanish term for "gang"; *salva*, short for "Salvadoran"; and *trucha*, slang for "watch out" and also the Spanish word for "trout," a fish that swims upstream and thus symbolizes the fight for survival.

S. Logan (2009) adopts the same meaning of *mara* as Vigil, but posits that *Salvatrucha* is a slang term for street smarts. Bruneau (2011, pp. 1–2) says that *mara* means a "fierce, tenacious type of Central American ant," that *salva* is for El Salvador, and that *trucha* "is something like 'reliable and alert' in Salvadoran slang." During the 1990s, fighting and control over drug turf in Los Angeles led to MS adding the "'13" to the end of their name to show affiliation with La Eme—the Mexican Mafia (Bruneau, 2011).

BRAZIL

Gangs in Brazil have been institutionalized in the *favelas* or slums since the 1960s (Hagedorn, 2008). In Rio de Janeiro, 700–800 *favelas* exist (Batista and Burgos, 2008). The city serves as an important transit point for cocaine distribution locally, as well as to Europe and South Africa (Hagedorn, 2008; United Nations Office on Drugs and Crime, 2011). Organized crime, drugs, gang culture, and homicide are all interrelated, and the *favelas* in cities like Rio and Sao Paulo are among the most dangerous to travel (Batista and Burgos, 2008). *Favelas* contain a variety of gang types (Batista and Burgos, 2008, p. 15):

- *facção*—armed group
- *quadhrilha*—gang or mob
- *bonde*—large and heavily armed group within a gang
- *o tráfico*—drug-trafficking group
- *o movimento*—a criminal movement
- *o coletivo*—a group that has things in common

Street and prison gangs have a tight connection. Hagedorn (2008) indicates that the military dictatorship once incarcerated gangs and revolutionaries together, from which they learned and adopted a more organized character. Nowadays, prison gangs control the flow of drugs through the streets, and they operate in a militaristic fashion in terms of attack and defense posturing and access to heavy firepower (Hagedorn, 2008). The *favelas* are built into the hillsides that skirt Rio, providing fortress-like qualities (Hagedorn, 2008). Hagedorn (2008) continues to note the power of the prison gangs. Once these gangs ordered all buses, schools, and manufacturing to shut down for one day in Rio. Although the prison gangs can be considered organized crime, the street gangs are decentralized networks—perfect for illicit drug selling (Hagedorn, 2008).

Caravalho and Soares (2013) closely examined drug-selling gangs in Rio. They utilized a relatively unique dataset from 2004, when a nongovernmental organization interviewed 230 youth ages 11 to 24 who worked for drug-selling gangs in 34 different *favelas*. The study also attempted to conduct follow-up interviews and collected death certificates over two years.

The authors found that members earned, on average, about $300 per month, which was only 23% more than youth not from gangs. To earn this much, the youth worked more than 10 hours per day and had only one day off every two weeks. Major risks were involved. At the first interview, half of the sample reported involvement in armed confrontations with rivals and two-thirds with the police. Also, 20% of the sample had been killed at the end of the two-year study. The upper levels of drug selling made 90% more (about $570/month) than those at the entry level, but they were likely to die within two years. Every year, the youth working for the gang received an increase in their wages of 10%. Any involvement in an armed conflict increased their wages by 5%. Those who violated a gang rule saw their wages drop by 17%.

The study examined the risk backgrounds of the youth as well as the intensity of gang membership. Young, black, illiterate individuals from poorer families and no religious affiliations were more likely to join gangs (see also Hagedorn, 2008). Those with problems in school and who used drugs early were more likely to be recruited at younger ages. Youth with weaker attachments to the gang and greater opportunities outside were more likely to leave. The future was not bright for those that remained. About a quarter of the youth reported gunshot wounds, and each gunfight over the two-year period increased their chance of death by 2%. Youth with anger and control issues were more likely to be killed. Despite these risks, many saw the drug gangs as their only viable source of earning money.

AUSTRALIA

The question of whether Australia has gangs similar to those in the United States has been examined extensively (McDonald, 2008; S. Perrone and White, 2000; R. White, 2002, 2006, 2008a, 2008b, 2009; R. White and Mason, 2006; R. White et al., 1999a, 1999b). In the 1990s, moral panics swept the nation, and earlier evidence suggests that the U.S.-style criminal street gangs were a media-generated myth (Perrone and White, 2000; R. White, 2006). A survey from law enforcement indicated 54 different gangs across the nation, but many were loosely connected groups of youth based on ethnicity or musical preference, or they were skinheads and graffiti artists (S. Perrone and White, 2000). Young people who hung around together and occasionally committed offenses did not perceive themselves as gangs (S. Perrone and White, 2000; R. White et al., 1999a, 1999b). Offending was limited and opportunistic and was done out of boredom, thrill seeking, and peer pressure (S. Perrone and White, 2000; R. White et al., 1999a, 1999b). Drug use and sales concerned marijuana, and no evidence emerged of gangs with national or international connections

(S. Perrone and White, 2000). Issues of territoriality were absent and intergroup violence was occasional and born out of racist conflicts (S. Perrone and White, 2000). S. Perrone and White (2000, p. 4) concluded

> that the expression youth "gangs" is generally not applicable in the Australian context, at least not as youth gangs are known in the United States. The research conducted to date consistently reinforces the picture of youth affiliations that are nonformalised and non-hierarchical in structure and certainly not purposely delineated along geographical territorial lines, nor formed specifically for large-scale criminal purpose. The spectre of threatening, violent gangs is, by and large, a myth perpetuated by the media.

While acknowledging that the term gang continues to lack a uniform definition in the Australian context, evidence of them is now found in many cities (McDonald, 2008; R. White et al., 1999a, 1999b, 2002, 2006, 2008a, 2008b). Immigration played a central role in their formation. Approximately a quarter of the Australian population are immigrants, and gangs are concentrated in Lebanese, Pacific Islander, Turkish, Somali, and Vietnamese communities because of unemployment, racism, language barriers, and geographic segregation (McDonald, 2008; R. White, 2006, 2008a, 2008b). R. White (2006) notes that the media's perception of a gang member was that of a young immigrant, leading to an increase in public fear toward and overpolicing within immigrant communities. Such reactions helped galvanize youth into forming gangs (R. White, 2006). Like the American context, ethnicity, violence, and gangs are intertwined (R. White, 2006, 2008a, 2008b).

R. White (2006, 2008a, 2008b) argues that ethnic similarities and solidarities form the core basis for the emergence of gangs, and violence was central to that culture. Mobbing and swarming are the Australian equivalents to getting jumped and group rumbles or riots. R. White (2006, 2008a, 2008b) indicates that gang violence was concentrated between different ethnic groups. In some cases, violence was intraethnic—within the same ethnicity. Different Asian populations, such as the Chinese and Vietnamese, fought one another, as did Tongans and Fijians.

Gangs are problematic in indigenous, nonwhite communities. McDonald (2008) discusses factions of warring Aboriginal gangs in the northern town of Wadeye that have adopted the names of heavy metal groups, wear military-style clothing, carry knives, and celebrate violence. He notes that gangs are concentrated in Aboriginal communities that were former religious missions. These missions controlled the Aboriginal people and forbade their customs and culture, disassociating them with their traditional ways of life. This led to the destruction of social structures and high rates of unemployment. Social exclusion and disorganization permeated their communities. Gangs emerged as an inevitable response, becoming "almost the only form of autonomous social organization among Aboriginal people" (McDonald, 2008, p. 10).

R. White (2009, p. 49) notes that Aboriginals were vulnerable to the victims of "overpolicing and exclusionary practices." The gang youth in R. White's (2009) study had similar chaotic family lives, as well as significant histories of racial discrimination. The shared narratives and real threat of victimization helped bond youth together—similar to immigrant gangs. They were territorial and defended their turf from racists trying to harm them. Much of their violence was racially motivated, and all Anglo-gangs felt targeted by gangs of Aboriginal youth because they were white (R. White, 2009). R. White (2009) sees racism as the core issue related to the emergence of Aboriginal gangs.

CHINA

The phrase *Bang Pai* roughly translates to gangs, although traditionally this term has referred to organized criminal syndicates and in more recent times to social groups with a common interest (V. J. Webb et al., 2011). A few researchers have found evidence of gangs in China (Lo, 2012; Pyrooz and Decker, 2013; V. J. Webb et al., 2011; L. Zhang et al., 1997). An earlier study by L. Zhang and colleagues (1997) conducted a survey of hundreds of young offenders who were also gang members in the city of Tianjin. For this study, the definition of gang employed in China referred to loosely connected groups of youth, ages 14–15, who were also co-offenders. L. Zhang et al. (1997) examined other characteristics and found that most had no names, rules, or organizational structure.

Another study employed the Second International Self-Report Delinquency in the city of Hangzhou and compared it with survey results in U.S. cities (V. J. Webb et al., 2011). The authors found that close to one in three of the youth surveyed (30%) reported that their group was a gang—five times the amount in the United States. A reason for this reporting could be a misunderstanding of the question and the significant differences between groups of youth who offend together and those who are part of a gang. How the Chinese youth interpret the word gang is different from Americans. Like evidence from the United States, members in Hangzhou were more likely to report lifetime involvement in a variety of offenses, including carrying a weapon, group fighting, and robbery. They were likely to experience victimization. Despite these findings, the authors indicate that radical differences between China and the United States help explain the overall lack of gangs in Hangzhou. These differences include the strength of family, school ties, lack of substance use, and overall racial homogeneity.

Lo (2012) focused on what he terms the triadization of youth into organized crime and that this process involves participation in gangs. Lo indicates that youth gangs have been a problem in Hong Kong for decades. He defines them "as a group of young people who have associations with a triad society and act collectively to achieve specific purposes, including the conduct of legal and illegal activities" (Lo, 2012, p. 558). Lo illustrates their role in triad-related crimes, as well as how they serve as a pool from which future triad members are recruited. Lo says that at the turn of the century, Hong Kong had just under 300 different youth gangs with more than 4,700 members that were linked to about 20 different triads. Youth were more likely to join gangs (as opposed to the less criminally inclined deviant youth groups) if triad societies operated in their neighborhoods. Lo employs the concept of triadization as a form of socialization and assimilation into triad society. Through this process, youth become more criminally involved and this phase of their lives serves as training grounds to be committed triad members. Lo describes membership on the way to becoming a triad as a spider's web: once in, escape becomes difficult.

Youth gangs and adult triads were linked through the Dai Lo-Lan Tsai (translation: Big Brother–Follower) connection. Prior to officially becoming a triad member, youth in gangs often had pre-established links. Despite this, most youth in Hong Kong are involved in routine, licit activities—hanging out and reading comic books (Lo, 2012). Illegality was a small part of their lives.

Pyrooz and Decker (2013) examined crime, violence, and gang membership among a school-based sample in the northern city of Changzhi. Of more than 2,000 youth, about 1 in 9 reported membership. The authors applied insights from major criminological theories in their analyses. They found that compared to other youth, gang youth had lower levels of self-control, were less attached to school, did not receive as much parental monitoring, and had peers who engaged in twice as many types of offending. No differences emerged between gang members and nonmembers in terms of parental education, single-parent family status, or rural characteristics. Like members in the United States, Pyrooz and Decker (2013) report that those in Changzhi were more likely to specialize in forms of violence and had higher frequencies of delinquency. Their findings offer evidence for the case that membership itself greatly increases youths' participation in crime and violence.

SUMMARY

Numerous countries now have criminal street gangs that are like those found in the United States. They emerged for comparable reasons and in some cases have a similar impact on rates of delinquency and violence as in the United States. These countries can begin to enjoy reviewing the same types of questions that American gang researchers and academics have entertained for decades, including What exactly is a gang? And What is the most appropriate response toward them?

The United Kingdom, more than anywhere else, has been a focus of gang research. The evidence for gangs in the United Kingdom was once limited, but nowadays evidence is everywhere. These gangs commit a variety of offenses, have fluid membership, lack organization, and frequently hang out and do nothing. The British government has an official policy to tackle gangs, and major cities have police units and specialized community organizations. The United Kingdom has something similar to gang injunctions. Although that country can learn a lot from the United States, perhaps Americans will also gain some insight into developing more effective approaches toward tackling the problem from the United Kingdom.

The Eurogang program has included cross-national research in Europe and other parts of the world. Their definition has proved to be a heuristic device for comparisons. Empirical research from scholars has noted the twin importance of immigration and ethnicity toward producing gangs. Nonwhite immigrants face discrimination and lack of opportunities. As a result, angry second- and third-generation youth form gangs as a way to protect themselves and profit through criminal activities. Immigration and ethnicity also shape the criminal patterns of local white skinhead gangs. Poor, unemployed, and undereducated youth feel frustrated and alienated and violently lash out at immigrants, blaming them.

Gangs in Latin America are different. Many Central and South American countries had street gangs similar to those in the United States. They were territorial based, engaged in petty crime, used soft drugs, and committed violence against other gangs. Over time, civil war, diasporas, corruption, mass influx of deportees, a shift in drug routes, dire socioeconomic conditions, and weak to ineffective responses culminated in the emergence of institutionalized drug gangs, or *maras*. They intermingle with the military and politics more than in the United States or Europe. Myths surround the amount of violence that the *maras* are responsible for. The information on the dangers associated with the drug gangs in the *favelas* is consistent.

Research has been extensive in Australia. Parallels can be drawn with the United States: immigration, segregation, media hype, public fear, and the overpolicing of minority communities. And like America, no consensus on the definition of gangs has emerged, leading to difficulties in precise numbers, comparisons, and approaches. Gang membership in China is high, but confusion surrounding the exact meaning raises questions about the accuracy of cross-national comparisons. Organized crime is closely linked with street gangs. Gang youth in China also have similar risk background characteristics in their lives prior to joining a gang and similar patterns of delinquency once they are a part of one.

CHAPTER REVIEW QUESTIONS

1. How were the groups of young offenders in B. Sanders's study similar to and different from U.S.-style gangs? Why did he fail to find gangs in London?
2. Gangs in the United Kingdom have been considered similar to those found in the United States. How so?
3. How are immigration and ethnicity interrelated to the emergence of gangs in various European nations?
4. How have some European gangs mimicked gang styles from the United States?
5. What did the Eurogang researchers find in terms of skinheads?
6. What are the consistencies in Central American countries in terms of their experience with *maras*? Why was the situation different for Nicaragua?
7. What are myths associated with the *maras*?
8. Describe the different kinds of gangs in Brazil. What are the risks and benefits of working for a drug gang in the *favelas*?
9. How do the gang findings in the Australian context compare and contrast to those within the Eurogang program?
10. What are the characteristics of Chinese gangs?

CHAPTER 13

SUPPRESSION, INTERVENTION, AND PREVENTION

KEY WORDS

Civil gang injunctions: Court-ordered restraining orders that prevent gang members from engaging in legal behaviors, such as wearing gang colors, flashing gang signs, hanging out with known gang members, and annoying others.

Community-based organization: An organization that attempts to help resolve locally based problems and/or provides a range of services for those in need. Gang interventionists are often housed in one of these organizations. The YMCA and Boys and Girls Clubs of America are examples, but others include the many smaller, independent agencies.

Community-wide approaches: These often involve some combination of suppression, intervention, and/or prevention techniques. These have often been expensive, complex to implement, and subject to fraud and waste, and it remains unclear whether they have impacted gangs, gang members, or gang crimes.

Diversion: A varied practice that attempts to redirect youth away from the justice system and provide supervision and treatment needs. Diversion can be a system of referrals to various service providers, a series of special courts, sporting events, and/or practices akin to restorative justice.

Intervention: A nebulous approach toward gangs that refers to programs that help young people get out of gangs. Some also offer preventive services. Interventions often work out of community-based organizations and offer a variety of referral services to employment, education, mental health, and substance abuse. Most gang interventions have not been measured and the ones that have offer mixed results at best.

Police gang units: Police officers who focus specifically on gangs. They provide intelligence, enforcement/suppression, investigation, and prevention in relation to gang crimes, gang members, and gang activity.

Prevention: Education. Gang prevention curricula are taught in schools over a period of several weeks. The focus is on youth before they become involved in gangs.

Suppression: Includes police gang units, specialized gang prosecutorial divisions, enhancements of community penalties if the offense is gang related, and civil gang injunctions that allow community members to sue gang members for particular infractions. The focus is on people who are already in gangs.

Chapter Learning Objectives

- Understand how gang prevention, intervention, and suppression are practiced.
- Discuss effective prevention, intervention, and suppression of gang efforts.
- Describe previous concerns and problems associated with such efforts.
- Outline the roles and responsibilities of gang interventionists.

INTRODUCTION

Approaches toward gangs include suppression, intervention, and prevention or a combination of all three.

Suppression tactics are laws that target members in two forms: gang enhancements that allow for increased community penalties and civil gang injunctions that restrict members' behaviors. Other tactics include diversion and gun control. Intervention is the most diverse approach. This practice often utilizes former gang members and/or offenders who have turned their lives around and now help youth who are still members and/or offenders or individuals heading in these directions. In the United States, gang prevention takes the form of education taught within the classroom. Another approach is an amalgamation of these efforts, coordinated on a citywide level. Funds are allocated to all three areas so that the police are arresting gang members, education is preventing youth from membership, and services are provided to help youth leave the gang.

The focus here is on gang-*specific* services. Some non-gang programs are mentioned because they have reduced gang crime. The first part of the chapter is about suppression, including gang legislation and injunctions, police gang units, firearm control, and diversion. The next section is about intervention, which refers to programs that attempt to help youth leave and/or desist from offending and prevent others from joining gangs. The history and role of the interventionist are discussed, as are major citywide programs, such as the Spergel model and the Comprehensive Strategy, and local ones, like Cure Violence and Homeboy Industries. The final part of the chapter examines prevention, with a focus on the only national program, the Gang Resistance Education and Training (G.R.E.A.T.) model.

SUPPRESSION

Most money directed toward gangs goes to suppression. The reasons for this include the overall lack of evidence of successful intervention programs, the increase in gangs and their perceived involvement in serious offenses, the moral panic resulting from a fear that innocent bystanders are harmed by members, the belief that gangs and drugs are closely linked, and a nationwide shift toward more conservative polices within the justice system (Brotherton, 2008d; Curry and Decker, 2003; Curry et al., 2013; Klein, 1995; Spergel, 1995). Suppression is law enforcement—the police and prosecution—and includes a variety of approaches. Many suppression tactics do not work (Bjerregaard, 2006; Fearn et al., 2006; Klein, 1995; J. W. Moore, 1991; Spergel, 1995). Whether the tactics work has been considered irrelevant because they are believed to have a deterrent effect (Howell, 1998; Klein, 1995).

GANG LEGISLATION

One aspect of gang legislation is a shift in the priorities or organization of the prosecution. In 1979, the Los Angeles District Attorney's Office created a unit that focused on gangs called Operation Hardcore (Howell, 1998, 2012; Klein et al., 1995; Klein and Maxson, 2006; Krisberg, 2005). Reduced caseloads, increased assistance and access, and victim support were its hallmarks. Although the program was positively evaluated for securing more convictions of serious crimes compared to other prosecutors, whether it impacted gang crimes was unclear (Howell, 1998; Klein, 1995). Operation Hardcore served as a model for the federal government's Habitual, Serious, and Violent Juvenile Offender Program (and several variations thereof; Krisberg, 2005).

Another aspect of legislation are statutes targeting gang members or their activity. These statutes can be grouped into two major categories (Bjerregaard, 2006; Fearn et al., 2006):

1. *Laws against those in gangs or gang-related offenses.* Gang enhancement laws—more penalties for individuals convicted of crimes if they are gang members or are found to have committed a crime in relation to the gang.
2. *Civil gang injunctions.* Remedies for victims of gangs, whereby average citizens can file lawsuits against members. These injunctions can prohibit gangs from activities such as hanging out together in public spaces (e.g., hanging out on the street).

California's Street Terrorism Enforcement and Prevention (STEP) Act of 1988—California Penal Code 186.22—is a well-known gang law (Bjerregaard, 2006; Fearn et al., 2006). Many other states have similar statutes. The STEP Act allows for enhanced community penalties for individuals convicted of gang-related offenses and for cities to use civil injunctions against gang members. To convict someone under the STEP Act, some interrelated facts must be established. The group must qualify as a criminal street gang, which is defined under the act as three or more people whose primary activities are the recurring committal of a series of predicate offenses. The accused must have committed the crime for "the benefit of, at the direction of, or in association with" the criminal street gang. The individual may or may not be a gang member.

Despite its popularity, it remains unclear whether such legislation works or is counter-productive (Brotherton, 2008d; Fearn et al., 2006; T. Hayden, 2005; Howell, 1998; Klein, 1995; Myers, 2008). Klein (1995) argues that the legislation may increase cohesion within gangs, which in turn leads to greater involvement in crime and violence (see also Hennigan and Sloane, 2013). Since legislation has been aggressively pursued, the prison population has swelled with gang members. Despite this, the belief persists that members on the streets continue to pose major threats to public order (Brotherton, 2008d).

CIVIL GANG INJUNCTIONS

Civil gang injunctions (CGIs) were first applied in California and now operate in other states (Arnold, 2011; Crawford, 2009; Grogger, 2002, 2005; Hennigan and Sloane, 2013; Maxson et al., 2005, 2006; Myers, 2008; Strosnider, 2002). This component of the STEP Act criminalized membership itself. CGIs are court-issued restraining orders that forbid members of criminal street gangs from engaging in a variety of behaviors, both legal and illegal. Under CGIs, they are not allowed to associate with other members, wear gang colors or clothing, make gang signs with their hands, annoy residents, or design methods to detect and flee from law enforcement (e.g., the use of lookouts). They also place members under curfew. The goal of CGIs is to prevent gang crimes by focusing on individuals within specific areas and interrupting routine activities (Maxson et al., 2006). Theoretically, social disorganization, deterrence, and de-individualization have been linked to CGIs (Maxson et al., 2005, 2006). Obtaining a CGI is an elaborate process involving collaborative efforts between the police and the prosecution and, on occasion, community members (Maxson et al., 2005, 2006).

The evaluations of the CGIs conflict with one another (Crawford, 2009; Hennigan and Sloane, 2013; Maxson et al., 2005). Crawford (2009) notes that the Los Angeles County Civil Grand Jury stated that the CGIs helped reduce crime and indicates that the LAPD reported significant reductions in gang-related offenses in the target areas. Grogger (2002, 2005) found a drop of between 5 and 10% in violent crime in the area where the CGI was implemented and no evidence of crime displacement. Maxson and colleagues (2005) only found reductions in the visible presence of gangs and the fear of them within the community. Hennigan and Sloane (2013) report that evaluations of CGIs suggest they help reduce crime and fear for up to six months to a year after being implemented, but results vary.

As with other suppression tactics, CGIs have been argued as strengthening the cohesion within gangs, leading to increases in gang-related crime (Decker, 1996; Hennigan and Sloane, 2013; Klein, 1971; Klein and Maxson, 2006). Hennigan and Sloane (2013) note that CGIs may reduce gangs through a deterrence effect (i.e., further exposure of the negative legal repercussions of gang membership), *decrease* cohesion, and weaken the individual's identification to the gang. The authors also note that the opposite might happen and that the difference between these outcomes depended largely on how the CGIs were implemented. They conducted a study that examined community responses and police implementation of CGIs in different areas. They reported that the tactics did *not* produce a deterrent effect (e.g., violence went up and down in the CGI areas just as it did across the city) and *increased* gang cohesion, but did help reduce the strength of individuals' identification with the gang, which in turn hypothetically lowered their levels of participation in crime and violence. Overall, the CGIs were a mix of positive and negative results.

The constitutionality of CGIs has been challenged (Arnold, 2011; Crawford, 2009; Hennigan and Sloane, 2013; Myers, 2008; Siegel, 2003; Strosnider, 2002). Saying "I'm a gang member" or other words associated with gangs, displaying hand gestures, and particular clothing exposes them to criminal prosecution. These aspects and others have been considered a violation not only of First Amendment rights—freedom of religion and expression—but also of the rights of the Fourth (unreasonable search and seizures), Fifth (due process), Ninth (fundamental rights), and Fourteenth (equal protection) Amendments (Bjerregaard, 2006; Crawford, 2009; Fearn et al., 2006; Myers, 2008; Siegel, 2003; Strosnider, 2002).

Gang injunctions are ambiguous. Crawford (2009) highlights the *Acuna* case and Justice Mosk's dissenting opinion in relation to vagueness, particularly the parts that criminalized associating with known members or behavior among them that could be considered annoying by average citizens (see also Siegel, 2003). People might have no idea whether others they are associating with are gang members. The concept of annoyance was also not clearly defined.

The American Civil Liberties Union has taken action against CGIs, challenging their constitutionality (Crawford, 2009; Siegel, 2003). In 2009, they successfully sued Orange County's gang injunctions for due process rights: individuals who had their cases dismissed were still listed on the injunctions.[1] This case helped highlight the fact that ex-members were often served injunctions, although they matured out long before, started their own families, and found employment. Crawford (2009) reports that no one has successfully had his or her name removed from the injunctions in Los Angeles.[2] Other names have been placed on them because the individuals live in gang neighborhoods (Crawford, 2009).

POLICE GANG UNITS

Police gang units or "gang cops" are another form of suppression (Howell, 1998, 2012; R. K. Jackson and McBride, 1996; C. M. Katz and Webb, 2006; Klein, 1995; Klein and Maxson, 2006; Krisberg, 2005; V. J. Webb and Katz, 2006). Los Angeles has CRASH—Community Resources against Street Hoodlums—which conducted "'gang sweeps,' 'hot spot targeting,' and 'intensified patrol' to apply 'excruciating pressure' on gangs" (Howell, 1998, p. 294).[3] Police-based suppression tactics have assumed a paramilitary stance (Brotherton, 2008d). These include ninja-like raids on gang-stronghold housing projects and the militarization of policing within their communities, such as the use of Checkpoint Charlies, low-flying helicopters, and tanks (Brotherton, 2008d; Krisberg, 2005). These tactics were ineffective (Howell, 1998; Klein, 1995; Krisberg, 2005).

---

1   For more on this story, visit http://www.streetgangs.com/news/051211_aclu_wins_gang_injunction#sthash .ZH47FrXA.dpbs/.

2   This began to change around 2007 and San Francisco and Los Angeles became the first cities in California to officially document ex–gang membership (Crawford, 2009).

3   A previous iteration of this unit implemented in East Los Angeles in the mid-1970s is TRASH—Total Resources against Street Hoodlums (Brotherton, 2008d).

A major problem was Operation Hammer, a CRASH-operated tactic that occurred in South Los Angeles in 1988. One thousand officers descended into the homes of suspected gang members and arrested close to 1,500 people, setting up a mobile booking station adjacent to the University of Southern California's Coliseum. All but about 100 of those arrested were released (many were not gang members), and about 30 were charged with felonies (Howell, 1998; Krisberg, 2005; Spergel, 1995). Klein (1995) notes that many of these types of police surges (although on a much smaller scale) have yielded similar, inefficient results (see also Krisberg, 2005). Operation Crown in New York City in the late 1990s involved the local police, federal immigration, and federal drug officers in the largest police sweep of that city since the anti-communist raids in the late 1910s (Brotherton, 2008d; Brotherton and Barrios, 2004). They harassed suspected members (mostly nonwhite, low-income males), recorded phone conversations, took photographic surveillance, and conducted police stings. Then Mayor Giuliani used this war on gangs to strengthen his public image (Brotherton, 2008d).

Heavy-handed tactics have had a history of backfiring and increasing crimes (Klein, 1995; Krisberg, 2005). Other strategies in Los Angeles, such as Operation Safe Streets, where sheriff's deputies interact on the streets with gang members in communities over time and are able to obtain sensitive information, have offered better results (Howell, 1998; R. K. Jackson and McBride, 1996; Klein, 1995).

Despite high-profile problems, gang units are important tools (Decker, 2007). They provide intelligence, enforcement/suppression, investigation, and prevention (R. K. Jackson and McBride, 1996; V. J. Webb and Katz, 2006). Intelligence is gathering and maintaining information on gangs, often through the use of a database. One method is the use of field interview cards (R. K. Jackson and McBride, 1996). Suppression, or enforcement, is patrolling known gang areas. Investigation was limited to serious crimes like murder, rape, and kidnapping. Prevention includes informing the public. J. V. Webb and Katz examined police units across the United States (C. M. Katz and Webb, 2006; J. V. Webb and Katz, 2006). They reported that the officers focused on these four aspects to varying degrees, with the least amount of time and effort spent on prevention and the most on enforcement and suppression. They found that the gang unit officers worked in secrecy.

Fearn and colleagues (2006) detailed community-oriented strategies toward policing gangs. They described the Anti-Gang Initiative (AGI) in the 1990s that operated within 15 cities. The goals of the AGI were to devise methods of reducing gang problems, particularly drug selling, and the fear caused in the community. The AGI received funding to improve data collection, link law enforcement with local service provision, and progress community policing. Although the AGI might have done these things, whether they contributed to a reduction in gang activity remains clouded (Fearn et al., 2006).

GANG COP MISCONDUCT

Police crackdowns have been linked with inappropriate conduct, illegal searches, and planting evidence (Krisberg, 2005). Chicago gang cops have been known to apprehend youth and then release them in the territory of rivals, increasing the chances of violent victimization (Klein, 1995; Krisberg, 2005).

Among the most well-known incidents of misconduct is the notorious Rampart Scandal of the CRASH unit in Los Angeles (see *Media Check!*).[4] In November 2000, the Los Angeles City Council approved one of the largest settlements in the city's history. The council voted unanimously to pay $15 million to Javier Ovando, who was shot several times by two LAPD officers, Raphael Perez and Nino Durden. Ovando was unarmed, but Perez later testified in court that the officers attacked and planted a gun on him. Ovando received a lengthy sentence. He served two and a half years in prison before his conviction was overturned. As a result of the Rampart Scandal, more than 100 cases have been reversed and hundreds more were tainted, most of them in which Perez and Durden were the arresting officers. Dozens of officers were under investigation for misconduct or for covering up. Many were never charged because of insufficient evidence or the expiration of statutory deadlines. Others, including sergeants, have been fired, suspended, or relieved of duty or they quit. About 140 civil cases were brought about, for which the total payout was estimated to be around $125 million.

Rampart is the name of a Los Angeles police division. Perez, an officer for 10 years, is the main whistleblower who exposed the division's excessive abuses. In 1999, Perez pled guilty to taking cocaine from an evidence locker. He bargained for a reduced sentence by agreeing to cooperate with the LAPD and district attorney. Perez said that innocent people had been charged with crimes they had not committed and were sentenced to prison. He admitted to hundreds of instances of false arrests, perjury, and the fabrication of evidence. He stole drugs from police evidence lockers and narcotics, guns, and cash from gang members—all of which he then resold on the streets. Perez testified in court that the officers aped the gangs they policed by appropriating specific tattoos, meaningful symbols, clothing styles, and their general demeanor.[5]

BOSTON GUN PROJECT

Although it is not a gang program, the Boston Gun Project has impacted gang-related crimes (Braga, 2014; Braga et al., 2006; Fearn et al., 2006; D. M. Kennedy, 1997, 1998; D. M. Kennedy et al., 1996). In Boston, gang members represented less than 1% of the overall youth population, but were responsible for about 60% of all youth homicides (Braga, 2014). The project operated by disrupting the gun market through various techniques and by threatening entire gangs with serious community penalties should any one of their members be suspected of involvement in a firearms offense. It served as a problem-oriented policing exercise that included collaboration among the police, gang interventionists, and various other community members (Braga, 2014; D. M. Kennedy, 2008). The project combines suppression with social intervention, opportunity provision, and community organization (Braga, 2014).

---

4   For more information on the Rampart Scandal, visit PBS Frontline: http://www.pbs.org/wgbh/pages/frontline/shows/lapd/scandal/cron.html/.

5   In 2012, several deputies within the Los Angeles Sheriffs' Operation Safe Streets Unit were suspended for the alleged involvement in the Jump Out Boys. This group also reportedly had their own tattoos and symbols (Faturechi, 2012).

The legacy of the project (later renamed Operation Ceasefire) was important because of its "pulling levers" approach, which is two pronged (Braga, 2014; D. M. Kennedy, 2008).[6] The first are the "levers," or legal available resources, including a specialized, collaborative team of police and parole officers alongside state and federal prosecutors. Violent and drug offenders were directly and repeatedly approached and reminded that they were under special surveillance and that all shootings would be dealt with using swift and certain punishments. The groups that stopped the killing would no longer receive intense scrutiny. Probation and parole officers enforced behavioral restrictions and curfews and regularly searched residences.

The second half of the project involved placing youth in contact with various services and informing them of the negative impact of violence as voiced by community members. To do this, the project convened a Ceasefire Working Group that held meetings with active gang members. The explicit message was that violence would not be tolerated. These meetings were frequent and ongoing and the messages were about the determination to stop violence (Braga, 2014). Violence was retaliatory, and if the Working Group could help establish a period of calm between warring factions, this might lead to the dissolution of the tit-for-tat cycle (Braga, 2014; D. M. Kennedy et al., 1996).

The program has been replicated in various cities, and evidence has emerged of its effectiveness. In Boston and Indianapolis, homicide rates fell by half, and young minority populations—those who the programs were directed toward—enjoyed the greatest relief (Braga, 2014; D. M. Kennedy, 2008). The Rampart Scandal affected the implementation of Ceasefire in Los Angeles, but reductions in violence, gang offenses, and gun crime were reported (Tita et al., 2003). In Stockton, Ceasefire was linked with a 42% decrease in gun homicides (Braga, 2014). A version of Ceasefire was implemented in Chicago called Project Safe Neighborhoods, which saw a 37% decrease in homicides (Papachristos et al., 2007).

DIVERSION

The aim of diversion is to redirect youth away from the justice system and provide supervision and treatment (Austin et al., 2005). Diversion includes late-night sporting events, drug and mental health courts, teen court, and restorative justice (see, e.g., Derezotes, 1995; Fielding et al., 2002; Godwin, 2000; McGarrell et al., 2000; M. E. Moore and Hiday, 2006). Diversion is a system of referrals from law enforcement to CBOs that provide services for substance use, employment, family conflict, education, mental health, religion, and/or recreational activities (see Boutilier and Cohen, 2009). Diversion programs have been argued as being effective at reducing recidivism (Krisberg and Austin, 1993; Shelden, 1999), but others say that they are ineffective and may increase future offending (Greenwood, 1996; Lipsey et al., 1981).

---

6   This is not to be confused with Operation Ceasefire in Chicago, which is a completely different approach toward reducing gang violence involving violence interrupters. Also, other Operation Ceasefires that once were or those that currently operate may or may not have anything to do with either the Boston ("pulling levers") or the Chicago (violence interruption) models. In Los Angeles, for instance, at least two different Operation Ceasefires have emerged: one based on the pulling-levers approach (e.g., Tita et al., 2003) and another the Southern California Ceasefire Committee.

Law enforcement in Los Angeles practices gang diversion. The Jeopardy Program operated by the Los Angeles Police Department has been around since the early 1990s. Anecdotes of positive results of participating in the program have been reported (e.g., Kleinbaum, 2006). The Los Angeles Sheriff's Department operates a diversion program at the Carson Sheriff's station: the Gang Diversion Team (GDT). Youth are referred to the GDT by schools, parents, or the police, where they meet with intake staff. They are then asked about their levels of gang interest or involvement, as well as about overall levels of crime and aggression, school performance, self-perception, and other measures. Staff probe the *intensity* of gang and criminal involvement. Based on these characteristics, youth are placed in one of four risk categories. Each category outlines specific activities and goals youth are to meet. If they meet the goals, they are considered to have successfully completed the program. GDT staff measure who completes the program. It operates on a shoestring budget, running at about $20,000 on average per year. Given all of these considerations, the following conclusions were made (B. Sanders, 2013, p. 49):

> The simple fact that the Los Angeles Sheriff's Department has something like the GDT is . . . commendable. . . . [A]nother noteworthy aspect . . . is that it provided measures of its efforts. In doing so, the evaluation component . . . has managed to provide what most gang programs in Los Angeles have not. The GDT makes no claims to have reduced crime or gang crime in the Carson area but rather indicates the percentage of youth at different levels that have completed targeted outcomes. Another commendable aspect of assessment and evaluation has to do with the GDT's attempt at identifying youth at different levels of risk for gang membership and/or involvement in offending . . . [t]he GDT has . . . potential savings . . . [t]he annual per bed cost of incarcerating juveniles at a probation-run camp in Los Angeles is over $30,000 . . . [i]f the GDT prevented one youth from entering the camp system every year, it would cover its operating costs for a year and a half.

Gang diversion programs operated by law enforcement can be found throughout the United States. It remains uncertain whether they have been evaluated.

INTERVENTION

Despite the vogue of suppression tactics, many researchers (and law enforcement) agree that without programs that remove the basis for membership, the situation is hopeless (Brotherton, 2008d; Fearn et al., 2006; Hagedorn, 1988; Howell, 1998, 2012; Huff, 1990; Klein, 1995; Klein and Maxson, 2006; J. W. Moore, 1991; Spergel, 1995). Programs or activities or institutions that help youth toward conventional, law-abiding pathways are considered interventions. Of all the approaches, intervention is the most capricious. Many young people join and leave in a short period of time, but how and why this happens is far from clear. Most gang interventions are atheoretical and have not been evaluated (Howell, 1998; Klein and Maxson, 2006). Intervention models often employ detached youth workers (aka gang interventionists, gang workers), and decades of programs have utilized such individuals (Klein, 1995; Spergel, 1995). Most models have been unable to provide evidence that they work and, in a few cases, they make things worse (for a list of programs and

outcomes, see Howell, 1998; Klein and Maxson, 2006). Some exceptions have emerged, which offer promising lines of inquiry.

THE CHICAGO AREA PROJECT

The Chicago Area Project (CAP) is the forefather of large-scale, community-wide efforts to reduce delinquency in general and gang membership in particular (Howell, 1998; Klein, 1995; Krisberg, 2005). This project is the brainchild of Clifford Shaw, who co-authored social disorganization theory. The CAP was based on that theoretical model, which attempted to improve the social structure to provide for the healthy socialization of youth. The program linked CBOs to formal agencies (e.g., schools, employment, welfare) and included community members at different levels. The results of the CAP have been mixed, although not positive (see Howell, 1998; Krisberg, 2005). An important legacy of the CAP was the idea that communities have the ability to effectively organize themselves and combat the conditions and processes that give rise to membership (Howell, 1998; Krisberg, 2005). Something like the CAP has been in effect in Chicago ever since (Howell, 1998). The CAP also introduced the concept of the detached youth worker (aka gang interventionist), which has since been a staple of intervention (Klein, 1995; Krisberg, 2005; Spergel, 1995).

INTERVENTIONISTS

Intervention is practiced in various ways and usually operates out of a CBO. Services offered by the CBOs include tattoo removal, counseling, education curricula, therapy, and/or referrals to education, employment, and mental health and substance abuse treatment. A critical component of these programs are gang interventionists (or detached youth workers or outreach workers or crisis interventionists or interrupters—these terms all generally refer to the same position). These individuals are often former (sometimes current) members and/or felons who now work on the streets with serious young offenders and hardcore gang youth. They are often from the areas in which they work and this, along with their criminal histories, provides them a "license to operate"—the credibility required to effectively engage active criminal street gang members and other criminally involved youth (Fearn et al., 2006). Interventionists have worked with youth who are members of the same gangs they were once a part of. This allows them to link youth to the services offered within the CBO. They provide "rumor control," "peace maintenance," and "street mediation" in attempts to quell violence (Arbreton and McClanahan, 2002; Cardenas, n.d.).

The use of detached youth workers has not proven to be effective—and in some cases it is counterproductive (Howell, 1998; although see Spergel, 2007). W. B. Miller (1962) found no reduction in key measures of delinquency when the Midcity Project in Boston operated in the 1950s. Klein (1971) reported that those youth who received services in the Group Guidance Project in Los Angeles became *more* involved. In most other cases, programs involving detached youth workers have not been assessed (Howell, 2012). Spergel's (1995) evaluation of the Crisis Intervention Services Project in Chicago was unique and promising in that a reduction in gang-related crimes was directly attributable to the efforts of the interventionists.

Gang intervention programs suffer from a high turnover of staff, low morale, limited funding, lack of direction, no understanding about the causes and correlates of gangs, crime, violence or drugs, and failure to record data (Shelden et al., 2001). Hostile relations between law enforcement and gang interventionists have been evident for a long time, but in some cases this has changed.[7] Several incidences of their suspected involvement in illegal behaviors have arisen in Los Angeles, including the following:

- A homicide detective warns about approaching a particular gang intervention program because their station suspects that the head of the organization is using the CBO they operate from to sell crack cocaine. Several other interventionists in the area claim the same thing.
- A young rising star interventionist at a well-known intervention agency has been arrested with a large amount of hard drugs. This is reported in the newspaper.
- An interventionist who has been paid a lot of money by a large city is found to still be an enforcer for a well-known organized criminal syndicate. His children, also interventionists, have tortured and murdered at least one person. This is reported in the newspaper.
- A major gang intervention agency has had several employees who are either the victims or the perpetrators or were somehow involved in various, unrelated homicides. This is reported in the newspaper.
- An interventionist tells me that he was incarcerated for several years for pistol-whipping a current gang member for disrespecting his family.
- An intervention agency cannot account for hundreds of thousands of dollars the city allotted them. In addition, sexual harassment claims are submitted against the agency. This is reported in the newspaper.

Despite these incidents, the job is important because, without interventionists connecting the most disaffected youth, services would be hindered (Spergel et al., 2006). Many programs across the United States continue to utilize their efforts and this is indicative of their overall importance. They have and continue to be critical components of community intervention strategies.

---

7   The views held by the chief of the LAPD as to the utility and opinion of the gang interventionists shifted around 2010, for instance.

What gang interventionists do is important to detail. One way to find out is when they offer stories about how they intervened in violent conflicts. Some of these stories emerge in the documentary *The Interrupters*. Stories from Skipp Townsend, a gang interventionist in Los Angeles, are paraphrased below:

> A large group of Bloods plan on attacking a small group of youths believed to be Crips at a cinema. In actuality, the groups of boys are not Crips, but do live in a community that is home to a large Crip set. The interventionist arrives prior to the Bloods. Soon, he sees about 25 or so Bloods heading toward him. The interventionist stands near the entrance of the cinema and tries to get the Bloods to calm down and not attack the group of youths they think are Crips. They ignore him and move around him. When the Bloods enter the cinema, they have the intention of attacking the groups of youth. The youths notice that they are heavily outnumbered. Many of them remove their baseball hats with insignias associating them with a Crip set. One of the youths does not do this but instead says, "No. I ain't hiding." The Bloods viciously attack him and the other youths. The interventionist jumps into the middle, grabbing Bloods off of the youth, saying, "I'm gonna call your fucken grandmamma and tell her what you're doing!" and "I was just on the phone with your auntie. She wanted me to help you. And here you come with this bullshit!" The Bloods do not strike him. The interventionist is able to separate the groups of youth from the Bloods and send them in different directions.

> A young man finds out that a member of a rival gang has just killed one of his friends. He is furious and bent on revenge and begins to make plans to violently retaliate. An interventionist is informed about the murder. He knows who the good friends of the victim are and is able to locate the young man seeking retribution. When he does, the interventionist notices that the young man has a large handgun. He clearly expresses his desire to commit murder. The interventionist walks with the youth, trying to calm him down. He makes calls to other interventionists, asking them to come. While talking, the interventionist casually places his hand alongside the hand of the youth. They are now both holding the gun and talking. Another interventionist arrives and the two are now able to coax the young man into a home of someone nearby. They then inform him about the consequences of retaliation and plead with him to reconsider. The young man agrees to leave the gun with the interventionist and retrieve it later.

The interventionists had a tragic story for every success story they told. Below are some direct quotes of these stories:

> A young man was just killed on Labor Day at [intersection]. Because of the yellow tape people were hanging around on [adjoining intersection] just on Monday. The young people they were hell bent on revenge and I wasn't able to stop them. They drove off and an hour later there was a homicide on [intersection]. And I know without a doubt that those young people did that. And what makes my stomach hurt was all the older people in the community high-fiving them, giving them the "Atta boy!" There was nothing I could do about it because the community supported that retaliation. I found out later it was a girl who they killed and she had three children. And I knew I was amongst the

killers right before they were about to kill and I was there when they returned. And that's a complete failure right there. I should've pulled everyone out of there and said, "Everyone's staying here." But it didn't work that way.

February of last year and I'm outta town. I get a call that there's a fight at a casino in [area #1] between two Blood gangs that normally get along. After the fight, the Blood gang from [area #2] shot and killed a couple of members of the Blood gang from [area #3]. Although I was out of town, it was in my heart and my mind to bring the two sides together. But while I was out of town I was told that one of my close friends from [area #2] who was 45 years old was killed as a result of the retaliation of the murders that happened at [area #3]. And in my mind, I knew for in order to bring peace, I would've brought that guy with me to [area #3] and be asking for peace. So I believe that I might have unknowingly put my own life in danger had I not been out of town. I'm thinking I would've gone to [area #2], grabbed two close friends who are older members, taken them over to [area #3], and tried to make peace. That's what I would've done if I was in town and I think that if I did that they would've shot and killed all three of us. Right when I got back, the other one I would've brought was shot in the stomach in a motel room. He didn't die. The war has gone on ever since and there's nothing I can do to stop it. . . . I've tried to bring peace and the son of my murdered friend says that he doesn't want it, that he doesn't want peace right now [because he is still seeking retaliation for his father's death]. So I have to sit back and wait. I don't know how long it's gonna take but at least they stopped shooting each other.

I am related to or know four of the victims or suspects in homicides this week alone. This is one of the worst weeks for me as an interventionist. Monday alone there were two people killed at about 2:30 in the afternoon. I knew one of the two of those killed and I went to start looking for their friends and I couldn't find them. The reason is because they were responsible. The young man [who was the shooter] threw his phone away. I went looking for them and at 8:00 another young man is shot and killed. That's when someone approached me and said that my nephew was involved. So I'm trying to get a hold of that and then another murder happened. So it's really painful. Then the group where the double homicide was were together and they started fighting. I can't trust anybody. The older folks don't condemn what happened. So I can't turn to them. The young folks are related to my relatives who did this. By the end of the week there were four more shootings in retaliation for the earlier ones. And on Saturday morning my friend who I grew up with was shot and killed in the alley. So I'm out there doing rumor control and do whatever I can to stop retaliation. The only thing I'm happy about is that it wasn't gang related. He got double tapped [i.e., shot in the head twice at close range] and gangs don't do that. That's military. This is a horrible week.

Let me give you the worst story I've ever heard. It didn't happen to me. It happened to M. M got a call that his son and his son's friends had went out and gotten into a shootout. In the middle of this, his son was shot in the side. The son said, "Don't take me to the hospital. Take me to my daddy." So M got him in the car and started asking him what happened. The son told him as he was going to the hospital. M starts getting on the phone, working intervention. The son is taking responsibility. M is working intervention, saying that his son was wrong, and that he was going to calm things on his side so there's no retaliation. M takes his son to the hospital while working intervention. He's at the hospital and tries to make this right, speaking with his son. While the son is in surgery, M is still on the phone working intervention, trying to keep the peace and stop retaliation. M's son dies in surgery. That was his second son that was killed. M has three sons that were killed. M was trying to stop the retaliation while his son died in surgery. I just can't get my head around that.

THE SPERGEL MODEL

The Comprehensive Community-Wide Approach to Gang Prevention, Intervention, and Suppression Program is known as the Spergel model after its architect, Irving Spergel (Fearn et al., 2006; Howell, 1998, 2012; Klein, 1995; Klein and Maxson, 2006; Spergel, 2007; Spergel et al., 2006). The model encourages community planning and coordination of resources for at-risk youth. It identifies various roles for different procedures and inter-organizational relationships are key features. Although the main focus is on intervention, the model also provides prevention and suppression strategies. This multifaceted approach is a reason others have considered it complex (Klein and Maxson, 2006). The model is theoretically grounded in the concepts of social disorganization, social learning, opportunities, strain, social control, and group processes (Spergel et al., 2006). It assumes gangs are loosely structured organizations that temporarily attract teenagers from disorganized and/or criminally involved families in socially and economically marginalized communities (Spergel et al., 2006). Five interrelated strategies make the model distinct from other approaches: community mobilization, social intervention, opportunity provision, suppression, and organizational change and development (Howell, 2012; Klein and Maxson, 2006; Spergel, 2007).

The Little Village Gang Project (LVGP) in Chicago is the prototype of the Spergel model and one of several sites evaluated across the nation (Klein and Maxson, 2006; Spergel, 2007; Spergel et al., 2006). It targeted about 200 of the main members of two gangs in a low-income, working-class Latino neighborhood with high levels of gang-related homicides. These members were responsible for about 75% of the felony violence. The LVGP objectives were twofold: (1) controlling violent youth through increased police and probation contacts; and (2) providing a variety of services so that youth could transition into productive, law-abiding citizens. The police and a CBO established for the purposes of the LVGP coordinated these efforts. Gang interventionists at the CBO played a key role in reaching out and interacting with members. The authors established control (i.e., youth from the same gangs who had also been arrested but were not included in the program) and quasi-control groups (i.e., youth from the same gangs who had also been arrested, but were offered only minimal services, largely those related to recreation).

An evaluation of the LVGP found decreases in violence and other incidents (Fearn et al., 2006; Howell, 1998, 2012; Spergel, 2007; Spergel et al., 2006). Arrests for gang-related violence increased more in the control area, and members reported fewer property, drug, and violent crimes as a direct result of their involvement in the LVGP (Howell, 1998;

Spergel, 2007; Spergel et al., 2006). Serious violence arrests for groups in the program declined significantly compared to the control and quasi-control groups. These findings are robust given the fact that the LVGP had such groups. Spergel et al. (2006) note an interrelationship among intensity of gang membership, employment referral and placement, and lower levels of violence and drug arrests. Youth who were successfully referred to or placed with jobs and those who received more services and contacts spent less time with gang friends. Those who reduced their affiliation also reported fewer drug and violence arrests.

The Chicago Early Warning System assisted in the LVGP (Howell, 1998). The police used this system and CBOs to help predict and prevent gang violence, including homicides. Spatial and geographic analyses help determine potential areas of conflict based on incidents and patterns of violence escalation, perpetration, and retaliation (Block and Block, 1993). Other successes of the LVGP were the interdisciplinary street team that provided a variety of integrated services: counseling, crisis intervention, employment and educational referrals, contact with family members, and warnings from law enforcement (Spergel, 2007; Spergel et al., 2006).

When examining all six sites where the model was employed, Spergel et al. (2006) identify several important aspects related to significant reductions in violence. These include governmental leaders committed to the model, the use of former members within an interagency street-based team, the interrelationship of intervention and suppression tactics, the offering of employment and educational opportunities by the interventionists and probation and police officers, and "optimal lead agency management capacity, with a substantial effort directed to the development of a steering committee" (Spergel et al., 2006, p. 217). Those sites that failed to implement any of these aspects were unable to report declines in violence among model youth or in targeted areas. Klein and Maxson (2006) highlighted some of the problems in sites outside of Little Village, arguing that the results at best were mixed and that often no reduction in the number of gang-related offenses was found. Klein and Maxson (2006) noted other problems, including the small and varied sample sizes, the lack of any noticeable effects on core versus fringe versus associate members, and no reductions in gang sizes or membership.

Additional problems have been noted with the Spergel model, including a lack of interagency collaboration, uneven evaluations, lack of comfort by collaborating agencies using gang interventionists, lack of monitoring by a central agency, and substandard data systems (Klein and Maxson, 2006). Spergel (2007) said that at times, what is adopted as the Spergel model in reality is far from it and shows no positive outcomes.[8] Klein and Maxson (2006) further scrutinize the model itself, including how unclear its operationalization was, what exactly it targeted, and the implementation of its concepts.

The most recent iteration of the model is called the Gang Reduction Program (GRP). A review of the GRP implemented in four cities across the United States echoes some of the

---

8   This is not limited to the Spergel model. For instance, an intervention in Los Angeles called Operation Ceasefire is completely distinct from both the Boston Gun Project and Cure Violence—both also called Operation Ceasefire. Another program called SafeFutures in St. Louis was actually not implemented, although it operated under this name and was evaluated as a SafeFuture's program (Klein and Maxson, 2006).

The Impact of Rampart in Movies and Television

The Rampart Scandal in Los Angeles reverberated not only within the LAPD, but also in Hollywood. This was a cash cow in terms of the fodder it provided for the movie and television industry. The movie *Training Day* (2001) and the television series *The Shield* (2002–2007) are inspired by its legacy. They have both won major awards. Several other movies and shows were also based on the scandal.

In *Training Day*, real-life gang members and gangsta rappers appear—and some served as consultants. Denzel Washington, as Senior Detective Harris, won an Oscar for his portrayal of the film's main antagonist, and Ethan Hawke, as Junior Detective Hoyt, was nominated for one as the main protagonist. The movie is set over a period of 24 hours—the training day of Hoyt by Harris—on how to be a gang cop in LA. This training starts off with Harris demanding that Hoyt smoke a marijuana joint. Hoyt does so reluctantly and is then told that he just smoked PCP (aka angel dust). Harris robs and sets up drug sellers, murders a former cop turned drug seller, and tries to have gang members kill his partner.

The Shield ran for several seasons and is about the life of Detective Vic Mackey. He leads the Strike Force, a hard-core gang crime unit in the ersatz Farmington district of LA. Mackey is dirty, but he gets the job done. He has no problem ignoring procedure. In the first scene, Mackey denudes a suspected drug dealer in broad daylight with onlookers and rips off a bag of cocaine taped to his crotch. By the end of the first episode, he has executed a cop. Mackey has a heart of gold; he gives money to a prostitute to get some food and see her kid. He even allows her to smoke crack in his office—crack he stole from the police evidence room. Mackey is the anti-hero of questionable moral character that everyone roots for.

Other one-line title movies that capture the essence of the scandal are *Dirty* (2005) and *Rampart* (2011). *Dirty* follows two gang officers, once former gang members—Cuba Gooding Jr. and Clifton Collins Jr.—on a journey as they kill gang members, steal drugs, and plant illegal evidence. Internal Affairs become interested and one thinks about rolling over on the other. The tension mounts as other variables are thrown in the mix, including the influence of a Canadian gang, and lines blur between the good guys and the bad. The singer and once Haitian presidential hopeful Wyclef Jean plays a notorious drug kingpin with a tantalizing offer for the officers. *Rampart* stars Woody Harrelson as a cop operating in the aftermath of the scandal. His involvement in another questionable incident of police abuse leads to his investigation. The officer leading this is played by O'Shea Jackson—otherwise known as the original gangsta rapper Ice Cube. Nearly 20 years prior, he debuted his acting chops as Doughboy, the crack-selling homie in *Boyz n the Hood*. Ice Cube was one of the main lyricists for the band NWA and penned the words to a street-classic song that expressed deep-seated antipolice sentiments

---

concerns mentioned earlier by Klein and Maxson (Cahill and Hayeslip, 2010). A few sites had trouble implementing the GRP model. In terms of outcomes, some showed reductions in violence and gang-related crimes associated with GRP. However, the report says that "the nature of the pre–post comparison group design . . . precludes concluding there were cause and effect relationships between GRP and the positive outcomes observed" (Cahill and Hayeslip, 2010, p. 14).

THE COMPREHENSIVE STRATEGY

The Comprehensive Strategy for Serious, Violent, and Chronic Juvenile Offenders (aka the Comprehensive Strategy) is based on the social development or risk factor or variables model (Hawkins and Catalano, 1992; Howell, 1998, 2012; Hughes, 2006). The theoretical underpinning of the Comprehensive Strategy is to mitigate the risks within young people's lives that increase their chances for membership; the strategy takes two approaches: prevention and intervention via graduated sanctions. A principal difference between the Comprehensive Strategy and the Spergel model is that the latter does not make the distinction between at-risk (who need delinquency prevention services) and delinquent youth (who need delinquency intervention services); the Spergel model combines approaches (Fearn et al., 2006).

Hawkins and Catalano's (1992) Communities That Care model is a blueprint from which the prevention component of the Comprehensive Strategy was drafted. This model targets various risk factors in young people's lives: individual, family, school, peer, and environment. Family-based programs include home-based training for expecting mothers (e.g., Nurse–Family Partnership; Olds et al., 1997) and parent-building skills (Howell, 1998, 2012). School-based programs include educational curricula (e.g., G.R.E.A.T.; Esbensen, 2006; Esbensen et al., 2012, 2014), instructional or organizational management, graduation incentives, and bullying programs (Howell, 1998). Peer and individual-level programs include employment and education training, conflict resolution, and alternatives to gang membership (Howell, 1998). Community-based components include developing social capital, community policing, empowerment and enterprise development, and developing stronger police/community relations (Howell, 1998, 2012).

Graduated sanctions are approaches toward juvenile offenders developed to be flexible to suit the needs of different types of young offenders, as well as the progress of individual ones (Krisberg, 2005). The approach provides a continuum of services within the juvenile system, from incarceration to intensive probation, reentry, and reform. A part of graduated sanctions are training programs—Aggression Replacement Training, Multisystemic Therapy, and Brief Strategic Family Therapy—all of which are used within juvenile justice—and have been applied to youth in gangs with positive results (Howell, 1998, 2012; Shelden et al., 2001; Valdez et al., 2013).

PROBLEMS WITH CITYWIDE APPROACHES

Some citywide approaches are riddled with problems. These include infighting, waste, fraud, a lack of accountability, an absence of scientific foundation, and criminal activity.

Klein and Maxson (2006) describe an example that happened in Los Angeles with LA Bridges. Given the amount of funding, number of youth targeted, collaboration of agencies, and academic input, LA Bridges was the nation's largest gang intervention/prevention program. It emerged in 1996 after the high-profile murder of a 3-year-old blue-eyed, blonde little girl killed in the crossfire of a gang shooting in 1995. The city council allotted $44 million to 29 designated high-crime areas. Bridges stressed prevention, accountability, and a continuity of funding for a minimum of four years to be operated by the Community Development Department (CDD).

Klein and Maxson (2006) noted problems from the start. The CDD allocated little money to middle schools in violent, gang-prone neighborhoods and more to those neighborhoods where employees of the CDD lived. Problems arise when trying to measure the program's impact on crime and gang crime—if they are already low, then reductions are unlikely. School principals at some locations had never heard of Bridges.

Another problem Klein and Maxson (2006) report concerns the request for proposals that the CDD sent out to attract CBOs and others at stake in the community. A total of 160 agencies were identified as the partners. The request for proposal stressed "youth development" and "youth at risk" with little to no mention of gangs, prevention, or intervention. The term "gang" only appeared six times in the 12 pages of orientation materials. The request for proposal left out any indication of needing programs that targeted gangs or of providing intervention. Many CBOs with little to no gang experience were recruited because they fit with the guidelines. Klein and Maxson (2006) said that if the numbers of gangs or their crimes failed to decrease, this could not be attributed to the CBOs, but to the CDD for mistaking the true target. This allowed the CBOs to receive funding to continue, despite their lack of focus on gangs. This program avoided specific gang-related issues.

Klein and Maxson (2006) posit that the Bridges program was clouded with confusion. The goals were unclear. Schools were not provided with adequate information. The focus was too much on schools and not enough on the community and street life. Nontraditional schools that gang members were more likely to attend were excluded. How the CBOs would link their services to youth and each other were concerns. Klein and Maxson also provided evidence of "creaming" and "net widening." Creaming occurs when a program selects the least troublesome youth—the cream of the crop—in terms of who participates. This increases their chances to show positive results. Net widening is similar and refers to increasing gang services to youth who were at a low risk of joining.

Rumors emerged about fraud and spin and no one applied to evaluate Bridges. Klein and Maxson (2006) say that in 2000, an audit by the city controller's office offered a damaging evaluation based on interviews and fiscal auditing. Two important findings came out. Bridges did not develop gang prevention efforts. The programs did not target the risk factors that give rise to gang youth. They also failed to assess reductions in gangs, gang behaviors, or gang participation. Financial and management irregularities were reported. Klein and Maxson note that the city controller recommended that Bridges funding cease, but the mayor thought otherwise and it continued for several more years, with an annual budget increase to $50 million.

HOMEBOY INDUSTRIES

Homeboy Industries is based in East Los Angeles and founded by Father Greg Boyle—aka G-Dog (see Franke and Leap, 2011; Fremon, 2006; Howell, 2012; Klein and Maxson, 2006). They train former members to work in the food industry, including operating restaurants—the Homeboy Diner and Homegirl Café—as well as the Homeboy Bakery and a farmers market. Homeboy tortilla chips and salsa can be bought at local supermarkets. They teach silk screening, make t-shirts, and sell them along with other merchandise with the Homeboy logo: *Nothing Stops a Bullet Like a Job* or *Jobs Not Jails*. Homeboy offers tattoo removal services. They were originally located in Boyle Heights, which has violent, large gangs that have been around for generations, including one of Los Angeles's chief *barrios* (Fremon, 2006). Homeboy headquarters now sits in a fantastic contemporary building near the California Endowment, a major shift from its humble beginnings. Father Boyle has been working with gangs and community members for decades. They provide substance abuse service and treatment and educational, employment, legal, and counseling services (e.g., domestic violence, anger management) and/or referrals.

Two evaluations of Homeboy Industries have emerged (Franke and Leap, 2011; Hunter and Huang, 2014). One is about the Substance Use Treatment and Reentry program that Homeboy was involved in because of a cooperative grant from the Substance Abuse and

Mental Health Services Administration. Hunter and Huang (2014) evaluated this program and reported fairly positive results. They said that more than 70% of participants who completed the longitudinal phase were still employed and that less than 15% had been rearrested. In relation to substance use, about 30% refrained from using drugs, and this number was stable over the course of the study. Substance use generally decreased over time (but did not necessarily stop). Franke and Leap's (2011) appraisal of Homeboy Industries offers vignettes of positive and struggling cases who have received services from Homeboy. The report indicates that some of them are doing well.

CURE VIOLENCE

Formerly called Ceasefire in Chicago, Cure Violence is the brainchild of epidemiologist Gary Slutkin. After working in African nations on AIDS and tuberculosis, he returned to the United States and began focusing on violence, applying epidemiological principles. He framed it as a disease and a major public health concern. Slutkin observed that homicide was concentrated in specific regions in Chicago and that what these areas had in common were cultures of violence. The transmission of violence in these communities is observing violence, being the victim of violence, and being informed that violence is acceptable. Cure Violence focused on the ways that violence was transmitted to interrupt its escalation or prevent it from happening in the first place.

Cure Violence did this using interrupters. Most of these individuals were former members or convicts—their histories provided them with a license to operate in some of the most violent neighborhoods. The interrupters located conflict and used techniques to help quell potential altercations. Hospitals contacted them if a patient was admitted with a penetration wound (e.g., knife or firearm) so that they could suppress any plans for retaliation. Outside of intervening in potential retaliatory conflicts, the interrupters tried to change the culture within the community. Violence has been an acceptable way of life for many years, and only through changing it can the underlying mechanisms that allow for violence be suppressed. These interrupters serve as ambassadors of peace within their neighborhoods and attempt to change the way the community thinks. An aim was to make it look like a less appealing type of behavior.

Cure Violence works (Picard-Fritsche and Cerniglia, 2013; Skogan et al., 2009; Webster et al., 2012). In Chicago, Skogan et al. (2009) reported that most communities had reductions in shootings that ranged from 41 to 73%. In more than half, retaliatory homicide dropped by 100%. Every area reported declines in the number of shootings, and the program has had a significant impact. The evaluation mentioned a drop in gang violence, including "significant shifts in gang homicide patterns in most of these areas . . . including declines in gang involvement homicide and retaliatory killings" (Skogan et al., 2009, p. iii). In Baltimore, Webster et al. (2012) found significant declines in the number of shootings or homicides. The interrupters were critical, and they were involved in 276 mediations (i.e., violence interruptions). Areas where they operated heavily reported better results. Community norms toward gun violence changed through word of mouth. The program impacted gang violence: of all 276 mediations, 3 in 4 involved members. In the Crown

Heights area of Brooklyn, New York, Picard-Fritsche and Cerniglia (2013) said the implemented version of Cure Violence was effective. Rates of shootings in the adjacent areas increased, but they went down in Crown Heights. Gun violence decreased by about one-fifth. The New York version also impacted gang violence: more than 9 in 10 of the participants were gang involved. The perception of gangs changed, with less believing it necessary to join one for protection.

TRUCES

Occasionally, gang truces brokered by intervention efforts have emerged. The House of Umoja that operated in Philadelphia in the 1970s was a sanctuary for youth, a place to get off the streets and be safe (Howell, 1998; Spergel, 1995). Programs provided counseling and educational and employment development. They had "gang summits" that led to truces between gangs responsible for a dramatic decrease in homicides (Howell, 1998).

Truces have occurred in Los Angeles. One was in Venice (Umemoto, 2006). Despite the affluent beach neighborhood, "the Oakwood corridor" has a long history of ganging. In the early 1990s, Venice 13, the Venice Shoreline Crips, and the Culver City Boys were involved in ongoing altercations. A fight between two individuals converted into a gang war that left more than 50 dead. This battle had an interethnic character, although most gang violence is among people of the same ethnicity. Umemoto describes how this conflict "morphed" into a larger issue of racial tensions between the police and the Latino and African American communities. She describes the roles of various mediators or "transpublics" in bringing peace between Latinos and African Americans in and around the Oakwood corridor, which culminated in a truce.

Another truce in Los Angeles occurred briefly between the Crips and the Bloods in the early 1990s (Brotherton and Barrios, 2004; T. Hayden, 2005; Rodriguez, 1993; Stoltze,

2012). The truce happened in the days prior to the Rodney King verdict in April 1992, which led to some of the worst rioting in the history of the United States. This truce was not between *all* Crip and Blood sets. The ceasefire agreement drawn up in 1949 between Israel and Egypt was used as a blueprint (Stoltze, 2012). Some Latinos followed suit and developed peace treaties (Rodriguez, 1993; Stoltze, 2012). Murders declined in Watts the following year, where the Crip and Blood truce originated (Stoltze, 2012).

PREVENTION

Gang prevention in the United States consists of education curricula taught in school settings, often elementary and middle schools. Gottfredson and Gottfredson (2006) conducted a nationwide study of more than 1,200 schools. They found that 7.6% of all males (and 3.8% of females) were in gangs; five percent of all principals said that gangs were a problem within their schools and about a third said that they were a concern in their communities. The gang youth were more likely to have lower educational expectations, experienced threats of victimization, used drugs, and carried a concealed weapon. Principals who said that gangs were a problem also reported more overall student victimizations, less safety, and poor administrative leadership. Gottfredson and Gottfredson's (2006) survey indicated 781,800 prevention activities and 159,700 interventions within all of the schools. Most targeted not gangs, but delinquency and problem behaviors more generally. These programs had different objectives and were implemented in various ways. They found major problems with the objectives offered and indicated that typical objectives do not "compare favorably with the characteristics of effective programs—for those kinds of programs that have been the subject of research" (Gottfredson and Gottfredson, 2006, p. 365). The authors report that members in secondary schools are the least likely to be involved in any prevention or intervention efforts.

GANG RESISTANCE EDUCATION AND TRAINING (G.R.E.A.T.)

Gang Resistance Education and Training is the nation's premiere and leading prevention program and is funded by the National Institute of Justice.[9] The program undergoes repeated evaluations by trained staff and experts (Esbensen, 2006; Esbensen et al., 2012, 2014).

G.R.E.A.T. was modeled after the Drug Abuse Resistance Education (D.A.R.E.) program, with "gangs" replacing "drugs" (Klein and Maxson, 2006). As with D.A.R.E., in G.R.E.A.T., uniformed police officers enter an elementary, middle, or junior high school once a week for several weeks. They inform students about the importance of making smart decisions and avoiding drugs and crime, although little is said about gangs. Early iterations of the G.R.E.A.T. program barely mentioned the term *gang* (Klein and Maxson, 2006). G.R.E.A.T.'s original nine lessons were as follows (Esbensen, 2006):

1. Introduction and program overview;
2. How crime and victimization impact school and their communities;
3. How culture shapes school and community experiences;
4. and 5. Conflict resolution;

---

9   For more on G.R.E.A.T., visit http://www.great-online.org/.

6. Meeting basic needs without the gang;
7. Drugs;
8. Responsibility; and
9. Setting goals.

Although G.R.E.A.T. was not theoretically driven—the authors did not use criminological theory when drafting this program—Esbensen (2006) stresses that the evaluation was. He argues that elements of social control and social learning theories were implicit. This version that operated from 1995 to 2001 was not related to a reduction in delinquency or membership. G.R.E.A.T. did not work, although short-term effects were noted (Esbensen, 2006; Klein and Maxson, 2006).

Based on these findings, the G.R.E.A.T. program went through several revisions that have improved its outcomes (Esbensen et al., 2012, 2014). The new G.R.E.A.T. added several topics and now focuses on developing realistic views about gangs and violence, improving communication and refusal skills, and anger management. The new objectives were to avoid gangs, violence, and crime and to develop positive relations with the police. As with their previous evaluation, the authors followed the students who received G.R.E.A.T. training in 7th grade into high school. Compared to students who were not in the program, G.R.E.A.T. students had more positive attitudes toward the police, less positive attitudes about gangs and lower rates of membership, more use of refusal skills, higher collective efficacy, less retaliatory violence (e.g., hitting), and less anger. A related study found G.R.E.A.T. students to be less self-centered, have more prosocial peers, and be better able to resist peer pressure (Esbensen et al., 2012). In both studies, these reductions were directly linked to aspects about the G.R.E.A.T. program, but G.R.E.A.T. was acknowledged to have a small to modest overall impact.

OTHER GANG EDUCATIONAL CURRICULA

One of the earlier school-based curricula prevention programs was Project BUILD (Broader Urban Involvement and Leadership Development). This project comprised a prevention curriculum, followed by an intensive after-school workshop on job training, sports, and educational and social skills; BUILD was marginally successful (Howell, 1998).

The Gang Alternative Program (GAP) in the Los Angeles area includes an educational curriculum for elementary and middle school students (i.e., grades 2, 4, and 6). It focuses on improving reading and writing, moral reasoning and problem solving, social and thinking skills, aspects of gang culture, such as graffiti, and the effects of membership. GAP educates youth about the negative impact that gangs have on families and futures. Students are introduced to positive alternatives and instructed on making healthy lifestyle choices. On completion, students are given certificates and t-shirts. They then pledge in front of others about living gang free. GAP includes after-school services for tutoring and homework assistance, as well as parent training sessions. GAP has been around for nearly 30 years and has served thousands of students. To examine its effectiveness, pre- and post-surveys ask questions such as, "If your friends joined a gang, would you?" and "Could your family get hurt if you joined a gang?" Success is measured by the increases in "correct" responses. GAP has demonstrated success.[10] Other GAP programs can be found across the nation.

GAP in North Carolina stands for Gang Alternative Principles. This program focuses on life skills training, developing leadership, anger management, and reducing substance use. Students in grades 7–10 attend sessions with a parent or guardian and then spend the next 10 Saturdays involved in various activities while wearing their GAP apparel. Each session ends with a meal and a game of basketball. Success was measured by the numbers of youth who did not recidivate; agreed that employment is important; and believe that gangs, drugs, and doing nothing are not conducive toward healthy lifestyles and/or progress. GAP students reported reductions in targeted problem behaviors.[11]

G.R.I.P. is a popular acronym related to various programs. G.R.I.P. can mean Gang Reduction and Intervention Program, Gang Reduction Is Paramount (in Paramount, California), Gang Reduction Intervention Partnership, Gang Response and Intervention Program, Gang Risk Intervention Program, and Gang Reduction Impact Partnership. G.R.I.P. is practiced in various ways in various states. In California, about two dozen cities offer G.R.I.P., each with its own focus and operationalization; more than $9.2 million was allocated for it in the 2012 fiscal year.

Testimonies have surfaced from participants about how the program benefitted them, and these often serve as the only indicators of the programs' successes. Third parties have evaluated G.R.I.P. In Paramount, the authors said that they were not able to determine any effects because several gang programs were operating in the city (Solis et al., 2003). They could not tell which program was related to which outcome because of their similarities (i.e., they focused on reducing gang crime, activity, and members). Other problems mentioned by Solis and colleagues (2003) were the transient nature of the population, the influence of gangs outside the target area, and inconsistent data collection across law enforcement agencies. Of approximately 900 children, about 80% said that G.R.I.P. helped them stay out of gangs.[12] Outside of gangs, G.R.I.P. has also been linked to decreases in community crime. In Richmond, Virginia, overall crime dropped by more than one-third and homicide was down 85%, but whether these declines can be directly attributable to G.R.I.P. is uncertain (Troutman et al., 2007). Many G.R.I.P. programs across the nation have not been evaluated (Klein and Maxson, 2006).

SUMMARY

Among all the approaches toward gangs, most of the money and effort has gone to suppression. Suppression tactics include enhanced penalties associated with gang-related offenses and civil remedies whereby members can be sued for hanging out and being

---

10 Visit http://notebook.lausd.net/pls/ptl/docs/page/ca_lausd/fldr_organizations/committee_main/committee_sshhs/committee_sshhs_agenda/4.%20%20gap%20(gap%20alternative%20%20%20program)%20briefing.pdf/ and http://www.laschoolboard.org/sites/default/files/5.%20GAP%20Board%20Presentation.pdf/.

11 Visit https://www.fbcwest.org/index.cfm/PageID/1673/index.html/.

12 Visit http://family1stcenter.org/grip/.

annoyances. Police and prosecutorial gang units exist that focus only on gang and gang-related crimes. Despite the problems, including corruption and the constitutionality of gang statutes, they are highly popular and universally deployed. Whether they are effective is irrelevant: they are believed to provide a deterrent effect because of the harsh punishments associated with them. Outside of gang laws or gang units, law enforcement has some lesser-known, inexpensive, and simple approaches that work.

Gang intervention is a hazy term; it refers to many types of approaches. These include the use of gang interventionists—individuals who work out of a CBO but engage youth in their own environments. Most of these individuals were once criminals and/or gang members. Interventionists have a long history of committing crimes and contributing to the delinquency of the gangs they work with. They have been key players within community-wide programs and have been credited with helping bring about significant declines in homicides.

Gang prevention is taught within schools. A few prevention programs have been positively evaluated as reducing the lure of gangs. Many others have not been evaluated or focus on issues other than gang involvement, crimes, or members. Many prevention curricula have a history of claiming that they focus on gangs when in fact they say little to nothing about them. Still others indicate they promote gang prevention but do nothing more than play sports and wear program attire.

CHAPTER REVIEW QUESTIONS

1. Describe the STEP Act.
2. What are civil gang injunctions? What are some problems that have emerged with them?
3. What are police gang units? What are some problems that have emerged with them?
4. What is the Boston Gun Project?
5. What are the pros and cons of gang interventionists?
6. What did Spergel et al. report about the Little Village Gang Project? What were some of its critiques?
7. How is the Spergel model different from and similar to the Comprehensive Strategy?
8. Describe the problems with LA Bridges.
9. According to Cure Violence, what is the transmission of violence? How do violence interrupters operate?
10. Describe the G.R.E.A.T. program, including whether it is found to be effective.

LINKS TO ARTICLES ON GANG SUPPRESSION, INTERVENTION, AND PREVENTION EFFORTS

Comprehensive gang model online overview
http://www.nationalgangcenter.gov/Comprehensive-Gang-Model/Online-Overview/

Assessment guide
http://www.nationalgangcenter.gov/Comprehensive-Gang-Model/Assessment-Guide/

Implementation manual
http://www.nationalgangcenter.gov/Comprehensive-Gang-Model/Implementation-Manual/

Best practices to address community gang problems: OJJDP's comprehensive gang model
https://www.ncjrs.gov/pdffiles1/ojjdp/231200.pdf/

Mobilizing communities to address gang problems
By J. C. Howell and G. D. Curry
http://www.nationalgangcenter.gov/Content/Documents/NYGC-bulletin-4.pdf/

Multidisciplinary gang intervention teams
By M. Arciaga
http://www.nationalgangcenter.gov/Content/Documents/NYGCbulletin3.pdf/

Street outreach and the OJJDP comprehensive gang model
By M. Arciaga and V. Gonzales
https://www.nationalgangcenter.gov/content/documents/street-outreach-comprehensive-gang
    -model.pdf

Gang prevention: An overview of research and programs
By J. C. Howell
https://www.ncjrs.gov/pdffiles1/ojjdp/231116.pdf/

Cure Violence
http://cureviolence.org/

G-Dog—The movie
http://gdogthemovie.com/

G.R.E.A.T. website
http://www.great-online.org/ (see also https://www.nationalgangcenter.gov/SPT/Programs/68/)

Evaluating G.R.E.A.T.: A school-based gang prevention program
https://www.ncjrs.gov/pdffiles1/198604.pdf/

APPENDIX

Beginning in Chapter Two and then continuing throughout the book are interview excerpts and other information gathered during what is referred to as the Los Angeles Study. Chapter Twelve presents similar data gathered during what is referred to as the London Study. The purpose of this Appendix is to describe the objectives and methodologies of both research projects.

THE LOS ANGELES STUDY

The Los Angeles Study focused on risk behaviors—drug use, violence, and unsafe sexual practices—among gang youth in Los Angeles and was conducted from 2005 to 2008.[1] Findings presented are from interview data from 60 members aged 16 to 25 years old from the eastern (Boyle Heights, Lincoln Heights, East Los Angeles), western (Culver City, Venice, Mar Vista), and southern (Inglewood, West Adams, Arlington Heights) parts of the city.

Youth were recruited from community-based organizations (CBOs), such as gang intervention agencies, employment centers, drug treatment programs, alternative schools, and youth community centers (e.g., Boys and Girls Club). All youth enrolled in the study self-identified as gang members. The adults who introduced the youth to the interviewer (B. Sanders) confirmed this identity. Others in senior positions at the CBOs referred these adults because they were believed to be the most knowledgeable about gangs. The strength of the claims of membership are this: the youth said they were members; the adults who worked with them said they were members; and others within the CBO said that those adults were the most knowledgeable about gangs.

Most interviews lasted from 1 hour to 90 minutes and were conducted in a private location within the CBO. Closed-ended questions captured epidemiological data about youths' risk behaviors (e.g., age of onset, frequency, duration), negative health outcomes

---

1 The methodology of this study is explained in more detail in B. Sanders et al. (2010), which can be found at http://www.ncbi.nlm.nih.gov/pmc/articles/PMC3176670/.

(e.g., injuries, addiction, STIs, including HIV/HCV), and health miscellanea (e.g., diet and exercise, health insurance, health access, awareness of service provision). Open-ended questions allowed for qualitative responses to emerge on the motivation, context, and environmental setting of risk behaviors. Other questions probed into everyday life, negative and positive aspects about the gang, and future prospects. Closed-ended responses were captured on a laptop computer with interview managing software and opened-ended responses were captured by a digital recording that was later transcribed verbatim. For their participation at the end of the interview, all youth received $20 in cash, a packet of condoms, and a referral sheet containing contact details for various health and social service providers in their area. All youth expressed appreciation for these incentives. The interviews occurred without incident. An institutional review board approved the research protocols.

Two important points emerged from this project. One is the difficult nature of locating active members to interview. It took about 18 months to find and interview 60 youth. The research did not unfold as first planned. The original design was to focus only on the western area of Los Angeles, to recruit an equal number of males and females, and to include white, black, Latino, and Asian youth. However, few organizations worked with gangs in western Los Angeles, and not enough members were introduced to the interviewer. Recruitment was broadened to other areas of the city to increase the sample size. A limited number of females were introduced to the study and, as a result, study findings are largely limited to males. Youth who were invited to participate identified as either Latino or black. Asian gang youth were not referred to the study and the only white gang member who was approached declined to participate. The intention was to stratify the sample by age within a range of 16 and 25 years old. However, few individuals age 20 to 25 were enrolled, and about 90% of the sample was 16 to 19 years old.

Recruiting youth into this study was related to the willingness of the gang interventionists or other adults at the CBOs to assist. About two dozen different CBOs across Los Angeles were approached and informed of the purposes of the research. Many expressed that the research was important. Of these organizations, some wanted to help, but declined because they did not have enough resources. Others agreed to participate and asked nothing in return. A third type of CBO became problematic because the interventionists requested large amounts of money. One wanted thousands of dollars to establish "collaboration" between their CBO and the project. Another wanted $100 per youth they introduced to the study. Individuals at these and other CBOs were suspected of being involved in criminal activity by those approached during the research, including youth workers, probation officers, homicide detectives, and other interventionists. A field note based on a conversation with a probation officer with 12 years of experience in the area captured this suspicion:

> She [expressed] that [gang intervention program] was a front for gang activity. She thought that the [community] center on [location] acts as a safe haven where gangsters sell drugs (crack), but that it's viewed as a youth center aimed at gang intervention. She was a bit upset that the City had allocated the money to the center, and then see it turn into such a

haven. She also [expressed] that the big guy . . . at the [organization's] meeting was, in fact, a member of [adult criminal syndicate]. She said that he was able to skirt around the gang injunction—where two members of the same gang cannot meet up—by saying that he is doing counseling for gang youth. . . . She doesn't believe any of it. (B. Sanders et al., 2010, p. 740)

A second important point of the methodology pertains to recruiting youth with differential levels of intensity or embeddedness within the gang (B. Sanders et al., 2010). This level was determined by the type of CBO from which they were recruited, as well as the location of that CBO. Those enrolled in the study from the alternative school, employment center, and drug treatment center were more heavily involved in risk behaviors than youth recruited from the youth and community centers. Also, youth from the eastern and southern areas of Los Angeles were more heavily involved in risk behaviors than youth in Western parts of the city. The CBOs that declined to participate because of their request for large amounts of money and/or those suspected of being involved in criminal activity had reputations for working hardcore gang youth (i.e., those with higher levels of participation in risk behaviors), as well as those in their twenties. Their assistance in recruitment would have resulted in the inclusion of more youth in the sample with higher levels of participation in risk behaviors.

The findings of this small, qualitative study do not lend themselves to generalizations. No claims are made that the sample are representative of gang members in Los Angeles or elsewhere. The veracity of interview responses can always be doubted. One factor indicating that youth were truthful is the similarity in their answers. Gang members across the city, from different ages and ethnicities, generally responded in the same way to the same questions.

THE LONDON STUDY

The London Study is based on a doctoral dissertation that sought to determine the presence of U.S.-style gangs in London, England (B. Sanders, 2005a; W. S. Sanders, 2002). The research was conducted between 1996 and 2002 in the borough of Lambeth, an inner-city area in the southern part of the city with some of the highest rates of crime and violence in the country at the time. One area in Lambeth in particular, Brixton, was synonymous with crime and disorder. In June 1996, the researcher (B. Sanders) moved to Brixton with the idea of befriending a group of young offenders, observing their interactions at close proximity, understanding how they made sense of their offending behaviors, and determining whether they were similar to gangs.

This approach did not work. Some progress in meeting a group of young offenders occurred, yet they consistently missed planned meetings. Another attempt included interviewing incarcerated youth at a local young offender's institution. Entry was rejected because there was a lack of sufficient staff. In the end, data for this study were based on six years of field notes of daily interactions in Lambeth and formal, in-depth interviews: 33 with young people with various histories of arrest and 67 with adults who worked with young offenders in different capacities, such as police and probation officers, youth and community workers, and detached youth workers. The youth were ages 14 to 22 and drawn from three pools: from an education center operated by juvenile probation, from a community center for at-risk youth, and through volunteering at a local CBO. All individuals approached throughout the research were informed about the research and its objectives. All participants agreed to be interviewed. No incentives were provided. With the exception of first names, no identifying information of the young offenders or those who work with them were collected.

Interview questions used the funneling approach to tease out the extent to which the groups the youth belonged to were gangs or whether the adults who worked with young offenders thought the groups were gangs.[2] Instead of directly asking "Are you in a gang?" the aim was to ask a broad range of questions about the group context of delinquency (e.g., "Do you hang out with a bunch of people?" or "Do you guys offend together?"). Questions were then narrowed to more specific gang-related ones (e.g., "Do you have a group name?" or "Do you have initiation or other ceremonies?"). The last questions were specifically about gangs (e.g., "Are you in a gang?" or "Do you consider your group a gang? Why/why not?"). All interviews were tape recorded and transcribed verbatim. Observations were generated from routine activities, such as working in a used clothing store, being a cover (i.e., substitute) teacher in schools throughout the borough, going to and from (e.g., university, shopping), and recreational activities (e.g., pubs, skateboarding, nightclubs). Observations were captured as field notes and stored in a single document on a computer.

After two years of data collection, the finding emerged that U.S.-style gangs were not apparent. Given this, determining whether this type of gang existed became a subplot of the research. The main focus became the various interpretations offered by young people of the offenses they committed, their relations with the police, and cultural aspects about their lives as they pertain to crime and delinquency.

This small pilot study operated with no budget. No claims were made that research findings were reflective of young offenders in Lambeth or elsewhere. The validity of interview responses is questionable. However, common patterns emerged between what the young offenders and those who work with them said about how offending was interpreted, including how its group context differed from that of gangs. Young people with a history of offending who were willing to be interviewed were difficult to find. Detached youth workers (the equivalent of a gang interventionist) were reluctant to introduce the youth they worked with to the interviewer. Had access been granted to interview such youth, study findings would be different.

---

2   The word "gang" was not introduced into the interview until the end so as not to prompt responses (see Klein and Maxson, 2006).

REFERENCES

Adamson, C. (2000). Defensive localism in white and black: A comparative history of European-American and African-American youth gangs. *Ethnic and Racial Studies, 23* (2), 272–298.

Adimora, A. A., and Schoenbach, V. J. (2005). Social context, sexual networks, and racial disparities in rates of sexually transmitted infections. *The Journal of Infectious Diseases, 191* (Suppl. 1), S115–S122.

Adler, F. (1975). *Sisters in crime: The rise of the new female criminal.* New York: McGraw-Hill.

Advancement Project. (2007). *A call to action: A case for a comprehensive solution to LA's gang violence epidemic.* Retrieved from http://www.advancementprojectca .org/sites/default/files/imce/p3_report.pdf

Agar, M. (1996). Recasting the "ethno" in epidemiology. *Medical Anthropology, 16,* 391–403.

Agnew, R. (1992). Foundation for a general strain theory of crime and delinquency. *Criminology, 30,* 47–87.

Akers, R. L. (1985). *Deviant behavior: A social learning approach* (3rd ed.). Belmont, CA: Wadsworth.

Akers, T. A., and Lanier, M. M. (2009). "Epidemiological criminology": Coming full circle. *American Journal of Public Health, 99* (3), 397–402.

Aldridge, J., and Medina, J. (2008). *Youth gangs in an English City: Social exclusion, drugs and violence.* Swindon, UK: Economic and Social Research Council.

Aldridge, J., Measham, F., Parker, H., and Williams, L. (2011). *Illegal leisure revisited: Changing patterns of alcohol and drug use in adolescents and young adults.* London: Routledge.

Aldridge, J., Medina, J., and Ralphs, R. (2008). Dangers and problems of doing "gang" research in the UK. In F. van Gemert, D. Peterson, and I-L. Lien (eds.), *Street gangs, migration and ethnicity* (pp. 31–45). Cullompton, UK: Willan.

Alexander, M. (2010). *The new Jim Crow: Mass incarceration in the age of colorblindness.* New York: New Press.

Allender, J. A., and Spradley, B. W. (2001). *Community health nursing: Concepts and practice* (5th ed.). Philadelphia: Lippincott.

Alleyne, E., and Wood, J. L. (2010). Gang involvement: Psychological and behavioral characteristics of gang members, peripheral youth, and nongang youth. *Aggressive Behavior, 36,* 423–436.

Alonso, A. (1998). *Urban graffiti on the city landscape.* Paper presented at the Western Geography Graduate Conference, San Diego State University, February 14, 1998. Retrieved from http://www.streetgangs.com/ academic/alonsograffiti.pdf/.

Alonso, A. (2004). Racialized identities and the formation of black gangs in Los Angeles. *Urban Geography, 25* (7), 658–674.

Alsaybar, B. D. (2002). Deconstructing deviance: Filipino American youth gangs, "party culture," and ethnic identity in Los Angeles. In P. G. Min (Ed.), *The second generation: Ethnic identity among Asian Americans* (pp. 129–151). Walnut Creek, CA: Altamira Press.

Anderson, E. (1990). *Streetwise: Race, class, and change in an urban community.* Chicago: Chicago University Press.

Anderson, E. (1999). *Code of the streets: Decency, violence and moral life in the inner city.* New York: Norton.

Anderson, J. (2007). *Gang-related witness intimidation.* Tallahassee, FL: National Gang Center.

Anti-defamation League. (2005). *Nazi Low Riders.* Retrieved from http://archive.adl.org/learn/ext_us/nlr.asp?xpicked=3&item=nlr#return1/.

Antrobus, S. (2009). *Dying to belong: An in-depth review of street gangs in Britain.* London. Center for Social Justice.

Aquilino, W. S., Wright, D. L., and Supple, A. J. (2000). Response effects due to bystander presence in CASI and paper-and-pencil surveys of drug use and alcohol use. *Substance Use and Misuse, 35* (6–8), 845–867.

Arbreton, A. J. A., and McClanahan, W. S. (2002). *Targeted outreach: Boys and Girls Clubs of America's approach to gang prevention and intervention.* Public/private Ventures: Philadelphia.

Armstrong, T., Bluehouse, P., Dennison, A., Mason, H., Mendenhall, B., Wall, D., and Zion, J. (1999). *Finding and knowing the gang Nayee—Field-initiated gang research project, the judicial branch of the Navajo Nation.* Washington, DC: Office of Juvenile Justice and Delinquency Prevention.

Arnold, E. K. (2011). Oakland gang injunctions: Gentrification or public safety? *Race, Poverty and the Environment, 18* (2), 70–74.

Artesi, A., Eatough, V., and Brooks-Gordon, B. (2010). Doing time and time: An interpretative phenomenological analysis of reformed ex-prisoners' experiences of self-change, identity and career opportunities. *Psychology, Crime & Law, 16* (3), 169–190.

Ashbury, H. (1927). *The gangs of New York.* New York: Knopf.

Auerswald, C. L., Muth, S. Q., Brown, B., Padian, N., and Ellen, J. (2006). Does partner selection contribute to sex differences in sexually transmitted infection rates among African American adolescents in San Francisco? *Sexually Transmitted Diseases, 33,* 480–484.

Austen, B. (2013). Public enemies: Social media is fueling gang wars in Chicago. *Wired* (September 17). Retrieved from http://www.wired.com/2013/09/gangs-of-social-media/all/.

Austin, J., Johnson, K. D., and Weitzer, R. (2005). *Alternatives to the secure detention and confinement of juvenile offenders.* Washington, DC: Office of Juvenile Justice and Delinquency Prevention.

Bailey, S., and Tarbuck, P. (2006). Recent advances in the development of screening tools for mental health in young offenders. *Current Opinion in Psychiatry, 19* (4), 373–377.

Ball, R. A., and Curry, G. D. (1995). The logic of definition in criminology: Purposes and methods for defining "gangs." *Criminology, 33* (2), 225–245.

Banks, R. R. (2003). Beyond profiling: Race, policing and the drug war. *Stanford Law Review, 56* (3), 571–603.

Bannister, J., Pickering, J., Batchelor, S., Burman, M., Kintrea, K., and McVie, S. (2010). *Troublesome youth groups, gangs and knife carrying in Scotland.* Edinburgh: Scottish Government Social Research.

Barnes, J. C., Beaver, K. M., and Miller, J. M. (2010). Estimating the effect of gang membership on nonviolent and violent delinquency: A counterfactual analysis. *Aggressive Behavior, 36,* 437–451.

Baron, S. (1997). Canadian male street skinheads: Street gang or street terrorist? *Canadian Review of Sociology and Anthropology, 34* (2), 125–154.

Barrios, L. (2003). The Almighty Latin King and Queen Nation and the spirituality of resistance: Agency, social cohesion, and liberating rituals in the making of a street organization. In: L. Kontos, D. Brotherton, and L. Barrios (Eds.), *Gangs and society: Alternative perspectives* (pp. 119–135). New York: Columbia University Press.

Barrios, L. (2008). Kingism. In: L. Kontos and D. C. Brotherton (Eds.), *Encyclopedia of gangs* (pp. 142–145). Westport, CN: Greenwood Press.

Baskin, D. R., and Sommers, I. B. (1997). *Casualties of community disorder: Women's careers in violent crime.* Boulder, CO: Westview.

Batista, A. S., and Burgos, M. D. (2008). Brazilian gangs. In L. Kontos and D. C. Brotherton (Eds.), *Encyclopedia of gangs* (pp. 15–20). Westport, CN: Greenwood Press.

Battin, S., Hill, K., Abbott, R., Catalano, R., and Hawkins, J. D. (1998). The contribution of gang membership to delinquency beyond delinquent friends. *Criminology, 36,* 93–115.

Battin-Pearson, S. R., Thornberry, T. P., Hawkins, J. D., and Krohn, M. D. (1998). *Gang membership, delinquent peers, and delinquent behavior.* Washington, DC: Office of Juvenile Justice and Delinquency Prevention.

Baugh, D. G. (1993). *Gangs in correctional facilities: A national assessment.* Laurel, MD: American Correctional Association.

Baumeister, R. F. (1991). *Meanings of life*. New York: Guilford Press.

Beaver, K. M., Wright, J. P., DeLisi, M., and Vaughn, M. G. (2008). Desistance from delinquency: The marriage effect revisited and extended. *Social Science Research, 37*, 736–752.

Beaver, K. M., DeLisi, M., Vaughn, M. G., and Barnes, J. C. (2010). Monoamine oxidase A genotype is associated with gang membership and weapon use. *Comprehensive Psychiatry, 51* (2), 130–134.

Becker, H. (1963). *Outsiders: Studies in the sociology of deviance*. New York: Free Press.

Beckett, K., Nyrop, K., and Pfingst, L. (2006). Race, drugs, and policing: Understanding disparities in drug delivery arrests. *Criminology, 44* (1), 105–137.

Bendixen, M., Endresen, I. M., and Olweus, D. (2006). Joining and leaving gangs: Selection and facilitation effects on self-reported antisocial behaviour in early adolescence. *European Journal of Criminology, 3* (1), 85–114.

Bennett, T., and Holloway, K. (2004). Gang membership, drugs and crime in the UK. *British Journal of Criminology, 44*, 305–323.

Bernburg, J. G., Krohn, M. D., and Rivera, C. J. (2006). Official labeling, criminal embeddedness, and subsequent delinquency: A longitudinal test of labeling theory. *Journal of Research in Crime & Delinquency, 43* (1), 67–88.

Bilchik, S. (1997). *1995 National Youth Gang Survey: Program summary*. Washington, DC: Office of Juvenile Justice and Delinquency Prevention.

Bjerregaard, B. (2006). Antigang legislation and its potential impact. In A. Egley Jr., C. L. Maxson, J. Miller, and M. W. Klein (Eds.), *The modern gang reader* (3rd ed.) (pp. 381–393). Los Angeles: Roxbury.

Bjerregaard, B. (2010). Gang membership and drug involvement: Untangling the complex relationship. *Crime & Delinquency, 56* (1), 3–34.

Bjerregaard, B., and Lizotte, A. J. (1995). Gun ownership and gang membership. *Journal of Criminal Law and Criminology, 86*, 37–57.

Bjerregaard, B., and Smith, C. (1993). Gender differences in gang participation, delinquency, and substance use. *Journal of Quantitative Criminology, 9*, 329–355.

Bjorgo, T. (1999). *How gangs fall apart: Processes of transformation and disintegration of gangs*. Paper presented at the 51st Annual Meeting of the American Society of Criminology, Toronto, CA, November 17–20.

Bjork, M. (2008). Wolves and sheepdogs: On migration, ethnic relations and gang–police interaction in Sweden. In F. van Gemert, D. Peterson, and I-L. Lien (Eds.). *Street gangs, migration and ethnicity* (pp. 241–254). Cullompton, UK: Willan.

Blackman, S. (2004). *Chilling out: The cultural politics of substance consumption, youth and drug policy*. Berkshire, UK: Open University Press.

Blatchford, C. (2009). *The Black Hand: The blood rise and redemption of "Boxer" Enriquez, a Mexican mob killer*. New York: Harper.

Bloch, H. A., and Niederhoffer, A. (1958). *The gang: A study in adolescent behavior*. Ann Arbor, MI: Philosophical Library.

Block, C. R., and Block, R. (1993). *Street gang crime in Chicago*. Washington, DC: National Institute of Justice.

Blonigen, D. M. (2010). Explaining the relationship between age and crime: Contributions from the developmental literature on personality. *Clinical Psychology Review, 30*, 89–100.

Blumstein, A., and Wallman, J. (2000). The recent rise and fall of American violence. In A. Blumstein and J. Wallman (Eds.), *The crime drop in America* (pp. 1–12). New York: Cambridge University Press.

Bolden, C. L. (2012). Liquid soldiers: Fluidity and gang membership. *Deviant Behavior, 33* (3), 207–222.

Booth, S. (2008). Gang symbols. In L. Kontos and D. C. Brotherton (Eds.), *Encyclopedia of gangs* (pp. 74–77). Westport, CN: Greenwood Press.

Borden, I. (2001). *Skateboarding, space and the city: Architecture and the body*. Oxford: Berg.

Bordua, D. (1961). Delinquent subcultures: Sociological interpretations of gang delinquency. *The Annals of the American Academy of Political and Social Science 1* (338), 119–136.

Bouchard, M., and Spindler, A. (2010). Groups, gangs, and delinquency: Does organization matter? *Journal of Criminal Justice, 38* (5), 921–933.

Bourgois, P. (1995). *In search of respect: Selling crack in El Barrio*. Cambridge, UK: Cambridge University Press.

Boutilier, A., and Cohen, M. (2009). *Diversion literature review*. Washington, DC: Office of Juvenile Justice and Delinquency Prevention.

Bowker, L. H., Gross, H. S., and Klein, M. W. (1980). Female participation in delinquent gang activities. *Adolescence, 15* (59), 509–519.

Bradshaw, P. (2005). Terrors and young teams: Youth gangs and delinquency in Edinburgh. In S. H. Decker and F. M. Weerman (Eds.), *European street gangs and troublesome youth groups* (pp. 193–218). New York: Altamira Press.

Braga, A. A. (2014). Focused deterrence strategies and the reduction of gang and group-involved violence. In C. L. Maxson, A. Egley Jr., J. Miller, and M. W. Klein (Eds.). *The modern gang reader* (4th ed.) (pp. 475–488). New York: Oxford University Press.

Braga, A. A., Hureau, D., and Winship, C. (2008). Losing faith? Police, black churches, and the resurgence of youth violence in Boston. *Ohio State Journal of Criminal Law 6*, 141–172.

Braga, A. A., Kennedy, D. M., and Tita, G. E. (2006). New approaches to the strategic prevention of gang and group-involved violence. In A. Egley Jr., C. L. Maxson, J. Miller, and M. W. Klein (Eds.). *The modern gang reader* (3rd ed.) (pp. 338–348). Los Angeles: Roxbury.

Braga A. A., Papachristos, A. V., and Hureau, D. (2010). The concentration and stability of gun violence at micro places in Boston, 1980–2008. *Journal of Quantitative Criminology, 26* (1), 33–53.

Brake, M. (1985). *Comparative youth cultures: The sociology of youth culture and youth subcultures in America, Britain, and Canada.* London: Routledge and Kegan Paul.

Brooks, R. A., Lee, S-J., Stover, G. N., and Barkley, T. W., Jr. (2009). Condom attitudes, perceived vulnerability, and sexual risk behaviors of young Latino male urban street gang members: Implications for HIV prevention. *AIDS Education and Prevention* (Suppl. B), 80–87.

Brooks, R. A., Lee, S-J., Stover, G. N., and Barkley, T. W., Jr. (2011). HIV testing, perceived vulnerability and correlates of HIV sexual risk behaviours of Latino and African American young gang members. *International Journal of STD and AIDS, 22*, 19–24.

Brotherton, D. C. (1996). "Smartness," "toughness," and "autonomy": Drug use in the context of female gang delinquency. *Journal of Drug Issues, 26*, 261–277.

Brotherton, D. C. (2008a). Beyond social reproduction: Bringing resistance back into gang theory. *Theoretical Criminology, 12* (1), 55–77.

Brotherton, D. C. (2008b). Gangs and the media. In L. Kontos and D. C. Brotherton (Eds.), *Encyclopedia of gangs* (pp. 85–87). Westport, CN: Greenwood Press.

Brotherton, D. C. (2008c). Street organizations. In L. Kontos and D. C. Brotherton (Eds.), *Encyclopedia of gangs* (pp. 234–238). Westport, CN: Greenwood Press.

Brotherton, D. C. (2008d). Police repression tactics against U.S. street gangs. In L. Kontos and D. C. Brotherton (Eds.), *Encyclopedia of gangs* (pp. 190–193). Westport, CN: Greenwood Press.

Brotherton, D., and Barrios, L. (2004). *The Almighty Latin King and Queen Nation: Street politics and the transformation of a New York City gang.* New York: Columbia University Press.

Brotherton, D. C., and Salazar-Atias, C. (2003). Amor de reina! The pushes and pulls of group membership among the Latin Queens. In L. Kontos, D. C. Brotherton, and L. Barrios (Eds.), *Gangs and society: Alternative perspectives* (pp. 183–209). New York: Columbia University Press.

Brown, G. C., Vigil, J. D., and Taylor, E. R. (2012). The ghettoization of Blacks in Los Angeles: The emergence of street gangs. *Journal of African American Studies, 16*, 209–225.

Brown, M. (2002). *Gang nation: Delinquent citizens in Puerto Rican, Chicano, and Chicana narratives.* Minneapolis: University of Minnesota Press.

Brownfield, D., Thompson, K. M., and Sorenson, A. M. (1997). Correlates of gang membership: A test of strain, social learning, and social control theories. *Journal of Gang Research, 4* (4), 11–22.

Bruneau, T. (2011). Introduction. In T. Bruneau, L. Dammert, and E. Skinner (Eds.), *Maras: Gang violence and security in Central America* (pp. 1–19). Austin: University of Texas Press.

Bucerius, S. M. (2008). German gangs. In L. Kontos and D. C. Brotherton (Eds.), *Encyclopedia of gangs* (pp. 113–118). Westport, CN: Greenwood Press.

Buettner, R. (2012). Court rules gang crime falls short of terrorism. December 11, *The New York Times.* Retrieved from http://www.nytimes.com/2012/12/12/nyregion/new-york-states-highest-court-rules-gang-crime-falls-short-of-terrorism.html?_r=0/.

Bullock, K., and Tilley, N. (2002). *Shootings, gangs, and violent incidents in Manchester: Developing a crime reduction strategy.* London: Home Office.

Bureau of Justice Assistance. (1998). *Addressing community gang problems: A practical guide.* Washington, D.C.: U.S. Department of Justice.

Burke, R., and Sunley, R. (1998). Post-modernism and youth subculture in Britain in the 1990s. In K. Hazelhurst and C. Hazelhurst (Eds.), *Gangs and youth subcultures: International explanations* (pp. 35–65). London: Transaction.

Burnette, M. (2006). *Fighting gangs the health way.* Retrieved from http://www.minoritynurse.com/community-health/fighting-gangs-healthy-way/.

Bursik, R. J., and Grasmick, H. G. (1993). *Neighborhoods and crime: The dimensions of effective community control.* New York: Lexington Books.

Byrne, J. M., and Hummer, D. (2007). Myths and realities of prison violence: A review of the evidence. *Victims and Offenders, 2*, 77–90.

Cahill, M., and Hayeslip, D. (2010). *Findings from the evaluation of OJJDP's Gang Reduction Program.* Washington, DC: Office of Juvenile Justice and Delinquency Prevention.

Caldwell, L., and Altschuler, D. M. (2001). Adolescents leaving gangs: An analysis of risk and protective factors, resiliency and desistance in a developmental context. *Journal of Gang Research, 8*, 21–34.

Camp, G. M., and Camp, C. G. (1985). *Prison gangs: Their extent, nature, and impact on prisons.* Washington, DC: U.S. Department of Justice.

Campbell, A. (1984). *The girls in the gang.* New York: Blackwell.

Campbell, A. (1992). *The girls in the gang* (2nd ed.). Cambridge, MA: Blackwell.

Canelles, N., and Feixa, C. (2008). Latin gangs in Barcelona. In L. Kontos and D. C. Brotherton (Eds.), *Encyclopedia of gangs* (pp. 151–153). Westport, CN: Greenwood Press.

Caravalho, L., and Soares, R. R. (2013). *Living on the edge: Youth entry, career and exit in drug-selling gangs.* Bonn, Germany: Institute for the Study of Labor.

Cardenas, T. (n.d.). *A guide for understanding effective community-based gang intervention.* Retrieved from https://cardenas.house.gov/sites/cardenas.house.gov/files/Community-Based%20Gang%20Intervention%20Model.pdf

Carson, D. C., Peterson, D., and Esbensen, F-A. (2013). Youth gang desistance: An examination of the effect of different operational definitions of desistance on the motivations, methods, and consequences associated with leaving the gang. *Criminal Justice Review, 38*, 510–534.

Caspi, A., Moffitt, T. E., Silva, P. A., Stouthamer-Loeber, M., Krueger, R. F., and Schmutte, P. S. (2006). Personality and crime: Are some people more crime prone? In R. A. Agnew and F. T. Cullen (Eds.), *Criminological theory: From past to present* (3rd ed.) (pp. 76–84). Los Angeles: Roxbury.

Castanon, J. (2008). Gang clothing. In L. Kontos and D. C. Brotherton (Eds.), *Encyclopedia of gangs* (pp. 59–61). Westport, CN: Greenwood Press.

Centers for Disease Control and Prevention. (2012). Gang homicides—Five U.S. cities, 2003–2008. *Morbidity and Mortality Weekly Report, 61* (3), 46–51.

Centers for Disease Control and Prevention. (2014). *National Health Interview Survey, Factsheet.* Retrieved from http://www.cdc.gov/nchs/data/factsheets/NHIS_2014.pdf/.

Cepeda, A., and Valdez, A. (2003). Risk behaviors among young Mexican American gang-associated females: Sexual relations, partying, substance use, and crime. *Journal of Adolescent Research, 18* (1), 90–107.

Cervantes, R. C., Duenas, N., Valdez, A., and Kaplan, C. (2006). Measuring violence risk and outcomes among Mexican American adolescent females. *Journal of Interpersonal Violence, 21*, 24–41.

Chesney-Lind, M. (2013). A feminist theory of female delinquency. In F. T. Cullen, R. Agnew, and P. Wilcox (Eds.), *Criminological theory: Past to present: Essential readings* (pp. 347–353). New York: Oxford University Press.

Chesney-Lind, M., Shelden, R. G., and Joe. K. A. (1996). Girls, delinquency, and gang membership. In C. R. Huff (Ed.), *Gangs in America* (2nd ed.) (pp. 185–204). Thousand Oaks, CA: Sage.

Chhuon, V. (2014). "I'm Khmer and I'm not a gangster!": The problematization of Cambodian male youth in US schools. *International Journal of Qualitative Studies in Education, 27* (2), 233–250.

Chibnall, S. (1977). *Law and order news: An analysis of crime reporting in the British press.* London: Tavistock.

Chin, K-L. (1990). *Chinese subculture and criminality.* Westport, CT: Greenwood Press.

Chin, K-L. (1996). *Chinatown gangs: Extortion, enterprise and ethnicity.* New York: Oxford University Press.

Chin, K-L. (2006). Chinese gangs and extortion. In A. Egley Jr., C. L. Maxson, J. Miller, and M. W. Klein (Eds.), *The modern gang reader* (3rd ed.) (pp. 176–184). Los Angeles: Roxbury.

Clark, L. F., and Humphries, M. (2013). Project AIM: Bringing evidence-based programs into community-based services. In B. Sanders, Y. Thomas, and B. Deeds (Eds.), *Crime, HIV and health: Intersections of criminal justice and public health concerns* (pp. 239–254). New York: Springer.

Clarke, J. (1976). Style. In S. Hall and T. Jefferson (Eds.), *Resistance through rituals: Youth subcultures in postwar Britain* (pp. 175–191). London: Routledge.

Cloward, R. A., and Ohlin, L. (1960). *Delinquency and opportunity: A theory of delinquent gangs.* New York: Free Press.

Coalition for Juvenile Justice. (2000). *Handle with care: Serving the mental health needs of young offenders.* The

16th Annual Report to the President, the Congress and the Administration of the Office of Juvenile Justice and Delinquency Prevention. Washington, DC: Office of Juvenile Justice and Delinquency Prevention.

Coffield, F. (1991). *Vandalism and graffiti: The state of the art.* London: Calouste Bulgenkian Foundation.

Cohen, A. K. (1955). *Delinquent boys: The culture of the gang.* New York: Free Press.

Cohen, A. K., and Short, J. F., Jr. (1958). Research in delinquent subcultures. *The Journal of Social Issues, 14* (3), 20–37.

Cohen, L. E., and Felson, M. (1979). Social change and crime rate trends: A routine activities approach. *American Sociological Review, 44* (4), 588–608.

Cohen, P. (1972). Sub-cultural conflict and working-class community. *Working Papers in Cultural Studies, 2,* 5–51.

Cohen, S. (Ed.) (1971). *Images of deviance.* Harmondsworth, UK: Penguin.

Cohen, S. (1972). *Folk devils and moral panics: The creation of the Mods and Rockers.* London: MacGibbon and Kee.

Cohen, S., and Young, J. (Eds.) (1973). *The manufacture of news: Deviance, social problems, and the mass media.* London: Constable.

Coleman-Jensen, A., Nord, M., and Singh, A., (2013). *Household food security in the United States in 2012.* Washington, DC: U.S. Department of Agriculture.

Collins, R. (2008). *Violence: A micro-sociological theory.* Princeton, NJ: Princeton University Press.

Conklin, J. (1972). *Robbery and the criminal justice system.* Philadelphia: Lippincott.

Conquergood, D. (1997). Street literacy. In J. Flood, S. B. Heath, and D. Lape (Eds.), *Handbook of research on teaching literacy through the communicative and visual arts* (pp. 354–375). New York: Simon & Schuster.

Conrad, P., and Leiter, V. (Eds.) (2003). *Health and health care as social problems.* Lanham, MD: Rowman & Littlefield.

Cook, P. J., Ludwig, J., Venkatesh, S., and Braga, A. A. (2007). Underground gun markets. *The Economic Journal, 117,* F558–F588.

Cooper, A., and Smith, E. L. (2011). *Homicide trends in the United States, 1980–2008: Annual rates for 2009 and 2010.* Washington, DC: Bureau of Justice Statistics.

Corcoran, P. (2013). Mexico's shifting criminal landscape: Change in gang operation and structure during the past century. *Trends in Organized Crime, 16,* 306–328.

Corrigan, P. (1979). *Schooling the Smash Street kids.* London: Macmillian.

Costanza, S. E., and Helms, R. (2012). Street gangs and aggregate homicides: An analysis of effects during the 1990s violent crime peak. *Homicide Studies, 16* (3), 280–307.

Coughlin, B. C., and Venkatesh, S. A. (2003). The urban street gang after 1970. *Annual Review of Sociology, 29,* 41–64.

Covey, H. C., Menard, S., and Franzese, R. J. (1992). *Juvenile gangs.* Springfield: Thomas.

Cox, A. (2011). Youth gangs in the UK: Myth or reality. *Internet Journal of Criminology.* Retrieved from http://www.internetjournalofcriminology.com/Cox_Youth_Gangs_in_the_UK_Myth_or_Reality_IJC_September_2011.pdf/.

Crawford, L. (2009). No way out: An analysis of exit processes for gang injunctions. *California Law Review, 97* (1), 161–194.

Critcher, C. (2008). Moral panic analysis: Past, present and future. *Sociology Compass, 2* (4), 1127–1144.

Cullen, F. T., Agnew, R., and Wilcox, P. (Eds.) (2013). *Criminological theory: Past to present* (5th ed.). New York: Oxford.

Cummings, S. (1993). Anatomy of a wilding gang. In S. Cummings and D. J. Monti (Eds.), *Gangs: The origins and impact of contemporary youth gangs in the United States* (pp. 49–74). Thousand Oaks, CA: Sage.

Cunningham, M. D., and Sorensen, J. R. (2007). Predictive factors for violent misconduct in close custody. *The Prison Journal, 87,* 241–253.

Curry, G. D. (1998). Female gang involvement. *Journal of Research in Crime and Delinquency, 35,* 100–118.

Curry, G. D., Ball, R. A., and Fox, R. J. (1994). *Gang crime and law enforcement record keeping.* Washington, DC: National Institute of Justice.

Curry, G. D., Ball, R. A., and Decker, S. H. (1996). Estimating the national scope of gang crime from law enforcement data. In C. R. Huff (Ed.), *Gangs in America* (2nd ed.) (pp. 21–36). Thousand Oaks, CA: Sage.

Curry, G. D., and Decker, S. (1998). *Confronting gangs: Crime and community.* Los Angeles: Roxbury Press.

Curry, G. D., and Decker, S. (2003). *Confronting gangs: Crime and community* (2nd ed.). Los Angeles: Roxbury Press.

Curry, G. D., Decker, S. H., and Pyrooz, D. C. (2013). *Confronting gangs: Crime and community* (3rd ed.). New York: Oxford University Press.

Curry, G. D., Howell, J. C., and Roush, D. W. (2000). *Youth gangs in juvenile detention and corrections facilities: A national survey of juvenile detention centers*. Washington, DC: Office of Juvenile Justice and Delinquency Prevention.

Curry, G. D., and Spergel, I. A. (1988). Gang homicide, delinquency, and community. *Criminology, 26* (3), 381–406.

Curtis, R. (2003). The negligible role of gangs in drug distribution in New York City in the 1990s. In L. Kontos, D. Brotherton, and L. Barrios (Eds.), *Gangs and society: Alternative perspectives* (pp. 41–61). New York: Columbia University Press.

David-Ferdon, C., Dahlberg, L. L., and Kegler, S. R. (2013). Homicide rates among persons aged 10–24 years, United States, 1981–2010. *Morbidity and Mortality Weekly Report, 62,* 545–548.

Davis, M. (2006). *City of quartz: Excavating the future in Los Angeles* (new ed.). New York: Verso.

Dawson, P. (2008). *Monitoring data from the Tackling Gangs Action Programme*. Home Office Crime Reduction Website. London: Home Office.

Debarbieux, E., and Blaya, C. (2008). Gangs and ethnicity: An interactive construction. The role of school segregation. In F. van Gemert, D. Peterson, and I-L. Liese (Eds.), *Youth Gangs, Migration and Ethnicity* (pp. 211–226). London: William.

Decker, S. H. (1996). Collective and normative features of gang violence. *Justice Quarterly, 13* (2), 243–264.

Decker, S. H. (2000). Legitimating drug use: A note on the impact of gang membership and drug sales on the use of illicit drugs. *Justice Quarterly, 17* (2), 393–411.

Decker, S. H. (2001). The impact of organizational features on gang activities and relationships. In M. W. Klein, H. J. Kerner, C. L. Maxson, and E. G. M. Weitekamp (Eds.), *The Eurogang paradox: Street gangs and youth groups in the US and Europe* (pp. 145–152). Amsterdam: Kluwer Academic.

Decker, S. H. (2003). *Policing gangs and youth violence.* Belmont, CA: Wadsworth.

Decker, S. H. (2007). Expand the use of police gang units. *Criminology & Public Policy, 6* (4), 729–733.

Decker, S. H., Bynum, T., and Weisel, D. (1998). A tale of two cities: Gangs as organized crime groups. *Justice Quarterly, 15* (3), 395–425.

Decker, S. H., and Curry, G. D. (2002). Gangs, gang homicides, and gang loyalty: Organized crimes of disorganized criminals? *Journal of Criminal Justice, 30,* 1–10.

Decker, S. H., Katz, C. M., and Webb, V. J. (2008). Understanding the black box of gang organization: Implications for involvement in violent crime, drug sales, and violent victimization. *Crime & Delinquency, 54* (1), 153–172.

Decker, S. H., and Kempf-Leonard, K. (1991). Constructing gangs: The social definition of youth activities. *Criminal Justice Policy Review, 5,* 271–291.

Decker, S. H., and Lauritsen, J. L. (2006). Leaving the gang. In A. Egley Jr., C. L. Maxson, J. Miller, and M. W. Klein (Eds.), *The modern gang reader* (3rd ed.) (pp. 60–70). Los Angeles: Roxbury.

Decker, S. H., and Pyrooz, D. C. (2011). Leaving the gang: Logging off and moving on. *Council on Foreign Relations Press.* Retrieved from http://www.cfr.org/counterradicalization/save-supporting-document-leaving-gang/p26590/.

Decker, S. H., and Pyrooz, D. (2014). Timing is everything. Gangs, gang violence, and the life course. In M. DeLisi and K. M. Beaver (Eds.), *Criminological theory: A life-course approach* (pp. 201–213). Burlington, MA: Jones & Bartlett Learning.

Decker, S. H., and Rosenfeld, R. (1995). "My wife is married and so is my girlfriend": Adaptations to the threat of AIDS in an arrestee population. *Crime & Delinquency, 41,* 37–35.

Decker, S. H., van Gemert, F., and Pyrooz, D. C. (2009). Gangs, migration, and crime: The changing landscape in Europe and the United States, *Journal of International Migration and Integration, 10,* 393–408.

Decker, S. H., and Van Winkle, B. (1995). Slingin' dope: The role of gangs and gang members in drug sales. *Justice Quarterly, 11,* 1001–1022.

Decker, S. H., and Van Winkle, B. (1996). *Life in the gang: Family, friends, and violence.* New York: Cambridge University Press.

Deflem, M. (1993). *Rap, rock, and censorship: Popular culture and the technologies of justice.* Paper presented at the annual meeting of the Law and Society Association, Chicago, May 27–30. Retrieved from http://www.mathieudeflem.net/.

de Jong, J. D. (2014). Typically Moroccan? A group dynamic explanation of nuisance and criminal behavior. In C. L. Maxson, A. Egley Jr., J. Miller, and M. W. Klein (Eds.), *The modern gang reader* (4th ed.) (pp. 244–252). New York: Oxford University Press.

Delaney, T. (2013). *American street gangs* (2nd ed.). Upper Saddle River, NJ: Prentice Hall.

De La Rosa, M., and Soriano, F. I. (1992). Understanding criminal activity and use of alcohol and cocaine derivatives by multi-ethnic gang members. In R. C. Cervantes (Ed.), *Substance abuse and gang violence* (pp. 24–39). London: Sage.

De La Rosa, M., Rugh, D., and Rice, C. (2006). An analysis of risk domains associated with drug transitions of active Latino gang members. *Journal of Addictive Diseases, 25* (4), 81–90.

Delor, F., and Hubert, M. (2000). Revisiting the concept of "vulnerability." *Social Science and Medicine, 50,* 1557–1570.

Densley, J. (2013). *How gangs work: An ethnography of youth violence.* London: Palgrave Macmillan.

Derezotes, D. S. (1995). Spirituality and religiosity: Neglected factors in social work practice. *Arete, 20* (1), 1–15.

Deschenes, E. P., and Esbensen, F-A. (1999). Violence and gangs: Gender differences in perceptions and behaviors. *Journal of Quantitative Criminology, 15,* 53–96.

Descormiers, K., and Morselli, C. (2011). Alliances, conflicts, and contradictions in Montreal's street gang landscape. *International Criminal Justice Review, 21* (3), 297–314.

DeSilva, D. (2014). Chart of the week: Is food too cheap for our own good? *Pew Research Center* (May 23). Retrieved from http://www.pewresearch.org/fact-tank/2014/05/23/chart-of-the-week-is-food-too-cheap-for-our-own-good/.

Diaz-Cayeros, A., Magaloni, B., Matanock, A., and Romero, V. (2011). *Living in fear: Mapping the social embeddedness of drug gangs and violence in Mexico.* San Diego: University of California, San Diego.

Dichiara, A. (2008a). Non-racist skinheads. In L. Kontos and D. C. Brotherton (Eds.), *Encyclopedia of gangs* (p. 177). Westport, CN: Greenwood Press.

Dichiara, A. (2008b). Skinheads. In L. Kontos and D. C. Brotherton (Eds.), *Encyclopedia of gangs* (pp. 217–218). Westport, CN: Greenwood Press.

Dimitriadis, G. (2006). The situation complex: Revisiting Frederic Thrasher's *The gang: A study of 1,313 gangs in Chicago. Cultural Studies, Critical Methodologies, 6* (3), 335–353.

DiPlacido, C., Simon, T. L., Witte, T. D., Gu, D., and Wong, S. C. (2006). Treatment of gang members can reduce recidivism and institutional misconduct. *Law and Human Behavior, 30,* 93–114.

Donnermeyer, J. F., Edwards, R. W., Chavez, E. L., and Beauvais, F. (1996). Involvement of American Indian youth in gangs. *Free Inquiry in Creative Sociology, 24* (2), 167–174.

Donziger, S. (1996). *The real war on crime.* New York: Basic Books.

Downes, D. (1966). *The delinquent solution: A study of subcultural theory.* London: Routledge & Kegan Paul.

Drury, A. J., and DeLisi, M. (2011). Gangkill: An exploratory empirical assessment of gang membership, homicide offending, and prison misconduct. *Crime & Delinquency, 57,* 130–146.

Dukes, R. L., Martinez, R. O., and Stein, J. A. (1997). Precursors and consequences of membership in youth gangs. *Youth & Society, 29,* 139–165.

Du Phuoc Long, P., and Richard, L. (1996). *The dream shattered: Vietnamese gangs in America.* Boston: Northeastern University Press.

DuRant, R. H., Altman, D., Wolfson, M., Barkin, S., Kreiter, S., and Krowchuk, D. (2000). Exposure to violence and victimization, depression, substance use, and the use of violence by young adolescents. *The Journal of Pediatrics, 137,* 707–713.

Durkheim, E. (1897). *Suicide: A study in sociology.* New York: The Free Press.

Egan, S. (2013). Why smoking rates are at new lows. *The New York Times* (June 25). Retrieved from http://well.blogs.nytimes.com/2013/06/25/why-smoking-rates-are-at-new-lows/?_php=true&_type=blogs&_r=0/.

Egley, A., Jr. (2000). *Highlights of the 1999 National Youth Gang Survey.* Washington, DC: Office of Juvenile Justice and Delinquency Prevention.

Egley, A., Jr. (2005). *Highlights of the 2002–2003 National Youth Gang Surveys.* Washington, DC: Office of Juvenile Justice and Delinquency Prevention.

Egley, A., Jr., and Howell, J. C. (2011) *Highlights of the 2009 National Youth Gang Survey.* Washington, DC: Office of Juvenile Justice and Delinquency Prevention.

Egley, A., Jr., and Howell, J. C. (2012). *Highlights of the 2010 National Youth Gang Survey.* Washington, DC: Office of Juvenile Justice and Delinquency Prevention.

Egley, A., Jr., and Howell, J. C. (2013). *Highlights of the 2011 National Youth Gang Survey.* Washington, DC: Office of Juvenile Justice and Delinquency Prevention.

Egley, A., Jr., Howell, J. C., and Harris, M. (2014). *Highlights of the 2012 National Youth Gang Survey.* Washington, DC: Office of Juvenile Justice and Delinquency Prevention.

Egley, A., Jr., Howell, J. C., and Major, A. K. (2006). *National Youth Gang Survey, 1999–2001.* Washington, DC: Office of Juvenile Justice and Delinquency Prevention.

Egley, A., Jr., Howell, J. C., and Moore, J. P. (2010). *Highlights of the 2008 National Youth Gang Survey*. Washington, DC: Office of Juvenile Justice and Delinquency Prevention.

Egley, A., Jr., and Major, A. K. (2003). *Highlights of the 2001 National Youth Gang Survey*. Washington, DC: Office of Juvenile Justice and Delinquency Prevention.

Egley, A., Jr., and Major, A. K. (2004). *Highlights of the 2002 National Youth Gang Survey*. Washington, DC: Office of Juvenile Justice and Delinquency Prevention.

Egley, A., Jr., and O'Donnell, C. E. (2008a). *Highlights of the 2005 National Youth Gang Survey*. Washington, DC: Office of Juvenile Justice and Delinquency Prevention.

Egley, A., Jr., and O'Donnell, C. E. (2008b). *Highlights of the 2006 National Youth Gang Survey*. Washington, DC: Office of Juvenile Justice and Delinquency Prevention.

Egley, A., Jr., and O'Donnell, C. E. (2009). *Highlights of the 2007 National Youth Gang Survey*. Washington, DC: Office of Juvenile Justice and Delinquency Prevention.

Egley, A., Jr., and Ruiz, C. E. (2006). *Highlights of the 2004 National Youth Gang Survey*. Washington, DC: Office of Juvenile Justice and Delinquency Prevention.

Eitle, D. (2010). General strain theory, persistence, and desistance among young adult males. *Journal of Criminal Justice, 38*, 1113–1121.

Eitle, D., Gunkel, S., and Van Gundy, K. (2004). Cumulative exposure to stressful life events and male gang membership. *Journal of Criminal Justice, 32* (2), 95–111.

Ericson, R. V., Baranek, P. M., and Chan, J. B. L. (1987). *Visualizing deviance: A study of news organization*. Toronto: University of Toronto Press.

Esbensen, F-A. (2006). The national evaluation of the Gang Resistance Education and Training (G.R.E.A.T.) program. In A. Egley Jr., C. L. Maxson, J. Miller, and M. W. Klein (Eds.), *The modern gang reader* (3rd ed.) (pp. 368–380). Los Angeles: Roxbury.

Esbensen, F-A., Brick, B. T., Melde, C., Tusinski, K., and Taylor, T. J. (2008). The role of race and ethnicity in gang membership. In F. van Gemert, D. Peterson, and I-L. Lien (Eds.), *Street gangs, migration and ethnicity* (pp. 117–139). Collumpton, UK: Willian.

Esbensen, F-A., and Deschenes, E. P. (1998). A multisite examination of youth gang membership: Does gender matter? *Criminology, 36*, 799–828.

Esbensen, F-A., Deschenes, E. P., Winfree, L. T., Jr. (1999). Differences between gang girls and gang boys: Results from a multi-site survey. *Youth and Society, 31* (1), 27–53.

Esbensen, F-A., and Huizinga, D. (1993). Gangs, drugs, and delinquency in a survey of urban youth. *Criminology, 31* (4), 589.

Esbensen, F-A., Huizinga, D., and Weiher, A. (1993). Gang and non-gang youth: Differences in explanatory factors. *Journal of Contemporary Criminal Justice, 9* (2), 94–116.

Esbensen, F-A., and Lynskey, D. P. (2001). Youth gang members in a school survey. In M. W. Klein, H-J. Kerner, C. L. Maxson, and E. G. M. Weitekamp (Eds.), *The Eurogang paradox; Street gangs and youth groups in the US and Europe* (pp. 93–114). Amsterdam: Kluwer Academic.

Esbensen, F-A., and Maxson, C. L. (Eds.). (2012). *Youth gangs in international perspective: Results from the Eurogang Program of research*. Springer: New York.

Esbensen, F-A., Peterson, D., Taylor, T. J., and Freng, A. (2009). Similarities and differences in risk factors for violent offending and gang membership. *The Australian and New Zealand Journal of Criminology, 42* (3), 310–335.

Esbensen, F-A., Peterson, D., Taylor, T. J., and Osgood. D. W. (2012). Results from a multi-site evaluation of the G.R.E.A.T. Program. *Justice Quarterly, 29* (1), 125–151.

Esbensen, F-A., Peterson, D., Taylor, T. J., and Osgood, D. W. (2014). Is G.R.E.A.T. effective? Results from the National Evaluation of the Gang Resistance Education and Training (G.R.E.A.T.) program. In C. L. Maxson, A. Egley Jr., J. Miller, and M. W. Klein (Eds.), *The modern gang reader* (4th ed.) (pp. 443–450). New York: Oxford University Press.

Esbensen, F-A., and Tusinski, K. E. (2007). Youth gangs in the print media. *Journal of Criminal Justice and Popular Culture, 14* (1), 21–38.

Esbensen, F-A., and Weerman, F. M. (2005). Youth gangs and troublesome youth groups in the United States and the Netherlands: A crossnational comparison. *European Journal of Criminology, 2*, 5–37.

Esbensen, F-A., and Winfree, L. T., Jr. (1998). Race and gender differences between gang and non-gang youth: Results from a multisite survey. *Justice Quarterly, 15* (3), 505–526.

Esbensen, F-A., Winfree, L. T., Jr., He, N., and Taylor, T. J. (2001). Youth gang and definitional issues: When is a gang a gang and why does it matter? *Crime and Delinquency, 47*, 105–130.

Erowid. (2009). *PCP—"embalming fluid"—"wet"—"fry": What is it and what do people think it is?* Retrieved from http://www.erowid.org/chemicals/pcp/pcp_info6.shtml/.

Evans, W., Albers, E., Macari, D., and Mason, A. (1996). Suicide ideation, attempts and abuse among incarcerated gang and non-gang delinquents. *Child and Adolescent Social Work Journal, 13*, 115–126.

Evans, W., Fitzgerald, C., Weigel, D., and Chvilicek, S. (1999). Are rural gang members similar to their urban peers? Implications for rural communities. *Youth and Society, 30*, 267–282.

Evans, W., and Mason, A. (1996). Factors associated with gang involvement among incarcerated youth. *Journal of Gang Research, 3*, 31–40.

Eyler, G. (2009). Gangs in the military. *The Yale Law Journal, 118*, 696–742.

Fagan, J. (1989). The social organization of drug use and drug dealing among urban gangs. *Criminology, 27* (4), 633–699.

Fagan, J. (1990). Social processes of delinquency and drug use among urban gangs. In C. R. Huff (Ed.), *Gangs in America* (pp. 183–219). Newbury Park, CA: Sage.

Fagan, J. (1993). Set and setting revisited: Influences of alcohol and illicit drugs on the social context of violent events. In S. E. Martin (Ed.), *Alcohol and interpersonal violence: Fostering multidisciplinary perspectives* (pp. 161–191). Bethesda, MD: National Institute on Alcohol Abuse and Alcoholism.

Fagan, J. (1996). Gangs, drugs, and neighborhood change. In C. R. Huff (Ed.), *Gangs in America* (2nd ed.) (pp. 39–74). Thousand Oaks, CA: Sage.

Farrington, D. (1986). Age and crime. In M. Tonry and N. Morris (Eds.), *Crime and justice: An annual review of research* (pp. 189–250). Chicago: University of Chicago Press.

Faturechi, R. (2012). 7 deputies from L.A. County sheriff's gang unit placed on leave. *Los Angeles Times*, May 17.

Fearn, N. E., Decker, S. H., and Curry, G. D. (2006). Responses to gangs: Evaluating the outcomes. In A. Egley Jr., C. L. Maxson, J. Miller, and M. W. Klein (Eds.), *The modern gang reader* (3rd ed.) (pp. 312–324). Los Angeles: Roxbury.

Federal Bureau of Investigation. (n.d.). *Black Guerilla Family part 1 of 3*. Retrieved from http://vault.fbi.gov/black-guerilla-family/black-guerilla-family-part-1-of-3/view/.

Federal Bureau of Investigation. (1982). *Aryan Brotherhood*. Retrieved from http://vault.fbi.gov/Aryan%20Brotherhood%20/Aryan%20Brotherhood%20Part%201%20of%201/view/.

Federal Bureau of Investigation. (2011). *2011 National gang threat assessment issued*. Retrieved from http://www.fbi.gov/news/pressrel/press-releases/2011-national-gang-threat-assessment-issued/.

Feixa, C. (2008). Mexican gangs. In L. Kontos and D. C. Brotherton (Eds.), *Encyclopedia of gangs* (pp. 162–174). Westport, CN: Greenwood Press.

Feixa, C., Canelles, N., Porzio, L., Recio, C., and Giliberti, L. (2008). Latin Kings in Barcelona. In F. van Gemert, D. Peterson, and I-L. Lien (Eds.), *Street gangs, migration and ethnicity* (pp. 63–78). Cullompton, UK: Willan.

Feixa, C., and Porzio, L. (2008). Spanish gangs. In L. Kontos and D. C. Brotherton (Eds.), *Encyclopedia of gangs* (pp. 226–234). Westport, CN: Greenwood Press.

Fellner, J. (2009). Race, drugs and law enforcement in the United States. *Stanford Law and Policy Review, 20* (2), 257–291.

Fernando, S. H. (1995). *The new beats: Exploring the music culture and attitudes of hip hop*. New York: Payback Press.

Ferrell, J. (1996). *Crimes of style: Urban graffiti and the politics of criminality*. Boston: Northeastern University Press.

Ferrell, J. (1999). Cultural criminology. *Annual Review of Sociology, 25*, 395–418.

Ferrell, J. (2008). Gang and non-gang graffiti. In L. Kontos and D. C. Brotherton (Eds.), *Encyclopedia of gangs* (pp. 56–59). Westport, CN: Greenwood Press.

Ferrell, J., Hayward, K., Morrison, W., and Presdee, M. (Eds.) (2004). *Cultural criminology unleashed*. London: Glasshouse Press.

Ferrell, J., Hayward, K., and Young, J. (2008) *Cultural criminology: An invitation*, London: Sage.

Ferrell, J., and Sanders, C. R. (1995a). Culture, crime, and criminology. In J. Ferrell and C. R. Sanders (Eds.), *Cultural criminology* (pp. 3–24). Boston: Northeastern University Press.

Ferrell, J., and Sanders, C. R. (1995b). Towards a cultural criminology. In J. Ferrell and C. R. Sanders (Eds.), *Cultural criminology* (pp. 297–326). Boston: Northeastern University Press.

Ferrell, J., and Websdale, N. (Eds.). (1999). *Making trouble: Cultural constructions of crime, deviance, and control*. New York: de Gruyter.

Finestone, H. (1957). Cats, kicks, and color. *Social Problems, 5*, 3–13.

Finn, P., and Healey, K. M. (1996). Preventing gangs and drug-related witness intimidation. *Issues and Practices*. Washington, DC: U.S. Department of Justice.

Fischer, D. R. (2002). *Arizona Department of Corrections: Security Threat Group (STG) program evaluation*. Washington, DC: National Institute of Justice.

Fleisher, M. S. (1998). *Dead end kids: Gang girls and the boys they know*. Madison: University of Wisconsin Press.

Fleisher, M. S. (2006). Youth gang social dynamics and social network analysis: Applying degree centrality measures to assess the nature of gang boundaries. In J. F. Short Jr. and L. A. Hughes (Eds.), *Studying Youth Gangs* (pp. 85–98). Lanham, MD: Altamira Press.

Fleisher, M. S., and Decker, S. H. (2001). An overview of the challenge of prison gangs. *Corrections Management Quarterly, 5* (1), 1–9.

Fleisher, M. S., and Krienert, J. L. (2004). Drug selling: A rational choice. In J. L. Krienert and M. S. Fleisher (Eds.), *Crime and employment: Critical issues in crime reduction for corrections* (pp. 192–210). New York: Altamira Press.

Flexon, J. L., Greenleaf, R. G., and Lurigio, A. J. (2012). The effects of self-control, gang membership, and parental attachment/identification on police contacts among Latino and African American youths. *International Journal of Offender Therapy and Comparative Criminology, 56*, 218–238.

Fielding, J. E., Tye, G., Ogawa, P. L., Imam, I. J., and Long, A. M. (2002). Los Angeles County drug court programs: Initial results. *Journal of Substance Abuse Treatment, 23*, 217–224.

Finn, P., and Healey, K. M. (1996). Preventing gang- and drug-related witness intimidation. *Issues and Practices*. Washington, DC: U.S. Department of Justice.

Fiori-Khayat, C. (2008). Ethnicity and juvenile street gangs in France. In F. van Gemert, D. Peterson, and I-L. Lien (Eds.), *Street gangs, migration and ethnicity* (pp. 156–172). Cullompton, UK: Willan.

Fong, R. S., and Buentello, S. (1991). The detection of prison gang development: An empirical assessment. *Federal Probation, 55*, 66–69.

Fong, R. S., Vogel, R. E., and Buentello, S. (1992). Prison gang dynamics: A look inside the Texas Department of Corrections. In P. J. Benekos and A. V. Merlo (Eds.), *Corrections: Dilemmas and directions* (pp. 57–77). Cincinatti, OH: Anderson.

Fong, R. S., Vogel, R. E., and Buentello, S. (1995). Blood-in, blood-out: The rationale behind defecting from prison gangs. *Journal of Gang Research, 2* (4), 45–51.

Foster, J. (1990) *Villains: Crime and community in the inner city*. London: Routledge.

Fox, K. A., Ward, J. T., and Lane, J. (2013). Selection for some, facilitation for others? Self-control theory and the gang–violence relationship. *Deviant Behavior, 34* (12), 996–1019.

Franke, T., and Leap, J. (2011). *Homeboy Industries—Los Angeles County Gang Intervention and Re-Entry Program. Second quarter report*. University of California, Los Angeles. Retrieved from http://zevyaroslavsky.org/wp-content/uploads/Homeboy-Industries-2nd-Quarter-Report-2011.pdf

Fremon, C. (2006). G-Dog and the homeboys. In A. Egley Jr., C. L. Maxson, J. Miller, and M. W. Klein (Eds.), *The modern gang reader* (3rd ed.) (pp. 325–337). Los Angeles: Roxbury.

Freng, A., Davis, T., McCord, K., and Roussell, A. (2013). The new American gang? Gangs in Indian country. *Journal of Contemporary Criminal Justice, 28* (4), 446–464.

Freng, A., and Esbensen, F-A. (2007). Race and gang affiliation: An examination of multiple marginality. *Justice Quarterly, 24* (4), 600–628.

Frost, N. A., Greene, J., and Pranis, K. (2006). *Hard hit: The growth of the imprisonment of women 1977–2004*. New York: Women's Prison Association.

Fryar, C. D., and Ervin, R. B. (2013). *Caloric intake from fast food among adults: United States, 2007–2010*. Hyattsville, MD: National Center for Health Statistics.

Gaes, G. G., Wallace, S., Gilman, E., Klein-Saffran, J., and Suppa, S. (2002). The influence of prison gang affiliation on violence and other prison misconduct. *The Prison Journal, 82*, 359–385.

Garcia, M. (2005). N.Y. using terrorism law to prosecute street gang. February 1, *The Washington Post*. Retrieved from http://www.washingtonpost.com/wp-dyn/articles/A52504-2005Jan31.html/.

Garfinkel, H. (1967). *Studies in ethnomethodology*. Englewood Cliffs, NJ: Prentice Hall.

Garot, R. (2007). Non-violence in the inner city: "Decent" and "street" as strategic resources. *Journal of African American Studies, 10*, 94–111.

Garot, R. (2010). *Who you claim: Performing gang identity in school and on the streets*. New York: New York University Press.

Gatti, U., Angelini, F., Marengo, G., Melchiorre, N., and Sasso, M. (2005). An old-fashioned young gang in Genoa. In S. H. Decker and F. M. Weerman (Eds.), *European street gangs and troublesome youth groups* (pp. 51–80). New York: Altamira Press.

Gatti, U., Haymoz, S., and Schadee, H. M. A. (2011). Deviant youth groups in 30 countries: Results from the Second International Self-Report Delinquency Study. *International Criminal Justice Review, 21* (3), 208–224.

Gatti, U., Tremblay, R. E., Vitaro, F., and McDuff, P. (2005). Youth gangs, delinquency and drug use: A test of the selection, facilitation, and enhancement hypotheses. *Journal of Child Psychology, 46,* 1178–1190.

Geller, A., and Fagan, J. (2010). *Pot as pretext: Marijuana, race and the new disorder in New York City street policing.* Retrieved from http://www.econ.brown.edu/fac/Glenn_Loury/louryhomepage/teaching/Ec%20137/Pot%20As%20Pretext_Submitted_JELS.pdf/.

George, N. (1998). *Hip-hop America.* New York: Viking.

Gibbons, D. (1973). *Society, crime and criminal careers.* Englewood Cliffs, NJ: Prentice Hall.

Gill, G., Burell, S., and Brown, J. (2001). Fear and frustration—The Liverpool cholera riots of 1832. *The Lancet, 358,* 233–237.

Giordano, P. C., Cernkovich, S. A., and Rudolph, J. L. (2002). Gender, crime, and desistance: Toward a theory of cognitive transformation. *American Journal of Sociology, 104,* 990–1064.

Glassner, B. (2000). *The culture of fear.* New York: Basic Books.

Glassner, B. (2002). Narrative techniques of fear mongering. *Social Research, 71* (4), 819–826.

Godwin, T. (2000). *National Youth Court Guidelines.* Washington, DC: Office of Juvenile Justice and Delinquency Prevention.

Goffman, E. (1967). *Interaction ritual.* Garden City, New York: Doubleday.

Goldstein, P. J. (1985). The drugs/violence nexus: A tripartite conceptual framework. *Journal of Drug Issues, 39,* 143–174.

Golembeski, C., and Fullilove, R. (2005). Criminal (in)justice in the city and its associated health consequences. *American Journal of Public Health, 95* (10), 1701–1706.

Golub, A., Dunlap, E., and Benoit, E. (2010). Drug use and conflict in inner-city African-American relationships in the 2000s. *Journal of Psychoactive Drugs, 42,* 327–337.

Goode, E., and Ben-Yehuda, N. (1994). Moral panics: Culture, politics, and social construction. *Annual Review of Sociology, 994* (20), 49–171.

Gordon, R. (2000). Criminal business organisations, street gangs and "wanna be" groups: A Vancouver perspective. *Canadian Journal of Criminology and Criminal Justice, 42* (1), 39–60.

Gordon, R. A., Lahey, B. B., Kawai, E., Loeber, R., Stouthamer-Loeber, M., and Farrington, D. P. (2004). Antisocial behaviors and youth gang membership: Selection and socialization. *Criminology, 42* (1), 55–87.

Gottfredson, G. D., and Gottfredson, D. C. (2006). Gang problems and gang programs in a national sample of schools. In A. Egley Jr., C. L. Maxson, J. Miller, and M. W. Klein (Eds.), *The modern gang reader* (3rd ed.) (pp. 361–367). Los Angeles: Roxbury.

Gottfredson, M. R., and Hirschi, T. (1990). *A general theory of crime.* Stanford, CA: Stanford University Press.

Gramsci, A. (1971). *Prison notebooks: Selections.* New York: International.

Grant, C. M., and Feimer, S. (2007). Street gangs in Indian Country: A clash of cultures. *Journal of Gang Research, 14* (4), 27–66.

Greenberg, A. (Ed.). (2007). *Youth subcultures: Exploring underground America.* Harlow, UK: Pearson Longman.

Greene, J., and Pranis, K. (2007). *Gang wars: The failure of enforcement tactics and the need for effective public safety strategies.* Justice Policy Institute Report, Justice Policy Institute.

Greenfeld, L. A., and Snell, T. L. (1999). *Women offenders.* Washington, DC: U.S. Department of Justice.

Greenwood, P. W. (1996). Responding to juvenile crime: Lessons learned. *The Future of Children: The Juvenile Court 6* (3), 75–85.

Greifinger, R. B. (2006). Inmates as public health sentinels. *Washington University Journal of Law and Policy, 22,* 253–264.

Griffin, M. L., and Hepburn, J. R. (2006). The effect of gang affiliation on violent misconduct among inmates during the early years of confinement. *Criminal Justice Review, 33,* 419–448.

Grisso, T., and Underwood, L. A. (2004). *Screening and assessing mental health and substance use disorders among youth in the Juvenile Justice System: A resource guide for practitioners.* Washington, DC: Office of Juvenile Justice and Delinquency Prevention.

Grogger, J. (2002). The effects of civil gang injunctions on reported violent crime: Evidence from Los Angeles County. *Journal of Law and Economics, 45* (1), 69–90.

Grogger, J. (2005). What we know about gang injunctions. *Criminology and Public Policy, 4* (3), 637–642.

Grund, T. U., and Densley, J. A. (2012). Ethnic heterogeneity in the activity and structure of a Black street gang. *European Journal of Criminology, 9,* 388–406.

Gunnison, E., and Mazerolle, P. (2007). Desistance from serious and not so serious crime: A comparison of psychological risk factors. *Criminal Justice Studies, 20,* 231–253.

Haegerich, T. M., Mercy, J., and Weiss, B. (2013). What is the role of public health in gang-membership prevention? In: *Changing course: Preventing gang membership* (pp. 31–49). Washington, DC: National Institute of Justice. Retrieved from http://nij.gov/publications/changing-course/Pages/public-health.aspx/.

Hagan, J. (1993). The social embeddedness of crime and unemployment. *Criminology, 31,* 465–491.

Hagedorn, J. M. (1994). Homeboys, dope fiends, and new jacks. *Criminology, 32* (2), 197–219.

Hagedorn, J. M. (1998). Gang violence in the post-industrial era. In M. Tonry (Ed.), *Crime and justice: A review of research, 24* (pp. 365–419). Chicago: University of Chicago Press.

Hagedorn, J. M. (2006a). Race not space: A revisionist history of gangs in Chicago. *The Journal of African American Studies, 91* (2), 194–208.

Hagedorn, J. M. (2006b). The global impact of gangs. In J. F. Short Jr. and L. A. Hughes (Eds.), *Studying youth gangs* (pp. 181–192). Lanham, MD: Altamira Press.

Hagedorn, J. M. (2008). *A world of gangs: Armed young men and gangsta culture.* Minneapolis: University of Minnesota Press.

Hagedorn, J. M., and Devitt, M. L. (1999). Fighting female: The social construction of female gangs. In M. Chesney-Lind and J. Hagedorn (Eds.), *Female gangs in America: Essays on girls, gangs and gender* (pp. 256–276). Chicago: Lake View Press.

Hagedorn, J. (with Perry Macon) (1988). *People and Folks: Gangs, crime and the underclass in a Rust Belt city.* Chicago: Lake View Press.

Hagedorn, J. (1998). *People and Folks: Gangs, crime and the underclass in a Rust Belt city (second edition).* Chicago: Lake View Press.

Hagedorn, J. M., Torres, J., and Giglio, G. (1998). Cocaine, kicks, and strain: Patterns of substance use in Milwaukee gangs. *Contemporary Drug Problems, 25,* 113–145.

Hall, G. P., Thornberry, T. P., and Lizotte, A. J. (2006). The gang facilitation effect and neighborhood risk: Do gangs have a stronger influence on delinquency in disadvantaged areas? In J. F. Short Jr. and L. A. Hughes (Eds.), *Studying youth gangs* (pp. 47–62). Lanham, MD: Altamira Press.

Hall, S, Critcher, C., Jefferson, T., Clark, J., and Roberts, R. (1978). *Policing the crisis: Mugging, the state, and law and order.* London: Macmillan.

Hall, S., and Jefferson, T. (Eds.) (1976). *Resistance through rituals: Youth subcultures in postwar Britain.* London: Routledge.

Hallsworth, S., and Young, T. (2004). Getting real about gangs. *Criminal Justice Matters, 55,* 12–13.

Hallsworth, S., and Young, T. (2008). Gang talk and gang talkers: A critique. *Crime Media and Culture, 4* (2), 175–195.

Hamm, M. S. (1993). *American skinheads: The criminology and control of hate crime.* Westport, CT: Praeger.

Hamm, M. S. (2008). *Prisoner radicalization: Assessing the threat in US correctional institutions.* Washington, DC: National Institute of Justice.

Hamm, M. S., and Ferrell, J. (1994). Rap, cops, and crime: Clarifying the "cop killer" controversy. *ACJS Today, 13* (1), 3–29.

Hammersley, R. (2011). Pathways through drugs and crime: Desistance, trauma and resilience. *Journal of Criminal Justice, 39,* 268–272.

Hammett, T. (2006). HIV in prison: Editorial introduction. *Criminology and Public Policy, 5* (1), 109–112.

Hamrin, V., Jonker, B., and Scahill, L. (2004). Acute stress disorder symptoms in gunshot-injured youth. *Journal of Child and Adolescent Psychiatric Nursing, 17* (4), 161–172.

Harper, G. W., Davidson, J., and Hosek, S. G. (2008). Influence of gang membership on negative effects, substance use, and antisocial behavior among homeless African American male youth. *American Journal of Men's Health, 2* (3), 229–243.

Harper, G. W., and Robinson, W. L. (1999). Pathways to risk among inner-city African American adolescent females: The influence of gang membership. *American Journal of Community Psychology, 27* (3), 383–404.

Harrell, E. (2005). *Violence by gang members, 1993–2003.* Washington, DC: U.S. Department of Justice.

Harris, M. G. (1988). *Cholas: Latino girls and gangs.* New York: AMS.

Harris, M. G. (1994). Cholas, Mexican-American girls, and gangs. *Sex Roles, 30* (3/4), 289–301.

Hartman, D. M., and Golub, A. (1999). The social construction of the crack epidemic in the print media. *Journal of Psychoactive Drugs, 31* (4), 423–433.

Haskins, J. (1974). *Street gangs: Yesterday and today.* Wayne, PA: Hastings.

Hawkins, J. D., and Catalano, R. F. (1992). *Communities that care: Action for drug abuse prevention.* San Francisco: Jossey-Bass.

Hayden, C. (2008). *Staying safe and out of trouble: A survey of young people's perceptions and experiences*. Portsmouth, UK: University of Portsmouth.

Hayden, T. (2004). *Street wars*. New York: New Press.

Haymoz, S., and Gatti, U. (2010). Girl members of deviant youth groups, offending behavior and victimization: Results from the ISRD2 in Italy and Switzerland. *European Journal on Criminal Policy and Research, 16* (3), 167–182.

Hebdige, D. (1979). *Subculture: The meaning of style*. London: Methuen.

Hendricks, L., and Wilson, A. (2013). The impact of crack-cocaine on Black America. *National Forum Journal of Counseling and Addiction, 2* (1), 1–6.

Hennigan, K. M., and Sloane, D. (2013). Improving civil gang injunctions: How implementation can affect gang dynamics, crime, and violence. *Criminology and Public Policy, 12* (1), 7–41.

Hill, K. G., Howell, J. C., Hawkins, J. D., and Battin-Pearson, S. R. (1999). Childhood risk factors for adolescent gang membership: Results from the Seattle Social Development Project. *Journal of Research in Crime and Delinquency, 36*, 300–322.

Hill, K. G., Lui, C., and Hawkins, J. D. (2001). *Early precursors of gang membership: A study of Seattle youth*. Washington, DC: U.S. Department of Justice.

Hindelang, M. J., Gottfredson, M. R., and Garofalo, J. (1978). *Victims of crime: An empirical foundation for a theory of personal victimization*. Cambridge, MA: Ballinger.

Hirschi, T. (1969). *Causes of delinquency*. Berkeley, CA: University of California Press.

Hodkinson, P. (2002). *Goth: Identity, style, and subculture*. Oxford, UK: Berg.

Holt, M. R., and San Pedro, V. (2014). Social media evidence: What you can't use won't help you—Practical considerations for using evidence gathered on the Internet. *The Florida Bar Journal, 88* (1). Retrieved from http://www.floridabar.org/DIVCOM/JN/JNJournal01.nsf/8c9f13012b96736985256aa900624829/78eec84889b66af085257c4a0073203a!Open Document.

Holvey, R. (2009). Prison managers are effectively fighting the proliferation of gangs in prisons. In A Soliz (Ed.), *Gangs* (pp. 99–106). Detroit: Greenhaven Press.

Hope, T. L., and Damphousse, K. R. (2002). Applying self-control theory to gang membership in a non-urban setting. *Journal of Gang Research, 9*, 41–61.

Horowitz, R. (1983). *Honor and the American dream: Culture and identity in a Chicano community*. Rutgers, NJ: Rutgers University Press.

Horowitz, R. (1990). Sociological perspectives on gangs: Conflicting definitions and concepts. In C. R. Huff (Ed.), *Gangs in America* (pp. 37–54). Thousand Oaks, CA: Sage.

Horowitz, R., and Schwartz, G. (1974). Honor, normative ambiguity and gang violence. *American Sociological Review, 39* (2), 238–251.

Howell, J. C. (1998). Promising programs for youth gang violence prevention and intervention. In R. Loeber and D. P. Farrington (Eds.), *Serious and violent juvenile offenders: Risk factors and successful interventions* (pp. 284–312). Thousand Oaks, CA: Sage.

Howell, J. C. (1999). Youth gang homicides: A literature review. *Crime and Delinquency, 45* (2), 208–241.

Howell, J. C. (2012). *Gangs in America's communities*. Thousand Oaks, CA: Sage.

Howell, J. C., and Decker, S. H. (1999). *The youth gangs, drugs, violence connection*. Washington, DC: U.S. Department of Justice.

Howell, J. C., and Egley, A., Jr. (2005). Moving risk factors into developmental theories of gang membership. *Youth Violence and Juvenile Justice, 3* (4), 334–354.

Howell, J. C., Egley, A., Jr., Tita, G. E., and Griffiths, E. (2011). *US Gang problem trends and seriousness, 1996–2009*. Washington, DC: U.S. Department of Justice.

Howell, J. C., and Gleason, D. K. (1999). *Youth gang drug trafficking*. Washington, DC: Office of Juvenile Justice and Delinquency Prevention.

Howell, J. C., and Moore, J. P. (2010). *History of street gangs in the United States*. Washington, DC: Office of Juvenile Justice and Delinquency Prevention.

Hser, Y-I., Longshore, D., and Anglin, M. D. (2007). The life course perspective on drug use: A conceptual model for understanding drug use trajectories. *Evaluation Review, 31*, 515–547.

Huebner, B. M. (2003). Administrative determinants of inmate violence: A multilevel analysis. *Journal of Criminal Justice, 31* (2), 107–117.

Huebner, B. M., Varano, S., and Bynum, T. S. (2007). Gangs, guns and drugs: Recidivism among serious, young offenders. *Criminology and Public Policy, 6* (2), 183–222.

Huff, C. R. (1989). Youth gangs and public policy. *Crime and Delinquency, 35*, 524–537.

Huff, C. R. (1990). Denial, overreaction, and misidentification: A postscript on public policy. In C. Huff (Ed.),

Gangs in America (pp. 310–317). Thousand Oaks, CA: Sage.

Huff, C. R. (1996). The criminal behavior of gang members and nongang at-risk youth. In C. R. Huff (Ed.), *Gangs in America* (2nd ed.) (pp. 75–102). Thousand Oaks, CA: Sage.

Hughes, L. A. (2006). Studying youth gangs: The importance of context. In J. F. Short and L. A. Hughes (Eds.), *Studying youth gangs* (pp. 37–45). Lanham, MD: Altamira Press.

Hunt, G. P., and Joe-Laidler, K. (2001). Alcohol and violence in the lives of gang members. *Alcohol Research and Health, 25* (1), 66–71.

Hunt, G., and Joe-Laidler, K. (2006). Situations of violence in the lives of girl gang members. In A. Egley Jr., C. L. Maxson, J. Miller, and M. W. Klein (Eds.), *The modern gang reader* (3rd ed.) (pp. 244–257). Los Angeles: Roxbury.

Hunt, G. P., Joe-Laidler, K., and Evans, K. (2002). The meaning and gendered culture of getting high: Gang girls and drug use issues. *Contemporary Drug Problems, 29,* 375–415.

Hunt, G., Joe-Laidler, K., and MacKenzie, K. (2000). "Chillin, being dogged and getting buzzed": Alcohol in the lives of female gang members. *Drugs: Education, Prevention, and Policy, 7* (4), 331–353.

Hunt, G., MacKenzie, K., and Joe-Laidler, K. (2005). Alcohol and masculinity: The case of ethnic youth gangs. In T. M. Wilson (Ed.), *Drinking cultures: Alcohol and identity* (pp. 225–254). Oxford: Berg.

Hunt, G., Moloney, M., Joe-Laidler, K., and MacKenzie, K. (2011). Young mother (in the hood): Gang girls' negotiation of new identities. In M. R. Pogrebin (Ed.), *About criminals: A view of the offenders' world* (pp. 145–157). Thousand Oaks, CA: Sage.

Hunt, G., Riegel, S., Morales, T., and Waldorf, D. (1993). Changes in prison culture: Prison gangs and the case of the "Pepsi Generation." *Social Problems, 40* (3), 398–409.

Hunter, S. B., and Huang, C. Y. (2014). *Substance Use Treatment and Reentry (STAR) Program: Final evaluation report.* Santa Monica: RAND Corporation.

Hutchinson, R. (1993). Blazon nouveau: Gang graffiti in the barrios of Los Angeles and Chicago. In S. Cummings and D. J. Monti (Eds.), *Gangs: The origins and impact of contemporary youth gangs in the United States* (pp. 137–171). Thousand Oaks, CA: Sage.

Hutson, H. R., Anglin, D., Kyriacou, D. N., Hart, J., and Spears, K. (1995). The epidemic of gang-related homicides in Los Angeles County from 1979 through 1994. *Journal of the American Medical Association, 274,* 1031–1036.

Hutson, H. R., Anglin, D., and Pratts, M. J. (1994). Adolescents and children injured or killed in drive-by shootings in Los Angeles. *The New England Journal of Medicine, 330,* 324–327.

Inciardi, J. A. (1990). The crack-violence connection within a population of hard-core adolescent offenders. In M. De La Rosa, E. Y. Lambert, and B. Gropper (Eds.), *Drugs and violence: Causes, correlates and consequences* (pp. 101–120). Besthesda, MD: National Institute on Drug Abuse.

Inciardi, J. A., Horowitz, R., and Pottieger, A. E. (1992). *Street kids, street drugs, street crime: An examination of drug use and serious delinquency in Miami.* Salt Lake City: Brooks/Cole.

Institute for Economics and Peace. (2013). *UK peace index 2013: Exploring the fabric of peace in the UK from 2003 to 2012.* New York: Institute for Economics and Peace.

Jackson, C. (2004) Nazi Low Riders boast over 1,000 members, most in prison. *Intelligence Report, 114.* Southern Poverty Law Center. Retrieved from http://www.splcenter.org/get-informed/intelligence-report/browse-all-issues/2004/summer/nazi-low-riders/.

Jackson, P., and Rudman, C. (1993). Moral panic and the response to gangs in California. In S. Cummings and D. J. Monti (Eds.), *Gangs: The origins and impact of contemporary youth gangs in the United States* (pp. 257–275). Albany: State University of New York.

Jackson, R., and McBride, W. D. (1992). *Understanding street gangs.* Placerville, CA: Copperhouse.

Jackson, R. K., and McBride, W. D. (1996). *Understanding street gangs.* Incline Village, NV: Copperhouse.

Jacobs, B. A. (1996). Crack dealers and restrictive deterrence: Identifying NARCS. *Criminology, 34* (3), 409–431.

Jacobs, B. A. (1999). Crack to heroin?: Drug markets and transition. *British Journal of Criminology, 39,* 555–574.

Jefferson, T. (1993). The racism of criminalization: Policing and the reproduction of the criminal other. In L. Gelsthorpe (Ed.), *Minority Ethnic Groups in the Criminal Justice System* (pp. 26–43). Cambridge, UK: University of Cambridge.

Jenness, V., Maxson, C. L., Matsuda, K. N., and Sumner, J. M. (2007). *Violence in California correctional facilities: An empirical examination of sexual assault.* Irvine: University of California, Irvine.

Joe, K. A., and Chesney-Lind, M. (1995). "Just every mother's angel": An analysis of gender and ethnic variations in youth gang membership. *Gender and Society, 9*, 408–430.

Joe, K. A., and Hunt, G. (1997). Violence and social organization in female gangs. *Social Justice, 24*, 148–169.

Joe-Laidler, K., and Hunt, G. (1997). Violence and social organization in female gangs. *Social Justice, 24* (4), 148–169.

Joe-Laidler, K., and Hunt, G. (2001). Accomplishing femininity among the girls in the gang. *British Journal of Criminology, 41* (4), 148–169.

Johnson, B., Goldstein, P. J., Preble, E., Schmeidler, J., Lipton, D. S., Spunt, B., and Miller, T. (1985). *Taking care of business: The economics of crime by heroin abusers*. New York: Lexington Books.

Johnston, L. D., O'Malley, P. M., Bachman, J. G., and Schulenberg, J. E. (2012). *Monitoring the future national results on adolescent drug use: Overview of key findings, 2011*. Bethesda, MD: National Institute on Drug Abuse.

Joseph, T., and Taylor, D. (2003). Native American youth and gangs. *Journal of Gang Research, 10* (2), 45–54.

Karberg, J. C., and James, D. J. (2005). *Substance dependence, abuse, and treatment of jail inmates, 2002*. Washington, DC: Bureau of Justice Statistics.

Kassel, P. (2003). The gang crackdown in the prisons of Massachusetts: Arbitrary and harsh treatment can only make matters worse. In: L. Kontos, D. Brotherton, and L. Barrios (Eds.), *Gangs and society: Alternative perspectives* (pp. 228–252). New York: Columbia University Press.

Katz, C. M., and Fox, A. M. (2010). Risk and protective factors associated with gang-involved youth in Trinidad and Tobago. *Pan American Journal of Public Health, 27* (3), 187–202.

Katz, C. M., and Webb, V. J. (2006). *Policing gangs in America*. New York: Cambridge University Press.

Katz, C. M., Webb, V. J., and Decker, S. H. (2005). Using the Arrestee Drug Abuse Monitoring (ADAM) program to further understand the relationship between drug use and gang membership. *Justice Quarterly, 22* (1), 58–88.

Katz, J. (1988). *Seductions of crime: Moral and sensual attractions in doing evil*. New York: Basic Books.

Katz, J. (2000). The gang myth. In S. Karstedt and K-D. Bussman (Eds.), *Social dynamics of crime and control: New theories for a world in transition* (pp. 171–187). Portland: Hart.

Katz, J., and Jackson-Jacobs, C. (2007). The criminologists' gang. In C. Sumner (Ed.), *The Blackwell companion to criminology* (pp. 91–124). Oxford: Blackwell.

Keiser, R. L. (1969). *The Vice Lords: Warriors of the streets*. New York: Holt, Rinehart, & Winston.

Keiser, R. L. (1979). *The Vice Lords: Warriors of the streets (Fieldwork edition)*. New York: Holt, Rinehart, & Winston.

Kelly, K., and Caputo, T. (2005). Linkages between street gangs and organized crime: The Canadian experience. *Journal of Gang Research, 13* (1), 17–32.

Kennedy, D. M. (1997). Pulling levers: Chronic offending, high-crime, settings, and a theory of prevention. *Valparaiso University Law Review, 31*, 449–484.

Kennedy, D. M. (1998). Pulling levers: Getting deterrence right. *National Institute of Justice Journal*, 2–8.

Kennedy, D. M. (2008). Operation Ceasefire. In L. Kontos and D. C. Brotherton (Eds.), *Encyclopedia of gangs* (pp. 178–180). Westport, CN: Greenwood Press.

Kennedy, D. M., Piehl, A. M., and Braga, A. A. (1996). Youth violence in Boston: Gun markets, serious youth offenders, and a use-reduction strategy. *Law and Contemporary Problems, 59*, 147–196.

Kennedy, L. W., and Baron, S. W. (1993). Routine activities and a subculture of violence: A study of violence on the street. *Journal of Research in Crime and Delinquency, 30* (1), 88–112.

Kent, D. R., and Felkenes, G. T. (1998). *Cultural explanations for Vietnamese youth involvement in street gangs*. Westminster, CA: Westminster Police Department.

Kerner, H-J., Reich, K., Coester, M., and Weitekamp, E. G. M. (2008). Migration background, group affiliation, and delinquency among endangered youth in a southwest German city. In F. van Gemert, D. Peterson, and I-L. Lien (Eds.), *Street gangs, migration and ethnicity* (pp. 173–191). Cullompton, UK: Willan.

Kessler, C. (2002). Need for attention to mental health of young offenders. *The Lancet, 359*, 1956–1957.

Kim, S. Y., Benner, A. D., Takushi, R. M. N., Ongbongan, K., Dennerlein, D., and Spencer, D. K. (2009). "It's like we're just renting over here": The pervasive experiences of discrimination of Filipino immigrant youth gang members in Hawai'i. *AAPI Nexus, 6* (1), 11–30.

Klein, M. (1995). *The American street gang: Its nature, prevalence and control*. New York: Oxford University Press.

Klein, M. W. (1971). *Street gangs and street workers*. New York: Prentice Hall.

Klein, M. W., Kerner, H. J., Maxson, C. L., and Weitekamp, E. G. M. (Eds.). (2001). *The Eurogang paradox; Street gangs and youth groups in the US and Europe*. Amsterdam: Kluwer Academic.

Klein, M. W., and Maxson, C. L. (1989). Street gang violence. In M. E. Wolfgang and N. Weiner (Eds.), *Violent crime, violent criminals* (pp. 198–234). Beverly Hills, CA: Sage.

Klein, M. W., and Maxson, C. L. (2006). *Street gang patterns and policies.* New York: Oxford University Press.

Klein, M. W., Maxson, C. L., and Miller, J. (Eds.) (1995). *The modern gang reader.* Los Angeles: Roxbury.

Kleinbaum, J. (2006). Knocking risk down: Jeopardy Program gives youths a way out. *Daily News,* March 7.

Killingbeck, D. (2001). The role of television news in the construction of violence as a "moral panic." *Journal of Criminal Justice and Popular Culture, 8* (3), 186–202.

King, J. E., Walpole, C. E., and Lamon, K. (2007). Surf and turf wars online: Growing implications of Internet gang violence. *Journal of Adolescent Health, 41,* S66–S68.

Kissner, J., and Pyrooz, D. C. (2009). Self-control, differential association, and gang membership: A theoretical and empirical extension of the literature. *Journal of Criminal Justice, 37,* 478–487.

Knox, G. (1997). The "get out of the gang thermometer": An application to a large national sample of African-American male youths. *Journal of Gang Research, 5* (1), 21–43.

Knox, G. W. (2000a). *An introduction to gangs* (5th ed.). Peotone, IL: New Chicago School Press.

Knox, G. W. (2000b). A national assessment of gangs and security threat groups (STGs) in adult correctional institutions: Results of the 1999 Adult Corrections Survey. *Journal of Gang Research, 7,* 1–45.

Knox, G. W. (2005). *The problem of gangs and security threat groups in American prisons today: Recent research findings from the 2004 Prison Gang Survey.* Peotone, IL: National Gang Crime Research Center.

Knox, G. W. (2012). *The problem of gangs and security threat groups in American prisons today: Recent research findings from the 2012 Prison Gang Survey.* Peotone, IL: National Gang Crime Research Center.

Knox, G. W., and Papachristos, A. V. (2002). *The Vice Lords: A gang profile analysis.* Peotone, IL: New Chicago School Press.

Knox, G. W., and Tromanhauser, E. D. (1991). Gangs and their control in adult correctional institutions. *The Prison Journal, 71,* 15–22.

Koniak-Griffin, D., Lesser, J., Uman, G., and Nyamathi, A. (2003). Teen pregnancy, motherhood, and unprotected sexual activity. *Research in Nursing and Health, 26,* 4–19.

Kontos, L. (2008). Latin King Bible. In L. Kontos and D. C. Brotherton (Eds.), *Encyclopedia of gangs* (pp. 153–155). Westport, CN: Greenwood Press.

Kornhauser, R. R. (1978). *Social sources of delinquency: An appraisal of analytical models.* Chicago: University of Chicago Press.

Krebs, C. P. (2006). Inmates factors associated with HIV transmission in prison. *Criminology and Public Policy, 5* (1), 113–136.

Krienert, J. L., and Fleisher, M. S. (2001). Gang membership as a proxy for social deficiencies: A study of Nebraska inmates. *Corrections Management Quarterly, 3* (1), 47–58.

Krisberg, B. (2005). *Juvenile justice: Redeeming our children.* Thousand Oaks, CA: Sage.

Krisberg, B. A., and Austin, J. F. (1993). *Reinventing Juvenile Justice.* Newbury Park, CA: Sage.

Krohn, M. D., Schmidt, N. M., Lizotte, A. J., and Baldwin, J. M. (2011). The impact of multiple marginality on gang membership and delinquency behavior for Hispanic, African American and White male adolescents. *Journal of Contemporary Criminal Justice, 27* (1), 18–42.

Kyriacou, D. N., Demetrios, N., Hutson, H. R., Anglin, D., Peek-Asa, C., and Kraus, J. F. (1999). The relationship between socioeconomic factors and gang violence in the City of Los Angeles. *The Journal of Trauma, Injury, Infection, and Critical Care, 46* (2), 334–339.

Lacourse, E., Nagin, D., Tremblay, R. E., Vitaro, F., and Claes, M. (2003). Developmental trajectories of boys' delinquent group membership and facilitation of violent behaviors during adolescence. *Development and Psychopathology, 15,* 183–197.

Lahey, B. B., Gordon, R. A., Loeber, R., Stouthamer-Loeber, M., and Farrington, D. P. (1999). Boys who join gangs: A prospective study of predictors of first gang entry. *Journal of Abnormal Child Psychology, 27* (4), 261–276.

Lam, K. D. (2012). Racism, school, and the streets. A critical analysis of Vietnamese American youth gang formation in Southern California. *Journal of Southeast Asian American Education and Advancement, 7,* 1–14.

Lane, J., and Meeker, J. W. (2000). Subcultural diversity and the fear of crime and gangs. *Crime and Delinquency, 46* (4), 497–521.

Lane, M. (1989). Inmate gangs. *Corrections Today, 51* (4), 98–99, 126, 128.

Lanier, M. M., Park, R. P., and Akers, T. A. (2010). Epidemiological criminology: Drug use among African American gang members. *Journal of Correctional Health Care, 16* (1), 6–16.

Laub, J. H., and Sampson, R. J. (2001). Understanding desistance from crime. In M. Tonry (Ed.), *Crime and justice* (pp. 1–69). Chicago: University of Chicago Press.

Laub, J. H., and Sampson, R. J. (2003). *Shared beginnings, divergent lives: Delinquent boys to age 70.* Cambridge, MA: Harvard University Press.

Lauderback, D., Hansen, J., and Waldorf, D. (1992). "Sisters are doin' it for themselves": A black female gang in San Francisco. *The Gang Journal, 1,* 57–70.

Lauritsen, J. L., Sampson, R. J., and Laub, J. H. (1991). The link between offending and victimization among adolescents. *Criminology, 29* (2), 265–292.

Lawson, W. A., and Lawson, A. (2013). Disparities in mental health diagnosis and treatment among African Americans: Implications for the correctional systems. In B. Sanders, Y. Thomas, and B. Deeds (Eds.), *Crime, HIV and health: Intersections of criminal justice and public health concerns* (pp. 81–91). New York: Springer.

LeBel, T. P., Burnett, R., Maruna, S., and Bushway, S. (2008). The "chicken and egg" of subjective and social factors in desistance from crime. *European Journal of Criminology, 5* (2), 131–159.

Lee, C.-Y. (1997). The role of the community health nurse in the provision of care to youth gangs. *Journal of Community Health Nursing, 14* (2), 111–117.

Lemert, E. (1967). *Human deviance, social problems and social control.* Englewood Cliffs, NJ: Prentice Hall.

Leovy, J. (2007). Homicides don't add up to a race war. *Los Angeles Times.* November 25.

Lerman, P. (1967). Argot, symbolic deviance and subcultural delinquency. *American Sociological Review, 32* (2), 209–224.

Lesser, J., and Escoto-Lloyd, S. (1999). Health-related problems in a vulnerable population: Pregnant teens and adolescent mothers. *Nursing Clinics of North America, 34* (2), 289–299.

Levitt, S. D., and Venkatesh, S. A. (2000). An economic analysis of a drug-selling gang's finances. *The Quarterly Journal of Economics, 115* (3), 755–789.

Levy, J. (2014). In U.S., uninsured rate lowest since 2008. *Gallup Well-Being* (April 7). Retrieved from http:// www.gallup.com/poll/168248/uninsured-rate-lowest-2008.aspx/.

Li, X., Stanton, B., Pack, R., Harris, C., Cottrell, L., and Burns, J. (2002). Risk and protective factors associated with gang involvement among urban African American adolescents. *Youth and Society, 34* (2), 172–194.

Lien, I-L. (2005a). Criminal gangs and their connections: Metaphors, definitions and structures. In S. H. Decker and F. M. Weerman (Eds.), *European street gangs and troublesome youth groups* (pp. 31–50). New York: Altamira Press.

Lien, I-L. (2005b). The role of crime acts in constituting the gang's mentality. In S. H. Decker and F. M. Weerman (Eds.), *European street gangs and troublesome youth groups* (pp. 105–125). New York: Altamira Press.

Lien, I-L. (2008). "Nemesis" and the Achilles heel of Pakistani gangs in Norway. In F. van Gemert, D. Peterson, and I-L. Lien (Eds.), *Street gangs, migration and ethnicity* (pp. 227–240). Cullompton, UK: Willan.

Lipset, S. M., and Raab, M. (1978). *The politics of unreason: Right-wing extremism in America, 1790–1977.* Chicago: University of Chicago Press.

Lipsey, M. W., Cordray, D. S., and Bereger, D. E. (1981). Evaluation of a juvenile diversion program: Using multiple lines of evidence. *Evaluation Review 5* (3), 283–306.

Lizotte, A. J., Tesoriero, J. M., Thornberry, T. P., and Krohn, M. (1994). Patterns of adolescent firearms ownership and use. *Justice Quarterly, 11,* 51–74.

Lo, T. W. (2012). Triadization of youth gangs in Hong Kong. *British Journal of Criminology, 52,* 556–576.

Loeber, R., and Farrington, D. P. (2000). Young children who commit crime: Epidemiology, developmental origins, risk factors, early interventions, and policy implications. *Developmental Psychology, 12,* 737–762.

Loeber, R., Farrington, D. F., Stouthamer-Loeber, M., and Van Kammen, W. B. (1998). *Antisocial behavior and mental health: Explanatory factors in childhood and adolescence.* Mahway, NJ: Erlbaum.

Logan, E. (1999). The wrong race, committing crime, doing drugs, and maladjusted for motherhood. The nation's fury of "crack babies." *Social Justice, 26* (1), 115–138.

Logan, S. (2009). *This is for the Mara Salavatrucha: Inside the MS-13, America's most violent gang.* Westport, CN: Hyperion.

Lopez, D. A., and Brummett, P. O. (2003). Gang membership and acculturation: ARSMA-II and choloization. *Crime and Delinquency, 49,* 627–642.

Luckenbill, D. F. (1977). Criminal homicide as a situated transaction. *Social Problems, 25,* 176–186.

Lyddane, D. (2009). The rap industry exacerbates the gang problem. In A. Soliz (Ed.), *Gangs* (pp. 73–79). Detroit: Gale Cengage Learning.

Lyman, M. D. (1989). *Gangland.* Springfield, IL: Thomas.

Lynskey, D. P., Winfree, L. T., Jr., Esbensen, F-A., and Clason, D. L. (2000). Linking gender, minority group status and family matters to self-control theory: A multivariate analysis of key self-control concepts in a youth-gang context. *Juvenile and Family Court Journal, 51* (3), 1–19.

MacDonald, N. (2001). *The graffiti subculture: Youth, masculinity and identity in London and New York.* New York: Palgrave.

MacKenzie, K., Hunt, G., and Joe-Laidler, K. (2005). Youth gangs and drugs: The case for marijuana. *Journal of Ethnicity in Substance Abuse, 4* (3–4), 99–134.

Main, F. (2012). Gangs using social media to spread violence. *Chicago Sun Times* (January 26). Retrieved from http://www.suntimes.com/news/metro/10256178-418/cyber-tagging-now-the-gang-graffiti-of-the-internet.html#.VFzzk4eFGgQ/.

Major, A. K., Egley, A., Jr., Howell, J. C., Mendenhall, B., and Armstrong, T. (2004). *Youth gangs in Indian country.* Washington, DC: Office of Juvenile Justice and Delinquency Prevention.

Mares, D. (2001). Gangstas or lager louts? Working class street gangs in Manchester. In M. W. Klein, H. J. Kerner, C. L. Maxson, and E. G. M. Weitekamp (Eds.), *The Eurogang paradox: Street gangs and youth groups in the U.S. and Europe* (pp. 153–164). London: Kluwer Academic.

Mares, D. (2010). Social disorganization and gang homicides in Chicago: A neighborhood level comparison of disaggregated homicides. *Youth Violence and Juvenile Justice, 8* (1), 38–57.

Marshall, B., Webb, B., and Tilley, N. (2005). *Rationalisation of current research on guns, gangs and other weapons: Phase 1.* London: University College London.

Martinez, J. F. E. (2008). Chavos banda in New York City. In L. Kontos and D. C. Brotherton (Eds.), *Encyclopedia of gangs* (pp. 21–24). Westport, CN: Greenwood Press.

Martinez, J. F. E., and Ramos, M. A. (2008). Crips. In L. Kontos and D. C. Brotherton (Eds.), *Encyclopedia of gangs* (pp. 43–46). Westport, CN: Greenwood Press.

Martinez, L. (2005). Gangs in Indian Country. *Law Enforcement Technology, 32* (2), 20–27.

Maruna, S. (2001). *Making good: How ex-convicts reform and rebuild their lives.* Washington, DC: American Psychological Association Books.

Maruna, S., LeBel, T. P., Mitchell, N., and Naples, M. (2004). Pygmalion in the reintegration process: Desistance from crime through the looking glass self. *Psychology, Crime and Law, 10* (3), 271–281.

Maruschak, L. M. (2006). *HIV in prisons, 2004.* Washington, DC: Bureau of Justice Statistics.

Maruschak, L. M. (2012). *HIV in prisons, 2001-2010.* Washington, DC: Bureau of Justice Statistics.

Massoglia, M. (2006). Desistance or displacement? The changing patterns of offending from adolescence to young adulthood. *Journal of Quantitative Criminology, 22,* 215–239.

Mata, A., Valdez, A., Alvarado, J., Cepeda, A., Cervantes, R., and Kaplan, C. D. (2002). Drug related violence among Mexican American youth in Laredo, TX: Preliminary findings. *Free Inquiry in Creative Sociology, 30,* 25–39.

Mateo, J. (2011). Street gangs of Honduras. In T. Bruneau, L. Dammert, and E. Skinner (Eds.), *Maras: Gang violence and security in Central America* (pp. 87–103). Austin: University of Texas Press.

Matsuda, K. N., Esbensen, F-A., and Carson, D. C. (2012). Putting the "gang" in "Eurogang": Characteristics of delinquent youth groups by different definitional approaches. In F-A. Esbensen and C. L. Maxson (Eds.), *Youth gangs in international perspective: Results from the Eurogang program of research* (pp. 17–33). New York: Springer.

Matza, D. (1964). *Delinquency and drift.* New York: Transaction.

Mauer, M. (2009). *The changing racial dynamics of the war on drugs.* Washington, DC: Sentencing Project.

Maxson, C. L. (1998). *Gang members on the move.* Washington, DC: Office of Juvenile Justice and Delinquency Prevention.

Maxson, C. L., Hennigan, K. M., and Sloane, D. C. (2005). "It's getting crazy out there": Can a civil gang injunction change a community? *Criminology and Public Policy, 4* (3), 577–598.

Maxson, C. L., Hennigan, K. M., and Sloane, D. C. (2006). For the sake of the neighborhood? Civil gang injunctions as a gang intervention tool in Southern California. In A. Egley Jr., C. L. Maxson, J. Miller, and

M. W. Klein (Eds.), *The modern gang reader* (3rd ed.) (pp. 394–406). Los Angeles: Roxbury.

Maxson, C. L., and Klein, M. W. (1990). Street gang violence: Twice as great or half as great? In C. R. Huff (Ed.), *Gangs in America* (pp. 71–102). Newbury Park, CA: Sage.

Maxson, C. L., and Klein, M. W. (1996). Defining gang homicide: An updated look at member and motive approaches. In C. R. Huff (Ed.), *Gangs in America* (2nd ed.) (pp. 3–20). Thousand Oaks, CA: Sage.

Maxson, C. L., Klein, M. W., and Gordon, M. (1985). Differences between gang and nongang homicides. *Criminology*, 23, 209–222.

Maxson, C. L., Whitlock, M. L., and Klein, M. W. (1998). Vulnerability to street gang membership: Implications for practice. *Social Service Review*, 70–91.

Mays, J. B. (1954). *Growing up in the city: A study of juvenile delinquency in an urban neighbourhood.* Liverpool: Liverpool University Press.

McCorkle, R. C., and Miethe, T. D. (1998). The political and organizations response to gangs: An examination of a "moral panic" in Nevada. *Justice Quarterly*, 15 (1), 41–64.

McDaniel, D. D. (2012). Risk and protective factors associated with gang affiliation among high-risk youth: A public health approach. *Injury Prevention*, 18 (4), 253–258.

McDaniel, D. D., Logan, J. E., and Schneiderman, J. U. (2014). Supporting gang violence prevention efforts: A public health approach for nurses. *The Online Journal of Nursing of Issues in Nursing*, 19, (1). Retrieved from http://nursingworld.org/MainMenuCategories /ANAMarketplace/ANAPeriodicals/OJIN/ TableofContents/Vol-19-2014/No1-Jan-2014/ Gang-Violence-Prevention-Public-Health-Approach .html/.

McDonald, K. (2008). Australian youth gangs. In L. Kontos and D. C. Brotherton (Eds.), *Encyclopedia of gangs* (pp. 8–10). Westport, CN: Greenwood Press.

McDonough, K. M. (2013). Combating gang-perpetrated witness intimidation with forfeiture by wrongdoing. *Seton Hall Law Review*, 43 (4), 1283–1313.

McGarrell, E. F., Olivares, K., Crawford, K., and Kroovand, N. (2000). *Returning justice to the community: The Indianapolis Juvenile Restorative Justice Experiment.* Indianapolis: Hudson Institute.

McPhail, M. (1991). *The myth of the maddening crowd.* New York: Aldine.

McVie, S. (2010). *Gang membership and knife carrying: Findings from the Edinburgh Study of Youth Transitions and Crime.* Edinburgh: Scottish Government Social Research.

Measham, F., Parker, H., and Aldridge, J. (2001). *Dancing on drugs: Risk, health and hedonism in the British club scene.* London: Free Association.

Measham, F., and Shiner, M. (2009). The legacy of "normalization": The role of classical and contemporary criminological theory in understanding young people's substance use. *International Journal of Drug Policy*, 20, 502–508.

Medina, J., Aldridge, J., Shute, J., and Ross, A. (2013). Measuring gang membership in England and Wales: A latent class analysis with Eurogang survey questions. *European Journal of Criminology*, 10, 591–605.

Melde, C., and Esbensen, F.-A. (2011). Gang membership as a turning point in the life course. *Criminology*, 49 (2), 513–552.

Melde, C., and Esbensen, F.-A. (2014). The relative impact of gang status: Identifying the mechanisms of change in delinquency. *Journal of Research in Crime and Delinquency*, 51 (3), 349–376.

Melde, C., Taylor, T. J., and Esbensen, F.-A. (2009). "I got your back": An examination of the protective function of gang membership in adolescence. *Criminology*, 47 (2), 565–594.

Mendoza-Denton, N. (2008). *Homegirls: Language and cultural practice among Latina youth gangs.* Hoboken, NJ: Wiley–Blackwell.

Merton, R. K. (1938). Social structure and anomie. *American Sociological Review*, 3 (5), 672–682.

Messerschmidt, J. W. (1993). *Masculinities and crime: Critique and reconceptualization of theory.* Lanham, MD: Rowman & Littlefield.

Messerschmidt, J. W. (1997). *Crime as structured action: Gender, race, class and crime in the making.* Thousand Oaks, CA: Sage.

Messerschmidt, J. W. (2000). *Nine lives: Adolescent masculinities, the body, and violence.* Oxford: Westview.

Messerschmidt, J. W. (2004). *Flesh and blood: Adolescent gender diversity and violence.* Lanham, MD: Rowman & Littlefield.

Metropolitan Police. (2006). *The Pan-London gang survey.* London: Metropolitan Police.

Mieczkowski, T. (1986). Geeking up and throwing down: Heroin street life in Detroit. *Criminology*, 24 (4), 645–666.

Miller, B. (2010). *Gang warfare in 18th century Boston.* Retrieved from http://outofthiscentury.wordpress.com/ 2010/02/16/18th-century-gang-warfare-in-boston/.

Miller, H. V., Barnes, J. C., and Hartley, R. D. (2011). Reconsidering Hispanic gang membership and acculturation in a multivariate context. *Crime and Delinquency, 53* (3), 331–355.

Miller, J. (1998). Gender and victimization risk among young women in gangs. *Journal of Research in Crime and Delinquency, 35,* 429–453.

Miller, J. (2001a). Young women's involvement in gangs in the United States: An overview. In M. W. Klein, H-J. Kerner, C. L. Maxson, and E. G. M. Weitekamp (Eds.), *The Eurogang paradox: Street gangs and youth groups in the US and Europe* (pp. 115–134). Amsterdam: Kluwer Academic.

Miller, J. (2001b). *One of the guys: Girls, gangs, and gender.* New York: Oxford University Press.

Miller, J., and Decker, S. H. (2001). Young women and gang violence: Gender, street offending, and violent victimization in gangs. *Justice Quarterly, 18,* 115–140.

Miller, J. A. (1995). Struggles over the symbolic: Gang style and the meanings of social control. In J. Ferrell and C. R. Sanders (Eds.), *Cultural criminology* (pp 213 234). Boston: Northeastern University Press.

Miller, W. B. (1958). Lower class culture as generating a milieu of gang delinquency. *Journal of Social Issues 14,* 5–19.

Miller, W. B. (1962). Impact of a total community delinquency control project. *Social Problems, 10,* 168–191.

Miller, W. B. (1973). The Molls. *Society, 11* (1), 32–35.

Miller, W. B. (1975). *Violence by youth gangs and youth groups as a crime problem in major American cities.* Washington, DC: Office of Juvenile Justice and Delinquency Prevention.

Miller, W. B. (1982). *Crime by youth gangs and groups in the United States.* Washington, DC: Office of Juvenile Justice and Delinquency Prevention.

Miller, W. B. (2001). *The growth of youth gang problems in the United States: 1970–1998.* Washington, DC: Office of Juvenile Justice and Delinquency Prevention.

Mills, A. (2013). UK youth street violence: An overview. In *EU street violence: Youth groups and violence in public spaces* (pp. 168–186). Paris: European Forum for Urban Security.

Minnis, A. M., Moore, J. G., Doherty, I. A., Rodas, C., Auerswald, C., Shiboski, S., and Padian, N. S. (2008). Gang exposure and pregnancy incidence among female adolescents in San Francisco: Evidence for the need to integrate reproductive health with violence prevention efforts. *American Journal of Epidemiology, 167* (1), 1102–1109.

Miranda, M. (2003). *Homegirls in the public sphere.* Austin: University of Texas Press.

Mock, B. (2006). Latino gang members in Southern California are terrorizing and killing blacks acting on orders from the Mexican Mafia. *Southern Poverty Law Center Intelligence Report, 124.* Retrieved from http://www.splcenter.org/get-informed/intelligence-report/browse-all-issues/2006/winter/la-blackout/.

Moffitt, T. (1993). Life-course-persistent and adolescence limited antisocial behavior: A developmental taxonomy. *Psychological Review, 100,* 674–701.

Moloney, M., Hunt, G., and Evans, K. (2008). Asian American identity and drug consumption: From acculturation to normalization. *Journal of Ethnicity in Substance Abuse 7,* 376–403.

Moloney, M., Hunt, G., and Joe-Laidler, K. (2010). Young mother (in the) hood: Gang girls' negotiation of new identities. *Journal of Youth Studies, 11,* 1–19.

Moloney, M., MacKenzie, K., Hunt, G., and Joe-Laidler, K. (2009). The path and promise of fatherhood for gang members. *British Journal of Criminology, 49,* 305–325.

Montgomery, M. (2009). Gangs are proliferating in prisons. In A. Soliz (Ed.), *Gangs* (pp. 89–98). Detroit: Greenhaven Press.

Moore, J. P., and Cook, I. L. (1999). *Highlights of the 1998 National Youth Gang Survey.* Washington, DC: Office of Juvenile Justice and Delinquency Prevention.

Moore, J. P., and Terrett, C. P. (1998). *Highlights of the 1996 National Youth Gang Survey.* Washington, DC: Office of Juvenile Justice and Delinquency Prevention.

Moore, J. P., and Terrett, C. P. (1999). *Highlights of the 1997 National Youth Gang Survey.* Washington, DC: Office of Juvenile Justice and Delinquency Prevention.

Moore, J. W. (1978). *Homeboys: Gangs, drugs and prison in the barrios of Los Angeles.* Philadelphia: Temple University Press.

Moore, J. W. (1985). Isolation and stigmatization in the development of an underclass: The case of Chicano gangs in East Los Angeles. *Social Problems, 33* (1), 1–12.

Moore, J. W. (1991). *Going down to the barrio: Homeboys and homegirls in change.* Philadelphia: Temple University Press.

Moore, J. W., and Devitt, M. (1989). The paradox of deviance in addicted Mexican American mothers. *Gender and Society, 3* (1), 53–70.

Moore, J. W., and Hagedorn, J. (1996). What happens to girls in the gang? In C. R. Huff (Ed.), *Gangs in America* (2nd ed.) (pp. 205–218). Thousand Oaks, CA: Sage.

Moore, J. W., Vigil, J. D., and Levy, J. (1995). Huisas of the street. *Latino Studies Journal, 6,* 27–48.

Moore, M. E., and Hiday, V. A. (2006). Mental health court outcomes: A comparison of re-arrest and re-arrest severity between mental health court and traditional court participants. *Law and Human Behavior, 30,* 659–674.

Moore, M. H. (1993). Violence prevention: Criminal justice or public health? *Health Affairs,* 34–45.

Moore, M. H. (1995). Public health and criminal justice approaches to prevention. *Crime and Justice, 19,* 237–262.

Morash, M. (1983). Gangs, groups, and delinquency. *British Journal of Criminology, 23,* 309–335.

Morbidity and Mortality Weekly Report. (1993) Gang-related outbreak of penicillinase-producing Neisseria Gonorrhoeae and other sexually transmitted diseases— Colorado Springs, Colorado, 1989–1991. *MMWR Surveillance Summaries, 42,* 25–28.

Morris, R. E., Harrison, E. A., Knox, G. W., Tromanhauser, E., Marquis, D. K., and Watt, L. L. (1995). Health risk behaviors survey from 39 juvenile correctional facilities in the United States. *Journal of Adolescent Health, 17* (6), 334–344.

Moser, C., and, Holland, J. (1997). *Urban poverty and violence in Jamaica.* Washington DC: World Bank.

Moule, R. K., Jr., Pyrooz, D. C., and Decker, S. H. (2014). Internet adoption and online behavior among American street gangs: Integrating gangs and organizational theory. *British Journal of Criminology, 2,* 199–221.

Muggleton, D. (2000). *Inside subculture: The postmodern meaning of style.* Oxford: Berg.

Murphy, J. (2008). *Tackling Gangs Action Programme: European Serious Organised Crime Conference.* London: Home Office.

Myers, T. A. (2008). The unconstitutionality, ineffectiveness, and alternatives of gang injunctions. *Michigan Journal of Race and Law, 14,* 285–306.

Nagin, D. S., and Paternoster, R. (2000). Population heterogeneity and state dependence: State of the evidence and directions for future research. *Journal of Quantitative Criminology, 16,* 117–144.

National Association for the Advancement of Colored People. (n.d.). *Criminal justice fact sheet.* Retrieved from http://www.naacp.org/pages/criminal-justice-fact-sheet/.

National Gang Center. (n.d.). *National Youth Gang Survey analysis.* Retrieved from https://www.nationalgang center.gov/survey-analysis/demographics

National Gang Intelligence Center. (2007). *Gang-related activity in the US armed forces increasing.* Retrieved from http://militarytimes.com/static/projects/pages/ngic_gangs.pdf/.

National Gang Intelligence Center. (2009). *National gang threat assessment 2009.* Retrieved from https://www.fbi.gov/stats-services/publications/national-gang-threat-assessment-2009-pdf

Needham, S., and Quintiliani, K. (2007). Cambodians in Long Beach, California: The making of a community. *Journal of Immigrant and Refugee Studies, 5* (1), 29–53.

Needle, J. A., and Stapleton, W. V. (1982). *Police handling of youth gangs.* Washington, DC: National Juvenile Justice Assessment Center.

Nurge, D. (2003). Liberating yet limiting: The paradox of female gang membership. In L. Kontos, D. Brotherton, and L. Barrios (Eds.), *Gangs and society: Alternative perspectives* (pp. 161–182). New York: Columbia University Press.

O'Connell, D. J. (2003). Investigating latent trait and life course theories as predictors of recidivism among an offender sample. *Journal of Criminal Justice, 31,* 455–467.

Ogden, C. L., Kit, B. K., Carroll, M. D., and Park, S. (2011). *Consumption of sugar drinks in the United States, 2005–2008.* Hyattsville, MD: National Center for Health Statistics.

Ohene, S., Ireland, M., and Blum, R. W. (2005). The clustering of risk behaviors among Caribbean youth. *Maternal and Child Health Journal, 9* (1), 91–100.

Okie S. (2007). Sex, drugs, prisons, and HIV. *The New England Journal of Medicine, 356* (2), 105–108.

Olate, R., Salas-Wright, C., and Vaughn, M. G. (2012). Predictors of violence and delinquency among high risk youth and youth gang members in San Salvador, El Salvador. *International Social Work, 55* (3), 383–401.

Olds, D. L., Eckenrode, J., Henderson, C. R., Jr., Kitzman, H., Powers, J., Cole, R., Sidora, K., Morris, P., Pettitt, L. M., and Luckey, D. (1997). Long-term effects of home visitation on maternal life course and child abuse and neglect: Fifteen-year follow-up of a randomized trial. *Journal of the American Medical Association, 278* (8), 637–643.

Olson, D., and Dooley, B. D. (2006). Gang membership and community corrections populations: Characteristics and recidivism rates relative to other offenders. In J. F. Short Jr. and L. A. Hughes (Eds.), *Studying Youth Gangs* (pp. 193–202). Lanham, MD: Altamira Press.

Olzak, S. (1989). Labor unrest, immigration, and ethnic conflict in urban America, 1880–1914. *American Journal of Sociology, 94* (6), 1303–1333.

O'Malley, P., and Mugford, S. (1994). Crime, excitement, and modernity. In G. Barak (Ed.), *Varieties of Criminology* (pp. 189–211). London: Praeger.

Omori, M. K. (2013). Moral panics and morality policy: The impact of media, political ideology, drug use, and manufacturing on methamphetamine legislation in the United States. *Journal of Drug Issues, 43* (4), 517–534.

Ompad, D. C., Strathdee, S. A., Celentano, D. D., Latkin, C., Poduska, J. M., Kellam, S. G., and Ialongo, N. S. (2006). Predictors of early initiation of vaginal and oral sex among urban young adults in Baltimore, Maryland. *Archives of Sexual Behavior, 35*, 53–65.

O'Neal, E. N., Decker, S. H., Moule, R. K., and Pyrooz, D. C. (2014). Girls, gangs, and getting out: Gender differences and similarities in leaving the gang. *Youth Violence and Juvenile Justice.* doi:10.1177/1541204014551426.

Orcutt, J. D., and Rudy, D. R. (Eds.). (2003). *Drugs, alcohol, and social problems.* Lanham, MD: Rowman & Littlefield.

Oualhaci, A. (2008). French gangs. In L. Kontos and D. C. Brotherton (Eds.), *Encyclopedia of gangs* (pp. 52–55). Westport, CN: Greenwood Press.

Oyserman, D., and Fryberg, S. (2006). The possible selves of diverse adolescent: Content and function across gender, race and national origin. In C. Dunkel and J. Kerpelman (Eds.), *Possible selves: Theory, research and application* (pp. 17–39). New York: Nova Science.

Oyserman, D., and Markus, H. (1990a). Possible selves in balance: Implications for delinquency. *Journal of Social Issues, 46* (2), 141–157.

Oyserman, D., and Markus, H. (1990b). Possible selves and delinquency. *Journal of Personality and Social Psychology, 59* (1), 112–125.

Padilla, F. (1992). *The gang as an American enterprise.* New Brunswick, NJ: Rutgers University Press.

Papachristos, A. V., and Kirk, D. S. (2006). Neighborhood effects on street gang behavior. In J. F. Short and L. A. Hughes (Eds.), *Studying youth gangs* (pp. 63–84). Lanham, MD: Altamira Press.

Papachristos, A., Meares, T., and Fagan, J. (2007). Attention felons: Evaluating Project Safe Neighborhoods in Chicago. *Journal of Empirical Legal Studies, 4*, 223–272.

Papachristos, A. V., Meares, T. L., and Fagan, J. (2012). Why do criminals obey the law? The influence of legitimacy and social networks on active gun offenders. *Journal of Criminal Law and Criminology, 102* (2), 397–440.

Park, R., and Burgess, E. W. (1925). *The city.* Chicago: University of Chicago Press.

Parker, H. (1974). *A view from the boys.* London: David & Charles.

Parker, H., Aldridge, J., and Measham, F. (1998). *Illegal leisure: The normalisation of adolescent recreational drug use.* London: Routledge.

Parker, H., Measham, F., and Aldridge, J. (1995). *Drugs futures: Changing patterns of drug use amongst English youth.* London: Institute for the Study of Drug Dependence.

Parker, H., Williams, L., and Aldridge, J. (2002). The normalization of "sensible" recreational drug use: Further evidence from the North West England Longitudinal Study. *Sociology, 36*, 941–964.

Paternoster, R., and Brame, R. (1997). Multiple routes to delinquency? A test of developmental and general theories of crime. *Criminology, 35* (1), 49–84.

Paternoster, R., and Bushway, S. (2009). Desistance and the "feared self": Toward an identity theory of criminal desistance. *Journal of Criminal Law and Criminology, 99* (4), 1103–1156.

Patrick, J. (1973). *A Glasgow gang observed.* London: Eyre Methuen.

Patrick, W. L. (2012). From the chat room to the courtroom: Social media postings as evidence. *California Bar Journal* (May). Retrieved from: http://apps.calbar.ca.gov/mcleselfstudy/mcle_home.aspx?testID=61/.

Patton, D. U., Eschmann, R. D., and Butler, D. A. (2013). Internet banging: New trends in social media, gang violence, masculinity and hip hop. *Computers in Human Behavior, 29*, A54–A59.

Pearson, G. (1983). *Hooligan: A history of respectable fears.* London: Macmillan.

Peisner, D. (2010). Jamaican dancehall: Gangster's paradise. *SPIN* (September 14).

Pelz, M. E., Marquart, J. W., and Pelz, C. T. (1991). Right-wing extremism in the Texas prisons: The rise and fall of the Aryan Brotherhood of Texas. *The Prison Journal, 71*, 23–37.

Pereira, M. A., Kartashov, A. I., Ebbeling, C. B., Van Horn, L., Slattery, M. L., Jacobs, D. R., and Ludwig, D. S. (2005). Fast-food habits, weight gain, insulin resistance (the CARDIA study): 15-year prospective analysis. *The Lancet, 365* (9453), 36–42.

Perrone, P., and Chesney-Lind, M. (1997). Representations of gangs and delinquency: Wild in the streets? *Social Justice, 24*, 96–116.

Perrone, S., and White, R. (2000). Young people and gangs. *Trends and Issues in Criminal Justice, 167*. Canberra: Australian Institute of Criminology.

Peterson, D. (2014). Girlfriends, gun-holders, and ghetto-rats? Moving beyond narrow views of girls in gangs. In C. L. Maxson, A. Egley Jr., J. Miller, and M. W. Klein (Eds.), *The modern gang reader* (4th ed.) (pp. 271–281). New York: Oxford University Press.

Peterson, D., Miller, J., and Esbensen, F-A. (2001). The impact of sex composition on gangs and gang member delinquency. *Criminology, 39* (2), 411–440.

Peterson, D., Miller, J., and Esbensen, F-A. (2006). The impact of sex composition on gangs and gang member delinquency. In A. Egley Jr., C. L. Maxson, J. Miller, and M. W. Klein (Eds.), *The modern gang reader* (3rd ed.) (pp. 206–221). Los Angeles: Roxbury.

Peterson D., Taylor, T. J., and Esbensen, F-A. (2004). Gang membership and violent victimization. *Justice Quarterly, 21*, 793–815.

Phillips, S. A. (1999). *Wallbangin': Graffiti and gangs in LA*. Chicago: University of Chicago Press.

Picard-Fritsche, S., and Cerniglia, L. (2013). *Testing a public health approach to gun violence: An evaluation of Crown Heights Save Our Streets, a replication of the Cure Violence model*. New York: Center for Court Innovation.

Pilkington, H. (2007). Beyond "peer pressure": Rethinking drug use and "youth culture." *International Journal of Drug Policy, 18*, 213–224.

Pitts, J. (2007). *Reluctant gangsters: Youth gangs in Waltham Forest*. Bedfordshire: University of Bedfordshire.

Pitts, J. (2008). *Reluctant gangsters: The changing face of youth crime*. Cullompton, UK: Willan.

Portillos, E. L. (1999). Women, men, and gangs: The social construction of gender in the barrio. In M. Chesney-Lind and J. Hagedorn (Eds.), *Female gangs in America: Essays on girls, gangs and gender* (pp. 232–244). Chicago: Lake View Press.

Preble, E. J., and Casey, J. J. (1969). Taking care of business: The heroin user's life on the street. *International Journal of Addictions, 4* (1), 1–24.

Presdee, M. (1994). Young people, culture, and the construction of crime: Doing wrong versus doing crime. In G. Barak (Ed.), *Varieties of Criminology* (pp. 179–187). London: Praeger.

Presdee, M. (2000). *Cultural criminology and the carnival of crime*. London: Routledge.

Produce for Better Health Foundation (2010). *State of the Plate: 2010 Study on America's Consumption of Fruits and Vegetables*. Retrieved from http://www.pbhfoundation.org/.

Pyrooz, D. C. (2012). Structural covariates of gang homicide in large U.S. cities. *Journal of Research in Crime and Delinquency, 49* (4), 489–518.

Pyrooz, D. C., and Decker, S. H. (2011). Motives and methods for leaving the gang: Understanding the process of gang desistance. *Journal of Criminal Justice, 39* (5), 417–425.

Pyrooz, D. C., and Decker, S. H. (2013). Delinquent behavior, violence, and gang involvement in China. *Journal of Quantitative Criminology, 29*, 251–272.

Pyrooz, D. C., Decker, S. H., and Fleisher, M. (2011). From the street to the prison, from the prison to the street: Understanding and responding to prison gangs. *Journal of Aggression, Conflict, and Peace Research, 3* (1), 12–24.

Pyrooz, D. C., Decker, S. H., and Moule, R. K., Jr. (2013). Criminal and routine activities in online settings: Gangs, offenders, and the Internet. *Justice Quarterly, 30* (3), 1–29.

Pyrooz, D. C., Decker, S. H., and Webb, V. J. (2014). The ties that bind: Desistance from gangs. *Crime and Delinquency, 60* (4), 491–516.

Pyrooz, D. C., Fox, A. M., and Decker, S. H. (2010). Racial and ethnic heterogeneity, economic disadvantage, and gangs: A macro-level study of gang membership in urban America. *Justice Quarterly, 27* (6), 867–892.

Pyrooz, D. C., and Sweeten, G. (2015). Gang membership between ages 5 and 17 in the United States. *Journal of Adolescent Health*. doi:10.1016/j.jadohealth.2014.11.018.

Pyrooz, D. C., Sweeten, G., and Piquero, A. R. (2013). Continuity and change in gang membership and gang embeddedness. *Journal of Research in Crime and Delinquency, 50* (2), 239–271.

Quicker, J. (1999). The Chicana gang: A preliminary description. In M. Chesney-Lind and J. Hagedorn (Eds.), *Female gangs in America: Essays on girls, gangs and gender* (pp. 48–56). Chicago: Lake View Press.

Quinones, S. (2013). Azusa 12 street gang leader, son sentenced to prison. *Los Angeles Times*, January 15. Retrieved from http://articles.latimes.com/2013/jan/15/local/la-me-0115-gang-sentence-20130115/.

Ralph, P. H., and Marquart, J. W. (1991). Gang violence in Texas prisons. *The Prison Journal, 71*, 38–49.

Ranum, E. C. (2011). Street gangs in Guatemala. In T. Bruneau, L. Dammert, and E. Skinner (Eds.), *Maras:*

Gang violence and security in Central America (pp. 71–86). Austin: University of Texas Press.

Reinarman, C., and Levine, H. G. (1997). The crack attack, politics and media in the crack scare. In C. Reinarman and H. G. Levine (Eds.), *Crack in America: Demon drugs and social justice* (pp. 18–51). Berkeley: University of California Press.

Reisig, M. D. (2002). Administrative control and inmate homicide. *Homicide Studies, 6*, 84–103.

Reiss, A., Jr., and Roth, J. A. (1993). *Understanding and preventing violence.* Washington, DC: National Academy Press.

Rennison, C. M., and Melde, C. (2009). Exploring the use of victim surveys to study gang crime: Prospects and possibilities. *Criminal Justice Review, 34* (4), 489–514.

Riveland, C. (1999). Prison management trends, 1975–2025. *Crime and Justice, 26*, 163–203.

Roberts, A. R., and Bender, K. (2006). Juvenile offender suicide: Prevalence, risk factors, assessment, and crisis intervention protocols. *International Journal of Emergency Mental Health, 8* (4), 255–265.

Robins, D. (1992). *Tarnished vision: Crime and conflict in the inner city.* Oxford: Oxford University Press.

Robinson, C. (2001). Methamphetamine use and sales among gang members: The cross-over effect. *Journal of Gang Research, 9* (1), 39–52.

Rocha, J. L. (2011). Street gangs of Nicaragua. In T. Bruneau, L. Dammert, and E. Skinner (Eds.), *Maras: Gang violence and security in Central America* (pp. 105–120). Austin: University of Texas Press.

Rodgers, W. (2008). Understanding the black-white earnings gap. *The American Prospect.* Retrieved from http://prospect.org/article/understanding-black-white-earnings-gap/.

Rodriguez, L. J. (1993). *Always running: La via loca: Gang days in LA.* New York: Touchstone.

Rohloff, A., and Wright, S. (2010). Moral panic and social theory: Beyond the heuristic. *Current Sociology, 58* (3), 403–419.

Rojek, C. (2000). *Leisure and culture.* London: Macmillan.

Roman, C. G., Cahill, M., Lachman, P., Lowry, S., Orosco, C., McCarty, C., Denver, M., and Pedroza, J. (2012). *Social networks, delinquency, and gangs: Using a neighborhood framework to examine the influence of network composition and structure in a Latino community.* Washington, DC: Urban Institute.

Romero, E. G., Teplin, L. A., McClelland, G. M., Abram, K. M., Welty, L. J., and Washburn, J. J. (2013). A longitudinal study of the prevalence, development, and persistence of HIV/STI risk behaviors in delinquent youth: Implications for health care in the community. In B. Sanders, Y. Thomas, and B. Deeds (Eds.), *Crime, HIV and health: Intersections of criminal justice and public health concerns* (pp. 19–62). New York: Springer.

Rose, T. (1994). *Black noise: Rap music and black culture in contemporary America.* Hanover, NH: Wesleyan University Press.

Rosenfeld, R., Bray, T. M., and Egley, A. (1999). Facilitating violence: A comparison of gang-motivated, gang-affiliated, and nongang youth homicides. *Journal of Quantitative Criminology, 15* (4), 495–516.

Ross, J. I. (2008). Gangs in prison. In L. Kontos and D. C. Brotherton (Eds.), *Encyclopedia of gangs* (pp. 98–101). Westport, CN: Greenwood Press.

Rowe, G. (2013). *Gods of mischief: My undercover vendetta to take down the Vagos outlaw motorcycle gang.* New York: Touchstone.

Rubio, M. (2011). Government responses and the dark side of gang suppression in Central America. In T. Bruneau, L. Dammert, and E. Skinner (Eds.), *Maras: Gang violence and security in Central America* (pp. 160–180). Austin: University of Texas Press.

Ruddell, R., Decker, S. H., and Egley, A., Jr. (2006). Gang interventions in jails: A national analysis. *Criminal Justice Review, 31*, 1–14.

Rudovsky, D., and Rosenthal, L. (2013). The constitutionality of stop-and-frisk in New York City. *University of Pennsylvania Law Review Online, 117*. Retrieved from http://www.pennlawreview.com/debates/index.php?id=49/.

Ruggiero, V. (1993). Brixton, London: A drug culture without a drug economy? *The International Journal of Drug Policy, 4* (2), 83–90.

Ruggiero, V. (2000). *Crime and markets: Essays in anti-criminology.* Oxford: Oxford University Press.

Ruggiero, V., and South, N. (1995). *Eurodrugs: Drug use, markets, and trafficking in Europe.* London: UCL Press.

Saad, L. (2012). Nearly half of American drink soda daily. *Gallup Well-Being* (July 23). Retrieved from http://www.gallup.com/poll/156116/nearly-half-americans-drink-soda-daily.aspx/.

Salagaev, A., Shaskin, A., Sherbakova, I., and Touriyanskiy, E. (2005). Contemporary Russian gangs: History, membership, and crime involvement. In S. H. Decker and F. M. Weerman (Eds.), *European street gangs and troublesome youth groups* (pp. 169–192). New York: Altamira Press.

Salazar, L. F., Crosby, R. A., DiClemente, R. J., Wingood, G. M., Rose, E., Sales, J. M., and Caliendo, A. M. (2007). Personal, relational, and peer-level risk factors for laboratory confirmed STD prevalence among low-income African American adolescent families. *Sexually Transmitted Diseases, 334* (10), 761–766.

Sampson, R. J., and Laub, J. (1993). *Crime in the making: Pathways and turning points through the life course.* Cambridge, MA: Harvard University Press.

Sampson, R. J., and Laub, J. H. (2005). A life-course view on the development of crime. *The Annals of Academy of Political and Social Science, 602* (12), 12–45.

Sampson, R. J., and Lauritsen, J. L. (1990). Deviant lifestyles, proximity to crime, and the offender–victim link in personal violence. *Journal of Research in Crime and Delinquency, 27* (2), 110–139.

Sampson, R. J., and Lauritsen, J. L. (1994). Violet victimization and offending: Individual, situation and community-level risk factors. In A. J. Reiss Jr. and J. A. Roth (Eds.), *Understanding and prevention violence,* Volume 3, *Social influences.* Washington, DC: National Research Council.

Sampson, R. J., and Lauritsen, J. L. (1997). Racial and ethnic disparities in crime and criminal justice in the United States. In M. Tonry (Ed.), *Ethnicity, crime and immigration: Comparative and cross-national perspectives* (pp. 311–374). Chicago: University of Chicago Press.

Sampson, R. J., Raudenbush, S. W., and Earls, F. (1997). Neighborhoods and violent crime: A multilevel study of collective efficacy. *Science, 277,* 918–924.

Sampson, R. J., and Wilson, W. J. (1995). Towards a theory of race, class, and urban inequality. In J. Hagan and R. D. Peterson (Eds.), *Crime and inequality* (p. 37–56). Stanford, CA: Stanford University Press.

Sanders, B. (2005a). *Youth crime and youth culture in the inner city.* London: Routledge.

Sanders, B. (2005b). In the club: Ecstasy use and supply in a London nightclub. *Sociology, 392,* 241–258.

Sanders, B. (Ed.). (2006a). *Clubs, drugs and young people: Sociological and public health perspectives.* Aldershot, UK: Ashgate.

Sanders, B. (2006b). Young people, clubs and drugs: In B. Sanders (Ed.), *Clubs, drugs and young people: Sociological and public health perspectives* (pp. 1–11). Aldershot, UK: Ashgate.

Sanders, B. (2012). Gang youth, substance use patterns, and drug normalization. *Journal of Youth Studies, 15* (8), 978–994.

Sanders, B. (2013). An overview of a gang diversion collaboration operated by the Carson Sheriff's Station in Los Angeles. *The Journal of Gang Research, 21* (1), 43–52.

Sanders, B. (in press). Ethnicity and drug use policy in the US. In T. Kolind, B. Thom, and G. Hunt (Eds.), *Sage handbook of drug and alcohol studies* (Volume I). Thousand Oaks, CA: Sage.

Sanders, B., and Lankenau, S. E. (2006). A public health model for studying gangs. In J. F. Short and L. A. Hughes (Eds.), *Studying youth gangs* (pp. 117–128). Lanham, MD: Altamira Press.

Sanders, B., Lankenau, S. E., and Bloom, J. J. (2010). Putting in work: Qualitative research on substance abuse and other risk behaviors among gang youth in Los Angeles. *Substance Use and Misuse, 45* (5), 736–753.

Sanders, B., Lankenau, S. E., and Jackson-Bloom, J. (2009). Risky sexual behaviors among a sample of gang youth in Los Angeles. *The Journal of Equity in Health, 2* (1), 61–71.

Sanders, B., Lankenau, S. E., Jackson Bloom, J., and Hathazi, D. (2008). Multiple drug use and polydrug use among homeless "traveling" youth. *Journal of Ethnicity in Substance Abuse, 71,* 23–40.

Sanders, B., Schneiderman, J. U., Loken, A., Lankenau, S. E., and Jackson-Bloom, J. (2009). Gang youth as a vulnerable population for nursing intervention. *Public Health Nursing, 26* (4), 346–352.

Sanders, B., Thomas, Y., and Deeds, B. (2013). Crime and public health in the United States. In B. Sanders, Y. Thomas, and B. Deeds (Eds.), *Crime, HIV and health: Intersections of criminal justice and public health concerns* (pp. 1–16). New York: Springer.

Sanders, B., Valdez, A., Hunt, G., Joe-Laidler, K., Molloney, M., and Cepeda, A. (2013). Gang youth, risk behaviors and negative health outcomes. In B. Sanders, Y. Thomas, and B. Deeds (Eds.), *Crime, HIV and health: Intersections of criminal justice and public health concerns* (pp. 113–127). New York: Springer.

Sanders, W. B. (1994). *Gangbangs and drive-bys: Grounded culture and juvenile gang violence.* New York: de Gruyter.

Sanders, W. B. (1997). Preliminary test of the theory of grounded culture and gang delinquency. *Free Inquiry in Creative Sociology, 25,* 59–64.

Sanders, W. S. (2002). "Breadren": Exploring the group context of young offenders in an inner city English borough. *International Journal of Comparative and Applied Criminal Justice, 26*, 101–114.

Sante, L. (1991). *Low life: Lures and snares of old New York.* New York: Vintage Books.

Schalet, A., Hunt, G., and Joe-Laidler, K. (2003). Respectability and autonomy: The articulation and meaning of sexuality among the girls in the gang. *Journal of Contemporary Ethnography, 32*, 108–143.

Schlosser, E. (1998). The prison–industrial complex. *The Atlantic Monthly* (December). Retrieved from http://www.theatlantic.com/magazine/archive/1998/12/the-prison-industrial-complex/4669/.

Schneider, E. C. (1999). *Vampires, Dragons and Egyptian Kings: Youth gangs in postwar New York.* Princeton, NJ: Princeton University Press.

Schoville, C. (2008). *Surenos: 2008.* Rocky Mountain Information Network: Phoenix. Retrieved from http://publicintelligence.net/ules-surenos-2008-special-gang-report/.

Schreck, C. J., Stewart, E. A., and Osgood, D. W. (2008). A reappraisal of the overlap of violent offenders and victims. *Criminology, 46* (4), 871–906.

Scott, G. S. (2004). Jabbing blow, pitching rocks, and stacking paper: How drug-selling street gangs organize the reentry of male ex-convicts into the community. In J. L. Krienert and M. S. Fleisher (Eds.), *Crime and employment: Critical issues in crime reduction for corrections* (pp. 106–140). New York: Altamira Press.

Scott, P. (1956). Gangs and delinquent groups in London. *The British Journal of Delinquency, 7*, 4–26.

Sela-Shayovitz, R. (2012). The impact of globalization, migration, and social group processes on Neo-Nazi youth gangs. In F-A. Esbensen and C. L. Maxson (Eds.), *Youth gangs in international perspective: Results from the Eurogang Program of research* (pp. 211–224). Springer: New York.

Sharp, C., Aldridge, J., and Medina, J. (2006). *Delinquent youth groups and offending behaviour: Findings from the 2004 Offending, Crime and Justice Survey.* London. Home Office.

Shashkin, A. (2008). Origins and development of racist skinheads in Moscow. In F. van Gemert, D. Peterson, and I-L. Lien (Eds.), *Street gangs, migration and ethnicity* (pp. 97–114). Cullompton, UK: Willan.

Shaw, C. R., and McKay, H. D. (1942). *Juvenile delinquency and urban areas.* Chicago: University of Chicago Press.

Shelden, R. G. (1991). A comparison of gang members and non-gang members in a prison setting. *The Prison Journal, 71*, 50–60.

Shelden, R. G. (1999). *Detention diversion advocacy: An evaluation.* Washington, DC: Office of Juvenile Justice and Delinquency Prevention.

Shelden, R. G., Tracy, S. K., and Brown, W. B. (2001). *Youth gangs in American society* (2nd ed.). Belmont, CA: Wadsworth.

Shildrick, T. (2002). Young people, drug use, and the question of normalization. *Journal of Youth Studies, 5* (1), 35–48.

Short, J. F., Jr. (1996). *Gangs and adolescent violence.* University of Colorado, Boulder: Center for the Study and Prevention of Violence.

Short, J. F., Jr. (2006). Why study gangs? An intellectual journey. In J. F. Short and L. A. Hughes (Eds.), *Studying youth gangs* (pp. 1–14). Lanham, MD: Altamira Press.

Short, J. F., Jr., and Strodtbeck, F. L. (1965). *Group process and gang delinquency.* Chicago: University of Chicago Press.

Shover, N. (1972). Structures and careers in burglary. *Journal of Criminal Law, Criminology, and Police Science, 63* (4), 540–549.

Shover, N. (1983). The latter stages of ordinary property offenders careers. *Social Problems, 31*, 28–218.

Shover, N., and Thompson, C. (1992). Age, differential expectations, and crime desistance. *Criminology, 30*, 89–104.

Shropshire, S., and McFarquhar, M. (2002). *Developing multi-agency strategies to address the street gang culture and reduce gun violence among young people.* Manchester: Shropshire and McFarquhar Consultancy.

Siegel, L. (2003). Gangs and the law. In L. Kontos, D. C. Brotherton, and L. Barrios (Eds.), *Gangs and society: Alternative perspectives* (pp. 213–227). New York: Columbia University Press.

Sikes, G. (1997). *Eight ball chicks: A year in the violent world of girl gangsters.* New York: Doubleday.

Simi, P. (2006). Hate groups of street gangs? The emergence of racist skinheads. In J. F. Short Jr. and L. A. Hughes (Eds.), *Studying youth gangs* (pp. 145–159). Lanham, MD: Altamira Press.

Simi, P. (2008). Racist skinheads in the US. In L. Kontos and D. C. Brotherton (Eds.), *Encyclopedia of gangs* (pp. 196–201). Westport, CN: Greenwood Press.

Sinclair, R., and Grekul, J. (2012). Aboriginal youth gangs in Canada: (De)constructing an epidemic. *First Peoples Child and Family Review, 7* (1), 8–28.

Singer, M., Clair, S., Schensul, J., Huebner, C., Eiserman, J., Pino, R., and Garcia, J. (2005). Dust in the wind:

The growing use of embalming fluid among youth in Hartford, CT. *Substance Use and Misuse, 40* (8), 1035–1050.

Skogan, W. G., Hartnett, S. M., Bump, N., and Dubois, J. (2009). *Evaluation of Chicago-Ceasefire*. Washington, DC: National Institute of Justice. Available at https://www.ncjrs.gov/pdffiles1/nij/grants/227181.pdf

Skolnick, J. (1990). The social structure of street drug dealing. *American Journal of Police, 9*, 1–41.

Slovic, P. (1987). Perception of risk. *Science, 236*, 280–285.

Smithson, H., Ralphs, R., and Williams, P. (2012). Used and abused: The problematic usage of gang terminology in the United Kingdom and its implications for ethnic minority youth. *British Journal of Criminology, 53* (1), 113–128.

Snyder, H. N., and Sickmund, M. (1999). *Juvenile offenders and victims: 1999 national report*. Washington, DC: Office of Juvenile Justice and Delinquency Prevention.

Solis, A., Schwartz, W., and Hinton, T. (2003). *Gang Resistance is Paramount (G.R.I.P.) program evaluation: Final report*. Los Angeles: University of Southern California.

Sommers, I., Baskin, D., and Fagan, J. (1994). Getting out of the life: Desistance by female street offenders. *Deviant Behavior, 15*, 125–149.

Song, D. H., Naude, G. P., Gilmore, D. A., and Bongard, F. (1996). Gang warfare: The medical repercussions. *Journal of Trauma, Injury, Infection and Critical Care, 40*, 810–815.

Sorenson, S. B. (2003). Public health and homicide. In C. R. Block and R. Block (Eds.), *Public health and criminal justice approaches to homicide research: Proceedings of the 2003 meeting of the homicide research working group* (pp. 5–11). Chicago: Homicide Research Working Group Publications.

Southgate, D. E. (2008). Rap music. In L. Kontos and D. C. Brotherton (Eds.), *Encyclopedia of gangs* (pp. 201–208). Westport, CN: Greenwood Press.

Sparks, R. (1992). *Television and the drama of crime: Moral tales and the place of crime in public life*. Philadelphia: Open University Press.

Spergel, I. (1964). *Racketville, Slumtown, Haulburg: An exploratory study of delinquent subcultures*. Chicago: University of Chicago Press.

Spergel, I. (1995). *The youth gang problem: A community approach*. Oxford: Oxford University Press.

Spergel, I. A. (2007). *Reducing youth gang violence: The Little Village Gang Project in Chicago*. New York: Altamira Press.

Spergel, I. A., and Curry, G. D. (1990). Strategies and perceived agency effectiveness in dealing with the youth gang problem. In C. R. Huff (Ed.), *Gangs in America* (pp. 288–309). Newbury Park, CA: Sage.

Spergel, I. A., Wa, K. M., and Sosa, R. V. (2006). The Comprehensive, Community-Wide Gang Program model: Success and failure. In J. F. Short and L. A. Hughes (Eds.), *Studying youth gangs* (pp. 203–223). Lanham, MD: Altamira Press.

Steffensmeier, D., and Schwartz, J. (2004). Trends in female criminality: Is crime still a man's world? In B. R. Price and N. J. Sokoloff (Eds.), *The criminal justice system and women: Offenders, prisons, victims and workers* (pp. 95–111). New York: McGraw-Hill.

Steinberg, J., Grella, C. E., and Boudov, M. R. (2013). Risky sexual behavior and negative health consequences among incarcerated female adolescents: Implications for public health policy and practice. In B. Sanders, Y. Thomas, and B. Deeds (Eds.), *Crime, HIV and health: Intersections of criminal justice and public health concerns* (pp. 63–79). New York: Springer.

Stelfox, P. (1998). Policing lower levels of organised crime in England and Wales. *The Howard Journal, 37* (4), 393–406.

Stephenson, S. (2008). Russian gangs. In L. Kontos and D. C. Brotherton (Eds.), *Encyclopedia of gangs* (pp. 214–216). Westport, CN: Greenwood Press.

Stephenson, S. (2011). The Kazan Leviathan: Russian street gangs as agents of social order. *The Sociological Review, 59* (2), 324–347.

Stephenson, S. (2012). The violent practices of youth territorial groups in Moscow. *Europe–Asia Studies, 64* (1), 69–90.

Stewart, D. G., Brown, S. A., and Myers, M. G. (1997). Antisocial behavior and psychoactive substance involvement among Hispanic and non-Hispanic Caucasian adolescents in substance abuse treatment. *Journal of Child and Adolescent Substance Abuse, 6*, 1–22.

Stewart, E. A., Schreck, C. J., and Simons, R. L. (2006). "I aint gonna let no one disrespect me": Does the code of the street reduce or increase violent victimization among African American adolescents? *Journal of Research in Crime and Delinquency, 43*, 427–458.

Stoltze, F. (2011). Federal indictment says Latino gang Azusa 13 targeted African-Americans. June 8, 2011. Retrieved from http://www.scpr.org/news/2011/06/08/27151/federal-indictment-says-latino-gang-targeted-afric/.

Stoltze, F. (2012). Forget the LA Riots—Historic 1992 Watts gang truce was the big news. May 4, *Off-Ramp*. Retrieved from http://www.scpr.org/programs/offramp/

2012/05/04/26351/forget-the-la-riots-historic-1992-watts-gang-truce/.

Stretesky, P. B., and Pogrebin, M. R. (2007). Gang-related gun violence: Socialization, identity, and self. *Journal of Contemporary Ethnography, 36* (1), 85–114.

Stringer, H. (2007). Gangs in the E.D.: Nurses ensure neutral turf. *Nurseweek, California Edition, 20* (19), 10–11.

Strosnider, K. (2002). Anti-gang ordinances after *City of Chicago v. Morales*: The intersection of race, vagueness doctrine, and equal protection in the criminal law. *American Criminal Law Review, 39,* 101–146.

Substance Abuse and Mental Health Services Administration. (2011). *Results from the 2010 National Survey on Drug Use and Health: Summary of national findings.* Rockville, MD: Substance Abuse and Mental Health Services Administration.

Substance Abuse and Mental Health Services Administration. (2012). *Results from the 2011 National Survey on Drug Use and Health: Volume I. Summary of National Findings.* Rockville, MD: Office of Applied Studies.

Sullivan, M. L. (1989). *"Getting paid": Youth crime and work in the inner city.* Ithaca, NY: Cornell University Press.

Sullivan, M. L. (2006). Are "gang" studies dangerous? Youth violence, local context, and the problem of reification. In J. F. Short and L. A. Hughes (Eds.), *Studying youth gangs* (pp. 15–35). Lanham, MD: Altamira Press.

Surette, R. (1992). *Media, crime and criminal justice.* Pacific Grove, CA: Brooks/Cole.

Sutherland, E. H. (1939). *Principles of criminology* (3rd ed.). Philadelphia: Lippincott.

Suttles, G. D. (1968). *The social order of the slum: Ethnicity and territory in the inner city.* Chicago: University of Chicago Press.

Swahn, M. H., Bossarte, R. M., West, B., and Topalli, V. (2010). Alcohol and drug use among gang members: Experiences of adolescents who attend school. *Journal of School Health, 80* (7), 353–360.

Sweeten, G., Pyrooz, D. C., and Piquero, A. R. (2013). Disengaging from gangs and desistance from crime. *Justice Quarterly, 30,* 469–500.

Sykes, G., and Matza, D. (1957). Techniques of neutralization. *American Sociological Review, 22* (6), 664–670.

Syme, S. L. (2000). Foreword. In L. F. Berkman and I. Kawachi (Eds.), *Social epidemiology.* New York: Oxford University Press.

Tannenbaum, F. (1938). *Crime and community.* Boston: Ginn.

Taylor, C. S. (1990). *Dangerous society.* East Lansing: Michigan State University Press.

Taylor, C. S. (1993). *Girls, gangs, women, and drugs.* East Lansing: Michigan State University Press.

Taylor, I., Walton, P., and Young, J. (1973). *The new criminology: For a social theory of deviance.* New York: Harper & Row.

Taylor, T. J., Freng, A., Esbensen, F-A., and Peterson, D. (2008). Youth gang membership and serious violent victimization: The importance of lifestyles and routine activities. *Journal of Interpersonal Violence, 23* (10), 1441–1464.

Taylor, T. J., Peterson, D., Esbensen, F-A., and Freng, A. (2007). Gang membership as a risk factor for adolescent violent victimization. *Journal of Research in Crime and Delinquency, 44* (4), 351–380.

Terry-McElrath, Y. M., O'Malley, P. M., and Johnson, L. D. (2009). Reasons for drug use among American youth by consumption level, gender, and race/ethnicity: 1976–2005. *Journal of Drug Issues, 39* (3), 677–714.

Tertilt, H. (2001). Patterns of ethnic violence in a Frankfurt street gang. In M. W. Klein, H-J. Kerner, C. L. Maxson, and E. G. M. Weitekamp (Eds.), *The Eurogang paradox: Street gangs and youth groups in the US and Europe* (pp. 181–193). Dordrecht: Kluwer.

Thompson, C. Y., Young, R. L., and Burns, R. (2000). Representing gangs in the news: Media constructions of criminal gangs. *Sociological Spectrum, 20,* 409–432.

Thompson, H. S. (1966). *Hell's Angels: The strange and terrible saga of the outlaw motorcycle gangs.* New York: Random House.

Thompson, K. M., and Braaten-Antrim, R. (1998). Youth maltreatment and gang involvement. *Journal of Interpersonal Violence, 13,* 328–345.

Thornberry, T. P. (1987). Toward an interactional theory of delinquency. *Criminology, 25* (4), 863–892.

Thornberry, T. P., Huizinga, D., and Loeber, R. (2004). The causes and correlates studies: Findings and policy implications. *Juvenile Justice, 9* (1), 3–19.

Thornberry, T. P., Krohn, M. D., Lizotte, A. J., and Chard-Wierschem, D. (1993). The role of juvenile gangs in facilitating delinquent behavior. *Journal of Research in Crime and Delinquency, 30,* 55–87.

Thornberry, T. P., Krohn, M. D., Lizotte, A. J., Smith, C. A., and Tobin, K. (2003). *Gangs and delinquency in developmental perspective.* Cambridge, UK: Cambridge University Press.

Thrasher, F. M. (2000). *The gang: A study of 1313 gangs in Chicago* (2000 ed.). Peotone, IL: New Chicago School Press. First published 1927.

Tita, G., and Abrahamse, A. (2004). *Gang homicide in LA, 1981–2001.* Perspectives on Violence Prevention. Sacramento: California Attorney General's Office.

Tita, G., Riley, K. J., Ridgeway, G., Grammich, C., Abrahamse, A., and Greenwood, P. (2003). *Reducing gun violence: Results from an intervention in East Los Angeles.* Santa Monica: RAND Corporation.

Toobin, J. (2014). This is my jail. *The New Yorker*, April 14.

Tokumatsu, G., and Bernstein, S. (2013). Hate crime laws bring down Azusa gang leader. *NBCLA.com,* January 17. Retrieved from http://www.nbclosangeles.com/news/local/Hate-Crime-Laws-Bring-Down-Gang-Azusa-Leader-187289771.html/.

Totten, M., and The Native Women's Association of Canada. (2010). Investigating the linkages between FASD, gangs, sexual exploitation and woman abuse in the Canadian Aboriginal population: A preliminary study. *First Peoples Child and Family Review, 5* (2), 9–22.

Toy, C. (1992a). A short history of Asian gangs in San Francisco. *Justice Quarterly, 9* (4), 647–665.

Toy, C. (1992b). Coming out to play: Reasons to join and participate in Asian gangs. *The Gang Journal, 1* (1), 13–29.

Troutman, D. R., Nugent-Borakove, M. E., and Jansen, S. (2007). *Prosecutor's Comprehensive Gang Response model.* Alexandria, VA: American Prosecutors Research Institute.

Trulson, C. R., Marquart, J., and Kawucha, S. (2006). Gang suppression and institutional control. *Corrections Today, 68,* 26–30.

Uman G. C., Urman, H. N., Malloy, C. L., Martinez, B., and DeMorst, L. (2006). *Pilot study on HIV among gang members.* Los Angeles: City of Los Angeles AIDS Coordinator's Office.

Umemoto, K. (2006). *The truce: Lessons from an L.A. gang war.* Ithaca, NY: Cornell University Press.

Umemoto, K., and Mikami, C. K. (2000). A profile of race-bias hate crime in Los Angeles County. *Western Criminology Review, 2* (2), 1–34.

United Nations Office on Drugs and Crime. (2010). *World drug report 2010.* Vienna: United Nations Office on Drugs and Crime.

United Nations Office on Drugs and Crime. (2011). *2011 Global study on homicide: Trends, context, data.* Vienna: United Nations Office on Drugs and Crime.

Valdez, A. (1999). Nazi Low Riders. *Police: The Law Enforcement Magazine, 23* (3), 46–48.

Valdez, A. (2003). Toward a typology of contemporary Mexican American youth gangs In L. Konton, D. Brotherton, and L. Barrios (Eds.), *Gangs and society: Alternative perspectives* (pp. 12–40). New York: Columbia University Press.

Valdez, A. (2005). Mexican American youth and adult prison gangs in a changing heroin market. *Journal of Drug Issues, 35* (4), 843–868.

Valdez, A. (2007). *Mexican American girls and gang violence: Beyond risk.* New York: Palgrave MacMillan.

Valdez, A., Cepeda, A., and Kaplan, C. (2009). Homicidal events among Mexican American street gangs: A situational analysis. *Homicide Studies, 13,* 288–306.

Valdez, A., Cepeda, A., Parrish, D., Horowitz, R., and Kaplan, C. (2013). An adapted Brief Strategic Family Therapy for gang-affiliated Mexican American adolescents. *Research on Social Work Practice, 23,* 383–396.

Valdez, A., Kaplan, C. D., and Cepeda, A. (2000). The process of paradoxical autonomy and survival in the heroin careers of Mexican American women. *Contemporary Drug Problems, 27* (1), 189–212.

Valdez, A., Kaplan, C. D., and Cepeda, A. (2006). The drugs-violence nexus among Mexican-American gang members. *Journal of Psychoactive Drugs, 38* (2), 109–121.

Valdez, A., Kaplan, C. D., and Codina, E. (2000). Psychopathy among Mexican American gang members: A comparative study. *International Journal of Offender Therapy and Comparative Criminology, 44* (1), 46–58.

Valdez, A., Kaplan, C. D., and Curtis, R. L., Jr. (2007). Aggressive crime, alcohol and drug use, and concentrated poverty in 24 US urban areas. *American Journal of Drug and Alcohol Abuse, 33* (4), 595–603.

Valdez, A., and Sifaneck, S. J. (2004). Getting high and getting by: Dimensions of drug selling behavior among Mexican gang members in Southern Texas. *Journal of Research in Crime and Delinquency, 41,* 82–105.

van Gemert, F. (2001). Crips in orange: Gangs and groups in the Netherlands. In M. W. Klein, H-J. Kerner, C. L. Maxson, and E. G. M Weitekamp (Eds.), *The Eurogang paradox: Street gangs and youth groups in the US and Europe* (pp. 145–152). Dordrecht: Kluwer.

van Gemert, F. (2005). Youth groups and gangs in Amsterdam: A pretest of the Eurogang Expert Survey. In S. H. Decker and F. M. Weerman (Eds.), *European street gangs and troublesome youth groups* (pp. 147–168). New York: Altamira Press.

van Gemert, F., and Fleisher, M. S. (2005). In the grip of the group. In S. H. Decker and F. M. Weerman (Eds.), *European street gangs and troublesome youth groups* (pp. 11–29). New York: Altamira Press.

van Gemert, F., Peterson, D., and Lien, I-L. (Eds.). (2008). *Street gangs, migration and ethnicity*. Cullompton, UK: Willan.

van Gemert, F., and Stuifbergen, J. (2008). Gangs, migration and conflict: Thrasher's theme in the Netherlands. In F. van Gemert, D. Peterson, and I-L. Lien (Eds.), *Street gangs, migration and ethnicity* (pp. 79–96). Cullompton, UK: Willan.

Venkatesh, S. A. (1996). The gang and the community. In C. R. Huff (Ed.), *Gangs in America* (2nd ed.) (pp. 241–256). Thousand Oaks, CA: Sage.

Venkatesh, S. A. (2008). *Gang leader for a day: A rogue sociologist takes to the streets*. New York: Penguin.

Vigil, J. D. (1988a). *Barrio gangs: Street life and identity in Southern California*. Austin: University of Texas Press.

Vigil, J. D. (1988b). Group processes and street identity: Adolescent Chicano gang members. *Ethos, 16* (4), 421–445.

Vigil, J. D. (2002). *A rainbow of gangs*. Austin: University of Texas Press.

Vigil, J. D. (2003). Urban violence and street gangs. *Annual Review of Anthropology, 32*, 225–242.

Vigil, J. D. (2007). *The projects: Gang and non-gang families in East Los Angeles*. Austin: University of Texas Press.

Vigil, J. D. (2008). Female gang members from East Los Angeles. *International Journal of Social Inquiry, 1* (1), 47–74.

Vigil, J. D., and Long, J. M. (1990). Emic and etic perspectives on gang culture: The Chicano case. In C. R. Huff (Ed.), *Gangs in America* (pp. 55–68). Newbury Park: Sage.

Vigil, J. D., and Yun, S. C. (1990). Vietnam youth gangs in Southern California. In C. R. Huff (Ed.), *Gangs in America* (pp. 146–162). Newbury Park, CA: Sage.

Voisin, D. R., Salazar, L. F., Crosby, R., DiClemente, R. J., Yarber, W. L., and Staples-Horne, M. (2004). The association between gang involvement and sexual behaviours among detained adolescent males. *Sexually Transmitted Infections, 80*, 440–442.

Wacquant, L. (2001). Deadly symbiosis: When ghetto and prison meet and mesh. *Punishment and Society, 3* (1), 95–134.

Waldorf, D. (1993a). Don't be your own best customer: Drug use of San Francisco gang drug sellers. *Crime, Law and Social Change, 19*, 1–15.

Waldorf, D. (1993b). When the Crips invaded San Francisco: Gang migration. *Journal of Gang Research, 1*, 11–16.

Waldorf, D., Hunt, G., and Joe, K. (1994). *Report of the Southeast Asian gangs and drugs study*. San Francisco: Institute for Scientific Analysis.

Waldorf, D., and Lauderback, D. (1993). *Gang drug sales in San Francisco: Organized or freelance?* Alameda, CA: Institute for Scientific Analysis.

Ward, T. W. (2012). *Gangsters without borders: An ethnography of a Salvadoran street gang*. New York: Oxford University Press.

Webb, G. (1998). *Dark alliance: The CIA, the Contras, and the crack cocaine explosion*. New York: Seven Stories Press.

Webb, V. J., and Katz, C. M. (2006) A study of police gang units in six cities. In A. Egley Jr., C. L. Maxson, J. Miller, and M. W. Klein (Eds.), *The modern gang reader* (3rd ed.) (pp. 349–376). Los Angeles: Roxbury.

Webb, V. J., Katz, C. M., and Decker, S. H. (2006). Assessing the validity of self-reports by gang members: Results from the Arrestee Drug Abuse Monitoring Program. *Crime and Delinquency, 52*, 232–252.

Webb, V. J., Ren, L., Zhao, J., He, N., and Marshall, I. H. (2011). A comparative study of youth gangs in China and the United States: Definition, offending, and victimization. *International Criminal Justice Review, 21* (3), 225–242.

Webster, D. W., Whitehill, J. M., Vernick, J. S., and Parker, E. M. (2012). *Evaluation of Baltimore's Safe Streets Program: Effects on attitudes, participants' experiences, and gun violence*. Baltimore, MD: John Hopkins University.

Weerman, F. M. (2005). Identification and self-identification: Using a survey to study gangs in the Netherlands. In S. H. Decker and F. M. Weerman (Eds.), *European street gangs and troublesome youth groups* (pp. 129–146). New York: Altamira Press.

Weerman, F. M., and Esbensen, F-A. (2005). A cross-national comparison of youth gangs: The United States and the Netherlands. In S. H. Decker and F. M. Weerman (Eds.), *European street gangs and troublesome youth groups* (pp. 219–255). New York: Altamira Press.

Weerman, F. M., Lovegrove, P. J., and Thornberry, T. (2015). Gang membership transitions and its consequences: Exploring changes related to joining and leaving gangs in two countries. *European Journal of Criminology, 12* (1), 70–91.

Weichselbaum, S. (2009). Gangs in New York talk Twitter: Use tweets to trash-talk rivals, plan fights. *Daily News*

(Saturday, November 28). Retrieved from http://www.nydailynews.com/news/crime/gangs-new-york-talk-twitter-tweets-trash-talk-rivals-plan-fights-article-1.414083/.

Weide, R. D. (2008). Gang graffiti: East coast vs. west coast. In L. Kontos and D. C. Brotherton (Eds.), *Encyclopedia of gangs* (pp. 64–67). Westport, CN: Greenwood Press.

Weisel, D. L. (2006). The evolution of street gangs: An examination of form and variation. In A. Egley Jr., C. L. Maxson, J. Miller, and M. W. Klein (Eds.), *The modern gang reader* (3rd ed.) (pp. 86–103). Los Angeles: Roxbury.

Weitekamp, E. G. M., Reich, K., and Kerner, H-J. (2005). Why do young male Russians of German descent tend to join or form violent gangs? In S. H. Decker and F. M. Weerman (Eds.), *European street gangs and troublesome youth groups* (pp. 81–104). New York: Altamira Press.

Welsh, B. C. (2005). Public health and the prevention of juvenile criminal violence. *Youth Violence and Juvenile Justice, 3* (23), 23–40.

Whitbeck, L. B., Hoyt, D. R., Chen, X., and Stubben, J. D. (2002). Predictors of gang involvement among American Indian adolescents. *Journal of Gang Research, 10* (1), 11–26.

White, H. R., and Gorman, D. M. (2000). *Dynamics of the drug-crime relationship* Retrieved from http://www.ncjrs.gov/criminal_justice2000/vol_1/02d.pdf/.

White, R. (2002). Understanding youth gangs. *Trends and Issues in Crime and Criminal Justice, 237,* Canberra: Australian Institute of Criminology.

White, R. (2006). Youth gang research in Australia. In J. F. Short Jr. and L. A. Hughes (Eds.), *Studying youth gangs* (pp. 161–179). Lanham, MD: Altamira Press.

White, R. (2008a). Weapons are for wimps: The social dynamics of ethnicity and violence in Australian gangs. In F. van Gemert, D. Peterson, and I-L. Lien (Eds.), *Street gangs, migration and ethnicity* (pp. 140–155). Cullompton, UK: Willan.

White, R. (2008b). Disputed definitions and fluid identities: The limitations of social profiling in relation to ethnic youth gangs. *Youth Justice, 8* (2), 149–161.

White, R. (2009). Indigenous youth and gangs as family. *Youth Studies Australia, 28* (3), 47–56.

White, R., and Mason, R. (2006). Youth gangs and youth violence: Charting the key dimensions. *Australian and New Zealand Journal of Criminology, 39* (1), 54–70.

White, R., Perrone, S., Guerra, C., and Lampugnani, R. (1999a). *Ethnic youth gangs in Australia. Do they Exist? Report #2, Turkish young people.* Victoria: Australian Multicultural Foundation.

White, R., Perrone, S., Guerra, C., and Lampugnani, R. (1999b). *Ethnic youth gangs in Australia. Do they Exist? Report #4, Somalian young people.* Victoria: Australian Multicultural Foundation.

Williams, T. (1989). *The cocaine kids: The inside story of a teenage drug ring.* Reading, MA: Addison–Wesley.

Willis, P. (1977). *Learning to labour: How working class kids get working class jobs.* Farnborough, UK: Saxson House.

Willis, P. (1978). *Profane culture.* London: Routledge & Kegan Paul.

Willmott, P. (1966). *Adolescent boys of East London.* London: Routledge & Kegan Paul.

Wilson, H., and Huntington, A. (2006). Deviant (m)others: The construction of teenage motherhood in contemporary discourse. *Journal of Social Policy, 35,* 59–76.

Wilson, S. (2012). *Jamiel Shaw, L.A. football star, murdered over his Spider-Man backpack, says D.A.; Shaw's gang affiliation won't factor into trial.* Retrieved from http://blogs.laweekly.com/informer/2012/04/jamiel_shaw_la_football_murdered_spider-man_backpack_da_gang_affiliation.php/.

Wilson, W. J. (1987). *The truly disadvantaged: The inner city, the underclass, and public policy.* Chicago: University of Chicago Press.

Winfree, L. T., Jr., Backstrom, T. V., and Mays, G. L. (1994). Social learning theory, self-reported delinquency, and youth gangs: A new twist on a general theory of crime and delinquency. *Youth and Society, 26,* 147–177.

Wingood, G. M., DiClemente, R. J., Crosby, R., Harrington, K., Davies, S. L., and Hook, E. W. III. (2002). Gang involvement and the health of African American female adolescents. *Pediatrics, 110,* 57–61.

Wolf, S. (2011). Street gangs of El Salvador. In T. Bruneau, L. Dammert, and E. Skinner (Eds.), *Maras: Gang violence and security in Central America* (pp. 43–70). Austin: University of Texas Press.

Wolfgang, M. E., and Ferracuti, F. (1967). *The subculture of violence.* London: Tavistock.

Wood J., and Alleyne, E. (2010). Street gang theory and research: Where are we now and where do we go from here? *Aggression and Violent Behavior, 15,* 100–111.

Wood, J., Foy, D. W., Goguen, C. A., Pynoos, R., and James, C. B. (2002). Violence exposure and PTSD among delinquent girls. *Journal of Aggression, Maltreatment and Trauma, 6* (1), 109–126.

Wood, R. T. (2006). *Straightedge youth: Complexity and contradictions of a subculture.* Syracuse, NY: Syracuse University Press.

Wooden, W. S. (1995). *Renegade kids, suburban outlaws.* Belmont, CA: Wadsworth.

Wooten, B. (1978). *Social science and social pathology.* London: Greenwood.

Wortley, S., and Tanner, J. (2006). Immigration, social disadvantage, and urban youth gangs: Results of a Toronto-area survey. *Canadian Journal of Urban Research, 15* (2), S18–S37.

Wortley, S., and Tanner, J. (2008). Respect, friendship, and racial injustice: Justifying gang membership in a Canadian city. In F. van Gemert, D. Peterson, and I-L. Lien (Eds.), *Street gangs, migration and ethnicity* (pp. 192–208). Cullompton, UK: Willan.

Xu, F., Town, M., Balluz, L. S., Bartoli, W. P., Murphy, W., Chowdhury, P. P., Garvin, W. S., Pierannunzi, C., Zhong, Y., Salandy, S. W., Jones, C. K., and Crawford, C. A. (2013). Surveillance for certain health behaviors among states and selected local areas—United States, 2010. *Morbidity and Mortality Weekly Report, 62,* 1–247.

Yablonsky, L. (1959). The delinquent gang as a near-group. *Social Problems, 7* (2), 108–117.

Yablonsky, L. (1962). *The violent gang.* Baltimore: Penguin.

Yablonsky, L. (1997). *Gangsters: Fifty years of madness, drugs, and death on the streets of America.* New York: New York University Press.

Yardley, E. (2008). Teenage mothers' experiences of stigma. *Journal of Youth Studies, 11* (6), 671–684.

Yoder, K. A., Whitbeck, L. B., and Hoyt, D. R. (2003). Gang involvement and membership among homeless and runaway youth. *Youth and Society, 34* (4), 441–467.

Young, J. (1971). *The drugtakers: The social meaning of drug use.* London: MacGibbon and Kee.

Young, J. (1999). *The exclusive society: Social exclusion, crime and difference in late modernity.* London: Sage.

Young, J. (2008). Moral panics. In L. Kontos and D. C. Brotherton (Eds.), *Encyclopedia of gangs* (pp. 174–176). Westport, CN: Greenwood Press.

Zahn, M., Hawkins, S. R., Chiancone, J., and Whitworth, A. (2008). *The Girls Study Group—Charting the way to delinquency prevention for girls.* Washington, DC: U.S. Department of Justice.

Zatz, M. S. (1987). Chicano youth gangs and crime: The creation of a moral panic. *Contemporary Crisis, 11* (2), 129–158.

Zatz, M. S., and Portillos, E. L. (2000). Voices from the barrio: Chicano/a gangs, families, and communities. *Criminology, 38* (2), 369–401.

Zhang, L., Messner, S., Lu, Z., and Deng, X. (1997). Gang crime and its punishment in China. *Journal of Criminal Justice, 25,* 289–302.

Zhang, L., Welte, J. W., and Wieczorek, W. F. (1999). Youth gangs, drug use, and delinquency. *Journal of Criminal Justice, 27* (2), 101–109.

Zhang, S. X. (2001). Chinese gangs: Familial and cultural dynamic. In C. R. Huff (Ed.), *Gangs in America* (3rd ed.) (pp. 219–236). Thousand Oaks, CA: Sage.

Zimring, F. E. (2006). *The great American crime decline.* New York: Oxford University Press.

Zohrabi, A. (2012). Resistance and repression: The Black Guerrilla Family in context. *Hastings Race and Poverty Law Journal, 9,* 167–190.

CREDITS

AUTHOR INDEX

SUBJECT INDEX